Integrated Advisory Service

Integrated Advisory Service

Breaking Through the Book Boundary to Better Serve Library Users

Jessica E. Moyer, Editor

AN IMPRINT OF ABC-CLIO, LLC
Santa Barbara, California • Denver, Colorado • Oxford, England

Library of Congress Cataloging-in-Publication Data

Integrated advisory service : breaking through the book boundary to better serve library users/Jessica E. Moyer, editor.

    p. cm.

  Includes bibliographical references and indexes.

  ISBN 978-1-59158-718-7 (acid-free paper) 1. Readers' advisory services—United States. 2. Libraries—Special collections—Audio-visual materials. 3. Audio-visual library service. 4. Audio-visual materials—Catalogs. 5. Fiction genres—Bibliography. 6. Popular literature—Stories, plots, etc. I. Moyer, Jessica E.

  Z711.55.I58   2010

  025.5'4—dc22   2010019748

ISBN 978-1-59158-718-7

14 13 12 11 10   1 2 3 4 5

This book is also available on the World Wide Web as an eBook. Visit www.abc-clio.com for details.

Libraries Unlimited
An Imprint of ABC-CLIO, LLC

ABC-CLIO, LLC
130 Cremona Drive, P.O. Box 1911
Santa Barbara, California 93116-1911

This book is printed on acid-free paper (∞)

Manufactured in the United States of America

Contents

Acknowledgments

This project would never have been possible without the hard work of all the contributors: Gary Warren Neibuhr, Jessica Zellers, Nanette Donohue, Rick Roche, Rollie Welch, Christy Donaldson, Kaite Dunneback, Mary Wilkes Towner, Heather Booth, Nicole Suarez, Kaite Mediatore Stover, and Rebecca Vnuk. Thanks so much for all your ideas, creativity, and willingness to revise and reformat, and meeting all the challenges of writing something completely new. Special thanks to Cassie Wagner for her many excellent suggestions of manga and graphic novels, especially in science fiction.

The Kent District Library's What's Next Web site was invaluable; without it, tracking down all the series information would have been next to impossible. Huge thanks to all the librarians at Kent District who put this amazing resource together and made it freely available online. The Menomonie Public Library kept me well supplied with new books, audiobooks, DVDs, and graphic novels; thanks to the circulation staff and especially Tim Fitzgerald for his help with interlibrary loans. Together you found me everything I needed for this project, an amazing feat for a small public library.

Without the excellent editorial guidance of Barbara Ittner, this project would never have happened. From the very beginning, your suggestions and comments provided significant assistance in creating the final manuscript. Special thanks to Kaite Stover for last-minute editorial assistance when I couldn't bear to re-read/re-edit any more chapters. Your suggestions were great, and as usual your editing skills were top notch.

Lastly I must thank my family who put up with me during the three long years of working on this book. The cats Mitt, Tiggy, and Smokey helped from the beginning, and newcomer Charlie is learning quickly how to be a useful writing assistant. My dog Callie as always encourages regular writing breaks and walks. Above all, my husband Christopher not only listened to me talk and talk and talk about this book in general, but also about crime and science fiction, despite his dedication to nonfiction reading. Without him to help out around the house, cook me wonderful dinners, and help take care of the pets, I never would have been able to give this project the concentrated efforts it required.

Introduction: Integrated Advisory

Introduction

As the public library has increasingly embraced its role as a resource for leisure activities, many libraries have expanded their collections beyond traditional print book collections. Today, graphic novels and manga are collected at most libraries, audiobooks continue to be a patron favorite, and videogames are starting to be collected and circulated by many libraries. Not to mention the increasing popularity of the film collections or new digital download services. In many libraries, the audiovisual (AV) collection gets as much as, or more use than, the fiction or nonfiction collections. June 2006 statistics from the Champaign Public Library revealed that 35 percent of total circulation came from the audiovisual collection.[1]

Many libraries that have invested in the new digital audiobook players, Playaways, have found them so popular that they circulate constantly and never sit on the shelves. Library programming is also expanding into new areas, especially in teen services, with gaming tournaments, manga discussion groups, and even online book groups.

Since the late 1980s, readers' advisory has enjoyed a renaissance, with increased visibility and services. Readers' advisory courses are increasingly being taught in LIS programs, readers' advisory-oriented continuing-education opportunities are common, and at the Public Library Association conferences, readers' advisory programs are some of the most popular. In the twenty-first century, readers' advisory services have become a central part of public services at most public libraries and are even making their way into school and academic libraries.

Initially, readers' advisory focused on fiction and was primarily aimed at adult leisure readers, but over the last several years, as we have become more comfortable with readers' advisory services, they have changed and expanded, first encompassing nonfiction and then readers' advisory services for teens. But that was just the beginning; as library patrons' expectations change and library collections expand beyond adult leisure reading books, readers' advisory services are also changing. It's about breaking down barriers and making new connections. In this book, we call this phenomenon integrated advisory, an approach to advisory services that integrates all aspect of modern public library collections: fiction books, nonfiction books, movies (entertainment and documentaries), videogames, graphic novels, manga, magazines, and even podcasts to help library patrons find the best match.

Defining Integrated Advisory

What is integrated advisory? It is a whole new way of looking at and thinking about library materials that incorporates the techniques of readers' advisory and the multiple media that make up modern library collections. It is a way for you and for library users to maximize your library's resources by finding connections between formats and genres.

Why another readers' advisory book? One, readers' advisory is changing and expanding beyond books and very little has been written about it, as compared to the literature on print-based readers' advisory. Readers' advisory was initially focused on print fiction, and has recently expanded to embrace nonfiction, but generally continues to ignore non-book media. For example, there are no dedicated tools for librarians that focus on audiobooks. Graphic novels are starting to get some coverage, but the guides generally tend to isolate them in terms of their illustrated format instead of considering them as a larger part of a genre.

Two, there are no printed or electronic tools that make explicit and continued connections between various types of media in a single genre. Some books have started on this, such as *Reading the High Country* (Libraries Unlimited, 2006), which covers westerns in book and movie form; *Hooked on Horror* (Libraries Unlimited, 2003) includes short film lists for each of the horror subgenres. Other guides sometimes note film versions. But this book goes much farther, with lists that include all types of media and formats.

This book breaks through format barriers with genre-focused chapters that include print fiction and nonfiction, audiobooks, graphic novels, manga, TV shows, movies, and even computer and videogames—all the materials that are not only found in today's libraries, but are popular with all types and ages of library users.

> Integrated advisory is a way of providing advisory services to library users that includes all different formats and media while staying focused around a genre.

The purpose of this book is to inspire librarians to think of their collections in new ways and support integrated advisory work in all types of school and public libraries, with both teen and adult library users. It is suggestive, rather than exhaustive, and will hopefully provoke thought and inspire new ways of handling library collections. It is meant for library staff to use when working with patrons, as professional reading and genre studies, and also for patrons to use on their own. It can be used either as a browsing guide or as a direct link. It's also a good source for display ideas.

For example, for a library user who has enjoyed a movie included in this book, locate the movie in the index and then find lists that include that movie among other media. Or if you're trying to help a library user find some new science fiction, flip to the science fiction chapter and browse for suggestions.

Patrons who may know exactly what they want to read next may have no idea how to select a satisfying audiobook or find a movie to enjoy over the weekend. They should be able to turn to a librarian and ask for assistance in the same way readers ask for help. Expanding readers' advisory does not mean excluding book readers or reading—we argue that there is the same value, in terms of leisure and entertainment, in watching a good movie as listening to a good book or reading a graphic novel or playing a favorite video game. Instead, this is a way for advisors to work with all of the library's collections and a way for patrons to access more of the library collections, not just the ones they know best. *Integrated Advisory* begins to answer to this problem. Just as *Genreflecting* (Libraries Unlimited) provided the first guide to genre fiction for readers' advisors when its first edition was first published in 1982, *Integrated Advisory* introduces the concept of cross-format advisory and gives advisors a resource to start this important work.

About This Book

One book can only be so long, and this is not meant to be a comprehensive guide to all genres and formats, but merely a starting place. Each chapter gives an overview of a genre and provides a variety of samples that help illustrate the concept of integrated advisory for that genre; together these can help both users and library staff find the next book, movie, audiobook, graphic novel, or video game. For library staff it will also be useful in getting into the integrated advisory mindset and understanding how the concept can work in various genres.

The following genres each have their own chapter: crime, fantasy, historical, horror, popular science, romance, science fiction, teen stories, urban lit, and women's stories. Within the chapters, fiction books, nonfiction books, graphic novels, manga, movies, TV shows, audiobooks, and video games can be found across the various lists. Due to size limitations, there are some genres that are not covered—notably mainstream fiction, thrillers, and westerns. However, rest assured that the principles of integrated advisory can be applied to virtually any genre or reading interest.

Each chapter was written by a genre expert (or experts) who selected their media based on their knowledge of the genre and overall availability in North American library collections. Out-of-print works that are still held in library collections are included, as are classics of the genre in addition to bestsellers and new releases. This lack of standard limitations was meant to allow contributors to create lists with a wide variety of materials representative of each genre. Overall, the annotated lists are designed to be illustrative rather than comprehensive, showcasing the concepts of integrated advisory.

Young adult titles have a separate chapter, and we have also marked titles that we think have the most appeal for younger readers with a YA designation throughout other chapters. This says nothing about age appropriateness or intended audience, it just notes which of the titles in any specific list are most likely to appeal to teen readers. Sometimes it indicates books that have been published as YA books, but is just as likely to indicate adult titles that have proven teen appeal, something that is common in genre fiction.

With print books, we have selected more from newer authors and titles to reduce duplication of previous print sources. Because of the lack of resources that include AV material, and make the connections between print and AV, availability is the only limit for inclusion for non-print titles.

Organization

This work is a contributed volume, with individual genre experts contributing to each chapter. Each expert offers their own interpretation of integrated advisory in their particular genre. Because of this fact and because each genre is unique, chapters are neither entirely consistent nor exclusive.

The book is organized around popular and well-known genres, as these are areas that are generally well known by both patrons and library staff. Genre fans always know the names of their favorites, and due to the increasing popularity of readers' advisory services in general, library staff are generally familiar with most genre terms, as both of the most well-known tools (which are also regularly assigned as texts in readers' advisory courses), Saricks' *Readers' Advisory Guide to Genre Fiction* (ALA editions) and *Genreflecting: A Guide to Reading Interests* (6th edition, Libraries Unlimited), are organized by genres. The entire concept of integrated advisory is new and may be slightly overwhelming to both staff and library patrons, but the use of familiar and well-known terms should help library staff and users become more comfortable with integrated advisory services.

The genres covered in this guide include crime, fantasy, historical, horror, popular science, romance, science fiction, teen stories, urban lit, and women's stories. Each chapter follows the same general format:

Part 1, Introduction: The introductory portion includes an overview of the genre, a definition of the genre, and a broad scan of the genre as it occurs in books, graphic novels, video and computer games, movies, and television shows. Information on integrated advisory and the genre is the focus. The final section of the introductory narrative highlights current and upcoming trends in subgenres, plots, characters, and formats.

Parts 2 to 5 include both narrative sections and annotated lists. Each list is organized alphabetically by main entry, with preference given first to series title (when available), author, and then title (most often for movies), and uses a variety of notations to provide additional information about formats and suggested reader or viewership.

Media noted include:

- BK: book—nonfiction is noted as NF BK
- MV: movie
- TV: television show
- CGM: computer game
- VGM: video game
- GN: graphic novel
- MN: manga
- AB: abridged audiobook
- UAB: unabridged audiobook
- PC: podcast

Other features that are noted with the annotations are:

- YA: recommended for teen readers
- SH: start here, best bet for readers new to this area/author/series, etc.
- CL: considered a classic by fans
- RS: rising star—the authors, books, TV, etc., to watch for in the next few years
- AP: chapter author pick

In addition to these notations, each entry includes the author and/or illustrator and title for books and graphic novels, the title for movies and television shows, as well as any series information. The first year of publication is also included for each entry. Series information is underlined, and titles are in italics.

Sample entry:

<u>Dresden Files</u>, Jim Butcher, *Storm Front* (2000) BK, UAB, GN, TV

This combination of fantasy and crime has been exploited by many storytellers. Jim Butcher's recent <u>Dresden File series</u> features Chicago P. I. Harry Dresden, who also happens to be a professional wizard for hire. These hardboiled crime stories are set in a world where Dresden needs to protect the innocent population from the magical elements of which they are ignorant, all while trying to make a living as a private investigator. The series began with *Storm Front* (2000) and the latest is *Changes* (2010). A thirteen-episode television series was filmed in 2007 with Paul Blackthorne as Dresden, and a graphic novel was released in 2008.

Explanation: Series is Dresden Files (indicated by underlining), author is Jim Butcher, and title of the first entry in the series is *Storm Front* (indicated by italics). The first series entry appeared in 2000 and entries are available as books (fiction), unabridged audiobooks, graphic novels, and as a television show. When there is more than one version (most often with movies), usually a specific one is suggested with information about the year of initial release.

Series information was obtained from the Kent District Library's *What's Next* online database. When that was not available or was incomplete, additional information was gathered from the author or publisher Web site, Amazon.com, the Internet Movie Database, and Wikipedia. These sites were also used, in addition to the Library of Congress Catalog and WorldCat, for all publication and format information included in the annotations.

Part 2, ''Plots,'' focuses on some of the current popular plot types for each genre. In addition to descriptions of the plot types, an annotated list of suggested titles in a variety of media is included for each type listed. These lists can be used by library staff advising patrons on what to read, watch, listen to, or play next.

Part 3, ''Characters,'' covers some of the most common or popular character types for the genres. Annotated lists with a variety of media accompany the character type descriptions.

Part 4, ''Theme.'' The unique nature of each genre takes center stage in this section, which highlights important themes. After defining and describing the theme and several related subthemes, contributors provide annotated lists for each subtheme. This section, unique to the integrated advisory approach, combines appeal factors of tone, style, and mood with the elements that set apart each genre.

Part 5, ''Making Connections.'' In addition to making connections within genres, advisors are encouraged to make cross-genre connections. This section attempts to make those connections, suggesting specific titles for readers of other genres, and highlighting both genre blends and titles with wide-ranging appeal. It is designed for users interested in exploring a new genre, as well as those looking to explore new areas. Descriptions of genre trends make this a great resource for library staff.

Part 6, ''Conclusion.'' Each chapter ends with a conclusion that summarizes and explores larger genre trends and discusses the future of the genre, including various formats.

Conclusion

We hope that you find this book useful working with library users. Integrated advisory is an exciting new concept that should greatly help in providing advisory services for all ages, and provide better access to the many formats in modern library collections.

Welcome to *Integrated Advisory*!

Endnote

1. Nanette Donohue, technical services manager, Champaign Public Library, June 2006 (personal e-mail to author).

1

Everything Crime Stories
Jessica E. Moyer and Gary W. Neibuhr

In this overview of the crime genre, crime covers all types of crime stories, including mysteries, crime thrillers, and true crime. Character types for crime include amateur detectives, lone wolf cops, partners, private and professional detectives, and criminals. The "Plots" section covers forensics, police procedurals, humor, and psychological thrillers (whydunits). The crime theme is settings and sense of place and has lists about Scandinavia, Between the Wars: 1918–1939, Across the Fifty States, and Around the World. The "Making Connections" section includes crime stories for fantasy fans, true crime for nonfiction lovers, and historical mysteries.

Introduction

Lost in humankind's history is a cave painting depicting the first recorded criminal behavior. Since that day, in all formats available, people have been recording acts against humanity.

Defining Crime Literature

The two elements a story must have to be included in this genre are:

- An element of crime
- An element of detection

Crime stories can generally be divided into two large categories: whodunit and whydunit. Each are discussed and defined below.

The whodunit is the classic puzzle of crime stories. It involves a person who acts as the detective, solving the crime before the reader or viewer can figure out the solution. The appeal of this type of story is in the game of playing along with the creator, using the clues provided, and trying to reach the correct resolution before it is revealed by the fictional detective. Within these stories, the detective characters and the plot in which they are embroiled are the major appeal elements.

The whydunit may have features of the whodunit contained within, but the thematic elements of the story are equally as important as the plot. Readers of these stories are as equally interested in the criminal characters as they are the detectives. The appeal of this type of story is in discovering the motivations behind the criminal act; the behavior of the criminal is the major appeal element.

Integrated Advisory, Crime Style

In the short story "Murder in the Rue Morgue," Edgar Allan Poe established the following conventions of the crime fiction genre:

- Eccentric detective main character
- Faithful partner and chronicler
- A murder that confuses with details
- Locked room puzzle
- Ineffectual police
- Wrongly suspected suspects

By writing two more short stories about the same character, he also invented the series detective. A great debt is owed to Edgar Allan Poe. The Mystery Writers of America recognize that by calling its annual award after this innovative writer.

The next peak in the popularity of crime fiction comes with the introduction and sustained love for the character Sherlock Holmes by Sir Arthur Conan Doyle. Eventually this character had an impact on the film industry as well. Holmes and his partner Watson featured in many short stories and novels and were beloved by readers who constantly clamored for more, to the dismay of Doyle, who hated writing Holmes books.

The golden age of mystery fiction is defined from the end of World War I to the end of World War II (1918–1945). During this period, crime fiction was dominated by the puzzle, which has the following characteristics:

- The reader is willing to play a game against the author.
- The author's job is to create a mystery puzzle with confusing details that the fictional detective will try to unravel.
- The author must "play fair."
- The author is allowed to lace the book with "red herrings."
- The author's fictional detective reveals the solution to the crime before the reader discovers the correct solution.
- The "gathering of the suspects."

The benchmark author in this period is Agatha Christie. By reading her Hercule Poirot or Miss Jane Marple series, both classic whodunit series, readers can gain an understanding of how the plot was the supreme element; and character, theme, and setting were less highly regarded.

After World War II, the introduction of psychological aspects into crime fiction transformed the genre from a plot-driven examination of "just the facts" to one that asked questions about why characters would behave in such bad ways. The works of Patricia Highsmith, one of the early innovators in this style, are intricate examinations of the characters that populate the worlds she created. By reading the adventures of the sociopath Tom Ripley, an understanding of how authors are making the motivations of the character equal to whatever actions the plot contains makes the tale.

In the latter part of the twentieth century and into the twenty-first century, all types of crime stories have flourished, making it one of the largest and most diverse genres. Crime stories, driven by the print market, have moved into movies, TV shows, graphic novels, and audiobooks. There is no format in which some type of crime story is not popular.

Hard-Boiled to Cozy

A key element of mystery stories is the spectrum of hard-boiled to cozy. Found in both classic puzzle mysteries as well as psychologically focused crime stories, the hard-boiled versus cozy spectrum often refers to the amount of violence, language, and sex. The closer to cozy, the more likely the violence is to occur off-scene and the characters to be repulsed and upset. The closer to hard-boiled, the more violence, language, and sex become part of the story. While this distinction is often classed as cozy = amateur and hard-boiled = PI, this is a false dichotomy as amateurs can be hard-boiled and some PI stories quite cozy. Most importantly, the hard-boiled versus cozy spectrum is best for understanding the tone and mood of crime stories. Over the years, the genre has tended to move from one side of the spectrum to the other, but neither side is ever completely missing.

Traditional Print Books

Mysteries and crime stories have been an important part of print books since the late nineteenth century and flourished in the golden age between the wars in both popular paperbacks and pulp magazines. Several of the most famous mystery magazines were founded during this time (*Ellery McQueen's Mystery Magazine*) that published short stories by popular authors. While short stories and magazines were significantly less popular in the second half of the twentieth century, in-print crime stories have continued to shine, with crime/thrillers consistently ranked as one of the favored genres of both male and female readers.[1] Print is a showcase of the crime genre, encompassing its depth and breadth, and showing off the full extent of crime stories and settings. All plot and character types can be found in print books, with police procedurals just as popular as cozies with amateur detectives. The strength and popularity of printed crime stories means that new trends are most likely to appear here first and then disseminate to other media.

Movies

Since the advent of film, the subject of criminal behavior has been shown on the silver screen. Early silent movies like *A Daring Daylight Burglary* (1903) or *The Great Train Robbery* (1903) demonstrate long-term appeal of crime stories.

In the 1910s and 1920s, an enthusiastic examination of the criminal life helped create a sentiment that the industry needed to rein in itself. The Hays Code, introduced in 1930, limited what could be shown on the screen and included a requirement that bad people in movies be punished for what they did. However, these restrictions did not keep the film industry from producing great crime films. The reigning master of the crime film was the Warner Brothers studio, which produced such crime classics as *Little Caesar* (1930), *The Public Enemy* (1931), and *Scarface* (1932).

The next trend in crime filmmaking was film noir, a film style first identified by French scholars; the term translates from the French as "black film." American film producers, searching for great crime stories and hoping to produce feature films on a limited budget, helped develop this style that is often identified by, but not limited to, the following:

- Film atmospherics that include the dramatic use of light
- A doomed protagonist, often linked to a femme fatale
- An urban location with a sense of a impending doom

Films such as *Double Indemnity* (1944), *Out of the Past* (1947), and *The Third Man* (1949) are great examples of films that are now categorized as film noir. The noir label has since been appropriated by print media and is a common description for some of the more hard-boiled types of crime stories.

Crime stories readily lend themselves to film, but certain plot types and characters are more likely to occur. Film noir continues to be an important subgenre as do stories about criminals like *The Untouchables* or *Bonnie and Clyde*. In addition to films based around real-life criminals, capers are also especially popular in film, as can be seen in the popularity of the Ocean's 11 series starring George Clooney and Brad Pitt. The more caper-oriented films often have a comic element and are action-oriented as compared to the darker and moodier film noir. Police procedurals have also found their way to film, but are not as common as they are on TV. Amateur detectives are less often seen in film, and cozy mysteries are the least common in the film format.

Television

The advent of television created a new venue for the crime story. Early crime television shows like *Dragnet* (1951–1959), *Perry Mason* (1957–1966), *Peter Gunn* (1958–1960), *The Untouchables* (1959–1963), and *77 Sunset Strip* (1958–1964) were prime-time examples of the popularity of the crime story. The advent of color did not significantly change the presentation of crime stories to a mass audience. *The Fugitive* (1963–1967), *Ironside* (1967–1975), and *Hawaii Five-0* (1968–1980) are examples of shows that drew on the tradition established by earlier black-and-white productions.

In recent decades, the introduction of cable television and such strong studios as Home Box Office (HBO) revolutionized the way that crime fiction was depicted on television. The freedom of cable allowed the development of such great crime series as *The Sopranos* (1999–2007), *The Shield* (2002–2008), and *The Wire* (2002–2008), which could depict more violence and stronger language than allowable on network television, leading to more realistic plots and characters.

Police stories continue to be one of the most popular genres for TV shows, from the lone wolf cop character of *Law & Order: Criminal Intent* to the ensemble cast productions typified in *Hill Street Blues* to the partners of Crockett and Tubbs in *Miami Vice*. Detective shows based on books are especially popular in the UK, where many series have been adapted, including Val McDermid's *Wire in the Blood* and M. C. Beaton's popular Highland village cop in *Hamish Macbeth*. Both hard-boiled and cozy series are popular on TV and have equally loyal audiences.

Graphic Novels

Crime comics had their heyday in the 1940s and 1950s when a blend of true crime and fictional stories were presented in this colorful format, which often featured lurid illustrations of graphic violence and mayhem. The industry drew the attention of the censors, and in 1954, the U.S. Congress convened the Senate Subcommittee on Juvenile Delinquency to investigate the comic book industry. The attention and wrath of Congress led the comic book industry to tame itself with a self-imposed code. This also tamed the crime story to the point where its popularity was supplanted by a focus on the superhero character. While some superheroes fight crime (that was the origin of Bat-Man), the formal crime focus faded.

In the late 1970s, the development of graphic novels intended to be issued as mass-market paperbacks began. *Road to Perdition* by Max Allan Collins and Richard Piers Rayner spawned a major feature-length film and a continuing series of stories related to the original publication. This was just the tip of the iceberg as graphic novels moved from edgy to mainstream in the 1990s and twenty-first century. As with any popular format, there are plenty of short crime stories, including short story collections like *Noir: A Collection of Crime Comics* and *The Mammoth Book of Best Crime Comics*. There are also plenty of longer graphic novel crime books, and while there are not yet as many crime stories in the graphic novel format as there are print books, this is a strong and growing area. Additionally, mainstream crime authors like Ian Rankin are beginning to not only embrace but also create original stories for graphic novels.

Computer and Video Games

Crime continues to captivate players as well as readers. The trend in video and computer games is generally games developed from popular TV shows such as *Law & Order* or *CSI*. Versions of the *Law & Order* video/computer game have existed since the mid-1990s, just another testament to the popularity of the franchise.

Original games also exist, but tend to be less focused on traditional mystery elements and more on larger issues of crime. *Grand Theft Auto*, now in multiple versions, is one of the best known, as the player gets to be a criminal stealing cars and generally delving into the underworld of various American cities. While video and computer games are huge in the mainstream world, they have yet to impact print publishing; while some books are made into games, as of yet, no games have produced spinoff crime books. This trend may be reflected in the generally older average age of crime readers; as the video game generation becomes older, expect to see more crime stories in the game format.

Trends

Trends in reader preferences are best reflected in the popular subgenres; today, international mysteries are all the rage, particularly those from Scandinavian countries, and historicals continue to have a strong audience, with the 1920s as the current favorite era. However, traditional subgenres like noir, police procedurals, and cozies with amateur detectives still have strong print audiences. TV shows are trending away from more traditional police procedurals to shows that embrace both crime and law enforcement, with HBO's award-winning show *The Wire* as the best example of this trend. However, forensic-based shows like *CSI* continue to have a strong audience, as does the long-running police and district attorney focused *Law & Order* franchise.

Crime stories have long been a staple of the audiobook market and continue to be one of the most popular audio genres. Many popular series have dedicated listening audiences and are read by some of the audio world's best narrators, such as Elizabeth

Peters's long-running Amelia Peabody series read by award-winning narrator Barbara Rosenblat. Crime and mysteries are common enough in audiobook formats that listeners who enjoy a series read by one narrator should have no problem finding others by that same narrator, such as Davina Porter who reads both McCall Smith's Isabel Dalhousie series and M. C. Beaton's Hamish Macbeth series. New formats in audio, such as the preloaded Playaway device, have an excellent selection of crime stories, and hundreds of new and backlist crime titles can now be found in digital format as audio pioneers Recorded Books and Books On Tape have digitized their extensive collections.

Characters

Characters are a key element of crime stories and often drive long-running series. Without unique and compelling characters, how many locked rooms or country-house murders would fans be able to stomach? Character variety helps distinguish between popular plots and attracts readers to continue with lengthy series.

The strength of characters is often one reason stories transition from print to television or movies or vice versa, as fans readily follow their favorites from format to format. Any true Kurt Wallander fan considers the recent BBC adaptation with Kenneth Branaugh as must watch, despite the fact that one of the weakest books (*Firewall*) was the first story filmed. Characters are also a key element in distinguishing types of crime stories as the type of investigator, amateur, private detective, or police detective is one of the major distinctions in crime.

Female Amateur Detectives

Not including law enforcement officials, how many people do you know who have solved a murder? If you are a fan of crime stories, the correct answer is hundreds. By definition, an amateur detective is a person who does not solve crimes for a living, but frequently finds him- or herself involved in murders, either at the behest of friends, because of their own nosy natures, or due to the perceived ineptitude of law enforcement. Since Miss Marple solved her first case from her cozy cottage in 1930, amateur detectives, whether busy running catering businesses or gossiping with fellow retirees, have thrived in print stories but are found less often in film.

Television, however, is home to one of the most famous of amateur detectives, Jessica Fletcher, a retired teacher and mystery writer living in coastal Maine. Despite the improbability of amateurs being around so many murders and being able to solve them better than the police, this is one of the most popular and enduring character types. As amateur detectives most often appear in the cozier stories, these can be good choices for younger readers just venturing into crime stories. Female amateurs are more common than men and popular as seen in the long-standing popularity of Jessica Fletcher and Miss Marple; the list below highlights the many amateur female crime solvers.

<u>Clare Fergusson</u>, Julia Spencer-Fleming, *In the Bleak Midwinter* **(2002) BK, UAB, SH, RS**
Clare Fergusson, an Army helicopter-pilot veteran, has found her strength by becoming an Episcopalian priest. However, that does not stop author Julia Spencer-Fleming from complicating Clare's life by plunking her down in an affair with Russ Van

Alstyne, the local police chief of Miller's Kill, New York. All of Claire's adventures are challenged by social issues and sometimes feature a thriller-like atmosphere.

Death on Demand, Carolyn G. Hart, *Death on Demand* **(1987) BK, UAB**
The Death on Demand mystery bookstore on Broward's Rock off the coast of South Carolina is the home of Annie Laurance and her partner Max Darling. At first just good friends, a romance between the two grows, and eventually consummates in a marriage that unites the bookstore owner and the private detective. Part of the fun of Hart's series is her use of the history of the mystery within her plots.

Faith Fairchild, Katherine Hall Page, *Body in the Belfry* **(1990) BK, UAB**
Katherine Hall Page's Faith Sibley Fairchild, a former caterer, is now married to a clergyman and living in a small Massachusetts town. Although she has given up the food industry, food has not given up her, and her adventures with murder also include recipes.

Meg Lanslow, Donna Andrews, *Murder with Peacocks* **(1999) BK, UAB, YA, AP**
Donna Andrews's series about the sculptor/blacksmith Meg Langslow incorporates humor into the investigation, a fact evident from the punny titles that head these works. Besides the intrusion of a crime into her life, Meg is constantly dealing with the challenges of her own family and their occasionally unusual behavior.

Miss Marple, Agatha Christie, *Murder at the Vicarage* **(1930) BK, MV, TV, CL, UAB**
The benchmark for amateur detectives is Agatha Christie's Miss Jane Marple. Featured in 17 titles starting with *Murder at the Vicarage*, this detective is the archetype for the "little old lady" sleuth character. With the novels predominantly set in the small English village of St. Mary's Mead, Miss Marple uses her network of social contacts to maintain the lines of communication when things go bad. Christie's use of the small village setting also established that location as a signature element of mystery fiction. (However, it does leave the authors with the conundrum that their amateur detectives reside in communities with the worst homicide rates in their nations.) Viewers can catch a Miss Marple film starring Margaret Rutherford in *Murder She Said* (1961) or the current television show with Julia McKenzie being shown on the BBC and A&E.

Mrs. Murphy, Rita Mae Brown and Sneaky Pie Brown, *Wish You Were Here* **(1990) BK, UAB**
Rita Mae Brown with her feline co-author, Sneaky Pie Brown, writes about the adventures of Mary Minor "Harry" Haristeen, the sleuthing cats, Mrs. Murphy and Pewter, and the corgi, Tee Tucker. All are set in a small town in the Virginia countryside. Mrs. Murphy, Pewter, and Tucker talk to each other, but not to humans, but nevertheless manage to help postmistress and divorcee, Harry, solve crimes.

Murder, She Wrote (1984–1996) TV, MV, BK, CL
The benchmark amateur detective who appears in a television show is Jessica Fletcher (Angela Lansbury) in *Murder, She Wrote* (1984–1996, plus four movie-length appearances). Jessica, a retired English teacher and a mystery novelist, always seems to be in the right spot to find a dead body, even when she is traveling; but when she is in her small hometown, Cabot Cove, Maine, residents beware.

Lone Wolf Cops

There are two types of police detective characters. The first is a regular officer who functions within the procedures of a police department. These are discussed in the plot section on police procedurals as the focus of these stories is not on character, but on the police dynamics and cases. The second type of cop character is more like a lone wolf, still carrying a badge, but working alone, similar to an amateur or private detective. The lone wolf cop rarely relies on his colleagues, often breaks the rules in his pursuit of justice, and has a tendency to go into dangerous situations without backup. These detectives also usually have unique and quirky characteristics that are accentuated by their lone wolf approach to life and work. The appeal of the lone wolf cop is long-standing in all formats, though there are many more male than female lone wolves.

Cold Case (2003–) TV, RS

Lilly Rush, played by Kathryn Morris, is the only female homicide investigator in Philadelphia but she finds her strength when she is assigned a cold case. This series debuted in 2003 and is still running strong. Working alone, Lilly is one of the few female lone wolves.

Columbo (1971–1978, 1989–1990) TV, CL

Columbo first utilized the lone wolf in the 1960s, but it was only when Peter Falk was cast as the odd detective who solved crimes that viewers responded. Early in the history of mystery fiction, a style of novel writing became known as the "inverted mystery," or a book in which the reader knows who committed the crime and then watches the detective try to put the clues together. Now there was a television show where the audience already knew the solution to the crime and rooted for the detective as he worked the clues. It ran from 1971 to 1978 and had a revival in 1989 and 1990.

Dirty Harry, *Dirty Harry* (1971) MV, CL, SH, AP

Viewers looking for movie-length lone wolf stories can't go wrong with Clint Eastwood's Dirty Harry series. As Inspector Harry Callahan, Eastwood is a dedicated cop who is disturbed by the lawlessness of 1970s (and 1980s) San Francisco and feels that the rules don't really apply to him. From *Dirty Harry* (1971) to *Dead Pool* (1988), Harry usually has a partner, but they rarely survive his no-holds-barred investigations of San Francisco's most vicious criminals, and he greatly prefers to work alone.

Harry Bosch, Michael Connelly, *The Black Echo* (1992) BK, UAB

Harry Bosch, a Los Angeles police officer with a troubling career path, takes center stage and finds it hard to play within the rules. His troubled past, including the murder of his mother and his Vietnam War experiences, leads him down a dark path from which it is hard for him to see the light

Inspector John Rebus, Ian Rankin, *Knots and Crosses* (1987) BK, UAB, CL

Ian Rankin's Rebus novels are powerful éxposes of the Scottish landscape, especially Edinburgh. Rebus, a prime example of the lone wolf cop, does not always work well with others. Yet his stunning ability to see through the veil of tears around a crime, past the political corruption that he must fight, and get to the essence of each mystery makes him a favorite with readers. There are 21 books in this series with the publication of Rebus' last case in *Exit Music* (2008).

Kinsey Millhone, Sue Grafton, *A is for Alibi* **(1991) BK, UAB, YA**
In 1982, Kinsey Millhone, the popular Santa Teresa, California, private eye, was created by Sue Grafton. With the publication of *U is for Undertow* in 2009, the series presumably has five more books to go. Kinsey, the traditional lone wolf detective, has an interesting support system in her relationship with her landlord Henry Pitts. As Kinsey ages approximately one year for every two books published, the series has slowly slid from contemporary to historical. Grafton has vowed that Kinsey will never appear on the silver screen or your television set.[2]

Prey, John Sandford, *Rules of Prey* **(1989) BK, UAB**
John Sandford's Lucas Davenport is a man slightly off-center in the beginning of this series as he is the only member of the police department's Office of Special Intelligence. Working alone, he chases serial killers of the worst variety. With the publication of *Wicked Prey* in 2009, there are now 19 novels in this series, and Lucas is now in the Minneapolis Bureau of Criminal Apprehension.

Sin City, Frank Miller, *Dark Horse Presents: Sin City* **(1991) GN, MV, YA**
Marv, a noir tough guy, finds the girl of his dreams, an incredible beauty named Goldie. But on their very first night together, Goldie is murdered. Marv sets out on a lonely mission to uncover her killer and avenge her, a journey that takes him through the bars and back alleys of the city.

Partners

Throughout the history of crime stories, relationships between two individuals have been a popular staple. While the relationship can be adversarial, as between detective and criminal, the focus is generally on the two detective partners who work together. Paired together in investigation after investigation, they find their individual skills are helpful but their pooled resources insure that justice is served.

The pattern was established early in the history of mystery with the idea that the great thinking detective needed a faithful partner and chronicler to tell his or her story. When Arthur Conan Doyle decided that Sherlock Holmes's stories would be relayed by Dr. Watson in five short story collections and four novels, he created a relationship that became as important to the series as the case that would be solved. Viewers of Sherlock Holmes adaptations know that there are many, including the recent film *Sherlock Holmes* with Robert Downey Jr. as the master detective and Jude Law as Dr. Watson, which focuses on their relationship. Cop partners have been a staple of television shows since its inception and often appear in movies as well as the many famous print partners.

Cagney and Lacey, **(1981–1988) TV**
Two female officers faced challenges from both the criminals and their department each week. Originally a "made-for-television" film in 1981 with Loretta Swit as Christine Cagney, the television series starred Sharon Gless as Cagney and Tyne Daly as Mary Beth Lacey. Dealing with crime and women's issues, the series was groundbreaking in both its attempts to show the pressure on women in the workforce but also on the issues that were affecting the country at the time.

Dalziel and Pascoe, Reginald Hill, *A Clubbable Woman* **(1970) BK, UAB, TV, CL**
Reginald Hill's series set in Yorkshire, England, features two officers of the law, Andy Dalziel and Peter Pascoe. To say that Dalziel challenges his contemporaries is an

understatement, but it is the long-suffering Pascoe who must deal with the situation and he provides the charm to the stories. Often involved in the cases is Pascoe's wife Ellie, who adds another dimension to the emotional challenges; she also occasionally contributes to the solving of the crime. Since 1996, there have been 12 television incarnations of this series, with Warren Clarke as Dalziel and Colin Buchanan as Pascoe.

Dragnet (1951–1959) TV

Joe Friday (Jack Webb) and Bill Gannon (Harry Morgan) of the LAPD starred in one of the earliest cop TV shows, *Dragnet* (1951–1959). The show featured their stoic attempt to disassociate their personalities from the search for "just the facts."

Inspector Morse, Colin Dexter, *Last Bus to Woodstock* (1975) BK, UAB, TV, SH

In *Last Bus to Woodstock* (1975), author Colin Dexter introduced Chief Inspector Morse and his faithful partner Sergeant Lewis. Morse, an intellectual with a complex personality not unlike Holmes, needs his Lewis for grounding and to keep him from getting into too much political trouble. Lewis keeps the investigation focused because he is from a working-class background that differentiates him from most of the people he encounters on their investigations in the Oxford environment. This pair's last print appearance was *The Remorseful Day* (1999). Television viewers can see John Thaw and Kevin Whately in 12 seasons of *Inspector Morse* and more of Sgt. Lewis in the spinoff production, *Lewis* (2006).

Lethal Weapon, *Lethal Weapon* (1987) MV, YA

For sheer laughs, the feature-length film adventures of Martin Riggs (Mel Gibson) and Roger Murtaugh (Danny Glover) in the four *Lethal Weapon* movies cannot be beat. These cop partners struggle to work together as each would rather be a lone wolf, but without each other they cannot solve the crimes.

Private and Professional Detectives: the Eccentric and Unusual

Somewhere between the police who should be solving crimes and the amateur who realistically should have nothing to do with a murder lie the private and professional detectives who legitimately have a reason to be within the circle of an investigation. With the freedom to act outside the normal police procedure, they are heroic individuals driven to find out who did it. Sherlock Holmes was one of the first professional detectives on the scene and still continues to be popular as evidenced by his hundreds of appearances in books, TV, and movies. This group includes private eyes, detectives for hire, consultants, bail bondsmen, and even judges—just about anyone with a legitimate reason to be involved in crime solving who is not a member of the local police force. And many private and professional detectives (just like Holmes) are a bit on the eccentric side. The list below features some of the more unusual characters found in crime stories.

Chet and Bernie, Spencer Quinn, *Dog On It* (2009) BK, UAB, YA, SH, RS, AP

One of the new dogs on the block is Chet the Jet, former police dog and partner in the Little Detective Agency with human Bernie Little. When a teenager named Madison goes missing, it is the special communication between man and canine that solves the mystery in this well-received first novel. The entire book is narrated by Chet and includes only his doggy point of view, which also stays true for the sequel, *Thereby Hangs A Tail* (2009).

Dresden Files, Jim Butcher, *Storm Front* (2000) BK, GN, TV, UAB, AP
As Chicago's only licensed wizard and PI, Harry has his hands full consulting for the Chicago PD and running his own business. Harry works for both the human and supernatural communities, and as the series progresses, he becomes more deeply involved with the local werewolves and vampires, not to mention his ever-helpful pixie informants. Adapted into a short-lived TV series, the Dresden Files has also been successfully turned into a series of graphic novels.

Monk, Lee Goldberg, *Mr. Monk Goes to the Firehouse*, (2002–2009) TV, (2006) BK, UAB
For one of the quirkiest characters to become a detective, viewers will want to sample *Monk* starring Tony Shalhoub as the damaged detective. Psychologically wounded by the death of his wife in a car bomb, Monk has retired from the police force, but is reluctantly coaxed back to solving crimes as a private detective. However, he is nearly overwhelmed by his own obsessive-compulsive disorder. Monk debuted in 2002 and its eighth and final season concluded on December 4, 2009.

***The Rockford Files* (1974–1980) TV**
For fans of the private detective, it does not get much better than *The Rockford Files* with James Garner as Jim Rockford. The television series (1974–1980) and subsequent made-for-television films featured a rather laid-back detective who lives in a trailer at the beach and still deals with his father's issues about parenthood.

Spenser, Robert B. Parker, *The Godwulf Manuscript* (1973) BK, UAB, TV, CL
Robert B. Parker's Spenser has become the modern male icon for the private detective. Set in Boston and featuring a cast of support characters that include the original bad-boy sidekick, Hawk, and the faithful companion, Susan, this series has now seen 36 entries with the publication of *Rough Weather* (2008). Viewers too can get their fill of Spenser; he has appeared on television in a number of formats, including *Spenser: For Hire* with Robert Urich (1985–1988) and some made-for-television movies that starred Urich and Joe Mantegna.

Stephanie Plum, Janet Evanovich, *One for the Money* (1994) BK, UAB, YA
When Stephanie Plum burst onto the crime fiction scene, it was like a breath of fresh air had energized the mystery. Funny yet slightly skewed, Janet Evanovich's character proved to be popular with readers as she faked her way through the bail bondsman industry while trying to balance a desire to be with two different men. Her quirky sidekicks and relatives also enliven the books.

V. I. Warshawski, Sara Paretsky, *Indemnity Only* (1982) BK, MV, UAB
While V. I. Warshawski made one film appearance in the rather pedestrian movie *V. I. Warshawski* (1991, with Kathleen Turner), Sara Paretsky's books are some of the best currently being published. V. I., a hard-boiled detective, often puts herself at risk to solve crimes. Her manner can even cause her loyal supporters, like Dr. Lotty Herschel, to question her ethics.

The Criminals

Some readers and viewers enjoy watching the exploits of those who commit the crimes rather than those assigned to catch them. English readers enjoyed the criminal exploits laid out in the pages of *Newgate Calendar*, an early tabloid that published the criminal exploits of the incarcerated. Some of the earliest written crime adventures were the memoirs of Eugène François Vidocq, a criminal who was the original "set a thief to catch a thief" detective when the French made him the first director of the *Sûreté Nationale*. In 1828, a four-volume autobiography detailed his life so far, but like many modern memoirs, it was semi-fictionalized. Vidocq's real-life exploits inspired a play by Balzac and Hugo's *Les Miserables* (1862), By the time the 1890s rolled around, the world was ready for a series of criminal adventures about the loveable A. J. Raffles, the gentleman thief created by E. W. Hornung. Stories of criminals can also be capers as they strive to commit their big jobs and get away from the cops. On the other side, just as many of these stories have a dark noir tone and a doomed protagonist.

Cain, James M., *The Postman Always Rings Twice* (1934) BK, UAB, MV, CL

Noir fiction features characters that are doomed from the beginning of the tale often because of one bad choice. The early master of this technique is James M. Cain. His novel *The Postman Always Rings Twice* tells the tale of a man whose open line is a classic: "They threw me off the hay truck about noon." The serendipity of his arrival at the right dinner where he meets the right woman to commit the right crime is legendary in the noir field. Filmed often, a great version to watch is the 1946 adaptation with John Garfield as Frank Chambers and Lana Turner as Cora Smith.

Dexter (2004) TV, BK, UAB, RS

The Dexter series, created by Jeff Lindsay starting with *Darkly Dreaming Dexter*, features a blood-splatter expert working for the Miami Metro Police Department. While that might normally get this character an entry in the private and professional detectives category, what keeps him here is that Dexter is also a serial killer. However, his redeeming quality is that he only kills people who are killers themselves. Filmed for Showtime as *Dexter* with Michael C. Hall as your favorite psycho, the show's fourth season aired in 2009 and a fifth was scheduled for 2010.

Double Indemnity (1943) MV, UAB

Insurance salesman Walter Huff arrives at the Nirdlinger household to renew a policy; he walks out immersed in a plot with the beauty Phyllis Nirdlinger to murder her husband for the double-indemnity funds in his insurance. The classic film noir version written by Raymond Chandler and directed by Billy Wilder was released in 1944 with Fred MacMurray and Barbara Stanwyck in the starring roles.

The Godfather, Mario Puzo, *The Godfather* (1969) BK, UAB, MV, SH

This best-selling novel told the story of Don Vito Corleone, the head of a mob family in New York. When this novel was adapted to the movies (*The Godfather*, 1972), the brilliance of Marlon Brando in the lead and the quality of the production surrounding him led to the film being considered one of the greatest movies ever made. Fighting the odds, the sequel (*The Godfather II*, 1974) is equally beloved. There is also a third film (*The Godfather III*, 1990) in the trilogy.

Hannibal Lecter, Thomas Harris (1981) BK, UAB, MV
Thomas Harris's Hannibal Lecter is better known as Hannibal the Cannibal. After his first appearance in *Red Dragon*, he catapulted to fame in 1988 in *The Silence of the Lambs*, and two more novels followed. The fascination with this serial killer has led to a number of films, including with *Manhunter* (1986, with Brian Cox as Hannibal); the Anthony Hopkins's roles in *The Silence of the Lambs* (1991, with an Academy Award to Hopkins as best actor), *Hannibal* (2001), and *Red Dragon* (2002); and the latest incarnation, *Hannibal Rising* (2007), with young actors playing a developing psycho.

Moore, Alan, *From Hell* (2000) GN (2002) MV
Moore's noir-laced crime graphic novel retells the story of Jack the Ripper, focusing on the events that led up to the murders in Whitechapel, as well as the subsequent cover-ups. Critically acclaimed among fans and critics, *From Hell* is considered a modern masterpiece.

***Ocean's Eleven* (2001) MV, YA**
Danny Ocean (George Clooney) gathers together a star-studded crew to pull off the greatest heist Las Vegas has ever seen—emptying the vaults of the three largest casinos of more than $150 million all at the same time. With quirky characters and plenty of humor, this action movie stands out from the crowd and is one of the better heist movies of the twenty-first century.

***Road to Perdition*, Max Allan Collins and Richard Piers Rayner (2002) GN, (2003) MV**
Based on a graphic novel by Max Allan Collins and Richard Piers Rayner, *Road to Perdition* is the story of a mob hit man who has to seek revenge when he finds himself on the outside of the protected circle of the family. Starring Tom Hanks as Michael Sullivan, the film also stars Paul Newman as John Rooney, the head of this family.

***The Sopranos* (1999–2007) TV**
For viewers who liked the Godfather movies, there is a logical successor: Tony Soprano (James Gandolfini) from the HBO series, *The Sopranos*, created by David Chase. From the very first episode where Tony seeks help from a psychiatrist, a new and modern twist is added to the classic mob tale. With great writing, the New Jersey setting, and a wonderful ensemble cast, this show shocks as well as entertains.

***Thomas Crown Affair* (1999, 1968) MV**
Pierce Brosnan and Rene Russo star in the modern-day remake of a wealthy man bored with his collections and money who manages to steal a valuable painting from a New York museum. But an art detective (Russo) is hot on his trail and may even be able to reveal his secret. The double dealing as Crown steals the painting, tries to outwit the art investigator, and then masterminds a complicated plan for its return make for a fascinating look into the criminal mind.

***The Wire* (2002–2008) TV, AP**
Although extensively about the police, *The Wire* (2002–2008) devotes as much time to the drug empire that plagues the people of Baltimore and the young men and women who work for them. Completed after five seasons in 2008, this award-winning series included many episodes written by big-name crime writers George Pelecanos and Dennis Lehane. One of the actresses, Felicia Pearson, has written a

memoir, *Grace After Midnight* (2008), about her real-life experiences growing up in Baltimore and her early involvement with gangs and violence.

Plots

In the days of the golden age of mystery fiction, the purpose of mysteries was to write a story with a well-constructed plot with lots of clues and some red herrings. While it is reasonable to say that most crime and mystery readers today read for character, there is still an expectation that some care will be given to presenting a baffling case with some clues for the reader to follow.

Forensics

Mysteries that focus on the forensic details and investigations are an important and popular subset. While the characters in these stories are often forensic examiners or other experts, the focus of the tale around the process of forensic investigation sets these stories apart and makes their plots unique.

CSI: Crime Scene Investigation (1999–) TV, SH
This popular TV series was first based in Las Vegas, but was so well received that spin-off shows taking place in New York and Miami have since been added. Each show details the work of a group of highly qualified forensic specialists as they tackle seemingly impossible crimes. Forensic technology and cutting-edge techniques are common elements.

Dr. Siri Paiboun, Colin Cotterill, *The Coroner's* Lunch (2004) BK, RS, AP
Outside of the United States, one of the most memorable medical examiners is Dr. Siri Paiboun, the reluctant but spry 70-something national medical examiner in 1970s Communist Laos. With few supplies and minimal training, Siri sets about his work with dedication and drive, and is assisted by an oddball cast as well as his own dreams and visions of ghosts.

Kay Scarpetta, Patricia Cornwell, *Post Mortem* (1993) BK, UAB, CL
With the advent of the Kay Scarpetta series by Patricia Cornwell, forensic evidence and those who work in that industry have become popular series heroes. Scarpetta begins her series as the chief medical examiner for the state of Virginia; but during the series, she lives in additional states while holding down a series of forensics-based jobs.

Quincy, M.E. (1976–1983) TV
Viewers who desire another forensic-viewing experience can turn to the *Quincy, M.E.* (1976–1983), which starred Jack Klugman as the coroner. Not unlike other detective heroes, it is Quincy's inability to look away from suspicious evidence and his dogged and determined investigations that eventually reveal the truth.

Roman Empire, Ruth Downie, *Medicus* (2007) BK, UAB, AP
Roman medical officer Gauis Russo takes a job in Roman Britain as a way to escape his ex-wife and his family debts. Soon after his arrival, Russo investigates the death of a barmaid, earning him the reputation of the doctor who likes to look at dead bodies. While not a certified forensic specialist or medical examiner, Russo is the

closest the Roman Empire has at the far reaches of the empire, and his new reputation ensures that all dead bodies come to his attention.

Temperance Brennan, Kathy Reichs, *Deja Dead* **(1998) BK, UAB, TV, SH, YA**
Another female forensics specialist, Temperance Brennan, was created by Kathy Reichs. Temperance, a forensic anthropologist, splits her time between Montreal and North Carolina, not unlike the author herself. She is often involved in crimes with multiple deaths and is occasionally assisted by love interest Detective Andrew Ryan. There are 11 books in this series with the publication of *Devil Bones* in 2008. When a decision was made to purchase the rights to Reichs' books for a television program called *Bones* (2005 to the present), Emily Deschanel was cast as Temperance.

Police Procedurals

For much of the history of crime fiction, the police were relegated to the role of the foiled sidekick, the ineffectual investigators one-upped by the amateur, or they were designed to function more like an independent or amateur detective. In the mid-1950s, Ed McBain (pseudonym of Salvatore Albert Lombino, later Evan Hunter) developed a police department on the island of Isola (a pseudonym for Manhattan) called the 87th Precinct. His intent in each of his 54 books was to have a police department solve multiple crimes using real police methods. This respectful innovation in crime fiction put "procedurals" on the map and led to a number of developments, including the police procedural as a fully fledged plot type that has never fallen out of favor with readers or viewers. As opposed to the lone wolf police discussed in character types, books with this plot type feature several police employees, with an ensemble-type case. The focus in these stories is not on one particular character or crime but on the entire cast of police officers, their lives at work and at home, and all the cases they are juggling as part of day-to-day police work.

Initially popular in print, this plot type soon became a staple of television as shows mirrored this ensemble approach to storytelling in *Hill Street Blues* (1981–1987), *Law & Order* (1990–), *NYPD Blue* (1993–2005), and *Homicide: Life on the Street* (1993–1999). This plot type has been less popular in movies, which may be due to the complex and serial nature of these stories.

The list below highlights a current trend in the police procedural staple: crime in the big city. While many of the titles are set in the city, others have a "big city" feel in the mood, tone, and crimes, as the "big city" crimes of drugs and violence spread into the countryside.

Detective Inspector Huss, Helene Tursten, *Detective Inspector Huss* **(2004) BK, YA, AP**
Helene Tursten's Swedish series has Detective Inspector Huss directing a dedicated police team and dealing with the crimes of modern Sweden, starting in *Detective Inspector Huss* (2004) and continuing in *Torso* (2006) when body parts start washing up in Sweden and Denmark. *Torso* has been adapted for TV in Sweden, but is not yet available in the United States.

Hill Street Blues **(1981–1987) TV, CL**
Viewers who enjoy procedurals rejoice at *Hill Street Blues*, a 101-episode series and a wonderful example of television done right. Following the daily lives of a precinct in an inner city, it featured the stories of multiple characters and many storylines.

Hollywood Station, Joseph Wambaugh, *Hollywood Station* (2006) BK, UAB, MV
Joseph Wambaugh, a career Los Angeles police officer for 14 years, turned to writing and became a best-selling author. With 14 police novels so far, including the three-part Hollywood Station series, he has set the bar for the realistic portrayals of police behaviors and mores. Six of his stand-alone novels have been filmed, including *Fugitive Nights* (1993) and *Echoes in the Darkness* (1987).

Inspector Lynley, Elizabeth George, *A Great Deliverance* (1988) BK, UAB, TV
Elizabeth George's Inspector Mysteries series has an ensemble feel to it because the stories often focus on either Chief Inspector Thomas Lynley or his sergeant Barbara Havers. While their cases are often convoluted and contain meaningful psychological motivation, they are reinforced by the backstory about the two police officers and their complicated personal lives. There are 15 books in the series, ending with *Careless in Red* (2008). For viewers, the BBC filmed *The Inspector Mysteries* from 2001 to 2007.

Inspector Van Veeteren, Hakan Nesser, *Mind's Eye* (2009) BK
Volatile and talented detective VV, as he is known to his fellow officers, leads a dedicated team of police officers as they hunt killers across modern-day Norway. VV is more likely to shout and rage than be depressed and glum, but his team knows his quirks and are happy to work with him. VV solves crimes only with the help of his entire team, and its characters are nearly as well developed as his. However, Nesser does not neglect the point of view of the criminals, and the interplay between the two makes for engaging plots.

Kurt Wallander, Henning Mankell, *Faceless Killers* (1997) BK, UAB, TV
Ystad, Sweden, is home of Detective Inspector Kurt Wallander. Henning Mankell's nine-book series offers a bleak and often-grim look at police work and modern society as Wallander, along with a dedicated team, copes with crimes against immigrants, intra-European Union smuggling of people and goods, and his own reluctance to accept the increased importance of women and technology in modern police work. Kenneth Branaugh stars in the new BBC miniseries adaption of series books *Firewall*, *One Step Behind*, and *Sidetracked*.

***Law & Order* (1990–) TV, SH, CL**
Law & Order is one of the longest-running TV shows and is about the police and district attorneys who attempt to solve crimes and convict criminals in New York City. Focusing on the homicide squad, the original show split the time fairly equally between the investigation by the police and the trial run by the district attorney. The Law & Order franchise has since expanded to include *Law & Order: Special Victims Unit*, with a focus on sex crimes and youth victims, and *Law & Order: Criminal Intent*, which is a Holmesian-inspired show with more of a whydunit than whodunit focus and a quirky-but-brilliant lead detective.

Logan McRae, Stuart MacBride, *Cold Granite* (2005) BK, AB, RS, AP
When readers first meet him in *Cold Granite* (2005), Logan McRae, a detective sergeant with the Aberdeen police, has just recovered from being stabbed 23 times. His cases involve the worse side of humanity, from child and prostitute murderers to arsonists and serial rapists. While challenged by his cases both physically and mentally, McRae manages to stay attentive to the job and loyal to his co-workers, despite the challenges of his two bosses, DIs Insch and Steele.

NYPD Blue **(1993–2005) TV**

NYPD Blue, another ensemble show with a strong cast of characters portrayed by great actors, was an early and groundbreaking procedural show. This show ran for 12 seasons from 1993 to 2005 and in its time was notorious for partial nudity in scenes that featured the home lives of the main characters.

<u>Powers</u>, **Brian Michael Bendis and Michael Avon Oeming,** *Who Killed Retro Girl?* **(2006) GN, YA**

Homicide detective Christian Walker is teamed up with a rookie to solve the mystery of the death of Retro Girl, one of the most popular superheroes of all time. With a hard-boiled tone and noir-style illustrations, this graphic novel is at its heart a police procedural, as Walker gives his all to solve the murder. It is an engaging mix of supernatural, noir, and fantasy crime fighting.

Humor

Is it disrespectful of the dead to make light of their fate? Writers have been finding humor in death since the inception of the crime story. The humor involves self-deprecation and irony and is usually found focused on the inept abilities of the detective hero and/or an eccentric cast of assisting characters. Humorous plots have long been popular with readers as they provide a lighter view of the worst sides of humanity. Humorous plots are often but not always found in cozies or with amateur detectives; black humor can also play an important role in caper and criminal stories. Humorous stories are just as likely to be on TV shows or in movies as printed books, showing its broad appeal as a plot type.

The Andy Griffith Show **(1960–1968) TV, CL**

How about the hometown wit of a small-town sheriff in *The Andy Griffith Show*? Spun around the idea that a strong personality can overcome any crime, the sheriff deals as much with the crooks as he does with his young son and his housekeeper. The ensemble cast includes a goofy deputy and some precious small-town characters whose strengths and flaws boosted the show's appeal.

Barney Miller **(1975–1982) TV**

The precinct, led by Captain Miller, featured the interaction between the cops on their shift with input from the criminals they are trying to take off the streets. While the intent of the series was to be humorous, the show was not shy about using more serious emotions to their proper effect.

Bernie Rhodenbarr, Lawrence Block, *Burglars Can't be Choosers* **(1977) BK, UAB, MV**

Bernie Rhodenbarr debuted in a series by Lawrence Block in *Burglars Can't be Choosers* (1977). Bernie extends the tradition of the gentleman thief forced to be a detective by occasionally finding a body for which he is not responsible at the scene of his latest burglary. As the series progresses, Bernie buys a bookstore but cannot leave his life of crime and murder. Viewers may be interested in seeing the only filmed version of this series by watching *Burglar* (1987) with Whoopi Goldberg as Bernice "Bernie" Rhodenbarr.

Hetty Wainthroppe Investigates **(1996–1998) TV**

Viewers who like the style of Precious Ramotswe would be well served to turn to *Hetty Wainthroppe Investigates*. Hetty is a PI in the tradition of the golden age of

British mystery stories. A pensioner who decides to redeem the life of a teenager by using him as a partner in her newly founded agency, she is so capable that she eventually converts her husband, who originally thought she was a lunatic to try to be a detective.

Meg Langslow, Donna Andrews, *Murder with Peacocks* (1999) BK, UAB, SH
Meg Langslow, Donna Andrews's amateur detective, shares the same humorous appeal as Janet Evanovich, including punny titles. Meg is a sculptor/blacksmith by trade but murder always finds a way to her doorstep. With a large extended family that challenges her, a love life that keeps her hoping, and a wild series of circumstances in each plot, readers will find plenty of laughs in this series.

Monk, Lee Goldberg *Mr. Monk Goes to the Firehouse* (2002–2009) TV, (2006) BK, UAB
The humor in this show comes from the fact that circumstances have made this former police detective a victim of obsessive-compulsive disorder. He continues to work as a private consultant with the hope of overcoming his disease and returning to the San Francisco police force. The irresistible weirdness of a character like Adrian Monk means that viewers will want more than the 119 episodes of the TV series. So they turn to novelizations and original stories produced by writers like Lee Goldberg who has written seven novels about Monk

Nursery Crimes, Jasper Fforde, *The Big Over Easy* (2005) BK, UAB, RS, AP
Detective Jack Sprat is happily married to his second wife (the first died of a heart attack because she "would eat no lean") and is partnered with Detective Sergeant Mary Mary, to solve the murder of Humpty Dumpty. This is a hilarious satire of classic crime novels, and Fforde also manages to concoct a clever (and rather unusual) mystery plot with fascinating characters. As head of the Nursery Crimes Division (NCD), Jack continues to investigate crimes against those of dubious reality in *The Fourth Bear*.

***Ocean's Eleven* (2001) MV, YA, SH**
The remake of the 1960 heist film stars Brad Pitt and George Clooney as leaders of an 11-man gang with a plan to empty the cash vaults of three Las Vegas casinos at the same time. They may be criminals but they are both likeable and funny and their exploits as they plan and attempt their caper will keep viewers smiling. This film spawned two sequels, *Ocean's Twelve* and *Ocean's Thirteen*.

Spellmans, Lisa Lutz, *The Spellman Files* (2007) BK, UAB, YA
The Spellman Files introduced readers to the crazed family of private investigators at Spellman Investigations. The focus is on Izzy Spellman, who started her detective career at age 12, but at age 28 would like to ease her way out of the business. Instead, she finds herself knee-deep in family related problems and clients who challenge her while making readers laugh out loud. With her precocious teenaged sister Rae (just one of many wacky family members), boyfriend problems, and even an arrest record, Izzy keeps readers laughing through *Curse of the Spellmans* (2008) and *Revenge of the Spellmans* (2009).

Stephanie Plum, Janet Evanovich, *One for the Money* (1995) BK, UAB
Out of desperation, Stephanie Plum forces her way into her cousin Vinnie's bail bondsman business as a bounty hunter. Having worked as a lingerie salesperson, she

has little experience but plenty of spunk; thus we have the comic element necessary to drive this series in best-seller-dom. For most of the series, Stephanie finds her heart bouncing back and forth between Ranger, the bad boy bounty hunter and the more stable Joe Morelli, a cop. Outrageous plots, comic relatives and a fast pace.

Whydunits, or Psychological Crime Stories

While series titles take on major issues and themes while developing characters over several books, stand-alone crime novels often have as one of their purposes an opportunity for their author to tackle a big picture issue that may overwhelm a series character. Readers can think of books like this not as whodunits but as rather whydunits. Some series books are also whydunits, but are much more rare than stand alone whydunits. Several of the authors who specialize in this plot type are highlighted in the list below. The pacing of these stories varies from leisurely to fast as the inside look into the lives of criminals, victims, and suspects creates an interior-oriented story.

Cracker (1993–1996) TV
For viewers of whydunits, the British show *Cracker* starring Robbie Coltrane as a forensic psychologist is a must-see. The show ran for four seasons from 1993 to 1996.

Cook, Thomas H. *The Chatham School Affair* (1996) BK, UAB, AP
Thomas H. Cook, a wonderful regional and historical writer, laces his novels with criminal issues. In print since 1980 with a total of 24 novels to his credit, Cook has been critically recognized numerous times for his stories. In the Edgar Award-winning *The Chatham School Affair* (1996), readers find a brilliant historical novel that observes how life in a Cape Cod town changes when a new schoolteacher arrives. One of these novels slowly peels away the layers until all is revealed.

Hammesfahr, Petra, *The Sinner* (2008) BK
German thriller writer Hammesfahr's American debut is a dark and gripping thriller about a seemingly normal young woman who suddenly stabs a neighbor at a local beach as her horrified family watches. Police officer Grovian is intrigued by the young woman and feels that there is something deeper; this drives his personal investigation into her murky past. Hammesfahr's *The Lie* is a less psychological but equally gripping story of two women who look eerily alike but whose lives have little in common.

McDermid, Val, BK, UAB, TV
McDermid is an excellent crime writer whose stand-alones are often award nominees and winners. Readers may wish to try *A Place of Execution* (1999). Journalist Catherine Heathcote interviews retired Detective Inspector George Bennett about the disappearance of a 13-year-old gil from a gated community in 1963. Thirty years have passed, but time does not keep the inspector from trying to find the truth behind the disappearance, nor does it mean the witnesses are any more willing to reveal their stories than they were during the original investigation. Viewers will be pleased to learn that British ITV filmed a three-part adaptation of this novel in 2008, with Juliet Stevenson as Heathcote. Readers may also enjoy McDermid's new stand-alone thriller, *A Darker Domain*, about a coal-mining community and another cold case.

Rendell, Ruth (Barbara Vine) BK, UAB, MV, CL
Having written 24 stand-alone novels under her own name and an additional 13 under the pseudonym of Barbara Vine, she has maintained the quality of her work by focusing on issues that echo the crime and present a theme without preaching. An example of this is an especially compelling book for all readers, *A Judgment in Stone* (1977). The opening line is a classic: "Eunice Parchman killed the Coverdale family because she could not read or write." Viewers can see either the British version *The Housekeeper,* which was released in the United States as *A Judgment in Stone* in 1986, or the French version, *Une Femme de Ménage* (2002).

<u>Tony Hill and Carol Jordan</u>, Val McDermid, *The Mermaids Singing* (1995) BK, UAB, TV, SH
Val McDermid has delivered hit after hit in a long career that includes series work and stand-alone novels. Her series fiction character, criminal profiler Tony Hill, often teamed with DCI Carol Jordan, is a fine hero in a series that emphasizes the why as much as the who. Viewers can enjoy this character as portrayed by Robson Green in the TV series *Wire in the Blood* (2002 to the present).

<u>Vik and Stubo</u>, Anne Holt, *What is Mine* (2006) BK, AP
Anne Holt's two-book series may initially appear to be a police story, but the focus is much more on the crimes, the criminals, and the victims. A master of the psychological thriller, only two of Holt's books have so far been translated into English; hopefully more will follow. In *What is Mine*, Joanne Vik, a former FBI profiler, works with Detective Adam Holt to solve a series of child kidnappings.

Walters, Minette, BK, UAB, TV
With 13 novels to her credit, Minette Walters has mastered psychological suspense; fans of Ruth Rendell's writing will also enjoy this author. Her 1993 book *The Sculptress*, a compelling novel of suspense, starts as a traditional story about a journalist who reluctantly agrees to interview a murderess. When Rosalind Leigh meets Olive Martin, she slowly becomes intrigued—and horrified. Ultimately, the nature of truth is up for debate in this novel. Viewers will revel in the wonderful BBC production with Pauline Quirke as Olive.

Theme: Settings and Sense of Place

True variety in modern mysteries comes in their settings. The best crime stories are able to combine a strong sense of place with a puzzling story and engaging characters. Settings can be modern day and range from your own background to the most distant of countries, or they can be set in any historical era. This dizzying array of options lends amazing variety to crime stories, and the unique nature of crime stories lends them well to stories that equally balance plot, characters, and sense of place.

Scandinavia

One of the most popular places for mysteries right now are the Scandinavian countries (Finland, Sweden, Norway, Denmark, and Iceland), which is fortunate as mysteries have a long tradition in these countries, and there are many great authors being translated for English readers. Despite the relative non-violent nature of Scandinavian society, many of these stories feature the most horrific crimes and staggering violence, and focus on issues of racism and poverty in countries with otherwise very high standards of living. Ystad, Sweden, home of Kurt Wallander, is not in fact one of the most violent small cities in Sweden; the amount of actual crime and violence is much lower, with relatively few murders, rapes, and kidnappings. The other theme in these stories is that of the other, whether a non-European immigrant, racism, religious intolerance, or the covering-up of poverty and loneliness, these stories all have a dark undertone that makes them unique and represents an important part of their appeal.

The immense and growing popularity of these stories can be seen in the recent move from books to other media, notably the BBC miniseries of Henning Mankell's *Kurt Wallander* series. Several of the other series have been filmed for European audiences, and English versions should soon become available for American fans. Graphic novel versions have yet to be produced, but the popularity of these settings and the illustrated format make them a good bet for the future.

Erlendur, Arnaldur Indridason, *Jar City* (2005) BK, AP
Iceland's answer to Kurt Wallander is Erlendur, a depressed, miserable, and overworked cop; his daughter is a junkie and his son is in jail. Erlendur solves uniquely Icelandic crimes in a country so small that not only does everyone know everyone else, they are likely related to each other as well. Murders are rare, especially those that can't be explained away by drunken fights or domestic violence, but disappearances are not; they are Erlendur's investigative specialty. Reading true crime accounts of missing people is his only hobby.

Harry Hole, Jo Nesbo, *Redbreast* (2007) BK, RS, AP
If Kurt Wallander was the trademark brilliant-but-flawed detective of the 1990s, then Harry Hole is his twenty-first-century counterpart. Working the mean streets of modern-day Oslo, Hole chases down serial killers all while battling a serious drinking problem. Throughout the series, Hole is searching for The Prince, an arms dealer who killed his partner, even as he faces the deep chill of winter or the overwhelming heat of summer. Hole's Oslo is a dangerous place, but also his beloved home. Harry's first case in *Redbreast* is a complex thriller and police procedural with ties to Norway's Nazi history.

Hoeg, Peter, *Smilla's Sense of Snow* (1993) BK, MV, CL
Half Danish, half Inuit Greenlander, Smilla Jasperson is spurred into action when the one person that she truly cares about, a small boy who lives in her apartment building, is found dead, apparently fallen off a roof. Smilla doesn't believe that it could possibly have been an accident and uses her father's money (that she otherwise refuses to touch) and her own intimate knowledge of snow and ice to discover the killer and uncover a conspiracy. Hoeg's beautiful and evocative descriptions of the changing winter weather conditions can make any reader chilly. The 2002 movie version received mixed reviews.

Inspector Sejer, Karin Fossum, *Don't Look Back* (2002) BK, UAB
Karin Fossum's Norwegian series is a thrilling combination of psychological crime story and police procedural, featuring tall, thin, and grieving widower Konrad Sejer and his assistant, Jakob Skarre. Devoting equal amounts of time to victims, criminals, and the police, Fossum's series explores the dark side of humanity and the impacts of tragedy upon the survivors. The sense of place comes less from the

descriptions of the settings (mostly small towns near Oslo) than its depiction of Norwegian society and culture. Several of the books have been serialized for TV in Norway.

Inspector Vaara, James Thompson, *Snow Angels* (2010) BK, RS, AP

The first book in a new series, *Snow Angels* introduces Inspector Kari Vaara, a small-town police chief in northern Finland, and his American wife, a ski-resort operator. With Finland as possibly the most exotic and unknown of the Scandinavian countries, especially the Lap culture of the far north, the point of view and questions from Vaara's wife will help American readers feel more comfortable. In *Snow Angels*, the characters struggle through the two weeks of complete darkness around the Winter Solstice, a time when the dark and brutal winter brings out the worst in people, including the brutal murder of a visiting young actress.

Kurt Wallander, Henning Mankell (1993) BK, UAB, TV, SH, CL

Kurt Wallander was the first Scandinavian detective many American readers met, and the diabetic, depressed, and driven detective was an immediate favorite. Mankell's novels have introduced millions to the bleak but beautiful countryside of Skane in southern Sweden as Wallander, head of the violent crimes unit of the Ystad, and his team travel the countryside in their investigations of horrific modern crimes. In his novels, Mankell not only evokes the landscape of Skane, but also reveals the plight of modern Swedish society, a welfare state and a monoculture suddenly forced to deal with non-European immigrants, racism, and violence. Kenneth Branagh skillfully portrays the moody Swede in a three-part miniseries for the BBC that was filmed in and around Ystad

Martin Beck, Maj Sjowall and Per Wahloo, *Roseanna* (1967) BK, UAB, TV, MV, CL

The first depressed Scandinavian detective for American readers, Martin Beck was a hit in Sweden in the 1960s and 1970s and has had a small American audience ever since. The breakout of Scandinavian crime stories in the 2000s has led to renewed interest in these classic police procedurals. Beck is constantly distressed by the modern crimes in his beloved Stockholm and leads a dedicated team of police officers in his unending quest for peace. Many of the 10 books in the series have been filmed or turned into TV shows in Sweden and Germany, and a few are available in the United States.

Millennium, Stieg Larsson, *The Girl with the Dragon Tattoo* (2008) BK, UAB

Despite his late entry into the American crime market, Larsson has managed to become one of the most popular and successful of the translated authors. Readers have flocked to the stories of prickly investigator Lisbeth Salander, starting with her investigation of a long-missing heiress that delves into modern Sweden's dark underbelly. While the talented journalist died shortly after completing the final book in the trilogy, Danish versions of all three books have already been filmed, and an American studio has optioned *The Girl With a Dragon Tattoo*. American fans won't have to say goodbye to Lisbeth at the end of *The Girl Who Kicked the Hornet's Nest* (2010).

Rebecka Martinsson, Asa Larsson, *Sun Storm* (2005) BK, UAB, YA

Overworked junior legal assistant Rebecka has never told her colleagues of her childhood in far northern Sweden, nor of her involvement in a fundamentalist church, but when a childhood acquaintance is murdered, she returns home. In midwinter, northern Sweden is perpetually dark and freezing cold, and Rebecka finds herself involved in a dangerous investigation of a charismatic preacher and the small town drawn into his hands.

Historical Crime Between the Wars: 1918–1939

The golden age of mystery writing is now a popular historical era. Stories set in the 1920s and 1930s are one of the most popular new subgenres in historical mystery. These interwar decades included both Prohibition and the Great Depression in America, plus post-war trauma and debt in Europe lent themselves well to mysteries, whether they tie into the lasting effects of the Great War like the Maisie Dobbs series or highlight the fast-living flapper lifestyle of Phryne Fisher. The rise of organized crime in the United States made for great movies like the classic *Bonnie and Clyde*.

Bonnie and Clyde (1967) MV, CL

A classic American film, this is the story of the bank-robbing couple Bonnie and Clyde and their gang. Set in the early 1930s, this slightly romanticized but basically true story of a young couple that falls in love and robs banks together has become an American legend. The movie version highlights the poverty, desperation, and lawlessness of the 1930s.

Daisy Dalrymple, Carola Dunn, *Death at Wentwater Court* (1994) BK, UAB

Daisy, an emancipated young woman in post-war Britain, begins work as a journalist only to stumble across a corpse while at a country house party, and so begin her adventures as an amateur detective in the 1920s, which have continued across 18 books. The dual ambience of the 1920s in Europe, the Great Depression, parties, unemployed and traumatized soldiers, and fast-living flappers come across strongly in this cozy series.

Jason, *The Left Bank Gang* (2005) GN, YA

In Jason's alternate world, novelists Ernest Hemingway, F. Scott Fitzgerald, and James Joyce are cartoonists, as comics are considered the ultimate art form. Set in 1920s Paris, Hemingway leads the group of Bohemian artists in a bank robbery that turns into a caper tale. Jason's illustrations make much of the 1920s setting and hint at a noir tone with subdued colors and spare drawings.

King, Laurie R., *Touchstone* (2008) BK, UAB

In this stand-alone novel set in 1926, U.S Department of Justice investigator Harris Stuyvesant comes to Britain in search of a terrorist behind a series of American bombings. Thick with period detail, the atmosphere is made even heavier as the threat of a general strike looms across England and violence threatens the country house where Harris is using his last resources to find the mastermind. Complex and thrilling with both social commentary and an exciting plot.

Maisie Dobbs, Jacqueline Winspear, *Maisie Dobbs* (2003) BK, UAB, RS

After working as a nurse at a casualty-clearing station in France, Maisie returns to college, finishes her studies, and apprentices with Maurice, a famous psychologist and detective much in demand by the British government. In 1929, Maisie strikes out on her own, starting her an investigative agency and moving into her own flat. Maisie's investigations are leisurely paced as she is a thoughtful and thorough detective, and nearly all her work ends up tying either directly into the war or the still-lingering aftermath.

Mary Russell, Laurie R. King, *Beekeeper's Apprentice* (1996) BK, UAB, YA

Mary Russell is only 15 when she meets the retired master detective Sherlock Holmes, but she helps revitalize his life, and he makes her a detective of note as he recognizes her as his intellectual equal. Working as a team, their cases are set in the 1910s and 1920s in England, the Middle East, India, and San Francisco.

Phryne Fisher, Kerry Greenwood, *Cocaine Blues* (1987) BK, UAB, SH, AP
Bored with English aristocratic country life after working as an ambulance driver during World War I, a pilot during the influenza epidemic and an artist's model in Paris, Phryne takes on work as a private detective and moves to Melbourne, Australia, in early 1928. After busting a cocaine ring, Phryne continues high-risk investigations using her skills from her days as an ambulance driver and a pilot, all while dressed in the height of fashion and enticing beautiful young men to her bed. The series highlights the flapper lifestyle with plenty of cocktail recipes and dress descriptions, but does not shrink away from the darker aspects of 1928 Australia, like racism and unemployment. All of Phryne's books are also available in outstanding audio versions read by Stephanie Daniel.

The *Untouchables* (1987) MV, CL, SH
This is a semi-fictionalized account of treasury agent Elliot Ness's battle against crime kingpin Al Capone. Set in 1920s Chicago at the height of Prohibition-motivated organized-crime warfare, Ness sets out to take down Capone with the help of an elite, handpicked team and little help from other agencies, as corruption is rampant at all levels of law enforcement in Chicago. With lots of action, this period piece plays up the 1920s setting with just the right cars and costumes and emphasizes the lawless nature of the Prohibition-era Chicago.

Across the Fifty States

Stories with a strong sense of place can be found in crime tales that feature the many different states and regions of the United States. Books series are especially popular, with multiple series set in just about every state in the nation. The list below highlights just a few of the best, with a focus on those that are strongest in their settings and sense of place. Fans enjoy reading and watching stories of their home locations, as well as places they have visited or hope to visit.

Anna Pigeon, Nevada Barr, *Track of the Cat* (1993) BK, UAB, SH, AP
Park ranger and law enforcement officer Anna Pigeon investigates crimes in national parks and forests across the United States. From her first murder in the Guadalupe Mountains of West Texas, to later investigations on Lake Superior, Ellis Island, and the caves of Lechuguilla, Anna's adventures take her to many of America's most beautiful locations. In each of her adventures, the unique features of the park play an important role in the mystery, leaving readers feeling as though they too have visited these special places. Viewers who enjoyed Ken Burns's recent documentary *National Parks* will like reading about many of the same places profiled in the series.

Dave Robicheaux, James Lee Burke, *Neon Rain* (1987) BK, UAB, MV, CL
James Lee Burke's series featuring Dave Robicheaux is a fascinating character study with a hard-boiled atmosphere. Initially moving to New Iberia, Louisiana, to escape the challenges that perplexed him as a police officer, Robicheaux soon decides that life as a lawman is for him, so he joins the sheriff's office. Each of his cases pits him against a hardened criminal and also against the social mores of his region. For

viewers, *Heaven's Prisoner* (1996, with Alec Baldwin as Robicheaux) and *In the Electric Mist* (2009, with Tommy Lee Jones as Robicheaux) have been filmed.

Homicide: Life on the Streets (1993–1999) TV, AP

Filmed in and around the Fells Point neighborhood of Baltimore, this was David Simon's first crime TV show to feature the rough-and-tumble life of the cops and criminals of Baltimore. With all of the shooting taking place on location, for viewers the sense of place is strong, both in the setting and the many characters with local accents

Joe Leaphorn and Jim Chee, Tony Hillerman, *The Blessing Way* (1990) BK, UAB

Set in the Four Corners area of the United States, the Joe Leaphorn and Jim Chee mysteries have long been a leader in mysteries with a strong sense of place. Leaphorn, a detective for the Navaho Tribal Police, is ably assisted by Chee, and their investigations are steeped in the southwestern setting and Navaho culture.

Lee, Harper, *To Kill A Mockingbird* (1960) BK, UAB, MV, CL, YA

Considering this is Lee's only book, it is an amazingly accomplished novel with its blend of coming of age, southern sensibilities, and courtroom drama. The novel deals with issues still in the forefront of our national debate about who we are: race, class, and the application of the law. Choosing to tell the tale from the perspective of a young child, Lee details all that an adult reader needs to know about what happened in Maycomb, Alabama, during that summer. When filmed (*To Kill a Mockingbird*, 1962) with Gregory Peck as Atticus Finch, the story only gained strength and the movie became an instant classic.

Nathan Active, Stan Jones, *White Sky, Black Ice* (2005) BK, RS

Alaskan state trooper Nathan Active is an Inuit born in the northwestern village of Chukchi but was raised by white parents in Anchorage and is dismayed to find his first trooper posting is his familiar home village. Northwestern Alaska, a dark, cold, and often stormy place, is beautifully rendered by Jones, both in terms of the locals who like living there and in Active's gradual acceptance of village life.

Spellman Files, Lisa Lutz, *The Spellman Files* (2007) BK, UAB, YA, RS

Twenty-year-old Izzy Spellman has been working for the family PI business since she was 12, and she thinks it might be time to move on (and move out—she lives in a tiny studio on the third floor of the family home). Hilarious and at times touching, the story of the crazy but close Spellman family, from youngest prodigy daughter Rae to the uncle who inspired the term "lost weekends," is set in San Francisco, a city clearly well known and loved by the author. Izzy's investigations take her across town and through the various neighborhoods on foot, by car, and via public transport.

The Wire (2002–2008) TV, AP

If *Homicide* was the crime show that first introduced viewers to Baltimore, then *The Wire* is the show that made Baltimore famous. Set not just in Fells Point, but across the entire city (and sometimes even into the suburbs), *The Wire* was filmed on location, and through the characters, their accents, and the uniquely Baltimorean story lines, viewers are treated to a TV series where the setting is a character in itself. Gritty and violent, but also realistic, *The Wire* is from the point of view of both the police (beat cops and detectives) and the people who run drug empires the police are trying to take down.

Around the World: International Crimes and Criminals

Despite Scandinavia being the most popular setting for international crime stories, there is no shortage of books, movies, and TV shows set in other parts of the world. These stories not only have the elements of a good crime story, but also introduce readers and viewers to exotic locales. Even though the settings may be unusual, many of the crimes and characters will be familiar to mystery fans. This is an emerging area and so far has mostly been limited to print; however, its burgeoning popularity means it is likely to be increasingly seen in other formats in the future. Audiobooks have already made the leap, with many titles already in audio versions and many more being released every year.

Aimee Leduc, Cara Black, *Murder in the Marais* (1999) BK, UAB, YA, AP

Twenty-something private investigator and computer expert Aimee Leduc, along with the help of impeccably dressed dwarf partner Rene, takes on cases that lead them into the secrets of each of Paris' neighborhoods, starting with the old Jewish quarter, the Marais. With the focus of each book on a single arrondissement, the sense of place is not only strong, but vivid, as each book includes maps of the featured district, and readers can follow Aimee street by street as she travels, always well dressed in high-fashion flea-market finds.

Chief Inspector Marion Silva, Leighton Gage, *Blood of the Wicked* (2008) BK

Set in modern-day Brazil, Chief Inspector Silva heads up a national crimes unit that investigates crimes that spread across local jurisdictions. Each book finds Silva and his team crisscrossing Brazil from the steamy jungles to the richest suburban enclaves in search of serial killers and kidnappers. Gage's series authentically portrays life in modern-day Brazil, and each book highlights another fascinating aspects of the largest country in South America.

Dr. Siri Paiboun, Colin Cotterill, *The Coroner's Lunch* (2004) BK, SH

Dr. Siri has been a lifelong and dedicated worker for the community cause in Laos and now that the war is finally over and the Communists are in charge, he hopes only for a quiet retirement. But resources are scarce in 1970s Communist Laos, and Dr. Siri is forced into accepting the job of national coroner despite his complete lack of experience. A partially burned (and badly outdated) French textbook and the coroner's assistants help out with the day-to-day work, and the job soon becomes a perfect excuse for Siri to investigate suspicious deaths. Since he also sees and sometimes talks to spirits, he feels compelled to uncover the real killers. His work as the only coroner in Laos takes him to all corners of this little-known country.

Faith Zanetti, Anna Blundy, *Bad News Bible* (2008) BK, RS

Faith Zanetti is a hard-boiled female foreign correspondent whose work takes her around the world, from Jerusalem to post-Soviet Russia. Each book introduces a new location for Faith, but her tough-as-nails attitude and hard-drinking lifestyle stay consistent. Here the sense of place comes through the crimes and informants that make each entry unique.

Hamish Macbeth, M. C. Beaton, *Death of a Gossip* (1985) BK, UAB, TV, CL, AP

M. C. Beaton's beloved Highland cop features in more than 25 books and multiple seasons of a TV show. Hamish loves his northwestern Scotland home, especially his home/police station in Lochduch. Since a promotion means having to move to dreadful Strathbane, Hamish does all he can to solve murders but still duck promotion.

Here the strong sense of place comes through in Beaton's loving descriptions of northwestern Scotland and in Hamish's actions to keep his home and job and preserve the safety of his village friends, many of whom (like Archie, the fisherman or Angela, the doctor's wife) appear in book after book.

Inspector Chen, Qui Xialong, *Death of a Red Heroine* **(2003) BK**
Detective Inspector Chen Cao, a poet and translator, was assigned to the police force during the years of Deng Xiaoping and gradually not only accepts his new job, but comes to love his work. The story is set in the mid-1990s and later a Shanghai setting as Communism moves into the modern era. As a highly trusted detective, Chen's cases often involve sensitive government issues and as such reflect life in one of modern China's largest cities. But the effects of the Cultural Revolution on Chen, his victims, and the suspects is never far from the surface.

Inspector Ghote, H. R. F. Keating, *A Perfect Murder* **(1964) BK, UAB, MV, CL**
Keating's highly acclaimed series was one of the first international mysteries to gain a large audience, and the first book, *A Perfect Murder*, has also been turned into a well-received movie. Keating's books are set in the second half of twentieth century in Bombay, where Ghote is a happily married, middle-class police detective. Despite being based entirely on research from England, his descriptions of Bombay and the overall sense of place are so strong that few readers believed that he had never visited Bombay until many years later.

Nergui, Michael Walters, *Shadow Walker* **(2009) BK**
Set in modern-day Mongolia, Walter's series features Nergui, a police officer working in administration on the hunt for a serial killer. In *Shadow Walker*, Walters introduces a story whose events are even more complex than they initially appear and a Harvard-educated investigator who is deeply in tune with his beloved country.

No. 1 Ladies Detective Agency, Alexander McCall Smith, *No. 1 Ladies Detective Agency* **(1998) BK, UAB, TV**
Precious Ramotswe runs Botswana's first and only ladies detective agency with the help of her secretary, Mma Makutsi, and an ever-growing cast of friends and family members. This cozy series faithfully and lovingly describes life in modern Botswana through the various cases taken on by the No. 1 Ladies Detective Agency. Sometimes criticized for lacking strong central mysteries, these character-driven stories are fun and enjoyable, even while falling on the light side. Lisette Lecat's readings of the audiobook are highly acclaimed as she reads in an atmosphere setting with a lilting African accent. The series has recently been filmed for TV.

Making Connections

The best authors make links with the stories that they tell. Throughout this chapter, connections have been made to elements of character, setting, plot, and theme that extend the experience of the story being told. In this section, you'll examine authors who blend elements from multiple genres to tell their stories. This section aims to help advisors make connections with readers new to crime or crime readers looking to expand their boundaries and explore new and related works.

Crime for Fantasy Fans

The recent merging of genres and genre blending has been especially popular in combinations of crime and fantasy. The overall popularity of fantasy and supernatural creatures has easily spread into the crime genre, as supernatural crimes and criminals are easy to imagine, as are fantasy crime fighters. The stories highlighted below include a mix of stories set in the real world, alternate worlds, and completely fantastical worlds. Those new to fantasy crime might want to start with the stories closest to their preferred genre, whether it is crime or fantasy. Not only is the genre blend currently popular, it is likely to stay so over the next few years. The stories have transitioned not only into other media, but into popular culture in general, as evidenced by the success of HBO's adaption of the Sookie Stackhouse/Southern Vampire series, a somewhat cozy series set primarily in northern Louisiana in a world where the invention of synthetic blood has allowed vampires to join mainstream society.

Batman (1939) GN, MV, TV

While often thought of as just a caped superhero, *The Bat-Man* originally debuted in Detective Comics #27. The caped crusader's original purpose was to defeat the criminal elements of Gotham City. Batman stood on the outside of all systems and was held in suspicion by the forces of the law. In comics since 1939, in graphic novels, in television programs, and through a series of films, this costumed character has sustained a long career as a crime fighter.

Dresden Files, Jim Butcher, *Storm Front* (2000) BK, UAB, GN, TV, SH, AP

Chicago PI Harry Dresden also happens to be a professional wizard for hire. These hard-boiled crime stories are set in a world where Dresden needs to protect the innocent population from the magical elements of which they are ignorant, all while trying to make a living as a PI. A 13-episode television series was filmed in 2007 with Paul Blackthorne as Dresden, and a graphic novel version of *Storm Front* was released in 2008.

Detective Inspector Chen, Liz Williams, *Snake Agent* (2005) BK

Wei Chen is assigned to the 13th precinct of Singapore 3 in an alternate world that allows free travel between heaven, hell, and Earth, which is why Chen is paired with demon detective Zhu Irzh to investigate a soul-trafficking scheme. Chen's also married to a demon, and while there are plenty of supernatural elements in this international mystery, modern Chinese culture and customs still shine through.

Gentleman Bastards, Scott Lynch, *Lies of Locke Lamora* (2006) BK, UAB, RS, YA, AP

Lynch's debut is the first in a projected trilogy about master thief and con artist Locke and his gang of street children. Despite living in a completely fantastical world, magic is basically nonexistent, and other than location names, there is little to distinguish this from any other Renaissance-era city. Locke is planning the biggest heist of his career, but falls afoul of the local crime lord. This caper story may seem light on the surface but has dark undertones that give depth and complexity to both the characters and the story.

Joe Grey, Shirley Rosseau Murphy, *Cat on the Edge,* (1996) BK, UAB, AP

When tomcat Joe Grey witnesses a murder, it shocks him into speaking English. Now he must rely on another speaking cat named Dulcie to save one of his lives and find the killer. She becomes his life partner, and when you add in Joe's bachelor human family, Clyde, and Dulcie's retired human, Wilma, the cast is complete. Joe, a hard-boiled detective, just happens to be a cat, but he's dedicated to solving crimes and says of himself in *Cat Playing Cupid*, "I'm just a cop in cat skin going under-cover," as he prepares to break into a suspect's home and toss it for clues.

Roger Rabbit, *Who Framed Roger Rabbit?* **(1988) MV**
Viewers who have never sampled the wild adventures of private detective Eddie Val-liant are in for a treat. While Valliant is human and the detective on the case, his client is the cartoon star, Roger Rabbit. This story exists in a world where cartoons are real, both as victims and as villains, even though they are forced to live in Toontown.

Sookie Stackhouse/Southern Vampires, Charlaine Harris, *Dead Until Dark,* **(2001) BK, UAB, TV, RS**
Sookie is a psychic cocktail waitress in a Louisiana town when a handsome vampire sweeps her off her feet and into many adventures with the undead, who desire to use her talents for their own agendas. Balancing humor, romantic suspense, and vampire action, these novels charm and captivate readers. Viewers were pleased when the series was brought to the small screen in the television series *True Blood* (2008 to the present) with Anna Paquin as Sookie.

True Crime for Nonfiction Readers

Nonfiction reader's advisory has become more popular in recent years. True crime is an important part of this, but also has had a long-term audience with crime readers in gen-eral. Since the late Victorian era, true-crime stories have entranced lovers of both crime and nonfiction.[3]

America's Most Wanted **(1988–) TV**
The television series *America's Most Wanted* (1988 to the present) recreates crimes in order to help police departments around the nation locate and apprehend criminals on the loose. It is hosted by John Walsh, a man whose personal story makes the show additionally compelling, who each week appeals to the viewers to help get these criminals behind bars.

Bendis, Brian Michael, *Torso: A True Crime Graphic Novel* **(1999) GN**
Federal agent Elliot Ness and his team investigate a series of killings that have resulted in headless torsos washing up on the banks of Lake Erie. While this true crime was never officially solved, Bendis offers an intriguing solution. In addition to Bendis's illustrations, a photo essay is included in the 2001 edition.

Berendt, John, *Midnight in the Garden of Good and Evil* **(1994) BK, UAB (1997) MV**
Midnight in the Garden of Good and Evil: A Savannah Story is a wonderful example of how a work of nonfiction can read like fiction, maintaining a high level of interest and producing as many appeal factors as its counterpart novels. The story of a 1981 incident in Savannah, Georgia, holds the reader in suspense regarding whether the action was one of self-defense or was murder. Its cast of characters equals any that would be developed by the skills of a novelist. The book uses its setting to perfection and delivers an evocative look at this wonderfully weird southern society. The 1997 film starring John Cusack and Kevin Spacey is equally enjoyable.

Capote, Truman, *In Cold Blood* (1966) BK, UAB, MV, TV, CL, SH

In Cold Blood: A True Account of a Multiple Murder and its Consequences is often cited as the first modern work of nonfiction that used a novelist's approach to relating the story. Imagined dialogue credited to characters based on interviews, as well as liberties with the portrayal of the events and the motivations behind them, may have undermined the integrity of the work, but no one can reject the power of the book as it was written. This stark story of a Kansas killing by two drifters still compels readers today. Viewers will enjoy the Richard Brooks film by the same title from 1967 starring Robert Blake and Scott Wilson as the two drifters. The story was retold in a 1996 television film starring Anthony Edwards and Eric Roberts as the murderers. Phillip Seymour Hoffman starred in the 2005 movie, *Capote*, which covers the writing of the book, among other things.

Cops (1989–) TV

True-crime fans can also get a dose of reality television by tuning in the long-running program *Cops* (1989 to the present). With camera crews ready to ride along with working members of various police departments around the nation, viewers get a firsthand account of the nature of the bad boys on the street.

Junger, Sebastian, *A Death in Belmont* (2007) BK, UAB

Journalist Junger delves into the mystery of the Boston Strangler after learning of family connections to the killer, including a possibly related death that took place in his own childhood neighborhood. Junger lays out all the evidence, but since DNA was never taken from the two suspects, and multiple confessions further muddy the waters, no one can ever be completely certain who really killed Junger's neighbor.

Larson, Erik, *Devil in the White City* (2003) BK, UAB

The Devil in the White City: Murder, Magic, and Madness at the Fair That Changed America by Erik Larson (2003) exemplifies how readers can be drawn into a story about crime yet experience a whole other subject. Most true-crime readers who gravitated to this book opened it because they were interested in H. H. Holmes, the infamous serial killer who roamed the United States plying his trade before settling down in Chicago during the World's Fair of 1893. What surprises readers about the work is that the building of the fair by architect Daniel H. Burnham is an equally interesting story. While the workers race against the clock and impossible odds to finish, they open a window into a world that shows the invention of items that we take as ordinary today. A major feature film based on this book is rumored to be in development.

Treasury of Victorian Murder, Rick Geary, *A Treasury of Victorian Murder* (1987) GN, YA

Geary recreates and investigates true crimes from the Victorian era in this graphic novel series. The first book is a collection of three stories, and later titles focus on famous criminals like Jack the Ripper and Lizzie Borden. His illustrations skillfully evoke the Victorian Era of contrasting grime and prudishness in black-and-white illustrations.

Mysteries for Fans of History

Lucky for their fans, historical mysteries have been a long-running popular trend. These stories combine historical detail and settings with traditional mysteries. Characters vary widely from private detectives to amateurs and even feature the occasional police officer. Historical mysteries have become so popular they can be found in all time periods from ancient Rome to Renaissance/Reformation Europe and throughout the nineteenth century. All fans need to do is identify their favorite period and they will have plenty of choices. With the abundance of historical mysteries, the list below reflects only a small selection.

Amelia Peabody Emerson, Elizabeth Peters, *Crocodile on the Sandbank* (1973) BK, UAB, CL, AP
Possibly one of the most popular historical-mystery series, the 18 (and counting) books cover more than 40 years in the saga of the ever-expanding Emerson family of Egyptologists, from Amelia and Emerson's first meeting and murder. Murder and violence always seem to show up, and Amelia never hesitates to investigate, whether it's their long-time rival Sethos, ever-present tomb robbers, or even bumbling fellow archeologists. With plenty of humor and mad-cap adventures, this series is set from 1880s through the 1920s in several different Egyptian locations. While all the stories include historical details, the books set during World War I are especially powerful (*The Golden One* and *Lord of the Silent*).

***Chinatown* (1974) MV**
If viewers wish to watch a popular historical-mystery movie in the noir tradition, a good candidate is *Chinatown* starring Jack Nicholson as private detective Jake Gittes and Faye Dunaway as the glamorous Evelyn Mulwray, who hires Jake to investigate her husband's extramarital affair. Set in Los Angeles during the heyday of the fictional private detective, it also tells the dark story of how Los Angeles acquired the water system it needed to become a major urban area. This movie placed nineteenth on the American Film Institute's original Top 100 American Films list.

Inspector William Monk, Anne Perry, *Face of a Stranger* (1990) BK, UAB
The William Monk stories feature a detective without a memory trying to solve crimes in Victorian England. His adventures begin with *Face of a Stranger* (1990); the latest is the eighteenth, *Execution Dock* (2009).

Mistress of the Art of Death, Ariana Franklin, *Mistress of the Art of Death* (2007) BK, UAB, SH
Twelfth-century England, ruled by King Henry II and Eleanor of Aquitaine, is a haven for Jewish coroner and unconventional woman Dr. Vesuvia Adelia Rachel Ortese Aguilar. Educated in Sicily, Adelia is first summoned to England to secretly discover who is killing Christian children in Cambridge. But Henry becomes fond of his secret investigator and Adelia discovers reasons of her own to stay in this foreign land.

Silver Rush, Ann Parker, *Silver Lies* (2008) BK, RS, AP
Inez Stannert came to Leadville, Colorado, with her husband, small son, and their partner to set up a saloon and profit from the 1879 silver rush. But her husband soon disappears and her son is unable to thrive in the harsh, high-altitude conditions. Left alone with African American Abe, Inez ably takes on the duties of running the saloon and even manages a high-stakes poker game for the city's most powerful men. But crime runs rampant during the silver rush, and in *Silver Lies*, Inez finds the body of a friend outside the back door of her establishment. The 1879 setting is both unique and clearly evoked from the snow in June to the dangerous and filthy work of mining.

Thomas and Charlotte Pitt, Anne Perry, *Cater Street Hangman* (1979) BK, UAB
One of the leading figures in historical mysteries is Anne Perry, who has made a number of efforts in various time periods that all illustrate the wonderful integration of fact and fiction. Her Thomas and Charlotte Pitt series begins with *The Cater*

Street Hangman and features the struggling police officer, Thomas Pitt, in late Victorian England. When he meets Charlotte Ellison, he finds a soul mate and investigative partner, and together they feature in 25 stories.

Toby Peters, Stuart Kaminsky, *Bullet for a Star* (1994) BK, UAB

Stuart Kaminsky is an author who has created numerous series characters, but when he began his career, he started with a humorous series starring a struggling PI named Toby Peters. While the style is humorous, what holds this series together is the historical setting of a 1940s Hollywood movie colony. Each of the books features one or more famous celebrities who have difficulties and need Toby's help. With its light, entertaining tone, the series begins with *Bullet for a Star* (1977, featuring Errol Flynn); the latest entry is *Now You See It* (2004, featuring Harry Blackstone).

World War I, Anne Perry, *No Graves as Yet* (2003) BK, UAB

Perry has also written five novels in a series that features the effects of World War I on England as much as it does the individual crimes in each book.

Conclusion

While the Scandinavian import craze will eventually wane, this is a subset of crime stories that is always likely to have a loyal audience, as Scandinavian crime writers are masters at their craft. Additionally, Scandinavian crime stories have a unique tone and mood that is related to, but not the same as, American or English noir or police stories. Readers who love these will continue to look for them; expect them also to be asking about movie and television versions, as many of the best series have been filmed in Europe.

International stories are also likely to become increasingly popular, and not just from Western European countries, but all over the world. Witness the attention and praise of Mario Silva's series set in Brazil (*Dying Gasp*, 2009) or Anna Blundy's *Faith Fairchild series* about a foreign correspondent. Expect English-speaking writers to increasingly use international settings and more international authors to be translated and published for the English-speaking market. E-books are making it easier for publishers to obtain English-language rights for multiple countries once the initial translation has been made.

Lastly, historical settings will likely continue their popularity, and while the current trend of stories set in the 1920s and 1930s will likely wane, another historical era will take its place. The popularity of an historical era tends to represent the current situation—the party atmosphere of the 1920s and the Depression of the 1930s may very well remind readers of the tech stock boom of the 1990s as well as today's recession.

In terms of formats, audiobooks will continue to be popular, and demand will probably only increase. Simultaneous release of print and audio versions is becoming increasingly common, and libraries need to be prepared for patrons who only listen to popular series. There is nothing to indicate that crime-related audiobooks will continue to be anything but the most popular genre in the years to come. Playaways, with their ease of use and library-friendly packaging, are becoming a must-buy format.

Graphic novels in particular and illustrated formats in general have started to become popular in crime publishing, and this is an area likely to see a great increase over the next few years as younger readers who have grown up reading and enjoying illustrated books become adult lovers of crime stories. The same goes for computer and video games—expect to see more versions and more demand.

There can be no doubt that crime stories are here to stay, whether in print, on the silver screen or the small, in graphic novels, or even computer and video games. Crime stories will always be with us for the simple reason that humans will always commit crimes and the rest of us will wonder about them.

Resources for Librarians

Cords, Sarah Statz. *The Real Story*. Westport, CT: Libraries Unlimited, 2006.
"Mystery Writers of America." http://www.mysterywriters.org/.
Niebuhr, Gary Warren. *Make Mine A Mystery*. Englewood, CO: Libraries Unlimited, 2003.
Niebuhr, Gary Warren. *Caught Up in* Crime. Englewood, CO: Libraries Unlimited, 2009.
"Stop You're Killing Me! A Web site to Die For . . . If you Love Mysteries." http://www.stopyourekillingme.com/.

Endnotes

1. Ross, Catherine Sheldrick. "Adult Readers" in *Reading Matters: What the Research Reveals About Reading, Libraries, and Community.*
2. "Sue Grafton: Interview." http://www.suegrafton.com/interview.htm.
3. Cords, Sarah Statz. "Chapter 3: True Crime," in *The Real Story*. Westport, CT: Libraries Unlimited, 2006.

2

Everything Fantasy
Jessica Zellers

In this chapter, Jessica Zellers covers the genre of fantasy. Defining fantasy as any story that includes a supernatural or magical element makes for a lengthy and wide-ranging chapter with broad appeal. The "Plots" section reviews traditional high fantasy stories, fairy tales, fables, myths, and relationship-driven stories. This chapter also has a special section on settings, a key appeal of fantasy, which includes medieval European-inspired settings, fantastic cities, and urban fantasy. In the "Characters" section, Jessica discusses the fantasy archetype of the "chosen one," spunky females, lone wolves, and sexy bad guys. The theme of the fantasy chapter is paranormals, which includes sections on vampires, witches, psychic phenomena, and talking animals. The final section, "Making Connections," suggests fantasy for science fiction, romance, historical fiction, and mystery.

Introduction

Fantasy is a genre that everybody loves. The earliest human stories have fantastic elements, as seen in creation stories throughout the world. The universal story types—myths, legends, and fables—all pay homage to the fantastic, and even in today's technologically advanced society, fantasy enjoys broad appeal. The first stories that we hear as children, fairy tales, are a subgenre of today's fantasy; the classics of children's literature are predominantly fantastic. Even adults, many of whom stop reading fantasy past their teens, love to explore the fantastic in video games and movies. It is a universally popular genre.

Definition of Fantasy

"All fiction is fantasy," writes James Cawthorn in his introduction to *Fantasy: The Best 100 Books*. "In all its forms, including the historically recent 'realistic' novel, it springs from the human urge to fantasize."[1] Susan Fichtelberg refutes this very broad definition in *Encountering Enchantment: A Guide to Speculative Fiction for Teens*, noting that "these kinds of imaginative literature [fantasy, science fiction, and horror] stretch so far beyond the boundaries of what is known, they require a willing suspension of disbelief exceeding that required for realistic fiction."[2] Fantasy, science fiction, and horror—three related genres known collectively as speculative fiction—each steps outside of reality in their own way. Many people enjoy the spectrum of speculative fiction without discriminating between the genres, which lend themselves nicely to genre blending.

But fantasy has its own distinct appeal. It necessarily includes something—a setting, a character, or an action—that could not occur in the past, present, or future of the world as we know it. Good fantasy ignites the imagination. It can offer an escape from reality and can throw reality into sharp relief, inviting critical thought about the real world. Fantasy can be straightforward and uncomplicated, with entertaining stories to delight and distract children and adults from the mundane trials of everyday life. It can also be sophisticated and complex; see, for instance, the play that is arguably the greatest work of literature in the English language, Shakespeare's *Hamlet*. Detractors of the genre will please note that Hamlet has a nice long chat with the ghost of his dead father. Fantasy strikes again!

No definition of fantasy is complete without a discussion of J. R. R. Tolkien. It's safe to say that if you haven't read his Lord of the Rings books, you're not a fantasy fan. LOTR is the quintessential fantasy story against which all others are inevitably judged, because all of the standard tropes of fantasy (the epic quest, the battle of good against evil, the medieval setting, and the abundance of orcs and dwarfs and elves) are here—in the original books, in Peter Jackson's magnificent film adaptation, and in the various computer and video games.

A common misperception of the fantasy genre, however, is that everything is derived from Tolkien. To be fair, many have imitated Tolkien—though who can blame them? It sells. Medieval settings, mythical tropes, quest stories, and powerful artifacts are the staples of high fantasy, the subgenre directly inspired by Tolkien. Because of Tolkien's tremendous influence, this particular type of fantasy is often conflated with fantasy as a whole—and make no mistake, it is a perennially popular subgenre. It has endured since the mid-twentieth century and shows no signs of waning.

But there are many other types of fantasy, as we shall see in the course of this chapter. Some writers, such as China Miéville, deliberately distance themselves from Tolkienesque elements that have, for better or worse, become clichéd. Others interpret fantasy very loosely, bending the rules and turning conventions on their heads. K. J. Parker, for instance, writes books that have no fantastic elements save for the imaginary setting (and if that setting strikes you as awfully similar to pre-Industrial Europe, you'd be right).

Perhaps more than any other genre, fantasy lends itself to integrated advisory. People enjoy fantasy because it tickles the imagination, because they get to explore new thoughts and ideas and to experiment intellectually—so getting them to extend the exploration and try various media can be a piece of cake. Furthermore, fantasy has a strong presence in all the various media, from movies and television to traditional books and graphic novels to computer and video games.

When practicing integrated advisory for fantasy lovers, no matter the medium, it's important to remember appealing characteristics and how they manifest in the genre and its subgenres. Most people want an interesting story—but do they want an epic quest, a fairy-tale retelling, a revenge story, or some other type of narrative? How about characters? Do they want the standard figures of high fantasy, or something less familiar? Do they want to race through the story, or luxuriate over details? Do they want lyrical, dazzling prose or a more straightforward style? For that matter, do they prefer familiar words, or do they enjoy new, creative vocabularies? (Or completely new words and languages? Thanks, Tolkien.)

And with fantasy, setting is supremely important. Without Hogwarts, there would be no Harry Potter; without Middle Earth, there would be no Lord of the Rings. Setting is so very important that it often achieves equal status with the plot, fusing with the storyline so that it is impossible to separate the two. The hybrid blend of setting and fantastical plot is often what distinguishes fantasy from other genres, and it is this blend that draws in readers, gamers, and movie watchers.

Trends

Make no mistake: Tolkienesque fantasy is here to stay. Even if all the fantasy novelists of the world suddenly decided to break from the Tolkien tradition (and there's no sign that this would ever happen), fantasy in movies, television, computer and video games, and other media continues to reflect Tolkien's influence. Tolkien-style fantasy is conflated with *all* fantasy in much of the popular consciousness. The perception is incorrect, but it's not going away. You can expect to see variations on the Tolkien theme for as long as people continue to enjoy stories of good triumphing over evil.

But dedicated fantasy readers know that the genre is changing, even if casual fans haven't realized it yet. Standard hallmarks that were once conventional are becoming optional. Although not endangered, "pure" fantasy is making room on the shelf for stories that liaise with horror, romance, mystery, suspense, science fiction, literary fiction, and even the western (consider Emma Bull's novel *Territory*). The fantasy landscape is shifting in new and exciting ways; it is deliciously impossible for fantasy fans to keep up with it all, but in particular, keep an eye out for these genre blends and genre trends:

Paranormal and Urban Fantasy

Similar to contemporary fantasy, this is a type of fiction that takes a perfectly recognizable Earth and populates it with witches, wizards, werewolves, shape-shifters, demons, gargoyles, and most especially vampires. Romance occurs fairly often; sex occurs almost invariably. We can thank Buffy (and, more recently, the Twilight series) for the meteoric rise in popularity of the subgenre. This is one to learn about as it draws a younger and non-traditional audience to fantasy.

Core and upcoming authors: Stephenie Meyer, Patricia Briggs, Jim Butcher, Charles de Lint, Christine Feehan, Neil Gagman, J. K. Rowling, Kim Harrison, Sherrilyn Kenyon, and J. R. Ward

Realistic Fantasy

A close relative of political fantasy, realistic fantasy usually features a setting that resembles our own world's history and environment. Magical elements may be few (even nonexistent!), and they do not overshadow the larger story. The action and story are deliberate, thoughtful, and nuanced; the style and tone are grim, dark, and gritty. Expect the characters to be exceedingly well developed and the moral questions to be ambiguous.

Core and upcoming authors: R. Scott Bakker, Stephen R. Donaldson, Jennifer Fallon, George R. R. Martin, K. J. Parker, and Jack Whyte

Literary Fantasy

Elegant prose, sophisticated symbolism, thought-provoking scenes, and cerebral allusions are present in literary fantasy, as one would expect with any subgenre of literary fiction—but the standbys of fantasy (the magical, the surreal, and the paranormal) are there, too. The literary fantasy subgenre (and its cousins from the magical realism and surrealism traditions) lures in book snobs who would otherwise ignore fantasy—and it offers a richly rewarding experience for fantasy fans looking for deeper fare.

Core and upcoming authors: Amy Bender, Jonathan Carroll, Michael Chabon, Susanna Clarke, Lev Grossman, Ursula K. Le Guin, Miranda July, Gregory Maguire, China Miéville, and Haruki Murakami

Bearing all this in mind, let's take a look at fantasy in different media.

Traditional Print Books

Fantasy has been around as long as the written word—longer, in fact: tales of the supernatural and the fantastic dominated traditional oral narratives such as Homer's *Odyssey*, the epic poem "Beowulf," and the *Mabinogion*. Likewise, it could be argued that the debut work of Gutenberg's movable-type printing press, a Latin-language Christian bible, contained an abundance of fantastic elements. (But readers beware: one person's fantasy is another person's religious dogma. It is in poor taste to casually refer to a sacred text as a work of fantasy, even if the text contains elements of the fantastic.)

As for fiction novels and short stories, fantasy permanently established itself as a genre with the publication of *The Lord of the Rings* in 1954–1955, though a good number of fantasy works enjoyed success prior to that (including Tolkien's own 1937 work *The Hobbit*). Jonathan Swift's *Gulliver's Travels* (1726) was arguably the first proper fantasy novel, and Mary Shelley distinguished herself from the overwhelmingly male circle of writers in 1818 with *Frankenstein*, a novel that blended fantasy, science fiction, *and* horror. Other notable pre-Tolkien writers included Robert Louis Stevenson, Jules Verne, H. G. Wells, and Edgar Rice Burroughs.

In the post-Tolkien era, fantasy has thrived in the book format. Though fantasy books do not typically dominate best-seller lists in the way that suspense, thrillers, and mystery genres do, there are some mega-best-selling exceptions—J. K. Rowling's Harry Potter series, Stephenie Meyers's Twilight series, and Tim LaHaye and Jerry B. Jenkins's Left Behind series—which in turn spawned a fantasy publishing frenzy. When fantasy goes mainstream, nothing can stop it. But even the fantasy titles that generate more modest sales figures have a strong following of readers. The traditional printed book is the heart of the fantasy genre: it is the perennial stalwart, the medium that lures in readers from early childhood, the springboard from which other media so often make their start.

Graphic Novels and Manga

The development of graphic novels and manga as a format fed the development of fantasy as a genre—or is it the other way around? Trying to separate one from the other is futile and, frankly, ridiculous. The two mesh together to form a perfect union: it's impossible to talk about one without acknowledging the other.

Superhero comics, a direct ancestor of today's graphic formats, offered a wealth of fantasy material for readers in the mid-twentieth century. Puzzlingly, these stories—the most widely recognized genre within the graphic format—were not typically marketed as fantasy, despite featuring two of the hallmarks of the genre: the characters had supernatural powers, and the stories focused on the conflict between good and evil. These features continue to characterize the superhero comics and graphic novels of the present, and though publishers still don't normally market the books as fantasy, librarians would be wise to recognize the huge overlap in appeal between traditional print fantasy and superhero books.

Now, as any long-suffering comics fan will tell you, probably in an exasperated voice, there is more to the graphic format than just superheroes. Superheroes sustained the medium from the Depression through World War II and into the Cold War, but Art Spiegelman's *Maus* introduced a new kid on the block and a new type of "comic book." Spiegelman's tale of his father's imprisonment in Auschwitz heralded the advent of the graphic memoir, which continues to dominate the nonfiction side of graphic materials and to rake in the awards: *Maus* won a special Pulitzer in 1992, Marjane Satrapi's *Persepolis* was named a *New York Times* Notable Book in 2003, and Alison Bechdel's *Fun Home* was the best nonfiction debut of 2006, according to Salon.com.

Nonfiction graphic novels showed the world at-large that comic characters do not necessarily wear spandex. And though superheroes are still going strong, fiction graphic novels, like nonfiction, have expanded into cape-free territory. But even with superheroes taken out of the equation, fantasy is a dominating force in the medium. The most feted, popular graphic series ever, Neil Gaiman's Sandman, is fantasy. (Also horror, science fiction, and literary fiction, if you're interested.) Jeff Smith's perennially popular Bone series is a quest fantasy. A plethora of manga series are fantasy, including D. N. Angel, Ranma 1/2, and Ceres, Celestial Legend. Other fiction genres do well in the graphic format, but fantasy is the star—possibly because the setting of a book, which is so often crucial to the quality of a fantasy story, can be depicted with images, colors, and shades on the page.

Movies and Television

Prior to the 1990s, the kindest way to describe fantasy on the screen would have been "niche." A more accurate description would have involved language such as "crappy special effects" or "melodramatic acting" or "hokey stories." There was some good stuff out there, though. *The Twilight Zone* made people think, and *The Wizard of Oz* is one of the most beloved films ever produced. But for the most part, fantasy television shows and movies were viewed only by people with a strong tolerance for camp.

In the 1990s, however, fantasy films and television shows began to edge into the mainstream. *Xena: Warrior Princess* and *Buffy the Vampire Slayer* each had a healthy dose of silliness, but they gradually lured in folks who had otherwise avoided fantasy. (Of course, it helped that the lead actresses were hot.) On the big screen, viewers flocked to the serious acting and rich storylines of movies such as *Ghost*, *Groundhog Day*, and *The Sixth Sense*. And in the 2000s, three classics of fantasy literature made it to the screen in a big way. Tolkien's Lord of the Rings, J. K. Rowling's Harry Potter, and C. S. Lewis's Chronicles of Narnia were all adapted to film. People who'd never read the books or watched fantasy movies flocked to the theaters, and a new group of fantasy lovers was born.

It's a shame that fantasy was such a late bloomer in television and movies. The screen is a powerful medium for the genre; as with graphic novels, the setting can be developed and explored in ways that move beyond the printed word. And with the special effects of movies and television, some of the most riveting moments of fantasy stretch the mind in powerful new ways.

Computer and Video Games

Pong was not a fantasy game, nor *Snake*, nor *Tetris*, nor *Pac-Man*. But after this first batch of computer games, fantasy found a home in the game world, and it hasn't left since. The Nintendo Entertainment System, the first video game console in America that became more than a passing fad, owed its initial success to the popularity of *Super Mario Bros.* (1985), a quest story featuring castles, otherworldly creatures, powerful artifacts, and a princess in need of rescue. Since then other genres have become popular in computer and video games, but fantasy maintains a strong following among gamers.

Within the fantasy genre, role-playing games (RPGs) are especially popular. Descendents of the game *Dungeons and Dragons*, which is played with other human beings, electronic RPGs can be played alone or with others. These RPGs typically have all the trappings of the Tolkienesque high fantasy: there's a quest, a battle between good and evil, a medieval setting, and a smattering of dwarves and elves. RPGs appeal to fantasy fans not just because of these characteristics, but because they develop sophisticated elements of setting and plot. With good animation, an RPG can create a breathtaking setting—and with good writers, an RPG can feature a story as engaging as anything found in a book.

Plots

Just about every fantasy story ever created explores the struggle between good and evil. Pare away the details, and you'll see why people love fantasy: they want to know if good will prevail. It is the details, however, that make fantasy so enticing. What supernatural artifacts, spells, entities, and powers will the good guys possess and use? (And a more interesting question: what supernatural toys will the bad guys have?). Many works of fiction touch on the question of good and evil, if only in the abstract; fantasy takes that question and makes it cooler by adding magic.

When considering plot, Tolkien makes for a good starting place. Some fantasy fans want stories that evoke Tolkien, while others seek stories that distance themselves from epic quests. Some people long for stories where the struggle between good and evil is easy to follow; others prefer moral ambiguity. Some crave action and bloodshed and adrenaline; others have a taste for storylines that gently provoke thought and contemplation.

Traditional High Fantasy: Swords, Sorcery, and Quests

Love it or hate it, traditional high fantasy is inextricably linked to the broader genre of fantasy in the popular consciousness. Its familiarity is a turnoff for some, a major selling point for others. Storylines in the traditional subgenre feature a struggle between good and evil, with plenty of magic, spell-casting, and enchanted artifacts to spice up the narrative—and there's almost always a quest thrown in for good measure.

Blade of the Immortal, Hiroaki Samura (1994–) MN, TV, YA

"Shady past" doesn't even begin to describe the background of our hero, Manji. Before he gave up his evil ways, he caused the deaths of 100 samurai. Now he's trying to make up for past misdeeds by killing 1,000 bad guys. It's a tough chore, but fortunately Manji has an edge: no injury can kill him. Swordcraft, quests, curses, and epic battles between good and evil in eighteenth-century Japan make for a captivating, fast-paced manga series by Hiroaki Samura—and be sure to catch the anime version, too.

Bone, Jeff Smith, *Bone: Out from Boneville* (1991) GN, CGM, YA
At first glance, Jeff Smith's series of graphic novels might seem childlike. The uncluttered images and the enjoyable characters—including a princess, wicked bad guys, and the Bone cousins—make it appealing to children, certainly, but there is depth here that will draw in adult readers, too. In the best tradition of epic quest fantasy, the *Bone* books feature complex characters, a sophisticated setting, a richly developed story arc, and a host of moral uncertainties. Read the series in order, starting with *Out from Boneville*, and then have a good time playing the computer game.

Bradley, Marion Zimmer, *The Mists of Avalon* (1982) BK, TV, UAB, CL
Most of the conventions are present and accounted for—the swords, the sorcery, the medieval European setting—but Bradley offers a most unusual take on the Arthurian legends, presenting them with a focus on women and women's issues. Morgaine (that is, Morgan Le Fay) is a sympathetic character, along with the other denizens of the female-only Avalon. Goddesses, paganism, and matriarchal attitudes do battle with patriarchy and the misogynist interpretation of Christianity that threatens the old order. It's a feminist book, no doubt about it, but don't worry: there's plenty of chest-thumping, bodice-ripping, blood-spilling action keeping company with the feminist agenda.

***Fable* and *Fable II*, Microsoft Game Studios (1996, 2008) CGM, VGM, YA**
In *Fable* and its sequel, *Fable II*, all of our favorite conventions of traditional fantasy are present and accounted for. Medieval setting? Check. Dungeons, crypts, and caves? Check. Quests, prophesies, and mythical bad guys? Check. A mysterious character of unknown origins, destined to save the world? But of course—that's where you come in, after all, in this sprawling role-playing game. Start with the original *Fable* to get a feel for the setting and mythos of the world of Albion, or plunge directly into *Fable II* for a dynamic, delightfully open-ended quest-based adventure.

Goldman, William, *The Princess Bride* (1973) BK, MV, CGM, YA, CL
There's a little something for everybody in this cult favorite. Meet Buttercup, a low-born girl who turns out to be a princess, a wicked despot who would make her his queen, and a farmhand who pledges eternal love to Buttercup, at least until he's killed by a pirate, sort of. There's a decades-long quest for vengeance, a formidable giant who likes rhyming games, a pack of R.O.U.S. (Rodents of Unusual Size), and a variety of perilous landscapes, including the Cliffs of Insanity, the Fire Swamp, and the Zoo of Death. Packed with action, romance, comedy, magic, and good old-fashioned questing, *The Princess Bride* is clean enough for kids and clever enough for adults. If you've only seen the movie, read the book; if you've only read the book, see the movie; and don't forget to try the computer game.

Homer, *The Odyssey* (eighth-century BCE; translation by Robert Fagles, 1999) BK, MV, CGM, GN, UAB, CL
If you struggled through *The Odyssey* in high school or college—if you weren't lucky enough to have a teacher who made it fun—then it's time for a reappraisal. The mother of all quest stories, *The Odyssey* follows the fortunes of Odysseus as he travels for 10 years to return his wife Penelope in Ithaca. You've got gods, an evil

sorceress, nasty monsters, and plenty of sword action in this pillar of Western literature. Homer's epic poem is thousands and thousands of years old, but it's still going strong; even if really long ancient Greek poems aren't your thing, there are plenty of variations to suit your fancy, from graphic novels to audio versions.

Jones, Diana Wynne, *Tough Guide to Fantasyland* **(2006) BK, YA**
Satire or sacrilege, satire or sacrilege: which is it? Is Diana Wynne Jones's send-up of high fantasy a tribute to the subgenre or a good-humored parody . . . or maybe a little of both? By including every cliché known to humankind (and elfkind and dragonkind, etc.) Jones pokes gentle fun at the conventions established by Tolkien, from the mystical artifacts to the caricatured mystical races. Hardcore fans of high fantasy will like this book if they have a sense of humor, while those who've grown tired of Tolkien and his heirs will delight in Jones's clever spin.

A Song of Fire and Ice, George R. R. Martin, *A Game of Thrones* **(1996) BK, GN, UAB**
Recently, it's been hard to find a new fantasy novel that doesn't boast a cover blurb comparing the author to George R. R. Martin. Martin is hugely popular, and for good reason; he has managed to take the ingredients of high fantasy—the swords, the sorcery, the medieval setting, the human and non-human races—and turn them into a marvelous epic, simply teeming with heady details, political intrigue, and richly crafted characters. Think Tolkien, but grittier, with more emphasis on politics and less on magic. At the time of this writing, the novels are a series in progress, with two novella prequels (*The Hedge Knight* and *The Sworn Sword*) available as traditional print and as graphic adaptations. HBO has begun casting for a pilot, so a TV series is likely in the near future.

Wheel of Time, Robert Jordan, *The Eye of the World* **(1990) BK, UAB, CGM, GN, SH**
Robert Jordan puts the "epic" in "epic fantasy." With 11 books written by Jordan, a final posthumous twelfth book (in three volumes!) to be finished by Brandon Sanderson, and a prequel, this is the ultimate indulgence for readers who want to lose themselves in a fantasy world. You've got the medieval setting, the warring factions, the magical powers, and the recurring theme of good versus evil, all related in intricate, densely layered storylines. This is not for the casual fantasy reader, but those who want to devote themselves to a brilliantly conceived new world will be in heaven.

Fairy Tales, Fable, and Myth

The stories that we heard as very young children—some of which have been passed from generation to generation for centuries—find new life when they are recast for adults. Sometimes the retellings comfort us, soothing us with faithful renditions of familiar tales; other times they challenge us to question the ideas we've always taken for granted.

The Fables Series, Bill Willingham *Fables: Legends in Exile* **(2002) GN, RS**
A dark menace has sent all the characters from the old stories into exile. In modern New York, they hide their existence from outsiders, but even in their own secluded community, all is not well. Enter Bigby Wolf (Get it? Big B. Wolf?), the semi-reformed bad guy whose rakish good looks and grumpy temperament make him the perfect noir investigator. He is called upon in the first book by mayor Snow White

to solve the murder of the party girl Rose Red. Continue with the series to meet such characters as the militant revolutionary Goldilocks and the spies Rodney and June, Geppetto's wooden children.

Gaiman, Neil, *American Gods* (2001) BK

To be honest, *any* Neil Gaiman title is going to have allusions to myths, fables, and fairy tales—just take your pick—but *American Gods* goes well beyond allusions: the characters are gods, walking-and-talking personifications of religious myths. Unfortunately for the deities, it's not a good time to be a god in America, since the modern United States is not a healthy place for keeping that old-time religion alive. Follow the mysterious hero Shadow as he uncovers their plan to restore themselves to power in this fascinating novel, steeped in religious and mythological references—and don't forget the semi-sequel, *Anansi Boys*.

InuYasha: A Feudal Fairy Tale, Rumiko Takahashi (1996–2008) MN, TV, MV, VGM, YA

Kagome Higurashi is a modern-day middle-school student in Tokyo. She also happens to be the reincarnation of Kikyo, avowed enemy of the half-demon InuYasha. Kagome discovers her past identity when she is yanked back to feudal Japan, where vengeance, romance, and complicated double-crossings combine to create a story of magic and high adventure. Traditional Japanese spirits and demons populate the story, making for an eclectic, compelling cast of characters; be sure to catch the original manga series by Rumiko Takahashi, as well as the anime series, the movies, and the video game.

Maguire, Gregory, *Wicked* and *Confessions of an Ugly Stepsister* (1995, 1999) BK, TV, UAB

Gregory Maguire does delightfully mischievous things with familiar stories. He's probably best known for corrupting—or, retelling—*The Wizard of Oz* in *Wicked*, but he's happily revised the stories of such characters as Snow White and the Tooth Fairy. In *Confessions of an Ugly Stepsister*, plain Iris and mentally challenged Ruth become stepsisters to the lovely Clara when their mother remarries. You'll recognize some of the elements—the eligible prince, the slipper, and the ball—but this novel definitely covers new territory with its fresh take on human emotions and motivations. Be sure to catch the television movie version, too.

McKinley, Robin

Traditional fairy tales come alive in marvelous new ways in Robin McKinley's capable hands. Try any or all of these four novels—and if you like them, continue exploring McKinley's other works for even more retellings:

- *Beauty* is a simple, lovely story, in which our heroine values her brains over her looks. It is faithful to the spirit and story of the Beauty and the Beast fairy tale. (1978) BK, YA, CL
- Likewise, *Rose Daughter* retells the Beauty and the Beast story, but it is a more challenging read. This is a sophisticated, elegant examination of the complicated characters of the heroine and her captor. (1997) BK, YA
- *Spindle's End*, as you might guess, retells the story of Cinderella, who in this treatment is a tomboyish young woman who talks with animals. She doesn't need a prince to rescue her because she's got a brain of her own—which she'll need if she's to escape the death curse that a bad fairy has cast upon her. (2000) BK, YA

- *Deerskin* is much darker than McKinkey's other books. Many fairy tales are sanitized so that young children don't get too scared, but McKinley pulls no punches with this disturbing take on the French fairy tale Donkeyskin. After being repeatedly raped by her own father, the king, Princess Lissar loses her memory and identity. This is a haunting novel with some very adult themes and scenes, but readers who can endure the heroine's psychological and physical trials will be rewarded with her transformation into a powerful young woman, aided by magic and true love. (1993) BK

Medley, Linda, *Castle Waiting* (2006) GN, YA
What happens after Sleeping Beauty awakes from her enchanted sleep? How does everyone else adjust after the main characters embark on their happily-ever-after lives? Linda Medley answers these questions with a delightful, inventive sequel to the Sleeping Beauty story in her gorgeous graphic novel *Castle Waiting*. With Sleeping Beauty out of the picture, the castle she inhabited has turned into a safe haven for characters from fairy tales, folktales, and nursery rhymes. A pregnant woman on the run, a knight with the head of a horse, a nun with a beard, and other assorted characters comprise the cast of this fanciful adventure, which is appropriate for younger readers but deep enough for adults.

Pratchett, Terry, *Witches Abroad* (1991) BK, CGM, GN, UAB
In Terry Pratchett's Discworld series, the stories we've cherished from childhood take on newer (and much funnier) meanings. In *Witches Abroad*, Pratchett lovingly satirizes "Little Red Riding Hood," *The Wizard of Oz*, and "Cinderella." (This last he pokes fun at repeatedly, to hysterical effect). Pratchett is insightful and sharp with his parody without ever being mean.

Shrek (1990) BK, MV, CGM, VGM, GN, UAB, YA, SH
A grumpy green ogre named Shrek is the star of a tremendously popular computer-animated series of movies based on the picture book by William Steig. In marvelous reversals of the traditional fairy tale trope, Shrek's one true love is not a beautiful human girl but a rather homely ogre princess, a fire-breathing dragon turns out to be a hero, the Big Bad Wolf is a swell guy, and the Headless Horseman wants to play the flute. The Shrek movies, books, and games endure in popularity not only because they are fun for children, but because they are packed with clever allusions to fairy tales and fables that appeal to adult sensibilities.

Romancing the Sorcerer's Stone: Relationship-Driven Fantasy
Sparks are flying, and not just from the tips of wizards' fingers. In these stories, sensual relationships are just as important as the elements of fantasy. Sometimes the stories will close with a happily-ever-after ending, while other times the relationships will be short-lived, but in any case the romantic chemistry between characters will keep you spellbound. (For a guaranteed happily-ever-after ending and a lighter dose of fantasy, see the "Fantasy for Romance Readers" list in Making Connections.

Corpse Bride, directed by Tim Burton (2005) MV, YA
Love triangles are never easy, especially if one of the people is dead. Victor and Victoria are engaged, but their marriage plans are derailed when Victor accidentally

places the wedding ring on a gnarly tree root that turns out to be the bony finger of Emily, a charming young woman—a charming young *dead* woman. Victor feels obligated to honor his accidental commitment to the corpse bride, though it means forsaking Victoria. It also means that he'll have to kill himself to join Emily in the afterlife. (Don't worry; true love eventually prevails). Superb stop-motion animation, a spooky atmosphere, and a madcap story line make this a darkly entertaining comedy of errors.

Dark, Christine Feehan, *Dark Prince* (1999) BK, UAB, GN

The Carpathians are basically a good lot. They have some creepy qualities—their life spans extend over hundreds of years, they can shift their shapes, and they drink human blood (but not to kill!)—but they're not vampires, which are evil soulless beings. Except that even the most noble of Carpathians do turn into vampires after centuries of no human companionship, and no females have been born in centuries. Will the Carpathians die out and/or turn into vampires? Or will a human woman named Raven, gifted with telepathy, offer the Carpathians a chance for a new start? Christine Feehan delivers a paranormal suspense series that is sensual, sexy, emotionally intense, and romantic; read the books in order, and don't miss the graphic novel series entry, *Dark Hunger*.

Dark-Hunter, Sherrilyn Kenyon, *Fantasy Lover* (2002) BK, UAB, MN, SH

Vengeance is sweet, but it comes with a catch—two catches, actually: the Greek goddess Artemis will give power to those who seek revenge, but they must sell her their souls, and on top of that, they must spend the rest of eternity hunting for soul-sucking vampires called Daimons. It's a steep price to pay, but worth it for those who choose to become Dark-Hunters. These immortal hunters and their quarry recur throughout the series, though it is not necessary to read the titles in order, as different characters take prominence in different books. What does not change from book to book is the romance element: each novel delivers a sensual, scorching romantic relationship.

Ghost (1990) MV

You're going to need tissues handy to watch *Ghost*, starting early on in the film when our hero Sam (Patrick Swayze) is killed before the eyes of his girlfriend Molly (Demi Moore) in a street mugging. But the murder was no random act of violence, realizes the newly deceased Sam, and the still-living Molly is in danger. So what if he's dead? He's got to save the woman he loves. With the help of a psychic named Oda Mae (Whoopi Goldberg), Sam is able to speak to Molly; in the most famous scene of the movie (get those tissues ready!), he's even able to touch her again. Suspense, action, and speculation into the afterlife make this worth watching, but it's the poignant, heartbreaking love between Molly and Sam that will stay with you.

Study, Maria Snyder, *Poison Study* (2005) BK, UAB

The good news is that the Commander has decided not to execute Yelena. The bad news is that she has to become his food taster: this is not a safe job, since plenty of people want the Commander dead. Certain people want Yelena dead, too, especially now that she's discovering her skills in magic. Author Maria Snyder develops intricate court politics and a finely crafted world of magic, but this is not just a political fantasy series. It's also a captivating romance series that follows the complicated relationship between Yelena and the Commander's spymaster, the aloof and alluring Valek.

Women of the Otherworld, Kelley Armstrong *Bitten* **(2001) BK, UAB**

Los Angeles, Anchorage, and Toronto—the various settings of the *Women of the Otherworld* series are just like what you'd find in real life, except that human beings are living alongside vampires, demons, and other supernatural creatures. Each book has a different focus—werewolves are prominent in some, witches in others—and a different woman, though recurring characters do link the books together. Discover Kelley Armstrong's compelling world of urban fantasy and indulge in the sizzling romance story lines that occur in each novel.

Settings

Criteria for inclusion in *The Dictionary of Imaginary Places* varied widely, but authors Alberto Manguel and Gianni Guadalupi "admit to having chosen certain places simply because they aroused in us that indescribable thrill that is the true achievement of fiction, places without which the world would be so much poorer."[3] Narnia and Camelot, Never-Never Land and the Land of Oz, Xanadu and Wonderland, Toad Hall and the Hundred Acre Wood—the world really would be poorer without them.

In most genres, attention to the setting is optional—it's great if it's developed, no great loss if it isn't—but in fantasy, the setting almost always plays an important role in the overall success of the story: all of the masterpieces of fantasy have memorable settings, and a good setting can transform an ordinary story into something truly magical. Sometimes people want a very specific type of setting (medieval Tolkienesque settings are popular); other times people do not care about the specifics, so long as the setting is developed with plenty of details and descriptions. Also bear in mind that some prefer settings that are entirely fantastic, while some prefer settings that take place in our own world.

Roughing It: Medieval Settings à la Middle Earth

Because of Tolkien, the quintessential fantasy setting is Middle Earth, a place that could be mistaken for medieval Europe if you could overlook the trolls and dragons and so forth. Though many fantasy writers create worlds that diverge from Middle Earth, medieval Europe (or something like it) is a frequently recurring setting. Life is harsh, the roads are dangerous, the countryside is uncivilized, and the cities are filthy—but chivalry is alive, the scenery is breathtaking, and there's an inn just through the woods where travelers are singing ballads.

Conan the Barbarian, originally created by Robert E. Howard (1935) BK, MV, TV, GN, UAB, CGM, VGM, YA, CL

After a great flood wiped out the city of Atlantis, the survivors and their descendents lost the sophistication and technology of their civilization, devolving into uncultured barbarians. In their primitive world, called Cimmeria, survival skills such as hunting and fighting reigned supreme. This hardscrabble environment was the perfect breeding ground for one of fantasy's most enduring characters, the sword-wielding Conan. At times a criminal, a pirate, and a mercenary, he's a rough character—but he's a hero nonetheless, a rescuer of princesses and a slayer of monsters. Many different creators have brought Conan and his Cimmeria to life; for a vivid visual depiction, try starting with Roy Thomas's graphic novel *The Chronicles of Conan*, or play the online role-playing game *Age of Conan*.

Deryni, Katherine Kurtz, *Deryni Rising* (1970) BK, UAB, GN

The Eleven Kingdoms are the foundation for Katherine Kurtz's sprawling, richly detailed fantasy series. Her world-building is superb, with stories that revolve around the political, cultural, and spiritual conflicts of the various peoples and races. The kingdom of Gwynedd frequently takes center stage; this medieval land features beautiful countrysides and several cities, each with its own distinct personality. Readers will in some ways be reminded of medieval Wales, though the magical powers of certain characters lend a sword-and-sorcery feel to the setting.

Ende, Michael, *The Neverending Story* (1983) BK, MV, YA

At the onset of Michael Ende's book, the setting is a far cry from Middle Earth: our young hero Bastian lives in a modern city from our world. But the book he starts reading features a place appropriately called Fantastica, with all the trappings of a medieval fantasyland. There is a human empress who rules over a variety of sentient races—dragons, werewolves, and people—who in turn dwell among a variety of fantastic settings—rural plains, a magical tower, and an enchanted waterfall. As Bastian becomes engrossed with his reading, he gradually leaves his own planet and enters Fantastica, where a quest to save the land awaits him. Read the novel first, then watch the 1984 film directed by Wolfgang Petersen; though it diverges from Ende's text, it is remarkable for the high-budget special effects of its time.

Godless World, Brian Ruckley, *Winterbirth* (2007) BK, RS

The Godless World is just that: a world abandoned by the gods, who took all the magic with them. There is a rugged beauty to the landscape, reminiscent of medieval Scotland, but it is not a pleasant place to be. Without the gods around, the remaining races are devolving into chaos and anarchy, with battles and bloodshed ruling the day. Brian Ruckley develops this harsh environment with sophisticated histories, politics, and religions; it is a violent setting, but rendered with precision and populated by memorable, lifelike characters.

Mice Templar, Bryan J. L. Glass, *The Prophecy* (2008) GN, YA, RS, SH

After seeing his mentor killed and his family enslaved by rats, a young mouse named Karic reluctantly begins studying the lost traditions of the Mice Templar, a now-defunct group of knights. His journey is beautifully rendered on the pages of this graphic novel, taking him from his home village through the savage wilderness to a corrupt medieval city. A story starring mice might seem childish, but although children with a stomach for violence (and lenient parents) can enjoy the *Mice Templar* series, it is a sophisticated work, rife with literary and mythical allusions, more suitable for young adults and adults.

Riftwar Cycle, Raymond E. Feist, *Magician: Apprentice* (1982) BK, GN

Midkemia is a standard medieval fantasy setting, with elves, dwarves, trolls, magicians, and princesses in occasional need of rescuing. But as a lowly apprentice named Pug discovers in the first book of the series, there is a rift in the fabric of existence: invaders from another world have ripped their way into Midkemia. Feist develops the cultures and characters of both worlds in several different series in the Riftwar Universe, with a whopping 25 novels at the time of this writing. Start with the first prose novel, *Magician: Apprentice*, or get maximum visual impact with the graphic-novel adaptation, *Magician: Apprentice, vol. 1*.

Willow, directed by Ron Howard (1988) MV, YA

A prophecy states that a newborn child will ultimately bring about an end to the tyranny oppressing the land, so evil queen Bavmorda does the only sensible thing: she rounds up all the pregnant women and resolves to murder the baby from the prophecy. But a clever midwife interferes, sending the marked newborn down a stream, where she is found by a group of dwarf-like people, the Nelwyns. One of these Nelwyns, Willow, resolves to restore the infant to the humans, and adventure ensues, replete with magicians, sorcerers, medieval castles, and unforgiving rural terrain. Watch this cult favorite to see the pioneering work of George Lucas's Industrial Light & Magic and see computer-generated imagery used for the first time to dazzling effect.

Emerald Cities and Metropolitan Jewels

Take a break from trudging through the countryside and step into the bustle and glamour of an imaginary city. A carefully constructed fantastic city is a joy to experience; it is a sophisticated act of world-building for a writer to attempt, but done properly, the city will take on a life of its own, becoming every bit as important as the characters who live there.

City Imperishable, *Trial of Flowers*, Jay Lake (2006) BK, SH, RS

The City Imperishable is anything but. Already it has decayed from its glory days, and new problems confront this ancient city. In the first book of the series, we find that the heir to the throne has vanished, the gods are wreaking havoc on the citizens, and the barbarians are at the gates. Jay Lake brings vivid details, unique characters, and elaborate political machinations to his troubled city. The result is a violent, edgy, beautifully crafted story of ambiguous morals and haunting imagery.

Discworld, Terry Pratchett, *Mort* (1989) BK, CGM, CN, UAB

"When a man is tired of Ankh-Morpork, he is tired of ankle-deep slurry." Discworld's busiest city has some sewage issues, but hey, every big city has problems. At least you can feel safe knowing you won't be murdered (unless the Assassins' Guild is after you) or robbed (unless you haven't paid your dues to the Thieves' Guild)—but if you are, the City Watch will investigate. Nearly all the books in the Discworld series mention Ankh-Morpork in some way (try *Unseen Academicals* to watch wizards play football for the city team, or *Feet of Clay* to understand the city's labor tensions), but if you'd like to start with one of the earlier books in the series to follow the city's development, try *Mort*, in which Death takes a holiday on the town, trying his immortal hand at line-dancing, short-order cooking, and serious drinking.

Gentleman Bastard, Scott Lynch, *The Lies of Locke Lamora* (2006) BK, UAB, RS

Locke Lamora is a liar, a criminal, a rogue, and a leader of a group called the Gentlemen Bastards—and bear in mind, he's the *good* guy. The bad guys are even worse, and their over-the-top villainy makes for a swashbuckling good read. The capers, assassinations, con jobs, and shenanigans of the characters are set against the backdrop of the island city of Camorr, reminiscent of a late medieval/early Renaissance Venice. With a rich sense of politics, history, mythology, and culture, Camorr is a vibrant, fully developed city; continue to the second book in the series, *Red Seas Under Red Skies*, to encounter Camorr's rival, the city-state of Tal Verrar.

Metropolis and Gotham City, DC Comics (1939) BK, MV, TV, CGM, VGM, GN, UAB, YA, CL

In the DC universe, Metropolis is the yin to Gotham City's yang. Like its most famous resident, Superman, Metropolis is bright, welcoming, wholesome, and clean. And Gotham City, like its most famous resident, Batman, is dark, dreary, edgy, and gritty. What they share in common is an uncanny tendency to attract supervillains and their heinous crimes. These cities crop up in innumerable graphic novels, movies, television shows, games, and books, but if you're looking for a good place to start, visit Metropolis in the 1978 film *Superman*, starring Christopher Reeve, and visit Gotham City in the 1989 film *Batman*, starring Michael Keaton.

Miéville, China, *The City and the City* (2009) BK, UAB

Somewhere in contemporary Eastern Europe, there's a city called Beszel, teeming with culture and history but down on its luck. There's also a city called Ul Qoma, likewise teeming with culture and history but thriving and affluent. In Miéville's utterly bizarre world, the two cities share the same physical geography but exist separately, with the citizens of each steadfastly refusing to acknowledge the other. Miéville's fans already know that he is brilliant at conceptualizing fantastic cities, though this novel departs somewhat from the urban fantasy subgenre and instead explores the police procedural crime novel.

<u>Shadowbridge</u>, Gregory Frost, *Shadowbridge* (2008) BK, UAB

Gregory Frost is a master of world-building. We learn about the details of his wildly inventive setting through the eyes of Leodora, a young woman who is a marvelous storyteller. (She's a little too good, actually; her growing skill is attracting dangerous attention.) The myths and histories that Leodora relates would themselves establish a captivating world, even if Shadowbridge were physically unremarkable, but in fact it is most unusual: the entire planet is covered in water, and its inhabitants—people, creatures, and gods—spend their time on bridges and in tunnels. Continue with the sequel, *Lord Tophet*.

There Goes the Neighborhood: Fantasy in the Real World

If Tolkien's Middle Earth represents all that is traditional in fantasy, then urban fantasy represents all that is new and fresh and different. Urban fantasies take place in modern, recognizable settings in our world, but with one major twist: here there are dragons (or vampires or werewolves or something of the sort). Urban fantasy is the fastest growing and arguably most popular subset of fantasy, with a wide readership among teens and adults. Charles de Lint and Neil Gaiman are often considered the forefathers of urban fantasy, and several of their books can be considered modern classics.

Bull, Emma, *War for the Oaks* (1987) BK, CL, SH

Take the movie *Bill and Ted's Bogus Journey*, lose the time machine and toss in some fairies, and you've got Emma Bull's *War for the Oaks*. Things aren't going well for singer/guitarist Eddi McCandry: her Minneapolis rock group is falling apart, and so is her relationship with her boyfriend. Oh, and she's being chased by the Unseelie Court, and the only person who can save her is an insufferable prankster faerie named Phouka. With high-stakes battles between the faerie courts, an unexpected romance, and a final rock-band showdown, this is one of the seminal novels of urban fantasy.

Gaiman, Neil, *Neverwhere* (1997) BK, TV, GN, UAB, CL

Sure, there are plenty of reasons to read, watch, and listen to Neil Gaiman's *Neverwhere*. The descriptions of normal London and its shadowy alternate London are vividly rendered; the magical and fantastical elements are superbly drawn; the spine-tingling, high-octane events are guaranteed to keep you up past bedtime. But the very best part of this urban adventure comes in the form of two magnificent bad guys, Croup—chatty, urbane, and utterly evil, and Vandemar—laconic, thuggish, and also utterly evil. Their goal in *Neverwhere* should be easy: all they must do is murder a young girl named Door, whose only defense comes in the form of the hapless human Richard Mayhew. Don't miss the audio version, narrated by the author himself in his dreamy English voice.

Her Majesty's Dog, Mick Takeuchi (2001–2006) MN, YA

Amane Kamori seems like a perfectly normal Tokyo high school student, though the other kids begrudge her for the undue attention she receives from the mega-hot Hyoue. What the others don't realize is that Hyoue is a shape-shifting supernatural being devoted to protecting Amane. And she certainly needs the help: as a psychic trying to hide her abilities in the modern world, she has a habit of getting into trouble. Part horror and part romance, this fantasy manga series by Mick Takeuchi is alternately dark and light-hearted, both fun and touching; start with volume one and read the books in order.

Highlander (1986) TV, BK, MV, CGM, VGM, GN

Pick your poison: *Highlander* can be enjoyed in dozens of ways, from the various television series to the novels and graphic novels to the games to the movies. To truly understand the mythos of epic universe, start with the first film, *Highlander* (directed by Russell Mulcahy), where we meet the sixteenth-century Scottish chap Connor MacLeod, who is an Immortal, a being who can only be killed by decapitation. Traversing the centuries and the globe sounds great until you realize that your mortal friends and lovers will die—and that the bad Immortals will stop at nothing to kill you.

Moonheart, Charles de Lint, *Moonheart* (1994) BK, UAB

Any of Charles de Lint's books will appeal to fans of urban fantasy, but try starting with *Moonheart*, the first of the series by the same name. Ottawa resident Sara Kendell and her uncle, Jamie Tamson, run an antiques store with a perfectly normal inventory—perfectly normal, that is, but for a few artifacts that hail from a different world altogether. Throw in a Druid, a biker, an inspector of the paranormal, and a gateway to ancient Wales, and you get a remarkable blend of mythical figures and magical happenings in two parallel worlds.

Characters

Like any genre, fantasy has its share of stock characters. Sometimes they are archetypes, especially in the early myths and legends of fantasy literature; other times they are merely stereotypical, especially those in Tolkienesque high fantasy. Among humans, there are male heroes (who are generally self-assured and good in a fight); secondary or tertiary females (usually playing the love interest of the male heroes, and not necessarily endowed with much in the way of personality); powerful wizards (ancient, wise, and bearded); and young males aspiring to be heroes (born on a farm, more often than not). Among mythical entities, there are dwarves (surly and aggressive), elves (beautiful and aloof), trolls, goblins, demons, and other bad guys (recognizable for their poor hygiene).

Some fans of fantasy cherish these familiar character types, while others recoil from convention. Either way, character is an extremely important consideration for many fantasy readers. Interactions between characters can drive an entire series: Will Hermione and Ron ever get together in Harry Potter? Will Edward and Jacob fight to the death in Twilight? And interactions *within* a character can drive a series: Will Gollum change his evil ways? Will Professor Snape?

These external and internal conflicts result in some of the best characters in all of fiction. In a fantasy story, characters are likely to face heavy decisions relating to honor, virtue, mortality, wisdom, sacrifice, and love. Regardless of whether they are clichéd or unusual, the characters of good fantasy are vivid, powerful, and unforgettable.

The Chosen One

The Chosen One is usually a character of lowly birth—not just poor or forgotten by those in power, but often the youngest, the most foolish, and naïve—someone who, under normal circumstances, has no chance of succeeding at anything. However, the Chosen One is always someone pure of heart. People love underdogs because they identify with them (most of us were *not* born into nobility or fame or money). It's always satisfying to see the little guy win the day, especially when he's fighting against the forces of ultimate evil.

<u>Chronicles of Prydain</u>, Lloyd Alexander, *The Book of Three* (1964) BK, MV, UAB, YA, CL, SH
Before there was Harry Potter, there was Taran, a young man whose origins are about as humble as it's possible to get: he's an orphaned *assistant* pig-keeper. Then a beautiful princess arrives on the scene: how is a commoner like Taran ever going to win her love? While he's busy trying to puzzle out the answer, he's also got to figure out how to save the kingdom. Meet Taran in *The Book of Three*, the first in Lloyd Alexander's marvelous *Chronicles of Prydain*, written for children but engrossing for adults—and while you're at it, don't miss Disney's animated version of the second book of the series, *The Black Cauldron*.

<u>Guards! Guards!</u>, Terry Pratchett (1989) BK, CGM, GN, UAB
Terry Pratchett delights in turning convention right on its adorable little head. In *Guards, Guards!*, the eighth book of the sprawling Discworld series, Pratchett presents a classic setup: there's a country bumpkin of unknown parentage who has just arrived in the city, which happens to be in need of rescuing. The citizens of Ankh-Morpork are being threatened by a dragon, exactly the type of critter who ought to be dispatched by a long-lost heir to the throne—though at present, Ankh-Morpork is ruled by a patrician, not by a monarchy. Could the guileless Carrot be the man destined to reclaim the throne? He *does* have a peculiar birthmark, but things in Discworld are never that predictable.

Harry Potter, J. K. Rowling, *Harry Potter and the Sorcerer's Stone* (1997) BK, MV, CGM, VGM, UAB, YA, CL

We know from the start of the Harry Potter series that Harry—born to wizards but raised by Muggles—is the Chosen One. It's hard to ignore the clues, such as the prominent scar on Harry's forehead, a token of his (temporary) triumph over the Dark Lord. But for someone whose destiny seems assured, there are still a lot of unanswered questions that run through the course of the series: Is Harry really supposed to kill You-Know-Who? (It couldn't be Neville instead . . . could it?) Is it even *possible* to kill Voldemort? And—gulp—is it possible to kill Voldemort without dying in the process?

Inheritance Cycle, Christopher Paolini, *Eragon* (2003) BK, MV, UAB

Like any other kid living on a farm in the middle of nowhere, Eragon likes spending time in the woods. While hunting one day, he picks up a shiny blue stone that catches his eye. A few days later, that stone turns out to be an egg, as evidenced by the dragon that hatches from it. Having a dragon around is pretty cool—there are elves to meet and magical studies to pursue—but a dragon can also draw the unwelcome attentions of a tyrant king, who is resolutely determined to prevent any upstart dragon riders from undermining his power.

Memory, Sorrow, and Thorn, Tad Williams, *The Dragonbone Chair* (1988) BK

At the start of *The Dragonbone Chair*, the first in Tad Williams's epic fantasy series, you might think you're reading a knockoff of *The Sword in the Stone*. There's a kid named Simon who does petty chores around the castle, and there's a wise old magician who begins to tutor him. But there's nothing derivative about this fine example of high fantasy. The familiar conventions are present, and yes—Simon *does* turn out to be the Chosen One—but Williams breathes new life into the tried-and-true quest story, mercilessly employing plot twists that will keep readers up way too late at night, racing to find out what happens next in this masterfully crafted universe.

Morrowind, Bethesda Softworks (2002) CGM, VGM, YA, CL

And the Chosen One is—you! No one believes it at first, though, because your character begins this epic game as a pathetic weakling; step into an innocent-looking stream, and you'll most likely be killed by a fish. But in this marvelously open-ended role-playing game, your character can improve him- or herself through countless quests. Spend enough time with *Morrowind* and after a while you'll have the skills, the spells, and the cool enchanted items you need to take down the evil god who's trying to take over the world. If that's not enough, try your hand at the next game in the series, *Oblivion*, set in the same medieval universe.

White, T. H., *The Sword in the Stone* (1939) BK, MV, UAB, YA, CL

Let's be honest here: a kid called Wart couldn't possibly be the Chosen One. Besides, the guy has nothing going for him: no money, no parents, and no friends. But then he meets a weird old guy named Merlyn, who just happens to be a wizard. Merlyn devises a variety of ways to impart knowledge to Wart—including turning his protégé into a variety of animals—and, in the process, Wart begins to look more and more like he might be the one to pull the fabled sword from the stone. Both the T. H. White novel and the Disney animated movie offer a charming, fun-filled introduction to King Arthur during an innocent stage of his life, before all the nonsense with Guinevere and Lancelot and Mordred.

The Spunky Female

Simply put, the spunky female kicks ass, takes names, and breaks hearts. Fantasy, especially traditional fantasy, is filled with the testosterone-driven, masculine posturing of men and (male) orcs and (male) dwarves. For a bit of relief from all the machismo, look to the ladies of fantasy, who do things their own way. Some of these damsels may be in distress, but they're quite capable of rescuing themselves.

Birds of Prey, DC Comics (1999) GN, TV, YA

Why settle for one kick-ass woman when you can have a whole team of them? In the television episodes and graphic novels of the Birds of Prey series, various super-heroines from the DC universe populate the cast, headed up by Oracle, née Batgirl, and known in real life as Barbara Gordon. Sure, she's in a wheelchair—but with brains, tech skills, and martial-arts savvy, she is more than capable of fighting crime and leading the other Birds of Prey, including Black Canary, Huntress, and Manhunter. Bookwise, any of the titles will appeal, but keep your eye out for those written by a real-life kick-ass woman, Gail Simone.

Buffy the Vampire Slayer (1992) BK, MV, TV, VGM, GN, YA, CL, SH

The film *Buffy the Vampire Slayer* was released in 1992, and the television series ended in 2003, but the Buffyverse shows no signs of slowing down—and how could it? Buffy's character is just too popular to fade away. Females in horror stories tend to sit about needing to be rescued, but this high school student (and later, college student) tackles supernatural demonic forces with her own strength—though granted, things get a bit tricky concerning the supernatural demonic force who happens to be her boyfriend. Joss Wheldon's creation has a huge following, and dedicated fans will want to indulge in the original movie, the television show (viewed in series order for maximum impact), and in the various computer games, video games, novels, and graphic novels.

Meyer, Stephenie, *Breaking Dawn* (2008) BK, MV, UAB, YA

It's almost cheating to call Bella Swan a spunky female. For the first three books of Stephenie Meyer's Twilight series, Bella does *not* kick ass (though she's definitely a pain in the ass). She does break hearts (including a vampire heart, a werewolf heart, and a human heart), but she's too busy getting herself rescued and botching up things to demonstrate any "grrrl power." But stick with the series through the fourth title, *Breaking Dawn*, and you'll find a bona fide strong woman who single-handedly saves the supernatural world.

Sailor Moon, Naoko Takeuchi (1992) TV, MN, YA

Serena Tsukino is, frankly, something of a loser. The Tokyo schoolgirl spends her time goofing off instead of concentrating on her studies, and she has an annoying tendency to cry when she doesn't get her way. Give her a magical brooch, though, and she turns into Sailor Moon, a soldier/princess who fights for peace. Experience the anime and manga in series order for maximum impact; though our heroine does have her irritating moments at the beginning, as things progress, she becomes a mature young woman who wields formidable supernatural powers to save the universe.

Thursday Next, Jasper Fforde, *The Eyre Affair* (2002) BK, UAB

In an alternate-reality England, where Big Brother is in and classic literature is the new religion, Thursday Next is fighting the good fight against corrupt government and literary crimes. This ex-military Shakespeare scholar works for the Special Operations forces, the elite secret police, as part of the LiteraTec Division, devoted to eradicating forged copies of original manuscripts. When the nefarious Acheron Hades kidnaps the heroine of *Jane Eyre*, only Thursday Next—armed with her heavy-duty weapons, brilliant mind, and pet dodo clone—stands a chance of preserving the beloved story. Thursday's adventures continue after she learns how to travel into the Book World and becomes a Jurisfiction Agent.

Wonder Woman, DC Comics (1941) GN, TV, YA, CL

In real life, spinning around three times does not transform the ordinary person into Wonder Woman (trust me, I've tried), but it works for Diana Prince. A mainstay of DC Comics since the 1940s, Wonder Woman is an Amazon whose props include a Lasso of Truth, bracelets that deflect bullets, and an invisible airplane. Deadly with her martial arts and weapons skills, and equally deadly with her ravishing good looks (both on the page and as played on television by Lynda Carter), Wonder Woman is one of the symbols of modern feminism, the first woman character to hold her own in a comics field dominated by men.

Xena: Warrior Princess (1995) TV, BK, GN, VGM, CGM, YA

Never mind Hercules; for kick-ass Greek warriors, Xena is where the action is. Though she got her start with a minor role in the television show *Hercules: The Legendary Journeys*, the character played by Lucy Lawless proved so popular that she became a star of the spin-off series *Xena: Warrior Princess*, replete with a dedicated cult following. Having moved swiftly from villain to hero, Xena became a feminist icon, a woman who used her brains, physical strength, and integrity to defeat bad guys and defend the innocent. Because of her enduring popularity, you'll be able to enjoy the Xenaverse not only with the television series, but also with novelizations, graphic novels, and computer and video games.

The Lone Wolf

Forming a fellowship with like-minded good guys is all well and good, but sometimes a hero has to take matters into his own hands. Those brooding, lonesome types would rather depend on their own brains and brawn to take care of business.

Batman, DC Comics (1939) BK, MV, TV, VGM, GN, MN, UAB, YA, CL

A cultural icon, Batman is one of the most recognizable lone wolves (lone bats?) in all of popular media. It's no wonder, as he shows up in nearly every medium you can think of, from movies (try *The Dark Knight*) to graphic novels (Frank Miller's *Batman: The Dark Knight Returns* is a classic) to television (if you haven't seen the 1960s series starring Adam West, you're missing out). It's true that Batman has a loyal friend in perennial sidekick Robin, but there's no escaping his essentially solitary nature. Traumatized as a child by seeing his parents murdered before his eyes, Bruce Wayne becomes obsessed with fighting crime in Gotham City. The result is Wayne's alter ego, Batman, a caped crusader who devotes himself to physical and intellectual self-improvement. Who can blame him if he gets moody now and again? Other superheroes have superpowers; Batman is just a normal guy with a seriously intense need to save the world.

The Chronicles of Thomas Covenant, the Unbeliever, Stephen R. Donaldson, *Lord Foul's Bane* (1977) BK, SH

It's difficult to claim that Thomas Covenant is a lone-wolf hero; it might be easier to call him a lone-wolf *anti*-hero. You will have to read the three sets of trilogies (starting with the first book, *Lord Foul's Bane*) to decide for yourself whether he counts as a good guy in the final reckoning. One thing is for sure, though: he doesn't have much in the way of friends, and his number-one interest is his own well-being. Because of Thomas's leprosy, it's inevitable that people shun him in the real world, but he can only blame his own selfish decisions for the enemies he makes in the fantastic alternate world, The Land. You may not like him—you probably *won't* like him—but Thomas Covenant remains one of the most compelling, fascinating, and lonely characters in all of fantasy literature.

Dark Tower, Stephen King, *The Gunslinger* (1982) BK, GN, UAB

"The man in black fled across the desert, and the gunslinger followed." If you've already read the seven Dark Tower books, chances are you've got a chill creeping up your spine just from reading that opening sentence. The man in black is a bad guy. The fellow chasing him is also a bad guy—or a good guy, if you're feeling charitable. Both hero and anti-hero, Roland the gunslinger is a morally complicated figure, one who will sacrifice anyone to bring him closer to his quest. Since he keeps killing off people he loves (girlfriends, children, best friends, pets), Roland is necessarily a solitary sort. But you can't help rooting for the grumpy, obsessive, determined star of Stephen King's series; he *is* trying to save the universe, after all. Don't miss the comic book prequels and adaptations, available in graphic-novel form, and keep your eyes out for a film adaptation.

Prince of Nothing, R. Scott Bakker, *The Darkness That Comes Before* (2004) BK, RS

You've got three lone-wolf heroes in R. Scott Bakker's hefty Prince of Nothing series. The star is Anasûrimbor Kellhus, a renaissance man in every way: he can do some of *everything*. Whether it's learning languages, casting spells, defeating armies, or studying theology, Kellhus excels at whatever he tries. But it's lonely at the top; when you're a god character, there's no one who can understand you. He keeps company with Cnaiur, a mighty warrior who has no real friends. (Possibly all his raping and pillaging has something to do with that.) Rounding out the uncomfortable alliance of protagonists is Drusas Achamian, whose lifestyle as a wizard spy makes it impossible for him to form any lasting relationships. Folks read Bakker's trilogy for lots of reasons—the intricate plot, the brilliantly developed setting, and the political intrigue—but for my money, the rich character development and the inherent unhappiness of those characters are the best reasons of all.

Sandman, Neil Gaiman, *Preludes and Nocturnes* (1991) GN, CL

He's grumpy. He's sullen. His hair is black, he dresses in black, and even his speech bubbles are black. The Sandman, also known as Dream, also known as Morpheus, is a classic loner. He does just fine without companionship, as we see at the start of Neil Gaiman's signature series of graphic novels, when we discover the Sandman patiently biding his time through 70 years of solitary imprisonment. Even after his escape, he's not the type of guy you expect to see at parties. He lives quietly, with only a librarian and a groundskeeper for company, and only with great reluctance does he occasionally interrupt his lifestyle to save the universe. Independent, introverted, and moody, the Sandman is mysterious and guarded—which, of course, makes readers race through the pages, hoping to glean more about the compelling title character.

Vampire Hunter, Hideyuki Kikuchi (2005) MN, BK, MV, VGM, YA

Vampire Hunter D presents readers and those who advise them a delicious dilemma: Do you start with the 1985 anime film? Perhaps with the first of the prose novels by Hideyuki Kikuchi, or the manga version of the same? Or should you just jump into the high-action video game? Wherever you choose to begin, you're in for an excellent story, with rich character development and nail-biting suspense. The setting is thousands of years in the future, in an apocalyptic nightmare world where vampires rule, where the only hope of justice comes from the mysterious vigilante D, a sexy but brooding half-human loner who derives his powers from his vampire lineage.

The Van Helsing Family, originally created by Bram Stoker (1897) BK, MV, TV, VGM, GN, MN, UAB

The various members of the Van Helsing family keep to themselves. It's only wise when your line of work involves hunting vampires and other nasty critters. The original Van Helsing, of course, was Dr. Abraham Van Helsing of Bram Stoker's novel *Dracula*. His wife is insane and his son is dead, so mainly he spends his time with his research, figuring out ways to vanquish vampires. He's been played on screen many, many times; look for Anthony Hopkins playing the role in *Bram Stoker's Dracula*, or watch Hugh Jackman bring the good doctor to life in *Van Helsing*. Then try your hand at playing Van Helsing's character in the video game *Van Helsing*. But don't forget Van Helsing's descendents; discover Rachel Van Helsing in the graphic novel series *The Tomb of Dracula*, and meet Integra Hellsing in the aptly named manga and anime series *Hellsing*.

Sexy Bad Guys

Sexy bad guys hold great appeal for readers. Works of fantasy depict the struggle between good and evil, so it stands to reason that a bad guy is going to be present. Since they're going to be around anyway, they may as well be sexy—but be careful: these charming baddies can be so sexy that you may end up rooting for the wrong side.

Basara Yumi Tamura (1990–1998) MN, TV, YA

With wavy dark hair, a very nicely defined chin, and regal bearing out the wazoo, Shuri the Red King is the dreamy son of the emperor in the manga and anime series *Basara*. He's a likeable guy, good at ruling his kingdom and brilliant with a sword. The young heroine has the hots for him, and the feeling is mutual; it seems like a perfect match. The thing is, Shuri is a bit of a despot. Woe betide anyone who stands against him—and therein lies the problem. The protagonist of the series is a survivor from the village that Shuri destroyed in his wrath. Shuri's cruelty marks him as the tyrant against whom the heroine must fight. But gosh, he's nice to look at.

Coldfire, C. S. Friedman, *Black Sun Rising* (1991) BK

Gerald Tarrant kicks off C. S. Friedman's Coldfire trilogy by murdering his wife and kids. Then he sets up house in a spooky old forest and takes up a new profession, killing innocent young girls. It's a peculiar career change for a fellow who used to be a church prophet. Everyone who knows him, or even knows *of* him, wants him dead—and yet there's something sexy about the guy. He's gorgeous to look at and has charisma off the charts. Even those who don't like Tarrant are compelled by him. Maybe it's something in his cologne?

Daredevil, Marvel Comics (1964) GN, MN, MV, CGM, VGM

Love it or hate it, you can't argue that the school of bad girl art in comics has produced some extraordinarily sexy characters. It's hard to say who's the sexiest, because all of the bad girls have perfect breasts and skimpy clothes, but a clear contender is Elektra. Created by Frank Miller for the Marvel universe, Elektra is the girlfriend of a good guy, Daredevil, but she herself is morally suspect. Occasionally she fights for the good guys, but her dark side is never far from the surface. She's an assassin, after all, conversant in crime and trained in ninja, and all the more deadly for her telepathic powers. What may be deadliest of all, however, is her luscious appearance. In her signature red outfit of supermodel proportions, every spectacular curve on her body is blissfully apparent. If the comic book version isn't enough for you, see if you can handle seeing Jennifer Garner bring the character to life in the movie *Daredevil*.

Final Fantasy VII, developed by Square (1997) CGM, VGM, YA, CL

Why is Sephiroth one of the most persistently popular video game baddies? Pure, unadulterated mojo, that's why. Sure, he's got a fascinatingly wicked personality; his scheme to deplete the world of energy in *Final Fantasy VII* just screams "evil genius." What makes him truly exceptional, however, is his sex appeal. He has the grace, speed, and strength of a warrior, bundled into a knockout package combining a lanky frame, green eyes, long silvery hair, and truly impressive shoulders. He carries a very long sword, but money says he's not compensating for anything.

Gormenghast, Mervyn Peake, *Titus Groan* (1946) BK, TV, CL

How can you not love a guy named Steerpike? To be sure, Mervyn Peake described him in physically unflattering terms in the Gormenghast series, but his sexiness lies in his character. He is a devious charmer with a sizzling intellect and political shrewdness, and he'll happily murder to achieve his ends. Not a good person, by any definition, but he has the Darth Vader complex: there's just something deliciously sexy about his evil nature. We can't help but lust for him, even though we know we shouldn't. And, lest his physique displease you in the books, just turn to the eye candy of Jonathan Rhys-Meyers as Steerpike in the BBC miniseries adaptation.

His Dark Materials, Philip Pullman, *The Golden Compass* (1995) BK, MV, UAB, YA, SH

Mrs. Coulter, of Philip Pullman's His Dark Materials series, is a power-hungry social climber who cheated on her husband. That's probably the best thing you can say about her personality. If you want to talk about her undesirable qualities, consider this: she kidnaps children in order to run experiments on them. Want the worst part? She kidnapped her own daughter. This is not a nice lady, not by anyone's standards. But it's so hard to say no to her because she's just so hot. She has a charming personality when she's not maiming anyone, and physically, she's a total knockout. This was apparent back when she was just a character in a book, but now we have the visual evidence in the movie to prove it. Thanks, Nicole Kidman.

Labyrinth (1986) MV, BK, MN, YA, CL

Some naysayers might not think David Bowie is hot, but that's only because they weren't fortunate enough to grow up in the 1980s. Jim Henson's *Labyrinth*, though released in 1986, endures as a cult classic, thanks in no small part to the big-haired allure of David Bowie as Jareth the Goblin King, who proves that men with bangs *can* have sex appeal. The Goblin King is a fiendish kidnapper who lives in a freaky castle and who displays a disturbing desire to rob the cradle. Not a nice guy, and quite possibly a pedophile, but if I'd been the nearly legal heroine, I would have eloped with him to the Labyrinth in a heartbeat.

Left Behind, Tim LaHaye and Jerry B. Jenkins, *Left Behind: A Novel of the Earth's Last Days* (1995) BK, MV, CGM, GN, UAB, AB

The baddest bad guy of them all is the ultimate charmer in the Left Behind series by Tim LaHaye and Jerry B. Jenkins. In this conservative Christian mega-hit, the Antichrist, Nicolae Jetty Carpathia, exudes charisma and charm. What's not to like? He preaches peace and world unity. It's technically true that he intends to destroy the world, but that's easy to miss behind his easy smile and remarkable good looks. He's a great conversationalist, a brilliant thinker, and a gifted athlete. Oh, and he's loaded. If you can overlook the bit about him wanting to conquer the world for Satan, he's a great catch, and very pleasant to look at on the screen as played by Gordon Currie.

Theme: It's Perfectly Paranormal

"Paranormal fantasy" is a bit redundant: the paranormal deals with the inexplicable, while fantasy deals with the inexplicable. As confusing as the wording may be, paranormal fantasy is the standard branding for a particular subgenre of fantasy, and we may as well get used to it, because this subgenre is hot.

Paranormal fantasy stories often take place in contemporary Earth settings, leading to a fair bit of overlap with a similar subgenre, urban fantasy; often the two are indistinguishable. Sometimes the stories include paranormal phenomena that have a colorful (if not scientifically verifiable) history on our own planet, including mind-reading, out-of-body experiences, and telekinesis. Other times the stories include phenomena that stray more into the truly fantastic: werewolves, talking animals, and vampires are perennial favorites, made all the more popular by another close genre relative, the paranormal romance. Distinctions among these subgenres (paranormal fantasy, contemporary fantasy, urban fantasy, and paranormal romance) are blurry: the thing to bear in mind is that they appeal to our interest in the improbable and the impossible while not straying too far out of our known world.

You Suck! Vampires in Fantasy

It's true that vampires prey on the innocent, drink the blood of humans, compromise the virtue of the pure, and generally act in ways that justify their eternal damnation, but can't we please look beyond all that? The important thing here is that they're hot—hot in the sexual sense, hot in popular culture, and a perennial favorite among fantasy fans.

30 Days of Night (2002) GN, MV

For fantasy fans who like plenty of horror in their stories, *30 Days of Night* fits the bill nicely. The premise is fabulous: a group of vampires have decided to relocate to a remote town in Alaska, where the sun goes down, and *stays* down, for a full month. It's not a bad solution for folks who normally turn to dust in sunlight, but the innocent townspeople don't think it's such a hot idea—not that many of them stay alive long enough to voice their opinions. Bloody, violent, and creepy, *30 Days of Night* is excellent both as a series of three graphic novels by Steve Niles, and as a movie starring Josh Hartnett as the man who tries to save the few survivors from the vampires.

Dark Shadows, created by Dan Curtis (1966–1971) TV, BK, MV, CL

Forget ordinary daytime soaps; for a soap opera that caters to fantasy fans, all you need is *Dark Shadows*. Though it aired from 1966–1971, there is nothing stale about this gothic drama, which still enjoys a devoted cult following. The vampire Barnabas Collins is an especially compelling figure, though other vampires, ghosts, werewolves, witches, etc., interact with the modern-day Collins family, who live in a creepy mansion called Collinwood. Watch the original series in order to indulge in the various story lines, and then catch the film versions. And those who can't get enough of the sweeping vampire saga should find the excellent the revival series from the early 1990s, along with the *Dark Shadows* novelizations.

Fox, Andrew, *Fat White Vampire Blues* and *Bride of the Fat White Vampire* (2003, 2004) BK, RS

Everyone knows that vampires are sexy and sophisticated and suave, right? It's common knowledge. But if you're tired of the same old sexy vampire shtick, look no further than Andrew Fox, author of *Fat White Vampire Blues* and its sequel *Bride of the Fat White Vampire*. The fat white vampire in question is Jules, an undead fellow of considerable girth. It's not his fault; he lives in New Orleans, where most of the pickings are themselves of sizable proportions—and anyway, people whose diets consist of tofu and lettuce taste absolutely dreadful. Fox's take on vampire lore is both refreshing and funny, supported by absolutely memorable characters (did I mention there's a New Age transvestite vampire sidekick?) and inventive, colorful storylines.

Moore, Christopher, *Bloodsucking Fiends: A Love Story* and *You Suck: A Love Story* (1995, 2007) BK, UAB

Christopher Moore is constitutionally incapable of writing anything remotely conventional, and that's why we love him. In *Bloodsucking Fiends* and its sequel, *You Suck*, meet Jody and Tommy, two perfectly normal young people who meet, fall in love, and spend their days trying to make ends meet. Except that, well, Jody actually spends her days *asleep*, seeing as sunlight would kill her. And there's also the matter of the string of murders in the neighborhood, which the police are trying to pin on Tommy. Plus there's a gang of vampire hunters on the loose. So maybe it's not your typical story of disaffected twentysomethings, but would we want it any other way? Read Moore for his excellent grasp of all things comedic, from absurdist humor to slapstick to deliciously subtle satire.

Stoker, Bram, *Dracula* (1897) BK, MV, CGM, VGM, GN, MN, UAB, SH

Okay, so Bram Stoker's classic book *Dracula* is more often thought of as a horror novel, but we here in fantasyland are proud to lay claim to it. If it weren't for the 1897 introduction of Count Dracula, and Bela Lugosi's sensual interpretation of the count in the 1931 film version, which made vampires sexy, vampires would remain an obscure monster in the public consciousness. Every vampire you've ever encountered, every bit of vampire lore you know, traces its lineage to Stoker. Don't miss out on the original novel; modern readers may have a difficult time adjusting to the Victorian prose, but the effort is well worth it. Then indulge yourself in the count's many appearances in popular media, either in adaptations of Stoker's novel (the 1931 film version with Bela Lugosi is a classic) or in stories that use the same character in a different setting; Elizabeth Kostova's interpretation of Dracula in her novel *The Historian* is excellent, as is the treatment of the count in the computer game *Dracula: Origin*, or even the family authorized sequel, *Dracula: The Un-Dead* (2009) by Stoker's great-nephew Dacre Stoker and Dracula historian Ian Holt.

Twilight, Stephenie Meyer, *Twilight* (2005) BK, MV, UAB, YA
Oh, those Cullens: they're the sexiest family alive, except that they aren't exactly alive. Sunlight doesn't hurt this family of vampires, and really, it's not fair to think of them as monsters; they've gone "vegetarian," choosing to drink blood only from animals. Several of them have psychic abilities: Alice can see into the future, Jasper can influence the emotions of people around him, and Edward—well, frankly, Edward is the reason to read Stephenie Meyers's series. He can read minds, he drives great cars, he's unbelievably gorgeous, and he's a total gentleman. Meet the Cullens, as well as various vampire enemies who aren't nearly so nice, in the four books of this fantasy/romance/horror series, and drool over Robert Pattinson as Edward in the movie.

Undead, Mary Janice Davidson, *Undead and Unwed* (2004) BK, UAB
Chick lit meets vampire horror in Mary Janice Davidson's fun, inventive series starring Betsy Taylor, who is the first to admit that "Betsy" is a ridiculous name for a vampire queen. It can't be helped, though: repeated attempts to kill herself, following her resurrection as a vampire, prove futile. Unwillingly forced into the undead existence, Betsy reluctantly accepts the challenges of being a vampire, though she refuses to surrender her fashion sense or to gracefully accept the advances of vampire Eric; he's a total jerk, after all, albeit a really sexy jerk.

Vampire Chronicles, Anne Rice, *Interview with the Vampire* (1976) BK, MV, MN, CL
Would that every first novel were as good as *Interview with the Vampire*! Anne Rice's hugely popular horror/fantasy debut features three deliciously complex vampire characters. Louis, weary of his long life and disillusioned with the nature of his existence, is the vampire being interviewed; the wild and reckless Lestat is the crazy foil to the more contemplative Louis; Claudia is the mature vampire woman trapped forever in a child's body. As always, Rice places her richly drawn characters in vivid settings, including a Louisiana slave plantation and a macabre Parisian theater. Indulge in Rice's novel or in the film version starring Brad Pitt as Louis, Tom Cruise as Lestat, and a shockingly young Kirsten Dunst as Claudia.

Sorcery and Witchery

Sorcerers and sorceresses, witches and wizards—these are the folks who practice magic with spells and charms, potions and chants. You'll find them everywhere, in traditional fantasy and in all the alternative subgenres, including the hugely popular urban fantasy and paranormal stories.

Bartimaeus, Jonathan Stroud, *The Amulet of Samarkand* **(2003) BK, UAB, YA, SH**
The three Bartimaeus books take place in our world, but you might have trouble recognizing it, because author Jonathan Stroud has tampered with history in one very significant way: he has injected magic into the course of human events. The British monarchy, for instance, is long gone, replaced by a ruling class of magicians. Magicians populate the common classes, too, along with non-magical people. And then there are demons and spirits, including a djinni named Bartimaeus. In the first book of this fun, high-adventure series, Bartimaeus and an arrogant but talented magician's apprentice named Nathaniel must defeat a wicked magician who is plotting against the government.

The Belgariad, David Eddings, *Pawn of Prophecy* **(1982) BK, UAB, CL**
In *Pawn of Prophecy*, the first of five books in an epic fantasy series by David Eddings, Garion is a nobody, a farmboy being raised by his Aunt Pol. An unlikely adventure lands in Garion's lap, though, when a storyteller called Mister Wolf mentions the theft of a valuable object. Garrion and Aunt Pol join Mister Wolf to hunt for the stolen object, and during the course of their quest, we learn that there may be more to Garrion than meets the eye. For that matter, Aunt Pol herself is hiding a few secrets about her magical talent. Sorcerers and sorceresses, both good and bad, vie for the fate of the world in this beloved fantasy adventure.

Bewitched **(1964–1969) TV, MV**
Poor, poor Darrin: his wife's family just doesn't like him. It's not Darrin's fault that he's an ordinary mortal, now is it? His wife is worth all the grief, though: the way Samantha twitches her nose is just too cute. Darrin and his witchy wife are perfectly happy together, but Samantha's magical family does its best to charm Darrin into leaving, episode after episode after episode. But, in the best tradition of romantic-comedy sitcoms, Samantha and Darrin always solve their problems, despite magical interference from the extended family. The original television show is wonderfully fun, as is the 2005 film of the same name.

Charmed **(1998–2006) TV, BK, YA**
Meet the Halliwells, three sisters in San Francisco who happen to be the world's most powerful good witches, The Charmed Ones. Prudence is telekinetic; Piper can freeze objects, and therefore time; Phoebe can see the future—and half-sister Paige, introduced midway through the series, has telekinetic orbiting powers. Through the eight seasons of the television series, and in the spin-off novels, the Halliwells fight demonic forces and evil incarnations while simultaneously making their way through the ordinary trials of life, such as careers and relationships.

Discworld, Terry Pratchett, *Equal Rites* **(1983) BK, UAB**
On the Discworld, men of magical talent go to Unseen University to become wizards, whereas women of magical talent skip all that academic nonsense and apply themselves directly to the practice of witchcraft. Wizards enjoy casting spells with shiny lights and loud noises, and they really do feel remorseful if they nearly destroy the universe, as they often do. Witches are a far more practical lot, preferring to forego the theatrics of sorcery for the subtle art of headology. Wizards and witches feature in many of Terry Pratchett's marvelous Discworld books; try *Witches Abroad* or *Maskerade* to read about witches, or *Sourcery* or *The Last Continent* for wizards,

or get a nice blend of both in *Equal Rites*, about a girl who is accidentally fated to become a wizard.

Earthsea, Ursula K. Le Guin, *A Wizard of Earthsea* (1968) BK, TV, UAB, YA, CL
Ursula K. Le Guin, one of the most lauded, well-regarded writers of fantasy, is perhaps best known for her Earthsea series. In the first book, *A Wizard of Earthsea*, readers meet a young boy from the boonies who unexpectedly develops a talent for magic. Talented but untrained, Ged hopes to hone his skills by serving as an apprentice to a magician—but when Ged leaves his master's safe environment to attend wizarding school, he accidentally summons an undead spirit that threatens his life. Throw in a dragon and a perilous natural environment, and Ged—despite his innate magical skill—finds himself fighting just to survive. Readers be warned: there is a television miniseries adaptation, but Le Guin does not endorse it.

Jones, Diana Wynne, *Howl's Moving Castle*, (1986) BK, MV, MN, UAB, YA
Sophie Hatter didn't mean to use her magical powers. She didn't even know she had magical talents, but when her accidentally enchanted hats incur the displeasure of a powerful witch, Sophie finds herself transformed into an old crone. Disgraced, she is forced to take the only job she can get, cleaning for the notorious wizard Howl. But all is not as it seems: Howl is not the creepy guy of his notorious reputation, and his home is a marvelous portal to other places. This captivating story by veteran fantasy writer Diana Wynne Jones is enjoyable in its original novel form, as an anime film, and as a manga adaptation by Hayao Miyazaki.

***Sabrina, the Teenage Witch* (1962) TV, BK, MV, GN, MN, YA**
Sabrina Spellman was only supposed to be a minor, one-time character in an *Archie* comic, but fans liked her so much that she got her own spin-off series—and that was just the start: since her initial appearance in the 1960s, the teenage witch has starred in three television series, a movie, and several novels, graphic novels, and manga books. Like other girls her age, Sabrina goes to high school and has a boyfriend—but unlike other girls her age, Sabrina happens to be a witch. The problem is that, even though she repeatedly uses her powers to help her friends and family, Sabrina can't tell anyone about her identity. The result is a fun, funny, enjoyable story of a good witch trying to make it in a normal world.

Psychic Phenomena

How can we explain the appeal of telekinesis and other mental tricks in fantasy? Maybe because, more than any other paranormal element of the genre, this one hits close to home. Face it, we'll probably never encounter a real troll or dragon or elf, but with a bit of imagination, we could place ourselves into the shoes of the characters who toy with the sixth sense.

Adams, Richard, *Watership Down* (1972) BK, MV, TV, CL
Richard Adams's classic adventure tale would have ended after approximately three pages if it were not for the prophetic visions of Fiver. Fiver, though weaker and smaller than other rabbits his age, can see the future—so when he senses that the warren is in grave danger, he and a handful of other rabbits escape in the nick of

time. (Later in the story, we learn that Fiver was right; the next day, the entire area was bulldozed.) As the rabbits journey toward a new home and work to establish a new life for themselves, Fiver's eerie ability to sense imminent danger rescues them time and time again. Discover this enchanting story in the original novel form or in the animated film version—and try to get your hands on the animated television series, which aired in Canada and the United Kingdom.

Clive Barker's Jericho (2007) CGM, VGM

Clive Barker, master horror and fantasy novelist, here turns his attentions to *Jericho*, a computer and video game in which the world's only defense against a supernatural evil comes in the form of the seven-member Jericho Squad. Fortunately, each person is prepared to duke it out with the bad guys, being armed not only with formidable weapons skills, but also with a paranormal talent; Captain Xavier Jones, for instance, is capable of astral projection, while Lt. Abigail Black is telekinetic. Violent, intense, and brimming with paranormal ass-kickings, the game is tremendous fun, but not for the faint of heart.

Dahl, Roald, Matilda (1988) BK, MV, UAB, YA, CL

Five-year-old Matilda is smart. Matilda is very, very smart. Matilda is so smart that that her brain, utterly bored with kindergarten, decides to amuse itself by learning telekinesis. Good thing, too: with uncaring, neglectful parents and a sadistic school principal named Miss Trunchbull (think Professor Umbridge from the Harry Potter books, only not nearly so nice), Matilda must resort to supernatural means to protect herself and to save the only person who acknowledges her intelligence, the sweet-natured Miss Honey. Like all of Roald Dahl's books for children, adults will find this an engaging story, and readers of all ages will delight in Matilda's bold use of telekinesis to save the day.

King, Stephen, Carrie (1972) BK, TV, MV, UAB, CL

If Matilda hadn't had a mentor like Miss Honey, she might have turned out like Carrie, the titular lead of the novel that made Stephen King famous. Psychologically, spiritually, and physically abused by her demented mother, Carrie harbors a dark rage within her—and as she is ridiculed by her classmates, she has no one to confide in. The rage explodes for the first time in the famous shower scene, when the onset of Carrie's first period opens the door to a previously unsuspected telekinetic power. But the minor damage in the school's shower room doesn't hold a candle to the telekinetic havoc that Carrie plans to unleash at the prom.

King, Stephen, The Shining (1977) BK, MV, TV, UAB, CL

Which version of *The Shining* is scariest, the novel by Stephen King, the film starring Jack Nicholson, or the miniseries starring Steven Weber? It's hard to say, but this much is certain: this horror/fantasy story would have been slightly creepy, at best, if not for the paranormal strains. When a family of three agrees to mind a sprawling Colorado hotel for the winter, it is the father's inclination toward seeing ghosts—and listening to them—that endangers his wife and child. And it is the son's ability to read minds—"the shine"—that offers his only protection against the monster his father has become.

McKinley, Robin, Sunshine (2003) BK

The title character of Robin McKinley's novel *Sunshine* can bake the best desserts in town; with skills like that, who needs other powers? But when Sunshine is abducted by vampires, her instinct for self-preservation reveals some very unusual paranormal capacities; with a lot of concentration, it turns out that she's able to protect a vampire ally from the sunlight. And Sunshine's not the only one who has a penchant for the paranormal in this urban fantasy ("Get a were-skunk mad at you and your life isn't worth living."). Unforgettable characters and an interspecies love triangle propel the story in this detailed, inventive world, where everyone seems to have an unusual mental talent.

Psychic Academy, Katsu Aki (1999–2003) MN, TV, YA

In an alternate contemporary Japan, certain people are blessed with aura power, which allows them to control a particular element, such as fire, earth, or lightning. Young people with aura power hone their skills at the Psychic Academy, but Ai Shiomi only enrolls with reluctance; he doesn't even know what his aura power is. He makes a few good friends at school, though, and eventually learns that he is gifted with the extremely rare light aura. Adventures, suspenseful moments, and romantic tensions abound throughout the series; enjoy *Psychic Academy* both as the anime television series and as the manga series by Katsu Aki.

The Sixth Sense (1999) MV, SH

Yeah, yeah, you've heard the famous line before: "I see dead people." Out of context, it's become something of a joke, but it's completely creepy when said by a child named Cole Sear (Haley Joel Osment) in M. Night Shyamalan's film *The Sixth Sense*. The question is, should his psychologist believe him? Dr. Malcolm Crowe (Bruce Willis) has dealt with a lot of troubled patients, but he slowly comes to believe what the audience has known all along: this little boy has the sixth sense in spades. He *does* see dead people, vivid, flesh-and-blood ghosts . . . and he's not the only one with a weird take on reality.

Anthropomorphism: Talking with Animals

Things have literally gone to the dogs in these stories. Animal stories grab us when we're young and never really let go. Anyone who's ever loved a pet will understand the appeal of a world where the animals can talk back.

Chronicles of Narnia, C. S. Lewis, *The Lion, the Witch, and the Wardrobe* (1950) BK, MV, TV, CGM, VGM, GN, UAB, YA, CL, SH

The country of Narnia is blighted by a terrible winter (with no possibility of Christmas!) and is ruled by a wicked queen. Lucy knows this, yet she can't help wanting to return; what little girl can resist a place where the animals talk? Some of them are just regular, non-speaking animals, but then others—including some beavers and a very significant lion—are fluent in English, as are the mythical half-human/half-animal creatures such as fauns and centaurs. For maximum impact, begin with *The Lion, the Witch, and the Wardrobe* (but be sure to go back later to catch the prequel, *The Magician's Nephew*). Enjoy these beloved children's classics in all their forms: as books, graphic interpretations, and audiobooks; as various movies and television adaptations (the BBC four-part series is especially good); and as computer or video games.

Dragonriders of Pern, Anne McCaffrey, *Dragonflight* (1968) BK, UAB, YA, CL

Science fiction fans would like to claim Anne McCaffrey's magnificent, multivolume series as their own, but we here in the fantasy camp refuse to yield: dragons feature prominently, and dragons mean fantasy. The dragons of Pern are not bad guys in the tradition of Tolkien's Smaug. Instead, they are intelligent companions to humans, and each dragon shares a lifelong telepathic link with one person. Introduce yourself to the series with *Dragonflight*, in which our human heroine Lessa must travel through time to locate some missing dragons, the only ones who can save the world from impending destruction.

Ghatti's Tale, Gayle Greeno, *Finders Seekers* (1993) BK
On the distant world of Methuen, an expedition of humans from Earth is unable to return home—but it's not a bad place to be stuck, especially if you're a cat lover. The planet is populated by the ghatti, a race of creatures that look like supersized house cats and who can share telepathic conversations with their favorite humans. In Gayle Greeno's first book, *Finders Seekers*, the human woman, Doyce, teams up with Khar'pern, a ghatta (that is, a female of the species), to solve a murder. Detailed world-building and an imaginative plot make this an enjoyable series for fantasy readers, especially cat-owning fantasy readers, who will feel validated by the ghattis' thoughts and behaviors; we always *did* suspect our cats were smarter than us.

***Kingdom Hospital* (2004) TV, BK, UAB, YA**
This quirky, unconventional, darkly funny (or is it lightly horrific?) television mini-series came to U.S. airwaves via the talented hand of Stephen King. Meet the denizens of the haunted Kingdom Hospital, including Dr. Hook (a human), Mary (formerly a human, now a ghost), and Antubis (not at all a human). At first glance, Antubis is your average ghost anteater, but his penchant for relaying the dead to the afterlife reveals him to be an incarnation of the Egyptian god Annubis. In any case, the giant anteater is the only hope for the hospital; without his guidance, the building will be consumed by an earthquake, and Mary's spirit will never find rest. Be sure to catch all 13 episodes, and don't miss the companion novel, *The Journals of Eleanor Druse*.

***Princess Mononoke* (1997) MV, MN, YA, CL**
To judge from San's behavior, you'd think she had been raised by wolves—and you'd be right. San's parents made the really bad mistake of damaging the forest, which in turn called down the wrath of the wolf goddess Moro. To save their own hides, San's parents offer their daughter to Moro, who raises the human as a wolf, and to great effect: San actually believes that she *is* a wolf. San, also known as Princess Mononoke, must reconcile her love of the forest with the complicated relationship she shares with Ashitaka, a human and therefore an enemy . . . or is he? Both the anime film and the manga adaptations are sure to delight.

The Wonderful Wizard of Oz, L. Frank Baum (1900) BK, MV, TV, VGM, GN, UAB, YA, CL
You have, of course, seen the classic 1939 film *The Wizard of Oz*, starring Judy Garland as Dorothy. (You *have* seen it, right?) The most notable talking animal is the Cowardly Lion, though the dog Toto communicates effectively in his own way, and frankly, it's a good thing that those flying monkeys *can't* talk. But if you want to explore the world of Oz from the eyes of the man who created it, turn to the wonderful series of novels by L. Frank Baum, starting with *The Wonderful Wizard of Oz* (sometimes titled *The Wizard of Oz*). Then read the subsequent novels, in which you'll find a wide assortment of talking animals, including an

animated sawhorse, a hen, a kitten, and various others. You'll also enjoy Oz in its many adaptations, including several movies, graphic novels, and television specials.

Making Connections

Fantasy has a lot going for it: exciting new worlds, memorable characters, and actions and events that stretch the mind. But some people may be reluctant to explore the genre, and to be fair, we must acknowledge the legitimacy of certain criticisms. Fantasy, especially traditional fantasy, can be derivative and stereotypical. Some fantasy stories rely too much on the *deus ex machina*, permitting a spell or a potion to magically whisk away a problem. For a story to be interesting, characters must depend on their intelligence and strengths to solve problems: this is true in every genre, and fantasy is no exception.

But those who hesitate to explore fantasy can be won over. As with every genre, fantasy includes some fluff. Look beyond that for stories that include powerful narratives, rich characters, strong world-building, and engaging prose: these are the traits that make fiction shine, no matter what its genre. Those who mistakenly assume that all fantasy is Tolkienesque will be especially delighted to discover the wealth of areas to explore.

Fantasy for Science Fiction Readers

Science fiction and fantasy are fraternal twins—they're not identical, but they have a lot in common. Both genres excite the imagination by asking "What if?" Engage fans of science fiction with fantasy works that don't stray too far into the realm of the impossible.

Engineer Trilogy, K. J. Parker, *Devices and Desires* (2005) BK, RS
In a world that strongly resembles pre-industrial Europe, technology has replaced religion, and a man named Vaatzes is sentenced to death for the crime of tinkering with the design for a mechanical doll. (That his tinkering resulted in an improvement is beside the point.) Fleeing to a neighboring, technologically backward country, Vaatzes begins to formulate his revenge by designing innovative new weapons that will bring the world to its knees. People who normally avoid fantasy will appreciate the complete absence of magic in K. J. Parker's trilogy, and science fiction devotees will love the meticulous attention to detail in the explanations and designs behind the technology.

Fullmetal Alchemist, Hiromu Arakawa (2001–) MN, BK, TV, MV, VGM, YA
Imagine a post-industrial world, similar to Earth, where alchemy is king among the sciences. Into this setting place two brothers, Edward and Alphonse, who suffer the loss of their mother at a young age. To try to bring her back to life, they attempt a dangerous alchemical experiment that goes horribly awry: their mother stays dead, Edward loses a leg, and Alphonse loses his entire body. Refitted with substitutes (Edward has an awesome prosthetic limb, and Alphonse now resides in a robot's frame), the brothers embark on a quest to restore their fully human forms. Hiromu

Arakawa's manga series (and its various adaptations into other media) combines a light fantastic touch with speculative science to create an engaging, adventurous, action-packed steampunk story.

Girl Genius, Phil and Kaja Foglio (2001) GN, YA, RS
It's the Victorian era here on Earth, only in this series of alternate-history graphic novels, science plays a much bigger role—*mad* science, to be precise. Robots, technology run amok, and scientists with astonishing powers dominate the setting. Our hero, Agatha Heterodyne, is a humble student at Transylvania Polygnostic University. At the start of the series, she has no idea that she is heir to a family of people with supernatural talents in physics—but she rapidly learns to come into her own scientific strengths when she is inadvertently thrust into an Industrial Revolution-style war. Light on the fantasy and heavy on the science, Phil and Kaja Foglio's series is a rollicking adventure with a strong female protagonist.

Juster, Norman, *The Phantom Tollbooth* (1961) BK, MV, UAB, YA, CL
A young man named Milo is on a quest to rescue two princesses—but this is no ordinary fantasy story. Though considered to be a classic of children's literature, Norton Juster's story is filled with so many wordplays and abstract concepts that it is more suitable for adults. There's a Mathemagician, a city called Digitopolis, and some Mountains of Ignorance to be conquered. Science fictions fans will love Juster's clever exploration of the tensions between rationality and imagination and his inversion of scientific truth.

L'Engle, Madeleine, *A Wrinkle in Time* (1962) BK, UAB, MV, YA, CL, SH
Fed up with the lack of women in science fiction, Madeleine L'Engle published her groundbreaking book in 1962, introducing the world to Meg Murray, an awkward teenage girl with a head for numbers. Meg comes by it naturally: her mother is a biologist, and her father is an astrophysicist—though no one's seen him for a long time. Turns out his experiments with the space-time continuum have landed him in distant dystopian planet, where he is being held captive. Meg must use the rational (science, logic, and math) and the magical (unicorns, witches, and telepathy) to rescue her father and save the universe.

Miéville, China, *Perdido Street Station* (2000) BK, UAB
Those who dislike the medieval settings, dwarves, sorcery, and assorted trappings of fantasy will find relief in the writings of China Miéville, who deliberately endeavors to work outside and against the Tolkien tradition. Blending fantasy, science fiction, horror, and literary fiction, Miéville's fiction aspires to something new, fresh, and innovative. Any of his works will appeal to science fiction readers, but try starting with *Perdido Street Station*, where magic exists alongside steampunk technology. The star is Isaac Dan der Grimnebulin, a semi-mad scientist who studies flying creatures to support his goal of regenerating the wings of a mutilated garuda, a predatory bird with eerily human qualities.

Fantasy for Romance Readers

Both romance and fantasy deal in magic—romance in the magic of love, fantasy in the magic of imagination (including, but not limited to, spells, sorcery, and potions). All but the bleakest examples of fantasy provide a happily-ever-after ending in the form of good triumphing over evil—and more often than not, the characters in fantasy find themselves in love. Move beyond the testosterone-drenched standards of traditional fantasy, and it's easy to find love stories that will appeal to romance readers.

Chibi Vampire, Yuna Kagesaki (2003–2008) MN, BK, TV, YA

If you're a teenage girl, how can you tell if you really like a guy? Nosebleeds, that's the ticket—at least if you're Karin Maaka. Karin is something of an oddball in her family of vampires: she can go out in daylight, she can sleep at night, and most notably, she can go without drinking blood. In fact, Karin has an abundance of blood: she actually has to bite others to release the excess, or else she'll suffer from nosebleeds. (Nosebleeds are actually a manga convention, indicating sexual arousal.) And every time she goes near a young man named Kenta Usui, her blood supply increases: yes, even vampires suffer from hormone problems. Yuna Kagesaki's manga series offers a light romance and a fun paranormal setting.

Kushiel's Legacy, Jacqueline Carey, *Kushiel's Dart* (2001) BK, UAB

Some folks like their romances to be chaste and demure, with tidy happily-ever-after endings. They are advised to stay well away from the Kushiel's Legacy series. These books are not traditional romances *per se*—romantic relationships abound, but they don't always end well—and they definitely aren't chaste. Those who enjoy steamy sensuality and complicated romantic entanglements, however, will be enraptured with the story of Kushiel, a woman destined from birth to serve as a courtesan. In Jacqueline Carey's alternate-history Renaissance Europe, religious worship takes the form of sex, so erotic encounters are frequent. But there's far more than sex in these books: suspense, espionage, intrigue, and magic, and rollicking high adventure fuse together into an epic, action-packed story.

Matheson, Richard, *Bid Time Return*, also known as *Somewhere in Time* (1975) MV, BK, MV, UAB, SH

Late-twentieth-century screenwriter Richard Collier has a celebrity crush based on a photograph of an actress popular in the 1800s, Elise McKenna. Not much chance of a relationship happening there, right? Wrong: Collier isn't going to let a disparity of decades prevent his wooing of the beautiful star. To make contact with Elise, Richard learns to self-hypnotize to the point where he can travel through time. Eventually he succeeds in reaching the nineteenth century, but get your handkerchief ready: some very difficult obstacles are going to interfere with the budding romance. Experience this beautiful, haunting story in book form, with Richard Matheson's novel (originally called *Bid Time Return*), and the film version, *Somewhere in Time*.

Outlander, Diana Gabaldon, *Outlander* (1991) BK, UAB

Diana Gabaldon's Outlander series defies easy categorization. It's a fantasy because it includes some mystical, magical elements, especially in the latter books of the series. It's science fiction because the main character, Claire Fraser, travels 200 years into the past from her starting point in World War II; it's historical because of the eighteenth-century Scottish and American settings. But without a doubt it's a romance series, because Claire falls for a Scottish clansman, her love for her twentieth-century husband notwithstanding. Steamy sex, powerfully emotional writing, and a love that withstands centuries of separation will appeal to anyone who enjoys romance.

Shakespeare, William, *A Midsummer Night's Dream* **(c. 1595) BK, MV, UAB, CL**
Romantic comedy simply does not get better than *A Midsummer Night's Dream*. At
the start of the play, there are several different couples that are obviously destined
for one another, but a few cases of seriously mistaken identity threaten to interfere
with the course of true love, and matters only become more complicated with the
advent of a bumbling group of amateur thespians. Even those who normally avoid
faeries (including Titania, Oberon, and the mischievous Puck) will find that Shakespeare's play is a guaranteed crowd pleaser, in print, on stage, or on screen.

<u>Sharing Knife</u>, Lois McMaster Bujold, *Beguilement* **(2006) BK, UAB**
In a departure from her typical approach to fantasy novels, Lois McMaster Bujold
here takes a light touch to her world-building and magical elements. She includes supernatural creatures and enchanted objects, but the main focus is on the unlikely
romance between Fawn, a farmgirl, and Dag, a sorcerer who saves her life early on
in the first book. Theirs is a poignant and lovely relationship, and while scenes of
action and magic use do occur throughout the series, it is the romance between Fawn
and Dag that will keep readers turning the pages.

Fantasy for Readers of Historical Fiction

All but the most resolute, "it must be absolutely historically accurate" fans of historical fiction can be enticed into loving fantasy. Because so many fantasy works have historical settings, it's easy enough to find examples of various times, eras, and settings. Some
fantasy books deliberately tamper with history in ways that will delight the imaginations of
historical fiction fans; some remain true to historical settings in spirit; and some lay a
veneer of magic atop settings that are historically accurate down to the last detail.

<u>The Camulod Chronicles</u>, Jack Whyte, *The Skystone* **(1996) BK, SH**
Bookstores and libraries sometimes shelve Jack Whyte's in the fantasy section, but
make no mistake: these novels are works of historical fiction that simply happen to have
a few supernatural elements. This is Whyte's magnificent vision of the story of King
Arthur, told in an entirely plausible way, enough to make the reader think it could have
really happened like this. All of the supernatural legends surrounding the Arthur myths—
the wizardry of Merlin, the enchantments of Excalibur, and the magic of Avalon—have
rational explanations. Read the books in series order to indulge in the savage medieval
setting, the epic character sagas, and the compelling story of Arthur's ascension and
fall.

Graham, Jo, *Black Ships* **(2008) BK, YA, RS**
Maybe you never made it through *The Aeneid*. That's okay: Jo Graham's retelling
of Virgil's epic poem will keep you enthralled. This is chiefly a work of historical
fiction, though there are paranormal elements, as we see when the heroine, Gull,
experiences a prophetic vision of black ships and a burning city. Those black ships
turn out to belong to Aeneas and the survivors of a ruined Troy. They also represent
a new direction for Gull, because Aeneas wisely chooses her as his new advisor. Experience the founding of Rome in this gorgeous, darkly atmospheric historical novel.

<u>Kristin Lavransdatter</u>, Sigrid Undset, *The Wreath* **(1920) BK, MV, CL**
Fourteenth-century Norway comes alive under the hyper-accurate attention of author
Sigrid Undset, replete with the deprivations, the travails, and the suffocating superstitions

of life in the Middle Ages. Smatterings of the supernatural in the form of witchcraft appeal to fans of paranormal fantasy, while anyone who likes a good story will enjoy the saga of Kristin, a young woman engaged to Simon but in love with Erlend. Catch it on film, or indulge in the three novels—just be sure to get the versions translated by Tiina Nunnally.

McCrumb, Sharyn, *Ghost Riders* (2003) BK, UAB
Rural Appalachia, 1862: a young man named Keith is drafted into the Confederate Army. His wife Melinda, determined to stay by his side, dresses in drag and enrolls as "Sam." Rural Appalachia, present day: Civil War re-enactors have outdone themselves; their dress and speech is so authentic, you'd think it was the real thing. Psychic Nora Bonesteel isn't fooled. She knows her community is being haunted by the ghosts of restless soldiers. Alternating between narrative threads in the past and the present, author Sharyn McCrumb delivers a ghost story of love, mystery, and romance.

Moore, Alan, The League of Extraordinary Gentlemen (1999) GN, MV
Blending historical fiction, literary fiction, and science fiction, Alan Moore's graphic novel *The League of Extraordinary Gentlemen* is a thumping good read, a dazzling mix of high adventure and literary allusions. In a steampunk-style Victorian England, a motley team of superheroes fights crime, but you won't recognize the characters from the pages of your comic book collection—you'll recognize them from the pages of your classic literature collection. Mina Harker (remember her from Dracula?) is the group's leader; other figures include Dr. Jekyll, Mr. Hyde, and Captain Nemo. This is an excellent choice for those who like the popular, social, and cultural sides of history.

A Song of Fire and Ice, George R. R. Martin, *A Game of Thrones* (1996) BK, GN, UAB
In the first pages of *A Game of Thrones*, we discover a scene of slaughter, where mythical, werewolf-like creatures have attacked some humans. But after this brief introduction, the magical elements of George R. R. Martin's series vanish for a good long while. Readers who prefer to avoid the heavy magic of traditional high fantasy will find that Martin doles out the supernatural sparingly through the course of his epic series. And though the narrative is set in a fictional world, fans of historical fiction will appreciate Martin's attention to the realistic details of the story: the politics, the conflicts and wars, the intense interpersonal relationships, and the gritty realism of life in a society that resembles medieval Europe.

Fantasy for Mystery Readers

People who enjoy mysteries like the standard features of the genre—the crimes, the puzzles, and the whodunit riddles—but that's only part of the story. Above and beyond the crime and the investigation, a mystery can feature interesting characters, well-developed settings, and good storytelling—characteristics that, fortuitously, can be found in abundance in fantasy fiction. The fantasy titles discussed here will please fans of mysteries for all these reasons; just don't be surprised if a dragon or a fairy gets involved.

The Dresden Files, Jim Butcher, Storm Front (2000) BK, TV, GN, UAB
Wisecracking Harry Dresden is your typical noir private investigator, a good guy who will break the laws and bend the rules to see that justice is served. He's also the

only practicing wizard in Chicago. Really: just look him up under "Wizard" in the Yellow Pages. Read and watch this series in order, to follow along with Harry's character development as he outwits vampires, double-crosses faeries, and battles werewolves.

Felix Gomez, Mario Acevedo, *The Nymphos of Rocky Flats* (2006) BK, UAB, RS
Private investigator Felix Gomez is pretty good at what he does. He's smart and savvy, and he's got some useful tricks up his sleeves: he can hypnotize people and erase their memories, he can levitate, and he can turn into a wolf. These skills aren't found in the typical repertoire of investigation techniques, but then most investigators aren't vampires. The mysteries that Felix solves are not necessarily run-of-the-mill (in the first book, for instance, he is hired to investigate an outbreak of nymphomania at the Department of Energy), but the stories are great fun, packed with action, outlandish adventures, and plenty of humor.

Garrett, PI, Glen Cook, *Sweet Silver Blues* (1987) BK
Ex-Marine Garrett is a tough guy with a taste for beer and women. He's a freelance investigator, quick to pick up on clues and even quicker with the one-liners. Underneath his macho exterior, he's got a keen sense of morality and compassion, so he kills only bad guys who really, really deserve it. But this is not your typical noir series, since Garrett lives in the fantasy city of TunFaire and regularly rubs elbows with trolls, elves, vampires, and wizards. Supernatural creatures and magical powers do have their place in Garrett's world, but the focus in each book is on the mystery. Read these in series order to follow Garrett's development.

Kitty Norville, Carrie Vaughn, *Kitty and the Midnight Hour* (2005) BK, UAB, RS
Kitty Norville is good at dispensing advice, so the job as a radio talk show host is perfect for her. Also, it's a night job, which suits Kitty's lifestyle; werewolves tend to be nocturnal creatures. She has no intention of becoming an investigator, but after the police learn of her supernatural identity, they engage her assistance in tracking down a serial killer. Fun, sexy, and suspenseful, this first book sets the stage for Kitty's amateur career in solving mysteries.

Rachel Morgan, Kim Harrison, *Dead Witch Walking* (2004) BK, UAB
After a plague nearly wiped out the humans and allowed the supernatural creatures to come out of hiding, law enforcement became a very complicated field. Now there's a special security service that exclusively employs non-humans, among them a witch named Rachel Morgan—and at the start of the first book, Rachel is bored silly with her job as a bounty hunter. Dismantling a drug operation will surely rejuvenate her career, provided she doesn't get killed in the process. Supernatural beings and magical powers abound, not to mention steamy romantic encounters, but the focus in each book is always on the crime that Rachel sets out to solve.

Sookie Stackhouse, Charlaine Harris, *Dead Until Dark* (2001) BK, UAB, TV, SH
Being a telepath is tough. The incessant intrusion of other people's thoughts can be a big disadvantage, especially in romantic situations, as waitress Sookie Stackhouse knows far too well. Cue the entrance of Bill, an eligible man whose mind can't be read because he is a vampire. Sookie is attracted to him, but just about the same time Bill shows up in town, a series of murders breaks out. Coincidence? Leave it to

Sookie to investigate! Read these mysteries in series order, and be sure to watch the HBO series adaptation, *True Blood*, starring Anna Paquin.

Conclusion: The Future of Fantasy

Fantasy is thriving. By some measures, it can be argued that fantasy is the most successful genre in mainstream culture; at the time of this writing, the second movie adaptation of Stephenie Meyer's Twilight series, *New Moon*, had shattered the opening-day box office record with a cool $72 million, and now holds the record for achieving $100 million in sales in just two days (just ahead of *The Dark Knight*, also a fantasy film, which took three days).

Throw another record-setting film into the mix—*Harry Potter and the Half-Blood Prince*, which holds the record for the best worldwide opening of a film (as of 2009)—and some trends are easy to spot. Urban fantasies that feature humans alongside supernatural creatures are the hottest thing going. Stories that are age-appropriate for teens while still appealing to adults are the most successful. And stories that translate into different media are the ones that will reach the widest audiences. Note that *Twilight* and *Harry Potter* started as print books, and that title character of *The Dark Knight*, Batman, started in a comic book; now all three are reaching fans in print, on screen, and in games.

The traditional epic quest, swords-and-sorcery subgenre remains strong, especially in print books and graphic novels, but the biggest areas of growth are in stories that have a contemporary feel and those that embrace several genres. Crossovers with romance are especially popular, though creators of fantasy are already beginning to experiment with variations on the crossover theme, as evidenced by the bizarre but strangely entertaining monster mash-ups that have entered the field lately. (See Seth Grahame-Smith's novel *Pride and Prejudice and Zombies*; the graphic novel and the film are both forthcoming). Today's fantasy might cause Tolkien to do a double take, but he would recognize in it the same qualities that have always made fantasy enjoyable: the imaginative storytelling, the strong characters and settings, and the tensions between good and evil.

Resources for Librarians

Turn to these resources for help when practicing fantasy integrated advisory.

Fantastic Fiction: http://www.fantasticfiction.co.uk/
    With an emphasis on writers of genre fiction, the Fantastic Fiction database is a wonderful resource that features author photos, brief author bios, book jackets, and plot summaries for more than 25,000 writers. Don't have time to linger? Search by author or title to get a quick bibliographical list of titles arranged in publication order.
Internet Movie Database: http://www.imdb.com
    IMDB is your one-stop shop for information on films and television. If a novel or short story has been adapted for the screen, even if the title has changed, you'll find it here. There's a wealth of information to be found, including plot summaries, movie stills, and extensive information on the actors and the people behind the scenes of any given production.

SciFan: http://www.scifan.com.

Web sites for readers of fantasy abound, but with more than 70,000 books and 20,000 writers, surely the most comprehensive is SciFan. Devoted to science fiction and fantasy books, the site includes information on new and upcoming releases while maintaining a staggering amount of information about older titles. When practicing integrated advisory, be sure to refer to their many thematic lists ("Crosswords," or "Steampunk" or "Indonesia," for instance).

Wikipedia: http://www.wikipedia.org.

Though the world's most famous online encyclopedia has its faults, it is often the best, fastest, and easiest (and sometimes only!) place to find information. (If reliability is crucial to your search, you can always confirm or deny the information from Wikipedia in a second source). When practicing integrated advisory, Wikipedia can be especially helpful because articles will typically indicate the different types of media to which a story has been adapted.

Endnotes

1. Cawthorn, James, and Michael Moorcock. *Fantasy: The Best 100 Books*. Philadelphia: Running Press, 1993.

2. Fichtelberg, Susan. *Encountering Enchantment: A Guide to Speculative Fiction for Teens*. Westport, CT: Libraries Unlimited, 2006.

3. Manguel, Alberto, and Gianni Guadalupi. *The Dictionary of Imaginary Places*. New York: Houghton Mifflin Harcourt, 2000.

3

Everything Historical (Fiction and Nonfiction)
Nanette Donohue

In this chapter, Nanette Donohue covers everything historical, including fiction and nonfiction, from prehistory through World War II, in all parts of the world. The "Characters" section includes eventful lives, famous characters revisited, family sagas and biographies, and English and French royalty. "Plots" covers two opposites, micro-histories and epics, as well as war and conflict and the westward movement in America. The featured theme for historical literature is era and settings, as these define the genre. The eras covered include prehistory, biblical stories, ancient Greece and Rome, early American history and the French Revolution. In the final section, you'll find historical titles for romance, fantasy, and mystery fans.

Introduction

Works about history speak to the human need to connect with our shared past. Humans have been captivated by history since ancient times, when historians such as Herodotus, Livy, and Thucydides wrote accounts of Greek and Roman history. Historical fiction found wide audiences in the nineteenth century, when popular authors of the era, including Sir Walter Scott (*Ivanhoe*, 1819), Charles Dickens (*A Tale of Two Cities*, 1859), Alexandre Dumas (*The Three Musketeers*, 1844), and Victor Hugo (*The Hunchback of Notre Dame*, 1831), produced epic novels set in the distant and not-so-distant past. With their combination of action, suspense, and romance, these novels became a sensation, and firmly cemented the popularity of historical novels for Western audiences. With the advent of film as popular entertainment, many historical works, both fiction and nonfiction, were adapted for the screen. A number of iconic films of the early-to-mid-twentieth century, including *The Four Feathers* (1939), *Ben-Hur* (1959), and *Cleopatra* (1963), were historical in nature.

Defining Historical Literature

Like any other genre, historical fiction is difficult to define, and readers may have different ideas of what constitutes a historical novel. The Historical Novel Society (HNS), an organization dedicated to the reading, appreciation, and support of the historical fiction genre, defines historical fiction as "written at least fifty years after the events described, or . . . written by someone who was not alive at the time of those events (who therefore approaches them only by research)."[1] The HNS also describes subgenres of historical fiction, including time-slip or time-travel novels, alternate histories, historical fantasies, and novels set in multiple time periods in their view of the genre. These are the definitions that are used in this chapter.

One essential feature of historical nonfiction is accuracy. A historical work can take years of research to produce, and this research tends to be meticulously documented. Reliance on source material is very common, as are lengthy bibliographies or source lists. While many historical fiction fans prefer that their novels be historically accurate, some readers are willing to let minor details slide if they get in the way of the story. Works about early history (prior to the Middle Ages) tend to be more speculative than novels about later eras, simply because the historical record is incomplete at best. It is easier to develop historically accurate fiction about prominent figures of any era, simply because information about these people has survived. For example, there is more documentation of the life and reign of Queen Elizabeth I than there is about one of her minor servants. This hasn't stopped authors from writing about Queen Elizabeth's servants, but these novels tend to include more speculation about what their lives may have been like.

Movies and TV

Historical film and television tend to be a mixed bag in terms of accuracy. Even works that are presented as historical nonfiction can be grossly inaccurate, while those presented as fictionalized accounts of historical events can illuminate new aspects of a well-known topic. Historical television programming is popular enough to support several cable television channels in the United States, including History, History International, and the Military Channel, and is a cornerstone of PBS programming as well. In general, historical films, including Academy Award Best Picture winners such as *Mutiny on the Bounty* (1935), *A Man for All Seasons* (1966), and *Gladiator* (2000), have been both popular and critically acclaimed. Some of the most successful historical films are adaptations of historical novels, nonfiction, or plays. For example, the 1977 eight-part television miniseries adaptation of Alex Haley's *Roots* was a smash hit, and its finale stands as the third-most-watched television program of all time in the United States.[2]

Books: Fiction, Nonfiction, and Graphic Novels

No easy generalizations can be made about people who enjoy historical works. Historical fiction and nonfiction are produced for audiences of all ages, and appeal to both genders. In its August 2008 issue, the *Historical Novels Review*, a quarterly magazine dedicated to reviews of current titles in historical fiction, published an article about trends in historical fiction for men. Ken Kreckel, the article's author, cites action and realism as key appeal factors for male readers of historical fiction and discusses the enduring appeal of war-themed historical fiction.[3] Print books continue to be the most popular medium for this genre, but fiction no longer dominates. Today, fiction and nonfiction are equally popular as narrative nonfiction writers have written stories that appeal to all readers, such as David McCullough's *1776* about the first year of the American Revolutionary War. Graphic novels are a tiny number of the historical titles published every year, although a few big titles in recent years like *300* indicate that there may be a market for historical graphic novels.

Integrated Advisory: Historical Style

Trends

When it comes to historical fiction, many readers prefer specific and often familiar characters or settings. The English royal court is a perennially popular setting for historical fiction. Readers seem to have an insatiable appetite for fiction about the Tudor era, although the Plantagenet era is rapidly gaining in popularity. Fiction about characters with a distant relationship to royalty (such as maids, servants, and distant relatives) gives authors a degree of freedom that writing about a well-known historical figure would not allow and provides different perspectives on famous historical events.

Even though well-known settings remain popular, the demand for books, both fiction and nonfiction, set in locales outside England, France, and the United States continues to increase. Another trend is an increase in genre blending. Historical novels with fantasy elements are on the rise, with authors like Neal Stephenson, Naomi Novik, Jo Graham, and Marie Brennan leading the way. The popularity of historical romance is likely to continue, as it is firmly established with readers. However, the content and tone of historical romance and historical fiction with romantic elements are changing as the romance genre expands. Erotic historicals and inspirational historicals represent opposite ends of the spectrum content-wise, but are major areas for growth in the fiction market.

Characters

By definition, historical literature is setting-based. However, character-driven novels and nonfiction works are currently very popular. Many historical works are character-driven, whether the character is the ruler of a multi-continent empire, a well-known politician or leader, or the keeper of a third-rate medieval inn. Characters provide readers with an entrée into a time other than their own, an identifiable focal point in an otherwise foreign world. Even though the customs, costumes, and conventions are different from the modern era, people still face the same struggles today as they did 500 years ago—thus ensuring that readers feel, in some way, like they are a part of something larger than their own small piece of history. Typical characters in historical works have some kind of special characteristic that sets them apart from the average person of their era. This characteristic may be something inherited, like a position in a royal court or a royal family, or it may be something developed over time, like a particular skill or personality trait.

In fictional books, movies, and television programs, historical characters may be real or imagined. Fictional works about true-life characters remain popular and show no signs of losing their hold on readers' and viewers' imaginations. For example, Philippa Gregory's best-selling *The Other Boleyn Girl* (2001) was so popular it was eventually adapted to both film and television. Works about England's Tudor dynasty, in fact, make up a good portion of the current historical works enjoyed by the English-speaking world. While many of the Tudor-era novels are fictionalized biographies of Anne

Boleyn or Queen Elizabeth, other authors have turned their attention to minor characters about whom little is known, or invented characters who live within the dangerous world of the Tudor court, such as the fictional Nell de Lacey in Ella March Chase's *The Virgin Queen's Daughter*. Historical entertainment is, by its very nature, grounded in reality, but authors and creators have ample opportunity to craft a fascinating story from the raw materials that have been provided.

Eventful Lives

Tales of characters who rise or fall from meager means to lives of wealth, comfort, and stardom have long captivated audiences. These works, which include an iconic American novel, as well as books about long-forgotten American icons, feature people whose circumstances rise and fall with the times.

Donnelly, Jennifer, *The Tea Rose* (2007) BK, RS
Fiona Finnegan is born into squalor. Her laborer father is killed for supporting a labor union, and her mother is murdered by the legendary scourge of 1880s Whitechapel, Jack the Ripper. All Fiona has is the love of her life, Joe Bristow, and a backbreaking job working for an unscrupulous tea merchant. As her London life falls apart, Fiona flees for the United States, gaining passage on a ship by posing as the wife of wealthy Nicholas Soames. Though she settles in and starts making her way in New York City, she never forgets her Whitechapel roots, and swears revenge for the injustices imposed on her family. Donnelly skillfully combines the history of fin de siècle London and New York City with a grand rags-to-riches tale of romance and revenge.

Holeman, Linda, *The Linnet Bird* (2006) BK, AP
When her father sells her into prostitution following her mother's death, 11-year old Linny Gow does what she has always done: she finds a way to survive. Convinced by her mother that she has noble blood, Linny determines to make something of her life. With the assistance of a kindly benefactor, she makes her way out of the slums and into a middle-class drawing room, but she knows that her fortune in England cannot last. When an opportunity to travel to India as a potential bride for a British colonist arises, she seizes her chance. Life in India brings her material wealth, but it also brings marriage to an abusive, angry husband. Linny's determination to survive despite her circumstances, combined with the raw and occasionally graphic descriptions of poverty and prostitution in Victorian London, make this a gripping though somewhat difficult read.

Mitchell, Margaret, *Gone with the Wind* (1936) BK (1939) MV, UAB, CL, SH
Originally published in 1936, the story of Scarlett O'Hara is such a part of American popular culture that most people are aware of it even if they have not read the book or seen the 1939 film adaptation; it has influenced the way many Americans view southern culture of the Civil War era. From her initial appearance as the spoiled, self-absorbed southern belle with a crush on Ashley Wilkes to her eventual comeuppance at the hands of Rhett Butler, Scarlett O'Hara's rise and fall is familiar to readers and cinephiles of all ages, and is one of the iconic American stories.

Uruburu, Paula, *American Eve* (2008) NF BK
Pittsburgh-born Florence Evelyn Nesbit was an astonishingly beautiful child—so beautiful that she is "discovered" in her early teens and asked to pose for a local

artist. After rapidly becoming a favorite among Pittsburgh's painters, she moves to New York City, where she becomes the toast of the town and the favorite of architect Stanford White, whose appetite for young women is insatiable. Nesbit's rise from poor, fatherless child to artist's muse to chorus girl to wealthy wife is rapid, and her fall, precipitated in part by the actions of her profligate husband, Harry Thaw, is just as quick. Though Evelyn Nesbit's story takes place at the turn of the twentieth century, the author could be describing the rise of any number of modern-day celebrities whose stars rise and fall before the age of 25.

Famous Characters Revisited

It's not uncommon for readers to want to spend more time with characters they have grown to love. Contemporary authors may write sequels or entire series centered on the same characters, but this is a fairly new development in the world of publishing. Most novels that we consider "classics" today were single volumes, therefore, the characters' story is finished at the end of the book. Works in this genre of historical fiction are often presented in one of three ways: as direct sequels of or continuations, as alternative retellings from the point of view of a different character, or as works inspired by another novel. They range from serious literary works to parodies to light romantic comedies.

Sequels to, continuations of, and works inspired by the novels of Jane Austen are especially popular. The first known novel inspired by Austen's works appeared in 1850, and their popularity has waxed and waned since. The Republic of Pemberley, a Jane Austen fan and information site, has a complete list of all known Austen sequels.[4] While *Pride and Prejudice* is, by far, the most popular novel for Austen sequels, all of the works in Austen's canon have been continued in some form or another.

Berdoll, Linda, *Mr. Darcy Takes a Wife* (2004) BK

This direct continuation of *Pride and Prejudice* steps behind the bed curtains of the newlywed Darcys, exploring the early years of their marriage in a way that Austen would never have imagined. Berdoll's novel contains a few troubling anachronisms, and Austen purists will scoff at some of the turns that the story takes, but as purely escapist reading, it's a good love story with a lot of spice. It is the first in an ongoing series of Austen sequels.

Brooks, Geraldine, *March* (2006) BK, UAB, YA

Mr. March, father of Louisa May Alcott's Little Women, is notably absent throughout that novel, leaving a blank canvas for author Geraldine Brooks to imagine his life and experiences during the U.S. Civil War. An ardent abolitionist, March serves as a Union chaplain during the war, where he is placed on a plantation that serves as a home for runaway slaves. The difficult choices made by many during the Civil War and its aftermath are explored. Brooks won the Pulitzer Prize for *March*, and it is a popular library book club selection.

Clinch, Jon, *Finn* (2008) BK, UAB

Clinch uses a minor scene from Mark Twain's *Adventures of Huckleberry Finn* as his entry into the world of "Pap" Finn. Huck's father is an unpleasant man, drunk, bigoted, and abusive; his daily life is a struggle. While it's a tough read for those who want their protagonists to be likeable and heroic, Clinch's novel gives readers a new perspective on the background of one of American literature's best-known characters.

Collins, Rebecca Ann, *The Pemberley Chronicles* **(2008) BK**
The first in a 10-book series of *Pride and Prejudice* sequels, it presents the story of Elizabeth, Darcy, and their children. Collins stays close to Austen in terms of style and presents a good deal of historical information about the era—much more than Austen would have included in her novels, which were contemporary for her original readers. Purists will appreciate Collins's light touch with Austen's beloved characters.

Hart, Lenore, *Becky: The Life and Loves of Becky Thatcher* **(2008) BK, YA**
Becky Thatcher, best known as Tom Sawyer's childhood girlfriend in Mark Twain's famous novel, looks back on her eventful life in this fictional memoir. Hart interweaves historical figures of the nineteenth century (including Twain himself) into Becky's tale of adventure, which follows her through the Civil War, the Gold Rush, and other events of the era.

McCaig, Donald, *Rhett Butler's People* **(2007) BK, UAB**
There are few sequels to and novels inspired by the much-beloved *Gone With the Wind*—probably because there are few authors willing to take a crack at one of the most enduring love stories in American popular literature, and because the few much-ballyhooed sequels, such as Alexandra Ripley's much-maligned *Scarlett* (BK 1991, TV 1994), was popular yet poorly received by critics. McCaig takes a different approach by focusing on the backstory of Rhett Butler, including several scenes from the original told from Rhett's perspective. Unlike some of the earlier companion novels, McCaig isn't trying to complete with *Gone With the Wind*, but to present one of its iconic characters in a different way.

Naslund, Sena Jeter, *Ahab's Wife* **(2009) BK, UAB, AP**
Captain Ahab's wife is mentioned only briefly in Herman Melville's American classic *Moby-Dick*; in this epic novel, Naslund provides her backstory. Raised in Kentucky by a strictly religious father, Una Spenser flees to Massachusetts, then escapes on a whaling ship by dressing as a boy. The ship wrecks, but the rescue leads her to Ahab, captain of the Pequot, whom she later marries. Naslund delves into the social issues of the era, including women's rights and slavery, through Una's story.

Families—Biographies and Sagas

Fictional family sagas wax and wane in popularity. Their last great heyday was during the 1980s, when 700+ page novels following generations of families became fixtures on the best-seller lists. Family sagas can be published in installments or as one long, self-contained novel. Family biographies are similar to family sagas in that they explore a family's history in detail, although they may or may not cover multiple generations. While most family biographies center around well-known historical figures, others may be based on "typical" families of a particular era.

Goldstone, Nancy, *Four Queens: The Provencal Sisters Who Ruled Europe* **(2008) NF BK, UAB**
In thirteenth-century Europe, the choices of women born to royal families were very limited: you married, hopefully into another royal family, and if you were very lucky, the marriage was happy and harmonious. The four daughters of the Count and Countess of Provence were extraordinarily lucky. Their politically astute and well-connected parents allowed them to rise above their station to rule as queens of

England, France, Germany, and Anjou. Rather than living as helpless queens under their husband's control, these four women ruled in their own right.

Gordon-Reed, Annette, *The Hemingses of Monticello* **(2008) NF BK, UAB**
Gordon-Reed's National Book Award-winning account of the Hemings family, whose lives she first explored in *Thomas Jefferson and Sally Hemings: An American Controversy*, traces the Hemings family tree to its roots: an English trading ship captain with the surname Hemings, and an African slave whose name has been lost to history. Gordon-Reed explores the history of the Hemingses in this intensively researched, complex, and detailed family biography, which includes the story of Sally Hemings as well as the stories of several other members of the family. There is also a film based on her story—*Sally Hemings: An American Scandal.*

*John Adams***, HBO (2008) TV**
The HBO miniseries chronicles the life of American patriot and politician John Adams from his days as a country lawyer through the dramatic days of the Revolutionary War and his time as a diplomat in France. Ending with his death in 1826, the series does not focus on Adams alone, but includes his wife, Abigail, and their children, including sixth president John Quincy Adams.

Lytton Family, Vincenzi, Penny, *No Angel* **(2003) BK**
The three novels that comprise Vincenzi's popular trilogy (*No Angel, Something Dangerous*, and *Into Temptation*) follow the lives, loves, and history of the fictional Lytton family, blue-blooded aristocrats who own a notable London publishing house. While the trilogy draws obvious comparisons to Barbara Taylor Bradford's *A Woman of Substance* (the same era, similarities in main characters, and the same glitz and glamour), Vincenzi's focus on the shift from Edwardian mores to modernity, as well as her descriptions of World War II-era London, keep the story grounded in a historical context.

Meacham, Leila, *Roses* **(2010) BK, AP, RS**
Meacham's first novel follows the life and loves of Mary Toliver, born into an east Texas cotton family at the turn of the twentieth century. Mary's life is one of privilege, but her love for the land above all else forces her to make decisions that will impact future generations of her family. This book is reminiscent of the great family sagas of the 1970s and 1980s.

Morland Dynasty, Harrod-Eagles, Cynthia, *The Founding* **(1981) BK**
Using the term "saga" to describe this sprawling series is a bit of an understatement. In the 31 novels that currently comprise this series, Harrod-Eagles follows the Morland family and its descendants from the War of the Roses and the reign of Richard the III through World War I. The series is scheduled to extend to 34 books, bringing the Morlands to World War II and covering approximately 500 years of British history.

Peebles, Frances de Pontes, *The Seamstress* **(2008) BK, RS**
This striking debut is set in 1930s Brazil, where political revolution has blossomed, movie stars are popular, and two orphaned sisters growing up in a rural Pernambuco state find their lives changed when a band of outlaws raids their village. Emilia is a dreamer who wants nothing more than to settle in the city with a handsome husband—goals that she achieves, but not without a price. Her sister, Luzia—known as Victrola

to the townspeople because a childhood injury has left her with a permanently disfig-ured arm—chooses to join the outlaws and becomes a legendary figure. The setting is unusual for American historical fiction, but de Pontes Peebles's descriptions of the Brazilian countryside will pique adventurous readers' interest.

Rashi's Daughters, Anton, Maggie, *Book One: Joheved* (2007) BK AP
The first novel in Anton's series about the daughters of eleventh-century French rabbi and Talmudic scholar Rashi focuses on Joheved, the eldest daughter, whose in-terest in and curiosity about Judaism inspires her father to take the unconventional step of teaching her about the Talmud. Anton's focus on this headstrong, unconven-tional, and bright young woman, and on Jewish life and tradition during the early medieval era, make this occasionally dense novel very rewarding. The story of Rashi's middle daughter, Miriam, was released in 2007; the final novel in the trilogy, about youngest daughter Rachel, was due in 2009.

Royalty

Many history buffs are attracted to larger-than-life characters, and what could be more extravagant and larger-than-life than royalty? The vast majority of historical fiction about royalty focuses on the English royal court, with the French court a close second. Favorite eras include the Tudor era, with the drama of Henry VIII and his revolving cast of wives, and the Restoration, featuring the bawdy court of Charles II. Pre-revolutionary France is also popular, with most English-language fiction focusing on the eighteenth cen-tury, after the construction of the palace at Versailles but before the revolution.

One benefit of writing about royalty is the historical record. The politics, drama, and excesses of kings and queens are well documented. While much historical fiction about royalty steps away from the king or queen to focus on a figure in their household (mis-tresses and ladies-in-waiting are popular), the royal personage tends to loom large in the background. In most historical novels, accurate history provides the groundwork for creative interpretation.

The English

While the English have had a royal family for over 1,000 years, certain eras have cap-tured readers' imaginations more than others. These tend to be eras of political conflict, powerful sovereigns, and cultural upheaval. The House of Plantagenet, especially Henry II and his wife, Eleanor of Aquitane, are at the center of most medieval-era English histor-ical novels.

The most popular English royal dynasty remains the Tudors. The larger-than-life per-sonalities of Henry VIII and Elizabeth I provide fertile ground for historians and histori-cal novelists, and the historical record from the era is significant enough that it is reasonably easy for authors to access. Of Henry's six wives, Anne Boleyn remains the most popular, with Katherine of Aragon running a close second.

The Restoration-era court of "merry monarch" Charles II is rising in popularity among readers, and the Regency period continues to be popular with novelists, particu-larly in romance and historical fiction with strong romantic elements.

Plantagenet, Lancastrian, and York England
While not as popular or accessible as the Tudor era, this period of English history (ranging from the twelfth through the fifteenth centuries) has no lack of drama or

larger-than-life figures. The Hundred Years' War and the War of the Roses took place during this era, and much of what readers think of when they think of the medieval era took place in England during this time.

Ball, Margaret, *Duchess of Aquitaine* (2006) BK

Ball's novel of the famous English queen begins with her youth as heiress to the wealthiest provinces of France. During an era when royal women were commonly used as pawns for men's political gain, Eleanor had the nerve to negotiate her own marriages—and to leave a marriage when it did not suit her. This particular treatment of Eleanor's story contains a strong focus on feminine/pagan magic, which may put off purists, but readers looking for historical fiction featuring strong female protagonists will find one of the greats in Queen Eleanor.

Braveheart (1995) MV

Winner of the 1996 Academy Award for Best Picture, this epic tale of the Scottish fight for independence from the oppressive rule of King Edward I stars Mel Gibson as William Wallace, whose battle cry that Scotland's enemies "may take our lives, but they'll never take our freedom" has become an iconic film quote, used and parodied in a variety of venues. While the historical accuracy of the film is questionable, and *Braveheart* has been criticized as being both Anglophobic and homophobic, it presents a popular, mythologized view of episodes in the long-running battle between England and Scotland.

Higginbotham, Susan, *The Traitor's Wife* (2009) BK, RS

Eleanor le Despenser, wife of Hugh le Despenser, played more of a role in the downfall of King Edward II that most readers realize—and she paid for it in spades. In her debut novel, Higginbotham, a scholar of the era, explores the life of Eleanor, who loved her husband unconditionally, despite the rumors of his affair with the king, and whose desire for survival helped her overcome the tragedies life imposed upon her.

The Lion in Winter (1968) MV, CL

Peter O'Toole and Katharine Hepburn star in this film adaptation of James Goldman's 1966 play about the marriage of Eleanor of Aquitaine and Henry II. Henry and Eleanor are in conflict over which of their children should be heir to the English throne, leading to a variety of political machinations. Hepburn's Eleanor is as steely as aficionados of the era expect, and she won a Best Actress Oscar for the role.

Penman, Sharon Kay, *When Christ and His Saints Slept* (1995) BK CL

Penman's Plantagenet trilogy opens with this epic novel, which focuses on Maude, daughter of Henry I, and her struggle for the English throne. As her father's last surviving child, Maude was to inherit the English throne, but her cousin Stephen challenges her inheritance, leading to a prolonged and bloody civil war. Maude's son, Henry II, meets and marries Eleanor of Aquitaine at the end of the novel, setting up the remainder of the trilogy. Penman is known for her dense-yet-engaging novels about royal struggles and conflicts, and though this is not her first novel, it has the earliest historical setting of all of her books.

Smith, Anne Easter, *A Rose for the Crown* (2006) BK, UAB

In her debut novel, Smith tells the story of Kate Haute, mistress of the much-maligned King Richard III and mother of his illegitimate children. Kate is born a peasant, but moves in with her mother's cousins, the noble Hautes, in order to serve as a companion for their daughter. Two unhappy marriages leave Kate with a fortune of her own, and a chance encounter with Richard, Duke of Gloucester, sparks an enduring romance. Smith goes well beyond the love story between Richard and Kate, describing the political turmoil of a very complex era in English history.

Worth, Sandra, *Lady of the Roses* **(2008) BK**
Worth's novel focuses on the War of the Roses through a woman's eyes. Isobel is a ward of Lancastrian Queen Marguerite, but the man she loves is a Yorkist—which makes him forbidden to her. Surprisingly, Marguerite allows the marriage, but at a price. While politics are against the couple, their love allows them to endure. Readers who enjoy historical fiction with strong romantic elements will enjoy Worth's romantic epic.

The Tudors

Despite its relative brevity, the Tudor dynasty, which lasted from 1485 to 1603, is one of the most written-about periods of English history. Full of colorful, larger-than-life characters, family drama, betrayal, deception, and romance, the reigns of Henry VIII, Mary I, Elizabeth I, and the other Tudor rulers are well suited to fiction and make for exceptionally engrossing nonfiction.

Barnes, Margaret Campbell, *My Lady of Cleves* **(2009) BK, CL**
Barnes's novel, originally published in 1946, has the distinction of being one of the few novels about Anne of Cleves, the decidedly unglamorous fourth wife of Henry VIII. Anne was dubbed "the Flanders Mare" by her husband, who quickly left her for a younger, more attractive woman. Though Anne lacked beauty and social graces, she was an intelligent woman who was not afraid to stand up to the often-tyrannical Henry, and was one of the few who survived her marriage to him. Barnes, who also wrote novels about Anne Boleyn and Elizabeth of York, gives this lesser-known queen her due.

Chase, Ella March, *The Virgin Queen's Daughter* **(2008) BK, UAB**
Precocious flame-haired Nell de Lacey first visits the Tudor court as a youth, and she is immediately drawn to the Princess Elizabeth, imprisoned in the Tower of London. She vows to return to London as an adult, and years later she does. Observers note that she bears a striking resemblance to the Virgin Queen in both appearance and manner—enough to arouse some curiosity about her parentage. Chase's debut features plenty of romance, as well as the standard court intrigue that readers have come to expect from Tudor-era novels.

Elizabeth **(1998) MV**
Cate Blanchett won her first Academy Award for her portrayal of England's Queen Elizabeth in Shekhar Kapur's 1998 film. *Elizabeth* opens at the early part of the new queen's reign, following several years of rule by her half-sister Mary. During the film, viewers watch Elizabeth mature into her role as Queen of England, defying all who doubt that a woman could rule one of the great world powers of the era. While liberties are taken with the history, Kapur's opulent vision of the Tudor court is a pleasure to see. The 2007 sequel, *Elizabeth: The Golden Age*, covered a later period of Queen Elizabeth's reign.

Gregory, Philippa, *The Other Boleyn Girl* (2004) BK (2007) MV, UAB, CL, YA
Gregory's best-selling novel (and popular book club pick) focuses on Mary Boleyn, Anne's older sister and Henry VIII's lover. Mary's legacy has been overshadowed by that of her tragic sister, but she was a force in her own right. Whether she was guided by her father's machinations to insinuate the Boleyns into the Tudor court or whether she was acting of her own volition is lost to history, but Gregory's version of Mary's story, with its sibling rivalry, torrid affairs, and power struggles, has helped set off the current craze for Tudor fiction. Gregory continues to turn to the Tudor court for subject matter; her other recent novels include *The Boleyn Inheritance* (about flirty Katherine Howard, Henry's fifth wife) and *The Constant Princess* (about Henry VIII's first wife, Katherine of Aragon). In 2007, *The Other Boleyn Girl* was made into a movie starring Scarlett Johansson and Natalie Portman. While the basic plot is the same, the narrative seems compressed significantly, and many of the details are lost in the translation from book to film.

olats

***Lady Jane* (1985) MV**
There were plenty of tragic heroines in Tudor England, but few were as tragic as Lady Jane Grey, Queen of England for a mere nine days before her untimely execution. Raised to the throne by her scheming family, Lady Jane was an innocent victim of the struggle for political power. The bright light in this sad story is Jane's relationship with her husband—presented here as an arranged marriage that leads to love. Lady Jane was reintroduced to the world by Helena Bonham Carter, who would become one of the great historical/costume drama actresses of the 1980s and beyond.

Lofts, Norah, *The Concubine* (2008) BK, CL
Lofts's 1963 novel, recently reissued to capitalize on the current mania for all things Tudor, remains one of the definitive novels about Anne Boleyn and Henry VIII. *The Concubine* follows Anne from her first encounter with the handsome English king through their early relationship and her eventual execution. Readers accustomed to racier novels about Boleyn may find Lofts' treatment somewhat tame, but the novel is well-grounded in historical fact and features all of the characteristics readers have come to expect from a book about one of England's best-known (and most notorious) queens.

Maxwell, Robin, *Mademoiselle Boleyn* (2007) BK, AP, YA
Maxwell, known for her historical novels about the Tudor era, focuses on Anne Boleyn's youth, particularly her time spent in France, in this novel. Anne is nine years old when her father is sent to France, and she quickly learns her way around the French court. Her sister, Mary, becomes King Francis's favorite mistress, but Anne's quick wit makes her a favorite of the courtiers. By focusing on a lesser-known period in Anne Boleyn's life, Maxwell's novel sets itself apart from the glut of historical fiction focusing on her reign as queen and her well-known downfall.

Miles, Rosalind, *I, Elizabeth* (2003) BK
Written as a first-person autobiography, this novel of the life and reign of Elizabeth I is comprehensive in scope and scrupulously researched. Elizabeth describes, in her own words, the life of a teenage princess, a fledgling monarch struggling to retain her power, and the powerful leader of a great empire. The first-person narration brings humanity and spark to the great queen.

The Tudors (2007) TV

With all of its glamour, deception, infidelity, and treason, the story of Henry VIII and his eight wives seems tailor-made for soap opera. While *The Tudors* isn't the first visual depiction of this popular era of English history, it's certainly one of the sudsiest. Jonathan Rhys-Meyers plays a young, strapping King Henry, and a series of beauties costar as his wives. *The Tudors* occasionally prizes style over substance, but it has obvious appeal to fans of the era.

Weir, Alison, *Innocent Traitor* (2007) BK, UAB, AP, YA

Weir, best known for her historical nonfiction, focuses on Lady Jane Grey, who reigned as Queen of England for nine days thanks to her family's political machinations—and lost her head as a traitor when their plot fell apart. *Innocent Traitor* uses a small group of narrators to follow Lady Jane from her birth through her childhood to her death at age 16. Weir is a historian's historical novelist. Her novel has a tremendous depth of research, yet is engaging and accessible. The subject matter certainly helps—there's plenty of plot to go around—but it isn't always easy to make historical detail sing in a novel.

Weir, Alison, *The Six Wives of Henry VIII* (1991) NF BK, CL

Popular historian Weir (who has also written biographies of Eleanor of Aquitaine and Katherine Swynford) turns her focus toward King Henry VIII and his wives. While numerous other biographies on this subject have been published, Weir's remains the gold standard for both its readability and the sheer exhaustiveness of her research. Weir is able to make history read like fiction—a good thing, since the political machinations and torrid love affairs of the notorious English monarch have the makings of a very engrossing novel.

Worth, Sandra, *The King's Daughter: A Novel of the First Tudor Queen* (2008) BK

Worth's novel is unusual in that it departs from the usual Tudor royals in favor of a lesser-known queen: Elizabeth the Good, wife of Henry VII and mother of Henry VIII. After a brief infatuation with her uncle, who later becomes Richard III, Elizabeth marries Henry Tudor, helping to found one of the great English royal dynasties. Though the players are not as well known, there's no lack of drama and intrigue, and readers may wonder why this reign isn't a more popular topic for historical fiction.

The Restoration

The period immediately following the restoration of the English monarchy is rapidly increasing in popularity among fans of historical entertainment. A number of colorful characters, including King Charles II, his mistress Nell Gwyn, and the diarist Samuel Pepys, make this time ripe for exploration.

Haeger, Diane, *The Perfect Royal Mistress* (2007) BK

The story of Nell Gwyn, favorite mistress of King Charles II, is one of the great rags-to-riches stories of all time. The daughter of a prostitute, Nell rose from working as an orange seller at the King's Theater to become one of the most famous comic actresses of her time. Though Charles was hardly faithful to one woman, his relationship with Nell was unique, and Haeger captures the complexity and drama of this grand and unexpected love story.

The Libertine (2006) MV

Teen-idol-turned-serious-actor Johnny Depp plays John Wilmot, Earl of Rochester, a dissolute, cruel, self-destructive noble who represents some of the worst of what Restoration society had to offer. Wilmot, previously banished from England, is welcomed back by King Charles II, who would like Wilmot to write a play glorifying his reign. He writes a play, all right—a satire of the king—which leads to Wilmot's second exile. In the process, Wilmot falls in love with a beautiful actress, contracts syphilis, and drinks himself to death. It's hardly uplifting, but it's a good reminder that the Restoration court wasn't all fun, games, and happy bed-hopping.

Pepys, Samuel, *The Diary of Samuel Pepys* (1825) NF BK

Sometimes the source material is just as fascinating and engrossing as a novel. Samuel Pepys is one of history's great diarists, and he recorded the events of his life, from the mundane to the history-making, on a near-daily basis from 1660 through 1669. His diary was first published in the nineteenth century, and his friendships with and descriptions of the history-makers of the time, including the king and his mistresses, make this an essential read for all Restoration buffs. Additionally, Pepys's diary is available online (in blog format!) at http://www.pepysdiary.com. One entry is posted each day.

Restoration (1994) MV

Based on Rose Tremain's novel of the same name, *Restoration* follows the life of physician Robert Merivel, who is summoned to the royal court to treat a patient but is thrust into a political (and sexless) marriage to one of the king's mistresses. Merivel's rise is rapid, but his fall is dramatic, and events of the era (including the Great Fire and the plague) add to the drama.

Scott, Susan Holloway, *Royal Harlot* (2007) BK, AP, RS

Scott's first biographical novel about the many mistresses of Charles II focuses on Barbara Palmer, the Countess Castlemaine, who ruled as the "uncrowned queen" of England for a number of years. Rather than treating Barbara as merely a cunning seductress, Scott gives her a mind and ambition—both of which would have been essential to keeping her alive at the cutthroat Restoration court. The follow-up novels, *The King's Favorite* (about Nell Gwyn) and *The French Mistress* (about Louise de Keroualle), continue in a similar vein.

Winsor, Kathleen, *Forever Amber* (1944) BK, CL

Originally published in 1944, Winsor's novel was an overnight bestseller and was banned by the city of Boston due to its frank sexual content. Though tame by contemporary standards, *Forever Amber* follows Amber St. Clare, a Nell Gwyn-style wit and beauty, as she charms her way into a life as the king's favorite mistress.

The French

French was the language of the European royal courts for centuries, and the beauty and glamour of France's royalty is legendary. While English-language works about French royalty tend to focus on seventeenth- and eighteenth-century royalty, there are a few works that describe earlier and later periods. Other works of interest to readers who enjoy French royalty can be found in the French Revolution section later in this chapter.

Carroll, Susan, *The Dark Queen* (2005) BK, TN
The first novel in Carroll's Dark Queen series, set throughout Renaissance Europe, takes place in France, where Ariane, one of the mystical Cheney sisters, finds herself entangled with Catherine de Medici. The combination of romance, political intrigue, and mysticism will appeal to historical romance and fantasy readers.

Fraser, Antonia, *Love and Louis XIV: The Women in the Life of the Sun King* (2007) NF BK, UAB, SH
British historian Fraser turns her sights back to France for this collective biography of the women who populated the life of Louis XIV. Covering everyone from his mother to his mistresses, Fraser explores the influence and relationships between one of France's most storied kings and the females who loved and challenged him. Like Fraser's other books, the research is extraordinary and the true story is as compelling as a novel.

Gulland, Sandra, *Mistress of the Sun* (2008) BK, UAB
Sandra Gulland returns to France with this account of the life of Louise de la Valliere, nicknamed "Petite." Unable to marry or join a convent, Petite joins the French court of Louis XIV as a lady-in-waiting, where she catches the king's eye and becomes his first mistress as well as the mother of several of his children. True to the usual "mistress story," Petite's life is full of intrigue, romance, and betrayal set against the glittering backdrop of one of history's most glamorous and decadent royal courts.

Haeger, Diane, *Courtesan* (2006) BK
The sixteenth-century reign of Francois I was full of intrigue and scandal, and Haeger's romantic historical explores one of its major scandals: the relationship between the widow Diane de Poitiers and Francois's son, the future King Henri II. Despite the obstacles to their relationship, including a political marriage to the legendary Catherine de Medici, Diane and Henri remained devoted to and passionate about one another throughout their lives.

<u>Josephine B.</u>, Gulland, Sandra, *The Lives and Secret Sorrows of Josephine B* (1999) BK
Gulland's three fictional diaries, inspired by the life of Josephine Bonaparte, follow Josephine from her youth in the Caribbean through her stormy and tempestuous marriage to Napoleon. Full of romance and political intrigue, Gulland's novels present Josephine as a heroine in her own right, rather than the wife of a conqueror.

Koen, Karleen, *Through a Glass Darkly* (1986) BK, AB, AP
Though chronologically the second in Koen's three-novel masterpiece, *Through a Glass Darkly* was the first to be published (in 1986) and presents the story of Barbara Alderly, a young woman who marries the man she loves only to find that he harbors a number of dark secrets. Set in both the English and French courts of the early eighteenth century, Barbara's story is absorbing and intelligent. The sequel, *Now Face to Face*, takes Barbara to the American colonies, and the prequel, *Dark Angels*, tells the story of Barbara's grandmother, Alice Verney, and her friendship and loyalty to Queen Catherine, long-suffering wife of England's Charles II.

Laker, Rosalind, *To Dance with Kings* (1988) BK
Originally published in 1988, Laker's family saga is about the lives, loves, and intrigues of four generations of women, all descendants of Marguerite, a peasant

woman who gives birth in the tiny village of Versailles in 1664. Through a number of twists of fate and chance encounters, Marguerite's descendants rise from poverty and find themselves living in the French royal court. While the main characters are fictional, the backdrop of the building of Versailles is well-researched and beautifully described.

Weber, Caroline, *Queen of Fashion: What Marie Antoinette Wore to the Revolution* (2007) NF BK
Countless books have been written about Marie Antoinette, but Weber takes a different approach, analyzing the life and activities of the queen through her fashion choices. It may sound like a frivolous tactic, but it's not—Marie lived in an era (similar to our own) where fashion choices, especially those of royalty, were scrutinized, criticized, and even politicized.

Plot

Usually, facts provide the underlying framework of a plot for a historical work. While creative interpretation of the historical record is possible (see the ending of Sofia Coppola's film *Marie Antoinette* for an example), deviating from the facts too much will likely alienate fans of the genre. This locks creators of historical works into a specific framework, but fortunately, there's usually ample source material to work with. To be specific, an author wouldn't write a novel in which Anne Boleyn and Henry VIII reconcile their differences and live happily ever after; but she could write a novel where Anne Boleyn's handmaiden and her Master of the Horse fall in love and live happily ever after, despite the fact that the handmaiden's mistress has lost her head.

War and Conflict

Plots may be ready-made in novels about war, but they represent some of the most creative and exciting works in the historical genre. Authors cannot tamper with the facts, but they can reinterpret events or introduce new and exciting characters. Historical works about war and conflict represent some of the earliest surviving literary works, including Homer's *Iliad*. They speak to our need to record the roots and outcomes of conflict in hopes of moving toward a more peaceful and just society.

Ellis, Warren, *Crecy* (2007) GN
This bloody, ribald graphic novel tells the story of the fourteenth-century battle at Crecy in Northern France. Part of the Hundred Years' War between the House of Plantagenet and the House of Valois, the Plantagenet English invaders slaughtered the Valois French due to superior firepower and strategy. Ellis's visual account of Crecy is shockingly brutal, and Ellis draws some parallels between warfare in the Middle Ages and modern warfare.

Frazier, Charles, *Cold Mountain* (1997) BK (2003) MV, UAB, AP
Cold Mountain focuses on the aftermath of war—the damage done to people after the fighting has ended. Inman, a wounded Confederate soldier, deserts the army and begins the long journey across the South to return to his home in the Blue Ridge Mountains. Meanwhile, Ada, the woman he left behind, struggles to keep her family's farm afloat. Frazier's gift for contrasting the natural beauty of nature with the coarse brutality of people helped make *Cold Mountain* an award-winning bestseller.

Glory (1989) MV, AP, YA
One of the classic films about the American Civil War, *Glory* tells the story of the 54th Regiment of the Massachusetts Volunteer Infantry, one of the few all-black regiments of the era. The men of the 54th show exceptional bravery throughout their service, even when embarking on a suicide mission to capture the Confederate Fort Wagner. Denzel Washington's portrayal of a runaway slave who joins the military won him a much-deserved Academy Award.

Horatio Hornblower, Forester, C. S., *Mr. Midshipman Hornblower* (1937) BK (1951) MV (1998) TV, UAB
Forester's Horatio Hornblower is one historical fiction's most popular and enduring characters. Hornblower is the protagonist of eleven novels and a number of short stories, and his naval career—from midshipman to admiral of the English navy—has inspired both film and television adaptations. The stories take place during the nineteenth century era of English naval supremacy, and feature action, exotic locales, and plenty of military suspense and drama.

Shaffer, Mary Anne, and Barrows, Annie, *The Guernsey Literary and Potato Peel Pie Society* (2008) BK, UAB, RS
Shaffer and Barrows' epistolary novel was one of the sleeper hits of 2008. During World War II, the British island of Guernsey was occupied by the Nazis, and the island's residents found small ways to rebel against the occupation—including, for some women, a book group. The authors explore the aftermath of war and occupation on the people living on the home front in an engaging style. This is a popular book club selection.

Sharpe, Bernard Cornwell, *Sharpe's Tiger* (1981) BK (1993) TV, UAB
Richard Sharpe is born of uncertain parentage in class-conscious eighteenth century England, and over the course of several novels and short stories, makes a name for himself as a distinguished military leader. Though the books were not originally published in chronological order, the majority of the Sharpe novels and stories take place during the Napoleonic Wars and are best enjoyed in chronological order. An ongoing television series parallels the Sharpe novels.

Tuchman, Barbara, *The Guns of August* (1962) BK, CL, UAB
Tuchman's nonfiction account of World War I focuses on the events that lead up to the war as well as the war's first month—watershed moments in world history that, to a great extent, dictated the course of twentieth-century European politics. Like most good historical nonfiction, Tuchman's work is as exciting as a novel, exhaustively researched, and extremely detailed.

Wood, Brian, *Northlanders* (2008) GN, YA
In the first two volumes of his ongoing graphic saga about Norse warriors (a third volume is expected in 2010), Wood introduces readers to Sven and Ragnar, two warriors living in different parts of the world (Sven in Constantinople, Ragnar in Ireland). Both protagonists defy the common stereotypes of Viking warriors as coarse, crude, and senselessly violent. This isn't to say that the stories aren't dark and violent—they certainly are—but they are more nuanced that most pop-culture portrayals of Vikings.

Pioneer and Frontier Life

Reader interest in novels about pioneers and frontier life waxes and wanes, and this once-popular subgenre of historical fiction is currently in a period of downtime. The exception is Christian fiction, where stories of American settlers and their journeys west are continually popular.

Bristow, Gwen, *Jubilee Trail* (1950) BK, CL

Romance and adventure combine in this classic novel of the Jubilee Trail, which leads to California. Garnet is a recent graduate of a New York boarding school who longs for adventure. When she marries Oliver Hale, a California rancher, her dream of travel becomes a reality. On the trail to California, Garnet meets Florinda, a glamorous woman with a mysterious past, and the two become fast friends. Bristow's other novel of frontier life, *Calico Palace*, is similar and also enjoyable.

Dallas, Sandra, *The Diary of Mattie Spenser* (1997) BK

Dallas's popular novel introduces Mattie Spenser, an idealistic young woman who unexpectedly finds herself married to Luke, her small town's most eligible bachelor—and traveling from her home in Iowa to a homestead on the Colorado frontier. Mattie and her new husband are virtual strangers, and their budding relationship is haunted by Luke's past and the hardships of the frontier.

Deadwood, HBO (2004) TV, AP

The HBO series *Deadwood* may be best known for its liberal use of profanity, but there's more to the story than blue language. Deadwood, South Dakota, is a boom town, settled after a gold rush, and it has attracted the colorful characters viewers would expect—sheriffs, saloon owners, and prostitutes—as well as a couple of real-life personages like Calamity Jane and Wild Bill Hickok. This series is more gritty and realistic than the television Westerns of earlier eras.

Mitchell, Shandi, *Under This Unbroken Sky* (2009) BK, AP, RS

This striking first novel tells the story of the Mykolayenko family, who escaped Stalin's hostile regime only to find a different kind of hostility on the Canadian prairies. Their battle against nature, inhospitable locals, and their own greed is described in unflinching, stark detail. Mitchell based this novel on her family's experiences settling the prairie provinces, and it's surprisingly hopeful, despite all of the turmoil.

Red River of the North, Lauraine Snelling, *An Untamed Land* (1996) BK, AB, UAB

The first in Snelling's popular Red River of the North series follows the Bjorklunds, a close-knit family of Norwegian immigrants, as they travel across the ocean to New York City, and then across the continent to South Dakota. The focus is not only on the struggles of the immigrants in an often-hostile country, but also on the struggles to maintain their strong Christian faith amid the tragedies and difficulties of pioneer life.

Roberts, David, *Devil's Gate: Brigham Young and the Great Mormon Handcart Tragedy* (2008) NF BK

The Mormons made up a large number of pioneers who traveled west during the nineteenth century as they fled religious persecution, pulling their worldly belongings in handcarts. Roberts tells the story of the Mormon emigration of 1856—a serious disaster in which numerous Mormon pioneers were killed en route to Utah. Roberts, a non-Mormon historian, describes the church politics behind the tragedy, blaming church elders' poor decisions for the deaths.

Turner, Nancy, *These Is My Words* **(1998) BK, YA**
Written in diary format, *These is My Words* tells the story of Sarah Agnes Prine, a pioneer woman in the Arizona Territories at the turn on the twentieth century. Sarah's challenges are typical of the era, and her diary shows how she grows and matures in a world that is as seductive as it is hostile.

Microhistory

Many historians specialize in a particular era, looking at a wide variety of influences, figures, and outcomes. Others choose instead to focus on one particular event, commodity, product, or cultural trend, following it through the ages and describing the unexpectedly long-ranging effects that something minor can have on society as a whole. This genre, sometimes called microhistory, has been particularly popular over the last 10 to 15 years. Microhistory is as effective in visual media as it is in print, and many titles of this genre are bestsellers. Stories of this type are most often nonfiction, but the best have exciting fiction-like narratives.

Baseball **(1994) TV**
Ken Burns is one of the best-known long-form documentarians in the United States, and *Baseball* is but one of his epic works. Like baseball itself, the documentary is presented in nine innings, following the sport from its early days in the mid-nineteenth century through its twentieth-century heyday. Burns focuses both on baseball as a national pastime and on the characters that made baseball what it is, providing not only a history of the sport but also a cultural history of the United States during a time of immense social change.

Kurlansky, Mark, *Cod: A Biography of the Fish that Changed the World* **(1998) NF BK, UAB, SH**
Who knew that the simple cod, a common fish of the Atlantic, had such a tremendous impact on Western history? Kurlansky, one of the preeminent authors of the genre (his book *Salt* is another well-known work) explores 1,000 years of cod fishing, from disputes between England and Germany to the role of cod as a food for American colonists to the current overfishing of cod in the Atlantic.

Petroski, Henry, *The Toothpick: Technology and Culture* **(2008) NF BK**
The toothpick is one of the lowlier of all consumer products—but, surprisingly, it's also one of the oldest and most storied. Petroski investigates the history of the toothpick in microscopic detail, from its origins among cave dwellers to its mass-produced modern incarnation, stopping along the way to revisit a number of historical events involving these small, yet useful, simple tools.

Winchester, Simon, *Krakatoa: The Day the World Exploded, August 27, 1883* **(2005) NF BK, UAB**
Winchester's great gift is his ability to take an event or a person, research it intensely, and present the result as an engaging, fascinating book. While most modern audiences have heard of Krakatoa, few are aware of the far-reaching effects of this volcanic explosion on a South Pacific island. Winchester weaves together several stories of Krakatoa into one narrative, and he makes the geological reality of a massive volcanic eruption just as fascinating as the human story.

Historical Epics

A number of historical fiction authors have made their name by chronicling the history of a place through time. In these works, setting (time and place) almost functions as a character of the story. James A. Michener was one of the first to make widespread use of this technique; the majority of his novels are lengthy sagas chronicling the people and the events of a specific geographic place. Other authors, including Edward Rutherfurd and Frank Delaney, use this technique as well. This style lends itself to lengthy works, and some authors break these epics into smaller chunks for easier reading. Generally fiction, these stories incorporate many historical elements, making them a good choice for nonfiction fans.

Delaney, Frank, *Ireland* (2008) BK, UAB
Delaney's novel weaves Irish stories and lore with history within a simple narrative framework: an itinerant storyteller shares his tales of the Emerald Isle with a nine-year-old boy. Delaney continues to write historical novels set in Ireland, and his most recent two novels, *Shannon* and *Tipperary*, are along the same lines.

Follett, Ken, *The Pillars of the Earth* (1989) BK, UAB, AP, CL, SH
Originally published in 1989, *The Pillars of the Earth* was a bestseller upon its release, and it gained an expanded audience when television talk-show host Oprah Winfrey selected it for her book club in 2007. The novel chronicles the building of a Gothic cathedral during the twelfth century, bringing together personal stories with the history of architecture and the medieval era. A 2006 board game based on *The Pillars of the Earth* has won several awards. A sequel, *World Without End*, set 200 years later, was published in 2007.

<u>Irish Century</u>, Morgan Llwelyn, *1916* (1998) BK, UAB
Llwelyn's series of novels chronicle the political and social history of Ireland during the twentieth century, focusing on several key events. The first novel, *1916*, describes the Irish Rebellion through the eyes of fictional character Ned Halloran, a survivor of the Titanic disaster whose friendship with a charismatic teacher brings him closer to his native culture. Other novels in the series take a similar approach to Irish history, framing it through the eyes of a main character that is involved in the events, including *1921, 1949, 1972,* and *1999*.

Michener, James, *Hawaii* (1959) BK, CL
James A. Michener's epic novel of Hawaiian history was originally published in 1959, the same year that Hawaii became a state. Beginning from the very beginning—a chronicle of the geological development of the islands—Michener proceeds through a number of eras in Hawaiian history, describing them through the eyes of families who lived through them. *Hawaii* is often regarded as the best of Michener's epic novels, which include *Alaska* (BK, 1988), *Chesapeake* (BK, 1978), *Poland* (BK, 1983), *Texas* (BK, 1985), and *Space* (NF BK, 1982).

Rutherfurd, Edward, *London* (2002) BK
Rutherfurd's 1,000-page novel chronicles the history of London, from the Druid and Roman settlements to the late twentieth century. Each segment focuses on a different event in the city's history, and members of one family recur throughout the novel, providing a bit of continuity through a lot of stories. Rutherfurd has also given England, Russia, Dublin, and New York similar treatment.

Tuchman, Barbara, *A Distant Mirror: The Calamitous Fourteenth Century* (1987) NF BK, UAB

Historian Tuchman (*The Guns of August*) chronicles the history of the fourteenth century in Europe in this sprawling, engaging history. Disasters and plagues flourished, religion changed, the Hundred Years' War and the Crusades raged, and the people of the era struggled to make sense of it all. Tuchman centers her story on Enguerrand de Coucy, a minor French noble who often found himself in the middle of the action. This true story reads like an epic novel.

Zinn, Howard, *A People's History of American Empire* (2008) GN, YA

Zinn, well-known for illuminating areas of American history that are undertaught or forgotten, takes his content into graphic novel format with the help of several fine artists. The focus here is on the modern era of American history, from approximately 1890 to the present. Zinn's work leans to the left politically, and therefore isn't for everyone, but readers who enjoy alternative viewpoints on American history will learn a lot from this book.

Theme: Era and Settings

Era and setting often go hand-in-hand in terms of reader appeal, especially with historical literature. Most historical entertainment fans gravitate toward the familiar rather than the exotic. England remains the most popular historical setting, especially for historical fiction, although works set in the United States and France also tend to do well. In terms of historical era, the formula for success seems to be a combination of an adequate historical record plus ample drama. This is why the Tudor era, with its legendary characters and intrigue, continues to be exceedingly popular, while the well-documented but comparatively drama-free Victorian era still hasn't captivated readers' interest to a great extent.

Prehistory

Fascination with prehistory begins as children, when we first learn about dinosaurs. For many, this transforms into an interest in human origins and the lives of our primitive ancestors. What we know of early peoples is based on the archaeological record, but many historians and novelists have taken these artifacts and speculated on what the lives of prehistoric humans were like.

10,000 BC (2008) MV

Movies with prehistoric settings have long been campy—the setting lends itself to fur bikinis and mammoth-stalking, grunting cavemen with large clubs and comparatively small brains. *10,000 BC* is no exception to this rule. The special effects are epic—director Roland Emmerich is the force behind several action-movie blockbusters, but the mishmash of history from different eras, including the titular 10,000 BCE as well as ancient Egypt, keep this one firmly in the campy special-effects spectacle realm.

Earth's Children, Jean Auel, *The Clan of the Cave Bear* (1980) BK (1999) TV, UAB, CL, YA

The first novel in Auel's popular Earth's Children series follows Ayla, an orphaned child rescued by the titular Clan of the Cave Bear. Auel's book explores the rivalry between the Neanderthals and the Cro-Magnons and the struggle faced by an outsider trying to make her way in the world. While the usual liberties have been taken with the actions of the characters, Auel's research into the era, particularly the culture and the medicine of the time, as well as the deft plotting and appealing characters, make this a classic of the prehistoric fiction genre.

First Americans, Sarabande, William, *Beyond the Sea of Ice* **(1987) BK**
Sarabande's series is often suggested as a read-alike for Jean Auel's popular Earth's Children series, although the two differ significantly in tone. Sarabande's vision of prehistory (approximately 40,000 years ago) is more violent and much less utopian. Like other books of this subgenre, it follows the migration of a tribe from Asia to North America, and features the usual trappings: ice-age intrigue, woolly mammoths, and a charismatic leader who guides his people to a new land.

First North Americans, Gear, W. Michael, and Gear, Kathleen O'Neal, *People of the Wolf* **(1992) BK, UAB**
The first volume of Gear and O'Neal's long-running, epic series introduces the titular People of the Wolf, who migrate from present-day Siberia through North America. Intended as a story of how the Native Americans arrived in North America, Gear and O'Neal borrow liberally from Native American religion and tribal customs, often pushing the novel into fantasy territory. The first four books follow the same group, while books five through 15 each follow different cultural groups across time.

Mithen, Stephen, *After the Ice: A Global Human History, 20,000–5,000* BC **(2006) NF BK**
Mithen's scholarly-yet-readable history of the Mesolithic and Neolithic eras covers 15,000 years of human existence via a narrative approach, centering around John Lubbock, a fictional Victorian-era gentleman scientist with a strong interest in prehistoric culture. The work is epic, but Mithen's choice of a narrative format ensures that the work is accessible to experts and dilettantes alike. Since our knowledge of these eras is based solely on the archaeological record, there is some speculation, but all of it is grounded in discoveries that have been made.

Quest for Fire **(1981) MV**
This 1981 film follows a small tribe of Cro-Magnons whose fire is stolen during an attack by a rival tribe. A small group is forced to go forth and seek more fire—a dangerous prospect in 80,000 BCE. The tribe members communicate in a manner that is likely realistic for the era, in a series of grunts, groans, and body language, and none of it is subtitled. Unlike most movies about the era, *Quest for Fire* steers clear of camp and focuses on the importance of community and collective experience—as well as life-sustaining fire—to our prehistoric ancestors.

Raising the Mammoth **(2000) TV**
The woolly mammoth is one of the great icons of prehistoric culture, and *Raising the Mammoth*, a Discovery Channel special, centers around a 1998 expedition into the Siberian permafrost in search of a fully intact woolly mammoth. Much of the drama involves the machinations surrounding the physical "raising" of the mammoth within its giant block of ice. While the audience never sees the mammoth, other than its tusks and some ruddy fur, the drama and excitement of scientific discovery are still exciting.

Biblical Retellings

Biblical fiction may be based on the events or characters of the Judeo-Christian bible, but because it deals with events that took place thousands of years ago, there is often a good deal of speculation involved. While there is some historical record of the late biblical era, it tends to be in the form of physical artifacts (such as containers or items intended for daily use) rather than written records, so many of the details of daily life and custom are lost to modern authors. One popular subgenre of biblical fiction focuses on the lives of biblical women, many of whom are mentioned only briefly in the text of the bible. Authors writing in this subgenre may be crafting an entire narrative from a brief story (sometimes as little as a single verse).

While biblical historical fiction is often popular with readers of Christian fiction and is frequently published by mainstream Christian publishers, there are also many popular works that take a critical or alternative viewpoint of biblical history. Some of these works may be controversial or even offend library patrons who take a literal view of the bible. A reader's advisory interview, including questions about other works in this genre that the reader has enjoyed and why they liked these works, can assist in determining readers' preferences.

<u>Canaan Trilogy</u>, Marek Halter, *Sarah* (2004) BK, UAB
French-Jewish author Halter explores the life of Sarah, wife of Abraham and matriarch of the Jewish people. Born Sarai, she is the daughter of a wealthy and powerful lord of the Sumerian city of Ur. Sarai rejects her arranged marriage and flees Ur, where she encounters Abram, a member of a nomadic tribe living outside the city walls. Though she is attracted to Abram, she chooses to return to her father's house, and she becomes the high priestess of the Sumerian goddess Ishtar. When Abram returns to Ur years later, she gives up her life in the city to join his tribe—and his faith. Later novels in Halter's Canaan trilogy focus on Zipporah and Lilah; his most recent work turns to the New Testament and Mary of Nazareth.

<u>Christ the Lord</u>, Anne Rice, *Out of Egypt* (2005) BK, UAB
When popular horror author Rice rediscovered the Catholic faith of her youth, she turned from novels about vampires to a multivolume biography of Jesus Christ. Rice's Christ the Lord series explores the areas of Jesus's life that are absent from the New Testament, particularly his youth and young adulthood. There are two novels in the series thus far—*Out of Egypt* and *The Road to Cana*.

Diamant, Anita, *The Red Tent* (1997) BK, UAB, AP, CL, YA
Focusing on the lives of Old Testament women, particularly on the custom of the "red tent," where women retreated when they were menstruating or giving birth, Diamant develops the story of Dinah, daughter of Jacob and Leah, whose mention in the book of Genesis is brief. Focusing first on the stories of Rachel and Leah, Jacob's two wives, to provide context for Dinah's actions and the women's culture that Dinah will soon join, readers experience the culture of the era, the differences between the inner and outer lives of the women, and the conflict between duty and desire. Diamant's novel is a popular, imaginative, and thought-provoking selection for book clubs.

Elliott, Elissa, *Eve: A Novel of the First Woman* (2009) BK, UAB
In her first novel, Elliott explores the story of Eve, the biblical "first woman"—a phrase she treats figuratively rather than literally by placing Eve and her family within the context of ancient Mesopotamia and treating her as the first woman to

worship Elohim. The narrative focuses on Eve and her three daughters: Aya, who is intellectually curious but significantly restricted by a club foot; Naavah, who is beautiful, ambitious, and conniving; and Dara, the youngest, who observes the action around her from a child's point of view. The conflict between Eve's family and the ruling class in the city, who worship differently, is at the heart of this imaginative, non-literal biblical reimagining.

Kohn, Rebecca, *The Gilded Chamber: A Novel of Queen Esther* **(2005) BK**
Kohn's biographical novel stays true to the biblical account of Esther, who rose from orphan to harem girl in the court of King Xerxes to Queen of Persia. Meticulously researched and strikingly detailed, this tale of a heroic queen who saves the Jewish people is often cited as a read-alike for *The Red Tent*.

The Last Temptation of Christ **(1988) MV**
Martin Scorsese's 1988 film (based on the novel of the same name by Nikos Kazantzakis) takes a markedly different view of Christ's passion—so different that biblical literalists consider it offensive. Drawing from the accounts of the crucifixion presented in the gnostic gospels, *The Last Temptation of Christ* presents Jesus as both divine and human, and the human side caused significant controversy upon the film's release. Kazantzakis and Scorsese's Jesus has doubts, insecurities, and even sexual desire. Viewers who are open to alternative viewpoints on the life and death of Jesus will seek out this film.

The Nativity Story **(2006) MV**
Library patrons familiar with director Catherine Hardwicke from her adaptation of the popular teen vampire novel *Twilight* and her troubled-teen drama *Thirteen* may be surprised that she also directed this gentle, restrained film about the birth of Jesus. The story is familiar to many, the acting is nuanced, and Hardwicke's version is reasonably true to the biblical account. While this wasn't an "event film" on the level of *The Passion of the Christ*, patrons looking for a biblical movie appropriate for families will find it appealing.

The Passion of the Christ **(2004) MV**
Director Mel Gibson's graphic depiction of the crucifixion of Jesus Christ closely follows the gospel accounts of the Passion and was embraced by evangelical Christians (and poorly received by film critics) upon its release. The dialogue is in Aramaic and Latin, with few subtitles, but as the story is well known to the intended audience, it isn't difficult to follow. Aside from the violence, the strongest criticism of *The Passion of the Christ* is that it is anti-Semitic, which Gibson has denied. It can be unrelenting and tough to watch, but that was most likely the director's point.

The Ten Commandments **(1956) MV**
The perennial favorite, which usually airs on U.S. network television near the Easter holiday, is an epic account of the biblical story of Moses and the Hebrew exodus from Egypt. While the movie (originally released in 1956) can be campy and overwrought, especially for contemporary audiences, it's a tradition for many, and is one of the best-known (and probably the most-watched) biblical historical films.

The Ancient, the Classical, and the Hellenic

While we have artifacts of earlier eras, ancient Egypt, Greece, and Rome are some of the earliest civilizations to have left a written record. Works about these civilizations still depend on a good deal of speculation, but enough history is definitively known to allow for a strong basis in fact. Works about this era include blends of fact and myth and tend to focus on well-known figures and events.

300 (1999) GN (2007) MV

A brief cinematic fad for all things ancient resulted in a few films about ancient Greece and Rome released within in a short period of time. The gory, intense *300* is one of the best of this bunch. Based on a graphic novel by Frank Miller and Lynn Varley, *300* tells the story of the Spartans' battle against Persia's King Xerxes at the strait of Thermopylae. There's a lot of blood and a lot of handsome, buff Greek warriors, and at times it stops just short of camp, but its translation of ancient history for modern sensibilities is surprisingly successful.

George, Margaret, *The Memoirs of Cleopatra* (1998) BK, UAB

George specializes in doorstopper-sized biographical fiction about well-known historical figures, and *The Memoirs of Cleopatra* is an exploration of the life, loves, and legacy of one of ancient Egypt's most familiar and least-understood rulers. Popular culture has long portrayed Cleopatra as a seductress who became a tool used by the men in her life; George gives us a much more balanced view of a ruler who is shrewd and diplomatic and who always had the best interests of her kingdom in mind.

Gladiator (2000) MV

The winner of 2001's Academy Award for Best Picture is a portrait of Maximus (Best Actor winner Russell Crowe), whose life has been destroyed by the emperor's son, Commodus. Forced into slavery, Maximus becomes one of the great gladiators of his time, all the while continuing to plot his revenge against Commodus. More violent and intense (and, therefore, more appealing to modern audiences) than the sword-and-sandals epics that preceded it, *Gladiator* sparked a renewed interest in the history and culture of ancient Rome.

Graham, Jo, *Hand of Isis* (2009) BK, AP, RS, YA

Graham's second novel is told from the perspective of Charmian, one of Cleopatra's handmaidens (and her half-sister—they share the same father). Cleopatra is a distant and unlikely heir to the Egyptian throne, and though she is well-educated and bright, few expect her to become more than a pawn in the marriage market. Cleopatra, Charmian, and Iras make a promise to the goddess Isis that they will always put Egypt first, and Isis blesses them by making Cleopatra the queen. Charmian is an engaging narrator whose life is as fascinating as Cleopatra's, and her view of key events in the Queen's life, such as Cleopatra's relationship with Caesar, allow for a bit more distance than an autobiographical novel would.

Le Guin, Ursula, *Lavinia* (2008) BK

In the Latin epic *The Aeneid*, Lavinia, daughter of King Latinus, never speaks. In this reimagining of the classic tale, Lavinia tells her life story. Despite her mother's wishes, prophecy declares that Lavinia will marry a foreigner—in this case, the hero, Aeneas—and that she will cause a civil war in the process. Told in poetic prose, Le Guin gives a voice to a woman whose legend has spanned centuries and whose story demands to be told.

Moran, Michelle, *Nefertiti* (2007) BK, UAB, AP, RS

History buffs are familiar with the ancient bust of Nefertiti, the Egyptian queen whose regal bearing and exquisite face have survived the ages. Nefertiti herself was no less powerful and regal, and Moran brings her to life through the eyes of her sister, Mutnodjmet. Nefertiti becomes the chief wife of the pharaoh as a teenager, and she and her husband make grand plans to build a city in the desert to honor the god Aten. Mutnodjmet, sensing trouble, attempts to advise her sister, but Nefertiti, driven by power and desire to leave a legacy, cannot be swayed. The relationship between the sisters will appeal to readers of women's fiction and remind us that rivalries between sisters are as old as, well, ancient Egypt.

Rome, HBO (2006) TV

HBO's epic series takes place during the fall of the Roman republic and follows both the elite of the day and the commoners, presenting a balanced, if sensationalized, view of Rome's transformation from republic to empire. There's as much nudity, sex, and violence as viewers of U.S. pay cable dramas expect, and the history isn't always completely accurate, but *Rome* is as provocative as the era upon which it was based.

Shanower, Eric, *Age of Bronze* (2001) GN, AP, YA

Shanower's epic tale (told over a projected seven volumes) tells the story of the Trojan War as readers have never seen it before—through words and images. His extensive research into everything from myth to architecture to costume lends a surprising amount of realism to this unique treatment of a well-known historical event.

Early American History

American history runs a distant second to English history as a popular setting for historical fiction and drama, but historical nonfiction about the United States continues to flourish. The most popular American setting for fiction is early American history, roughly from the European discovery of the North America in the fifteenth century through the War of 1812, with a particular focus on the colonial and revolutionary eras. Some novels in the Western genre could also be considered American historical fiction, particularly those with a focus on historical accuracy.

Interest in American history tends to be cyclical, coinciding with major historical anniversaries. The bicentennial celebrations in 1976 brought about a burst of interest in Revolutionary War, and Abraham Lincoln is currently a particularly hot topic in American history, due to the 2009 celebrations of the bicentennial of his birth.

John Adams, HBO (2008) TV, AP, SH

Based on the best-selling biography by historian David McCullough, John Adams follows the life of the second president of the United States from his early days as a Boston patriot. As expected, the bulk of the eight-hour miniseries focuses on Adams's political life, including his work on the Declaration of Independence, the U.S. Constitution, and his ambassadorships to France and the Netherlands during the early days of American independence. Paul Giamatti portrays Adams as both a loving husband and a shrewd politician, and like McCullough's book, Adams's faults are not sugarcoated. American history buffs will appreciate the accuracy of the settings and costumes, and viewers whose interest in American history is marginal at best will find themselves drawn into the life story of one of the great founders of the United States.

McCullough, David, *1776* (2006) NF BK, UAB

To many Americans, 1776 means one thing: the year that the Declaration of Independence was signed, giving birth to the United States of America. Noted historian

McCullough focuses instead on the military history of that year, where the momentum of the war turned toward the Americans. Like McCullough's other works, it is scrupulously researched, yet accessible to leisure readers, and it presents well-known historical figures in a new (and sometimes unexpected) light.

Seton, Anya, *The Winthrop Woman* (2006) BK, CL
Originally published in 1958, Seton's second bestseller (after her classic romance *Katherine*, BK 1954) explores the life and loves of Elizabeth Winthrop, nee Fones, who married into the family of Massachusetts' colony governor John Winthrop. Elizabeth's independent-mindedness causes friction with her husband's family, and her tendency toward compassion for others sets her apart from some of the other colonists, who demand retribution for a variety of infractions. The *Winthrop Woman*'s depth and historical accuracy appeals to those who enjoy lengthy, detailed epics.

Sharratt, Mary, *The Vanishing Point* (2006) BK, AP
May Powers leaves her sister, Hannah, and emigrates from England to the colonies in the early 1690s so she can marry her father's cousin. May's promiscuous behavior has rendered her unmarriageable at home, and though she and her sister are close, Hannah stays behind to care for their aging father. When he dies, Hannah travels to America in search of her sister, but upon her arrival, she makes a gruesome discovery: the plantation that May described in her letters has been abandoned. May is gone, and her grief-stricken husband, Gabriel, is the only person in the house. Independent-minded Hannah finds herself on a quest to discover what fate befell her sister while trying to settle into the new, strange land. Details of seventeenth-century medicine add a unique angle to this suspenseful story.

Vowell, Sarah, *The Wordy Shipmates* (2008) NF BK, UAB, YA
Popular NPR commentator Vowell journeys into the minds, hearts, and faith of the Puritans, who fled religious persecution in England to found the Massachusetts colony. By focusing on the major names and events of seventeenth-century New England, Vowell gives readers an overview of early American history. While considered by many as "history lite," and Vowell's frequent (and often humorous) editorial interjections may vex history purists, this is a good layperson's introduction to some of the philosophical forces that shaped early America and continue to influence American morals and thought.

<u>Wilderness Saga</u>, Donati, Sara, *Into the Wilderness* (1998) BK, UAB
The first novel in Donati's ongoing early American saga introduces Elizabeth Middleton, an Englishwoman of genteel upbringing who travels to upstate New York in the early 1790s to become a teacher. Paradise, the town where she settles, is the frontier, and tensions between the Native Americans and the settlers are high. When Elizabeth meets Nathaniel Bonner, a backwoodsman with strong ties to the Mahican people, she recognizes a kindred spirit, and as she gets to know Nathaniel, they find love. Though it is billed as a sequel (of sorts) to James Fenimore Cooper's *Last of the Mohicans*, readers who are unfamiliar with Cooper's work will easily pick up the details necessary to enjoy this book.

The French Revolution

There are few historical events that capture the imagination as the French Revolution does. The power of common people to engineer the fall of the excessive, profligate French nobility has appealed to readers for ages. Works about the French Revolution tend to focus on one side or the other—either the nobles or the common people. The figure that looms largest in works about the era is the glamorous queen, Marie Antoinette, who lost her head to the guillotine.

Delors, Catherine, *Mistress of the Revolution* (2008) BK

Delors's debut is the story of Gabrielle de Montserrat, a French noblewoman forced into an abusive marriage with a fellow noble, despite her love for a commoner. When her husband dies, Gabrielle and her daughter arrive at the court of Louis XVI at an inopportune time—just before the dawn of the revolution. Readers familiar with the French Revolution will find numerous familiar figures, and Gabrielle herself is a sympathetic character thrust into situations well beyond her control.

Dickens, Charles, *A Tale of Two Cities* (1859) BK, TV, MV, CL, AB, UAB

If you read this classic novel in high school and gave up on it (or hated it), give it another try. You might find yourself pleasantly surprised. This epic, regarded by many as one of Dickens's greatest, follows a number of characters as they navigate the complex political and personal landscapes of Paris and London during the French Revolution. You'll never forget Madame Defarge, the tricoteuse, knitting away as the guillotine claims another victim. There have also been a few movie versions and a Masterpiece Theatre version; an audio version read by Simon Vance is highly recommended.

Fraser, Antonia, *Marie Antoinette: The Journey* (2002) NF BK, UAB

Well-known historical biographer Fraser takes on the much-maligned Marie Antoinette in a sympathetic, balanced account of her life and times. Readers used to the shallow, petty side of Marie may be surprised at the depth of her dignity and compassion and her love of her family and the French people. As with Fraser's other works, the depth of research is exhaustive, and the writing is never dull.

Marie Antoinette (2006) MV, YA

An overabundance of style wins out over substance in Sofia Coppola's 2006 adaptation of Antonia Fraser's *Marie Antoinette: The Journey*. Marie Antoinette, played by Kirsten Dunst, is a giddy, fish-out-of-water teen princess thrust into the unfamiliar territory of the French court. One key criticism of the film is Coppola's use of modern music rather than the music of the era, as well as other modern touches (Marie wears Converse sneakers in one scene). Most viewers are likely familiar with how Marie's story ends, which is good, since this version ends with Marie and Louis escaping Versailles in a carriage, with nary an inkling of their true fate. Historical accuracy aside, it's fun to watch, and makes a statement about celebrity and royalty that transcends a specific time period.

Naslund, Sena Jeter, *Abundance* (2006) BK, AP, UAB

Marie Antoinette's story is well known, and Naslund's take may be one of the finest fictional accounts of the life of the doomed queen of France. Opening with Marie's journey from her home and family in Austria, Naslund explores Marie's inner life and struggles, presenting a queen who can be petty, is often troubled, and is surprisingly human. The final section of the novel, with an imprisoned Marie making a case for her life, is especially memorable.

Piercy, Marge, *City of Darkness, City of Light* (1997) BK

Well-known feminist author Piercy takes on the French Revolution with this portrait of three women of varying social circumstances attempting to survive the bloody terror. Unlike many other novels of this era that focus on everyday people, Piercy keeps the focus directly on women in the revolution, bringing to light the little-known and oft-forgotten, yet important, role that they played.

Tipton, James, *Annette Vallon* **(2008) BK**
Tipton's novel centers on the titular Annette Vallon, lover of the English Romantic poet William Wordsworth and inspiration for several of his best-known works. Annette, a Frenchwoman, meets and falls in love with Wordsworth during the turbulent revolutionary era. When her lover is forced to flee France, Annette is left alone and pregnant and must find a way to survive. The blend of romance and history will appeal to a variety of readers.

Making Connections

Historical Entertainment for Romance Readers

Romance fiction and historical fiction are closely related. One of the most popular genres of romance fiction is the historical romance, and historical romance novels tend to be as meticulously researched as historical fiction. There are a few distinctive differences, though. Historical romance is almost always told from a third-person point of view, while historical fiction can be told from any point of view. One question to ask a historical romance reader before recommending a non-romance historical novel is if he or she has a strong preference for the third-person point of view. There are romance readers who do not enjoy first-person novels. The second difference is that the love story is always central to a historical romance. Most if not all of the conflict, character, and plot development is related to the love story. In non-romance historical fiction, this may not be the case.

The following novels and authors have strong crossover appeal for romance readers, although there are many other historical works with strong romantic elements listed in this chapter that romance readers would certainly enjoy.

Beau Brummell: This Charming Man **(2006) TV**
Brummell is a stock character in Regency romance novels—the legendary man of fashion who sometimes appears to help an ugly-duckling protagonist make her debut to society in a most smashing way. This BBC documentary introduces viewers to the real Beau Brummell—a man both fashionable and clever, whose fondness for hygiene (thankfully) became a Regency trend.

Gregory, Philippa. *The Other Boleyn Girl* **(2004) BK (2007) MV, CL, YA, UAB**
Gregory's best-selling novel (and popular book club pick) focuses on Mary Boleyn, Anne's older sister and Henry VIII's lover. Mary's legacy has been overshadowed by that of her tragic sister, but she was a force in her own right. Whether she was guided by her father's machinations to insinuate the Boleyns into the Tudor court or whether she was acting of her own volition is lost to history, but Gregory's version of Mary's story, with its sibling rivalry, torrid affairs, and power struggles, has helped set off the current craze for Tudor fiction. Gregory continues to turn to the Tudor court for subject matter; her other recent novels include *The Boleyn Inheritance* (about flirty Katherine Howard, Henry's fifth wife) and *The Constant Princess* (about Henry VIII's first wife, Katherine of Aragon). In 2007, *The Other Boleyn Girl* was made into a movie starring Scarlett Johansson and Natalie Portman. While the basic plot is the same, the narrative seems compressed significantly, and many of the details are lost in the translation.

Heyer, Georgette. *The Conqueror* **(1931) BK**
Georgette Heyer published a number of deftly plotted, intensely researched historical romance novels set during the Regency period, but she also published several works

of historical fiction, many of which have been re-released. *The Conqueror*, her tale of England's first king, William the Conqueror, is no exception. All of Heyer's works feature her trademark wit and dialogue, which some critics have likened to the works of Jane Austen. Many romance readers will be familiar with Heyer's Regencies, but her historical fiction is lesser known (but no less enjoyable).

Mitchell, Margaret. *Gone with the Wind*, (1936) BK (1939) MV, CL, SH, UAB
The Pulitzer prize winning book, originally published in 1936 became an award winning and classic American movie with the 1939 adaption. Scarlett, the headstrong daughter of a Georgia plantation owner and Irish immigrant, comes of age just as the Civil War begins and the book and movie follow her over many years from her initial appearance as the spoiled, self-absorbed southern belle with a crush on southern gentleman Ashley Wilkes through the war, and Reconstruction and her marriage to handsome scoundrel Rhett Butler.

<u>Outlander</u>, Gabaldon, Diana, *Outlander* (1992) BK, AP, CL, SH, UAB, GN
The first installment in Gabaldon's epic time-slip saga focuses on Claire Randall, who finds herself transported back 200 years in time to 1743 Scotland. Once Claire moves past the fish-out-of-water sensation of moving from post-World War II Britain, where she worked as a professional nurse, to the clan battles of eighteenth-century Scotland, where expectations for women were significantly different, she grows to love her new home—not to mention Jamie Fraser, an archetypally handsome and virile Scottish clansman. While some readers may be put off by the fact that Claire is a married woman engaging in a relationship with another man, others will be immediately swept in to Gabaldon's meticulousl researched historical detail and sweeping love story. A graphic novel, *The Exile* set in the Outlander world, is forthcoming.

<u>Pink Carnation</u>, Willig, Lauren, *The Secret History of the Pink Carnation* (2005) BK, YA, UAB
The Pink Carnation is one of history's most elusive spies, and the subject of PhD student Eloise Kelly's dissertation. Eloise is determined to unmask the Napoleonic-era spy, and her research leads her to the private papers of Arabella Selwick-Alderly. During her stay at the Selwick home, Eloise encounters Arabella's infuriating nephew, Colin. The novel alternates between Eloise's point of view and that of Amy Balcourt, a feisty young woman who may (or may not) be the Pink Carnation. The Regency era is one of the most popular in romance novels, and the dual love stories, lighthearted humor, and smart, snappy heroines will be familiar to romance readers.

<u>Roselynde Chronicles</u>, Gellis, Roberta, *Roselynde* (1978) BK, CL
Roberta Gellis's six-volume Roselynde Chronicles were first published in the 1970s and have been marketed as both historical fiction and romance. Set in medieval England, the series follows the heirs to Roselynde, a feudal estate, from the reign of King John through the reign of Henry III. Peppered with real-life royal personages and historical events and dramatic love stories, these novels will appeal to readers who enjoy historical fiction with strong romantic elements.

Seton, Anya, *Katherine* and *Green Darkness* (1954, 1972) BK, CL, YA
Anya Seton's novels were bestsellers in the mid-twentieth century. Each of her works focuses on a woman of a specific era, ranging from fourteenth-century England (*Katherine*) to 1930s America (*Foxfire*). Though some of Seton's novels are closer to traditional romance than others, each features a prominent love story and a

historically accurate plot. *Katherine* (BK, 1954) and *Green Darkness* (BK, 1972) are the most likely to appeal to romance readers.

Historical Fiction for Fantasy Readers

Though historical fiction and fantasy may not seem to have much in common on the outside, many of the appeal factors that attract readers to these genres are similar. Like historical readers, fantasy readers tend to be patient with epic novels—it isn't uncommon to see novels in both genres that are more than 600 pages. Careful world-building is also critical in both genres. Readers want to be immersed in the world of the novel, whether it's a fantasy world, a historical setting, or a blend of the two. Many fantasy authors borrow from history or historical events as a basis for their worlds, and historical fantasy, a blended genre featuring fantastic events in real-world settings, is becoming more common. The following list includes historical fantasy novels, as well as historical novels featuring characteristics that appeal to readers of fantasy fiction.

300 (2007) MV, GN

A brief cinematic fad for all things ancient resulted in a few films about ancient Greece and Rome released within in a short period of time. The gory, intense *300* is one of the best of this bunch. Based on a graphic novel by Frank Miller and Lynn Varley, *300* tells the story of the Spartans' battle against Persia's King Xerxes at the strait of Thermopylae. There's a lot of blood and many handsome, buff Greek warriors, and at times it stops just short of camp, but its translation of ancient history for modern sensibilities is surprisingly successful.

<u>Avalon</u>, **Marion Zimmer Bradley**, *The Mists of Avalon* (1982) BK, TV, UAB

Marion Zimmer Bradley's epic retellings of the King Arthur legends, starting with *The Mists of Avalon*, have expanded upon and described the years before the Roman invasion, the Roman years, and the years after the Romans left, all key time periods in British history. Bradley's series takes a feminist view of history and sees the King Arthur tale as the story of the conflict between Druidism and Christianity, themes that are expanded on in all the books of the series.

<u>Baroque Cycle</u>, **Stephenson, Neal**, *Quicksilver* (2003) BK, AB

Stephenson, previously known for his "cyberpunk" novels of the 1990s, makes his second foray into historical fiction (after *Cryptonomicon*) with this three-novel series set in the seventeenth century. Blending science, adventure, and history, the three volumes in the series are both an old-fashioned epic and a very modern look at Europe during the Age of Reason.

Brennan, Marie, *Midnight Never Come* (2008) BK, YA

Brennan, a folklorist, presents an alternate history of the Tudor court of Elizabeth I, where a "shadow court" led by Invidiana, queen of the fey, co-rules England. When Invidiana's power grows too strong, it is up to Lune, a fairy banished from Invidiana's court, and Michael Deven, a minor gentleman, to find a way to break her rule and restore harmony to the fey and human courts. Brennan deftly combines folklore with fact in a novel that readers of historical novels and fantasy novels will both enjoy.

Graham, Jo, *Black Ships* **(2008) BK, AP**

Graham's powerful debut focuses on the events of Virgil's Aeneid through the eyes of Gull, a young woman crippled at a young age whose mother leaves her with the Oracle of the Lady of the Dead. When Gull experiences a vision of nine black ships sailing toward the city, the Oracle recognizes her abilities and trains her to become the next Pythia. When Aeneas arrives seeking advice from Pythia, Gull chooses to travel with him and the last surviving residents of the city of Wilusa to find refuge and a place to rebuild. The ensuing adventures are as epic as anything you might read in high school Latin class, yet significantly darker and bleaker. While the historical research behind *Black Ships* is well-informed, the epic characteristics and strong, powerful, forthright female heroine will appeal to fantasy readers who enjoy works similar to Jacqueline Carey's Kushiel series.

Temeraire, Novik, Naomi, *His Majesty's Dragon* **(2006) BK, YA, UAB**

Described by reviewers as "Patrick O'Brian with dragons," Novik's series follows Will Laurence, a British sea captain of the Napoleonic era, and his dragon Temeraire, who he discovers on a French ship captured by the British navy, as they train and fight as members of an elite group of dragon-handlers known as aviators. The history in the series is accurate, but the presence of the dragons adds a fantastic element to the story.

Historical Fiction for Mystery Readers

Historical mysteries are a popular subgenre for mystery readers. A number of well-known mystery series are set in the past, and others use real-life historical or cultural figures, such as Queen Elizabeth I or Jane Austen, as amateur sleuths. Historical mysteries may be set in any geographic locale or time period, but like historical romance, the most popular settings for English-language historical mysteries are England and the United States. Historical fiction readers who enjoy mysteries will be interested in the works of authors such as David Liss (early American), C. J. Sansom (Tudor England), or Ellis Peters (medieval England).

Clark, Clare, *The Great Stink* **(2006) BK**

Clark's debut takes the reader inside the stinking, dilapidated Victorian sewer system for a unique look at the denizens of a world that is truly underground. The main character, William May, is a veteran of the bloody, brutal Crimean War who now works as an engineer in the sewer system. May witnesses a murder in the sewer system, and his knowledge of the crime makes him a prime suspect. Readers have compared Clark's novel to the works of Charles Dickens, both because of the era that she describes and because of the view of a segment of humanity that is foreign to most.

Cox, Michael, *The Meaning of Night* **(2006) BK, UAB, AP**

When Edward Glyver makes a chance discovery about the circumstances of his birth, it leads him on a quest for the truth and inflames his desire to reclaim the birthright that was stolen from him by his long-time rival, the poet Phoebus Daunt. Set in mid-Victorian England, Cox's debut novel contains numerous elements that appeal to mystery readers, including an amateur sleuth, a quest for a solution, and plenty of suspects with reasons to conceal the truth. The sequel, *The Glass of Time*, continues, deepens, and solves some of the lingering threads from the first novel.

History Detectives, **PBS (2003–) TV**
Since 2003, the 70-plus episodes have covered such diverse topics as Bonnie and Clyde, George Washington's portrait, and Doc Holliday's watch. A treat for mystery fans, this show delves into a wide range of American historical mysteries focusing on historical objects. The investigative team's traditional and modern techniques will be familiar to mystery readers.

History's Mysteries, **History Channel (1998–) TV**
A long-running and popular TV series, it covers diverse historical subjects, including the Manhattan Project, Hitler's secret diaries, and the Loch Ness monster. Multiple viewpoints from scholars and enthusiasts show both sides of controversial topics, along with trivia and commentary provided by the show's host.

Pears, Iain, *An Instance of the Fingerpost* **(1998) BK, AB**
Set in Oxford in 1663, this epic historical mystery focuses on four views of the same crime: the murder of Dr. Robert Grove, presumably by poison. Each of the four characters provides his own version of the events leading up to the crime. Pears blends history and fiction effectively, and there's enough accurate historical content to please history buffs, yet the mystery is good enough for fans of the genre.

Phillips, Christi, *The Rossetti Letter* **(2008) BK**
The first in Phillips's ongoing series combines seventeenth-century Venetian politics and twenty-first-century academic politics, contrasting the tale of courtesan Alessandra Rossetti, author of a letter that exposed a conspiracy to the tale of Claire Donovan, a modern graduate student whose dissertation is in peril thanks to a fellow researcher's work. Phillips moves back and forth between the time periods effectively, and there's a strong element of suspense throughout the work.

Conclusion

While the popularity of specific topics within the historical fiction genre waxes and wanes, the genre as a whole has been popular for hundreds if not thousands of years, and readership has grown with time.

The popularity of television programs like *The Tudors* and *John Adams* proves that there is an audience for history-as-entertainment, and historical documentaries, both lightweight and serious, have numerous outlets on U.S. television. Historical film still leans toward the highbrow, and while some historical movies are more eye-candy than mind-candy, the majority of history-based films are serious works that are acclaimed by critics and celebrated by viewers for their historical accuracy. While historical films will likely never reach the volume of viewers as summer blockbusters or superhero movies, they are far from a niche product.

As long as people continue to be curious about their past, historical entertainment will endure—and flourish.

Resources for Librarians

There are a number of books and periodicals dedicated to history and historical entertainment. These publications can be used for collection development as well as for current awareness.

Adamson, Lynda G. *American Historical Fiction: An Annotated Guide to Novels for Adults and Young Adults.* Phoenix, AZ: Oryx, 1998.

> This update of Virginia Brokaw Gerhardstein's classic guide to historical fiction is one of the primary resources for older historical novels (especially those published prior to 1995). Coming in 2010: *Literature Links to World History, K–12* and *Literature Links to American History.*

Cords, Sarah Statz, and Robert Burgin. *The Real Story: A Guide to Nonfiction Reading Interests.* Westport, CT: Libraries Unlimited, 2006.

> This guide to readers' advisory for nonfiction readers was the first of its kind and remains an excellent source for nonfiction reader's advisory in all genres. Several chapters include historical nonfiction content.

Historical Novels Review and *Solander*. http://www.historicalnovelsociety.org.

> Published by the Historical Novel Society, these publications are the best sources for reviews and commentary on current historical fiction. Both publications routinely include articles discussing historical films and television programming, as well as articles geared toward authors of historical fiction. *Historical Novels Review* is a quarterly publication focusing mainly on reviews, and *Solander* appears biannually and focuses on in-depth criticism of historical fiction. Both publications cover works published or released in the United States and the United Kingdom.

Hooper, Brad. *Read On: Historical Fiction.* Westport, CT: Libraries Unlimited, 2006.

> Hooper, the Adult Books editor at *Booklist*, compiled this thematic collection of historical fiction organized by appeal factor rather than era or type of book. The unique arrangement makes it easier for readers' advisory staff to recommend books based on factors other than era or setting. Though some of the combinations seem like a stretch, the extensive annotations make the case for grouping particular titles together.

Johnson, Sarah L. *Historical Fiction: A Guide to the Genre.* Westport, CT: Libraries Unlimited, 2005, and *Historical Fiction II: A Guide to the Genre.* Westport, CT: Libraries Unlimited, 2009.

> Johnson, a librarian, prolific book reviewer and noted historical fiction expert, provides a series of booklists for readers of historical fiction and the libraries that help them find the next book to read. The first volume focuses on novels published between 1995 and 2004, and the second focuses on novels published between 2004 and 2008—the most recent surge in historical fiction's popularity. The lists are organized by type of novel, then by place and era.

Endnotes

1. Historical Novel Society Web site. http://www.historicalnovelsociety.org/definition.htm.
2. "Top 100 TV Shows of All Time." Variety Web site. http://www.variety.com/index.asp?layout=chart_pass&charttype=chart_topshowsalltime.
3. "Make War Not Love: Trends in Men's Historical Fiction." *Historical Novels Review*, Issue 45 (August 2008): pp. 5–7.
4. The Republic of Pemberley. http://www.pemberley.com.

4

Everything Horror
Jennifer Brannen

In this chapter, Jennifer Brannen covers the horror genre in books, movies, television shows, and graphic novels. After defining horror, she discusses horror integrated advisory and then covers plots, characters, and theme and connects horror to other genres. In "Plots," Jennifer includes comic horror, extreme horror and splatterpunk, science gone wild, and comic horror. "Characters" includes serial killers, vampires, zombies, and werewolves, all currently popular characters. In "Theme," everyday horror covers psychological horror, small town horror, and killer critters. Finally, in the "Making Connections" section, you'll find horror for science fiction, mystery, and nonfiction fans.

Introduction

What scares you? Is it that thing that goes bump in the night? Or gets your pulse racing with adrenaline? Or is it something that lets you work through your fears or feel better about your life? Or is it a lens through which you can view and critique the society around you? In horror, the answer is yes. Horror is all of those things and more. From the visceral to the intellectual, horror is all about the response.

Horror thrives across media and has always seemed to leap from medium to medium as new ones are created. Trends from one medium frequently fuel another in this genre, which can actually ease the plight of the librarian-advisor in figuring out what a patron really wants. Now we find horror in print and electronically, in movies, in manga and graphic novels, and in video games. The chances are pretty good that it will be an early genre adopter in whatever the next medium is. So it's a natural for integrated advisory.

Film is another medium key to understanding the horror genre, and this can work for you in advisory services. Familiarity with one format can inform an understanding in another. Trying to ascertain how much gore is too much for your patron, and they haven't read any of the authors you suggest? Try movies. Or TV. There's a good chance that even if they haven't seen the movies or shows you mention that they'll have at least seen previews or read about them. Are they more comfortable with *The Sixth Sense* or *The Others*? Or do their preferences lean toward Rob Zombie flicks and the *Saw* franchise? That can make the difference between recommending Shirley Jackson or Poppy Z. Brite.

What Is It? Definition of Horror

Horror can be a challenging genre to get a handle on when it comes to advisory services. It is innately subjective, yet it pervades our popular culture. Horror is what Saricks refers to as an emotion-based genre.[1] What this means is that horror is more about the emotions it evokes rather than how it evokes them. Another reason it's so hard to define is that it is by sheer necessity broad and diverse. Different things scare different people, and even more universal tropes in the genre, such as the Boogeyman, may scare people for different reasons, so the genre has to be flexible to accommodate that.

One of the big questions that comes with this genre more than most others is "Why would anyone want to read/watch that?" What do horror fans get from the genre? On a basic level, they're looking for an emotional response; they want to be scared, surprised, or thrilled. They might enjoy the adrenaline rush that comes with a good scare. They may want to escape from the drudgery of daily life with over-the-top thrills or action. They may be looking for critiques of social mores and conflicts. Or they may be looking for a way to work through their own fears. Horror provides an outlet for all of these things and more.

Horror has deep roots in literature, and many authors in the Western canon have written in it. From Jane Austen and Nathaniel Hawthorne to Toni Morrison and Cormac McCarthy, well-respected authors have experimented with and contributed to the genre. Why? Because in many ways, it gets at the root of human experience, or at least the dark side of it. There is love, joy, generosity, and hope, but there is also anger, fear, grief, and madness. Each speaks to us in varying degrees and deserves to be explored. Some of the greatest stories in literature can be considered horror: *House of the Seven Gables*, *Wuthering Heights*, *A Christmas Carol*, *Heart of Darkness,* and *Beloved*.

Horror clearly reflects the culture that generates it. It's hardly a coincidence that it tends to thrive in times of societal unrest. The late 1960s through the mid-1970s was not only a period of great turmoil and social uncertainty (the Vietnam War, the civil rights movement, and the assassinations of prominent political and social leaders), it was a heyday for horror. In film, George Romero reinvented the zombie, using it to take jabs at racism and consumer culture. We saw our first *Texas Chainsaw Massacre*, which introduced the figure of "the final girl." John Carpenter turned independent film on its head with *Halloween* (at the time, the highest-grossing indie film in history). It also saw the launch of some of the most prominent writers in the genre, such as Anne Rice (*Interview with the Vampire*, 1976), Stephen King (*Carrie*, 1974, *'Salem's Lot*, 1975), Peter Straub (*Marriages*, 1973, *Ghost Story*, 1980) and Dean R. Koontz (writing as Brian Coffey, *Wall of Masks*, 1975, *The Face of Fear*, 1977), and Ramsey Campbell (*The Doll Who Ate His Mother*, 1976, though his first collection of short stories was published in the 1960s).

The economic downturn of the 1980s fomented the popularity of several slasher franchises and the rise of splatterpunk. Key genre writers such as Clive Barker and Poppy Z. Brite launched their careers, while stalwarts such as King, Rice, and Koontz thrived.

It comes as no surprise that with social, political, and economic tremors of the 2000s, there's been a resurgence of the popularity of horror throughout popular culture.

This has been most readily apparent in movies. Some are political allegories (*28 Weeks Later*, 2007), some emphatically not (*Saw*, 2004). Remakes of seminal horror films abound: *Halloween* (2007), *Last House on the Left* (2009), *Friday the 13th* (2009), *The Texas Chainsaw Massacre* (2003), and the *Wolf Man* remake (2010). Don't forget television either. *Buffy the Vampire Slayer*, *Angel*, *Supernatural*, *True Blood*, and *Dexter* are all proof that horror thrives on the small screen as well.

Horror may not always be what you think. It's not all monsters and gore, though those have their place. An example is psychological horror, which blurs the lines between what is real and what's in the narrator's mind, leaving the reader entertained but uncertain. Horror is also a frequent player in genre blends. Horror crosses over easily and frequently with fantasy, romance, science fiction, thrillers, and mysteries, to name just a few.

Traditional Print Books

As with other genres, novels have dominated the genre. Early gothics such as *The Monk* or *The Castle of Otranto* contain some elements of horror, but *Frankenstein* is the generally agreed-upon turning point, where the gothic transformed into what we now recognize as the modern horror novel. Horror thrived in the Victorian era, with Bram Stoker and Robert Louis Stevenson, among others.

Another key period to remember is the pulp magazines and novels of the 1930s, 1940s, and 1950s. H. P. Lovecraft helped usher in this era. His fascination with and stories about the Old Gods and the Cthulhu were an entirely new sort of horror. Although long deceased, he continues to wield significant influence on writers within the genre, such as Ramsey Campbell. Arkham House was founded in 1939 by August Derleth and Donald Wandrei in order to keep Lovecraft's stories in print, and over the years many famous writers in the genre have published with Arkham.

In horror, it is essential to recognize the importance of short stories and novellas. Most horror writers write short, medium, and long form. The history of the genre encouraged this since many earlier twentieth-century horror writers of note got their start writing for magazines (think Bradbury, Ellison, etc.). It can be easier to experiment and take risks in short stories, so it makes sense that trends in the genre are most readily tracked in its short fiction. By extension, anthologies are key to print horror advisory. They are frequently published, can expose readers to a wide variety of writers and styles within the genre, and can be an excellent introduction to an author's body of work when a single writer is anthologized. As print magazines go increasingly by the wayside, anthologies are where new voices are being heard.

Short stories and anthologies are especially important to grasping this genre, and not just in print. Many classic TV shows were horror or speculative anthologies—*The Twilight Zone*, *The Outer Limits*, and *Tales from the Crypt*. Even horror movies indulge in small-form anthologizing. Think Vincent Price in *Tales of Terror* (1962) or in *Twice-Told Tales* (1963); Christopher Lee in *Doctor Terror's House of Horrors*; or more recently, *Twilight Zone: The Movie* (1983).

Aside from the major names and crossover authors, horror doesn't garner a lot of review space and is often only selectively released by the major publishing houses. Yet some of the most prolific and profitable authors of the past several decades have been horror writers, such as Stephen King, Anne Rice, Thomas Harris, and Dean Koontz. Because of this, independent presses are integral to the genre, enabling it to thrive and grow. Arkham House was a progenitor for today's independent horror publishers.

Knowledge of these presses and who they publish is helpful for both advisory and collection purposes. Independents are where the newest writers and trends in the genre get the greatest exposure. They are often home to the smaller or more extreme subgenres as well.

And speaking of those big names in horror, as prolific as most of them are, as readers' advisors, it's important to move beyond them. Fans will burn through their oeuvres with surprising rapidity and want more or different things from the genre.

Graphic Novels and Manga

Horror comics have a long history. The comics of the 1930s and 1940s introduced any number of supernatural plotlines, heroes, and villains. But it wasn't until 1946 that the first true horror comic came out, *Eerie*. The 1950s saw both a horror comic boom and the introduction of government censorship of comics of all sorts. The horror comics of the 1950s contained a surprising amount of gore and violence. Gore and humor were often combined to good effect in comics such as *Tales from the Crypt* (1950–1955). Horror comics found their way back in the 1970s. With this background, today's graphic novels and manga are logical extensions of their horror comic predecessors.

More recently, Neil Gaiman's *Sandman* series, *30 Days of Night* (2002/2003), *Preacher* (1995/1996), *Hellboy* (1994/1997), *Hellblazer* (1988/1992), *Swamp Thing* (1983, 1998), and *The Walking Dead* (2003/2004) are all notable horror graphic novel series. Print authors such as Stephen King (*The Secretary of Dreams*, 2006) and Clive Barker (*Clive Barker's Hellraiser*, 2002) have tried their hands at the medium as well. The Graphic Classics series has adapted the works of such classic authors such Bram Stoker (various stories, 2004) and Edgar Allen Poe (various stories, 2006).

Manga (Japanese comics) have a thriving subset of horror series as well, tackling everything from vampires (*Vampire Hunter D*, 2005) and zombies (*Black Sun, Silver Moon*, 2007) to demons (*Mark of the Succubus*, 2005) and exorcists (*D. Gray-man*, 2006). Manga titles to watch out for include *The Hino Horror* series (2004–) by Hideshi Hino and *D. Gray-man* (2006) by Katsura Hoshino.

Magazines

Magazines such as *Weird Tales* were seminal to the development of the horror genre, publishing famous authors early on and even throughout their careers. They were often the first to publish short stories, which are especially important in horror. There are far fewer magazines today, and the ones remaining are often published in print less frequently or are publishing only electronically. The big title to watch for these days is *Cemetery Dance*, which still publishes bimonthly; others to consider include *Dark Discoveries*, *Horror Fiction Review*, *Bare Bone*, and *Dark Wisdom*.

Movies and Television

As previously noted, movies are especially important to horror and have influenced writers from early in the history of the medium. They are quick to reflect trends and societal concerns and issues (though sometimes very obliquely). They also bring a wider audience to the genre.

Television shows such as *Buffy the Vampire Slayer*, *Angel*, *The X-Files*, and *Supernatural* continue to be popular on television both in first run and in syndication. In some cases they are pioneering new ways of telling stories within the medium. *Buffy* episodes "Hush" (1999), "The Body" (2001), and "Once More with Feeling" (2001) are all good examples of this. These series regularly build complicated internal mythologies that explore the nature of good and evil, truth and lies, juxtaposed with a selective monster of the week and a short storytelling arc.

Computer and Video Games

Some of the most seminal computer games of the past 10 to 15 years have been rooted in horror (*Doom, Resident Evil*, and *Silent Hill*, to name a few). *Doom* in particular raised the bar on computer graphics and introduced the concept of the first-person shooter into active gaming vernacular. And in one of those lovely postmodern twists, these same games are now being made into horror movies.

Trends in Horror

Vampires were the red-hot ticket for many years (and will doubtless be eternally popular), but they are currently taking a backseat to zombies. What may slow down this particular undead juggernaut are the challenges inherent in writing a successful zombie romance. However, the wildly unexpected success of *Pride and Prejudice and Zombies* certainly suggests that authors are willing to try to mix the two.

That title also exemplifies another trend, which is the mash-up between horror and classic literature. Mash-ups have been common in recent years with music and increasingly with videos, but popular print has been something of a latecomer to this cultural trend.

As the lines between horror and other genres continue to blur, we see horror successfully crossing over into more genres than ever before. One of the most prominent crossovers continues to be with romance; paranormal romances have been established as a thriving and expansive subgenre. Crossovers with fantasy continue to be common as well, as epitomized by urban fantasy from authors such as Laurell K. Hamilton and Kim Harrison. But horror has also found its way into science fiction, thrillers, mysteries, historical fiction, and even the occasional western.

YA Trends

Perennially popular with tweens and teens, horror is currently experiencing something of a heyday in young adult literature. Recently, there has been a lot of creative exploration, reworking, and reinventing of the genre in young adult lit. Libba Bray reinvented the gothic for a new generation with *A Great and Terrible Beauty* (2003) and its two sequels (*Rebel Angels*, 2005, and *The Sweet Far Thing*, 2007). Katie Maxwell and Julie Kenner have married supernatural romance and humor to great effect, with titles such as *Got Fangs?* (2005) and *The Good Ghoul's Guide to Getting Even* (2007). Neal Shusterman blurs the boundaries between genres; his titles include urban horror (*Red Rider's Hood*, 2005), eerie supernatural settings (*Everlost, 2006*), and dystopian visions of teens being grown in order to harvest body parts (*Unwind*, 2007). Many of these titles have significant crossover appeal for adult readers, as evidenced by the wide-ranging appeal of Stephenie Meyer's Twilight series.

Other writers have tackled vampire mythology successfully but to very different effect than the Twilight series. Thirsty series (1997) by M. T. Anderson, *Peeps* (2005) by Scott Westerfeld, and *Sweetblood* (2003) by Pete Hautman all have darker, vastly different takes on the undead. For the undead hitting high school, try *Vampire High*

(2003) by Douglas Rees or *The Chronicles of Vladimir Tod* (2007) by Heather Brewer. Cynthia Leitich Smith took on both vampires and werewolves in *Tantalize* (2007).

Zombies are seeing a surge in popularity in YA lit as well, spanning the gamut from humor to bleak zombie apocalypses with titles such as *The Forest of Hands and Teeth* (2009), *You Are So Undead to Me* (2009), *Generation Dead* (2008), *Soulless* (2008), and *Zombie Queen of Newbury High* (2009).

Plots

Horror has a raft of plot and character tropes to play with, which makes sense since it takes a wide variety things to scare a wide variety of people. Here is where horror's ability to cross over into a variety of genres becomes readily apparent. Many of the plots commonly explored in technology or science-based horror could just as easily belong in science fiction (or sometimes the morning paper). Sometimes the path to the scare is direct (extreme horror), sometimes it's insidious (possession), and sometimes it ambushes you with a smile on its metaphorical face (humor). The only safe bet in horror when it comes to plotting and storytelling is to strap in and to expect the unexpected.

Laugh, I Nearly Died: Comic Horror

Horror is a genre that can laugh at itself and its audience. From the crude humor of Freddy in the Nightmare on Elm Street movies to the elaborate farcical humor of Christopher Moore, being able to laugh at our fears disarms them. (Could a supernatural serial killer who makes such rotten jokes really be a threat?) Inversely, it can soften up the reader or viewer so that the scares have an even greater impact (think the black humor of *American Psycho*). In humorous horror, the setups to create the humor help make distinctive plots and characters. Fundamentally, the use of humor allows writers to stand horror conventions upside down (monsters running in fear from a petite blonde teenager) and to create wonderfully unexpected plot twists (*A Dirty Job*).

This mixture thrives across media. *Buffy the Vampire Slayer* and *Supernatural* both rely regularly on humor to humanize and develop their stories. (Though even more poker-faced shows such as *The X-Files* and *Angel* had their moments.) And don't forget the Crypt Keeper from *The Tales of the Crypt*, whose jokes were the setup to that episode's gore-fest. Movies such as the original *Buffy*, *Shaun of the Dead*, *Zombieland*, *Bubba Ho-Tep*, *The Mummy* (remake), and *The Evil Dead* all take full advantage of the contradictions and plot twists generated by introducing humor into horror.

Brown, S. G., *Breathers: A Zombie's Lament* (2009) BK

Just as vampires have recently been rehabilitated into sympathetic characters, so zombies are now expanding their horizons from brain-eating automatons to the misunderstood undead. Andy Warner is, or rather was, the everyman, boy-next-door, until he died and wouldn't stay dead. His transition into zombie-hood isn't the smoothest—his parents are angry with him, his living friends don't call anymore, and he isn't too popular in society as a whole. So Andy starts attending Undead Anonymous meetings, where he meets and befriends the lovely Rita, who has a penchant for formaldehyde-laden cosmetics, and Jerry, the car-crash victim with the exposed brain. Things are starting to come together until the group meets a rogue zombie who teaches them a taste for human flesh.

Bubba Ho-Tep (2002) MV
What happens when you mix Elvis, President John F. Kennedy, and an evil Egyptian mummy? *Bubba Ho-Tep*. Elvis is whiling away his golden years in an East Texas nursing home having survived his "death" in remarkably good condition. He's friends with Jack, who thinks that he's America's favorite dead president. Life's pretty quiet until an evil Egyptian "soul-sucker" decides to move in and harvest the residents' souls. Will Elvis triumph over evil? The movie is based on a short story by Joe Lansdale, who's no stranger to mixing horror and humor.

Carey, Mike, *The Devil You Know* (2007) BK
The life of a freelance exorcist has its amusements and compensations, especially if said ghostbuster happens to live in London—a city host to many forms of fun and restless spirits. Sooner or later, though, even the best exorcist is outmatched, and Felix Castor is no exception. While he's trying figure out what new trade he might ply his rather specific skill set in, Felix takes on a last job. It was *supposed* to be a bread-and-butter, pay-the-bills exorcism in an appropriately shadowy London museum. The project takes a nasty turn however, and Castor finds himself the unfortunate prize in an informal contest to see who—or what—can kill him first.

Grahame-Smith, Seth, *Pride and Prejudice and Zombies* (2009) BK, YA
It is a truth universally acknowledged that a little zombie mayhem will certainly liven up a village fete. Elizabeth Bennett and her family live in the small village of Meryton, being shepherded along by an egregiously marriage-minded mama with big plans and few manners. When Mr. Darcy and Mr. Bingley arrive with their entourage to take up residence in a local manor, matchmaking Mrs. Bennett goes into overdrive. Sister Jane and Mr. Bingley appear quite smitten with each other, and sparks that fly between Elizabeth and Mr. Darcy cannot be solely attributed to dislike. The dance of her prejudice and his pride (or perhaps vice versa) gets sidelined when the unmentionables (that's Regency for zombies) start to crash the parties and picnics, leaving bloody mayhem and disrupted engagements in their wake. Will true love conquer not only pride and prejudice, but the undead menace?

Kenner, Julie, *Carpe Demon: Adventures of a Demon-hunting Soccer Mom* (2005) BK
Life in San Diablo is pretty normal for soccer mom Kate Connor until the day a demon follows her home from a grocery trip. Her demon-hunting days are back with a vengeance, and Kate's juggling play dates, carpools to the mall, and creatures from hell. This while trying to keep her family in the dark *and* throwing the perfect dinner party for her husband, who's aspiring to local political office. Returning to work as a demon hunter is as hard on her housekeeping as it is on her nerves. Can she keep her toddler placated, her teen out of trouble, and her house from crashing down around her while she makes sure that San Diablo stays a family-friendly (and human-friendly) place to live? Also look for others in series, including *California Demon*, *Demons Are Forever*, and *Deja Demon*.

Martinez, A. Lee, *Gil's All Fright Diner* (2005) BK, YA
Earl (as in Earl of the Vampires) and Duke (as in Duke of the Werewolves) have been hired by the not-to-be-trifled-with Loretta (as in the owner-operator of the

all-night diner in question) to do a little cleaning up. She and the town of Rockwood are being plagued by various bits of cosmic weirdness, and it's starting to get inconvenient. The latest manifestation? A zombie attack on the diner while Earl and Duke are just trying to grab a bite. Loretta hires Earl and Duke to take care of it for $100. They don't anticipate much trouble with the zombies (they aren't really noted for their brains, after all). The one-time gig turns into a full-time job, though, as Earl and Duke face the real problem—who or what is raising the dead and apparently trying to end the world? And what have they got against the best little all-night diner in Texas? Martinez frequently turns speculative fiction tropes on their heads, so if you enjoy this one, also check out his others: *In the Company of Ogres* (2006), *A Nameless Witch* (2007), and *The Automatic Detective* (2008).

Moore, Christopher, *A Dirty Job* **(2006) BK, SH, UAB**
The author who epitomizes the overlap between horror and humor is Christopher Moore, who is, to say the least, in a class by himself. Master combiner of humor and horror, Moore is an author with unique appeal. In *A Dirty Job*, Charlie meets Death (yes, the real guy) on the day his daughter is born and his wife dies; he finds that few things are as he had always thought. Why exactly have hellhounds moved in his house? And why can he see glowing red in the thrift shop? Is a new job in Charlie's future? Armed with the *Big Book of Death*, Charlie reluctantly embarks on his destiny in true beta-male fashion—it's a dirty job but somebody's got to do it. Other good books by Moore are *Blood-Sucking Fiends: A Love Story* and *Practical Demonkeeping: A Comedy of Horrors*.

Prill, David, *Serial Killer Days* **(1996) BK**
Standard Springs, Minnesota, is home to the Anti-Claus. The Anti-Claus is the serial killer who has terrorized the town for the past 20 years, claiming a victim on the same day in July each year. This could be the kiss of death for some small towns, but not this one. They start an annual festival called Serial Killer Days. In the midst of these cheerfully morbid tourist festivities, the unfortunately well-adjusted Debbie Sue Morning is doggedly trying to win the Scream Queen Pageant; the town council is trying to rename Standard Springs to Serial Killer, Minnesota; and everyone wants to know the identity of the man in Mrs. Flatwire's apple orchard.

Shaun of the Dead **(2004) MV**
Shaun and Ed are British slackers with dead-end jobs, roommate issues, and disgruntled girlfriends. Well, at least Shaun had a girlfriend, until she dumped him for flaking on their anniversary. So immersed are they in their own problems that Shaun and Ed completely fail to notice a zombie uprising surging through London. Moping over pints and then heading home for the inevitable hangover, they remain oblivious until zombies attack in the back garden the next morning. Improvised tools, an obnoxious zombie roommate, and a suitably dramatic rescue of the ex-girlfriend combine to create a wonderful parody of just about every zombie movie convention you can think of.

Completely Over the Top: Extreme Horror and Splatterpunk

What drives the plots in splatterpunk is excess. The need to go over the top (presumably to see what's on the bloody other side) is integral to splatterpunk storytelling. Control is overrated, and nothing succeeds like excess in descriptions, in language, in

characterization, and most definitely in plotting. Familiar characters such as serial killers, werewolves, and vampires are ramped up into over-the-top creations who revel in
their actions. Gore, violence, torture, graphic sex (often non-consensual), and pungent
language are hallmarks. No detail is too gratuitous. It's more than just gross-outs
though. Many writers are making a point either by exploring (and exploiting) the pruri-
ence of the reader or the flaws in society as a whole.

Splatterpunk is a smaller part of the overall horror genre, but it continues to gain
ground in movies. Think of any film Rob Zombie has ever made (*House of 1,000 Corpses* and *The Devil's Rejects*), *Hostel*, the Saw franchise, *Grindhouse* by Robert Rodri-
guez and Quentin Tarantino (especially *The Planet Terror* feature), *The Hills Have
Eyes* (the original and the remake), and *The Last House on the Left* (the original and the
remake). The violence may be cartoonish (*Planet Terror*) or deeply disturbing (*The Last
House on the Left*), but it's integral the plot of the movie.

Barker, Clive, *Books of Blood* (1998) BK, MV, SH

These were a series of six books of short stories and novellas released from 1984 to
1988 that have since been reprinted in several different combinations. These are
arguably Barker's earliest, most intense, and bloodiest work. The stories are usually
in contemporary, often urban, settings, and the protagonists are normal people who
suddenly find out in the worst ways that the world is very different from what they
thought. Though extremely dark, Barker does lace some tales with perverse humor.
Several of the stories have been adapted into movies for both television and the
big screen. The story "The Forbidden" was the basis of the 1992 film *Candyman*,
and "The Last Illusion" was filmed as *Lord of Illusions* in 1995. Barker is considered one of the key writers in this subgenre, though he also writes fantasy and even
YA novels.

Brite, Poppy Z., *Exquisite Corpse* (1996) BK

With a pair of serial-killing gay necrophilic cannibal lovers as your protagonists, what
can possibly go wrong? Andrew Compton is a British serial killer who has killed a
couple of dozen young boys. He's finally caught in the United States but escapes and
makes his way to New Orleans, the capital of decadent excess. There he meets dashing
young serial killer Jay Compton. The two hit it off and indulge in a spree of over-the-
top violence, punctuated with necrophilia and cannibalism. It's also a love story as
bloodlust begets lust in a gory romance. Reveling in the detritus of decay and dismem-
berment, Brite's prose is stomach-churning but almost poetic in its transgressive glee.
Brite is also noted for her vampire novels *Lost Souls* and *Drawing Blood*.

The Devil's Rejects (2005) MV, RS

Torture, gore, murder, mayhem, and revenge are all in Rob Zombie's film about a
family of sadistic serial killers who've hit the road in this sequel to *House of 1,000
Corpses*. Baby, Otis, and Captain Spaulding are on the run and being pursued by the
righteously vengeful Sheriff Wydell. The sheriff tracks them through the destruction
and mangled bodies left in their wake. Extraordinarily violent but leavened with surprising moments of very dark humor, this movie has a timeless feel to it and could
just as easily come out of the 1970s as the 2000s.

Ellis, Bret Easton, *American Psycho* (1991/2000) BK, MV

In this satire of the 1980s, a wealthy and successful investment banker epitomizes
the yuppie. He is materialistic, greedy, callous, and appearance-oriented in all things.
What sets him apart from his peers? His penchant for murder. The book dwells in

loving detail on, well, the details. Whether its Patrick Bateman's inventive use of a nail gun or the attention he pays to the brand and cut of his suit, for Pat, the devil is cheerfully, malevolently in the details. The book caused a stir upon publication and even got dropped by the initial publisher. The movie is considerably less overt in its depictions of gore and violence, though it manages to communicate the novel's perverse humor quite well.

Jacob, Charlee, *This Symbiotic Fascination* (2002) BK
Nominated for a Bram Stoker award, this novel tells the twisted love story of a vampire and a shape-shifter. Let go of any preconceptions you might have from that scenario, though. Two immortals, Tawne Delaney and Arcan Tyler, meet and become friends, protecting each other and staving off loneliness. The shape-shifter takes up a career of serial rape and torture, while a Nosferatu bites Tawne, changing her from a simple immortal into a sexual and bloodthirsty predator. Now more than a match for Arcan, the two join together in bloodlust, devastation, and, of course, death.

Ketchum, Jack, *The Girl Next Door* (1989/2007) BK, MV
When Meg and Susan first move in with their Aunt Ruth and their cousins, everything is fine. They settle in and start making friends in the neighborhood. The local kids hang out at Ruth's house a lot because she is permissive and will let them roughhouse and even drink sometimes. Soon, though, things take a turn for the worse as Ruth starts to verbally and then physically abuse her nieces and even encourages their neighborhood friends to participate. Eventually, the brutality escalates to unspeakable acts, and the question is will someone do something to stop the violence before it's too late? Unfortunately, this book is loosely based on the true story of Sylvia Likens, who was murdered by her aunt in 1965 in Indiana.

Moody, David, *Hater* (2006) BK
Danny McCoyne is a nice enough guy, though his life is filled with the stresses of a modest-paying job as a low-level parking bureaucrat in some unnamed and presumably British city. He works hard and takes care of his wife and kids as best he can. He sees a number of violent attacks and begins to wonder what's going on. People are fine one day and then are prone to acts of brutality and homicidal mania against family, friends, neighbors, and random strangers. Nobody can figure out why people are turning into Haters, but these brutal attacks are increasing all over the country to the point where the stability of society is threatened. Danny thinks that there's something bigger at work, but should he pursue it or keep his head down and his family safe?

Saw (2004) MV
This surprising indie film hit has a simple yet grim premise: What would you do to survive? Two men, Adam and Lawrence, wake up chained in a dirty bathroom, prisoners of the mysterious serial killer Jigsaw. They've been drafted into a sadistic "game," where losing means violent death and winning comes at a horrific cost. The rules? Adam must escape, while Lawrence must kill him or lose his life and those of his wife and daughter. Their tools for survival? Two hacksaws.

Science Gone Wild: Human Hubris and Horror

When it comes to horror, science is not always our friend, and progress may come with a price. The granddaddy of this plot is actually the novel that helped transition the genre from the gothic to the beginnings of the modern horror, *Frankenstein* by Mary Shelley. Though clearly influenced by ancient legends about the Golem, the subtitle was "The Modern Prometheus," a clear acknowledgment of the injudicious use of knowledge and science. This staple plot of the genre has seen the development of many variations in recent years, from the fear of what we'll really find in space (or worse yet, what may find us) to Mother Nature biting back with ecological terrors. History has proven that advances in science and technology can outpace humankind's ability to truly understand their ramifications or use them wisely. These days it's less often a vengeful monster resulting from technology run amuck, than the groundwork for the apocalypse that results from science gone wrong. Think of books and movies such as *Twelve Monkeys*, *Children of Men*, *The Stand*, *The Andromeda Strain*, *I Am Legend*, *28 Days Later*, and *The Morning-star Strain*.

The Fly (1986) MV

The original version of *The Fly*, released in 1958, starred Vincent Price. It ended with the classic scene of a fly with a human head crying, "Help Me!" as it struggled in a spider's web. David Cronenberg's 1986 remake is an entirely different animal, yet is still an exercise in exploring the dark side of unchecked scientific curiosity. The scientist, Seth Brundle, has created two pods that should allow for teleportation. When he uses himself as a test subject, there is a small glitch—a fly is in the other pod, and Seth's cells merge with it. Initially everything appears fine, but of course it's not, as Seth graphically transforms into a grotesque human-fly hybrid, dropping body parts along the way and gaining new inhuman skills.

Koontz, Dean R., *Watchers* (1987/1988) BK, MV

A classic Koontz mix of supernatural mayhem and all-too-human evil, *Watchers* features an emotionally wounded loner on the mend in the form of Travis Cornell. Hunting in the southern California mountains, he comes across a golden retriever snarling at the Other. Travis decides to vacate and takes the otherwise amiable dog, whom he names Einstein, with him. The dog is frighteningly smart and has something of a sense of humor and is generally far more than he seems. The Other, who is grotesque, bred to kill, and very angry with the world in general and Einstein in particular continues to track the dog, as do a violent mobster and a ruthless KGB agent. Not surprisingly, blood and extraordinary violence follow in their wakes, as Travis, Einstein, and love-interest Nora flee to San Francisco, scene of the inevitable final showdown. The novel contains more than a few nods to *The Island of Doctor Moreau* and *Frankenstein*.

McCarthy, Cormac, *The Road* (2006/2009) BK, MV

Set in a post-apocalyptic America, this is a grim story of a father and son journeying across the country in an effort to reach the sea. The implied but unstated cause of the apocalypse is nuclear warfare and the resulting nuclear winter. The scarcity of resources has led to violence and cannibalism. The father and son know they can't survive much longer in their current location and they hold out hope for a better place near the ocean, despite the dangerous traveling conditions. The father is constantly on guard to protect his son from starvation, the elements, and most especially the other people they meet on the road. *The Road* was adapted into a movie that hews closely to the novel.

Preston, Richard, *The Hot Zone* (1994) NF BK

A classic tale of a barely averted outbreak of the feared Ebola virus near a major metropolitan area in America, this book is terrifying because it's true. This close call happened in Reston, Virginia, where an Ebola variant burned through the primate population at an Army research facility. In order to prevent it from spreading to other labs or crossing over into the general human population, scientists undertook an operation unlike any they'd ever tackled before. And failure—or even a small mistake—could have devastating consequences. Preston's 1997 novel, *The Cobra Event*, is a chilling tale of biological terrorism.

The Terminator (1984) CG, CL, MV, TV,

It's not a contagion but a self-aware computer network that sows the seeds of mankind's destruction in this story. The invention of artificial intelligence was seen as a boon to the military industrial complex, until Skynet's computer network decides to launch a nuclear war and eradicate the human race. In the aftermath, the world is run by machines and only a handful of human survivors, led by John Connor, are left to resist. Skynet sends a Terminator back in time to kill Connor's mother Sarah, and a resistance fighter, Kyle Reese, is sent back to protect her. What follows is an intense series of violent chases and battles as Kyle and Sarah battle the killer cyborg. Not surprisingly, the movies spawned several arcade and computer games. A relatively short-lived television series on Fox explored Sarah and John's adventures between *Terminator 2* and *Terminator 3* in *The Sarah Connor Chronicles.*

Wells, H. G., *The Island of Doctor Moreau* (1896) BK, MV

Shipwreck survivor Edward Prendick is picked up by a passing ship and taken to an island belonging to the mysterious Dr. Moreau. The young naturalist soon finds out that everything is not what it seems as Moreau's horrible experiments come to light. The not-so-good doctor's goal? To cross humans with select animals to create a race of beast-men. Neither the animals nor the humans fare well, and the hybrid results who live in their own compound are very unhappy indeed. This is a classic mad-scientist tale. Several movie versions have been made. Try the *Island of Lost Souls*, released in 1932.

When the Devil Comes Knocking: Possession, Satanism, and Demons

Even in these times, when superstition is scorned and most beliefs are held up to the hard light of day and scientific scrutiny, the very idea of the devil still has the power to terrify. Evil incarnate with the power to exploit human weaknesses and create chaos for his own amusement, he's nobody you want to tangle with, much less make a deal with. And yet, people do, whether to save someone else ("Take me") or for their own pleasure or benefit. There's also something truly disconcerting about the idea of possession, about being an involuntary human portal for chaos. Cursed objects and dark rituals also tend to abound in these stories, and these elements may often found in combination.

Barker, Clive, *The Hellbound Heart* (1986/1987) BK, MV

At the center of this short novel is a mysterious puzzle box that is purported to be a gateway to an array of carnal pleasures for anyone who solves it. Unfortunately for Frank, the man who opens it, it is a portal to hell instead and lets the sadistic demons known as Cenobites into the world, even as Frank is sucked into hell. Filled with Barker's trademark gore and violence, *The Hellbound Heart* explores morality in the face of temptation and terror. This story was the basis for the original *Hellraiser* movie, which was written and directed by Barker (as well as the lesser sequels, which he had nothing to do with).

Blatty, William Peter, *The Exorcist* **(1971/1973) BK, CL, MV**
Inspired by a short article in the *Washington Post*, *The Exorcist* has become the gold standard of possession stories and films. Twelve-year-old Regan isn't herself anymore—thrashing, spouting obscenities, and apparently speaking in a variety of languages. Her worried mother, Chris, takes her to a number of medical specialists, but nothing works. As a last resort, she contacts a priest, Father Karras, who's forced to consider the unthinkable; demonic possession. Joined by another priest, the two attempt an exorcism in an effort to save Regan's body and soul. William Friedkin directed the 1973 movie, which remains one of the highest-grossing horror films ever made and a still-terrifying classic.

Hellblazer, Jamie Delano and others, *Hellblazer: Original Sins* **(1988–) GN, MV**
Published by Vertigo/DC Comics, the long-running *Hellblazer* series features John Constantine, con-man/detective/exorcist. Every inch the anti-hero, he frequently works for the greater good in the worst possible way, conning, misdirecting, and endangering his friends even as he tries to save individuals and score points on hell and its minions. It's an uphill battle, and his wins come at a terrible cost and are often all too fleeting. The Hellblazer series has been gathered into numerous collections; the first, *Hellblazer: Original Sins*, was published in 1992. *Constantine*, the 2005 movie adaptation starring Keanu Reeves, was surprisingly enjoyable as it captured the feeling of the comics, if not always the specifics.

Johnson, Maureen, *Devilish* **(2006) BK, YA**
What does it look like when a high schooler sells her soul to the devil? Good hair, fashionable clothes, surprising academic skills, and of course, popularity. Best friends Jane and Allison have never been popular but they've always had fun and each other. After an epic social disaster, Allison comes to school a whole new girl—chic, popular, and speaking Latin fluently. And also ignoring Jane completely. Jane doesn't understand what's happening until freshman Owen explains that Allison sold her soul to the devil. Not quite buying it, Allison finds that there may be more to it than she thought. But can she save her friend before the biblical disaster of the Poodle Prom?

Levin, Ira, *Rosemary's Baby* **(1967/1968) BK, MV, UAB**
Newlyweds Rosemary and Guy Woodhouse move into the Bramford apartment building to start their lives together. The old building has a dark past, though. The neighbors, especially the old couple next door, are friendly, possibly too friendly. Guy's acting career suddenly starts to blossom though he's starting to become a bit distant from Rosemary. One night, Rosemary's romantic interlude with her husband fades into a bad dream, and she wakes up covered in scratches. Soon she discovers she is pregnant, and soon after that she finds that, courtesy of her satanically inclined next-door neighbors, the father may not be her husband. When the baby is born, the coven is prepared to take it away, but Rosemary will have none of it, because it's still her child, even if he does "have his father's eyes." Both the book and the 1968 Roman Polanski film are equally funny and insidious.

Supernatural **(2005–) TV**
The brothers Winchester (Sam and Dean) are hunters and travel across the country fighting monsters, urban legends, and evil in all forms. But their underlying mission is to find and kill the demon that murdered their mother when Sam was only six months old. It turned the Winchesters' lives upside down as revenge became their

father's only goal. The family discovers that demons are everywhere, able to possess almost anyone, and that there may be a much larger endgame than they realized and that Sam may just be the key to the apocalypse. This complicated mythology and the mixture of humor and emotion keeps *Supernatural* from being a simple monster-of-the-week show.

Characters

When people think horror, they often think monsters: vampires, zombies, and were-wolves, oh my! Monsters take many forms, though, so the range of scary characters is broader and more unnerving than that classic array. (Though classic monsters are classics for a reason.) Monsters can be animals (*Jaws* or *Cujo*), children (Gage in *Pet Sematary,* the ominous towheaded tots of *Village of the Damned*), the boogeyman (insert your favorite serial killer here), or even your friends and neighbors ("The Lottery" by Shirley Jackson).

Plot twists are common in horror, and this extends to characterization as well. Characters are often not what they seem, and character types can be stood on their heads with little warning. From the friendly neighbor as serial killer to the werewolf as anti-hero, characters as individuals and tropes in horror are subject to change. The disruption of old stereotypes often leads to the creation of new ones, though. Witness the reinvention of the vampire as predator (Nosferatu) to the vampire as troubled romantic lead (Edward Cullen is only the latest in this line of undead babes).

Tensions between characters and *within* characters drive plots. In horror, conflict is as likely to be within a character as between them. Heroes may be flawed or do the right things the wrong way or wrong things for the right reasons. Monsters may exhibit unexpected humanity or mercy. In this way, characterization drives the plot, action, and even the tenor of the narrative.

Serial Killers: Free-Floating Evil and the Psychopath Next Door

Do serial killers belong in horror? Of course they do. They are the personification of evil for its own sake in the most human of forms. Hannibal Lecter is a horror icon on par with Dracula, Frankenstein, the Wolf Man, or George Romero's zombies. But serial killers are not a recent phenomena, nor strictly an American one (although Americans do have something of a knack for generating them and writing about them). They have been part of the long tradition in storytelling in Western culture. Think Charles Perrault's "Bluebeard" or the Grimm Brothers' "The Robber Bridegroom." Even some of our favorites monsters have their origins in serial killers past: Gilles de Rais, who was the original Bluebeard; Elizabeth Bathory, the Blood Countess who spawned many tales of female vampires; Vlad the III of Wallachia inspired Stoker's *Dracula*, and more recently Ed Gein, who served as the inspiration for *Psycho*.

In this horror subgenre, non-fiction can be just as important as fiction and it can certainly be just as horrifying, if not more so. True crime provides a bounty of real-life brutality. Ann Rule, a doyenne of true crime and serial killers, has written about Ted Bundy, the Green River Killer, the I-5 Killer, and more. And then there are the profilers. Brought to prominence by *The Silence of the Lambs*, the FBI's Investigative

Support Unit has produced a spate of retired agents-turned-writers: *Mindhunter* by John E. Douglas, *Whoever Fights Monsters* by Robert K. Ressler, and *The Evil That Men Do* by Stephen G. Michaud and Roy Hazelwood.

Bloch, Robert, *Psycho* (1959) BK, CL, MV

Many credit this novel with launching serial killers into the character pantheon of horror. Unassuming Norman Bates lives with his mother in an ominous-looking house behind the Bates Motel. Mary Crane is on the run from a crime and looking for shelter from a storm. When Norman meets Mary, bad things happen. And when the sheriff is finally called in, the big question is, who wielded the knife? Norman or his mother? Alfred Hitchcock based his excellent movie of the same name on this book and skillfully managed to imply startling levels of violence. Even though this movie has been used as template many times over, it still has the power to keep viewers on the edge of their seats.

Cain, Chelsea, *Heartsick* (2007) BK

Detective Archie Sheridan spent more than a decade tracking the prolifically murderous Beauty Killer, but in the end, the trail of over two dozen bodies didn't lead Archie to the killer; it led the killer to him. Claiming him as her ultimate trophy, Gretchen Lowell captured Archie and kept him for 10 torture-filled days. Then for reasons that no one, least of all Archie, understands, she called 911, saved his life, and turned herself in. The scars Archie bears from the encounter go far beyond the physical and include a wrecked marriage and a lingering addiction to painkillers. When a new serial killer takes to Portland's rainy streets, Archie is called out of semi-retirement to head up the task force and enters a complicated and lethal dance with the new killer, a local reporter, and Gretchen herself. As with *Silence of the Lambs*, this story plays up an unhealthy relationship between an officer of the law and a serial killer; but after that, things take a very different turn.

Criminal Minds (2005–) TV

The Behavioral Analysis Unit in *Criminal Minds* is a highly fictionalized version of the FBI's real-life Investigative Support Unit. Capitalizing on an ongoing fascination with serial killers as well as psychological profiling, this ensemble drama essentially follows a serial-killer-of-the-week format. It's a crime procedural that owes a fair amount to *CSI*, among others. The stories feature a surprising amount of gore and violence for prime-time network television but are compelling enough that the occasional stiffness of the writing or characters can easily be overlooked.

Harris, Thomas, *Silence of the Lambs* (1988) BK, MV, SH

This seminal novel in the serial killer subgenre pits young FBI trainee Clarice Starling against notorious serial killer (and cannibal) Dr. Hannibal Lecter. The goal? To garner the information necessary to catch serial killer Buffalo Bill (so named because he "skins his humps"). The ante gets upped as his latest victim is a senator's daughter. The dance between Clarice and Dr. Lecter gets increasingly intimate and dangerous as he exchanges information on the case for personal information about her. In the end, one killer escapes and one goes free. Lecter first appeared in Harris's earlier book *Red Dragon,* and appeared again with Clarice in *Hannibal*, whose controversial ending left many fans outraged. *Silence of the Lambs* introduced psychological profiling into popular culture. The film adaptation is emotionally faithful, award-winning, and unnerving, as the protagonists in the film as deftly portrayed by Jodie Foster and Anthony Hopkins have a surprising chemistry.

Lindsay, Jeff, *Darkly Dreaming Dexter* (2004) BK, TV

Dexter Morgan is a serial killer with a mission—to target other serial killers. His adopted father, a police officer, recognized early on what Dexter would one day become and taught him to channel it for the greater good. Dexter is the ultimate modern anti-hero, a serial-killing crime fighter. His day job is a forensic specialist in blood spatter for the Miami Metro Police Department. His consuming hobby off the job: tracking the unindictable and even undiscovered bad guys in Miami and making them pay for their crimes with careful and creative brutality. Add into the mix Dexter's police rookie sister, a clever serial killer sending Dexter an invitation to the dance, and a nemesis in the form of Sgt. James Doakes. The novel is extremely gory and laced with a large amount of black humor. *Dexter* is also a deeply funny and gruesome cable television series featuring Michael C. Hall as the lead character. After the first season, the series departs significantly in plot from Lindsay's books.

Moore, Alan, *From Hell* (1999/2001) GN, MV

Originally published in serial form, this complex and thought-provoking graphic novel about Jack the Ripper is one of the most original takes on his story. Detailed black-and-white drawings depict a Victorian London that is often far more than it seems. Detective Inspector Frederick Abberline is on the trail of the Ripper, but the more he finds out, the less he seems to know. At heart, the plot involves a royal conspiracy surrounding the birth of an illegitimate child fathered by Prince Albert Victor, grandson of Queen Victoria. When the royal physician, Sir William Gull, confesses to the crimes, the cover-up begins. This dense and textured graphic novel was loosely adapted into a mediocre movie of the same title.

Rule, Ann, *The Stranger Beside Me* (1980) NF BK, TV

In the early 1970s, former police officer Ann Rule lived in Seattle. She volunteered at a local rape crisis hotline where she made friends with a nice young man as a series of murders and disappearances of young brunette women was wracking the area. Fast forward a few years and Rule is under contract to write a book about the Seattle killings. So imagine her surprise when she sees a picture of the prime suspect on the news and recognizes her old friend Ted Bundy from the volunteer hotline. Such is the setup for this in-depth look at one of the most notorious serial killers in American history—Ted Bundy. This insider's look at the killer is also the story of the author's reluctant acceptance that her friend was in fact the worst kind of stranger. The book was later adapted into a television movie.

Vampires: Bloodlust, Anti-Heroes, and the Reinvention of the Predator

The vampire started out as a predator, pure and simple, with no real charm or beauty to smooth his way. A good depiction of this is Nosferatu in the 1922 movie of the same name. Then Dracula came along. Still a predator, he had learned to cloak his intentions and nature with a patina of sophisticated charm. (It's worth noting that the charm and the beauty were more prone to slip in the original book than in all of the movies that followed.) Since then, the vampire has been reinvented as a misunderstood object of desire in large part thanks to the handiwork of Anne Rice. At this point, hundreds of vampire romances have been written, and readers devour them with great pleasure. But the vampire as predator has never really left the horror pantheon, even as it took a backseat to its more media-friendly romantic counterpart. And the two aren't mutually exclusive by any means, as *Dracula* amply demonstrates. The modern-day vampire takes many forms in its predation, from bloodsucker to parasite and even to virus carrier, but not all are unsympathetic, like the relatively friendly vampires of the Sookie Stackhouse novels and the *True Blood* TV show.

Ajvide Lindqvist, John, *Let the Right One In* (2007) BK, MV

Call this a murder mystery with fangs or a chilling fairy tale. Either way, this compelling read lands somewhere between Clive Barker and Neil Gaiman in its humane depiction of the inhuman among us. Oskar is a 12-year-old boy living in suburban Stockholm in the early 1980s. Lonely and picked on, his wish for a friend seems to come true when 12-year-old Eli moves in next door. Soon after, a gruesome series of murders starts and Oskar begins to wonder—is his best friend (and hopefully soon-to-be girlfriend) Eli a vampire? And if she is, does he really care? The movie, though more condensed, is every bit as good as the book. (The book was originally published under the title *Let Me In*.)

Del Toro, Guillermo, and Chuck Hogan, *The Strain* (2009) BK, YA

A plane lands at JFK Airport in New York City and within minutes is completely dark on the tarmac. As the plane is neither transmitting nor responding to radio hails, officials cautiously approach it. What they find is a plane full of people who died so swiftly that they didn't even have time to panic. A special task force from the CDC boards and finds four amnesiac survivors, but they carry the strain, a vampire virus that is highly transmissible, as it kills and then turns its hosts into mutated parasitic vampires with stingers to paralyze their prey. Ugly and very dangerous, these new vampires are emotional blanks with one mission aside from the kill—to return home to their loved ones. This is the first in a projected trilogy.

King, Stephen, '*Salem's Lot* (1975) BK, MV, TV

After the death of his wife, writer Ben Mears decides to return to his tiny rural hometown of Jerusalem's Lot, Maine. With plans to write about an old mansion that cast dark shadows on his childhood, he starts making friends and forms a romantic connection with Susan. The mansion with a grim past is bought by the mysterious Mr. Straker and Mr. Barlow. Soon after, disappearances and deaths begin. A once-thriving town is soon reduced to a ghost town, and Ben, Susan, the town doctor, and a few others form a small group that try to prevent the town from being completely overrun by vampires. '*Salem's Lot* was reissued in 2005 with 50 extra pages and was adapted into television movies in 1979 and 2004 and even a BBC radio series in 1995.

Matheson, Richard, *I Am Legend* (1954) BK, GN, MV

Robert Neville is the last man on Earth. Or at least the last one that hasn't been turned into a vampire by an epidemic. He spends his days dispatching the undead and looking for a cure. But everything may not be as it seems, and the plot turnabout is a kicker. The germ-born apocalypse plot in horror owes a lot to this novel even though it's mostly been rolled in with the zombie subgenre. And there's a lot of crossover potential with science fiction, as Matheson is best known for his science fiction. Several movie versions of varying quality have been made of the story (*The Last Man on Earth*, *The Omega Man*, and most recently, *I Am Legend*, starring Will

Smith). The book was also successfully adapted into a graphic novel by Steve Niles entitled *Richard Matheson's I Am Legend*.

Nosferatu (1922) CL, MV

Nosferatu was a silent German Expressionist film released in the early 1920s. Drawing heavily upon *Dracula*, it depicts a very different sort of vampire. Count Orlok, the Nosferatu in question, is unattractive with no pretense at charm or seduction. His features are almost bat-like with elongated ears and noticeable fangs. He is a predator, and death and plague follow in his wake, as he prefers killing over creating new vampires. Werner Herzog remade the film as *Nosferatu the Vampyre* with Klaus Kinski in the lead role. The year 2000 saw the release of *Shadow of the Vampire*, which was a fictionalized story of the making of *Nosferatu* that posited that the lead actor was actually a vampire, cast for the sake of verisimilitude.

Penzler, Otto, ed., *The Vampire Archives: The Most Complete Volume of Vampire Tales Ever Published* (2009) BK, SH

This wonderfully thorough anthology features over 80 stories from writers as diverse as Lord Byron and Ray Bradbury. All of the familiar names are here and as well as some unexpected ones. From pre-*Dracula* stories and poetry to psychic vampires and modern classics, there's something for anyone with a penchant for the undead. One particularly special feature: a gloriously comprehensive vampire bibliography that clocks in at more than 100 pages.

Wilson, F. Paul, *Midnight Mass* (2004) BK

Vampires are overrunning the world, and now they've hit the shores of the eastern United States. They kill brutally and are ruthlessly efficient in preventing unnecessary turnings by beheading victims. The vampires hire turncoat humans to round up people for food, paying them off with promises of eternal life. Into this battle ready to wage guerilla warfare against the undead step our heroes: a rabbi, a nun, a niece, and a priest. Their ultimate goal? Killing the vampire king of New York. The 2003 movie version is loosely adapted and is not recommended.

Zombies: The Other Undead

Zombies tend to fall into two categories: pre-Romero and post-Romero. Before George Romero got a hold of the zombie, they were very different. Less monsters than victims of villainy, zombies were originally the victims of some Hollywood-ized voodoo potion or ceremony often because of a love triangle gone wrong. Emotionless, lacking will, and usually quite alive, the zombies of such Hollywood classics as *White Zombie* and *I Walked with a Zombie* didn't engage in rampant decay or cannibalism. Cures were usually effective, and true love won the day. (The closest rendering we've seen of the old-school zombie is Wes Craven's *The Serpent and the Rainbow*, which had more to do with politics in modern Haiti than love, but it did have zombie powder.) Post-Romero zombies are whole other creatures, just as mindless but monstrous, messy, and really, really hungry.

Unlike other characters in horror, zombies almost never stand alone. Where there's one, there's likely to be dozens more in various states of decay and hunger. This doesn't leave much room for character development, but even if they lack personality or the ability to speak, zombies are the great commentators of horror. Writers and filmmakers alike use zombies as a decaying lens through which to view politics and society. Zombies have become critical shambling metaphors for conformity, civil rights, war, scientific hubris, materialism, and more. They are currently undergoing something of a renaissance across popular culture. From the classic lurchers of *Night of the Living Dead* to the rage-fueled speed zombies of *28 Days Later,* there is an intriguing variety in the uses and depictions of the other undead.

28 Days Later/28 Weeks Later (2002/2007) MV, GN

The rage virus has been loosed on London by animal-rights activists raiding a lab; it is instantly infectious and immediate in effect, as mere days pass between the initial infection and a decimating epidemic. Transmitted by blood, the virus changes its victims into red-eyed rampaging monsters with an uncontrollable urge toward murderous violence. Jim wakes up from a coma disoriented and more than a little confused in a deserted hospital and city, but it doesn't take long to encounter the infected as well as a handful of other survivors. As Jim and his companions try to escape London, it becomes unclear whether life outside the city gates is any safer. The first movie was followed up with a graphic novel, *28 Days Later: The Aftermath*, which explored the virus's origin as well as the spread of the epidemic in greater depth.

Adams, John Joseph, ed., *The Living Dead* (2008) BK

This anthology is crammed with wonderful short stories about the undead that range from gruesome to funny to weirdly beautiful. There will be many familiar names (Clive Barker, Stephen King) and titles in it, but the editor's stated intent was to gather up excellent and compelling but less-familiar stories. From the literally visceral "Calcutta, Lord of Nerves" by Poppy Z. Brite, to the unnerving beauty of David Schow's classic "Blossom," to the black humor of John Langan's "How the Day Runs Down," the stories encompass quite a range of zombies. Look for contributions by some unexpected writers such as Sherman Alexie, Nina Kiriki Hoffman, and Harlan Ellison. This is a good introduction for zombie neophytes and very enjoyable for zombie fans.

Brooks, Max, *World War Z: An Oral History of the Zombie War* (2006) BK, RS, UAB

Author of the wonderfully pokerfaced *The Zombie Survival Guide*, Max Brooks channels Studs Terkel as he imagines a truly worldwide zombie apocalypse. The narrator is writing from a world where humanity has just barely triumphed over the zombie horde after a decade of brutal combat and tremendous losses. From its origins in rural China to the devastated postwar landscape, the history of the zombie plague is reconstructed though a series of "oral histories" taken from a worldwide cross-section of people. This is a nerve-wracking and more traditional portrayal of zombies, written on an epic scale with grace notes about politics, disease, global community, and what it really means to be human. The audiobook is well worth checking out as the oral-history format of the story lends itself well to an audio version.

Doom (1993) CG

This is the first-person shooter game that spawned a legion of sequels and imitators, such as *Resident Evil* and *Left for Dead*. The premise is simple: the player is an anonymous lone space marine on Mars who is fighting off a seemingly endless stream of zombies and demons in an effort to survive. Hugely popular, the game represented a phenomenal leap forward in graphics and gaming technology and really brought the first-person shooter concept to the forefront of computer gaming. It's popularity led to a handful of novelizations, some comics, and even a movie.

Keene, Brian, *The Rising* (2004) BK
Winner of the Bram Stoker Award for Best First Novel, *The Rising* offers a new and discomfiting twist on the zombie myth. What if the undead were just as dead and just as hungry, but were smart? When a scientist accidentally opens an interdimensional rift, it allows demons to pour through and possess the dead. The result is a rapidly spreading zombie plague, and the resulting undead are smart, able to use weapons, set traps for human survivors, and even drive. Jim Thurmond emerges from his bomb shelter to trek across the country to save his son. Along his violent journey, he is joined by a preacher, an ex-prostitute, and a scientist, even as he dodges an army and national guard running amuck.

Monster Trilogy, Wellington, David, *Monster Island* (2006) BK, RS
Manhattan has turned into the titular monster island of the first book in this zombie apocalypse trilogy. Populated by voracious and cannibalistic hordes of the decaying undead, it's no place for the few human survivors of a global plague of disastrous proportions. But an expedition from Africa consisting a former UN weapons inspector and several teenage girl soldiers arrives at Ellis Island in pursuit of medication. In a twist unique to Wellington, a couple of zombies on the island have retained their mental faculties and even gained some mysterious psychic powers. The New York backdrop is integral to the story and is host to many gripping battles and chases. The second in the trilogy is a prequel, while the third takes place 12 years later. Each book has a different tone, and the final book starts to veer into fantasy territory.

Night of the Living Dead/Dawn of the Dead/Day of the Dead (1968/1978/1985) CL, MV, SH
George Romero introduced the zombie as we now know it into popular culture. His zombies are relentless, mindless, and crave human flesh, especially brains. They are quite dead (often sloughing body parts), slow moving, and can be someone you know. The only way to stop them is a gunshot or decapitating blow to the head. Their origins are murky but man-made. The original film, *Night of the Living Dead*, is surprisingly bloodless but violates a number of taboos (a zombie child eating her mother) as well as commenting not so obliquely on race in the 1960s. Gorier and more graphic, *Dawn of the Dead* tackles materialism with gleeful black humor as the dead gravitate toward a giant shopping mall.

The Walking Dead, Robert Kirkman, *The Walking Dead, Vol. I* (2003–) GN, TV
Reminiscent of Romero's zombie movies, this series focuses on Rick Grimes, a small-town police officer from Kentucky. In a coma when the zombie outbreak began, he awakens to a very changed world. Everywhere he turns there are zombies with a taste for human flesh roaming and lurking, the streets are empty, and information is scarce. Rick sets off in search of his family and other survivors. The focus of the story line is less all-zombie action than how the characters survive, develop, and interact around the collapse of society. Another issue the survivors have to contend with: the plague isn't infectious so much as inevitable, and everyone who dies with an intact brain will return as a zombie. Currently, there is a television adaptation in development.

Werewolves: Getting to Know the Beast in the Mirror

Tragic victim, slavering beast, grouchy anti-hero, serial killer, confused teenager next door. Werewolves have been all of these things and more. The werewolf is an excellent metaphor for the dark side of humanity or our inner beasts. But they have also been used to great effect to explore coming-of-age issues and even feminist empowerment. Though stories of were-creatures and werewolves in particular have been around for centuries, they continue to appeal and have relevance in the modern world. Society may change, but human nature does not so much; we'll always want to look at that beast in the mirror.

An American Werewolf in London (1981) CL, MV

Justifiably considered a cult classic, this movie epitomizes the marriage of horror and humor. Two college students on a backpacking trip across England get caught out after dark on the moors. Against the cryptic advice of the locals, they strayed from the road and stayed out until the full moon rose. They are attacked by a large howling animal (any guesses?) and Jack is killed. Three weeks later, David wakes up in a London hospital, healed but confused and suffering advice-laden visits from the revenant of his maimed friend Jack, who warns of his impending transition. David remains sympathetic even after his first kills and the inevitable unhappy ending gains some gravitas from that fact. The special effects won an Oscar and changed the course of special effects in film. Also note the nicely ironic use of music throughout the film.

Barlow, Toby, Sharp Teeth (2008) BK, YA

This is an award-winning novel in verse about werewolves in Los Angeles. With that as a set up, what's not to love? This noir verse is a wink and a nod to epic poems of the past while evoking in grittily bleak terms life in postmodern Los Angeles. An ancient race of shape-shifters has survived into the modern day and takes up residence in Southern California. The werewolves are bent on dominating L.A.'s underworld and are not above involuntary recruiting from the down-and-outs of L.A. This mix of lycanthropy, gang warfare, tacos, crystal meth labs, and surfing is a Los Angeles of urban legend. Meshing the plotlines together is a surprisingly tender love story between a dog catcher who falls (unknowingly) in love with a female werewolf who has abandoned her pack.

Hayter, Sparkle, Naked Brunch (2003) BK

In this darkly humorous tale of female empowerment in the big city, Annie Engel is a put-upon secretary with a small apartment, self-centered friends, and no love life. But Annie hasn't been feeling quite like herself lately. Waking up several mornings a month with the mother of all hangovers, she has no idea what she's been up to. It turns out that her weird dreams and hangovers are remnants of Annie's four-footed nightlife in New York City each month during the full moon. As Annie's lupine escapades start to draw attention, she finds herself more popular than ever with a love life that's no longer DOA.

Krause, Annette, Blood and Chocolate (1997) BK, MV, YA

In this complex and rich coming-of-age story, a young werewolf girl faces hard choices about where she belongs and who she can love. Sixteen-year-old Vivian is still reeling from grief at the death of her father, and her pack is in disarray. Unimpressed with her age-mates in the pack, deeply lonely, and in a mood to defy her mother, she crushes on a "meat-boy," a non-lycanthrope named Aiden. Will she pursue her heart and a life outside of the pack and its violent power struggles, or will she accept her role as a future queen and pair up with dominant pack member Gabriel? Rich with plot, complex characterization, and evocative language, this novel is more than the sum of its parts and is a classic in YA lit. The 2007 movie is a rather loose adaptation of the book.

Krinard, Susan, *To Tame a Wolf* (2005) BK

This novel stands at an interesting between intersection romance, westerns, and horror, and as unruly as that sounds, Krinard makes it work. Tally Bernard is a widow with a bleak past, who now runs a ranch (incognito as a young man) with her brother and several friends. When her brother disappears, she hires Simeon Kavanaugh to track him. Unknown to her, he's a shape-shifter who's using his wolf senses to track. As they travel together in search of her brother, they find that the path may lead to love as well as redemption.

Pekearo, Nicholas, *The Wolfman* (2008) BK

Marlowe Higgins, dishonorably discharged Vietnam vet, lives a rough-and-tumble life in and out of prison, moving from town to town. He has to keep moving because every time there's a full moon, he kills someone. He's not particularly happy about this but he does the best he can, killing only the really bad people. But eventually life on the road gets old, so Marlowe decides to settle down in the small town of Evelyn, where he works as a short-order cook and becomes buddies with a local police detective. Small-town life develops some unexpected complications because another monster has also decided to call Evelyn home—a serial killer, who is the obvious "really bad person" to put on Marlowe's to-do list for the next full moon. But in keeping with the rest of Marlowe's life, things start to go drastically wrong no matter how many good intentions he has.

Streiber, Whitley, *The Wolfen* (1978/1981) BK, MV

This 1978 novel reinvented the concept of the werewolf and then dropped it into the urban wastelands of certain New York City boroughs in the 1970s. Rather than being lycanthropes, Streiber's wolves are actually an advanced species of wolf—extremely smart, canny, and strong. They also possess almost hand-like claws and astonishing senses of smell and hearing. The pack has been successfully living undetected in New York City when they make the strategic error of killing two police officers. Detectives Becky Neff and George Wilson are on their trail, and the wolves return the favor as it becomes a race to see whose trap will spring first. Wolves and detectives alike are portrayed sympathetically, with certain parts of the story told from the wolves' point of view. The movie is a solid adaptation that merits viewing.

The Wolf Man (1941) CL, MV

Larry Talbot returns to his ancestral digs in England for a funeral after living for years in America. Deciding to stay on for a while, he encounters a pretty village shopgirl and a mysterious old gypsy. Soon after, Larry manages to defeat a werewolf with his silver cane, but not before it bites him, changing Larry's life forever. Now it's his turn to run wild beneath the full moon. This Universal Pictures classic cherry-picked through a wide variety of European folklore to create the now-familiar mythology of the modern wolf man. It explicitly depicted its titular character as a tragic hero doomed through no fault of his own, basically creating the trope of the tragic werewolf with a good heart. This is a classic well worth watching. Universal Pictures released a remake of this film starring Benicio del Toro.

Theme: Everyday Horror

Often the scariest, most unnerving sort of horror is everyday horror. It can take many different forms, from the uncanny horror of the mundane to the various permutations of everyday life going very, very wrong.[2] In many ways, there's nothing more frightening than the familiar going suddenly askew, leading to the realization that everything you know is wrong. This everyday horror is found all over the genre. It can be falling down the rabbit hole (*John Dies at the End*), the insidious pervading wrongness of *Invasion of the Body Snatchers*, or the realization that your neighbors aren't who you thought they were ("The Lottery"). The changes can be subtle with a building sense of paranoia (*The Stepford Wives*) or they can be sudden and terrifying—the one wrong turn that changes your life forever (*Cujo*).

For many of us, the most ubiquitous things in our lives are the person we see in the mirror, our homes and communities, family and friends, neighbors, and even pets. When they turn against us, the world becomes a very scary and unfamiliar place indeed.

It's All in Your Head . . . Or Is It?: Psychological Horror

Sometimes the everyday becomes horrific, but it's not reality's fault. Rather than the monster under the bed, it's the monsters in someone's head who take center stage. These often take the form of guilt, fear, rage, or sadness. Consuming memories and emotions can tip into instability with devastating consequences. Since the monster is internal, these stories rely upon atmosphere to help build frissons of fear. It's about what isn't seen as much as what is seen. There can be a dreamy, hallucinatory feel as the boundaries between reality and the mind become increasingly unclear to the characters and the readers alike. But sometimes things are real and someone or something is giving our protagonists a helping hand in their descents into madness. For obvious reasons, there's a lot of crossover with stories of hauntings, ghosts, and possession. Many well-respected writers have delved into this darkness and several classic pieces of literature have resulted.

The Blair Witch Project (1999) MV
Three film-school students set off into the backwoods of Burkittsville, Maryland, in pursuit of a local legend: the Blair Witch. They disappear and a year later much of their equipment and footage has been found. Many groundbreaking aspects of the film will seem familiar now: the jerky camerawork, the participants filming themselves into the story, the film as "documentary," the indie film budget that leads to a surprisingly old-school solution of implying rather than showing. Once you get used to the jerky camerawork, which effectively builds atmosphere, you have a movie with two different faces. Are these college kids succumbing to their own fears and fueling each other's hysteria? Or are they actually being haunted by an evil presence that is picking them off one by one in the woods?

DuMaurier, Daphne, *Rebecca* (1938/1940) BK, CL, MV

"Last night I dreamt I went to Manderley again." So starts a classic novel that typifies this subgenre. Told in an extended flashback, the narrator is a new bride, married after a brief and intense courtship to widower Max de Winter. At Manderley, the de Winter home, she immediately runs into trouble with the formidable housekeeper Mrs. Danvers, who remains obsessively loyal to her dead mistress, Rebecca. Mrs. Danvers continually undermines the new Mrs. de Winter, eroding her confidence in her abilities and her marriage and leaving her wondering if she and the house both are being haunted by Rebecca. The equally atmospheric and classic movie released in 1940 was directed by Alfred Hitchcock.

Gilman, Charlotte Perkins, *The Charlotte Perkins Gilman Reader: The Yellow Wallpaper and Other Stories* (1980) BK, CL, MV, TV, UAB

Originally published in the 1890s, "The Yellow Wallpaper" was Perkins' only dabbling into the horror genre, but its potency remains undiminished by time. The narrator tells her story in a series of ever-more-erratic journal entries. She's been forced into a rest cure by her physician husband for her depression and mild hysteria and is locked in a room with yellow wallpaper in a vacation home with absolutely nothing to do except stare at the walls, which seem to have a woman behind them staring back at her. She hates the wallpaper and becomes convinced that it's moving around and that there is something moving behind it. The story is both an important piece of early feminist writing and a succinctly harrowing descent into madness. It continues to resonate and has been adapted into radio plays, audiobooks, a British television film, and a movie.

Gran, Sara, *Come Closer: A Novel* (2003) BK

Amanda, the book's narrator, is a promising young architect in a happy marriage. Suddenly things aren't quite right: there are odd noises in home, she's not getting along with her husband, and she starts smoking. When she mistakenly receives a book in the mail, on demonology instead of architecture, she takes a quiz inside, "Are You Possessed by a Demon?" and if her answers are anything to go by, then yes she is. Demonic possession explains the inexplicable like her recent out-of-character actions such as sending obscene notes to her boss and stealing. But is she really possessed by the demon Naamah or is she simply coming undone?

Oates, Joyce Carol, *Beasts* (2002) BK

This short novel tackles gothic conventions in a modern setting. The result is an exercise in psychological discomfort and suspense. Set in the 1970s at a small all-girls college in New England, it follows poetry major Gillian Brauer, who along with the rest of the girls in her class is in emotional and intellectual thrall to their charismatic poetry teacher, Andre Harrow, who ratchets up sexual tension with erotic poetry readings and subtly inappropriate nicknames. Gillian is chosen as one of his special girls and fancies herself in love with him, but she is also fascinated by his sculptor wife, Dorcas, who specializes in unnerving totems representing the bestial side of human sexuality. All is not well as a rash of fires start, on campus and students become suicidal. In the midst of this, Andre forces the girls in his special writing group to read their journals out loud, revealing private thoughts best left unconfessed.

Small-Town Horror

Whether you're born there or are a recent arrival, small-town life isn't always everything that it's cracked up to be. Getting to know your neighbors and having them know you can be downright dangerous. Even passing through town can pose problems for the unwary traveler. Sometimes the menace wears a human face, as in "The Lottery," and sometimes it's unabashedly supernatural in nature ('*Salem's Lot* and pretty much any small town in Maine that Stephen King has a hand in). The inhabitants of these small towns make urban life look more appealing with every read.

Burnside, John, *The Glister* (2009) BK, UAB

Innertown is dying. Once a small but thriving industrial town, after the local chemical plant was abandoned, the population started to decline. The town falls somewhere between ghost town and post-apocalyse as those left behind are being poisoned by mysterious chemicals leaching into the water and soil from the shuttered plant. Even as death, deformity, and mutations abound, there's another more subtle threat plaguing the town, as teenage boys disappear roughly once a year. Fifteen-year-old Leonard is worried and suspicious and wants to know what's happening to his friends. He knows they aren't leaving town as much as they might want to. So if they haven't run away, where are they and who—or what—has them?

Hardy, Robin, and Anthony Shaffer, *The Wicker Man* (1978/1973) BK, MV

Lt. Howie arrives on the remote Scottish island of Summerisle to follow up an anonymous letter detailing the disappearance of a local girl. Though otherwise fairly friendly, the islanders stonewall him about the girl. He comes to believe the worst has happened and that there is an island-wide cover-up led by the local laird Lord Summerisle. Howie is a good Christian and the longer he stays on the island, the more he catches whiffs of distinctly pagan beliefs and practices. He confronts the community during their harvest festival only to face a most unexpected turnabout. The first movie was made in 1973 and is a scary cult classic. The 2006 remake is at best considered inferior to the first film.

Jackson, Shirley, *The Lottery and Other Stories* (1949) BK, CL, SH, TV

The title story caused tremendous controversy when it was published in *The New Yorker* in 1948. Equal to the controversy was the critical aclaim it received; a genuine American classic, it's also a really scary story and a scathing commentary on the perils of conformity. Set in a small town, the community members gather for the annual lottery. The head of each family draws a slip. When an unlucky family is chosen, those family members draw again and the loser is turned over to the community and promptly stoned to death by everyone in order to ensure the ongoing prosperity of all. There have been many adaptations for radio and television over the years.

Langan, Sarah, *The Missing* (2007) BK, RS

Corpus Christi is an affluent small town in the middle of Maine. It's also lucky, remaining untouched by the environmental mayhem that wrecked nearby Bedford after a fire at the Clott Paper Mill. When Lois Larkin takes her third-grade class on a field trip to the ghost town of Bedford, everything changes. One her charges goes astray in the nearby woods and digs up a virulent plague whose victims become inhuman beings crazed with anger and hunger. The contagion spreads and no one sleeps through the night anymore. Will anyone in the town survive to warn the outside world?

Levin, Ira, *The Stepford Wives* (1972/1975) BK, MV

The small buccolic town of Stepford seems like the perfect escape from the big city. When Joanna Eberhart moves there with her family, she's looking forward to quieter living and getting to know her neighbors. But most of her women neighbors seem too busy to get to know her as they lavish all of their time and energy on housecleaning and pampering their husbands; the women's club fades away even as the men's club meets almost daily. They also tend to have unnaturally perfect physiques. Joanna and a couple of other newcomers seem impervious to the local strain of hyper haus-frau-ness but that starts to change. Are the wives of Stepford being brainwashed? Or is it something much worse? The book has a healthy dollop of dark humor and is more open-ended than the two film adaptations that have been made (in 1975 and in 2004). The most recent film plays it overtly for laughs and is chock full of big names.

Man's Best Friend? Maybe Not

Animals. Boon companions and helpmeets of humankind? Sometimes. But when they decide to cut loose, people don't have very good odds. Animals are part of our daily lives, whether they take the form of pets, birds in the park, the gerbil in the classroom, or the livestock on the farm. Some animals in these stories we've never considered friends, though we might be fascinated (sharks), but others are part of our everyday lives, which makes their dark turns all the more horrifying (dogs). From the relentless rogue shark of *Jaws* to the Saint Bernard that you feel sorry for even as he menaces a mother and child in *Cujo*, animals have the power to terrify us on a most primal level.

Benchley, Peter, *Jaws* (1974/1975/2009) BK, MV, SH, UAB

The story is classic: small-town police chief battles a rogue shark terrorizing his town and the local politicians who want to deny the shark's existence. Round it out by adding three men battling the sea and a sea monster. Benchley's original novel was in many ways a darker work than the movie it spawned, laced with class issues and infidelity, and the characters are more complex but not as likeable. Spielberg streamlined the story and crafted a movie that is still filled with jolts and just enough gore to provoke the imagination.

The Birds (1963) CL, MV

By the end of this Hitchcock film, you'll think twice next time you take a walk in the park or go to a playground. After meeting in a pet shop over a pair of lovebirds, a wealthy young socialite pursues a man who caught her interest to his small coastal hometown of Bodega Bay, California. A surprise attack by a single seagull sets the stage for increasing number of violent attacks by the ever-growing bird population. No one is safe, from children in school to a hapless caller trapped in a phone booth. The movie was based on a short story by gothic favorite Daphne DuMaurier.

King, Stephen, *Cujo* (1981/1983) BK, MV

In a relatively unsupernatural turn (though there are hints of the demonic), King's villain in this piece is also something of a victim. Cujo, a cheerful Saint Bernard, gets bitten on the nose by a rabid bat. As the infection overtakes the dog, he becomes increasingly odd and reactive until he is fully rabid. Then all bets are off as he goes on a killing spree in the much beleaguered town of Castle Rock, Maine (setting for other King novels). A neighbor is the first to die followed by one of his owners. But the crux of the book is the standoff between Cujo and a woman and child trapped in a broken-down car on an isolated farm.

Lee, Edward, *Slither* (2006) BK

Even the lowly, unassuming worm can take on a monstrous aspect. When a team of scientists travels to an isolated Florida island to study a rare worm, they get more than they bargained for. Mutant flesh-eating worms to be exact, along with a mysterious assemblage of dead bodies. Soon enough, the scientists start behaving oddly because it turns out these worms are also parasites.

Willard (1971) MV

Willard is a shy underachiever who lives a circumscribed life. He suffers through miserable workdays only to return home to a bitter mother. When he meets a pack of rats, it is the answer to a couple of different issues: loneliness and the desire for revenge. Willard befriends the rats and trains them to go after his enemies. But the friendship doesn't end well as the rats eventually turn on him. The movie's famous theme song is performed by Michael Jackson. There was a remake in 2003 (somewhere between homage and parody) that starred Crispin Glover.

Wyndham, John, *Day of the Triffids* (1951/2003) BK, CL, MV, TV

More killer critter than killer animal, triffids are rather sizeable alien plants who've taken up residence on Earth. Able to uproot and perambulate, they pose a definite danger as they have a taste for human flesh. And living is easy for the triffids because the majority of people on the planet have been blinded by a mysterious celestial event. Throw in a plague and the fact that the sighted survivors are mentally breaking down and the survival of humankind is far from assured. A natural science fiction/horror crossover, it's been made into a movie and television mini-series.

Making Connections

Horror has permeated just about every aspect of popular culture from books and movies to music and computer games. It's not surprising, therefore, that aspects of horror can be found lurking in many other genres. In recent years, horror has had a considerable impact on the romance genre, spawning a new and thriving subgenre: paranormal romance. Horror has always had a place in science fiction, where humankind's exploration of the great unknown or the final frontier opens doors to its greatest nightmares and most formidable monsters. Horror has even found its way into mysteries both in the form of supernatural crime-solvers and crimes that may have only paranormal solutions.

Horror for Science Fiction Fans

Science fiction and horror cross over frequently and easily. Our fascination with space has always been tempered with a certain fear about what we might find there. Or what might come and find us. Likewise, near-future and dystopian stories often have horror elements and characters as part of an overall collapse of society.

Alien/Aliens/Alien 3/Alien Resurrection (1979/1986/1992/1997) CL, MV

The tagline sums it up: "In space, no one can hear you scream." The crew of a commercial spaceship is awakened from stasis sleep to investigate a mysterious signal from a nearby asteroid. This sets up the first of many encounters between humans and a voracious, parasitic, and incredibly aggressive alien race. The aliens lay their eggs inside of people, and when the alien hatches, it bursts through the chest. Paranoia, violence, and gore abound as the crew led by Lt. Ellen Ripley fights off the alien even as they wonder who else may have been infected. The literally visceral fear of becoming a human hatchery/carrier drives all of the films.

Finney, Jack, *Invasion of the Body Snatchers* **(1955/1956/1978) BK, MV, SH, UAB**
Originally published in 1955 as *The Body Snatchers*, this science fiction classic by Jack Finney has been made into multiple films and more recently into a wonderfully unnerving audiobook. The premise is simple: One day the people around you start behaving a little differently; they're not quite right. You start thinking that they're not really your friends, family, and neighbors at all. And of course, when you try to tell the police or the family doctor or your girlfriend, no one believes you. For the extra kicker, you start finding the pod people, who are perfect physical replacements of the victims. And it turns out the pods can form only when the intended victim is sleeping. And everybody has to sleep some time. Whether it's set on a military base, in a small town, or in the big city of San Francisco, the paranoia and the fear ratchet up just as inevitably.

Lumley, Brian, *Necroscope* **(1986) BK**
Vampires have been reinvented as the Wamphyrii in the Necroscope universe (there are multiple sub-series). These vampires are not just evil, as they have the usual taste for human blood (and flesh), they are parasitic. Standing against them is the necroscope of the title, Harry Keogh, who communicates with the dead and the undead. Vampires are mixing it up in human politics and have plans to use the Soviet Union and the KGB to come to power. Started in the mid-1980s, the early series reflects Cold War concerns and machinations with a science fiction and horror twist. As the series evolves, Lumley plays with the complicated and mysterious Mobius Continuum, multiple time streams, and alien invasions by parasitic vampires.

Threshold **(2005–2006) TV**
This short-lived TV series is well worth checking out on DVD. A strong ensemble cast paired with a well-rendered concept of subtle alien invasion is chilling. The invasion is transmitted through infection and there may be human collusion. The government team of scientists assembled to identify and fight this invasion is in an involuntary lockdown, which amplifies personality clashes and ramps up the paranoia. There is a nod to *Invasion of the Body Snatchers* because the alien infection isn't obvious until the person starts acting out of character. Even the team isn't immune, and the question becomes: is it just the stress or is the infection running rampant here, too?

Wells, H. G. *The War of the Worlds* **(1898/1953) BK, CL, MV, Radio UAB**
This granddaddy of alien invasion terror is set in late Victorian England as Martians brutally invade Earth. The narrator spends the novel trying to reunite with his wife even as he witnesses Martians conquering parts of England. A radio play broadcast in 1938 adapted the novel into a series of news bulletins and was so terrifyingly effective that it convinced some listeners that it was actual news coverage. The book has been adapted (sometimes quite loosely) into several movies, the most recent of which was Steven Spielberg's 2005 special-effects extravaganza.

Horror for Mystery Fans

Mysteries come in a wide variety of forms, as do the detectives who solve them. In some of these mysteries, it appears that the only solution may be a supernatural one. In others, the supernatural element is the detective solving the case.

Doyle, Arthur, Conan, *The Hound of the Baskervilles* **(1922/1939/1988/2009) BK, CL, GN, MV, TV**
This classic Sherlock Holmes mystery plays with the paranormal throughout the story. The foggy, dangerous moor with the screams of wild ponies dying in the mire. The almost ghost story about the evil ancestor Hugo Baskerville, whose actions brought about the curse of the hound. The footprints of a gigantic hound found glowing near Baskerville Hall. All of these unite to create an atmospheric and creepy tale where even the reasoning skills and intellectual acumen of Sherlock Holmes face an uphill battle against the forces of darkness. Many movie versions have been made as well, but the Granada Television version with Jeremy Brett is one of the best.

Jack Fleming/*The Vampire Files***, Elrod, P. N.,** *Bloodlist* **(1990–) BK**
Ace journalist Jack Fleming wakes up on the shores of Lake Michigan to discover that reports of his death were unfortunately *not* exaggerated. It turns out his most recent paramour was a bit more than she seemed, and now so is Jack. A vampire journalist is going to have a challenging time of it in 1930s Chicago, so he puts his investigative skills to a different use and becomes a private detective. His first case? Trying to figure what he did to upset the mob so much that they had him killed. His next? Trying to find the mysterious woman whose disappearance led him to Chicago in the first place. The mysteries are interesting, the sense of place and time evocative, and the detective surprisingly down to earth as he tries to understand his new state.

Mercedes "Mercy" Thompson, Briggs, Patricia, *Moon Called* **(2006–) BK, YA**
Shape-shifter coyote Mercy Thompson tries to lead a normal life, working as a mechanic and trying to get by. But if you were raised by werewolves, are friends with a vampire, and have a nose for magic, normal can be a pretty tall order. Mercy finds herself caught in the middle of mysteries that have her running afoul of witches, vampire queens, and even gremlins. Add in the romantic tension of having two competing werewolf love interests, and Mercy's life is never dull.

The Parasol Protectorate, Carriger, Gail, *Soulless* **(2009) BK**
Alexia Tarabotti is a Victorian spinster with a penchant for treacle tart and an elaborate parasol of her own devising that she carries everywhere. It's an unfashionable accoutrement at a ball but an undeniably useful one when she is set upon by a vampire. Alexia is more than she seems though; she was born without a soul. This makes her a preternatural, a person capable of negating supernatural powers. When vampires begin disappearing soon after Alexia's fatal set-to with the vampire at the ball, she becomes the likely suspect, so it's up to her to solve the mystery of what's actually happening to London's high society—both mortal and supernatural.

Reaves, Michael, and John Pelan, eds., *Shadows Over Baker Street* **(2003) BK**
In an unlikely juxtaposition that works surprisingly well, the 18 stories in this anthology mesh the universe of Sherlock Holmes (Victorian London, logic, mystery solving, and familiar characters) with the Cthulhu universe of H. P. Lovecraft (monstrous old gods, the macabre, and supernatural chaos). Stories range from Neil Gaiman's "A Study in Emerald," where the mystery of royal blood becomes sanguinary indeed, to "The Terror of Many Faces" by Tim Lebbon, in which Dr. Watson witnesses a particularly brutal murder apparently committed by his friend Sherlock Holmes. Lovecraftian darkness permeating the innate reason of Holmesian crime-solving makes for a wide range of successful and disconcerting stories.

Vicky Nelson, Huff, Tanya, *Blood Price* (1991) BK, TV
Sometimes the detective is human but the victims of the crimes are not. Vicky Nelson is a former Toronto homicide detective who resigned from the police force and is now working as a private detective. Her first case is a murder that appears to be supernatural in origin. Over the course of the investigation, she teams up with Henry Fitzroy, historical romance author, vampire, and bastard son of Henry VIII. As the supernatural killings continue, she reaches out to her former partner, Detective-Sergeant Mike Cellucci, for help. In the ensuing novels and stories, this threesome solve crimes involving vampires, werewolves, and many creatures in between; the series is best read in order. This was made into the TV series *Blood Ties*.

Horror for Fantasy Fans

Fantasy, much like romance, is having a crossover heyday with horror. The phrase "fantastic fiction" takes on a wonderful variety of nuances when fantasy and horror intersect. This is best exemplified by the subgenre of urban fantasy that rolls in elements from both and often has romance as well. Urban fantasy often mixes anti-heroes, or at least conflicted and ambivalent heroes, with classic fantasy elements such as fairies and dragons in grittier-than-not urban settings. These fantastical creatures can be mythical in origin or take the form of more familiar horror characters such as vampires and demons recast in less horrific settings.

Buffy the Vampire Slayer/Angel (1997–2003/1997–2004) TV, BK, GN (1997–), SH, YA
Sunnydale seems like a perfectly nice place to live. It lives up to its sunny name and has nice neighborhoods and good schools. The problem? Sunnydale is on the Hellmouth, which makes it a focal point for supernatural bad guys of all sorts, from demons who gamble for kittens to vampires who want to end the world. Enter Buffy the Vampire Slayer, a mediocre high school student and superlative hero, her erudite Watcher, the high-school librarian, and her faithful friends, Willow and Xander. Over the course of high school and college, they save the world several times, Willow becomes a witch, and Xander falls in complicated love with a former vengeance demon. Buffy's love life has issues since her true love is a vampire with a soul that takes the maxim of "opposites attract" to the limit.

Datlow, Ellen, et al., eds., *The Year's Best Fantasy and Horror* (1988–2008) BK, SH, YA
These anthologies reflect the wonderful diversity that can be encompassed by the darker shades of fantastic fiction. Unknowns are mixed with notable authors in both genres, and poetry is mixed with fiction. YA authors such as M. T. Anderson, Holly Black, and Garth Nix are also frequently included. Sadly, this longstanding anthology series has ceased publication, though its previous editions are well worth checking out.

The Hollows, Harrison, Kim, *Dead Witch Walking* (2004–) BK, UAB, YA
Kim Harrison's rich urban fantasy world features Rachel Morgan—bounty hunter, private investigator, and witch. She works with a vampire and a rather menacing pixie to keep the supernatural inhabitants of Cincinnati in-line and from harming innocents. Mystery, action, and humor abound; some titles in the series are more romance-heavy than others. Several of the series are audiobooks. Most of the titles are nods to Clint Eastwood movie titles.

Sookie Stackhouse, Harris, Charlaine, *Dead Until Dark* (2001) BK, TV
When psychic Sookie Stackhouse meets vampire Bill Compton in the small-town bar where she is a waitress, she is intrigued by him because his mind is silent to her. Few people know about Sookie's abilities, but the invention of synthetic blood has allowed vampires to come out in the open, and they are intrigued by Sookie and her talents, just as she is drawn to their silent minds. With Bill's help, Sookie undertakes solving a series of murders plaguing her hometown of Bon Temps after Sookie's brother Jason becomes the main suspect. Alan Ball and HBO have adapted the Sookie Stackhouse novels into the popular television series *True Blood.*

Horror for Non-Fiction Fans

Call it the fascination of forensics, but true crime fascinates. Think of it as the horror of real life. Often the gorier and more outrageous it is, the more it draws us in, in a confusing welter of curiosity, schadenfreude, and morbid fascination. Reading stories of how other people's friends, neighbors, and families go off the rails, disappear, or die bloodily can reassure us about our own safety, or it can lead us to wonder why our next-door neighbor is so fond of gardening at night. The growing interest with forensic science and forensic psychiatry over the past decade has only fueled the boom in true crime. Guaranteed to be discomfiting, the following stories demonstrate how the truly horrifying can be going on behind the scenes in everyday life.

Brown, Arnold R., *Lizzie Borden: The Legend, The Truth, The Final Chapter* (1991) BK
"Lizzie Borden took an axe and gave her mother 40 whacks. When she saw what she had done, she gave her father 41." Or did she? Contrary to the famous jump-rope rhyme, author Brown believes that Lizzie never took up that axe and, in fact, went to great lengths to assume the blame for someone else. Who? Her illegitimate younger brother. Using courtroom documents and newspaper stories, Brown effectively constructs a very different version of the crime. Not everyone believes his theory, but his research and attention to detail make for an intriguing read on one of the most famous and gruesome domestic murder cases in American history.

Craig, Emily, *Teasing Secrets from the Dead: My Investigations at America's Most Infamous Crime Scenes* (2004) BK
Murder from the ground up, often literally. This forensic anthropologist's memoir explores grisly crimes in equally grisly detail, from identifying individuals in the aftermath of 9/11 to domestic crimes in the boondocks of her home state of Kentucky. Vivid and descriptive writing makes the crimes gripping and brings the victims to life. As gruesome as it gets (decayed tissue is compared to chocolate pudding) with a plethora of maggots and ugly insights into human behavior, Craig always comes across as innately humane and empathetic. For her, the dead will always carry the faces of the living.

Ruddick, James, *Death at the Priory: Love, Sex, and Murder in Victorian England* (2001) BK
Unsolved murder, spousal cruelty, and poison combine dramatically in the 1876 case of Charles Bravo. His young wife, Florence Ricardo, was widowed and came into possession of a sizable fortune after her abusive first husband's death. Threat of social scandal drove her into the marital arms of Charles Bravo, who also turned out to be

abusive. After a few months of marriage, he became very ill and eventually died after three agonizing days. Suspicion soon fell on Florence and the housekeeper, Mrs. Cox. But the story is filled with suspects: jilted lovers, unhappy servants, as well as the husband and wife. Nothing was ever successfully proven against Florence or any of the servants, making this domestic crime a favorite of amateur detectives.

Summerscale, Kate, *The Suspicions of Mr. Whicher: A Shocking Murder and the Undoing of a Great Detective* **(2008) BK**
Murder most foul occurred at an English country home in 1860, and Detective-Inspector Jonathan Whicher from Scotland Yard was brought in to investigate after the local constabulary found little in the way of clues. The victim was three-year-old Saville Kent, found in a servant's privy with his throat slashed open. With little evidence and no confession to support his belief that Constance Kent, the half-sister, was responsible, Whicher returned to London in disgrace, stonewalled by the Kent family, and an object of community outrage. Five years later, he was proved right as the killer confessed and a lurid trial followed. Whicher is famous for being the inspiration for several fictional detectives.

True Crime, **Harold Schechter, ed. (2008) BK, SH**
This is an impressive compendium of American true-crime writing that encompasses the past 300 years. It includes everything from murder ballads to magazine articles with some very familiar names from the literary world making appearances (including Theodore Dreiser, Nathaniel Hawthorne, Robert Bloch, Zora Neale Hurston, and Ambrose Bierce). Expect the usual crimes of Ed Gein, Charles Manson, and the Son of Sam, but also some less familiar ones, like the Cleveland Butcher. This anthology includes some of the most notorious cases in American history and makes for compelling reading and analysis of crime writing over the centuries.

Conclusion

The horror genre always meets the society that generates it more than halfway. If you want to understand what scares people individually and collectively, horror will hold up that mirror. The reflection is always changing, as it should be, with characters and tropes evolving as social concerns and conditions shift.

Sometimes these trends are simple to spot: the evolution of the vampire into a sympathetic character and the subsequent resurgence of all things zombie. Sometimes they're more complex or darker, with an amorphous uneasiness. Think of the growing popularity of horror laced with humor juxtaposed with the thriving violence of extreme horror.

Film will continue to be a key component in horror advisory. Independent presses are almost certain to continue to be a rich source of new writers and trends in the genre, and electronic publishing will likely prove a boon to the genre as well, enabling it to thrive even if mainstream publishing continues to be cautious in its horror choices.

The key is not to be afraid of horror. It can be a complicated genre to advise around because it's so tied to emotions; fears are personal to the individual, which can make them hard to describe. But cross-media advisory is a natural for this genre and even a tool for the willing librarian (films and video games can both be used to ascertian acceptable levels of violence and gore).

In a wonderful contradiction, what scares us makes us happier, and maybe even more resilient. By vicariously engaging with and often conquering our fears in the pages of a scary book or in a darkened theater, we arm ourselves and disarm what frightens us. Maybe it's the reassurance that monsters really can be killed. Or perhaps it's a matter of perspective: What's scarier? Rising gas prices or zombie hordes?

Resources for Librarians

Castle, Mort, ed. *On Writing Horror: A Handbook by The Horror Writers Association.* Rev. ed. Cincinnati, OH: Writer's Digest Books, 2007.
> This tackles the genre from the perspective of the writer rather than the reader/consumer, but it has rich insight for the librarian who wants a more in-depth understanding of the genre and the motivations of those who write within it.

Fonseca, Anthony J., and June Michelle Pulliam. *Hooked on Horror III: A Guide to Reading Interests.* Westport, CT: Libraries Unlimited, 2009.
> Part of the Genreflecting series, this is one of the definitive resources for horror advisory. One of its special strengths is how it addresses the importance of film to the horror genre and makes film suggestions for every subgenre. The content changed significantly from the second edition to the third, and the authors themselves recommend using the two editions in conjunction for the broadest coverage.

Joshi, S. T., ed. *Icons of Horror and the Supernatural: An Encyclopedia of Our Worst Nightmares, 2 vols.* Westport, CT: Greenwood Press, 2007.
> More of an academic exploration of the archetypes of horror, most of these essays are quite readable and interesting, addressing everything from vampires to sea serpents. Most of the contributors discuss horror in film as well as in print. It is also a good source of insight into the appeal of the genre and specific subgenres or archetypes.

King, Stephen. *Danse Macabre.* New York: Everest House Publishers, 1981.
> This is a classic exploration of the genre by the biggest writer in the genre. Something of a period piece, it was written relatively early in King's career. Even so, he gives a lot of thought about what makes for good horror and what makes for tripe and why people read it. It is opinionated and often rather funny.

Monsterlibrarian.com: http://www.monsterlibrarian.com.
> This Web site is by a librarian for librarians and others interested in horror. It is filled with book reviews on titles from mainstream *and* independent publishers, booklists, genre news, and even collection-development ideas. It can be challenging to navigate but the content is well worth it.

Pulliam, June Michelle, and Anthony J. Fonseca. *Read On . . . Horror Fiction.* Westport, CT: Libraries Unlimited, 2006.
> Instead of a focus on subgenres with extensive annotations that are the hallmark of *Hooked on Horror*, the authors explore the genre through a wide variety of appeal factors, from the use of language and how an author builds atmosphere to plot types and settings.

Saricks, Joyce G. *The Readers' Advisory Guide to Genre Fiction.* 2nd ed. Chicago: American Library Association, 2009.
> This is a general text on RA, but the horror chapter is concise and insightful, intended to explain horror to the non-genre reader. As always, Saricks excels at finding links between the genres, finding entre into other genres for horror readers and vice versa.

Spratford, Becky Siegel, and Tammy Hennigh Clausen. *The Horror Readers' Advisory: The Librarian's Guide to Vampires, Killer Tomatoes, and Haunted Houses.* Chicago: American Library Association, 2004.

This is a concise take on the genre and tackles it with humor and affection. It breaks down horror into several subgenres and provides mini-essays with annotated lists for each. Additionally, it covers how to conduct an RA interview for the genre, the various awards, collection development, and marketing the collection. It is well worth checking out.

Endnotes

1. Joyce G. Sarricks, *The Readers' Advisory Guide to Genre Fiction*, 2nd ed. Chicago: American Library Association, 2009, 4, pp. 113–114.

2. Anthony J. Fonseca and June Michelle Pulliam, *Hooked on Horror III: A Guide to Reading Interests*. Westport, CT: Libraries Unlimited, 2009, pp. 343–345.

5

Everything Popular Science
Rick Roche

In this chapter, Rick Roche covers the world of popular science. "Plots" covers discoveries, inventions, conflicts, mistakes, and science that saved the world. "Characters" reviews contemporary and everyday scientists, pioneers, controversial figures, and mad scientists. The theme of this chapter is the world around us, which includes nature stories, animals both wild and companion, food and eating, humans, our world, and evolution. In "Making Connections," Rick suggests science titles for mystery, adventures, history, and literary fans.

Introduction

Is popular science a misnomer? How can science be popular when many readers do not like science? In the opening pages of her book *The Canon: The Whirligig Tour of the Beautiful Basics of Science*, Natalie Angier reports that many adults claim to dislike science, which they equate with dull classes, heavy textbooks, assignment deadlines, and dreaded exams.[1] Remembering how they suffered through high school or college biology, chemistry, physics, and algebra, they are unwilling to repeat the ordeal. Yet these same people enjoy a good medical story, follow the space program, visit zoos, build their own computers, seek rare garden plants with long names, and cook with the exacting care of a chemist. They debate the age of the universe, the existence of global warming, and the merits of good and bad cholesterol. Without cognition of the discipline, they surround themselves with science.

What is Popular Science?
Perhaps the confusion originates in the definition of "science." To many, science is simply test tubes, formulas, and supercomputers. In its broadest definition, however, it is "knowledge gained through experience."[2] Those experiences include observation, identification, description, testing, and theorizing. Seen this way, prehistoric humans who painted images of mastodons surrounded by hunters onto cave walls were applying science to their everyday lives. Their paintings may have helped them understand and plan their activities. They may also have pointed to the images as they told stories about their

hunts. The role of popular science literature is much the same today: people tell the stories so others may better understand the world around them.

If you accept that popular science is science topics presented in a style and at a level of sophistication that is palatable to general readers, it is everywhere. It is not often even labeled as "science" and is probably in narrative form. Books, magazines, newspapers, television, radio, movies, and the Internet present science narratives to eager consumers, who see them simply as "news" or "stories." Astute publishers and retailers effectively market their science literature to people with specific interests, such as healthy living, wildlife, space exploration, dinosaurs, or advanced technology. With new discoveries daily, science authors always have new stories to tell to the ready market. The keys to sales and devoted readership are the same as with any genre—good stories with identifiable characters and interesting themes will sell popular science to readers.

Having popular science collections offers libraries these readers' advisory opportunities:

- Readers who shun fiction, particularly men, and who enjoy nonfiction, are often drawn to popular science literature. They appreciate the implied emphasis on truth and practicality. These materials help them understand and adapt to the evolving world.
- Readers who follow news and current affairs demand up-to-date and relevant materials. A library that can build and maintain an up-to-date popular science collection can win the patronage of these readers.
- A library with a good popular science collection can distinguish itself as a valuable community resource as science topics become newsworthy and topics of public debate.

Despite its aura of modernity and its concern for the future, popular science literature has a long and illustrious past.

History and Development of Popular Science Literature

The origins of popular science and its literature are obscure. Science has always been a popular concern, as anonymous people developed crops, designed tools, watched the stars, and sought herbs with which to heal the sick. Without publishing and a culture trained to the scientific method, however, knowledge was passed orally. Technology and the quality of life improved very slowly. For Western culture, the big breakthrough was the development of the printing press by German goldsmith Johannes Gutenberg around 1439, which allowed for the dissemination of scientific findings. The first scientific bestsellers were treatises by Sir Isaac Newton, including *Opticks: Or a Treatise of the Reflections Inflections and Colours of Light* and *Principia: Mathematical Principles of Natural Philosophy*.[3] Printing allowed Newton's theories to be communicated throughout Europe and even to the colonies in America. Of course, with illiteracy high in the seventeenth century, it is a stretch to call these titles "popular science."

Gutenberg's printing press came at a good time. The fifteenth through seventeenth centuries saw the forming of learned societies in the wake of the European Renaissance. Scholars, nobles, and newly empowered merchants began to be interested in mathematics, astronomy, and natural sciences, and they came together as Sodalitas Litterarum Vistulana in Poland, Accademia dei Lincei in Italy, L'Académie Française, and the Royal Society of London. The first such society in America was started by Benjamin

Franklin in Philadelphia in 1743.[4] Qualifications for joining these societies varied, and they were never truly representative of populations, but they did spread the interest in reading and discussing science far beyond universities.

From the learned societies arose three traditions that underlie the culture of popular science: the publishing of papers, the public lecture, and the veneration of celebrity scientists.[5] The papers transformed into journals and books. The lectures eventually became radio, television, and film documentaries. Early celebrity scientists, such as Newton and Franklin, gave way to Albert Einstein, Carl Sagan, and Bill Nye the Science Guy.

Integrated Advisory: Science Style

Humans have always needed to communicate what they have discovered with others. Oral instruction gave way to print. Mechanized print has led to various forms of electronic media. Science communications have naturally been on the leading edge, adopting each new media for professional and then mass-market distribution.

Traditional Print Books

The first true scientific publications may have been the astronomical reports of fourth century BCE Babylonians found on cuneiform tablets discovered by British archeologists in the nineteenth century CE. These documents, which were lost for more than 2,000 years, however, may not be called popular science, as they were not widely disseminated. Second-century BCE Greek historians might get a nod for writing early popular science as they wrote about Thales of Miletos, a sixth-century BCE philosopher who is credited for discovering electricity and magnetism, refining geometry, predicting eclipses, and arguing that the moon reflects the light of the sun. Unfortunately, none of Thales's writing survived.[6] Greek philosophers, including Leucippus (c. 440 BCE), Democritus (c. 420 BCE), and Epicurus (342–270 BCE), sought to explain natural history and even proposed that all matter was composed of tiny particles called atoms. They did not, however, have the means to prove their theories, and Aristotle's theories regarding chemistry and the four elements (e.g., earth, air, fire, and water) prevailed in Europe through the Dark and Medieval Ages, a long period of scientific dormancy.[7]

As mentioned in the previous section, the development of the printing press by German goldsmith Johannes Gutenberg around 1439 was essential to the development of science literature, and Sir Isaac Newton was the first celebrity scientist. Many books followed Gutenberg's invention, though only a few have survived and continue to be read as science or history. These include:

- *On the Revolutions of the Heavenly Spheres* by Nicolaus Copernicus (1543)
- *Epitome of Copernican Astronomy* by Johannes Kepler (1618)
- *Dialogues Concerning Two New Sciences (On the Shoulders of Giants)* by Galileo Galilei (1638)
- *Elements of Chemistry* by Antoine Lavoisier (1789)
- *Principles of Geology* by Charles Lyall (1830)
- *The Voyage of the Beagle* by Charles Darwin (1839)
- *Personal Narrative of a Journey to the Equinoctial Regions of the New Continent* by Alexander von Humboldt (1851)

- *On the Origin of Species* by Charles Darwin (1859)
- *The Meaning of Relativity* by Albert Einstein (1922)

Most of these books are fairly academic and not "popular" by today's standards. A modern list of popular science classics to be found at libraries and bookstores would include some of the following titles:

- *A Brief History of Time: From the Big Bang to Black Holes* by Stephen Hawking (NF BK 1988, UAB)
- *Cosmos* by Carl Sagan (NF BK 1980, TV 1980)
- *The Double Helix: A Personal Account of the Discovery of the Structure of DNA* by James D. Watson (NF BK 1968)
- *Gorillas in the Mist* by Dian Fossey (NF BK 1983, DVD 1999)
- *How We Die: Reflections on Life's Final Chapter* by Sherwin B. Nuland (NF BK 1993, AB)
- *Lives of a Cell: Notes of a Biology Watcher* by Lewis Thomas (NF BK 1978)
- *Never Cry Wolf* by Farley Mowat (NF BK 1963)
- *A Short History of Nearly Everything* by Bill Bryson (NF BK 2003, AB)
- *Silent Spring* by Rachel L. Carson (NF BK 1962, UAB)
- *Six Easy Pieces: Essentials of Physics Explained by Its Most Brilliant Teacher* by Richard P. Feynman (NF BK 1994, UAB)

At this point in time, there are popular science books for nearly every taste, as the lists in this chapter will prove. Just do not call them science, and more library users will enjoy them.

Magazines

As mentioned in the previous section, the formation of learned societies led to communications between its members. Letters, reports, and treatises were distributed among members in increasingly standardized publications, which developed into modern scientific periodicals. From the viewpoint of popular science, a milestone was the formation of the National Geographic Society by 33 members of the Cosmos Club of Washington, DC, in 1888. Though these men were all social elites, they had more democratic ideals than their European predecessors and sought to form an organization that any American could and would want to join. Replacing academic writing with journalistic reports, they began publishing *National Geographic* magazine. Most importantly, the magazine's editors pioneered the use of color photography, and it eventually became the first magazine to adopt a full-color format. The effort was an immediate and continued success, as interested readers became members to read reports on natural wonders and exotic locations in the last great age of exploration.[8]

National Geographic is not our country's oldest continuous science publication. In August 1845, inventor Rufus Porter produced a four-page newsletter about inventions, which he called *Scientific American*. Porter's weekly publication caught on quickly, and within a year, he sold it to the publishing firm of Munn & Company, which expanded the publication to eight pages and began adding general science news. By 1848, there were 10,000 subscribers eager to learn about the latest patents and the promise of science to improve their lives and fortunes.[9]

A third venerable and still popular science publication is *Audubon*, which began its life in 1887 as a membership publication for the National Audubon Society, which was denouncing the use of feathers in lady's fashions and educating the public to the dramatic decline in bird populations. From a newsletter printed on brown paper devoted to birds, the publication has developed into a colorful magazine devoted to a broad range of conservation and environmental issues.[10]

In the twenty-first century, readers are still interested in a wide range of popular science and technology publications, many of which can be found at libraries, at bookstores, and on the Internet. Popular titles include the following:

COMPUTERS AND ELECTRONICS
iCreate
Laptop
Mac Life
Macworld
Make: Technology on Your Time
PC Magazine
PC World
Wired

CONSERVATION/ENVIRONMENT/NATURAL HISTORY
Audubon
Birds and Blooms
E: The Environmental Magazine
National Geographic
National Geographic Adventure
National Parks
National Wildlife World Edition
Natural History
Sierra

GARDENING
American Gardener
Better Homes and Gardens
Fine Gardening
Herb Quarterly
Horticulture
Mother Earth News
Organic Gardening

HEALTH
Body and Soul
Consumer Reports on Health
Diabetes Forecast
Fitness
Harvard Health Letter
Health
Johns Hopkins Medical Letter
Mayo Clinic Health Letter

Medical Tourism
Men's Health
Nutrition Action Health Letter
Prevention
Tuft's University Health and Nutrition Letter
University of California at Berkeley, Wellness Letter
Women's Health

PETS/ANIMALS
Aquarium
Bark
Bird Talk
Cat Fancy
Dog Fancy
Equus
Horse Illustrated
Tropical Fish Hobbyist

PSYCHOLOGY
Psychology Today
Scientific American Mind

SCIENCE AND TECHNOLOGY
Air & Space
American Heritage's Invention and Technology
Aviation Week and Space Technology
Discover
Popular Mechanics
Popular Science
Science
Science News
Scientific American
Seed
Skeptic
Technology Review
Wired Magazine

Television and Movies

For many people, science needs to be seen to be understood. Before the advent of film, the best way to present science was the live demonstration. The Montgolfier brothers (Joseph and Jacques) sailed their hot air balloons over Lyon and Paris. Robert Fulton demonstrated his steamboats on the Hudson River in New York City. Pioneers of surgery performed their operations for their colleagues in surgical theaters. Members of learned societies worldwide demonstrated their experiments at society meetings. These events were exciting, but viewers had to meet at specific times and places to witness the demonstrations.

In the nineteenth century, the development of photography led to magic lantern shows. While they tended to be travelogues featuring exotic locations to people before the age of easy travel, they included images of ecosystems, unknown animals, volcanoes, glaciers, and other features of scientific interest. Likewise, early motion picture documentaries, such as *Nanook of the North* (1922) and *In the Land of the Headhunters* (1914), which were more social science than physical science, paved the way for greater use of film for education. An instructional film industry developed to supply schools with films to support their curricula. While science films never flourished in movie theaters, the educational film industry has expanded and transformed itself in the age of digital media and the Internet.

When radio debuted in the 1920s, the American Museum of Natural History and the Smithsonian Institution recognized the educational possibilities of the medium. They developed popular science lectures to broadcast to listeners in their area. National radio networks in need of appealing content noticed and began broadcasting science programs across the United States. When television began to reach American homes in the late 1940s and 1950s, it followed radio's lead, airing science programs, including *John Hopkins Science Review* (Dumont), *Adventure* (CBS), *Watch Mr. Wizard* (NBC), and *Animal Clinic* (ABC).[11] Science programs have since mostly disappeared from network television, but they proliferate on public television and cable networks.

Today, many popular science programs may be viewed on television, DVD, or the Internet. Leading producers of these programs are the National Geographic Society, the Discovery Channel, and the Public Broadcasting Service and its stations, such as WNET and WGBH. Other producers whose DVDs of science television series can be found in retail stores and in libraries include the BBC, A&E Network, CNN, the History Channel, HBO, Animal Planet, and Reader's Digest. Some programs, such as PBS's *Nature* or *NOVA*, come packaged as individual episodes, while others, such as the BBC's *Life of Birds* with David Attenborough or the History Channel's *Engineering An Empire*, are packaged as entire seasons or series.

Graphic Novels and Illustrated Books

Like films, graphic novels try to communicate as much to consumers through images as through narration. Also like film, the cartoon-like form of the graphic novel has more often been applied to instruction of science students than to narration of true science stories for pleasure reading. Because of the school market and for parents hoping to stimulate their children's study, there are many illustrated curriculum titles, such as *The Cartoon Guide to Chemistry* by Larry Gonick and Craig Criddle and *The Stuff of Life: A Graphic Guide to Genetics and DNA* by Mark Schultz. While these books may be entertaining, they are not entertainment.

Finding true popular science graphic novels is difficult. There are very few in *500 Essential Graphic Novels* by Gene Kannenberg Jr., *The Rough Guide to Graphic Novels* by Danny Fingeroth, and *Graphic Novels: Beyond the Basics* by Martha Cornog. Search "graphic novel" with "science" in a library catalog, in database, or on the Internet, and you will find many science fiction titles. The few graphic novels you will find will be either biographical or historical. A look through nonfiction graphic novel lists in books, on Web sites, and in *NoveList* reveals a growing number of graphic novel memoirs about living with diseases, such as *Epileptic* by David B. or *Mom's Cancer* by Brian Fies. Martha Cornog and Steve Raiteri confirm this observation in their column "Graphic Novels" in the July 2009 issue of *Library Journal*. Interesting as they are, calling these disease memoirs "popular science" would be a stretch of the definition, for they focus more on human experience than on medicine.

The graphic novel is shown to be a powerful storytelling tool in works by Jim Ottaviani. Working with a variety of illustrators, he tells in-depth stories of rivalry between paleontologists in *Bone Sharps, Cowboys, and Thunder Lizards* and of rivalry between nations in *T-Minus: The Race to the Moon*. Few science authors, however, will turn to the graphic novel format until it becomes more popular with nonfiction-reading adults.

Podcasts

Descended from radio and television but free of broadcast times, the science podcast is a new entry into the world of popular science literature. Podcasts are audio or video files that can be downloaded from the Internet for playing either on a computer or a handheld player. As with radio in the 1920s, scientific organizations and broadcast media are working together to develop the field. Each has entertaining formats with regular hosts and weekly features. A look at the pages of the iTunes Store from Apple Computers shows a number of podcasts from trusted names in science: *Scientific American*, NOVA, NASA, the *New England Journal of Medicine*, and the McDonald Observatory. Despite being accessed through a "store," these podcasts are all free of charge. Fans can subscribe, and they will be delivered to iTunes automatically. Video podcasts are noted, while all others are audio.

Here are some of the more popular podcasts, according to the iTunes Store:

ASTRONOMY
Astronomy Cast with Fraser Cain and Dr. Pamela Gay
HD—NASA's Jet Propulsion Laboratory (Video)
Hidden Universe HD: NASA's Spitzer Space Telescope (Video)
Hubblecast (Video)
NASACast: Space Shuttle and Space Station (Video)
StarDate from the McDonald Observatory

COMPUTERS AND ELECTRONICS
Cranky Geeks MP3 Audio
FLOSS Weekly
MacCast—For Mac Geeks, by Mac Geeks
MAKE Magazine: MAKE Podcast (Video)
TED Talks (Video)
Tekzilla (Video)
Wired's Gadget Lab Video Podcast (Video)
Xbox Live's Major Nelson Radio

CONSERVATION AND ENVIRONMENT
Living Green: Effortless Ecology for Everyday People
Nature Podcast
NPR: Climate Connections Podcast
NPR: Environmental Podcast
TERRA: The Nature of Our World (Video)

HEALTH AND MEDICINE
Fitness Rocks
Mayo Clinic—Medical Edge Radio
NEJM This Week from the New England Journal of Medicine
NPR: On Health Podcast
Vital Signs from Discover Magazine

PETS AND ANIMALS
2GB: The Pet Vet
Pet Hour from XM Radio
The Petcast with Steve Friess and Emily Richmond
PetLifeRadio
Petspeak with Jana Sellers

Speaking of Pets with Mindy Norton
Talking Animals with Duncan Strauss

PSYCHOLOGY
60-Second Psych from Scientific American
All in the Mind from ABC Radio
Psychology in Everyday Life with Michael Britt
Psychology Podcast from Texas Tech University

SCIENCE AND TECHNOLOGY
60-Second Science from Scientific American
Brain Stuff with Marshall Brain
Naked Scientists Naked Science Radio Show
NOVA Science Now
NOVA Vodcast (Video)
NPR: On Science Podcast
NPR: Science Friday Podcast with Ira Flatow
Science Times from the New York Times
Scientific American Podcast
Skeptic's Guide to the Universe
WNYC's Radio Lab with Jad Abumrad and Robert Krulwich

Trends

Despite the tendency of many readers to say that they do not care for science, which was noted at the beginning of this chapter, popular science will continue to flourish. And because popular science readers are the first to embrace new technologies, they will be ahead of the curve to adopt new gadgets and protocols for disseminating new literature. Look for more popular science titles in formats for audio players, handheld readers, and online devices.

The economic downturn starting in 2008 may suppress the spread of popular science literature temporarily. Publishers will put out fewer books aimed at what they feel are niche markets. Some magazines will fail. Free broadcast television will eventually disappear as advertisers realize consumers have gone to cable or the Internet. The readers' desire for stories, however, will remain. Authors will turn more to innovative media distributed through the Internet to economically reach their readers. Electronic books and online magazines that may be downloaded along with audio and video podcasts will gain a market advantage when consumers warm to them. Most importantly, popular science literature will survive as a thriving genre because its titles collectively tell an essential story of human history.

Plots

Though science is sometimes viewed as a dispassionate quest for knowledge involving very disciplined researchers in laboratories, scientific history has its periods of great drama when the course of human events is changed. The books in this section are grouped around frequent science story lines, such as discovery, invention, and the need to save the world.

Discovery

Throughout human history, there have been mysteries to solve. Why do apples fall from trees? Where does the sun go at night? For as long as people have been reading, they have enjoyed stories about how the mysteries were solved. The following titles recount how scientists dramatically overcame difficulties to make great discoveries that reveal the nature of the universe and the life within.

Berlinski, David. *Newton's Gift: How Sir Isaac Newton Unlocked the Systems of the World* **(2000) NF BK**
Isaac Newton laid the foundation for all future scientific inquiry with his mathematical theories of physical mechanics. In *Newton's Gift*, novelist and mathematician David Berlinski describes a gentleman scientist who never left his native England. This book will appeal to readers who want to understand Newton without having to know complicated math.

Bodanis, David. *Electric Universe: The Shocking True Story of Electricity* **(2008) NF BK, UAB**
Human understanding of electricity is historically recent, dating back only to the 1790s, when Alessandro Volta accidentally discovered how to make a small battery. In *Electric Universe*, popular science author David Bodanis weaves together the stories of Joseph Henry, Samuel Morse, Thomas Edison, Allen Turing, and others to tell how the discovery of electricity has transformed human life. This book would be good company for a commuter.

Cutler, Alan. *Seashell on the Mountaintop: A Story of Science, Sainthood, and the Humble Genius Who Discovered a New History of the Earth* **(2003) NF BK**
The ancient Greeks knew why seashells were found inland, but medieval theology insisted that the fossils were evidence of the biblical flood. Though he knew how Galileo had been punished for his championing science that contradicted Catholic doctrine, Danish anatomist and priest Nicholas Steno published a small book that refuted church sanctioned historical timelines. In *The Seashell on the Mountaintop*, geologist Alan Cutler profiles the quiet priest who founded modern geological science.

***Elegant Universe*, WGBH Boston (2003) TV (1999) NF BK, SH**
Author Brian Greene hosts a bright, colorful program based on his book by the same title about the continuing discovery of how the universe works. He starts with Newton and his apples and ends with an 11-dimensional world composed of superstrings that bridge the theories of gravity and electromagnetism. The visual models remind viewers of Monty Python animations.

Kluger, Jeffrey, *Splendid Solution: Jonas Salk and the Conquest of Polio* **(2004) NF BK, UAB**
When Jonas Salk became a doctor, he disappointed his mother who planned for him to become a rabbi. He made amends by becoming a prominent medical research scientist. In *Splendid Solution*, author Jeffrey Kluger chronicles the education and work of a headstrong scientist who, by rejecting the methods and conclusions of his older colleagues, developed an effective polio vaccine.

Lemonick, Michael D., *The Georgian Star: How William and Caroline Herschel Revolutionized Our Understanding of the Cosmos* **(2009) NF BK, AP**
In late eighteenth-century England, astronomy was the pastime of royals, nobles, and academics until a German-born musician became a stargazer. Unable to buy telescopes,

William Herschel built his own and drafted his sister Caroline as his assistant. In the dual biography *The Georgian Star*, Lemonick recounts how the duo discovered Uranus, improved telescope design, remapped the night sky, coined the term "asteroid," and redefined the field of astronomy.

McGrayne, Sharon Bertsch, *Nobel Prize Women in Science: Their Lives, Struggles, and Momentous Discoveries.* **2nd ed. (1998) NF BK, YA, SH**
Throughout the twentieth century, women found few opportunities for careers in science. Only the most persistent and brilliant women overcame discrimination in universities, government, and industry to win jobs, much less fame. In *Nobel Prize Women in Science*, McGrayne profiles 10 Nobel winners and five women whom she believes should have won awards that were instead given to men. Readers interested in women's studies will enjoy these personal stories of scientists. Family photographs and technical illustrations accompany the stories.

Meyers, Morton A., *Happy Accidents: Serendipity in Modern Medical Breakthroughs* **(2007) NF BK**
Though they try very hard, some medical researchers cannot find what they seek. Ironically, they sometimes notice something else unrelated that turns out to be far more important, such as how to make penicillin or that common aspirin reduces colon cancer risks. In *Happy Accidents*, Morton A. Meyers tells the stories of dozens of alert researchers who discovered drugs, treatments, and prevention methods that have improved our health.

Morell, Virginia, *Ancestral Passions: The Leakey Family and the Quest for Humankind's Beginnings* **(1995) NF BK, CL**
Working in East Africa, anthropologists Louis S. B. Leakey, his wife Mary, and son Richard revolutionized scientific understanding of human origins. In *Ancestral Passions*, science journalist Virginia Morell candidly recounts how the Leakeys survived field work in the Olduvai Gorge in Tanzania, attacks by conservative scientists, and even family fights. A compelling family portrait, this book will likely appeal to general readers.

Quammen, David, *The Reluctant Mr. Darwin: An Intimate Portrait of Charles Darwin and the Making of his Theory of Evolution* **(2006) NF BK, UAB**
Charles Darwin studied and perfected his theory of evolution for many years before announcing it to the public. Only the threat of Alfred Russel Wallace reporting his finding first convinced the cautious Darwin to publish. *The Reluctant Mr. Darwin* starts after Darwin returns from his travels on the HMS *Beagle*, describes his career, explains his theories, and discusses his private life. A little knowledge of evolutionary theory will help when reading this detailed account aimed at the naturalist's admirers.

Invention

One of the common assumptions of most people is that science and invention improve our lives, making them more pleasant and longer. Grateful readers have long enjoyed learning how their lives were made easier and better. These titles recount the histories of inventions ranging from the screwdriver to the Hubble Space Telescope.

Carlisle, Rodney, *Scientific American Inventions and Discoveries: All the Milestones of Ingenuity from the Discovery of Fire to the Invention of the Microwave Oven* **(2004) NF BK**
From the days of the ancient Egyptians to today, every civilization has had its signature inventions that help define its age. Also, in every time, some great ideas go

unrecognized only to resurface when society is ready for them. Rodney Carlisle cites the origins of many inventions, technologies, and sciences in *Scientific American Inventions and Discoveries*. Readers may spend many evenings engrossed in this epic history.

George, Rose, *The Big Necessity: The Unmentionable World of Human Waste and Why It Matters* (2008) NF BK
Four in 10 people on Earth have no access to toilets, outhouses, latrines, or even family buckets. Sanitation is a privilege, not a claimable right in some cultures. In her compelling book *The Big Necessity: The Unmentionable World of Human Waste and Why It Matters*, Rose George recounts her world travels to see the sewers, toilets, and other structures of sanitation.

Rybczynski, Witold, *One Good Turn: A Natural History of the Screwdriver and the Screw* (2000) NF BK
Without the humble screw and the screwdriver with which to embed and extract it, many of the machines that we rely on today would not exist. Journalist Witold Rybczynski tells an entertaining story that includes science luminaries Archimedes and Leonardo da Vinci in *One Good Turn*.

Sagan, Nick, Mark Frary, and Andy Walker, *You Call This the Future? The Greatest Inventions Sci-Fi Imagined and Science Promised* (2007) NF BK, YA, SH
From where have ideas for new gadgets come? Leonardo da Vinci, for sure, but also from *Star Trek*, Ian Fleming's James Bond, and George Orwell's *1984*. In *You Call This the Future?*, the authors report on the first sightings, histories, and current realities of dozens of technologies, like cell phones, jetpacks, terra forming, bionic humans, invisibility cloaks, and time travel.

Spignesi, Stephen J., *American Firsts: Innovations, Discoveries, and Gadgets Born in the U.S.A.* (2004) NF BK
We take so much for granted. Who would even think that someone had to invent the mail drop box and that it came long after postal service was established? Who would guess that the microwave oven, on the other hand, was invented in the 1940s? In *American Firsts*, Spignesi has created an entertaining dictionary of American inventions that will make readers notice and appreciate the innovations around them.

Technology Review MZ (magazine)
From the Massachusetts Institute of Technology, *Technology Review* is a colorful periodical filled with inventions in the fields of computing, communications, energy, biomedicine, industry, and material science. It is a must for readers who want to know what's really new.

Wired's Gadget Lab Video Podcast, PC
New devices ranging from pocketknives to handheld computers are reviewed by the editors of *Wired* magazine. Reports on a cell phone made from recycled materials and an infrared hot dog cooker are among the innovative stories.

Zimmerman, Robert, *The Universe in a Mirror: The Saga of the Hubble Space Telescope and the Visionaries Who Built It* (2008) NF BK
Built decades after it was conceived, the Hubble Space Telescope has often been in peril. Funding challenges, bad mirrors, and early retirement threatened to shut down

what has become the most famous piece of astronomical equipment in history. Robert Zimmerman recounts the improbable story in *The Universe in a Mirror*.

Conflict

Men and women of science do not always work together cooperatively. Disagreeing about scientific theory is only part of the problem; they also seek fame and fortune. Does competition help or hamper scientific advancement? Read these books for answers to this question or for good fight stories.

Dobbs, David, *Reef Madness: Charles Darwin, Alexander Agassiz, and the Meaning of Coral* **(2005) NF BK**
In the wake of the early debates over evolution, in which Charles Darwin's theories won acclaim over the discredited ideas of noted naturalist Louis Agassiz, his son Alexander Agassiz sought to disprove Darwin's account of how coral reefs formed. Matters of science were only part of the battle that pitted incompatible men with differing views of nature and religion. In recounting the contest, author David Dobbs reveals how both Darwin and the young Agassiz contributed to modern oceanography.

Hardesty, Von, and Eisman, Gene, *Epic Rivalry: The Inside Story of the Soviet and American Space Race* **(2007) NF BK**
National security meant more than scientific advancement to U.S. and Soviet government officials in the 1950s. Neither country wanted to lose an edge in the nuclear balance of power. When the Soviets launched their Sputnik satellite in 1957, the United States had to respond with its own space effort. With new information from Soviet archives and historic photos, Von Hardesty and Gene Eisman recount the race to the moon.

Jonnes, Jill, *Empires of Light: Edison, Tesla, Westinghouse, and the Race to Electrify the World* **(2003) NF BK**
Three industrious men believed that electricity could replace candles and gaslights, making cities brighter, cleaner, and safer. They did not agree, however, on how to build the power network to bring this light to the public. These three men also had their fortunes and egos to protect. Jill Jonnes describes the great late-nineteenth-century contest in her compelling history.

Marriott, Edward, *Plague: A Story of Science, Rivalry, and the Scourge That Won't Go Away* **(2003) NF BK**
Though it is thought by many as a medieval act of God, bubonic plague is still a menacing disease. In *Plague*, Edward Marriott reveals how in two cases in two centuries the wrong scientist with the wrong answer was praised by public officials for discovering the disease's cause. This is a perfect book for readers skeptical of the wisdom of governments.

Miller, Arthur I., *Empire of the Stars: Obsession, Friendship, and Betrayal in the Quest for Black Holes* **(2005) NF BK, AP**
In a rivalry that was colored by the decline of the British Empire, physicists Subrahmanyan Chandrasekhar and Sir Arthur Eddington publicly sparred over the existence of black holes created by the collapse of dying stars. Arthur I. Miller shares an important story about how scientific progress was subverted by the Englishman's need to prevail over a scientist from the colonies in *Empire of the Stars*.

Ottaviani, Jim, and Big Time Attic, *Bone Sharps, Cowboys, and Thunder Lizards: A Tale of Edward Drinker Cope, Othniel Charles Marsh, and the Gilded Age of Paleontology* **(2005) GN, YA**
Paleontologists were more likely to be ridiculed than revered in the late nineteenth century, especially in the wild frontier of the American West. Jim Ottaviani shows how bone-seeking dinosaur hunters made it even worse with their bitter rivalry in *Bone Sharps, Cowboys, and Thunder Lizards.*

Slack, Charles, *Noble Obsession: Charles Goodyear, Thomas Hancock, and the Race to Unlock the Greatest Industrial Secret of the Nineteenth Century* **(2002) NF BK, UAB**
In the nineteenth century, scientists knew that rubber promised to be valuable industrial material if it could be stabilized. American Charles Goodyear and Englishman Thomas Hancock shared an obsession to be the scientist to discover the secret process to make rubber useful. In *Noble Obsession*, Charles Slack recounts the conflict that resulted in a famed trial on which the fortunes of the rubber industry depended.

Susskind, Leonard, *Black Hole War: My Battle with Stephen Hawking to Make the World Safe for Quantum Mechanics* **(2008) NF BK, RS**
Theoretical physicist Stephen Hawking has held the spotlight in the debate over the shape of the universe for decades, but his theories have been disputed. He publicly retracted some assertions after a challenge by Leonard Susskind. Susskind presents his opposing theories in *Black Hole War.*

White, Michael, *Acid Tongues and Tranquil Dreamers: Eight Scientific Rivalries That Changed the World* **(2001) NF BK**
Bitter contests between rival scientists have spurred some of histories greatest discoveries. Michael White recounts fights involving Sir Isaac Newton, Joseph Priestly, Nikola Tesla, and Bill Gates.

Mistakes

Even when scientists rigorously apply scientific method, they make mistakes. When one trusted scientist reaches an erroneous conclusion, many others may follow. Corrections may be made decades later. These investigative tales reveal the need for constant scientific verification and reassessment.

Colapinto, John, *As Nature Made Him: The Boy Who Was Raised as a Girl* **(2000) NF BK, UAB YA**
In the 1960s, medical journals reported that an anonymous boy was being successfully raised as a girl after his penis had been damaged and removed. These reports were often cited as proving that sexual identity was taught and not instinctive. Though the experiment failed early in the 1970s, it was 1997 before the story broke. In *As Nature Made Him*, journalist John Colapinto thoughtfully documents the case to tell an unusual tale about a man who continues to struggle with self-image.

Garwood, Christine, *Flat Earth: The History of an Infamous Idea* **(2007) NF BK, AP, SH**
Scholars of the Middle Ages have been falsely accused of ignorance. Ironically, the idea that people believed that the Earth was flat came out of the Age of Reason and was spread by the Victorians. Science historian Christine Garwood reveals the culprits, including the humorist Washington Irving, in the entertaining *Flat Earth.*

Hooper, Judith, *Of Moths and Men: An Evolutionary Tale: The Untold Story of Science and the Peppered Moth* **(2002) NF BK**
For decades, science textbooks pointed to the findings of moth hobbyist H. B. D. Kettlewell as solid proof of natural selection in action. His story about the dark and light varieties of peppered moths made Darwinian sense. But Kettlewell's data was exaggerated. In *Of Moths and Men*, Judith Hooper recounts from the beginning the science community's slow but eventual exposing of a myth.

Jones, Sheilla, *The Quantum Ten: A Story of Passion, Tragedy, Ambition, and Science* **(2008) NF BK, SH**
Contrary to popular belief, the great physicists of the twentieth century never fully discovered the nature of subatomic particle behavior. They have never found the unified theory to explain the discrepancies between classical and quantum physics. Science writer Sheilla Jones focuses on 10 physicists who attended the 1927 Solvay Conference, including Albert Einstein and Neils Bohr, in her microhistory for lay readers.

Lindley, David, *Degrees Kelvin: A Tale of Genius, Invention, and Tragedy* **(2004) NF BK**
In *Degrees Kelvin*, David Lindley asserts that physicist William Thomson was brilliant in his youth, solving mathematical puzzles and inventing many useful devices. In middle age, however, he denied the existence of atoms and radioactivity and publicly ridiculed Darwin's theories of evolution. This story of an obstinate man who relied too much on his past achievements is a cautionary tale for all readers.

Ohanian, Hans C., *Einstein's Mistakes: The Human Failings of Genius* **(2008) NF BK**
Nobody's perfect, not even Einstein. Hans C. Ohanian limits his review of Einsteinian miscalculations and errors of judgment to the great physicist's papers, excluding his personal affairs. An understanding of physics will help with this critical and yet sympathetic look at Einstein's career.

Stross, Randall, *The Wizard of Menlo Park: How Thomas Alva Edison Invented the Modern World* **(2007) NF BK**
Thomas Alva Edison was a brilliant inventor but a poor businessman. With a self-defeating inclination to manage his companies alone, dismissing the advice of consultants, he made a series of terrible decisions, such as manufacturing concrete furniture. In *The Wizard of Menlo Park*, Randall Stross tells a fascinating story of genius sometimes wasted.

Saving the World

With global warming, pollution, desertification, loss of resources, virulent diseases, and a population explosion posing threats to life on the planet, scientists have become key players in the fight to save the Earth. The odds are long and the opposition is often strong. Books, films, and other media about science in defense of the planet are often filled with passion and rhetoric. These titles are recommended for discussion groups and students, as well as nonfiction readers looking for hot-topic stories.

Barcott, Bruce, *Last Flight of the Scarlet Macaw: One Woman's Fight to Save the World's Most Beautiful Bird* **(2008) NF BK, YA**
Introduce a dedicated environmentalist to an investigative reporter and put them in a beautiful developing country where multinational corporations envision unrestricted profits, and you are bound to find a dramatic story. Bruce Barcott recounts the fight

between "Zoo Lady" Sharon Matola and a Canadian power company wanting to flood a nature reserve in *The Last Flight of the Scarlet Macaw*.

Bonner, Jeffrey P., *Sailing with Noah: Stories from the World of Zoos* (2006) NF BK, SH

The role of zoos has changed from amusing visitors to preserving the biodiversity of the planet. In *Sailing with Noah*, St. Louis Zoo director Jeffrey P. Bonner tells behind-the-scenes stories from his and other zoos that are involved in saving the lives of animals in captivity and in the wild.

Chivian, Eric, and Aaron Bernstein, eds., *Sustaining Life: How Human Health Depends on Biodiversity* (2008) NF BK

The current rate at which natural habitats and species are disappearing is unprecedented. Missing are some plants and animals whose genes could have helped cure diseases in the near future. In *Sustaining Life*, more than 100 eminent scientists weigh in on how to protect and improve human life by conserving species and ecosystems.

Gore, Al, *An Inconvenient Truth: The Planetary Emergency of Global Warming and What We Can Do About It* (2006) MV, NF BK, UAB, SH

Former vice president Al Gore claims that global warming is real. In this companion book to his film of the same title, he presents many facts through story and graphic illustrations. He mixes personal observations with current events in his call for international policy change in regards to the consumption of fossil fuels.

Melville, Greg, *Greasy Rider: Two Dudes, One Fry-Oil-Powered Car, and a Cross-Country Search for a Greener Future* (2008) NF BK, YA

Greg Melville and his friend Iggy modified a 1985 Mercedes to run on used cooking oil, avoiding fossil fuels and reducing their carbon emissions. In *Greasy Rider*, they beg, steal, and borrow oil to drive from Vermont to California, proving their idea works.

***NPR Environmental Podcast*, PC**

National Public Radio is known for on-the-spot reporting that includes the sounds around the news. A report on a dam, for example, will include the sound of the water through the floodgates. Once a week, the editors at NPR release a podcast repeating its most important environmental stories of the week.

Sierra Magazine

Sierra is an advocacy magazine printed on recycled paper that has become hip in its presentation. Every issue has stories about the struggle to save the environment. The January-February 2009 issue focuses on the carbon footprint of the average family home and includes its popular Outings Guide, listing adventure and service vacations.

Characters

The people who choose to be scientists are often remarkable characters who forsake common comfort and safety to pursue their work. Their relationships with family, friends, and colleagues are often unconventional. They are typically men and women of great intelligence and ahead of their times, a condition that often leads them to be criticized or even attacked by the forces threatened by change. Their stories are often inspiring.

Contemporary Scientists

Scientists are not as a profession regarded as attention-seekers. Many spend years of study in isolated labs or in remote locations. Some, however, feel the need to bring their messages to the public. Occasionally, the public is fascinated, and a celebrity is born. These books recount the work and lives of scientists who became widely known and followed in the news by fans.

Attenborough, David, *Life on Air: Memoirs of a Broadcaster* (2002) NF BK

BBC science broadcaster David Attenborough has not always had adequate funds to produce lavish television series, such as *The Private Life of Plants* (1995, TV) or *Living Planet* (1984, TV). In *Life on Air*, he recounts with amusing grace his career from the scrape-by-as-you-can days to the days of international fame and acclaim. He always has a good plant or animal story to share. Viewers who enjoyed seeing him hang from tropical canopies on television will enjoy his memoirs.

Clarke, Arthur C., *Greetings, Carbon-Based Bipeds! Collected Essays, 1934–1998* (1999) NF BK, CL

Early in his career as a writer, Arthur C. Clarke focused mostly on space and interplanetary travel, but by his sixth decade as an author of fiction and essays, he had written also about art, literature, and the world of knowledge, always with a touch of science and a grand vision of the future. *Greetings, Carbon-Based Bipeds!* will entertain fans who enjoy elegant essays from a distinctive voice.

Cousteau, Jacques Yves, and Scheifelbein, Susan, *The Human, the Orchid, and the Octopus: Exploring and Conserving Our Natural World*, (2007) NF BK, UAB

Published in English a decade after his death, *The Human, the Orchid, and the Octopus* tells how Cousteau became an advocate for the Earth and its seas. He remembers his many research quests and resulting films, and he describes how people must change to reverse the course of history.

Feynman, Richard, *Surely You're Joking, Mr. Feynman: Adventures of a Curious Character* (1985) NF BK, UAB, CL, YA, SH

Richard Feynman was not the kind of scientist you would expect to have worked on the Manhattan Project. He was outrageous, outspoken, and liable to irritate serious characters. Still, he was acclaimed as one of the great physicists of his time. In *Surely You're Joking, Mr. Feynman*, he recounts many of his scrapes and triumphs.

Gould, Carol Grant, *The Remarkable Life of William Beebe: Explorer and Naturalist* (2004) NF BK, AP

Before there was Jacques Cousteau, there was William Beebe, thrilling radio listeners with his ocean adventures. Long before the television age of David Attenborough, Beebe traveled to remote jungles seeking out rare and new species of animals and plants for his magazine articles and books. Carol Grant Gould tells how, as the first ornithologist for the Bronx Zoo, the energetic scientist collected and studied birds from around the globe.

Isaacson, Walter, *Einstein*: *His Life and Universe* (2007) NF BK, UAB, AP, SH

In 1905, Albert Einstein, a low-paid patent clerk, published five brilliant articles that challenged Newtonian physics and became the basis of the science of quantum physics and the concept of relativity. From this start, he became a key figure in international science and politics. In *Einstein: His Life and Universe*, Walter Isaacson describes how the physicist struggled to live an ethical life. Readers do not have to understand the science to enjoy this epic biography of an unlikely celebrity.

LaFollette, Marcel Chotkowski, *Science on the Air: Popularizers and Personalities on Radio and Early Television* (2008) NF BK
Radio was the iPod of the 1920s. Science organizations, such as the American Museum of Natural History and the Smithsonian Institution, recognized the cool of the new technology and quickly adapted their popular lecture series for broadcast into homes across the country. Marcel Chotkowski LaFollette recounts the exciting early days of broadcast science.

Poundstone, William, *Carl Sagan: A Life in the Cosmos* (1999) NF BK
Through books and television programs, astronomer Carl Sagan led a popular and almost hopeless search for extraterrestrial life. In the 1970s and 1980s, he was a frequent spokesperson for a movement demanding more exploration of space. In *Carl Sagan: A Life in the Cosmos*, author William Poundstone profiles the exobiologist as a passionate man in pursuit of an idea. No scientific background is needed to read this admiring biography.

Schwartz, Joe, *Einstein for Beginners* (1979) GN
It helps to have pictures when the theories of Einstein are being explained. Author Joe Schwartz and illustrator Michael McGuinness think pictures also help tell the scientist's story. Their book looks like a cross between clip art and Monty Python.

Everyday Scientists

A trend in the literature of biography and memoir is to feature people who are not famous. As part of this movement, books and media about on-the-frontline scientists are proliferating. Why would anyone want to work in an office shuffling papers when the career of scientist is available? Even the run-of-the-mill, everyday scientist encounters mysteries and adventure if the authors of these books and television series are to be believed.

Big Cats WNET (2005) TV
From the Emmy award-winning television series *Nature*, two episodes recount the lives and characters of wildlife filmmakers in Africa. Testing state-of-the-art cameras and building their own equipment, they put in long hours both day and night. Viewers join in the excitement of the chase.

Brazaitis, Peter, *You Belong in a Zoo! Tales from a Lifetime Spent with Cobras, Crocs, and Other Creatures* (2003) NF BK, YA
At age 12, Peter Brazaitis took a $10 correspondence course in taxidermy that changed his life. His hobby and his collection of unusual pets taught him enough animal anatomy to get job at the Bronx Zoo right out of high school. Brazaitis recounts his strange encounters with reptiles in *You Belong in a Zoo!*

Coffey, Patrick, *Cathedrals of Science: The Personalities and Rivalries That Made Modern Science* (2008) NF BK
Science, politics, war, and everyday human emotions drove the work of 13 men and one woman who shaped the field of chemistry. Historian Patrick Coffey presents important scientific discoveries in the context of late nineteenth- and early twentieth-century international affairs in *Cathedrals of Science*.

Fortey, Richard A., *Dry Storeroom No. 1: The Secret Life of the Natural History Museum* **(2008) NF BK**
In his natural history of the Natural History Museum in London, longtime employee Richard A. Fortey tells revealing behind-the-scenes stories featuring a cast of dedicated curators. While many of them take place in the labyrinth of labs and storerooms, they also take readers to exotic field operations around the world. *Dry Storeroom No. 1* will please curious people who enjoy reading engaging anecdotes.

Manning, Philip, *Grave Secrets of the Dinosaurs: Soft Tissues and Hard Science* **(2008) NF BK**
Paleontologists work in extreme heat and cold to unearth fossils that reveal the evolutionary past of our planet. In *Grave Secrets of the Dinosaurs*, Philip Manning takes readers both into the field and back in time with enthusiastic scientists who share their daily grind and the excitement of dinosaur discoveries.

Sobel, Dava, *Longitude: The True Story of a Lone Genius Who Solved the Greatest Scientific Problem of His Time* **(1995) NF BK, UAB**
John Harrison was a carpenter and clockmaker who sought to win a prize of £20,000 from the British Parliament for inventing a device or method to measure meridians of longitude. Harrison perfected a clock that would keep correct time at sea, unaffected by the motion of waves, but Parliament failed to award him the prize. Dava Sobel recounts a story of science and class prejudice in *Longitude*.

Sutherland, Amy, *Kicked, Bitten, and Scratched: Life and Lessons at the World's Premier School for Exotic Animal Trainers* **(2006) NF BK, YA**
Ever enjoy a dolphin show at an aquarium or an animal act at the circus? Wonder where you could get training to handle wild and dangerous animals? Amy Sutherland describes her year of following brave students in the Exotic Animal Training and Management Program at Moorpark Community College in the entertaining *Kicked, Bitten, and Scratched*.

Science Pioneers

One of the big debates in scientific history is who were the first scientists? While many ancient figures contributed to human knowledge, many are ruled out because they did not adhere to scientific methods in their research. Many of their conclusions have later been easily disproved. The following titles identify characters that hold strong claims to be pioneers in their respective fields.

Aczel, Amir D., *Pendulum: Leon Foucault and the Triumph of Science* **(2003) NF BK**
Because French physicist Leon Foucault was self-taught, many of his peers considered him insignificant and dismissed many of his theories. In 1853, however, he demonstrated beyond a doubt that the Earth revolves on an axis. Amir D. Aczel recounts the life of a brilliant scientist who struggled to be heard.

Brian, Denis, *The Curies: A Biography of the Most Controversial Family in Science* **(2005) NF BK**
Chemists and physicists Marie and Pierre Curie never fully realized the dangers of working with radioactive materials, nor the opposition they would face for their political ideas. The devoted couple passed on their lack of regard for safety and public opinion to their children. Denis Brian examines several generations of hot-tempered lives.

Clegg, Brian, *The First Scientist: A Life of Roger Bacon* **(2003) NF BK, AP**
Roger Bacon became a Franciscan monk to assure his livelihood and to gain access
to the religious order's library. The position, however, did not protect him from
charges of violating church dogma. In *The First Scientist: A Life of Roger Bacon*,
Brian Clegg describes Bacon, who should be credited with the development of scientific method, as a man far ahead of his time.

Google Boys, **A&E (2006) TV, SH**
The cable network A&E profiles Sergey Brin and Larry Page, the Stanford computer
scientists who created the Google search engine and from there an empire of innovative Internet tools. Information science mixes with business theory in this light
biography.

Nicholl, Charles, *Leonardo da Vinci: Flights of the Mind* **(2004) NF BK**
Leonardo was interested in every subject known to Renaissance scholars. Anatomy,
botany, astronomy, mechanics, and architecture were his everyday interests. Charles
Nicholl draws heavily from Leonardo's notebooks to show how the brilliant scientist
worked in the detailed biography *Leonardo da Vinci: Flights of the Mind.*

Sale, Kirkpatrick, *The Fire of His Genius: Robert Fulton and the American Dream*
(2001) NF BK
Robert Fulton's torpedo demonstration in 1807 had been an entertaining and embarrassing failure, and "Fulton's Folly" was already a familiar phrase on lips and in
newsprint. Later that year, the steamship *North River* performed well at a speedy
four miles per hour, and the sometimes-ridiculed maritime engineer was proclaimed a
hero. In *The Fire of His Genius*, Kirkpatrick Sale portrays Fulton as a flawed individual whose inventions helped his country but who died in financial distress.

Tobin, James, *Great Projects: The Epic Story of Building America, from the Taming of the Mississippi to the Invention of the Internet* **(2001) NF BK, YA**
Some engineers whose dreams transformed our country have been nearly forgotten.
James Buchanan Eads, John Bloomfield Jervis, and J. C. R. Licklider are not household names despite the impact of their work on modern life. Historian James Tobin
tells their incredible stories in highly illustrated *Great Projects.*

Tobin, James, *To Conquer the Air: The Wright Brothers and the Great Race for
Flight* **(2003) NF BK**
When Wilbur Wright and Orville Wright first flew at Kitty Hawk, North Carolina, in
1903, many more famous and better-funded inventors were unwilling to recognize the
accomplishment. The brothers had to defend their claims with public demonstrations,
which they did repeatedly until 1910, when they were awarded the Langley Medal. In
the elegantly written *To Conquer the Air*, James Tobin intimately describes the close
but sometimes prickly working relationship of the ambitious brothers in the context of
the contest for scientific achievement.

Controversial Figures and Reexaminations

Whether scientists are perceived as heroes or villains often depends on the cultural and
political tenor of their times. Discoveries that threaten the established thought of the
period may be condemned. Likewise, their powerful new inventions may be diverted

from good to evil. In these books, authors reevaluate the deeds and reputations of controversial scientists.

Bird, Kai, and Sherwin, Martin J., *American Prometheus: The Triumph and Tragedy of J. Robert Oppenheimer* **(2005) NF BK, UAB**
Atomic physicist J. Robert Oppenheimer regretted his role in the Manhattan Project. His public stance that atomic weapons, which he helped to create, endangered the country and needed to be eliminated proved to be political suicide in 1950s America. In *American Prometheus*, authors Kai Bird and Martin J. Sherwin profile the scientist and policy advisor as a man of conscience in a dark period of American history.

Eminent Lives, Kramer, Peter D., *Freud: Inventor of the Modern Mind* **(2006) NF BK**
Psychiatrist Peter D. Kramer chronicles the life and career of Sigmund Freud, showing how the learned man's personal experiences colored his research results and interpretations. In *Freud: Inventor of the Modern Mind*, Kramer shows Freud to be less as a god of psychological science and more as a fallible scholar, who still contributed significantly to our understanding of human behavior.

Hager, Thomas, *The Alchemy of Air: A Jewish Genius, a Doomed Tycoon, and the Scientific Discovery That Fed the World but Fueled the Rise of Hitler* **(2008) NF BK**
The consequences of scientific discovery and manufacturing applications are sometimes shocking. What can save lives can also kill. Thomas Hager reexamines the lives of chemists Carl Bosch and Fritz Haber, whose development of powerful fertilizers enabled the company IG Farben to become a munitions manufacturer. Readers interested in World War II will want this revealing book.

Maddox, Brenda, *Rosalind Franklin: The Dark Lady of DNA* **(2002) NF BK**
Rosalind Franklin was a respected microbiologist with many friends in her field, but colleague James Watson attacked her work as mediocre. Biographer Brenda Maddox ironically reveals that Watson and Francis Crick relied heavily on Franklin's research findings and her photographs of DNA in their work. In this sympathetic account for readers who like stories about heroic women, Maddox restores the reputation of a brilliant scientist and mountain climber who should be acclaimed for her breakthroughs on DNA.

Neufeld, Michael J., *Von Braun: Dreamer of Space, Engineer of War* **(2007) NF BK**
Wernher von Braun was a rocket specialist who designed missiles for the German Army in World War II before surrendering to Allied troops at the end of the war. He then became a key figure in the American space effort, despite his shadowy Nazi past. In *Von Braun: Dreamer of Space, Engineer of War*, author Michael J. Neufeld weighs the Jekyll-and-Hyde aspects of von Braun's life.

Pringle, Peter, *The Murder of Nikolai Vavilov: The Story of Stalin's Persecution of One of the Great Scientists of the Twentieth Century* **(2008) NF BK**
While other scientists abandoned Russia during the Bolshevik Revolution, plant geneticist Nikolai Vavilov stayed to work for Vladimir Lenin's agricultural initiative, eventually becoming director of the Bureau of Applied Botany. There he established a seed bank from which he hoped to improve Soviet crop species, but Joseph Stalin's collectivization of farming sabotaged his work. Unable to please Stalin, Vavilov was

sent to prison, where he starved to death. Peter Pringle documents a dark time in Russian history in *The Murder of Nikolai Vavilov*.

Tesla, Master of Lightning, PBS (2007) MV
While Nicola Tesla lost the battle for fame and fortune to Thomas Edison, a century later he is being recognized as a genius whose inventions led to many of our modern appliances and communications devices. Tesla is portrayed as an idealist in this docudrama.

Winchester, Simon, *The Man Who Loved China: The Fantastic Story of the Eccentric Scientist Who Unlocked the Mysteries of the Middle Kingdom* (2006) NF BK, UAB, RS
It was adultery that led biochemist Joseph Needham to China, but he stayed for the science. He verified the history of Chinese scientific firsts, such as the first magnetic compass, crossbow, and suspension bridge. Braving the Japanese invasion, the Cultural Revolution, and dangerous single-engine planes, he made many trips to remote corners of the country. In *The Man Who Loved China*, Simon Winchester recounts the uncommon life of a scientist and lover.

Zinsser, Judith, *La Dame d'Esprit: A Biography of the Marquise Du Chatelet* (2006) NF BK
Gabrielle Emilie le Tonnelier de Breteuil, the marquise Du Chatelet, was not your typical eighteenth-century French lady. She wrote treatises on mathematics and physics, translated Sir Isaac Newton's work into French, and started a love affair with the great author Voltaire. She even described the relationship of energy to matter more than 150 years before Albert Einstein! Author Judith Zinsser recounts the exciting life of an unconventional woman.

Mad Scientists

The idea of the mad scientist predates Mary Shelley's *Frankenstein* (1818). Throughout the Middle Ages and the Renaissance, scientists such as Roger Bacon, Johannes Kepler, and Galileo were often depicted as heretics and sorcerers. In modern times, some scientists continue to step outside the lines of socially accepted behavior.

Blum, Deborah, *Love at Goon Park: Harry Harlow and the Science of Affection* (2002) NF BK
Experimental psychologist Harry Harlow of the University of Wisconsin was a solitary scientist who isolated young monkeys in cages to study to their need for affection. In *Love at Goon Park*, Deborah Blum sympathetically examines the life of an obsessive professor who lost his wife and family while becoming an advocate for love.

Galileo's Battle for the Heavens: Mathematician, Philosopher, Astronomer, Heretic, Father, PBS (2006) MV
Actor Simon Callow narrates a two-hour documentary based on Dava Sobel's book *Galileo's Daughter*. Actors reenact some scenes of the scientist's life, including his heresy trial.

Goodchild, Peter, *Edward Teller: The Real Dr. Strangelove* (2004) NF BK
To whom did Stanley Kubrick refer in his film *Dr. Strangelove*? Was it physicist Edward Teller? Journalist Peter Goodchild claims the similarities between fact and fiction were quite striking. In *Edward Teller: The Real Dr. Strangelove*, Goodchild recounts the

controversial Hungarian scientist's story and points out that Teller was not the man of peace he purported, always opposing test-ban treaties and actively planning the next war.

Hoffman, Paul, *The Man Who Loved Only Numbers: The Story of Paul Erdos and the Search for Mathematical Truth* **(1998) NF BK**
Hungarian mathematician and scholarly nomad Paul Erdos constantly visited other mathematicians around the globe, accepting their generous hospitality. With only a few clothes in his battered suitcase and his notebooks in a shopping bag, he would suddenly appear and then be off again in days. In his humorous *The Man Who Loved Only Numbers*, Paul Hoffman traces the physical and mathematical journey of a prolific genius.

Jago, Lucy, *The Northern Lights* **(2001) NF BK**
In 1899, geophysicist Kristian Birkeland led a team of observers in a blizzard up Haldde Mountain in northern Norway to test his theories about the aurora borealis. Subsequently, he endured extreme weather to visit stations in the Arctic Ocean and in the Egyptian desert to witness other celestial events. These and other dangerous explorations cost him his marriage, reputation, and health. In *The Northern Lights*, author Lucy Jago tells a classic tale of a man seduced by science and obsessed with finding answers.

Nasar, Sylvia, *A Beautiful Mind: A Biography of John Forbes Nash, Jr., Winner of the Nobel Prize in Economics* **(1994) NF BK, UAB, MV, AP**
The source of mathematician John Forbes Nash Jr.'s genius was also the source of his madness. In flashes, he saw solutions to complex problems in the fields of game theory, computer architecture, and geometry, but he also saw extraterrestrials and a messianic mission that would make him a prince of peace. In a sympathetic and admiring biography, economics reporter Sylvia Nasar chronicles how Nash woke from a 30-year delusion to recover his cognitive abilities and win a Nobel Prize in Economics.

Silverman, Kenneth, *Lightning Man: The Accursed Life of Samuel F. B. Morse* **(2003) NF BK**
Samuel F. B. Morse was a talented painter, early photographer, and inventor. His greatest fame came from his development of the telegraph—an idea he stole. However, he lacked good business sense, offended many people, and repeatedly found himself in court defending patents and trying to hold off bankruptcy. In the candid biography *Lightning Man*, Kenneth Silverman shows Morse as an advocate of technical progress who exhibited all that was good and bad about society during the Industrial Revolution.

Theme: The World Around Us

Like other types of literature, there are recurring themes sought by the readers of popular science. Many correspond with readers' own personal interests, such as observing nature, raising pets, or taking care of their own health. In these mostly narrative books and media, many somewhat autobiographical, authors connect very personally with their readers.

A Walk in the Woods

The idea that science takes place only in a laboratory is dispelled by professional and amateur naturalists, who take to the field in all weather. They may also face vicious animals and dangerous people. These stories take place in woods, on mountains, in deserts, and even in Central Park in Manhattan.

Berger, Joel, *The Better to Eat You With: Fear in the Animal World* **(2008) NF BK**
It is better to eat than be eaten. Avoiding violence is essential for survival. Animals learn from the mistakes of others. These are the tenets that wildlife conservator Joel Berger examines in his journey to preserves around the world.

Dempsey, Luke, *A Supremely Bad Idea: Three Mad Birders and Their Quest to See It All* **(2008) NF BK**
For those who have never tried it, birding is seen as a tranquil hobby, which at worst might require tolerating a little bad weather. Luke Dempsey dispels this notion with his account of long weekends and vacations braving harsh weather, rough terrain, swarms of insects, dangerous people, and grouchy friends in *A Supremely Bad Idea*.

Exploring the Deserts of the Earth **(2004) TV, NF BK, (2007)**
Photographer Michael Martin and filmmaker Elke Wallner spent 900 days on a motorcycle exploring in the deserts of the world to create the 12 30-minute episodes for this series. Stark landscapes and the people who can survive them are featured. Martin's photography is the also the basis for their book *Deserts of the Earth*.

Helferich, Gerald, *Humboldt's Cosmos: Alexander Von Humboldt and the Latin American Journey That Changed the Way We See the World* **(2004) NF BK**
In the early nineteenth century, Alexander von Humboldt and his companion Aimé Bolpland traversed the Amazon and the Andes in search of plants and other wonders. Gerald Helferich recounts five rugged years through jungles and over mountains.

Storm Shooter, **National Geographic Channel (2003) TV**
New Zealand TV cameraman Geoff Mackley routinely gets in the way of volcanoes and hurricanes to get dramatic images for television news programs. In a dramatic episode of *Dangerous Jobs*, National Geographic Channel video shows Mackley at work chasing Hurricane Isodore. http://channel.nationalgeographic.com/channel/videos/player.html?channel=60850

Trauth, Joy, and Aldemaro Romero, Eds, *Adventures in the Wild: Tales of Biologists of the Natural State* **(2008) NF BK**
Biological fieldwork can be hazardous. In addition to poisonous plants and dangerous animals, biologists sometimes find criminals and rebel militias when they wander into jungles. More than a dozen field biologists tell why they take risks in *Adventures in the Wild*.

Todd, Kim, *Chrysalis: Maria Sibylla Merian and the Secrets of Metamorphosis* **(2007) NF BK**
As a child in mid-seventeenth-century Frankfurt, Maria Sibylla Merian loved insects, especially moths and butterflies, and was encouraged by her stepfather, the still-life painter Jacob Marrel, to draw and paint them. This was the start of an obsession that would slowly lead her away from the traditional roles as wife and mother and toward the company of amateur naturalists. In *Chrysalis*, Kim Todd recounts how Merian left her comfortable life and sailed to Surinam at age 52 to spend two years studying and illustrating flora and fauna of the South American rainforest.

Winn, Marie, *Central Park in the Dark: More Mysteries of Urban Wildlife* **(2008) NF BK, AP, YA**
Deep in the heart of Manhattan, Central Park has long been a habitat for wildlife. With crime down, people are returning to the park, even in the dead of night. In *Central*

Park in the Dark, Marie Winn recounts some of her adventures spotting a variety of remarkable creatures.

Wild Animals

The telling of incredible animal stories has spawned many books and films. Americans love animals so much that they support a cable television channel dedicated solely to stories of wild animals and pets, Animal Planet. The following books and DVDs feature a variety of wild animals.

Grizzly Man (2005) MV

After spending 13 summers in Alaska filming bears, amateur naturalist Timothy Treadwell was mauled to death by one of his subjects. With over 100 hours of Treadwell's video, director Werner Herzog tells a story of misplacing trust in the predictability of bear behavior.

Life in Cold Blood, BBC Video (2008) TV, NF BK

Amphibians and reptiles used to rule the planet. Enthusiastic host David Attenborough narrates five episodes featuring these cold-blooded creatures. Viewers will enjoy learning all about the lives and habits strange creatures living in remote settings, from lizards to crocodiles.

The Life of Birds (2003) TV, NF BK, SH

With his camera crew, David Attenborough travels to the remotest places on Earth and to backyards to film amazing birds and their little-known behaviors. Attenborough has recruited legions of bird watchers with this series, which chronicles the lives and great diversity of birds.

Lloyd, John, and John Mitchinson, The Book of Animal Ignorance (2007) NF BK

Who's ignorant? Not the animals! John Lloyd and John Mitchinson seek to end human misconceptions about our earthly companions who have developed many unique behaviors to survive and multiply. *The Book of Animal Ignorance* is a fun book to read to friends and family. Tell them how many lice they harbor.

March of the Penguins (2005) MV, AP, YA

Emperor penguins are more than stylish-looking birds that waddle. They are determined, heroic parents who march long distances and suffer great cold in their traditional breeding grounds in Antarctica. Actor Morgan Freeman narrates an epic story of love and valor in *March of the Penguins*.

Microcosm (1996) MV

Time-lapse photography reveals the remarkable lives of insects, species that many people hardly notice, yet that shape our environments tremendously. The cinematography won acclaim in many film festivals in the 1990s.

Moss, Stephen, Remarkable Birds: 100 of the World's Most Notable Birds (2008) NF BK

In a world full of beauty, many birds stand out for their grace and color. Others are remarkable for their size, odd bills, mating dances, and great migrations. Stephen Moss combines stunning photographs with insightful profiles in a book that would look good on any coffee table or nightstand. *Remarkable Birds* is an excellent companion to Attenborough's BBC series *The Life of Birds*.

The Rhino with Glue-On Shoes and Other Surprising True Stories of Zoo Vets and Their Patients (2008) NF BK

Getting a zoo veterinarian to come to your party must insure fun for all. They have such entertaining and unusual stories to tell about their work with animals. In *The Rhino with Glue-On Shoes*, readers will find 28 spellbinding stories from vets from zoos, aquariums, and nature preserves.

Rinella, Steven, *American Buffalo: In Search of a Lost Icon* (2008) NF BK

The survival of the American bison is an often-mentioned conservation success story filled with many myths. Few people ever question the genetic integrity of contemporary herds. In *American Buffalo*, Steven Rinella tells his own buffalo tales, examines bison history, and contemplates the animal's future with little open range.

Rossellini, Isabella, *Green Porno: A Book and Short Films* (2009) NF BK, DVD

Despite the title, this humorous book and DVD set is not pornographic. In the short films, Isabella Rossellini dons absurd costumes to describe the sex lives of marine animals. She follows each act with an environmental message.

Rothenberg, David, *Thousand Mile Song: Whale Music in a Sea of Sound* (2008) NF BK

After playing clarinet for and with birds, David Rothenberg pursued a gig with humpback whales. In *Thousand Mile Song*, he describes his travels and research into the singing of the whales. A compact disc with the resulting music is included.

Schutt, Bill, *Dark Banquet: Blood and the Curious Lives of Blood-Feeding Creatures* (2008) NF BK, YA

In *Dark Banquet*, fearless biology professor Bill Schutt takes readers into woods and swamps in the dark of night in search of blood-sucking creatures like vampire bats, leeches, and ticks. His up-close descriptions and gentle humor make these field trips fun. For those who think staying home is safer, he also describes bedbugs.

Stolzenburg, William, *Where the Wild Things Were: Life, Death, and Ecological Wreckage in a Land of Vanishing Predators* (2008) NF BK

Early in Precambrian times, multicellular creatures peacefully ate microscopic life, but as true animals appeared, predation began. Carnivorous species began to stalk and attack vegetarians. William Stolzenburg takes readers around the world to learn the history of predation and its role in keeping ecosystems healthy.

Domestic Animals

It seems that whenever people gather, they eventually talk about their pets. Coming-of-age memoirs almost always have poignant pet stories. Animal Planet runs many series about people and their pets. Why is there such a universal interest in our animal companions? The following entertaining books examine the nature of pet-human relationships.

Brown, Bradford B., *While You're Here, Doc: Farmyard Adventures of a Maine Veterinarian* (2006) NF BK

Bradford B. Brown began his veterinary career in rural Maine in the 1950s. When he drove to distant farms, he often administered his services to a variety of domestic animals, pets, and owners. Filled with many humorous incidents, Bradford's memoir *While You're Here, Doc* is in the tradition of the animal tales of James Herriot.

Dog Whisperer (2006) TV, YA

Three seasons of Cesar Millan's popular television series about rehabilitating dogs with behavioral problems are available on DVD. Of course, the problems lie as much in the dog owners as the dogs themselves. Millan teaches viewers to establish rule by being top dog.

Forbes, Harrison, *Dog Talk: Lessons Learned from a Life with Dogs* (2008) NF BK

Harrison Forbes, the host of the radio program *Pet Talk*, has trained dangerous dogs for more than 20 years. In *Dog Talk*, he deftly recounts his most difficult and illuminating cases, including dogs that have attacked humans. These well-told stories will help readers understand dog behavior and motivation.

Katz, Jon, *A Dog Year: Twelve Months, Four Dogs, and Me* (2002) NF BK

When Jon Katz adopted a high-strung border collie named Devon, it upset the social balance of dogs and people in his house. With patience and understanding, he set out to improve the situation. In *A Dog Year*, he describes the dynamics of animal-animal and animal-human relations while telling an engaging story.

MacPherson, Malcolm, *The Cowboy and His Elephant: The Story of a Remarkable Friendship* (2001) NF BK

American cowboy Bob Norris had a menagerie on his ranch before he adopted an orphaned elephant named Amy. Drawing from his experiences as a horse trainer, he successfully raised Amy to adulthood, at which point she joined a circus. Later she was returned to the wild in Africa. Malcolm MacPherson tells an unusual story of human-animal understanding.

Nature, PBS, *Why We Love Cats and Dogs* (2009) TV, AP

PBS *Nature* airs an episode about pets nearly every year. In the 2008–2009 season, that episode was *Why We Love Cats and Dogs*, which featured intimate conversations between pet owners and behavioral scientists. Some of the humans sacrificed their homes and careers to care for their ailing pets in this moving documentary.

O'Brien, Stacey, *Wesley the Owl: The Remarkable Love Story of an Owl and His Girl* (2008) NF BK, YA

Wesley the Owl would have died in the wild. He was only four days old when biologist Stacey O'Brien rescued the injured orphan. O'Brien recounts her demanding 19-year relationship with her devoted bird friend in *Wesley the Owl*.

Rivas, Mim Eichler, *Beautiful Jim Key: The Lost History of a Horse and a Man Who Changed the World* (2005) NF BK

Between 1890 and 1920, the second most famous horse in the world (behind only the fictional Black Beauty) was Beautiful Jim Key, a horse that could read, spell, do math, and make change. Millions of people took the Beautiful Jim Key pledge to treat all animals humanely. Mim Eichler Rivas recounts Jim's training and life in *Beautiful Jim Key*.

Food and Eating

Eating is not only a necessity, it is also an obsession. Consider the fact that there is an entire television network devoted to food! In the profusion of books, articles, and programs about food and eating, many nutritional myths are spread. As the authors of these books and media about the science of food reveal, it is unhealthy to ignore the basic science behind eating.

Chen, Joanne, *The Taste of Sweet: Our Complicated Love Affair with Our Favorite Treats* **(2007) NF BK**
Long ago, humans developed the taste of sweet to help them select foods when foraging. Now that finding foods is easy, the sense is less critical for survival, but its impact of food desire is still strong. Joanne Chen combines social history and science in this compelling book about the sweet things that we eat.

Food, Inc. **(2009) MV, NF BK**
Based on the book by the same name by Eric Schlosser, this film takes viewers on location to see how their food is produced. The results are unnerving. Many outspoken food-industry critics appear in this provocative film.

Good Eats with Alton Brown, **Food Network (1998–) TV**
Chef Alton Brown appears to be at home in his own kitchen in many of the episodes of his television series *Good Eats*. While he entertainingly demonstrates cooking, he deftly explains a lot of food science with helpful props and diagrams.

Kingsolver, Barbara, with Stephen L. Hopp and Camille Kingsolver, *Animal, Vegetable, Miracle: A Year of Food Life* **(2007) NF BK, UAB, YA, SH**
Barbara Kingsolver and her family committed to eating mostly local foods for a year, not an easy task when most of the items in supermarkets are grown and processed in distant states and countries. Growing their own crops and finding local farmers' markets, the family mostly succeeded. They tell how they fared in *Animal, Vegetable, Miracle*, a narrative with recipes.

Murray, Sarah, *Moveable Feasts: From Ancient Rome to the 21st Century, the Incredible Journeys of the Food We Eat* **(2007) NF BK**
The commerce of food items between distant nations is not just a recent trend. The ancient Greeks and Romans were among the many societies that learned to preserve and package foods such as olives, cheeses, and fish for international trade. Sarah Murray recounts how food trade has shaped human history in *Moveable Feasts*.

Pollan, Michael, *Omnivore's Dilemma: A Natural History of Four Meals* **(2006) NF BK, UAB**
American consumers have strayed far from the food of their ancestors and hardly recognize good food when they see it. In *Omnivore's Dilemma*, Michael Pollan exposes how industrial agriculture and government have worked together to lead eaters to artificial, adulterated, and hollow foods. In his sequel *In Defense of Food* (2008), he gives advice on reconstructing good eating habits.

Ronald, Pamela C., and Raoul W. Adamchak, *Tomorrow's Table: Organic Farming, Genetics, and the Future of Food* **(2008) NF BK**
To feed the world well, humans cannot return to a time before designer crops and industrial agriculture, but they can conserve soil and reduce their use of chemicals. A geneticist and an organic farmer describe a future that embraces the best of the old and new.

Schlosser, Eric, *Fast Food Nation: The Dark Side of the All-American Meal* **(2001) NF BK, UAB, MV, YA, RS**
Most American consumers never think about the source of the foods that they eat on the run. In *Fast Food Nation*, Eric Schlosser takes readers behind the scenes to witness

the horrors of meatpacking plants, supermarket warehouses, and restaurant kitchens across the country. You may not want to eat out again.

Humans

What are the most difficult subjects for objective scientific study? What types of study are most prone to be questioned for accuracy and ethics? I nominate medicine and psychology, the sciences that examine the human body and mind. Both at times threaten preconceived beliefs and social values. People do not read these books with disinterest.

60-Second Psych from Scientific American, PC, http://www.sciam.com/podcast/.
Once a week, *Scientific American* releases a one-minute podcast on an intriguing human behavior or emotion. While many of the topics sound like stories for the tabloid press, science reporters succinctly present empirical data and psychological explanations. These quick introductions may compel listeners to learn more from books, magazines, or the Internet.

B., David, *Epileptic* (2005) GN
David B. is a French illustrator who witnessed his brother suffer epileptic seizures. In this acclaimed graphic novel-like memoir, he describes the disease, its impact on his family, and the many medical treatments tried.

Engel, Jonathan, *American Therapy: The Rise of Psychotherapy in the United States* (2008) NF BK
Forget Sigmund Freud and psychoanalysis. Psychotherapy is now the psychiatry of choice. Jonathan Engel describes its transition from an elite treatment available only to the wealthy to more pragmatic and affordable therapy in his lucid microhistory.

Garavaglia, Jan, *How Not to Die: Surprising Lessons on Living Longer, Safer, and Healthier from America's Favorite Medical Examiner* (2008) NF BK
Whenever someone in the Orlando area dies mysteriously, Jan Garavaglia finds the body on her autopsy table the next morning. In *How Not to Die*, Garavaglia recounts strange cases and the autopsies that solved them. In the process, she offers readers life-saving advice.

Kurson, Robert, *Crashing Through: A True Story of Risk, Adventure, and the Man Who Dared to See* (2007) NF BK, UAB
Mike May is not only fearless, he was also blind until he had radical eye surgery. Still he skied and tried other dangerous sports. Robert Kurson describes May's courageous life in a book filled with revelations about the physical and psychological aspects of sight.

Martensen, Robert, *A Life Worth Living: A Doctor's Reflections on Illness in a High-Tech Era* (2008) NF BK
Physician and bioethicist Robert Martensen has cared for many terminally ill patients in his long career. The rise in medical technology has not, he regrets to say, fulfilled its promise of providing dignified palliative care. In his quick read *A Life Worth Living*, he recounts cases that illustrate the problems and possibilities facing the critically ill, their families, and physicians.

Roach, Mary, *Bonk: The Curious Coupling of Science and Sex* (2008) NF BK
Many layers of desire and expectations influence human sexual performance. Can it all be understood? As Mary Roach shows in this lighthearted book, there is much more

scientific research being conducted on human sexuality than most people would ever imagine.

Shubin, Neil, *Your Inner Fish: A Journey into the 3.5 Billion-Year History of the Human Body* (2008) NF BK, UAB
"What does the body of a professor share with a blob?" This is not Neil Shubin's first question in *Your Inner Fish*, but by the time he asks, the reader knows to expect an entertaining answer using clear examples from daily life and pop culture that elucidate the history of human development.

The World and Natural Phenomena

Closed inside our homes, offices, and automobiles, we sometimes forget that we live in a world that is vast and dangerous. When a tremendous storm disrupts our routine, we notice the great forces of nature as though they were new. The books and media in this list seek to explain these forces and how they shape our lives even when we do not notice.

***Blue Planet: Seas of Life* BBC (2007) TV**
Over two-thirds of the Earth's surface is covered by water. Led by narrator David Attenborough, viewers visit remote coasts and the depths of the seas to learn about powerful natural forces and the diversity of life. Every habitat has unlikely creatures. The cinematography is stunning.

Carson, Rachel, *The Sea Around Us: An Illustrated Commemorative Edition* (2003) NF BK, CL
Biologist and advocate Rachel Carson loved the oceans for their abundance of life and the mysteries that lay deep below the waves. In *The Sea Around Us*, she beautifully describes the geophysical forces and human dependence on the seas. In an introduction to the commemorative edition, oceanographer Robert D. Ballard profiles Carson and updates the discoveries that followed the original publication of this classic.

Diclaudio, Dennis, *Man vs. Weather: How to Be Your Own Weatherman* (2008) NF BK
Author and comedian Dennis Diclaudio has written a primer to weather with a comic attitude. He wittily explains the hydrologic cycle, development of storms, instruments of atmospheric measurement, and dangers that individuals face if they are not vigilant in their dealings with the weather. He claims that *Man vs. Weather* might even save your life.

Ehrlich, Robert, *Nine Crazy Ideas in Science: A Few Might Even Be True* (2001) NF BK
Does our solar system have two suns? Are there particles that move faster than light? Is time travel possible? These are three of the nine questions that physicist Robert Ehrlich examines in his lighthearted *Nine Crazy Ideas in Science*. If you like these, he has more in *Eight Preposterous Propositions*.

Friedman, John S., *Out of the Blue: A History of Lightning: Science, Superstition, and Amazing Stories of Survival* (2008) NF BK
The power of lightning is tremendous and unpredictable. Surprisingly, most people struck by lightning do not die. John S. Friedman recounts many survival stories in this microhistory of the phenomena.

***Planet Earth*, BBC (2007) TV, AP, YA, SH**
With some of the most stunning nature cinematography ever produced, *Planet Earth* is a detailed overview of the many different environments and species that populate our planet. Famed naturalist David Attenborough narrates and directs this fabulous

epic of nature TV across 12 one-hour episodes. *The Living Planet* (1984) is an older 12-part series that features a younger and livelier Attenborough as narrator and host trekking across the planet and visiting some of the world's most unusual plants and animals.

Science Book: Everything You Need to Know About the World and How It Works (2008) NF BK

Produced by the editors of *National Geographic*, *Science Book* is a big and beautiful reference book designed for people who enjoy learning about nature, geology, astronomy, physics, and chemistry. Knowledge hounds will spend hours browsing the colorful illustrations and photographs.

Seife, Charles, Sun in a Bottle: The Strange History of Fusion and the Science of Wishful Thinking (2008) NF BK

For more than 50 years, the promise of unlimited energy from atomic fusion has been touted as the key to a clean and prosperous future, but this promise is to date unfulfilled. In *Sun in a Bottle*, Charles Seife chronicles both billion-dollar projects and amateur experiments that have fused atoms but failed to produce power.

Ulin, David L., The Myth of Solid Ground: Earthquakes, Prediction, and the Fault Line Between Reason and Faith (2004) NF BK

On what can you rely if the very ground under your feet may rise and throw you? Recounting his own earthquake stories, California resident and science reporter David L. Ulin examines efforts to predict quakes and minimize their physical and psychological damage.

Evolution

"Nothing endures but change," said the Greek philosopher Heraclitus. This is especially evident in science and technology. Almost every aspect of life has been altered by the inventions and industrial applications of the past centuries. The authors of the following books and media show that change is a central scientific and societal force.

Blumburg, Mark S., Freaks of Nature: What Anomalies Tell Us About Development and Evolution (2009) NF BK

"Freak" and "monster" are unkind words to describe people or animals that shock us by having extra arms or heads. In his thoughtful microhistory of genetic variations, psychobiologist Mark S. Blumburg asserts that mutations are natural phenomena that reveal the methods of evolution.

Charles Darwin and the Tree of Life (2009) TV

David Attenborough narrates a beautifully photographed program that is both a biography of Charles Darwin and an explanation of evolutionary theory. Attenborough's take is that with many environmental problems to solve, belief in Darwinian principals is more important than ever.

Hedeen, Stanley, Big Bone Lick: The Cradle of American Paleontology (2008) NF BK

There was great demand for the gigantic bones found at Big Bone Lick in the eighteenth century. Benjamin Franklin wanted some, as did Thomas Jefferson. Science societies in America, Great Britain, and France bought them. In the quick read *Big Bone Lick*, author Stanley Hedeen recounts the excitement that the famous fossils stirred and their role in advancing the study of extinct species.

Life After People, History Channel (2008) TV

What would happen to cities, houses, and the countryside if all people disappeared from the Earth? Would pavement crumble, buildings fall, and wildlife return? In the

DVD *Life After People*, History Channel producers mix clever animated projections with actual films from the ghost towns of Chernobyl to show the fragility of human structures against the power of nature.

McCalman, Iain, *Darwin's Armada: Four Voyages and the Battle for the Theory of Evolution* (2009) NF BK
Charles Darwin was not alone in drawing evolutionary conclusions from exploration of exotic lands. Iain McCalman recounts the travels and writings of Darwin, Joseph Hooker, Thomas Huxley, and Alfred Russel Wallace and their contributions to science in this collective biography.

Mindell, David P., *The Evolving World: Evolution in Everyday Life* (2006) NF BK
The theory of evolution may still be challenged by some religious sects, but its precepts have been applied far beyond the developmental history of plants and animals. Author David P. Mindell shows how evolutionary processes explain the rise of societies, cultures, and religion. He also discusses how human action has itself become an evolutionary force in the selection of species.

NPR: Science Now Podcast, **PC, AP**
Every Friday, NPR science correspondent Ira Flatow interviews scientists from the fields of nature, space, physics, math, and technology about their new discoveries. What will become of us seems to be a constant question. Each compelling segment from the two-hour program becomes a separate podcast that may be downloaded for on-demand listening.

Science Talk, **PC**
For well over 100 years, *Scientific American* has been a trusted source for in-depth reporting on scientific discovery. In weekly half-hour episodes available as podcasts, host Steve Mirsky interviews newsmakers in various fields of science and technology.

Scott, Rebecca, *Darwin and the Barnacle* (2003) NF BK
While some historians think Darwin's eight-year study of barnacles delayed his announcing his theories of evolution and natural selection, author Rebecca Scott argues that the naturalist used the time to solidify his confidence and prepare a defense of his work. In *Darwin and the Barnacle*, she shows how he was able shake the world of science from an isolated country estate.

***The Way We Will Be 50 Years from Today: 60 of the World's Greatest Minds Share Their Visions of the Next Half Century* (2008) NF BK**
Experts from the fields of science, medicine, government, and philanthropy have different visions of the future. News correspondent Mike Wallace collects 60 provocative forecasts from modern innovators in *The Way We Will Be 50 Years from Today*.

Making Connections

Readers do not usually think of themselves as devotees to only one genre of literature, so they are willing to cross the somewhat artificial boundaries that are sometimes drawn for them in bookstores and libraries. The following lists suggest materials that may be considered popular science that will interest readers who tend toward other genres.

Science for the Mystery Reader

Without the sense of mystery or puzzles to be solved, there would never have been any science. What the scientist does is try to solve mysteries. It is fitting that there are many popular science books that appeal to some mystery fans.

Blake, Rich, *The Day Donny Herbert Woke Up: A True Story* (2007) NF BK, UAB

Fireman Donny Herbert had been in an unusual vegetative state for more than nine years, ever since a snow-covered roof had fallen on him in 1995. Then he woke up. For a decade, his wife Linda had insisted physicians try new treatments that might rouse her unresponsive husband, and she had repeatedly taken him on family outings in his wheelchair. Journalist Rich Blake tells the story of Herbert, who suddenly spoke for 19 hours straight, and then slipped back into a coma. Fans of true-life mysteries will likely enjoy this strange story.

Bombs, Bullets, and Fraud (2009) TV

The U. S. Postal Service is on the frontline of the war against crime. Many illegal and dangerous items are posted every day. Smithsonian reporters show the science used to discover these items, protect postal employees, and catch the crooks.

Brier, Bob, and Jean Pierre Houdin, *The Secret of the Great Pyramid* (2008) NF BK, YA

How the Great Pyramid at Giza was built has always been a great mystery. Scholars have argued that either long or spiraling ramps outside the pyramid would have been necessary to accomplish the feat, but there is no physical evidence to support these theories. In *The Secret of the Great Pyramid*, Egyptologist Bob Brier and architect Jean Pierre Houdin reveal that the pyramid was built from the inside! Their persuasive book includes many computer-generated illustrations aimed to sway the doubting reader.

Carroll, Sean B., *The Making of the Fittest: DNA and the Ultimate Forensic Record of Evolution* (2006) NF BK

The analysis of DNA evidence can do much more than identify criminals. In *The Making of the Fittest*, geneticist Sean B. Carroll explains DNA analysis through a series of curious stories about natural mysteries being solved by genetic study.

Hayes, Bill, *The Anatomist: A True Story of Gray's Anatomy* (2008) NF BK

Who was Henry Gray (1827–1861)? Though he wrote the original *Gray's Anatomy* and was elected a Fellow of the Royal Society, few personal details of his life were recorded until Bill Hayes discovered a diary by the textbook's illustrator, Henry Vandyke Carter. Readers will enjoy this entertaining investigative biography.

Larson, Erik, *Thunderstruck* (2006) NF BK, UAB, RS, SH

The setting is London and the surface of the northern Atlantic Ocean in the early part of the twentieth century. Italian Gugliemo Marconi is trying to perfect his wireless radio and establish a network of receiving towers to link the Europe with America. Meanwhile, Hawley Harvey Crippen is murdering his wife and trying to escape with his mistress. In *Thunderstruck*, Larson weaves the unrelated lives of these two unhappy, scheming, newsworthy men to depict their technologically energetic and socially unsettled time.

Martin, Russell, *Beethoven's Hair: An Extraordinary Odyssey and a Scientific Mystery Solved* **(2000) NF BK**
Why did Beethoven die? When a good-sized twist of this hair was sold at Sotheby's in 1994, scientists wanted to see it. In *Beethoven's Hair*, author Russell Martin alternates chapters on the history of ownership and scientific analysis of the composer's lock of hair with chapters about Beethoven's life, death, and legacy.

Psychology Today **(magazine)**
Mystery novels rely on interest in human psychology to attract readers. Behind every good mystery story is a puzzle involving human motivations. *Psychology Today* shows that real humans are just as difficult to comprehend.

Seventy Great Mysteries of the Natural World **(2008) NF BK, YA**
Why did the dinosaurs die? Why do continents move? How do bees communicate? These are only three of the mysteries explained in *The Seventy Great Mysteries of the Natural World*, a colorful collection of stories about geology, biology, and environmental science. This large volume is suitable for the coffee table or the desk.

Science for the Adventure Reader

Science is not always nine-to-five work in a lab type of job. Sometimes scientists have to venture to remote and dangerous locations to observe the plants and animals, find fossils, and measure the power of storms. Here are stories about brave, and perhaps foolhardy, scientists that will appeal to adventure readers.

Conant, Jennet, *Tuxedo Park: A Wall Street Tycoon and the Secret Palace of Science That Changed the Course of World War II* **(2002) NF BK, AP**
Handsome millionaire stockbroker Alfred Lee Loomis, like a character from a comic book, kept a secret laboratory in his fabulous mansion where he met with great scientists to invent devices to save the world from the Nazis. When he wasn't at a nightclub or on his yacht with attractive women, he was designing radar and atomic bombs with Albert Einstein, Niels Bohr, or Enrico Fermi. Jennet Conant recounts an entertaining and adventurous double life in *Tuxedo Park*.

Croke, Vicki Constantine, *The Lady and the Panda: The True Adventures of the First American Explorer to Bring Back China's Most Exotic Animal* **(2005) NF BK, UAB**
As late as the 1930s, no explorers had captured a panda, but former dressmaker and New York socialite Ruth Harkness succeeded where seasoned hunters had failed. In *The Lady and the Panda*, Vicki Constantine Croke tells how Harkness brought two pandas to the Brookfield Zoo and the change of heart she felt afterward. Armchair travelers and animal lovers will relish this story.

HD—NASA's Jet Propulsion Laboratory, **PC, http://www.jpl.nasa.gov/.**
Using high-definition video, NASA scientists take viewers across the solar system and into deep space, showing what their unmanned probes have revealed. Many episodes include late-breaking news with dramatic images, guaranteed to excite armchair space travelers.

Hollingshead, Mike, and Eric Nguyen, *Adventures in Tornado Alley: The Storm Chasers* **(2008) NF BK, YA, SH**
Instead of seeking shelter when tornados form, Mike Hollingshead and Eric Nguyen try to place themselves where they can get the most dramatic photos. They revel in the dust, wind, and hail. *Adventures in Tornado Alley* is their photo-filled diary of their chases across the American Midwest.

James, Jamie, *The Snake Charmer: A Life and Death in Pursuit of Knowledge* **(2008) NF BK**
Joe Slowinski was a herpetologist determined to find the most rare and deadliest snakes on the planet. He had won coveted appointments and large grants, but later he carelessly stuck his hand into a wiggling sack containing a deadly Burmese krait. Author Jamie James vividly recounts the bold life of adventuring scientist.

Johnson, Kirk, *Cruisin' the Fossil Freeway: An Epoch Tale of a Scientist and an Artist on the Ultimate 5,000-Mile Paleo Road Trip* **(2007) NF BK**
Dinosaurs have always been cool. Kirk Johnson and Ray Troll raise the bar of cool in *Cruisin' the Fossil Freeway*, a science adventure with underground comics-like illustrations. Dinofans of all ages will enjoy this crazy, colorful book.

The Long Way Round: The Ultimate Road Trip **(2005) NF BK, TV, SH**
How can two young men travel between London and New York on motorcycles? In *The Long Way Round*, actors Ewan McGregor and Charley Boorman ride their motorcycles across Europe, Russia, Alaska, Canada, and into the United States to show that it could be done. In their sequel *The Long Way Down* (2007, TV), they take their bikes from Scotland to South Africa.

National Geographic Adventure **(magazine)**
Geographic adventure has been democratized. Anyone with the desire and a little extra cash can now venture to the remotest parts of the globe, trek across deserts, climb mountains, and meet people of different cultures. *National Geographic Adventure* tells would-be explorers how to get there and what to do.

Prager, Ellen, *Chasing Science at Sea: Racing Hurricanes, Stalking Sharks, and Living Undersea with Ocean Experts* **(2008) NF BK**
Since the days of Jacques Cousteau, magazine readers and television viewers have closely followed the work of marine biologists. In *Chasing Science at Sea*, Ellen Prager describes the daily work and recounts exciting adventures in the dangerous waters of the Earth's oceans.

Preston, Diana, and Michael Preston, *A Pirate of Exquisite Mind: Explorer, Naturalist, and Buccaneer: The Life of William Dampier* **(2004) NF BK, AP**
Not many scientists double as true-life pirates. The hydrologist and naturalist William Dampier (1651–1715) was such a man, a charming buccaneer who charted ocean currents and described exotic birds when not attacking Spanish treasure ships. Diana and Michael Preston recount his adventures.

Williams, Stanley, and Fen Montaigne, *Surviving Galeras* **(2001) NF BK**
Because the eruption of volcanoes is difficult to predict, geologists are always at risk when they climb onto their cones. Author Stanley Williams is the sole survivor of a team that ventured onto Galeras in Columbia in 1993. Williams describes the eruption and his rescue in his memoir.

Worster, Donald, *A River Running West: The Life of John Wesley Powell* **(2001) NF BK, UAB**
As a child, John Wesley Powell studied rocks, shells, and plants. He was an experienced naturalist by the time he led a bold exploration of the Colorado River and Grand Canyon, a dangerous adventure that featured scientific discovery, scarce supplies, and mutiny. In *A River Running West*, author Donald Worster chronicles the evolution of a conservationist who helped spark the American parks movement.

Science for the History Reader

Scientific and technological advances preceded many of the political, cultural, and economic changes in history. Recently, these science-history relationships have been featured in a flood of popular science microhistories. Here are some titles that will appeal to armchair historians.

Archaeology (magazine)

Archeologists are like detectives trying to uncover historical truth that has long lay hidden. They now apply many high tech tools to the work, pointing sonic devices into the earth, measuring radioisotopes, and scanning aerial images into analyzing computers. *Archaeology* is filled with stories and glossy photographs that take readers onto the frontlines of research about ancient and modern civilizations.

Aveni, Anthony, *People and the Sky: Our Ancestors and the Cosmos* (2008) NF BK

Because of the pervasiveness of artificial light, most people can see few stars at night. As a result, they have lost their ability to read the night sky. In *People and the Sky*, Anthony Aveni reveals that our ancestors not only knew the stars, but depended on their cyclic patterns to inform them how to navigate the seas and when to plant crops, hunt game, and celebrate holy days. Stargazers will enjoy this reflective history.

Barrow, John D., *Cosmic Imagery: Key Images in the History of Science* (2008) NF BK

That every picture tells a story is an old saying. In *Cosmic Imagery*, every picture has a story. In this attractive history, author and mathematician John D. Barrow recounts the impact of each of the most important illustrations in science, from drawings by Leonardo to photographs from the Hubble Space Telescope.

Bryson, Bill, *Short History of Nearly Everything* (2003) NF BK, UAB, SH

Is there a subject that does not interest Bill Bryson? Is there a reader whom he cannot charm? The prolific author addresses the history of science in his ambitious *A Short History of Nearly Everything* and transforms familiar facts and dates into compelling human-interest stories and lucid explanations of scientific processes. Skillfully read by Richard Matthews, the audio version will ease weeks of commuting.

Carlsen, Spike, *A Splintered History of Wood: Belt Sander Races, Blind Woodworkers, and Baseball Bats* (2008) NF BK

Throughout history, humans have turned to wood and products made from bark or pulp to meet their needs for warmth, shelter, food, transportation, and entertainment. In his entertaining anecdotal history, *A Splintered History of Wood*, Spike Carlsen explains why humans love and prefer wood to newer materials that might serve well.

Connections, Ambrose Video (1978) TV, NF BK, CL

Though produced in 1978, the premise behind this stylish television series is still valid—every bit of technology that we now take for granted has a surprising legacy of discovery. Author and narrator James Burke connects the stories from the past to those of the present and the future. Viewers may also marvel at the absence of personal computers and cell phones in what was thought to be a totally modern society.

Dyson, Freeman, *From Eros to Gaia* (1992) NF BK, CL

Freeman Dyson was a rare individual capable of working in the high-tech world of physics while still being able to write for the lay reader. *From Eros to Gaia*, which selectively collects his essays from over six decades, serves as a "you were there" history of twentieth-century science and public policy. Included are intimate profiles of important figures such as J. Robert Oppenheimer and Richard Feynman.

Ferris, Timothy, *Coming of Age in the Milky Way* **(1998) NF BK, CL**
Ancient Sumerian, Chinese, Korean, and Egyptian astronomers thought the stars and planets moved in a single field. Copernicus recognized space as three-dimensional. Science writer and astronomer Timothy Ferris recounts the long and sometimes contentious history of human understanding of the universe.

Humphries, Courtney, *Superdove: How the Pigeon Took Manhattan . . . And the World* **(2008) NF BK**
Visit nearly any city in the world and you will find flocks of lead-colored pigeons in city squares and parks. You will also find divided sentiments over the birds. While some people feed them, others call for their extermination. In her microhistory, science reporter Courtney Humphries reveals centuries of good and bad human-pigeon relationships.

Marling, Karal Ann, *Ice: Great Moments in the History of Hard, Cold Water* **(2008) NF BK**
From ice cubes to icebergs, ice sculpture to ice palaces, frozen water has played an important role in the development of human societies, culture, and technology. Karal Ann Marling examines that role in her engaging microhistory. This quick read requires no scientific knowledge.

Ottaviani, Jim, et al., *Fallout: J. Robert Oppenheimer, Leo Szilard, and the Political Science of the Atomic Bomb* **(2001) GN**
After World War II ended, physicist J. Robert Oppenheimer was a hero for leading the Manhattan Project, but he misread the political climate and became a target of right-wing politicians for recommending arms control. His colleague Leo Szilard harbored regrets for designing weapons that could eliminate life on Earth. With the help of a team of illustrators, Jim Ottaviani recounts their struggles in the graphic novel *Fallout*.

Time Team America **(2009) TV, AP**
The premise of *Time Team America* is that almost any historical project can be helped by a team of top-flight archeologists with the latest scientific equipment. However, the team gets only three days to help. Viewers will enjoy watching the archeologists fight the weather and difficult terrain to locate remnants of missing buildings.

Science for Literary Readers

Precise language and philosophical observations attract many serious readers. The titles in this section show that popular science can compete with poetry and literary fiction for eloquent expression.

American Earth: Environmental Writing Since Thoreau **(2008) NF BK**
Readers who enjoy fine essays about nature history, conservation, and environmental protection will appreciate this massive collection of works by writers as diverse as Walt Whitman, John Muir, P. T. Barnum, Barbara Kingsolver, Wendell Berry, and Alice Walker.

Ehrlich, Gretel, *John Muir: Nature's Visionary* **(2000) NF BK**
John Muir was a wanderer and a truant. He spent much of his life outdoors, examining rocks, plants, and wildlife and writing about his love of nature. In the attractively

illustrated *John Muir: Nature's Visionary*, poet Gretel Ehrlich tracks the first president of the Sierra Club through the woods and mountains of California and on voyages around the world.

Hurd, Barbara, *Walking the Wrack Line: On Tidal Shifts and What Remains* (2008) NF BK, AP, SH
The wrack line is the high water mark that tides leave on beaches. In *Walking the Wrack Line*, poet and naturalist Barbara Hurd recounts her visits to beaches worldwide to see and muse about what washes up from the sea. These elegant essays foster contemplation about nature and the human experience.

Johnson, Steven, *The Ghost Map: The Story of London's Most Terrifying Epidemic— and How It Changed Science, Cities, and the Modern World* (2006) NF BK
It may seem hard to believe now, but in the middle of the nineteenth century, most people, including scientists, had no idea how cholera spread. Steven Johnson takes readers back to the London of Charles Dickens and other reformers in *The Ghost Map*.

Nadkarni, Nalini M., *Between Earth and Sky: Our Intimate Connection to Trees* (2008) NF BK
Though Inuits and some desert dwellers never see them, most people have both practical and emotion relationships with trees. Nalini M. Nadkarni examines the tree-human bond in *Between Earth and Sky*, a natural history filled with poetry and literary quotes.

***TERRA: The Nature of Our World*, PC, http://www.lifeonterra.com.**
Video podcasts from LIFEONTERRA are independently produced and distributed free on the Internet. These short films incorporate nature photography, music, poetry, and interviews to tell stories about places around the world.

Zimmer, Carl, *Microcosm: E. Coli and the New Science of Life* (2008) NF BK
Scientists discovered the world of microscopic life in the nineteenth century. Science reporter Carl Zimmer reveals how their study of bacteria and other small creatures has led scientists and philosophers to alter their definition of life in his eloquent meditation.

Resources for Librarians

Adamson, Lynda G. *Thematic Guide to Popular Nonfiction*. Westport, CT: Greenwood Press, 2006.

Angier, Natalie. *The Canon: The Whirligig Tour of the Beautiful Basics of Science*. New York: Houghton Mifflin, 2007.

Berlinski, David. *Newton's Gift: How Sir Isaac Newton Unlocked the Systems of the World*. New York: Free Press, 2000.

Cords, Sarah Statz. *The Real Story: A Guide to Nonfiction Reading Interests*. Westport, CT: Libraries Unlimited, 2006.

Cornog, Martha. *Graphic Novels: Beyond the Basics*. Westport, CT: Libraries Unlimited, 2009.

Cornog, Martha and Raiteri, Steve. "Graphic Novels." *Library Journal* (7/09): 76.

Kannenberg, Gene Jr. *500 Essential Graphic Novels: The Ultimate Guide*. New York: Collins Design, 2008.

LaFollette, Marcel. *Science on the Air: Popularizers and Personalities on Radio and Early Television*. Chicago: University of Chicago Press, 2008.

Lerner, K. Lee. "Introduction: 2000 B.C. to A.D. 699" in *Science and Its Times: Understanding the Social Significance of Scientific Discovery*. Farmington Hills, MI: Gale Group, 2000, pp. xiii–xv.

McClellan, James E. *Science Reorganized: Scientific Societies in the Eighteenth Century*. New York: Columbia University, 1985.

Roche, Rick. *Real Lives Revealed: A Guide to Reading Interests in Biography*. Westport, CT: Libraries Unlimited, 2009.

Steinhart, Peter. "The Longer View." *Audubon* (3/87): 10–13.

Wyatt, Neal. *The Readers' Advisory Guide to Nonfiction*. Chicago: American Library Association, 2007.

Endnotes

1. Angier, Natalie. *The Canon: The Whirligig Tour of the Beautiful Basics of Science*. New York: Houghton Mifflin, 2007.

2. "Science." *American Heritage Dictionary*, 1,560.

3. Berlinski, David. *Newton's Gift: How Sir Isaac Newton Unlocked the Systems of the World*. New York: Free Press, 2000.

4. Wheatley, Steven C. "Learned Societies" in *Dictionary of American History*, 3rd ed. New York: Charles Scribner's Sons, 2003, pp. 66–68.

5. McClellan, James E. *Science Reorganized: Scientific Societies in the Eighteenth Century*. New York: Columbia University, 1985.

6. McCue, J. J. G. "Science (In Antiquity)" in *New Catholic Encyclopedia*. Farmington Hills, MI: Gale Group, 2003, pp. 799–807.

7. Lerner, K. Lee. "Introduction: 2000 B.C. to A.D. 699" in *Science and Its Times: Understanding the Social Significance of Scientific Discovery*. Farmington Hills, MI: Gale Group, 2000, pp. xiii–xv.

8. Gianoulis, Tina. "National Geographic" in *St. James Encyclopedia of Popular Culture*. Farmington Hills, MI: Gale Group, 1999, pp. 484–85.

9. Schafer, Elizabeth D. "Scientific American" in *St. James Encyclopedia of Popular Culture*. Farmington Hills, MI: Gale Group, 1999, pp. 334–35.

10. Steinhart, Peter. "The Longer View." *Audubon* (March 1987): 10–13.

11. LaFollette, Marcel. *Science on the Air: Popularizers and Personalities on Radio and Early Television*. Chicago: University of Chicago Press, 2008.

6

Everything Romance
Katie Dunneback and
Mary Wilkes Towner

In this chapter, Katie Dunneback and Mary Wilkes Towner offer an overview the vast world of romance, including some background history and the roots of modern romance. "Plots" includes romantic suspense, paranormal romance, fairy tales and mythology, and GLBT romances. The "Characters" section covers lords, ladies, gypsies, damsels in distress, sports players and agents, African American stories, bad boys and girls, alpha heroes, real women, and widows and widowers. The theme of this chapter is the many varieties of love, which include romantic comedies, romantic stories, gentle love, and erotica. In the "Making Connections" section, you'll find suggested romance for mystery, fantasy, and western fans, and romances for men.

Introduction

The Romance Writers of America (RWA) defines a romance novel as a story with "a central love story and an emotionally satisfying and optimistic ending."[1] This basic definition serves the romance genre of all media well. However, different degrees of success have been achieved in conveying a romance through different media.

It's also important to distinguish between "romance" and "romantic." In Nora Roberts' *The Pagan Stone*, when the heroine, Cybil, is asked if she is looking for romance, she replies, "Everyone is. It's the personal definitions thereof that vary." Awareness of the variations in definition is crucial to providing excellent advisory services to a romance fan. A long-time romance genre reader may demand that anything called a romance adhere to the RWA definition. Others may treat anything that has any kind of emotional or sexual relationship develop between characters as being a romance. The primary key in the development of the following lists is that the definition of "romance" requires the development of the romantic relationship as the primary plotline. In contrast, the term "romantic" allows for the development of a romantic relationship to be an integral part of the plot, but not the primary one.

Defining genres is an eternal struggle for anyone dealing with any specific genre, from librarians, writers, and scholars to publishers and readers. In romance, the two generally accepted main criteria as mentioned in the RWA definition above are constantly discussed, fought over, and refined. Throughout most of the history of the romance genre, the required ending was borrowed from fairy tales: "and they lived happily ever after." Preferably, explicitly married. With children. The "happily ever after" or HEA ending ruled the genre. "Good" girls got married. ("Bad" girls presumably died or went away.)

However, a culture is built on its mores, and as mores shift, so does the culture. In the last 15 to 20 years, American culture, which is the predominant informant of the romance genre, has changed to a general acceptance of couples living together without the cultural trappings of marriage. This is, in turn, reflected in the acceptance by readers of the "happy for now" or HFN ending in romance novels. A number of readers have stated in public blog conversations that they find an HFN ending more believable than an HEA, especially if the time line of the story is compressed. However, they demand at least an HFN ending if a novel is to be marketed as a romance. There is no faster way for an author, and potentially a publisher, to lose a reader than to not deliver on the promise of a happy romantic resolution if the novel is implicitly, if not explicitly, marketed as romance.

Many movies fit within the definition of "romantic" rather than "romance." The most common subgenre of movie that the stricter definition of "romance" can be applied to is romantic comedies. However, there is more latitude given to what may fall under the romance genre classification of movies, including ones where the primary characters do not even achieve a "happy for now" ending, let alone a "happily ever after." Television shows also usually suffer from a lack of the resolution to the romance plotline due to their serial nature and the need to continue dramatic tension when and where possible.

Ultimately, a person searching for romance entertainment provides the definition of romance at that point in time for herself or himself, no matter what the medium preferred.

Building from the basic definition of romance, romance still lies within the hearts of individual readers. It takes two to create a successful romance novel—the author and the reader. Authors provide the story that lets the reader become lost in the romance. And they provide a lot. According to the Romance Writers of America 2007 Romance Literature Statistics, romance was the biggest fiction category published that year—8,090 individual titles were published![2]

In the end, each reader brings his or her own definition of what is romantic to each book he or she reads. And what's romantic to one reader may not be as fulfilling to another. In addition, the well-known readers' advisory appeals of plot, characters, pacing, setting, and mood most definitely come into play here.

Appeal of Romance

Just by choosing to read a romance or a book with a strong romantic element, the reader has already decided to read about love and a relationship as part of the story. This is an experience the reader seeks.

"Happily ever after"/"happy for now" may be the most important component of the romance. We want to know there's closure—even if brief—and that the two main characters will live that moment of their lives in bliss ever after. Their love is a success story suspended in time. Their happiness makes us happy. As readers, we can forget our own lives briefly and revel in vicarious pleasure.

How we get there involves a multiplicity of choices. Some readers appreciate books with strong characters. If they're engaging or multilayered or strike a chord within us so we identify with them, the book comes alive.

Plot can also be of great importance. Why have scrumptious characters if they don't have something exciting to do? What creates the tension that will draw the two lovers together?

Love Costa Rica or Regency England? Romances can put you right there, alongside your favorite characters. Do you like excitement? Do you prefer to stand back and examine the scene, pondering each occurrence? Romance novels can provide swift or contemplative reading experiences for your pleasure. Are style and eloquence of thought a major draw? There are romances for you.

Of course, just as in any genre, some works are crafted more expertly than others. Sometimes exciting plots and characters are enough. The variety of romance authors and their blending of styles and plots ensure that the perfect romance is out there for any readers, no matter what mood they might be in at the moment.

Mood is an especially important appeal in providing a successful romantic reading experience. It is transient and not the same for each reader. One of the successes of the romance industry is that it provides many types of reading experiences for all types of readers and all types of moods. Publishers realize that our mood triggers what we'll buy—that's why so many romances are published and sold each year.

Roots of Romance

Since the beginning of myth and oral tradition, romance has lived in people's imagination, along with tales of war and religion and magic. How else would we know of Penelope's dogged determination to wait for her beloved Ulysses or of Paris's lust for the beauteous Helen of Troy? Romance and love are celebrated in the bible's Song of Solomon. "I am my beloved's, and my beloved is mine. . . ."

Given this long history, it's not at all surprising that today's romance novels—and movies or TV shows or audiobooks—are so popular. They're just continuing the trend. Over the past few centuries, certain romantic tales have provided great enjoyment to their readers and have been significant milestones in the genre. These have been cited over and over again in books and articles about the romance genre. We've read the ones listed below and totally agree. Many of these have inspired filmmakers to adapt the stories to a different medium. All still provide unique and important reading experiences for romance fans and reflect the reading trends of their times.

Early stories such as epistolary tale *Pamela, or Virtue Rewarded* (1740) by Samuel Richardson are important foundations for expressing woman-man relationships, but one significant romance novel is still revered today—Jane Austen's *Pride and Prejudice* (1813). Readers thrill to the restrained romance between prideful Elizabeth Bennet and prejudiced Mr. Darcy. While a contemporary novel, authors of Regency novels today celebrate the same time and society in their tales. Sequels and reimaginings abound. Visual adaptations have appeared on screen and television. Devotees can enjoy 2004's *Bride and Prejudice: The Bollywood Musical*, featuring Aishwarya Rai, or thrill to the new paranormal print mash-up, *Pride and Prejudice and Zombies* (2009).

Many novels published in the 1800s highlighted contemporary society or history. *Ivanhoe* (1819) by Sir Walter Scott explored the age of the Crusades. *Jane Eyre* (1847) by Charlotte Bronte was a fine, suspenseful gothic tale.

The twentieth century produced a number of important authors and titles. Romances continued to gain in popularity. *The Scarlet Pimpernel* (1905) by Baroness Orczy recounted the French Revolution and exploits of heroic British noblemen. E. M. Hull's *The Sheik* (1919) provided moments of forbidden passion to its readers. Well-known authors such as Georgette Heyer and Barbara Cartland started publishing their historical novels in the 1920s. It's hard to select just one representative book by the revered Heyer, who, through her meticulous research and engaging plots, set the standards for all later Regency novelists. The middle part of the century provided romantic suspense, lush historical, and gothic novels. Representative titles include *Rebecca* by Daphne Du Maurier (1938), *Forever Amber* (1944) by Kathleen Winsor, *Katherine* (1954) by Anya Seton, and *Mistress of Mellyn* (1960) by Victoria Holt. *Forever Amber*—a meticulously researched bestseller from the 1940s—was perceived as scandalous, but is a lush blend of sex, romance, and historical fiction.

The publishing house Harlequin was founded in Ontario, Canada, in 1949. It started buying the rights to reprint romances published in the UK by Mills and Boon. These short, simple tales highlighting individual love stories became incredibly popular, especially since they were published in inexpensive paperback format. Specific titles might not be standouts, but the type of reading experience provided promoted the romance reading experience and opened readership and publishing conduits for later titles. Harlequin remains a major publisher today.

Kathleen Woodiwiss' sensual novel, *The Flame and the Flower* (1972), published as a stand-alone paperback original, is notable for being one of the first in which the heroine acknowledged her sexuality and femininity, and was a key early book in the 1970s and 1980s historical fiction craze. This was followed shortly after by Rosemary Rogers' *Sweet Savage Love* (1974). One of the first "bodice-rippers," the basic plot of this novel involves innocent Virginia Brandon's forceful introduction into womanhood by macho Steve Morgan. This historical novel is intense and not for everyone, and is certainly not politically correct today, but was influential at the beginning of the development of modern erotic romance.

These titles provided the background in plots, characters, and settings for the romances we read and watch today.

Integrated Advisory: Romance Style

Romance is emotion. Those who engage with the genre want to be transported to another world through their emotions. Different media engage the senses in different ways and thereby the consumer's emotions. In traditional print books, an author uses words to paint the developing relationship and name thoughts and emotions that, for some, are unnamable in the real world. Graphic novels add the visual layer of illustration to further explore how characters interact with each other. Movies and television combine the visual and audio experience to evoke the intimate dance of falling in love and learning to live with each other. In video games like *The Sims*, players can replicate the real world as they create characters who engage in romantic relationships. When determining the media experience the patron is looking for, it is important to consider how the patron wants to interact with the media and respond accordingly.

Traditional Print Books

Publishers are well aware that their romance readers want to escape, so they provide the means. And they are increasingly providing the means in print and in media formats to feed this need. In an April 8, 2009, article in the *New York Times*, Motoko Rich states, "Recession fuels readers' escapist urges . . . In a recession, what people want is a happy ending. At a time when booksellers are struggling to lure readers, sales of romance novels are outstripping most other categories of books and giving some buoyancy to an otherwise sluggish market."[3] The article goes on to state that the romance category in adult fiction sales was up 7 percent during the recession, including both print and e-books. Retailers, publishers, and libraries are reaping the benefit.

Harlequin is a perfect example. Every month, Harlequin publishes 10 imprints with more than 40 series. A variety of titles are also available as e-books and in large print. There is certainly an appeal there for every reader. And Harlequin is only one publisher of romances.

Media

Just as the genres are changing, the medium of presentation also is in flux. Digital methods of presentation are taking their place next to print and large print. The romance genre is the recognized leader among genre fiction for the adoption of the electronic format, especially among readers of erotica, as paper availability has long been limited. Ellora's Cave is one example of an e-publisher; their books are available for download, to be read either on computer or transferred to one of the many e-book reading devices. With the popularity of the Sony Reader and the Kindle rising rapidly, more and more mainstream romance will become available in digital format.

Books on audio are incredibly popular. This is one area in which romance needs to expand. Publishers are providing romance on audio, but not as copiously as in print format, nor in quantities equal to those published in other popular genres. And, truthfully, listening to romance is a very different experience than reading it. Not all romance novels translate well into being read aloud. "Kiss me, you beauteous creature, kiss me" sounds rather silly when hearing it. Audio formats are flourishing but fluctuating. While audiotape is dying out, books on CD are still the standard. Playaways—small, self-contained, battery-driven player/audio units—are the current rage in many public libraries. The Playaway front- and backlists aren't huge at the moment, but publishers are continuing to issue more titles as the popularity grows. Downloadable audio is becoming one of the hottest trends. Not only are there a number of companies selling downloadable audio, but many public libraries are contracting with businesses such as Overdrive, Books on Tape, or NetLibrary to provide access for their patrons. Digital rights management (DRM) issues have hindered some of these initiatives, but many are now working on platforms that will provide both MP3 and iPod versions of the products.

Graphic Novels and Manga

Romance lends itself well to a visual format. Graphic novels and manga abound. These formats have increased in popularity immensely the past few years. Harlequin briefly published the Harlequin Pink & Harlequin Lavender (Ginger Blossom manga) lines, producing a dozen or so print titles between 2006 and 2008. Digital Manga Publishing just announced that they'd be adding more than 20 new Harlequin Manga titles to their eManga.com online manga rental Web site beginning in November/December 2009.[4] Some of these, such as *The Sheik's Reluctant Bride* by Teresa Southwick (with art by Ayumu Aso), are available as downloadable apps on iTunes. Several of the Harlequin romance manga titles are now available at the Kindle store on Amazon.com.

Romance is particularly popular in Japanese manga (*manhwa* in Korean and *manhua* in Chinese; the Japanese market is discussed here). As with most other genres of manga, the two prominent divisions are *shôjo* and *shônen*, which refer to girls and boys respectively. According to Jason Thompson in *The Complete Guide to Manga*, romance is the dominant genre in *shôjo* manga. There are numerous further subdivisions that are primarily along demographic lines. A popular subgenre of *shôjo* is *yaoi*, which refers to "boys' love." In perusing a general bookstore, what becomes apparent is that the majority of manga titles that may appeal to romance readers generally feature middle and high schoolers as the main characters. This is primarily due to the fact that *shôjo* romance is generally about the discovery of first love. The subdivision of manga that may better appeal to older audiences is *jôsei*, but Thompson notes that relatively few of these titles have been translated into English.[5]

It should be noted that graphic novels can refer either to a collection of comics, or chapters, in a series or to a self-contained story. Romances as self-contained graphic novels do not appear to be especially popular at the moment; however, there seems to be an emerging trend of adapting popular novels into comic-formatted series. These have primarily been in the fantasy genre, but one of the most notable adaptations has appeal to romance readers: the Anita Blake series by Laurell K. Hamilton. This is an area that bears watching as a nascent market.

In many Spanish-speaking communities, fotonovelas are wildly popular. Fotonovelas are small-sized comic books published in Spanish. The stories are told in photos, with brief text. The cover art can be quite suggestive or provocative, although the content may not deliver such a spicy read. Universally read by both women and men, the tales are often romantic in tone and certainly fit our media discussion, although there isn't an English equivalent at this time. Collection-development policies are important here. Not all titles may be suitable for public libraries. In 2005, the Denver Public Library reconsidered several series due to explicit sexual content and suggestions of violence toward women.[6]

Games

More and more libraries are starting to embrace games and gaming in their programming and collection development. Will love stories be an important recreational element to consider? Can reader identification translate successfully into another format? Romance seems not to have caught on yet in the gaming community. Role-playing endeavors provide one outlet. For those who seek, there can be quite a bit of romance—or sexuality—in the realm of virtual reality, such as Second Life. A romp through the Internet does reveal some romantic games out there (which we haven't played), such as *"Bliss*, a computer romance game for married lovers"* (or *"Renai*, an interactive computer game based on themes of love and sex.").[7] In December 2009, it was announced that the first in Nora Roberts' Bride Quartet, *Vision in White* (2009), would be adapted into a video game by iPlay, the company that has adapted works by James Patterson and Agatha Christie.[8] These all seem to be more appropriate for home use rather than library offerings.

In her article "Romance in the Computer Game Industry," Lauren E. Darcey suggests some reasons why romance may not yet have conquered the gaming world.[9] Three conference participants in a panel discussion considered difficulties in creating a game containing a love story. In a typical romance, the ending is known in advance. So while plot and emotions could be used to differentiate the game experience, the "chance" aspect would be hindered by the ultimate outcome. The future of romance in games may be as a subplot or emotion incorporated into a larger whole. This is something for us librarians to be aware of down the road, especially if the new Nora Roberts game proves popular.

Movies

Romance and romantic plotlines are powerful sources of dramatic tension. The added depth of the visual medium creates its own tension unlike that found in books because the visual depiction of the characters and scenes are created for the viewer. Romantic comedies have been a part of movies since the early era of silent films. Classics include *They Would Elope* (1909), *A Girl of Yesterday* (1915), and *It* (1927). The American Film Institute, when creating its Top 10 lists, recognized romantic comedies as one of the main movie genres. Unlike in books, films outside of romantic comedies rarely have a romantic plotline as the main plot and with a positive resolution to the developing relationship. The majority of films with romance plots are best described as romantic rather than romances for this reason.

Each generation is dominated by film actors and actresses who specialize in romance. Many popular actors and actresses who play romantic leads often have long and successful film careers. In recent years, the mantle of favored romantic actresses has passed from Meg Ryan and Julia Roberts to Kate Hudson, Reese Witherspoon, Drew Barrymore, and Katherine Heigl for romantic comedies. Keira Knightly is building a strong reputation for historical romantic dramas. Diane Lane is a favored actress for older romantic roles. Male actors tend to have a longer shelf life for romantic leads. Current favorites include Brad Pitt, Gerard Butler, Colin Firth, Matthew McConaughey, Steve Carrell, and Vince Vaughn. Like the directors from the days of the studio contract system, today's directors do not seem to be as identified to specific genres of film. Directors of today who have seen success with romantic and romance movies include Ang Lee, Judd Apatow, the Farrelly brothers, and Mike Newell.

Movies with strong romantic plots continue to be popular, though they are not dominant at the box office. As of November 23, 2009, only three movies of the top 25 for box office receipts in 2009 could be termed as having a strong romantic plot as the primary or strong secondary plot (*The Proposal*, *The Twilight Saga: New Moon*, and *Couples Retreat*).[10] A number of foreign-language films such as *Amelie* and *Eat, Drink, Man, Woman* provide a strong romance plot, but usually due to cultural differences as to what constitutes "romance," these may or may not fully satisfy.

Television Shows

Television, as a format, may be considered by some to be better suited than movies to the development of characters' relationships because of the time available to explore the developing relationship. However, this serialized nature is also a drawback. If a couple does get together, it usually marks the end of the series or they will soon find themselves breaking up. It's hard to create dramatic tension if everyone is happy. However, television is the home of many of American culture's more famous fictional couples: Luke and Laura of *General Hospital*, Ross and Rachel of *Friends*, Susan and Mike of *Desperate Housewives*, and Ted and the mother of his children of *How I Met Your Mother*.

In television, romance is rather ubiquitous, appearing in cop shows and reality TV as well as in sitcoms, because it creates conflict and character-development opportunities. However, it is rarely the primary plot. The genres where it can most often be found as a primary plot or a strong subplot are in sitcoms and soap operas. The hybrid of "made for TV" movies is where the romance genre has found its niche on television. Currently, the Lifetime and Oxygen networks predominate, and DVD library copies are fertile areas for media collection development. "Made for TV" shows are frequently based on popular romance novels, such as the BBC's adaptations of Barbara Cartland's historical romance novels (*The Flame of Love*, *A Hazard of Hearts*, *The Lady and the Highwayman*, etc.), Danielle Steel miniseries from the early-1990s (*Jewels*, *Palomino*, *Daddy*, *Kaleidoscope*, etc.), and, more recently, *One Special Moment* from BET (2001), based on the novel of the same name by Brenda Jackson, and *Maneater* from Lifetime (2009), based on the novel of the same name by Gigi Levangie.

Since the early 1990s, adaptations of a number of Harlequin novels have found their way onto the airwaves, such as *At the Midnight Hour* (1994), based on the novel of the same name by Alicia Scott, and *Broken Lullaby* (1994), based on the novel of the same name by Laurel Pace. In 2007, Lifetime aired adaptations of four of Nora Roberts' romantic suspense novels (*Angels Fall*, *Carolina Moon*, *Blue Smoke*, and *Montana Sky*) with another four airing in March and April 2009 (*Midnight Bayou*, *High Noon*, *Northern Lights*, and *Tribute*). With the success of these television movies and those adapted from other popular women's fiction titles, there may be an increase in novels adapted for television in the coming years. Another area to watch is the adaptation of book series into television series. Until now, mysteries have been most successful in this arena, but that doesn't rule out popular romance and strong romantic book series.

Fans of the television series *Ugly Betty* may not realize it, but they're watching a telenovela—American style. (*Yo soy Betty, la Fea* was originally produced in Colombia in 1999 as a telenovela. The concept was adapted into a weekly series in the United States.) Long a staple in Spanish-speaking communities throughout the world, telenovelas are passionate, serial melodramas similar to soap operas. The major differences are that the telenovelas are finite—often six months to a year—the plots wrap up, and the episodes are usually shown five days per week. As in soap operas, the plots frequently involve or totally revolve around romances. Telenovelas are currently broadcast on Univision and Telemundo in the United States. English-language telenovelas have not met with success so far. In 2005, MyNetworkTV debuted, featuring two telenovelas each night and a weekend summary. Viewership declined, and after a couple years, MyNetworkTV switched to different programming.[11] However, abridged telenovelas with English subtitles are available via Lionsgate Home Entertainment for those interested in collection development in this area.[12]

Subgenres

Statistics are one way of analyzing the popularity of the various romantic subgenres. Once again, Romance Writers of America is a reliable source for this 2007 information on subgenres:[13]

- Contemporary series romance: 25.7 percent of romance releases in 2007
- Contemporary romance: 21.8 percent
- Historical romance: 16 percent
- Paranormal romance: 11.8 percent
- Romantic suspense: 7.2 percent
- Inspirational romance: 7.1 percent
- Romantic suspense (series): 4.7 percent
- Other (chick-lit, erotic romance, women's fiction): 2.9 percent
- Young adult romance: 2.8 percent

There is no consensus indicating one subgenre over another as a favorite among romance readers, as 50 percent of romance readers are somewhat or extremely likely to try a new subgenre in the next 24 months.[14]

Trends

However, statistics tell only part of the story and change constantly. The romance genre does not remain static. Category romances, Regencies, gothics, and lush historicals have all had their times of popularity. Chick lit was robust at the beginning of the twenty-first century, but seems to be on the downswing now.

What are today's trends? Those working in libraries have a good idea; the topic was discussed during April 2009 on the Fiction_L mailing list, and those ideas pretty much mirror what we've observed.[15] Paranormal titles of all types remain popular—vampires, were-wolves, shape-shifters, psychics, and time travel. Historical romances and romantic suspense maintain a good audience. Urban fiction is big, though not all titles are true romance. GLBT titles are starting to grow in request and publication rates. But it seems the biggest trends right now are genre blending and the polar opposites of erotica and gentle reads.

Genre blending is a concept that's been around for a long time, though we librarians have only recently started using that term. As the word implies, genre-blended books contain multiple, major elements. Many are grounded in historical fiction. Leon Uris's *Exodus* (1958) detailed the birth of the state of Israel, along with the growing attraction between Palestinian Ari Ben Canaan and nurse Kitty Fremont. More recently, romance has danced with mystery, speculative fiction, and inspirational fiction. J. D. Robb's *In Death* series (1995–) series combines science fiction with mystery and romance. Caroline Stevermer and Patricia C. Wrede's *Sorcery and Cecelia, or The Enchanted Chocolate Pot* (2003) merges Regency, magical, romantic, and young adult facets. Iris Johansen's stories about forensic sculptor Eve Duncan pull together romantic suspense and terror. Beverly Lewis's gentle Amish titles featuring love and lifestyle have an enthusiastic readership. Suzanne Brockmann's strong heroes are men of action. We learn all about their Navy SEAL adventures. But we also experience their love stories.

Gentle fiction can either be sweet tales without too much sex and violence or books of faith in which the main characters investigate their beliefs. Sometimes these elements blend into the same title. There's a growing audience for such tales. More and more patrons have been asking for books on the Amish, for example, and publishers have been responding. Overall, religious publishers such as Bethany House, Thomas Nelson, and Zondervan are all doing well. Harlequin has several lines in its inspirational Steeple Hill imprint.

Erotic fiction is getting hotter and more explicit. The trend started with titles available in downloadable format, but now has made its way to print. Mainstream publishers carry some lines that have more detailed sexual content, such as Harlequin's Blaze or Spice imprints and Kensington's Aprhodisia. Electronic publishers that specialize in erotic include Ellora's Cave, Samhain, Phaze, and Siren, among others. All subgenres and settings have their equivalents in erotic romance. What's considered pushing the envelope today would have been considered pornography 30 years ago. A recent line offers books in which the characters comport with multiple sex partners. While library patrons are interested in these titles, purchasing them for a collection can be problematical. How much is considered too much? Sarah Wendell and Candy Tan, the Smart Bitches, Trashy Novels bloggers, present this opinion in their book *Beyond Heaving Bosoms*:

> "... romance novels are one of the very few genres that examine sex for its own sake, and explain it often in marvelously precise detail. So while some readers embrace the sexual education inherent in romance novels, and others decry it as perversity, or sexual miseducation, the root of the turgid truth is simple: romances are about intimacy. Intimacy often includes sex. There is absolutely nothing wrong with that."[16]

Authors

Here are some contemporary authors to know about, because romance fans enjoy their books and read them with romance in mind.

Christian Fiction or Gentle Reads

- Dee Henderson
- Karen Kingsbury
- Beverly Lewis
- Lori Wick

Contemporary/Humorous

- Jennifer Crusie
- Susan Elizabeth Phillips
- Nora Roberts

Erotic

- Virginia Henley
- Robin Schone
- Bertrice Small

Historical

- Diana Gabaldon
- Philippa Gregory

Paranormal

- Christine Feehan
- Susan Grant
- Sherrily Kenyon
- Susan Krinard
- J. R. Ward

Regency

- Mary Balogh
- Georgette Heyer
- Eloisa James
- Stephanie Laurens
- Barbara Metzger

Romantic Suspense

- Suzanne Brockmann
- Sandra Brown
- Mary Higgins Clark
- Iris Johansen
- Jayne Ann Krentz
- Nora Roberts

Multicultural

- Donna Hill
- Brenda Jackson
- Beverly Jenkins
- Francis Ray
- Zane

Plots

Despite the necessity of a HEA or HFN ending, plots in romances have a wide variety, and many fans enjoy or will consume only certain plot types, while others read widely but want to make sure to avoid some specific plot types. In the end, like everything else, it comes down to the preference of the reader/listener/viewer. This next section highlights several plots types that are currently popular but is not intended as an overview of all the plot types found in romance stories.

Suspense

Suspenseful situations create enforced intimacy, driving people to learn a lot about the other people they are in the situation with in order to survive. Often, the hero or heroine is involved in law enforcement or the military. The immediacy of the situation allows the reader or viewer to quickly immerse themselves in the characters' stories. Romantic suspense grew out of the gothic tradition and continues in popularity today. Romantic suspense lends itself well to the movie format as the generally fast pace of the stories translates relatively well to the screen. Readers may guess the ending; the thrill of how they get there with the authors and characters is what they seek.

Brennan Allison, *Killing Fear* (2008) BK
Businesswoman and former stripper Robin McKenna is moving on with her life when an earthquake rips through the San Francisco area. The quake damages the walls of San Quentin prison, allowing the man she helped send to death row for murder to escape. Theodore Glenn is on a mission that will only end when everyone who helped put him away is dead, and Robin is his ultimate target. Robin turns to her former lover, and the cop who investigated the murders, for protection. The embers of their former passion flame high as the killer closes in on them. Brennan provides a taut story of rediscovering trust in a former loved one in the face of returning danger.

Howard, Linda, *Mr. Perfect* (2000) BK, CL, UAB, AP
It was the result of a Friday after-work happy hour. Too bad the "Mr. Perfect" list started making national headlines. Jaine Bright turns to her sexy new neighbor, and undercover cop, Sam Donovan, for help when someone insulted by the list starts killing off her friends. Snappy dialogue and the sharp characterizations of Sam and Jaine have created a touchstone book among Howard's legions of fans.

McKenna, Shannon, *Return to Me* (2004) BK, RS
Simon Riley has ridden back into the town he swore he'd left behind for good 17 years ago. His uncle's sudden death has lured him back. He gives in to temptation and seeks out the woman he'd thought he lost when he left. Ellen Kent's not ready to welcome

him back with open arms, but she can't resist the chance to prove whether he's her knight in tarnished armor or not. Unfortunately for them, a killer's on the loose and would rather the past stay buried. McKenna's darkly sensual story pulls no punches.

Mr. and Mrs. Smith (2005) MV, AP
Overshadowed by the Hollywood scandal of its costars, Angelina Jolie and Brad Pitt, this movie is an interesting exploration of a long-married couple discovering the secrets behind their spouse. They must each decide if they can live with those secrets, because if they can't, they'll find themselves on the wrong end of a bullet. Romance fans will especially love the flashbacks to the beginning of the couple's relationship.

Roberts, Nora, *Northern Lights* (2004) BK, TV, MV, AP, UAB, SH
Lunacy, Alaska, is Nate Burke's last hope for sanity. Welcomed as the town's new chief of police, he's slowly getting to know all of its characters, especially bush pilot Meg Galloway, when a long-dead body is discovered on a search-and-rescue mission. The body is Meg's father, Pat, whom the whole town had assumed just up and left when he disappeared. It's clear Pat Galloway hadn't left on his own, as an axe is found buried in his chest. When the body of another prominent town resident is found, it seems the killer is cleaning house; Nate must discover the killer's identity before Meg becomes the next victim. Roberts excels with this book with the stark portrayal of small-town life in Alaska. This will also greatly appeal to those who enjoy seeing the romance hero as the protagonist.

Rose, Karen, *Die for Me* (2007) BK, SH, RS, UAB
A grid of graves is discovered on the outskirts of Philadelphia, and Detective Vito Ciccotelli recruits archaeologist Sophie Johannsen for the excavation. Quickly realizing they've interrupted a serial killer at work, they must work to uncover his identity before more graves are filled. Sophie wants to keep their relationship strictly professional, but Vito's seen enough as a cop to know he can't waste time when he's found the right woman. When the killer targets Sophie, Vito's never been more afraid of failing at his job. Rose perfectly marries the romance and suspense plotlines to create a dark and tense story that will keep the reader on the edge of her or his seat.

The Thomas Crown Affair (1968, 1999) MV, CL, SH
Thomas Crown is a man who has seemingly everything and loves living on the edge. His latest start is participating in the perfect crime. The lovely insurance investigator on his tail may be his undoing. Both versions recommended for their portrayal of strong heroines who must walk the tightrope of their moral codes.

Vampires, Witches, and Werewolves, Oh My!

Paranormal romance covers a wide range of tropes, from time travel to vampires to fairies to ghosts to magic and beyond. The fantasy elements provide for escapist fantasies beyond the everyday. Paranormal characters such as vampires and werewolves also enjoy a high level of popularity due to their appeal as alpha heroes and heroines. While the romance novel market seems to have reached the saturation point for paranormal, there is a shift in it toward the genre-crossing market of urban fantasies. Movies such as *Underworld* and books like Patricia Briggs' Mercy Thompson series are examples of this.

Bast, Anya, *Witch Fire* (2007) BK
A sacrifice is demanded by a demon. All that's needed is a rare Air Elemental witch, and the target is Mira Hoskins. Mira, orphaned as a baby, was raised by her aunt. Her

parents had been killed as part of the last sacrifice, and her aunt believed the only way to keep Mira safe was to hide the truth from her. Fire Elemental witch Jack McAllister rescues Mira in the middle of a kidnap attempt and must keep her out of the hands of those wanting to kill her. He can't seem to keep his own hands off of her. Mira's only chance at surviving is discovering and mastering her hidden self. With her background in erotic romance, Bast provides the strong story of a woman exploring a previously hidden part of her nature with a very spicy romance.

Black Dagger Brotherhood, J. R. Ward, *Dark Lover* **(2005) BK, CL**
Wrath, the Black Dagger Brotherhood's leader, is intent on vengeance for his long-dead parents, but promises a dying comrade he will look after the vampire's half-breed daughter. Beth Randall's world is turned upside down when the most gorgeous man she has ever met shows up in the middle of the night, making her think he's there to kill her. She's unprepared for the lust that grips the both of them and his revelation that she's really half-vampire. Ward's storytelling is widely considered to be addictive and usually evokes strong love/hate reactions in readers. *Dark Lover* is the first in a best-selling series that becomes less romance and more urban fantasy as it progresses.

Furumiya, Kazuko, *Bloody Kiss* **(2009) GN**
Kiyo has inherited her grandmother's house along with its two resident vampires, Kuroboshi and Alshu. Things get interesting when Kuroboshi decides to make Kiyo his bride.

Kurland, Lynn, *Stardust of Yesterday* **(1996) BK, SH, AP, CL**
Kendrick de Piaget has waited centuries for a Buchanan to sign over control of Seakirk Castle to him. So what if he's the ghost of a thirteenth-century warrior? He was cursed at the point of death by a witch to forever wander the halls of the castle, and Genevieve Buchanan of California is his last hope. Once Genevieve overcomes the surprise of inheriting a battalion of ghosts along with the castle, she finds Kendrick impossible to resist and loses her heart to him. A threat from his distant past is determined to have the final word and banish Kendrick from both the ghostly and Earthly realms forever. This book will greatly appeal to romance readers who want paranormal romance without the vampires and shape-shifters, those who like the bedroom door closed for the most part, and those who enjoy richly detailed plots.

Love at Stake, Kerrelyn Sparks, *Vamps and the City* **(2006) BK**
Darcy Newhart, show director at an all-vampire television network, brainstormed the best idea for a reality television show: "The Sexiest Man on Earth: Vampire vs. Human." Problem number one: she has to rig the show for the vampire. Problem number two: she finds the human contestant, Austin Erickson, is "dead" sexy. Problem number three: he's a vampire slayer. This second humorous entry in Sparks's Love at Stake series explores the tension of human and vampire relationships and the choice of turning from one to the other.

Singh, Nalini, *Slave to Sensation* **(2006) BK, SH, RS**
On the trail of a murderer, changeling Lucas Hunter must infiltrate the world of the Psy. Psy Sascha Duncan fears she's losing control of her mind. If she shows anything but the iciest control, it's incarceration in the "rehabilitation" center for her. Sascha is Lucas' entry into the Psy's world, but he may be her salvation by helping cut her loose. This is an intriguing alternative to the widely popular fantasy-based paranormal, and Singh crafts a fully-realized world for her strong characters.

Splash **(1984) MV, CL, SH**
This classic tale of lovers from two different worlds helped put both Tom Hanks and Daryl Hannah on the map. Allen Bauer (Hanks) thought he was done for after a boating accident, when a lovely mermaid (Hannah) saves him. When she appears on land to return his wallet, he must decide if this woman of his dreams is the real thing. This sweet romantic comedy provides some suspenseful moments, but makes the watcher believe in love that was meant to be.

Underworld **(2003) MV**
Selene (Kate Beckinsale) is an enforcer for the Vampires and is sent to find out why the Lycans—werewolves—have taken such an interest in lowly medical student Michael Corvin (Scott Speedman). She soon discovers that the Lycans see Corvin as their potential savior in the fight with the Vampires, as he carries the blood of the founding family of both the Lycans and Vampires. In her fight to save Michael from both her enemies and her friends, she discovers he is the one who may save her soul.

Fairy Tale and Mythology Retellings

Mythology has a rich tradition of stories of lovers. These enduring stories are often a writer's first introduction to the idea of romance. Fairy tales also have many tales of lovers populating their ranks. Through the years, this genre of fairy tale has moved from a set of cautionary yarns to almost-epic fables of love conquering all. Authors often cannot resist the lure of recreating these timeless narratives with their own twists.

Cast, P. C., *Goddess of the Rose* (2006) BK, SH
Mikki Empousai doesn't understand the family tradition of the secret blood sacrifice for their roses, but when she wakes up in a dream realm with the Beast from her favorite statue standing over her, she's sorry she ever indulged in the practice. By touching the statue with her bloody hand, she woke the Beast, the goddess Hecate's Guardian. He had been cursed to remain in the realm of the mortals until called forth by the High Priestess, the Empousa of Hecate. Mikki's not sure if she's ready to take on the mantle of the Empousa, and she's definitely not ready for the feelings the Guardian, who's haunted her dreams, inspires in her. Cast's lyrical use of language captivates readers.

Dark Hunters, Sherrilyn Kenyon, *Acheron* (2008) BK, AB, CL, UAB
If it were not for the many machinations of both Atlantean and Greek gods and goddesses, Acheron may have lived a life of pleasure instead of one of constant pain and betrayal. The leader of the Dark Hunters comes to terms with his past and discovers the woman meant to live by his side in Kenyon's magnum opus. Richly detailed, readers should be prepared to spend many hours with this tale. This is also a good suggestion for urban fantasy readers.

Ever After (1998) MV, AP, SH
A subversive retelling of the Cinderella fairy tale, Drew Barrymore stars in this movie that is lush but realistic to the time period. Angelica Huston and Dougray Scott costar.

Joyce, Lydia, *Voices of the Night* (2007) BK, SH
Charles Crossham, Lord Edgington has wagered that he can turn Maggie of King Street into a lady within a month's time. The streets aren't ready to give up Maggie, and it's a race to see who will claim her, the man ready to offer her the world on a

plate or the world she's fought hard to leave behind. Fans of *My Fair Lady* and *Pygmalion* will greatly appreciate this interpretation.

Kaufman, Donna, *The Cinderella Rules* (2004) BK

Darby Landon isn't quite Cinderella. At least she doesn't have to worry about wicked stepsisters and stepmothers. But she does have three fairy godmothers determined to make her over and present her to Prince Charming, Shane Morgan. Only there may well be another Prince Charming waiting in the wings, and the course of true love never runs smoothly. Kaufman's upbeat and comedic voice also appeals to fans of chick lit.

Yun, Mi-Kyung, *Bride of the Water God* (2007) GN

In order to end a drought, Soah has been sacrificed by her village to be the bride of the water god, Habaek. Habaek is suffering under a curse where during the day he appears to be a boy, but is returned to his adult form at night, which he hides from Soah. Soah must find her way through the world of the gods and goddess as the boy-god's human wife as she begins to fall in love with the darkly mysterious god, Miu (Habaek in adult form), at night.

GLBT Romance

Romance novels today aren't just about the love between a man and woman. Gay and lesbian couples figure more prominently in romances of their own, providing characters readers can relate to. And these are true romances, with the same appeals as any romance. The ending may not always be happy, but the love portrayed is very real. Just like more traditional novels, the plots and conflicts vary, the degree of sexuality ranges from sweet to steamy, and the quality of writing of some can be better than of others. Novels cover a range of subgenres, from historical to contemporary. Short collections are popular.

Kristin Ramsdell says it well in the "Gay and Lesbian Romance" chapter:

> "The gay or lesbian romance offers an alternative to heterosexual status quo—a love story that assumes the validity of the gay or lesbian lifestyle and proceeds from there. . . . These stories may also be of interest to heterosexuals who have an interest in the gay lifestyle. The likelihood of crossover readership is especially enhanced by books that contain both gay and straight characters and portray them all with realism, openness, and warmth."[17]

One decision point for libraries collecting gay and lesbian romance novels is where the items should be shelved. They fit within the romance collection, but will interested patrons browse there? It's up to librarians to provide many access points to make this collection findable. We need to make sure the titles are fully cataloged and provide bibliographies and displays to highlight them.

The Romance Writers of America has recently established a brand new chapter, the Rainbow Romance Writers, an LGBT special-interest group of authors.[18] Two of the organization's goals are:

- To promote excellence in gay, lesbian, bisexual, and transgender romances
- To be a resource to our members and others on writing and the publishing industry

The Web site http://www.rainbowromancewriters.com/ provides reviews, news, award-winners, and a lengthy, clickable list of GLBT publishers. This will be an excellent collection-development resource for librarians seeking current lesbian and gay romance titles.

Girolami, Lisa, *Love on Location* **(2008) BK**
Hollywood producer Kate is in a relationship with gorgeous movie star Hannah. On location in Florida, Kate meets Dawn, her beauteous art director. Florida isn't all that's steamy. Instant attraction leads to an instant triangle. Whom will Kate choose?

Herendeen, Ann, *Phyllida and the Brotherhood of Philander* **(2008) BK, AP**
This traditional Regency novel with a twist features Andrew Carrington, a handsome, wealthy, and decidedly gay nobleman. Andrew must remain scandal-free and must have an heir. Marriage is the answer, but not any woman will do. She must be well bred and of good family. By a stroke of luck, Andrew discovers and marries Phyllida Lewis. Phyllida accepts Andrew's lifestyle, and the two find their own form of passion. Recovering from the betrayal of his longtime lover, Andrew meets a new man, Matthew, who becomes part of the family. But both Phyllida and Andrew have secrets, and enemies out to blackmail them. What will triumph—ruin or fulfilling love?

La Cage aux Folles **(1978) MV**
La Cage aux Folles, and its remake, *Birdcage* (1996), feature a gay nightclub owner and his long-time drag queen partner. For the love of their son, who is bringing his fiancée and her straight-laced parents home to meet his folks, the couple pretends to be straight. Hysterical situations ensue, but the family love and acceptance of individuals is the core message.

Man of My Dreams **(2004) BK**
This anthology from Kensington Books, a publisher of many romance novels and similar heterosexual anthologies, contains four happy-ending romantic short stories: "Out of Bounds" by Dave Benbow; "Sex and the Single Rock Star" by Jon Jeffrey; "Spanish Eyes" by Ben Tyler; and "Bad Boy Dreams" by Sean Wolfe.

Merrick, Gordon, *The Lord Won't Mind* **(1970) BK, CL**
Charlie and Peter meet, falling instantly into lust, then love. Unable to commit fully to the relationship, Peter breaks up and finds a wife in Hattie. Peter moves on to another. The attraction remains, but the two stay apart until a shocking event reunites them. This novel features handsome characters and explicit sex scenes. Merrick wrote two other books in the trilogy—*One From the Gods* and *Forth Into Light*.

Queer As Folk **(2000–2005) TV** and *The L-Word* **(2004–2009) TV**
These two television series made their mark by detailing the everyday lives of their gay and lesbian characters.

Radclyffe, *The Lonely Hearts Club* **(2008) BK**
Liz, Brenda, and Candace are best friends, having shared secrets and breakups for almost 10 years, creating their own sort of family along the way. Now Liz is pregnant with her first child. And a chance meeting brings new love interest—Reilly, a physician. How will the dynamics of the group change as this new relationship grows?

Rule, Jane, *Desert of the Heart* **(1964) BK, MV, CL**
Professor Evelyn Hall leaves her unhappy marriage and goes to Reno, Nevada, for a divorce. She meets the free-spirited Ann. Can Evelyn break free from the conventions of her life to accept a new concept of love? *Desert Hearts* (1985), featuring Helen Shaver and Patricia Charbonneau, is the acclaimed film based on this book. The concept of the movie is less introspective than the novel, but the plot of two finding each other remains.

Scott & Scott, *Surf 'N' Turf: A Romentics Novel* **(2006) BK**
The book's blurb states, "Through both tragedy and comedy, these modern-day star-crossed lovers get ready to rumble for true love." Bookstore owner Robert comes to spend the summer at resort town of Seaside. He's just broken up with his work/life partner of 13 years and wants time to reevaluate his life. Southerner Blakely, too, has split from his boyfriend, and arrives in Seaside, where there are boys and jobs. They find each other and hot sex, but will the gangs ruling the town let them stay together?

Victor Victoria **(1982) MV, AP**
This hilarious musical comedy explores sexual identity. Set in 1930s Paris, the film introduces us to Victoria (Julie Andrews), whose singing career is going nowhere. Aided by her proudly gay friend, Toddy (Robert Preston), who poses as her lover, Victoria triumphs as nightclub sensation "Count Victor," thus becoming a woman pretending to be a man who is a female impersonator. But then Victoria meets gangster King Marchand (James Garner). The attraction is mutual. Can King deal with his feelings for a man? And will his bodyguard (Alex Karras) make a life revelation of his own? Love overcomes all in this uplifting film.

Warren, Patricia Nell, *The Front Runner* **(1974) BK, CL**
Harlan Brown, a college track coach, conceals the fact that he's gay so he doesn't lose his job. Billy, an openly gay runner on his team, has a shot at competing in the Olympics. Love grows between the two and they marry, relying on their strong relationship throughout Billy's quest to join the Olympic team. Their love is a triumph, in spite of tragedy. *Harlan's Race* is the sequel.

Characters

Characters play an important role in romance stories as readers frequently identify and empathize with the lead characters. Readers often have strong opinions on the types of characters they will or will not read; some readers love anachronistic historical heroines, and others can't stand stories that feature children as characters. As characters are such an important element, there are nearly as many character types as there are books. This next section highlights a few of the more popular and enduring characters.

From Lords and Ladies to Gypsies and Damsels in Distress

Historicals have long enjoyed a firm place in romance. Over the past 20 years, many have decried the decline of the historical romance in literature, but it is one of the more firmly entrenched subgenres. The resurgence of television and movie adaptations of Jane Austen's novels has helped to keep the historical setting prominent in the public's consciousness. The wide range of types of characters, in terms of societal function and the opportunities available to them, provides readers almost an unlimited choice of romantic fantasy.

A return to classic novels by authors such as Austen and the Brontë sisters is being fueled by a number of factors, including reissues of the original texts, reimaginings of the original story (*Pride and Prejudice and Zombies*), and tie-ins to popular series (*Wuthering Heights: Bella and Edward's Favorite Novel*).

In recent years, there has been an expansion of the historical genre in regard to time periods. For many years, the predominant time and location was Regency England. While this is still a popular sub-subgenre, Georgian and Victorian set novels are seeing a rise in popularity. Due to the typical publication schedule of books (generally two years from the time of contract offer to release, not necessarily including the time it takes to write the book), there may be an uptick of Tudor-set novels in the near future linked to the popularity of Showtime's TV series *The Tudors* starring Jonathan Rhys Meyers as King Henry VIII. As to location setting, England and the continent remain popular, but it is likely more exotic settings will filter into the subgenre. American historicals will probably remain a small section of the market with loyal readers unless there is a breakout novel using the location. American-set historical movies with a strong romantic plot are more likely to be popular than novels as *Titanic* remains the dominant box-office winner in the last 25 years, and, adjusted for inflation, *Gone With the Wind* is the movie with the largest box-office receipts.[19] The largest shift in historicals, however, is in the characters portrayed. The historical is no longer the purview of the high aristocracy. While there is still a strong interest in this population, there is a definite increase in the more common man and woman, as well as grittier issues facing those from all walks of life, such as Lisa Kleypas' inclusion of Gypsies as heroes in her recent Hathaway series and Sherry Thomas' selection of a cook as the heroine and a lawyer as the hero of *Delicious*, a Library Journal Best Book of 2008.

Bourne, Joanna, *The Spymaster's Lady* (2008) BK, CL, RS, SH, AP, AW
Annique Villiers is on the run from her French spymasters as they want her dead. She has known no other life beyond spying, growing up in revolutionary France with a father who was a revolution martyr and a mother known as one of the best spies in France. Sick of the slaughter she has witnessed over the years, she is on her way to England when she helps to liberate two English spies. Robert Grey, the British Head of Section, knows he has an invaluable asset in Annique and refuses to let her go. This is an instant classic due to the author's ear for language. It is set in early 1800s France and England.

Cornick, Nicola, *Deceived* (2006) BK, RS
Isabella never thought she'd face the threat of winding up in debtor's prison, nor did she imagine it would bring her face to face with the man she'd been forced to abandon at the altar 12 years before. Marcus Stockhaven is in Fleet incognito searching for information regarding a criminal mastermind. He has never been able to forget the beautiful Isabella and isn't about to let her slip through his fingers once more. The book is set in 1816 England. Reunited lovers and witty dialogue make this an entertaining read.

Inne, Lora, *The Dreamer: The Consequence of Nathan Hale, vol. 1* (2009) GN, YA, AP
Bea Whaley is a typical twenty-first century 17-year-old girl, with loyal friends, a teasing cousin, aspirations to become an actress, and a longtime killer crush on handsome Ben Cato. But when she dreams, she finds herself transported into the life of colonial officer Alan Warren and into the times of the American Revolutionary War. Which life is real? *The Dreamer* combines the best of romance, historical fiction, and attractive art.

James, Eloisa, *Duchess by Night* (2008) BK, SH, AP
A take-off of *Twelfth Night*, Harriet, Duchess of Berrow, attends a house party dressed as a man at the home of the scandalous Lord Strange. She is finally putting the suicide of her husband behind her and coming out of mourning. Looking at the

adventure as only a lark, she doesn't expect to fall in love with the mysterious Lord Strange or his lonely young daughter. The book is set in 1784 England. James creates richly layered characters in a time period not often seen in historicals.

Mori, Kaoru, *Emma* (2002) GN, YA
In a romanticized version of Victorian England, Emma is a maid in the household of a former governess. When one of the governess's former charges comes to visit, a young Mr. William Jones, sparks fly between them.

Tarr, Hope, *Enslaved* (2007) BK
Years ago, orphan Gavin Carmichael promised little Daisy Lake that he would forever protect her. When he is taken away from the orphanage by his grandfather, he is forced to leave behind the only friends he's ever known and the little girl who owns a piece of his heart. One night, when at an East End supper club with friends, he discovers that the enticing seductress on stage, one Delilah du Lac, star of Montmartre, is his little Daisy. When past and present collide, Gavin must reconcile himself to the woman Daisy has grown to be if he is to win her heart for good. Set in 1891 London and darkly sensuous, this will appeal to readers who like stories outside of the *haut ton*.

Thomas, Sherry, *Delicious* (2008) BK, RS, SH, UAB
To Stuart Somerset, one meal was the same as the next, until he inherited his late brother's cook, Verity Durant. She is as tempting as the food she serves up. Verity has been greatly burned by love in the past and isn't willing to lose her heart to a man with a bright and shining future in politics. The past has a way of returning, catching the both of them by surprise. This book is set in 1890s England and will appeal to those who enjoy richly detailed storytelling and liberal use of flashbacks.

It's All in the Game: Players and Agents
Susan Elizabeth Phillips has said at various appearances over the years that she was told she would never be able to sell a book set in the world of football. It was "common knowledge" that sports stars, along with rock stars, were unsellable in romance, as the fantasy of creating a lasting romance with that type of hero was too unrealistic. Phillips' Chicago Stars series of books has taken her to the *New York Times* bestsellers list a number of times. Phillips is not an isolated case, though. A number of authors have found success in mining characters from the world of sports. Harlequin, the world's largest publisher of romance, has a miniseries dedicated to portraying characters involved with NASCAR. The primary appeal of the sports player, or sports agent, is one of power. The sports player is at the peak of his or her physical fitness. The sports agent is one whose mental game must always be in top gear. The flipside to this is the exploration of what happens when that person is falling from grace and how he or she deals with the loss of power. While male athletes very much qualify for the title of "alpha hero," they are also unique in that athletes often have been training since childhood for their current positions and that formative mental and emotional development can present emotional conflict not easily explored with other character types. The world of professional sports is one few people inhabit, and participating in some way is a common fantasy for many.

Britton, Pamela, *To the Limit* (2007) BK, SH
Aerospace engineer Kristen McKenna has been offered what once was her dream job by her boss, who recently bought a racing team: design a better race car. Matthew

Knight knows he's got one of the best engineers on his team. Only they both seem to have a hard time remembering the line between boss and employee. Fans of NASCAR will appreciate a behind-the-scenes look at the sport, and non-fans will appreciate the depiction of a strong, highly intelligent heroine.

Chicago Stars, Susan Elizabeth Phillips, *Match Me If You Can* (2005) BK, AP, SH, CL, UAB
Matchmaker Annabelle Granger has truly met her match in celebrity sports agent Heath Champion. Heath has hired her to find him the perfect trophy wife. With every candidate Annabelle guides Heath's way, Heath comes to realize the woman of his dreams may very well be the woman in front of him. The attraction of opposites and Annabelle's non-conforming to ideal beauty enriches an entertaining story. Part of the loosely connected Chicago Stars series.

***Fever Pitch* (2005) MV, AP**
This very humorous, though loose, adaptation of Nick Hornby's *Fever Pitch* starring Jimmy Fallon and Drew Barrymore explores what it means to love twice, equally and deeply, and have to choose between those loves, even when you're the one who is forcing the choice. This fabulous and fun movie also unwittingly documented the Boston Red Sox's historic 2004 World Series season.

Gibson, Rachel, *See Jane Score* (2003) BK, CL, AP
Jane Alcott leads a secret life. During the day, she covers the exploits of Seattle's hockey team, the Chinooks. At night, she lets her alter ego of "Honey Pie" take over, creating scandalous stories that set tongues wagging. Luc Martineau is the Chinooks star goalie and often tells reporters where they can stick their questions. Before he knows it, a spunky girl reporter has gotten inside his defenses, and he's unsure quite how to get her out or if he even wants to. This is a fun read from one of the original stars of romantic comedies.

Jenkins, Beverly, *Deadly Sexy* (2007) BK, SH
When sports agent JT Blake is rescued on the side of the road by trucker Reese Anthony, she doesn't realize it's a role he's destined to repeat. JT's played hardball with the best in the business, but a shadowy enemy from her past is determined to make her pay. Reese's skills extend beyond the cab of a semi and the case he's covertly investigating places him squarely in JT's way. It's a place he's more than happy to occupy, even if JT isn't as thrilled. A strong female lead and taut suspense provide readers with a high-octane read.

***Jerry Maguire* (1996) MV, CL, AW**
A man who must reinvent himself after a dramatic revelation, Maguire (Tom Cruise) cannot lose his final star player (Cuba Gooding Jr.). It's with the faith of his secretary (Renee Zellweger) and her son (Jonathan Lipnicki) where he learns it's not the job that makes the man, but the man who makes the job. A remake of a 1941 movie, *Here Comes Mr. Jordan*, this is a perfect mix of romance and sports.

McCarthy, Erin, *Flat-Out Sexy* (2008) BK, AP, SH, RS
All NASCAR widow and academic Tamara Briggs wants out of her next relationship is a safe and steady partner who will help raise her two children. Instead she falls head over heels in lust with rookie driver Elec Monroe. With a family feud between his family and her deceased husband's, along with their six-year age difference, Tamara can't believe there's a future in store for them. It will take everything Elec has to convince her otherwise. A fast-paced, sexy read, this story realistically addresses the issues older women sometimes face when dating younger men.

New York Blades, Deirdre Martin, *Power Play* (2008) BK, AP, RS, CL
Soap star Monica Geary is desperate to retain her status as one of the divas of daytime TV, no matter the scheme. She's had to fake numerous love scenes over the years, so being caught kissing the hottest hockey player in town should be no big deal. When defenseman and number 40 on *People's* list of hottest bachelors Eric Mitchell joins the set for a cameo, he can't wait to get his hands on Monica, the woman whose exploits he's watched religiously for years. Soon, Monica's no longer acting, and Eric realizes that beauty is often accompanied by brains. Martin deftly fleshes out what could have been two stereotypical lead characters and delivers a story made all the more fun for its seemingly unbelievable situations.

White, Pat, *Got a Hold on You* (2003) BK
As the accountant for the family business, WHAK, Wrestling Heroes and Kings, Frankie McGee is roped by her uncle into stepping into the shoes of Tatiana the Tigress in order to help boost attendance. Not only does she attract the notice of the fans, but also of Black Jack Hudson, the current title belt holder and wannabe retiree. Black Jack thinks he's finally found the love of his life, but the league's prissy accountant isn't spilling the beans on Tatiana's identity. It's shaping up to be the throw-down of his life. This is a humorous read, especially for those who grew up watching both men's and ladies' wrestling.

African American Family and Friends

African American romances aren't usually just the story of the relationship, as romances are traditionally defined. While primarily character-driven, they frequently highlight other elements that are important in African American communities and that give the books depth. The heroine is often a strong professional woman who's made a success out of her life. Family and friends play an important part in the stories, just as they do in real life. Because of this, series are prevalent. Religion and faith are important in many of these books. The road to love is not always easy; usually there is an obstacle to overcome, or forgiveness to accept. The sexual element varies depending on the book and author. Interracial relationships are another recurring theme.

One unique appeal of this subgenre is that men can be presented in a positive light. Moreover, there are a number of male authors writing romantic tales, furthering their plots from the male point of view. Their books may not always be traditional romances, but men are presented as strong role models or men who are redeemed. Eric Jerome Dickey and the late E. Lynn Harris are two of the best-known authors. E. Lynn Harris was gay, and his books often featured gay main or secondary characters, sometimes on the down low.

African American literature today includes mainstream authors such as Terry McMillan and Toni Morrison, as well as gritty urban literature and romance. Sometimes it's hard to distinguish among them, as publisher marketing has targeted the community of their readers as a whole. These titles can all provide snippets or a full meal of traditional love stories, urban romance, or extremely spicy reads, depending on the author and the taste of the reader. Some are true romances; some are just romantic. While these different focuses probably appeal to different readerships, there are no statistics to confirm who the readers are and what and how much they read. It looks like this will soon change. According to Patrick Huguenin, writing for the *New York Daily News*, in his story "African American Romance Writers Come Into Their Own":

> Just before Christmas, the Book Industry Study Group, the organization that assigns genre codes used by publishers and booksellers, approved specific codes for African

American erotica, mystery, contemporary women's writing, faith-based writing, and "urban life."

This summer, Nielsen Bookscan, which monitors 70 percent of the sales data in the book world, will begin tracking African American-authored romances as a specific sub-segment of the romance genre.

The behind-the-scenes changes are a sign that the book business has caught on to the popularity of African American writing, and wants to keep up.[20]

There's been a significant increase in publishing houses promoting African American literature. Harlequin has the Kimani imprint, which produces several series, including Arabesque and Sepia. Genesis Press has Indigo. And Zane has her own publishing company, Strebor Books.

Beauty Shop (2005) MV, AP

Hairstylist Gina moves from Chicago to Atlanta to pursue her career. After an unsatisfying job with diva boss Jorge, she quits and manages to open her own salon, a comfy neighborhood place that attracts a variety of hairstylists and customers. It's not easy, but Gina finds success and love with African electrician Joe. Queen Latifah reprises her role in this sequel to *Barbershop 2: Back in Business*. Alicia Silverstone shines in a secondary role as a stylist. The characters are quirky, the situations are humorous and believable, and love triumphs. This is a feel-good movie immersed in the neighborhood.

Harris, E. Lynn, *Just Too Good To Be True* (2008) BK, UAB

While this is not a true romance in the happily-ever-after sense, all the characters in the book are driven by love. Carmyn, a successful beauty shop owner, loves her son Brady, a Heisman Trophy candidate, so she hides her past and denies her love for Sylvester. Barrett/ Raquel, a gorgeous con-woman who is trying to manipulate Brady into signing with a certain shady sports agent, loves him and hopes to make a life with him. Lowell, a professor unwisely attracted to one of his male students, mentors his godson Brady. Brady, because he loves his mother and it means so much to her, tries very hard to live up to his vow of celibacy. The plot is intricate and involves secrets, family, relationships, and friendship.

Jackson, Brenda, *Irresistible Forces* (2008) BK, AP, UAB

Successful businesswoman Taylor Steele wants a baby but not a husband. Moreover, she's picky. She doesn't want just anyone to be her baby daddy. She wants someone handsome, healthy, and wealthy. And Dominic Saxon fits the bill. One of her clients, he's part African American and part French. He doesn't want marriage, but he would like a child, and she's willing to share. The plan for the merger? Spend a weeklong "procreation vacation" in the Caribbean. Will their very hot retreat lead to a more lasting relationship?

Jenkins, Beverly, *Sexy/Dangerous* (2006) BK

Romantic suspense with rottweilers! The rottweilers belong to Max Blake, former marine and NIA agent, who takes the dogs with her everywhere as part of her team when on assignment. Her mission is to safeguard eccentric professor Dr. Adam Gary. Masquerading as his housekeeper, Max must keep Adam's prototype energy-producing invention from falling into the wrong hands. But she finds it harder to keep from falling into Adam's welcoming and passionate arms.

Madaris Friends and Family, Brenda Jackson, *Surrender* (2001) BK

Netherland "Nettie" Brooms is the proprietor of Sisters, a popular restaurant and gathering place for women in downtown Houston. An Army brat, Nettie has sworn never to get involved with a military man. But stunning Marine Colonel Ashton Sinclair, half African American and half Cherokee, has a vision that foretells their future together. She's stubborn, he's persistent, and along the way three other couples flirt with romance. Veteran author Jackson displays her skill at intertwining current tales with continuing characters, and a handy genealogy chart is included in the Kimani Press 2008 reissue. The Madaris family has become so popular that Jackson has created her own publishing company, Madaris Publishing, which will feature books based on secondary characters introduced in the Madaris books. And for the past several years, fans have been able to join together on the Madaris Family Reunion Cruise that Jackson sponsors.

Never Knew Love Like This Before **(2007) BK**
Publisher Urban Soul presents this anthology of three short stories by Maxine Thompson, Michelle McGriff, and Denise Campbell, focused around women living their lives and facing decisions. There are some sexy scenes, but the emphasis in this collection is on relationships.

Reed, Vashti Ann, *Trust In Love* **(2008) BK**
This appealing contemporary romance features Danita and Cullen, administrators of two charities vying against each other for a grant. Instant attraction is tempered by the need to compete for desperately needed funding. The tension of the romance frames the stories of the other characters. Danita works with seniors; Cullen provides hope for amputees. Cullen is a widower who is close to his mother-in-law. Family and personal obligations are at the core of this novel.

Sex Chronicles **(2008) TV**
In the fall of 2008 Cinemax Cable network premiered the 12-episode first season of *Sex Chronicles*, sexy vignettes based on two urban tales by Zane—*The Sex Chronicles: Shattering The Myth* and *Getting' Buck Wild: The Sex Chronicles 2*. Five friends find release from the day-to-day stresses of their lives and relationships by reading steamy stories published by Zane on her blog. Think of an even more erotic *Sex and the City* a la Zane. This series embodies that goal in a romantic and erotic way. Others agree; a second season of the television program will be produced. This is for mature audiences only.

Zane, *The Heat Seekers* **(2002) BK**
Zane's books are compelling, sensual reads. Word-of-mouth has increasingly brought patrons in to public libraries to just to check out her books. *Heat Seekers* starts with the voices of four young African American adults searching for a hot time. Galpals Tempest and Jenessa go clubbing, where they meet Geren and Devonté. Jenessa and playa Devonté hook up, while Tempest and Geren form a deeper bond. Tempest has a secret, one that's led her to work with pregnant teens. And when Jenessa discovers she's having a baby, Tempest must take her relationship with Geren to the next step of trust.

Bad Boys and Girls

The bad boy, or girl, from the wrong side of the tracks has an appeal that is hard to resist. They often live outside the boundaries of conventional society. There is a wildness to their psyches that the everyday heroine or hero wants to explore. A true antihero or -heroine is rare to come by in romance because they must be redeemable to the reader in some way. They may still be outside of society's boundaries, but they must be worthy of their mate and be willing to protect and love that person into the future. Generally, readers are more likely to find an atypical hero or heroine than the true antihero or -heroine.

Chase, Loretta, *Lord of Scoundrels* (1995) BK, AP, SH, CL
Sebastian Ballister, the Marquess of Dain, lives his life as he pleases, and he pleases a great deal. Miss Jessica Trent is determined to see her brother fall in line, and out of Dain's circle, so she can get on with her plans of opening an antiques shop. She has no use for the dissolute Dain, but he realizes she just may be his salvation. A forceful heroine and a devil-may-care hero create a highly charged story.

Goodman, Jo, *The Price of Desire* (2008) BK, AP, SH, RS
Griffin Wright-Jones, Viscount Breckenridge, runs one of the most notorious gambling halls in London. He's under suspicion of the murder of his wife, though he knows she's hiding from him somewhere. When Olivia Cole is offered to him as a marker for her brother's debt, he's reluctant to take possession of her, but she is the only thing of value her brother has to offer. Living outside of society's rules has hardened Griffin to the many vagaries of the upper class, but the unveiling of Olivia's secret past rocks even his cynical outlook as he tries to save her. Highly detailed storytelling gives readers much into which to sink their teeth.

Howard, Linda, *Death Angel* (2008) BK, AP, UAB
Drea Rousseau has cultivated the persona of the perfect mistress: vapid and beautiful. She wears the mask over her high intelligence very well, until her lover gifts her to his pet assassin Simon as payment for a job. His only reason for asking for a few hours alone with Drea was to see how badly her lover wanted him for this job. He must make a choice between his career and Drea when her lover changes the hit to Drea. On the run, Drea must choose between the lifestyle she constructed for herself or returning to the one she had been destined for as a child. Very dark and sensual, this book may appeal to those looking for an unconventional romance.

Langtry, Leslie, *Stand By Your Hitman* (2008) BK
Single mom and assassin Missi Bombay is stuck in Costa Rica on the set of a hit reality show. She's there to scope out her next target, but keeps getting distracted by her hot-as-the-dickens partner, Lex. Soon, it takes all of Missi's skills to survive the sabotaged challenges and convince Lex she isn't the one behind them. The story is humorous with a balanced mix of romance and mystery.

Metzger, Barbara, *The Hourglass* (2007) BK, SH, AP
Sir Coryn of Ardsley has six months to win his bet with the devil. The former minion of the Angel of Death is dropped into the aftermath of the Battle of Waterloo and fights his former compatriots with the help of a disgraced battlefield widow, Imogene Macklin. In his search to regain his humanity, Sir Coryn may be overlooking the key to it. Metzger, a past master of the Regency romance, delivers once more with this rich and engaging story.

Stuart, Anne, *Black Ice* (2005) BK, SH
Chloe Underwood gets roped by her roommate into translating an importers' business meeting in the French countryside. Unfortunately for linguistically talented Chloe, the importers are drug runners and they realize she understands more than for which they hired her. She's swept off the estate by the man ordered to kill her. Bastien Toussaint had thought his heart had iced over long ago, allowing him to do his many jobs

efficiently and with little emotion. Chloe warms him in a way he never expected, and his record of perfect service is about to go down the drain. Stuart delivers on her trademark inscrutable hero in this dark, taut, and suspenseful book.

Sugisake, Yukiru, *D. N. Angel* (2004) GN, YA
Daisuke Niwa has fallen in love. Unfortunately for him, this triggers a curse: the transformation into the master thief, Dark. To break the curse, Daisuke must have his love returned. As the object of his affections has fallen in love with Dark, this may be nearly impossible.

Alpha Hero

To many romance readers, an alpha hero is catnip. They can't get enough. Others can handle only so much before they start searching out a guy they're not likely to want to smother in his sleep. Very often these heroes are involved in law enforcement, the military, intelligence, or firefighting. There are also the alphas of the business world, CEOs. These professions tend to draw men with a take-charge attitude, high intelligence, and a strong sense of personal ethics. With the possible exception of CEOs and intelligence operatives, they are also relatively easy to portray as heroes as there is cultural goodwill already in place. There is a fine line between an alpha hero and a jerk, and readers are often vocal about characters who toe the line.

Emery, Lynn, *Tell Me Something Good* (2002) BK
CEO Noel St. Denis is used to getting what he wants, and what he wants now is art consultant Lyrissa Rideau. Lyrissa's got better things to worry about than keeping the well-known playboy's hands off of her, namely reclaiming a family heirloom that was stolen decades ago. It soon becomes apparent that she can't resist the sexy player's charm, but she's determined to show him how much fun being a one-woman man can be. This book is for readers who enjoy characters with strong family values as well as those who like reading about lovers overcoming perceived class differences.

Gerard, Cindy, *To the Edge* (2005) BK
After a lifetime of being surrounded by bodyguards, Jillian Kincaid refuses to submit to that lifestyle again. When she begins receiving death threats, her father goes behind her back and hires the services of Nolan Garrett, former military special operative. Nolan expects to receive trouble from a pampered princess, and instead finds a woman determined to take care of herself on her own terms. This story is fast-paced and suspenseful with well-developed, intelligent characters.

In Death, J. D. Robb, *Naked in Death* (1995) BK, CL, SH, AP, UAB
Lieutenant Eve Dallas is on the hunt to find a serial killer of prostitutes before he fulfills his promise of killing six of them. Each murder scene she comes across is bloodier and more violent than the last, and she knows while he may change his method, he'll never stop at just six. With each step in the investigation, she's led to power magnate Roarke. Eve knows she's being fed the information by the killer, but her gut instinct isn't going to be enough to clear Roarke in the eyes of her superiors, especially if they find out about her growing relationship with a suspect. Fiery, intelligent characters as well as a finely crafted mystery plot make this compelling; it is the first book in the series.

Kleypas, Lisa, *Someone to Watch Over Me* (1999) BK, AP
Rescued from the Thames, a woman is told she's one of London's most notorious courtesans, Vivien Duvall. Bow Street runner Grant Morgan is assigned to her protection,

but he can't get past the fact this woman, while looking like Vivien, acts nothing like the woman he knows. While trying to untangle what happened to put her in the Thames, the two of them give in to their growing attraction, knowing it may be the worst thing they could do. This is an intriguing look into the development of modern policing in England as well as characters outside of the norm.

Troubleshooters, Suzanne Brockmann, *The Unsung Hero* (2000) BK, CL, AP, SH, UAB
Once the town bad boy, Commander Tom Paoletti is back home on enforced medical leave. Going about his business, he spots a man he believes to be the terrorist he's been chasing for most of his Navy SEAL career. When his superiors write off his concerns as being caused by his head injury, he recruits his own counterterrorist team, including the girl he loved from afar in high school, Dr. Kelly Ashton. Told with flashbacks to a related World War II romance, this book kicked off Brockmann's highly successful Troubleshooters series. This story is for readers who prefer strong, detailed plots with multiple character storylines.

Real Women

The appeal of the "real" woman in romance is widespread. Readers want to have someone they can identify with in some way. If an author does his or her job correctly, he or she will create a heroine whom the reader can like. However, many heroines are explicitly or implicitly on the smaller end of the size scale. Even if they're not, they are often in a state of exceptional fitness. Readers read genre fiction for escapism, and don't necessarily want to read about the health issues often related to excess weight. But there is truth to the saying "big girls need love, too." The desire for "real" women is not restricted to larger women, but also includes those who do not fit the traditional ideal of beauty. In the visual media of movies and television, finding a heroine who is not of the thin variety is almost impossible. You are more likely to find an actress who possesses an unconventional type of beauty. What you will often find, no matter the media, is an exploration of the main character's sense of self and body acceptance and the idea that beauty is in the eye of the beholder.

Donovan, Susan, *He Loves Lucy* (2005) BK, SH, AP
Lucy Cunningham can't believe she's been roped into the latest marketing plan her firm has contracted. She's got one year to lose as much weight as she can with the guidance of her trainer, Theo Redmond. All this while checking in on TV, and trying not to drool over Theo, and resisting the lure of Milk Duds. When it becomes clear that Theo's interested in her too, is it because he really likes her or is it because she's getting thinner and thinner? This is for those who enjoy novels where the story is as much about the heroine learning to love herself as the hero.

***Head Over Heels* (2001) MV, AP**
Needing a place to live in New York, art restorer Amanda answers an ad only to find that it's the former closet of four aspiring runway models. They find her way of life just as fascinating as she finds theirs, and they all find the exercise-prone hottie across the way mouthwatering. With suspense elements reminiscent of *Rear Window* and heavy doses of humor, this is an underrated and entertaining movie.

Linz, Cathie, *Big Girls Don't Cry* (2007) BK, SH
Leena Riley expected never to return to her hometown again. If she absolutely had to, she expected to return as the cover model of a national magazine. Her agent has fired

her though, and the former plus-sized model is licking her wounds after being called "thunder thighs" by her last boyfriend. The person she least expects to fall for is her new boss Cole Flannigan, the town's vet, one of Pennsylvania's sexiest bachelors, and the boy she once knocked out on the playground for making fun of her. This is a breezy story of returning to your roots and accepting yourself as you are.

MacAlister, Katie, *The Corset Diaries* (2004) BK

Tessa Riordan can't believe she agreed to take over the role of the American heiress who marries a duke for a British reality television show featuring what life was like in 1879. Especially after she gets a look at the original person in the role, who is significantly smaller than Tessa's own voluptuous curves. But there is a $10,000 payment for appearing on the show. And it's only for four weeks. And the man playing the duke is extremely good looking. Told in the first person, this book is for those who enjoy older and larger heroines or those who may like the shows *Manor House*, *Colonial House*, and *Frontier House* on PBS.

The Matchmaker (1997) MV, SH, AP, AP

Marcy Tizard (Janeane Garofalo) is sent to Ireland by her boss, a Massachusetts senator seeking reelection, to search out his Irish ancestors so he can align himself more closely with the Kennedy legacy. She lands in the town of Ballinagra in the middle of a matchmaking festival. Trying to spend her time only on doing her job, she gets swept up in the town's enthusiasm for finding love. Sweet and savvy, this will especially appeal to fans of tales of fish out of water and movies like *Waking Ned Devine* for the scenery.

My Big Fat Greek Wedding (2002) MV, CL, AW, SH

Toula Portokalos (Nia Vardalos) decides she needs to make over her life, and meets the non-Greek Ian Miller (John Corbett) after she begins working in her aunt and uncle's travel agency. She knows Ian is the man for her, but can he survive her proudly Greek family? This ugly-duckling tale is full of both the humor and frustrations that come from dealing with large, close, and fiercely heritage-proud families.

Yagami, Chitose, *Fall in Love Like a Comic* (2004) GN

Rena Sakura navigates the trials and tribulations of high school while hiding a secret: she's a famous mangaka (manga artist). One of the most popular boys in her school finds out, though. In a bid to bring a more realistic sensibility to her stories, she asks him to be her boyfriend, never expecting to fall in love for real.

Second Time Around: Widows and Widowers

The hero or heroine as a widow or widower in romance is often contending with the ghost of their lover's previous spouse. In historicals, because marriages were often done for the advancement of social standing, estate holdings, or both, the widow or widower may have had little feeling one way or another for the previous spouse, but the deceased's family members may still be in the picture. Character development usually involves the surviving spouses needing to create a sense of closure on this phase of their lives before they can move on to a healthy relationship with a new love.

Dan in Real Life (2007) MV, SH

Newspaper columnist Dan Burns (Steve Carrell) is not sure how to deal with the trials of raising three girls without his late wife, despite being the expert on the topic in print. On a family vacation to his parents' cottage, he meets a bookstore clerk,

Marie (Juliet Binoche) and feels an instant attraction. Unfortunately for him, he discovers Marie has been dating his younger brother Mitch (Dane Cook) and will be spending the vacation with them. This low-key movie looks at how family dynamics effect the development of new romantic relationships.

Hoyt, Elizabeth, *To Taste Temptation* (2008) BK, AP, SH, RS

Lady Emeline Gordon is preparing to marry her childhood friend, Lord Vale, when an American colonist presumes upon his acquaintance with her deceased brother to hire her to present his sister to London society. As she gets to know Samuel Hartley better, she is torn between the society she grew up in and planned to raise her son in and a second chance at love. Artful descriptions, strong characterization, including a few realistically dealing with post-traumatic stress disorder (at that time unknown), and an intriguing premise will hook readers looking for a break from typical Regency-set historical romance.

Kelly, Carla, *Beau Crusoe* (2007) BK, SH, YA

Susannah Park has built a quiet life for herself and her son after the death of her husband. It's as quiet a life as she can manage living with her eccentric parents and bitter sister. James Trevenen is to receive an award from the Royal Society for his treatise on a unique species of crabs he studied while shipwrecked in the Pacific. Susannah is to guide James around London, and they begin to fall in love. James's past will not rest, and they must discover why he cannot remember what happened to the only other man who survived the sinking of their ship and the lifeboat drifting to the island from which James was rescued. This is a sweet romance with well-rounded, believable characters.

Michaels, Lynn, *Return Engagement* (2003) BK

At the age of 18, Lindsey West left the world of Hollywood celebrity to marry her childhood sweetheart. Seventeen years later, she's widowed and raising her son in the town where she grew up. Finally giving in to her sister's desire to stage a play at the regional theater, she is shocked to discover that her new costar is the man who rose to fame with her as her TV boyfriend. Noah Patrick knows the play is his last shot at putting his life back together, sober. Unfortunately for them, Lindsey's high-powered Hollywood agent of a mother is still pulling strings to get what she wants, even though all Lindsey and Noah seem to want is each other. Redemption in the wake of a seemingly failed life, and an appreciation of former love, makes this a sweet read.

Quinn, Julia, *When He Was Wicked* (2004) BK, UAB

Michael Stirling enjoys his life as a rake, but is ready to give it up the moment he catches sight of Francesca Bridgerton. Too bad for him, he meets her at the celebration dinner of her upcoming nuptials to his cousin. When his cousin dies two years later, Michael flees to India rather than being near a mourning and single Francesca. He finally returns to London, only to discover Francesca on the hunt for a new husband, and he's determined she not overlook him. These sympathetic characters fight their attraction in the belief that they're each dishonoring their deceased loved ones by pursuing a relationship before coming to realize they're both worthy of the other's love.

Uncommon Heroes, Dee Henderson, *True Devotion* (2000) BK, YA, AB

During a search-and-rescue operation, lifeguard Kelly Jacobs lets her guard fall with Lieutenant Joe Baker, her best friend and her deceased husband's former commander. They can't go back to being just friends, but can they deal with being more than friends? Especially when the killer of Kelly's husband has come to settle some scores? This is an action-packed romantic suspense and an examination of finding new love with an old friend with a strong Christian sensibility. This is the first in the Uncommon Heroes series.

Theme: The Many Ways of Love

Love has many guises. Sometimes it's a feeling, sometimes it's humorous, and sometimes it is love come again. Love can be intense; love can be sweet. There are many choices to fulfill your favorite romantic experience.

Romantic and Screwball Comedy

In the late-1990s and early-2000s, there was a boom in romantic comedy novels with the increase in single titles, the debut of the "cartoon" covers, and the creation of the Harlequin Flipside and Duets lines. The boom crashed in the mid-2000s, and Flipside and Duets closed their doors. The cartoon covers were not as prevalent. However, romantic comedy has survived as one of the staple niche markets of contemporary single titles. Comedy has had a place in the romance world for what seems like time immemorial. Almost all of Shakespeare's comedies revolve around the farce that relationships can be. Romance movies have been and are most typically romantic comedies. What this all means is that romantic comedy may be the easiest area of romance in which to provide integrated advisory services. However, librarians will find that readers' or viewers' senses of humor can be a minefield.

Cabot, Meg, *Boy Next Door* (2002) BK, SH, AW, UAB

Melissa Fuller really wants to write harder news stories than the Page 10 gossip column. When she discovers her neighbor knocked unconscious by an intruder, she thinks there's a story there, but her boss disagrees. She's taken over walking her neighbor's Great Dane until the woman's nephew returns to town. When he does, Melissa can't take her eyes off of him. John Trent is doing a favor for his best friend, Max, by impersonating Max until Max's aunt and Mel's neighbor wakes up from her coma. All he has to do is take care of the woman's dog and apartment and somehow ignore the good-looking Mel. Told in epistolary format using e-mail, this is a witty beach read.

Coupling (2000–2004) TV, CL, AP

Sometimes called the BBC's version of *Friends*, this raunchy and insightful series follows the evolution of the relationship of Steve Taylor (Jack Davenport) and Susan Walker (Sarah Alexander). Along for the ride is Steve's ex-girlfriend Jane Christie (Gina Bellman), Susan's ex-boyfriend Patrick Maitland (Ben Miles), Susan's best friend Sally Harper (Kate Isitt), who can't seem to decide if she wants to sleep with womanizer Patrick or not, and Steve's best friend Jeff Murdock (Richard Coyle), who has a very interesting take on women and relationships. This show is an honest look at how men and women view relationships and their development.

How I Met Your Mother (2005–) TV, AP, SH

This series primarily follows the romantic intrigues of architect Ted Mosby (Josh Radnor) as he searches New York City for the woman he wants to marry. The main supporting cast includes Ted's best friend, aspiring lawyer Marshall Eriksen (Jason Segel), his fiancée/wife and kindergarten art teacher Lily Aldrin (Alyson Hannigan), Ted's other best friend and womanizer Barney Stinson (Neil Patrick Harris), and Ted's girlfriend/ex-girlfriend and news reporter Robin Scherbatsky (Cobie Smulders). This show features self-aware characters who aren't afraid to go the distance for the ones they love.

How to Lose a Guy in 10 Days (2003) MV, SH

Andie (Kate Hudson) has bet her boss that if she can write an article on how to lose a guy in 10 days, she can write meatier reporting articles. Ben (Matthew McConaughey) has bet his two coworkers that he can make a woman fall in love with him in 10 days; if he wins, he gets the advertising account for which they're all competing. Ben's coworkers know about Andie and choose her as the woman he has to seduce. Sparks fly as the two match wits to win their respective bets. This movie is sharply funny in exploring the dynamics of how men and women interact while in the courting stages of a relationship.

Howard, Linda, *To Die For* (2005) BK, CL, SH, UAB, AP

Southern belle and former cheerleader Blair Mallory's life is going perfectly even if she sometimes misses male companionship. But other than that, and an irritating client that imitates how she does her hair and dresses, life is good. However, the client is shot to death outside of Blair's business, and the responding detective is Lieutenant Wyatt Bloodworth, a man who left Blair after three hot and heavy dates, saying she was high maintenance. This story, told in first person, involves a heroine who acknowledges the stereotypes of blonde former cheerleaders and uses them to her advantage.

Sweet Home Alabama (2002) MV, AP

Melanie Smooter (Reese Witherspoon) has met the man of her dreams, Andrew Hennings (Patrick Dempsey), and is getting ready to marry him. Only she still needs to divorce her childhood sweetheart, Jake Perry (Josh Lucas), who she left behind in Alabama. Rediscovering her roots might mean rediscovering love. Sweet and at times sarcastic, this is a fun movie about the rediscovery of lost love.

Thompson, Vicki Lewis, *Nerd in Shining Armor* (2003) BK, AW (Reading with Ripa)

Genevieve Terrence has been stranded on a remote Pacific island with her sexy boss, whom she'd been hoping to have a weekend alone with, and the company's nerdy computer programmer, Jackson Farley. Only her boss is an embezzling weasel and Jack's brains are coming in mighty handy for surviving the island. Opposites attract in this self-effacing and quick read.

Romantic, Not Romance

As we've expressed earlier, true romance novels focus on relationships and provide satisfying and optimistic endings. But there are many books that do not fit within this narrow definition that are equally enjoyed by romance readers. These are the "romantic" novels, which the Romance Writers of America defines as "fiction in which a romance plays a significant part in the story, but other themes or elements take the plot beyond the traditional romance boundaries."[21] Definitions in the *Oxford English Dictionary* shed additional light on the term "romantic." One, although given as a musical meaning, fits quite well for our purpose—"Characterized by the subordination of form to theme, and by imagination and passion."[22] The romantic novel may not have the technically correct form of the romance novel, but it has all the passion and imagination of love, along with a story. In these novels, the focus on the romance is secondary, but it's there, lurking under what's going on. And as long as there is a strong romance in the mix, the characters can display many other elements.

"Romantic" books are good stepping-stones for introducing non-romance readers to the genre as a whole. Men in particular might be attracted to these titles, as the stories are far more sweeping and intricate. While the love story is one of the plotlines, more intricate plots, strong characters, and well-detailed settings might capture and maintain their interest.

Allen, Sarah Addison, *Garden Spells* (2007) BK, UAB, AP, AW

Bascom, North Carolina, contains a strong-willed and prophetic apple tree. Its owners, the Waverleys, have always been viewed askance by the community because of their unusual magical gifts. Claire and Sydney Waverley, abandoned by their mother, view their hometown differently. Claire feels safe and has become a caterer, preparing dishes from special flowers and herbs. Sydney fled, but 10 years later returns to hide from an abusive relationship, bringing her own daughter, Bay. Can the sisters reconnect in spite of their family history? And can they let go of their pasts enough to let the men who love them into their lives? This novel will appeal to fans of magical realism, as that aspect is strong. Small town southern life, supporting characters with substance, and romantic relationships will also draw readers.

Bujold, Lois McMaster, *Shards of Honor* (1986) BK, CL, AP, UAB

Cordelia Naismith is a survey captain for the peaceful Beta colony when her landing party is driven off by mutinous Barrayaran soldiers and she is captured by their former leader, Aral Vorkosigan, also known as the Butcher of Komarr. As Aral and Cordelia trek through the wilderness, they come to understand each other and fall in love. After their respective home planets declare war, is there any chance for their relationship? Regency lovers may want to read *A Civil Campaign: A Comedy of Biology and Manners* (1999), which is about Aral and Cordelia's son Miles.

McEwan, Ian, *Atonement* (2001) BK, MV, AB

Atonement is not a love story—it is a story of requited but unfulfilled love. In 1935, young Briony Tallis witnesses a love encounter between her sister, Cecelia, and Robbie, the son of a family servant who has been mentored by Briony and Cecelia's father. Briony misunderstands what is happening and later accuses Robbie of a crime. Set against the backdrop of World War II, the book's theme of love and longing underscores all that happens. The historical elements are strong, as are the characters and Briony's need to express her regret and somehow atone for her actions. Keira Knightley and James McEvoy bring Cecelia and Robbie to life in the superbly imaged 2007 motion picture.

Mitchell, Margaret, *Gone With the Wind* (1936) BL, CL, MV, AP, UAB

Who can forget the tortured love of Rhett Butler for the oblivious Scarlet O'Hara? Sweeping stories of the American Civil war and the Reconstruction are interspersed between vignettes of hardship in the South. The characters and the Georgian atmosphere elevate *GWTW* far beyond the typical historical novel. While this isn't technically a romance, romance readers revere it as part of the genre. The iconic 1939 motion picture starring Clark Gable and Vivien Leigh delivered even more fans and remains a popular film today, particularly in the newer full-color versions.

Outlander, Gabaldon, Diana, *Outlander* (1991) BK, CL, AP, UAB

British nurse Claire Randall and her husband Frank take a second honeymoon in Inverness after the end of World War II. Exploring the countryside, Claire visits a stand of historic stones and is transported to eighteenth-century Scotland. Great confusion reigns on both sides, as Claire tries to orient herself and as those she meets are scandalized by her mode of dress and wonder if she's a spy with her British accent. Then Claire encounters Jamie, her enduring love. The tale begins, unfolding into complexity and building the sort of detailed world enjoyed by fantasy fans. *Outlander* has something for every reader, including six sequels. Fans of time travel, magic, historical fiction, erotic love scenes, the battle of Culloden, herbalism, and witchcraft will all discover satisfaction, as will readers interested in what happens happily ever after as the sequels cover more than 30 years of Claire's life.

Wittig, Laurel, *The Secret History of the Pink Carnation* (2005) BK, UAB, AP

This novel within a novel is the first of five sequential titles framed around the grad school exploits of Eloise Kelly as she tries to track down dissertation information about the Pink Carnation, a British spy who flourished during the 1789–1815 wars with France. Arriving in England on a shoestring budget, Eloise soon discovers a noble family hording a treasure trove of old letters and journals that might hold the clue to the identity of the elusive spy. The son of the house, the very attractive Colin, is skeptical of Eloise's purpose. But as Eloise delves further and further into her primary documents, the nineteenth century comes to life. Readers entranced by spies, Napoleonic wars, the Regency period, and action will enjoy the historical setting of this series, as will fans who like romance that happens when opposites attract.

Gentle Love

Romance novels can take many roads on the trip to their happy endings. Not everyone wants to travel the same path. There is a large readership looking for softer, gentler love stories, with a minimum or lack of explicit sex or violence. Some prefer novels with an inspirational element. They want their heroes and heroines to have character, or to star in meaningful stories. The Christian fiction market is particularly robust. The February 23, 2009, online edition of *Publisher's Weekly* notes that, "In recent years, the market for Christian fiction has been so successfully cultivated by a handful of evangelical Christian publishers, such as Nelson, Tyndale, Bethany House, Zondervan, and Barbour, that even large, otherwise secular houses have formed their own Christian imprints"[23].

Annie's People, Beverly Lewis, *The Englisher* (2006) BK, UAB

In this second of Lewis' popular modern Amish series, Annie Zook has given up her art as she promised her father. But when handsome Ben Martin moves to town, Annie discovers a mutual attraction. Is there a future for them? Or will secrets and Annie's heritage intervene?

Browne, Hester, *The Little Lady Agency* (2005) BK

Hilarity abounds in this chick lit romance, the first of a series. Melissa Romney-Jones is a perfectly nice British girl. She just hasn't been successful at doing anything significant. This annoys her bizarre upper-middle-class family, especially since her father is a member of Parliament. But then Melissa discovers a niche—she can use her social skills to help others who aren't quite so adept at life—clueless bachelors! She helps them shop, prepare for social engagements, buy gifts, goes with them to important functions as an appropriate companion, and does almost everything a wife might. To keep from embarrassing her family, who might get the wrong idea, Melissa adopts the sobriquet of "Honey" and dons an expensive blonde wig to match. All is going well until Honey meets American businessman client Jonathan Riley, but Melissa is the one who falls for him. Innuendos, but any action is offscreen.

Circle of Friends (1990) BK (1995) MV, AP, AB

Circle of Friends by Maeve Binchy was made into a delightful film starring Minnie Driver and Chris O'Donnell. Set in 1950s Dublin, the tale introduces us to Benny Hogan, who's heading off to college. Benny falls in love with Jack Foley. But he disappoints her when he's trapped into an engagement with one of Benny's friends, a girl who wasn't as good as she should have been. This charming story is well told, tasteful given the central dilemma, and has a happy ending with a moral.

Doyle, Marissa, *Bewitching Season* (2008) BK, YA

It's 1837, and identical twins Persephone and Penelope Leland are excited—and apprehensive—that they're soon going to London for their social debut. The two can hardly wait to meet Princess Victoria, as they share her birthday. But Persy and Pen have a secret—they can perform magic—a heritage that women in their family have shared before them. Persy is attracted to a handsome neighbor, Lochinvar, but must conceal her powers. When Persy and Pen's governess Ally disappears, the twins intertwine their social season with the search to find her. While marketed to teens, the romance and social milieu are strongly reminiscent of Regency and other romances detailing the British upper class that fans of gentle reads enjoy. There's just a little magic thrown it.

Henderson, Dee, *Danger in the Shadows* (1999) BK, AB

Sara Walsh is a respected author. But as a child, she was victim of a kidnapping case in which her twin died. The kidnapper is still out there waiting to kill Sara, forcing FBI protection. Fate—a stalled elevator—introduces Sara to Adam Black. As their relationship intensifies, it's harder and harder for Sara to hide, for Adam is a professional athlete with a very high profile. Will Sara keep running, and will Adam sacrifice his career to be by her side? Or will she take a stand? This romantic suspense novel is a prequel, and introduces one of the characters in the first O'Malley series book, *The Negotiator*. The whole series is a complete blend of worthy characters, suspense, and belief.

Love Comes Softly (2004–2009) MV, BK, UAB

The Hallmark channel filmed and aired the first six of Janette Oke's popular western Christian fiction series. These are now available on DVD. The last two films in the series were released in April 2009. The series covers the lives of several generations of pioneers on the prairie. The first movie, starring Katherine Heigl, introduces us to the family matriarch. Marty, widowed due to an accident, is forced into a marriage of convenience with Clark, a widower who has a young daughter. These films will thrill fans of the books and will appeal to anyone who enjoys simple stories of faith and characters who grow together.

Shaffer, Mary Ann, and Annie Barrows, *The Guernsey Literary and Potato Peel Pie Society* (2008) BK, UAB, AP

This charming romance unfolds entirely in letters. It's 1946, and Juliet Ashton, an English writer who covered the lighter side of World War II, wants to turn to a more serious topic for her next book. One day she receives a letter from Dawsey Adams, a man who lived through the German occupation on the island of Guernsey. Thus begins Juliet's fascination with the isle, its complex residents, tragedies the war created, and the "book club" started to hide a live pig from the Germans—the Guernsey Literary and Potato Peel Pie Society.

Wick, Lori, *Bamboo and Lace* (2001) BK, AB

Having spent most of her life in a remote Asian country with her strict missionary father, Lily Walsh is overwhelmed by vast new experiences awaiting her when she visits her brother Jeff in Oahu. Called away unexpectedly, Jeff entrusts Lily to the care of his best friend Gabe Kapaia and Gabe's extended family. Can sheltered Lily overcome her upbringing and find true love without shaming her father's honor?

Erotica

Erotica, while closely tied to romance, has very fine distinctions from its "sister" genre. It is becoming harder to distinguish the two with the growing popularity of the erotic romance subgenre. The main element to keep in mind when trying to distinguish between the three is the focus of the story. Romance features the development of a romantic relationship and the positive resolution of such. Erotic romance also focuses on the development of the romantic relationship, but the graphic depiction of the sexual relationship is used to highlight the arc of the romantic one. The focus in erotica is primarily on how the main character's sexual life impacts his or her world and is used to highlight the main character's development through the story.

Review sources can be hard to use, especially as erotica is a highly personalized form of storytelling. What one reader connects with may turn off the next. Erotica and erotic romance are currently undergoing an explosion of growth, primarily thanks to the e-book and online bookstore markets. Traditional publishers have also embraced the genres; however, they have decreased production since the initial, enthusiastic entrance into the market. Erotica is generally not accepted in wide-release films and rarely receives the popularly acceptable R-rating due to the sexual content. Advising in this area can also be a minefield due to the conflation of erotic fiction and erotic movies with pornography. At the same time, due to individual sensibilities, one person's erotica will be another's pornography.

Da Costa, Portia, *Gothic Blue* (1996) BK

Trapped by a broken-down car at a remote, seemingly abandoned priory, Belinda Seward and Johnathan Sumner take shelter inside. They meet the owner of the priory, a nobleman who seems to be of a different era. Soon the atmosphere of the priory affects them and they explore their sexual limits. This is an atmospheric, sensual adventure with a paranormal twist, especially for those who like Victoria Holt and Mary Stewart.

Hart, Megan, *Broken* (2007) BK, AP, AB

Sadie meets Joe for lunch once a week and he spins tales of his sexual exploits for her. Sadie lets herself imagine what it would be like to be each woman Joe describes. It is her most consistent sexual outlet since her husband Adam was paralyzed from the neck down in a skiing accident. The longer she meets with Joe, though, the harder she tries to convince herself they're only friends. This is a journey through the sexual expression of relationships and how the ability, or not, to communicate in that way affects relationships.

Kozak, P. F., *Sins and Secrets* **(2006) BK**

In late-Victorian England, Pamela Kingston has decided she is done waiting for her guardian to recognize her as a grown woman. Finally home from school, she chooses to seduce him. How she goes about it is up to the reader. This is an adult version of the Choose Your Adventure books.

Secretary **(2002) MV, AW, CL**

Lee Holloway (Maggie Gyllenhall) is released from a mental hospital after a suicide attempt. Her first job interview is with lawyer E. Edward Grey (James Spader), who hires her ostensibly for her phenomenal keyboarding abilities. It is during the interview that both begin to realize the other is the one who can satisfy their complementary sexual needs. A highly atmospheric exploration of the psychology behind sadomasochism, this film won a special jury prize at its 2002 Sundance film festival debut. Atmospheric and fine acting help create an emotionally resonant film.

Secrets, *Red Sage Publishing* **(1995–) BK**

Secrets is a series of anthologies from one of the first publishers to focus on the genre of erotic romance. Each anthology contains four to six stories and covers every romance subgenre, from contemporary to historical to paranormal. Many authors such as MaryJanice Davidson and Angela Knight got their publishing start in these anthologies. This is a perfect series for those wanting to explore the range of erotic romance stories.

Walker, Saskia, *Double Dare* **(2006) BK, AP**

Abby Douglas takes no prisoners in her life and enjoys her reputation as a ballbuster. When she meets the sexy Zac Bordino, something about him intrigues her and she tells him she's a receptionist instead of the investment advisor she is. Zac discovers Abby is not who she says she is and must decide whether to reveal the secrets he's kept from her. A relationship they both believed to be only sexual quickly becomes deeper, and each must deal with their perceptions of the other. This book features strong-willed characters with sizzling chemistry and is especially for those who prefer a British voice.

Making Connections

Romance for Mystery Readers

The most obvious subgenre from which to draw suggestions for mystery readers is that of romantic suspense. There is also a grey area of blending of the genres that a number of authors seem to inhabit, most notably Tami Hoag, Sandra Brown, Kay Hooper, Iris Johansen, and J. D. Robb. All of these authors received their starts rooted firmly in the romance genre but have drifted to the mystery end of the spectrum as their careers have grown. With many mysteries containing romantic entanglement plotlines, there is most likely already an acceptance of the romance genre with readers.

Dodd, Christina, *Thigh High* **(2008) BK**

Recruited by the mysterious Jeremiah McNaught to help with his investigation of bank robberies, straitlaced Nessa Dahl revels in an adventurous side she'd feared to let loose until she finds out he believes she's involved in the crime. It becomes a race to prove her innocence and save herself from heartbreak. This book is for those who enjoy heroines who are dropped into unexpected situations and need to rely on their wits and friends to help them.

Jackson, Lisa, *Twice Kissed* **(1998) BK, SH**
To search for her missing twin, Maggie McCrae takes on her identity and discovers a dark side she hadn't known existed. Hidden family secrets and betrayals meet her every move, and the man she once loved will either be her salvation or her damnation. The story is dark and menacing and for those who enjoy emotional stories and characters overcoming trust issues in a high-stakes environment.

Lowell, Heather, *No Escape* **(2004) BK, SH**
Prosecutor Kelly Martin has taken the word of a teenage runaway and begins court proceedings that could have some very nasty results. When her star witness disappears into the Los Angeles underworld, she calls on the help of private investigator Luke Novak. This is a fast-paced suspense story with strong characters.

Peterson, Jenna, *Seduction is Forever* **(2007) BK**
Part of a secret cadre of lady spies, Emily Redgrave is given her next assignment after almost meeting her maker at the hands of an infamous assassin. She is to guard Grant Ashbury. Unknown to her, he has his own orders: guard her with his life. It's a task he relishes. This is the final in a trilogy, but all can be read alone. Described by the author as *Charlie's Angels* in Regency England, this book is for those who like reading about secret agents who must prove themselves worthy of the work.

Romance for Science Fiction Readers

In the past, readers of science fiction were not likely to find romance novels that would appeal to their genre sensibilities. The examples of science fiction romance were few and far between. Often, the closest approximation they could achieve were time-travel romances and, as the modes of time travel usually were not scientifically based, those novels still may have fallen short. With Susan Grant's RITA award-winning novel *Contact*, science fiction romance began to break into the ranks of established subgenres. The subgenre continues to grow and evolve as more and more readers read across genres.

2176, Kathleen Nance, *Day of Fire* **(2004) BK, AP**
In the post-apocalyptic year of 2176, Canadian mountie Day Daniels must partner with an enigmatic government agent in her quest to uncover the source behind treasonous broadcasts and a possible new epidemic. Canada has survived and thrived since it closed itself off from the rest of the infected world more than 100 years ago. The threat to her country is just as treacherous as the threat to Day's heart. This futuristic suspense explores the threat of biological warfare and is the second of part of the five-book 2176 series by Susan Grant, Patti O'Shea, and Liz Maverick.

CLAMP, *Chobits* **(2002) GN**
Chobits is a world where humanoid computers, known as persocoms, interact with their masters, often resulting in the formation of romantic entanglements.

Grant, Susan, *Contact* **(2002) BK, AW, SH**
Flying a 747 over the Pacific, pilot Jordan Cady is unnerved when what appears to be a storm on the radar materializes before the plane, swallowing it whole. Moments after landing somewhere, the captain suffers a heart attack and dies, leaving Jordan in charge of

the fate of almost 300 people in what turns out to be an alien abduction. Surviving their new circumstances, the passengers and crew rise to the occasion, and Jordan finds her heart slowly stolen by the alien commander, Kào. This is for fans of first-contact stories.

Sams, Candace, *Electra Galaxy's Mr. Interstellar Feller* (2008) BK

Policewoman Sagan Carter is prepared for the chaos that is an intergalactic beauty pageant. What she isn't prepared for is being the liaison to an extremely good-looking undercover alien investigator. Sparks fly between them, and it's a race to find the alien arms smugglers before Captain Keir Trask has to answer the final interview question in this humorous tale of interplanetary politics.

Sinclair, Linnea, *An Accidental Goddess* (2005) BK, SH

Put into stasis more than 300 years ago, Gillaine Davré wakes up to find herself anointed as a goddess. Admiral Mack Makarian believes the unknown woman to be a smuggler rather than the goddess his entire space center, including himself, worships. When an enemy from her past threatens her home once more, Gillaine must rise to the power accorded to her. This is for fans of the space opera subgenre of science fiction.

Romance for Fantasy Readers

With the growing convergence of genres and genre blending, many fantasy readers are likely to find a romance that speaks to their personal tastes. A lot of romance authors are also fans of the fantasy genre and find ways to incorporate elements into their romance novels. Fantasy readers can find nearly everything they look for in fantasies in fantasy romances, including elves, quests, magic, faeries, time travels, dragons, and more. An interesting convergence is the development of the urban fantasy subgenre. A section of it has great appeal to romance readers despite not necessarily being romances. This is due to the growth of the paranormal romance genre. Some people may prefer to call this newish section paranormal fantasy rather than urban fantasy to distinguish it between romance genre-influenced novels from the tradition of urban fantasy made popular by Emma Bull and Charles de Lint.

Cooke, Deborah, *Kiss of Fire* (2008) BK

Attacked on her way home from her job at her aunt's New Age bookstore, Sara Keegan can't believe her eyes when her rescuer turns out to be a dragon. Quinn Tyrrell has lived a life of anonymity for the last few centuries, but he knew his time of mating had finally come and he would need to protect his mate from those who would use her, well-intentioned and not. This is for fans of secret societies of shape-shifters or dragons in general.

Galenorn, Yasmine, *Witchling* (2006) BK, UAB

Three half-fairy, half-human sisters have been sent to Earth to act as operatives for the Otherworld Intelligence Agency (OIA). When one of their fellow operatives, a giant, is found murdered, they team up with a human detective to find out who is attacking OIA agents. Told in the first person, this book is for fans of lightly voiced urban fantasy such as Kim Harrison's Rachel Morgan series.

Gleason, Colleen, *The Rest Falls Away* (2007) BK, RS

In the ballrooms and streets of Victorian England, vampires stalk the humans. Called to take on her family's legacy of slaying, debutante Victoria Gardella Grantworth must choose between it and her burgeoning love with London's prime catch of the season, the Marquess of Rockley. Urban fantasy tropes in this book's historical setting.

Liu, Marjorie, M., *The Iron Hunt* **(2008) BK, RS, SH, AB**
Maxine Kiss lives with a legacy passed from mother to daughter. She was born to hunt demons, and demons live on her skin in the form of tattoos. She's got the itch to leave Seattle, partially because a man is breaking through her defenses, making her vulnerable. Before she can run, however, the fight comes to her. Told in the first person, this dark fantasy tone combines with classic urban fantasy.

Moning, Karen Marie, *Bloodfever* **(2007) BK, SH, UAB**
MacKayla Lane is on a quest to discover a book for which her sister died. If she doesn't find it, the curtain between that of the Fae and human worlds will be forever torn, to the detriment of humans. Helping her in her quest are two men, one human and one Fae. Mac will need to discover each man's motive if she is to survive. Told in first person, this book is for those looking to explore the urban fantasy subgenre.

Wilson, C. L., *Lord of the Fading Lands* **(2007) BK, RS, UAB**
The first in the Tairen Soul quadrology, Rain Tairen Soul, King of the Fey, has arrived in the city-state of Celieria looking for his true mate. He finds her in Elly-setta Baristani, the daughter of a woodcarver. The ancient Mage wars are threatening to erupt once more, and Ellie discovers she is not only the future queen of the Fey, but also the key to ending the wars once and for all. This book would be especially appealing to fans of traditional high fantasy.

Romance for Western Readers

The western is a genre that offers truly American settings and characters or events recognizable as part of our heritage. The western blends well with romance because they share similar archetypes. The strong, male knight-like cowboy meets the equally strong, independent woman, and the two forge a life together in the face of adversity. Or not, if the cowboy must ride off alone into the distance. But the love is there. Because the blend between the two genres is already in place, readers of traditional westerns might very well enjoy stories with a western setting that just happen to be marketed as romance. The love element might be a little more prevalent, but much of the action and storylines are just as satisfying.

The Big Country (1958) MV, AP
Gregory Peck stars in this William Wyler action film as James McKay, a retired sea captain come to join his fiancée Patricia (Carroll Baker) on her father's enormous ranch. Upon arrival, he discovers that his future father-in-law is embroiled in a range war over water rights. Julie (Jean Simmons), a schoolteacher, is caught in the middle of the fight. She owns the Big Muddy, a ranch desired by both sides, as it is the only source of water. Julie sells the Big Muddy to McKay, a neutral party. While the movie deals with feuds, what desperate men will do, and personal honor, the romantic element shines through. McKay loves his fiancée, but is attracted to Julie. Foreman Steve (Charlton Heston) loves Patricia and cannot understand her attraction to James. The swelling movie score by Jerome Moross and the spectacular scenery help make this a truly exceptional western.

Garlock, Dorothy, *Train from Marietta* **(2007) BK**
In the deepest depression of the 1930s, rich society girl Kate Tyler fulfills her dream to become a nurse and make a difference. She heads west by train to a California hospital. Along the way, she's kidnapped because her father's business partner needs the

ransom money. Rancher/skilled tracker Tate Castle, a fellow train traveler, answers the call to retrieve the attractive blonde. Finding Kate is easy, but the escape through the wilderness and the bonding together against the villains create the true story.

Gentry, Georgina, *To Seduce A Texan* (2009) BK, AP

It's Civil War days in Kansas, and five Texas rebels are on a mission to rob a bank and gain much-needed funds for the confederates. Their plans are stymied and the fallback plan is to kidnap the banker's daughter and hold her for ransom. Little do they know that Rosemary is the greedy banker's stepchild, and he'd be overjoyed for her to disappear. Rosemary isn't the typical western heroine. She's clumsy and "plus-sized," with a tendency to daydream. Sergeant Waco has a dilemma—can he fight off the powerful attraction developing between him and Rosemary and at the same time obtain the money he and his men need? Well-drawn characters, an unusual plot, and humor and action all blend to make this an excellent choice for western lovers and romantics alike. If this tale is intriguing, and you like extended series, check out others by Gentry. All of her books connect in some way through their characters.

Greenwood, Leigh, *Texas Tender* (2007) BK

Idalou's one chance to save her failing ranch is to sell her bull. But he's gone missing— a neighbor has hidden it in hopes that Idalou will be forced into bankruptcy. Extraordinarily handsome Will Haskins discovers that Idalou is far more appealing than the bull he was sent to purchase. Will his Texas visit turn into a courtship instead? Leigh Greenwood, one of the few male romance writers, provides a tale with complex characters and a growing relationship.

Kelton, Elmer, *The Pumpkin Rollers* (1996) BK, UAB

Trey McLean is the hero of this traditional western coming-of-age story. Leaving the family homestead, he heads west to learn the cattle trade. Along the way, he meets farm girl Sarah Stark. Sarah follows Trey; they marry young, but with much love. Together, the two grow up, face adversity on the frontier, and make a life for themselves.

<u>Only</u>, Elizabeth Lowell, *Only You* (1992) BK, UAB

Colorado, 1867: Eve bets herself as collateral in a poker game. Besides seeking revenge against the killer at the table, she needs the money. But the wrong man wins the hand—and the girl. When Eve takes off with the winnings, Matt goes after her to claim his prize. Together, the two set off on a steamy, dangerous adventure in search of a treasure in gold. This is the third book in Lowell's Only series.

Outsider (2002) TV, BK

Widow Rebecca (Naomi Watts), a member of an Amish-type religious sect, nurses a wounded gunslinger (Tim Daly) back to health after he's been shot. Will she give in to the attraction she feels for him and risk being ostracized by her friends and family? This is based on the novel by Penelope Williamson.

<u>Whispering Mountain</u>, Jodi Thomas, *Texas Rain* (2006) BK

Former Texas Ranger Travis McMurray is intrigued by green-eyed Rainey Adams even though she's stolen his horse. Rainey notices the tall stranger and wishes it were another time or place—he'd be a man worth knowing. But she can't stay. She's taken well-earned money and is fleeing a strict, vengeful father who's arranged an inconvenient marriage. Family is important in this tale, which focuses more on character than violent action. Will the hero get his girl in the end? Read this first in the Whispering Mountain series and find out.

Romance for Men

We librarians are aware that men do read romance and that this is a trend that's increasing. We mentioned earlier the two Romance Writers of America studies that confirm this suspicion.

But very few of us know men who admit to reading romance, much less ones who ask for suggestions. While there are male authors who write romance, very few, if any, traditional romances are specifically written for and marketed to men. (Gay romance and erotic romance for men is much more prominent, including publishers such as Alyson Books and Romentics.)

Romance reference interviews can be tricky, and with male patrons could be even more so. This certainly is an area in which librarians can confidently recommend books that are romantic, but aren't specifically written as romances. Luckily, many mainstream and genre novels contain strong romantic elements that will satisfy. One useful strategy is to find out the type of book the male reader is looking for and connect him with an author of that type who features romance in his plot. Once you do the usual round of questioning and have a comfortable give and take going with the patron, you can ask what sort of plot dynamic he enjoys—straight action, one that focuses on a relationship, or one with colleagues working together. This can give some clues as to how much romance, if any, the patron is looking for. The answer might also provide an idea of the level of sensuality acceptable.

Crusie, Jennifer, and Bob Mayer, *Agnes and the Hitman* **(2007) BK, AP, UAB**
Agnes is a cook with an anger-management problem and one heck of a frying-pan swing. Shane is a hitman. They come together in South Carolina in an improbable tangle of quirky characters, weddings, hot sex, and 5 million missing bucks. Black humor and romance blend together here in a satisfying collaboration of authors.

Donati, Sara, *Into the Wilderness* **(1998) BK, AB**
In the late 1700s, spinster Elizabeth Middleton joins her father in the remote frontier of New York, leaving her comfortable home in England to teach school. Her father has other plans—a timely betrothal to the local doctor would solve his financial woes. But Elizabeth is drawn to frontiersman Nathaniel Bonner, friend of the Mohawk, and son of Hawkeye and Cora, first introduced in James Fenimore Cooper's *The Last of the Mohicans*.

***Last of the Mohicans* (1992) MV, BK, AP, UAB**
James Fenimore Cooper's wordy tale of the French-Indian wars in the eighteenth century translates well into film in this version. Hawkeye, adopted by the Mohican tribe as an orphan, is a crack shot and strong frontiersman. Against the backdrop of the war, a luminous love story of mutual attraction between Hawkeye and the colonel's daughter Cora Monro unfolds. Male viewers will enjoy the tale, the action, and the beautiful North Carolina scenery. The rest of us will listen to the haunting musical score and remember why this is the most romantic movie ever made—"Stay alive. I WILL find you." Daniel Day-Lewis and Madeleine Stowe are the perfect Hawkeye and Cora.

McCaig, Donald, *Rhett Butler's People* **(2007) BK, UAB**
Picture the classic American historical novel, told from the man's point of view, highlighting characters on his side of the tale. Rhett is the real romantic hero in this story, loving Scarlett intensely. "Scarlett O'Hara was pure yearning. She and he were two of a kind, but she didn't know it and she never would." Rhett forges his own way after the war, and strives to find a way he and Scarlett can be together.

Niffenegger, Audrey, *The Time Traveler's Wife* **(2003) BK, MV, UAB**
Librarian Henry suffers from an unusual "disease"; he is an unwilling time traveler. Henry loves his wife Clare, but his unpredictable trips complicate his marriage. True romance can survive—Henry and Clare prove it. A motion picture version of this film was released in summer 2009.

Phillips, Susan Elizabeth, *Natural Born Charmer* **(2007) BK, UAB, AP**
How often do you see a girl walking out in the middle of nowhere and dressed in a beaver costume? Not all that often, which is why quarterback Dean Robillard stops and offers a ride to Blue Bailey. Dean is rich, famous, and a chick magnet. Blue is broke, stranded, and dumped by her latest boyfriend. Somehow, Blue winds up with a gig decorating Dean's Tennessee farmhouse. Opposites attract, but in a quite delightful way.

Conclusion

Romance novels and their readers have suffered wrongfully from negative opinion for years. Not everyone appreciates romance. That's okay; everyone is entitled to his own personal taste. But naysayers should read a romance before forming an opinion. The reality is that romance is a well-appreciated, vibrant genre.

Romance fiction annually captures the largest share of the retail book market; thousands of titles are published. While readers are primarily women, men also indulge. Readership of the genre covers all age groups and educational levels. The variety of subgenres is vast to meet the wide diversity of readers' interests.

What does this mean for librarians?

1. Serve the needs of your patrons by carrying the romances they want to read.
   Know your communities and collections to determine what subgenres are desired and appropriate, and then commit to buying them. Don't rely on donations. Make sure to consider series and characters.
2. Stay current in the genre.
   The number of subgenres is vast and ever evolving; trends change constantly. Talk to fans about what they enjoy. Read reviews in library journals, popular magazines, and specialty magazines such as *RT Book Reviews*. Subscribe to the RWA's quarterly *Romance Sells*, a catalog of upcoming romance releases. Take advantage of conferences to talk to publishers about trends. Utilize all the wonderful and informative blogs and Web sites on the Internet. Romancing the Blog, Smart Bitches, Trashy Books, and All About Romance are excellent examples of what's out there for librarians to consult.[24]

Yes—and here's my suggestion:
Make romance accessible to your patrons.

Don't denigrate anyone's reading taste by making romances "giveaways" or an "honor collection." Your patrons want to read these books. What do they think if we consider romance unimportant and not worthy of our effort? Romance novels are a significant and legitimate segment of the publishing industry, and, as such, we should collect, shelve, and promote them. Give all romances full cataloging, including series tracings and subject headings. Either create a romance section or clearly label the romances so that they can be easily browsed by readers.

Make sure you carry romance in a variety of formats, as available and requested by your patrons. At conferences, lobby with large print and media publishers or your sales reps to promote increasing the number of romance titles they produce.

Romance is here to stay. Whether in print or audio or on the screen, romance is a major part of your libraries' collections and a major focus of interest for your patrons. Embrace, enhance, and promote romance in your library.

Resources for Librarians

"All About Romance." http://www.likesbooks.com/.

Juarez, Vanessa. "Bold, Beautiful, and Totally Bizarre," *Entertainment Weekly* (January 16, 2009): 40–44.

Logan, Robert. "How to Bring Fotonovelas Into Your Library." *Criticas* (June 1, 2002). http://www.schoollibraryjournal.com/article/CA6257851.html.

Logan, Robert; updated by Ospina, Carmen. "How to Bring Fotonovelas Into Your Library." *Criticas* (September 15, 2005). http://www.schoollibraryjournal.com/article/CA6257851.html.

Ramsdell, Kristin. *Romance Fiction: A Guide to the Genre*. Englewood, CO: Libraries Unlimited, 1999.

Ramsdell, Kristin. "Romance Through the Ages." *Romantic Times Magazine* 191 (February 2000): 12–15, 107.

Regis, Pamela. *A Natural History of the Romance Novel*. Philadelphia: University of Pennsylvania Press, 2003.

"Romancing the Blog." http://www.romancingtheblog.com/blog/.

Wendell, Sarah, and Candy Tan. "Smart Bitches, Trashy Books." http://www.smartbitchestrashy books.com/.

Wendell, Sarah, and Candy Tan. *Beyond Heaving Bosoms: The Smart Bitches' Guide to Romance Novels*. New York: Simon & Schuster, 2009.

Endnotes

1. Romance Writers of America. "About the Romance Genre." http://www.rwanational.org/cs/the_romance_genre.

2. Romance Writers of America. "About the Romance Genre: Industry Statistics." http://www.rwanational.org/cs/the_romance_genre/romance_literature_statistics/industry_statistics.

3. Rich, Motoko. "Recession Fuels Readers' Escapist Urges." *New York Times*, April 8, 2009. http://www.nytimes.com/2009/04/08/books/08roma.html.

4. Aoki, Deb. "About.com Guide to Manga: Digital Manga Adds New Harlequin Graphic Novels to eManga." http://manga.about.com/b/2009/11/04/digital-manga-adds-new-harlequin-graphic-novels-to-emanga.htm.

5. Thompson, Jason. *The Complete Guide to Manga*. New York: Ballantine, 2009.

6. "Denver Reconsiders Fotonovela Collection." *American Libraries* (August 12, 2005) http://www.ala.org/ala/alonline/currentnews/newsarchive/2005abc/august2005abc/fotonovela.cfm; Independent Television Service. "Independent Lens: What is a Foto-novela?" http://www.pbs.org/independentlens/fotonovelas2/what.html.

7. Romance Between the Lines. "Bliss: Computer Game for Married Lovers." http://www.romancebetweenthelines.com/site/476224/page/675168; Buzzle.com. "Renai Games—Romance and Sex in Virtual Reality." http://www.buzzle.com/editorials/5-17-2006-96398.asp.

8. Staskiewicz, Keith. "Nora Roberts to Release a Downloadable Game Based on Her Book." *EW's Shelf Life*, http://shelf-life.ew.com/2009/12/08/nora-roberts-to-release-a-downloadable-game-based-on-her-work/.

9. Darcey, Lauren E. "Romance in the Computer Game Industry" *Mamlambo* (March 2004). http://www.mamlambo.com/writing/articles/000013.html.

10. Box Office Mojo. "2009 Domestic Grosses." http://boxofficemojo.com/yearly/chart/?yr=2009&p=.htm.

11. Dempsey, John. "Soaps Not Sudsy for MyNetwork TV: Network Revamps its Schedule." *Variety.com*, http://www.variety.com/article/VR1117958532.html?categoryid=14&cs=1.

12. Lionsgate. "Lionsgate and Xenon Pictures Announce New Home Entertainment Distribution Agreement." http://bit.ly/JgsyI.

13. Romance Writers of America. "About the Romance Genre: Romance Literature Statistics: Overview." http://www.rwanational.org/cs/the_romance_genre/romance_literature_statistics.

14. Romance Writers of America. "About the Romance Genre: Romance Literature Statistics: Readership Statistics." http://www.rwanational.org/cs/readership_stats.

15. Fiction_L Archives. "Romance and Women's Fiction Publishing Trends." http://www.webrary.org/MaillistF/msgcur/2009/4/Re.RomanceandWomensFictio.html.

16. Wendell, Sarah, and Candy Tan. *Beyond Heaving Bosoms: The Smart Bitches' Guide to Romance Novels*. New York: Simon & Schuster, 2009, p. 167.

17. Ramsdell, Kristin. "Gay and Lesbian Romance" in *Romance Fiction: A Guide to the Genre*. Englewood, CO: Libraries Unlimited, 1999. http://www.readersadvisoronline.com.

18. "Rainbow Romance Writers." http://www.rainbowromancewriters.com/.

19. Box Office Mojo, "All Time Adjusted Grosses." http://boxofficemojo.com/alltime/adjusted.htm.

20. Huguenn, Patrick. "African-American Romance Writers Come Into Their Own." *New York Daily News*, May 23, 2009. http://www.nydailynews.com/entertainment/arts/2009/05/24/2009-05-24_africanamerican_romance_writers_come_into_their_own.html?page=0.

21. Romance Writers of America. "About the Romance Genre: Romance Genre: Romance Literature Subgenres." http://www.rwanational.org/cs/romance_literature_subgenres.

22. "Romantic." Oxford English Dictionary Online.

23. February 23, 2009, edition of *Publisher's Weekly* http://www.publishersweekly.com/article/CA6639008.html.

24. "Romancing the Blog." http://www.romancingtheblog.com/blog/;
Sarah Wendell and Candy Tan. "Smart Bitches, Trashy Books." http://www.smartbitchestrashybooks.com/; "All About Romance." http://www.likesbooks.com/.

7

Everything Science Fiction
Jessica E. Moyer, Christy Donaldson, and Cassie Wilson

In this chapter, Jessica Moyer and Christy Donaldson overview science fiction with a wide variety of books, movies, graphic novels, manga, video games, and television shows. In "Plots," they cover near aliens and invasions, colonies and the new frontier, dystopias and disasters, and space operas. The "Characters" section includes lists for leaders and the law, unstoppable heroines, rogue good men and women, and cats and dogs. The theme for this chapter is technology, and it covers cyborgs, computers, robots that come alive, portal and time travel, the big question of what it means to be human, and cyberpunk and steampunk. In the "Making Connections" section, you'll find near future thriller suggestions for action and adventure fans, science fiction for fantasy and romance, and literary science fiction.

Introduction

Science fiction is one of the most exciting genres because it is the genre of the future. Science fiction is especially exciting when it comes to integrated advisory because there are nearly as many movies, TV shows, video games, manga, and graphic novels as there are print fiction books. Additionally, science fiction movies and television shows tend to be more well known and have more of a mainstream audience, and science fiction today is not heavily influenced by print, but new trends draw equally from all formats. Also, science fiction fans are just as likely to enjoy good science fiction shows as they are books, making it especially easy to conduct integrated advisory.

Definition of Science Fiction

What is science fiction? In *Genreflecting* (Libraries Unlimited, 2006), science fiction is defined as "a genre driven by 'what if' questions, science fiction thrives on new and provocative ideas relating to science, technology, and society, and their interrelationships."[1]

In this chapter, we use a similar definition, defining science fiction as the literature of the future, ranging from stories set so far in the future that Earth is lost (*Battlestar Galactica*) to near-future stories set only a few years from now (*40 Days of Rain*). Science fiction is stories about space, stories about technology, and stories of bleak, post-apocalyptic futures. In the broadest sense, science fiction stories are speculations on the future of humanity, based on extrapolations of current science and society. Science fiction stories all ask "what if?"

Most readers have probably already read science fiction and not even realized it. Several literary fiction authors regularly write science fiction, such as Margaret Atwood's *Handmaid's Tale* (1986) or *Oryx and Crake* (2003), both near-future science fiction stories. Classics such as *1984* (1949) or *A Brave New World* (1932) are also science fiction, again both near-future stories, which is also the subgenre of Cormac McCarthy's post-apocalyptic tale *The Road* (2007), a 2008 Oprah Book Club pick and a movie starring Viggo Mortensen.

Science fiction is one of the easiest genres for integrated advisory. People enjoy science fiction because it tickles the imagination, because they get to explore new thoughts and ideas and experiment intellectually—so getting them to extend the exploration and try various media can be a piece of cake. Furthermore, science fiction has a strong presence in all the various media, from movies and television to traditional books and graphic novels to computer and video games, and many science fiction fans will be just as likely to watch science fiction as read it or listen to it.

When practicing integrated advisory for science fiction fans, no matter the medium, it's important to remember appealing characteristics and how they manifest in the genre and its subgenres. Science fiction is actually no stranger or more difficult to understand than any other genre of popular fiction, but finding the right titles and authors for new readers can be a bit tricky. Many science fiction novels assume that readers have background knowledge, usually in math or science. There are also traditions of science fiction that portray settings totally unfamiliar to readers, such as cyberpunk, steampunk, or even post-apocalyptic stories. Perhaps most confusing, science fiction does not have a standard plot formula like those shared by other popular genres, such as romance or mystery, but instead sprawls across many different plot and character types, all while tackling big philosophical questions.

Trends and Subgenres

Several trends and subgenres currently stand out in science fiction, and each of these is highlighted and discussed below, along with a list of the current and upcoming authors. Cyberpunk, while still around, has lately been evolving into steampunk, which is appealing to a larger audience and is not driven by print books but rather popular culture in general. Hard science fiction, long a staple, continues to thrive as a subgenre, with a small but loyal audience. Space opera, once derided, is now the most popular and fastest growing and is a great place for those new to science fiction to get started. Lastly, stories set in the near future and/or featuring a post-apocalyptic setting are once again gaining an audience; this subgenre is especially popular in YA books.

Cyberpunk and Steampunk

Cyberpunk may have been all the rage in the 1990s but today steampunk is the newest and most popular subgenre. Combining science fiction and alternate history, as compared to the tech-heavy cyberpunk, steampunk has a slightly different appeal and isn't necessarily set in the future so much as an alternate past or present, although the focus on technology is still a key element.

Current and upcoming authors: Neal Stephenson, China Mieville, Scott Westerfelt, Gail Carriger

Hard Science Fiction

Hard science fiction comes from a long tradition of using fictional stories to explore and contemplate developments in science. This subgenre has been an especially important part of the genre since the 1940s, when the great scientific breakthroughs of World War II and the subsequent space race inspired many writers. In hard science fiction, the emphasis is on technology, new scientific breakthroughs, or other life-changing developments around which the author builds a story. Suggesting titles to readers in this area can be tricky, as plenty of technical and scientific knowledge is often assumed on the part of the reader, while plot, characterization, and story lines vary from novel to novel. Male characters tend to dominate these stories, and the few female characters tend to be cardboard-cutout stereotypes, although this is changing in more modern stories. The good news about introducing hard science fiction to new readers is that the science in many classic novels has become everyday reality in the twenty-first century, not to mention the fact that hard science fiction provides the basis for popular movies such as *2001: A Space Odyssey*.

Current and upcoming authors: Robert Charles Wilson, Charles Stross

Space Opera

Originally one of the most derisive things that could be said about a science fiction book, space opera was meant to imply that the stories were pulpy trash no better than the horse operas (westerns) of early film and radio. Now space opera is more commonly used to describe any adventure, military, action, romance, mysteries, or other stories that take place in space, usually in the far future. There are lots of women in space in the future, a noticeable difference from the harder science fiction stories. While technology abounds in all of these stories, it does not have to be the emphasis. Those ready to make the leap into outer space will find plenty of stories friendly to new fans, even those without a strong interest in science or math, and this is one of the fastest growing and most popular areas of science fiction.

Current and upcoming authors: John Scalzi, Catherine Asaro, Sandra McDonald, Mike Resnick, David Weber, Elizabeth Moon

Near Future and Post-Apocalyptic

Historically, many of these stories were called dystopias for their negative views of our future, and the negative emphasis still lingers. Post-apocalyptic stories about life after nuclear war were especially common during the Cold War; now stories of the disasters caused by global warming or a meteor knocking the moon off its orbit have added depth to this traditional subgenre. This subgenre has recently seen a strong resurgence in young adult publishing, and these dark stories of struggle and survival appeal to teens.

Current and upcoming authors: Susan Beth Pfeffers, Kim Stanley Robinson, Suzanne Collins, Philip Reeve

Traditional Print Books

Science fiction has been an important part of print publishing since the early twentieth century, when popular fiction made big gains with the proliferation of dime novels and pulp magazines. In the early years, short stories dominated and were published in *Amazing Stories* or *Astounding Stories* (now *Analog*), but as the century progressed, full-length novels gradually overtook short stories, and *Amazing Stories* ceased printing in 2005.[2]

The 1930s and 1940s science fiction books came into their own with popular authors like Robert A. Heinlien, Isaac Asimov, and Arthur C. Clarke. Since the 1950s, print books have continued to be a mainstay of science fiction, and the topics have gradually expanded, as has the number of authors writing and the number of readers consuming. Today, science fiction books have a strong place in the market, and while many stand alone, there is a large audience for books that tie into popular movies and TV shows like *Star Wars* or *Star Trek*.

E-books are also important to science fiction as science fiction readers also tend to be early adopters of technology. Baen Books has had an e-book story and Web library of free e-book titles for many years and has been a leader in accessible and affordable e-books.[3] As more and more science fiction readers get e-book readers, expect more demand for science fiction e-books, especially from readers accustomed to the ease of use of the Baen Free Library. Many older science fiction titles are in the public domain, and large collections of classic science fiction are now available at very low prices.

Graphic Novels and Manga

Graphic novels and manga have gradually become an important market for science fiction stories. Manga has a longer history with science fiction as science fiction stories have been popular in the manga format for many years. While many of these stories have only recently become available in the United States, there are still plenty to choose from. As several of the more popular or critically acclaimed manga have been made into anime movies (another format with increasing popularity in the United States), the demand for science fiction manga is likely to increase. Nearly all of the lists below include some manga titles, many part of long series with multiple volumes.

Graphic novels have only recently moved into science fiction stories, just as they have moved into mainstream literature. Some classic stories like *Ender's Game* are now being adapted to the graphic format and sometimes all-new stories are being written. Expect to see more graphic novel science fiction stories as younger patrons who have been brought up on graphic novels are introduced to science fiction.

Movies and Television

Since the 1950s, science fiction has been a staple of movies, but it wasn't until George Lucas created *Star Wars* that science fiction movies moved into mainstream culture. Since then, some of the biggest movies have been science fiction, from the blockbuster Terminator series to the most recent mega-hit, *Avatar*.

On television, science fiction has also long had a place, but it was more a niche audience for network TV. *Star Trek* has always had a fan base, but it wasn't until the growing cable audience in the 1980s and 1990s led to the creation of the Sci-Fi Channel that science fiction found a regular TV home. Since then, in addition to *Star Trek*, several science fiction shows have had big and somewhat mainstream success, notably the Stargate franchise and, more recently, *Battlestar Galatica*.

Computer and Video Games

Science fiction-influenced video games have existed since nearly the beginning, with *Space Invaders* as an early classic. Since then, science fiction games have continued to prosper both in computer and video games. Games tied into book or movie series tend to have the most popularity; there have been some kind of *Star Wars* video games since the early days. More recently, the trend has reversed, with games inspiring books, such as the *Halo* game leading to a series of Halo books. As media merges and science fiction continues to be popular, expect to see more games and more links between games, books, movies, and more.

Plots

Without certain plot elements, science fiction wouldn't be the same, and in fact it might not even be science fiction. Plots that involve space, space exploration, colonization, and adventures in space are all popular and long, enduring plot types that pervade all formats of science fiction storytelling.

Aliens and Invasions

When aliens invade Earth, it is just as likely to be funny and peaceful as it is dark and violent, as can be seen in two classic alien invasion stories. *War of the Worlds* tells of a violent, world-destroying invasion that threatens all of humanity, whereas *E. T.* is a sweet and gentle story about a friendly alien who wants only to return to his distant home.

3rd Rock From the Sun (1996–2001) TV
Three aliens come to Earth to study our customs and culture and in order to blend in, take the shape of humans and live as a human family. Unfortunately, they don't really understand their new bodies or roles, which leads to many humorous situations. This was not only a sitcom, but a commentary on modern America.

Alien (1979) CL, MV
In this terrifying space story, a mining ship stops at a distant planet to investigate an SOS only to discover an alien life form that takes over the bodies of humans. Starring Sigourney Weaver and directed by Ridley Scott, this was a response to *Star Wars* and provided a much grimmer and darker view of space adventure and alien life. The original spawned a series of sequels.

Ender, Orson Scott Card, *Ender's Game* (1985) YA, SH, BK, GN
At six years old, child genius Ender Wiggins is sent to a military academy to learn to fight the Buggers, aliens who invaded Earth many years ago and will soon return in force. Ender's story is continued in *Ender in Exile* and in a related series from the point of view of Bean, a fellow Battle School classmate. Together, their story is currently being told in graphic novel format. Originally an adult novel, it has become a teen favorite.

Men in Black (1997) YA, MV
Will Smith and Tommy Lee Jones star as federal agents working in a secret agency that protects and liaises with the many alien life forms that secretly live on Earth, "Protecting Earth from the Scum of the Universe." All goes well until aliens threaten to blow up

Earth and agitate the local population. This movie is humorous and full of action, with lots of wacky alien life forms.

Mars Attacks! (1996) MV
One of the funniest and most violent science fiction movies, Martians attack Earth— their only goal: total destruction. Thanks to old country songs, video game-playing kids, and the resourceful president's daughter (Natalie Portman), they manage to defeat the Martians, but only after most of the adults have been killed or captured.

Parasyte, Hitoshi Iwaaki (2007) MN
Aliens have invaded Earth and taken over people's minds and bodies. Unfortunately, no one but teenager Shinichi seems to know it. With the help of his alien symbiote, Shinichi sets out to save the world from the alien menace in a story that is by turns suspenseful and humorous.

Safehold, David Weber, *Off Armageddon Reef* (2005) AP, BK, UAB
The Gbaba are vicious aliens intent on destruction of all other sentient species, including humanity. When they make the final attack on Earth, a desperate plan is hatched to preserve humanity, and a small group is sent away to start a secret low-tech colony. Lt. Alban finds herself the guardian of the colony when her personality is implanted into her human-appearing robot body and she awakes 800 years after settlement. Her mission: prepare the remnants of humanity for the final fight with the Gbaba; but the technology backslide has been worse than she expected—they barely have working muskets.

Wilson, Robert Charles, *Spin* (2004) BK
When the sun goes black, and the moon and stars disappear, Tyler, Jason, and Diane soon realize that the darkness has been caused by aliens who have set up an artificial barrier that will cause the sun to be permanently extinguished in less than 40 years.

Colonies

As the human population grows and exceeds the capacity of Earth, humanity begins to create new places to live. The earliest colonies are always those closes to us: the moon and Mars, but soon technological advances make it possible to colonize the nearer star systems. Even as these early colonies develop and thrive, other early colonial efforts are lost in the depths of space. Some are rediscovered, but others are never found, and their human populations live and struggle in isolation.

Early Colonies

Baker, Kage, *Empress of Mars* (2008) RS, AP, SH, BK
Mary Griffith and her daughters live in a Mars colony dominated by the British Arean Company, which has declared Mary redundant, but not given her any way to get home. Ever resourceful, Mary and her daughters, now dedicated to life on Mars, start the first Martian bar, the Empress of Mars. Mary's watering hole becomes the gathering place for the variety of characters who are dedicated to life on Mars and the center of an independence movement.

Freedom, Anne McCaffrey, *Freedom's Landing* (1995) BK
Kris, a college student at the University of Denver, struggles to survive when she and a few hundred other humans are kidnapped by aliens and dumped on a new planet to test its prospects as a colony. But the humans are not alone; Zainal, a Catteni alien noble,

has also been dumped as punishment, and as Kris is one the few humans who will work with him, they gradually develop a close relationship.

Heinlein, Robert, *The Moon is a Harsh Mistress* (1966) BK, UAB, CL

Heinlien's classic colony story is also an exploration of libertarian ideals. The moon has become a penal colony of sorts where undesirables are shipped off for a permanent new life. As the original settlers marry, procreate, and begin their new lives, Earth sends more and more new residents and attempts to control all aspects of the lunar lifestyle. With the help of the colony computer, the settlers organize a revolt for lunar independence. "No Such Thing As A Free Lunch" or NSTAFL becomes the colony slogan, expressing the harsh lunar life and their philosophy of governance.

Planetes, Makoto Yukimura (2003) YA, MN

As humanity pushes out into the solar system, it leaves lots of things behind. Lots of tiny pieces of trash are left in orbit around Earth, where they are a serious hazard to orbiters and outward-bound spacecraft. Hachimaki and the rest of the crew of the *Toybox* have the totally non-glamorous but extremely important task of clearing the debris. They're space garbage collectors. But for Hachimaki this is just a stepping-stone. He doesn't want to be a garbage man his whole life. He dreams of being selected for the first mission to Jupiter and trains obsessively to reach his goal. Life has some surprises for Hachimaki, though, and over the course of the series he learns more than just the technical skills he will need to make it to Jupiter.

Lost and Abandoned Colonies

Darkover Marion Zimmer Bradley, Deborah J. Ross, Adrienne Martine-Barnes, and Mercedes Lackey (1958) CL, BK

Since the late 1950s, the late Marion Zimmer Bradley and her collaborators have written more than 25 full-length novels and dozens of short stories set on Darkover, a lost and then rediscovered colony. In thousands of years of isolation, it developed a complex culture and mythology that includes a wide variety of psychic abilities caused by Darkover's unique flora, interbreeding with the elusive and indigenous cheiri, and a draconian breeding program between the most highly gifted. *The Bloody Sun*, originally written in 1964 and rewritten in 1979, is a good choice for new readers, as it is set only a short time after Darkover is rediscovered by the Terran Federation; the culture clash is an important series theme. Readers who wish to start at the beginning would want *Darkover Landfall* (1972), about the crash landing and the first terrible years in Darkover's brutal climate.

Dragonriders of Pern, Anne McCaffrey, Dragonsdawn (1989) YA, BK, UAB

Dragonsdawn chronicles the initial arrival of settlers from Earth and their first few idyllic years. Then comes the arrival of the deadly Thread, and the settlers' struggle to find a way to survive in their new home as there is no way to return to Earth. This is also a good place to start reading McCaffrey's extensive Dragonriders series, since it explains the scientific origins of the dragons.

Ringworld, Larry Niven, *Ringworld* (1970) BK, UAB, VG, CL

A mixed group of humans and aliens sets sail to find a new home world and discover the Ringworld, an enormous hollow circular tube that sits in a planetary orbit, previously only a remote theoretical possibility. Inside the ring the explorers discover a habitat perfectly set up for humanity and their allies.

Scalzi, John, *The Last Colony,* **(2007) RS, SH, BK, UAB**
Third in the series Old Man's War, John and his wife Jane and their adopted daughter Zoe and her alien bodyguards volunteer to settle Roanoke, a new colony, despite the galactic ban on colonization. To preserve their safety, all communications are shut off and the colony becomes completely isolated.

Dystopias and Disasters

Since Sir Thomas Moore wrote *Utopia* in the sixteenth century, writers have been exploring alternate societies, usually set in the future. From the early years of science fiction, dystopias have been popular fare; *1984* by George Orwell and *A Brave New World* by Aldous Huxley are seminal classics of this popular plot. These stories can be broken down into nuclear and non-nuclear disasters.

Non-Nuclear Disasters

Butler, Octavia, *Parable of the Sower* **(1995) BK, UAB**
A classic near-future dystopia, in 2025 society is physically divided as the few with money live in well-guarded fortresses while the rest struggle to survive, as paying jobs are few and far between. Preacher's daughter Lauren is psychically sensitive, she can feel the pain of others in her body, and as she leads a group of refugees north toward rumors of paying jobs, she begins her own religion, Earthseed.

Collins, Suzanne, *Hunger Games* **(2008) BK, UAB, YA, SH, AP, RS**
On the future Earth there has been a great war in North America and those in the Capitol won, but it's not in Washington, DC, but in a well-defended part of the continent surrounded by mountains. The other districts that it defeated must now live by Capitol rules. The Capitol hosts the Hunger Games each year, which is like a reality TV show combined with real gladiators. Throw in some high-tech environmental manipulations and gene splicing manipulation to produce the ultimate animal threats, and you've got the Hunger Games: a boy and girl from each district get thrown in an arena each year and only one of them walks out alive. There's politics, young love, amazing costumes, blood, death, family drama, and food to make you hungry for more.

de Crecy, Nicolas, *Glacial Period* **(2007) AP, GN**
A team of explorers on a frozen world discovers the perfectly preserved Louve under snow and ice. They try to reconstruct the history of mankind from the works of art on display with opinions that differ wildly from our interpretations of the same works.

Doctorow, Cory, *Little Brother* **(2008) BK, YA, SH**
Set only a few years in the future, Cory Doctorow's latest novel is the story of Marcus, a teenaged hacker and games player who was skipping school to play an Internet-based scavenger hunt when terrorists attacked San Francisco, and he and his friends were picked up and interrogated by Homeland Security. Upon his release, Marcus finds that everything he does is now monitored, so he uses his computer skills to develop a covert communication network and coordinate a movement to push back against the new authoritarian safety measures. While the slogan, "don't trust anyone over 25" may put off some older readers, others who remember the 1960s will find it especially appealing. Marcus's conversations with his parents, both 1960s radicals who never left the Bay Area, are one of the strengths of the book, as the effects on his parents show the impact of the terrorist attacks on the entire population.

Farmer, Nancy, *The House of the Scorpion* (2002) YA, BK, UAB
The border region between the United States and Mexico is a separate country controlled by drug lords and is the home of Matt, a clone of the 142-year-old drug lord, El Patron. But clones are raised for one purpose only—to serve as replacement bodies for the very rich and powerful, and it is nearly too late when Matt realizes his intended fate.

<u>Mad Max</u>, *Mad Max* (1979) MV, CL, AP
Mel Gibson's breakout role features a very young Mel as a family man and cop who works in a dangerous and violent crumbling society. As resources get tighter and tighter, the cops are increasingly fighting a losing war, especially against the road gangs that dominate the highways of the Australian outback. *Mad Max 2 (The Road Warrior)* is an even bleaker story as a lone Max drives through the desert fighting off bandits.

***Nausicaa of the Valley of the Wind* (1984) MV**
Mankind clings to life on an Earth covered with poisonous fungus. A young girl sets out to learn more about the widely scattered people and the dangerous world in which they live. Along the way, she sees both beauty and violence and learns about the essential nature of the planet and humanity. Written and drawn by Hayao Miyazaki, the creator of such classic films as *Spirited Away* and *My Neighbor Totoro*.

Pfeffer, Susan Beth, *Life as We Knew It* (2006) BK, UAB, YA
The story of 16-year-old Miranda and her family's challenges in the catastrophic year after a meteor hits the moon. Miranda chronicles the increasingly difficult struggle to survive in their small town in northern Pennsylvania as society breaks down and atmospheric and climatic changes wreak havoc across the planet.

Stewart, George, *Earth Abides* (1949) CL, BK, UAB
Isherwood Williams has spent the last several weeks in a mountain cave recovering from a snakebite, which is why he is one of the few survivors of a plague that has decimated humanity. Gathering together the few survivors, he is pained to learn that they care little for learning—they would rather scavenge from the remnants of civilization than learn how to read.

<u>To Terra . . .</u>, Keiko Takemiya (2007) MN
After pushing the world to the edge of environmental collapse, humanity begins the era of Superior Domination, where all decisions are controlled by the specially educated elite and a powerful supercomputer called Mother. Life is perfect and everything is perfect, unless you step out of line.

<u>Transmetropolitan</u>, Warren Ellis, *Back on the Street* (1998) GN
A Hunter S. Thompson-esque journalist takes on an overcrowded, polluted, and hopelessly corrupt world with his laptop, attitude, and bowel disruptor. With his two faithful assistants, Spider Jerusalem attacks monsters at all levels, including a newly elected president.

<u>Uglies</u>, Scott Westerfeld, *Uglies* (2004) BK, UAB, YA
Fifteen-year-old Talia is anticipating her final months as an ugly before her sixteenth birthday and the mandatory plastic surgery that will make her a pretty. Talia lives several hundred years in the future in a world with no petroleum-based products, which were all destroyed by the ending of the Rusty culture, resulting in massive changes in human culture and society.

Wood, Brian, *Channel Zero* (2000) GN

The United States has passed the Clean Acts, which limit speech to that approved by a Christian, conservative government, and has sealed itself off from the corrupting influence of the rest of the world. Inside the United States, guerilla broadcaster Jennie Zero hijacks the airwaves to encourage people to think for themselves.

Y: The Last Man, Brian K. Vaughn, *Unmanned* (2003) GN

A mysterious disease/event/smiting sweeps the planet and kills all the males of every species except for unemployed magician Yorick Brown and Ampersand, the helper monkey he is trying to train. Paired up with a scientist and a secret agent, Yorick embarks on a journey to save humanity, find his girlfriend, and generally survive in a world that is slowly putting itself back together.

Life After Nuclear Disaster

A subset of near-future stories is life after nuclear disasters. Especially popular during the Cold War when nuclear war seemed likely, this specialized subgenre still prospers and is remarkably popular in YA books.

Akira, Katsuhiro Otomo (2000) MN

Years ago, after an explosion leveled most of Tokyo, the world fell into a nuclear war. Now a battered Neo Tokyo fights with teenaged delinquents and violent gangs. Deep within the ruins at the center of the city, the Japanese military continues to experiment in an attempt to create new superweapons. And they hold what might be the most powerful weapon of all: Akira.

Book Of Ember, Jeanne DuPrau, *City of Ember* (2004) BK, UAB, MV, YA

After a nuclear disaster, the survivors move underground. Some 241 years later, 12-year-old Lina learns about the history of the City of Ember and yearns to venture aboveground.

The Hungry City Chronicles, Philip Reeve, *Mortal Engines* (2004) BK, YA

After nuclear war has destroyed civilization, the cities of Europe go on the move. As the great traction cities chase each other across the plains, playing by the rules of municipal Darwinism, the mayor of London plots to do more than just recycle smaller cities for power, threatening a new nuclear disaster.

Moore, Alan, *V for Vendetta* (1988) GN, MV, AP

A nuclear war has destroyed most of the world. Somehow Great Britain has survived, but this may not be for the best. Led by a fascist government, postwar Britain is a land of surveillance, governmental abuse, and concentration camps. Into the storm strides V, a man who hides behind a Guy Fawkes' mask and strives to bring his vision of anarchy—where each individual has the freedom and power to decide on his future for himself—to the land.

Terminator, *Terminator 1* (1984) MN, TV, CL, SH

When Skynet becomes self-aware, it takes over the world's weapons systems, and once it has determined humanity to be the greatest threat to its existence, Skynet launches nukes on all the major cities of the world. The few survivors huddle underground where the resistance is led by John Connor. Throughout the series, Skynet attempts to manipulate history to remove John and his mother Sarah through the use of time-traveling killer cyborgs, Terminators.

Space Opera

Space opera may be one of the most derisive terms in the science fiction world, but it's too good a term to dismiss. Evolving from the horse operas and soap operas of the 1950s, today space operas are stories that focus on action, adventure, and drama and just happen to take place in space. With the focus on a good story and a compelling plot, not only are these fun to read for science fiction readers, but the lack of overwhelming technical jargon can make these great intros to science fiction for teen or adult readers.

The Star Trek franchise has been one of the most popular science fiction shows (and books and movies) since it premiered in the 1960s. Star Trek is the perfect example of the action and space-adventure aspect of space opera, but it also illustrates another key element that is often overlooked in space opera: big philosophical issues are not ignored, but are neatly woven into the plot and action.

Library users ready to make the leap into outer space will find plenty of stories friendly to new fans, even those without a strong interest in science or math. This is one of the fastest growing and most popular areas of science fiction.

Andromeda (2000) TV, AP

Star Trek's Gene Rodenberry left some storylines that, after his death, his wife produced as this television series. Set in the far future, the story revolves around a ship stranded at the edge of a black hole being towed back into the time line. The ship's captain, Dylan Hunt, along with the ship itself, *Andromeda*, whose powerful artificial intelligence is also a main character in the series, are salvaged by a crew of misfits who join Dylan's cause and try to bring peace to the universe by creating a new commonwealth of nations. Of course, it's not an easy road with several different races across different galaxies. The alien characters are interesting, with well-developed worlds and backgrounds. It is an interesting ride that takes us through the long night where, "on the starship *Andromeda*, hope lives again."

Farscape (1999) TV, AP

When an experimental space mission goes badly wrong, astronaut John Crichton finds himself far, far, from home, flung through a wormhole to the far side of the galaxy and in the middle of an intergalactic conflict. Multiple alien races, armed with deadly weapons, including a militant species hunting just for Crichton, make this an exciting TV series.

Heris Serrano/Esmay Suiza, Elizabeth Moon, *Hunting Party* (1993) BK, SH

The first in a series about middle-aged and unemployed Heris Serrano, who takes the job as the captain of a rich elderly woman's private yacht out of desperation after losing her military career, only to find civilian life much more interesting than she ever thought when a group of young people are the prey in an exclusive and private hunting party.

Jodenny Scott and Terry Myel, Sandra McDonald, *Outback Stars* (2007) BK, RS

Humanity moves into space after Australian astronauts discover the Alcheringa—an interstellar pathway that links Earth with seven planets perfect for human habitation. Logistics officer Lt. Jodenny Scott works for Team Space, the company that controls all movement and commerce, and takes the first available berth after recovering from injuries sustained in the destruction of her previous ship. However, something is not right on the *Aral Sea*, and Jodenny is worried about another deadly accident. The story is fast-paced and laced with elements of Australian culture and Aboriginal mysticism.

Lt. Leary, David Drake, *With the Lightnings* (1998) BK, UAB
Drake's Lt. Leary series draws on the same historical inspiration as Weber's Honor Harrington books, but is more upbeat and presents less-serious issues. Leary is an easygoing officer with an amazing ability to land on his feet, and his sidekick is Adele, a deadly librarian and information officer. Many of Leary's crew are regulars and appear in each of his adventures.

Sinclair, Linnea, *An Accidental Goddess* (2005) BK
Captain Gilliane Davre wakes up after a 350-year sleep to discover that she's been turned into a goddess. In this fun and sexy space opera, Davre also has to face an enemy from her past.

Stellvia, Xebec (2005) MN
This is a humorous look inside a school for budding space pilots.

To Terra . . . , Keiko Takemiya (2007) MN
In the far future, humanity has split into "normal" humans and the psychic Mu. There is much mutual distrust as the Mu journey across space to reclaim their place on Earth.

Virga, Karl Schroeder, *Sun of Suns* (2006) BK, UAB
Admiral Chaison Fanning is the leader of the Slipstream fleet and the conqueror of the nation of Aerie in the first volume of this futuristic adventure series. Hayden Griffin, orphaned in the conquest, travels to the city of Rush to seek revenge.

Characters

In science fiction, characters can be just as important as plots or technology, and the best science fiction stories find a balance between the three. In this section, we explore several popular and enduring characters, the kind that draw fans from page to screen to graphic novels and beyond.

Leaders and the Law

Leaders and law enforcers are just as important in science fiction as they are in other genres, sometimes even more important as some of the colonies or post-apocalyptic settings can be lawless places similar to the Old West. What all these characters have in common is their ability to lead and inspire others.

Battlestar Galatica (2004) AP, TV, BK, UAB
Admiral Adama is the undisputed leader of the ship *Battlestar Galatica*, but he's not the only leader of the ragtag band of survivors his ship is escorting. He has to contend with the civilian leadership, first in the person of President Laura Roslyn, then President Gaius Balter, who doesn't give him as much of a personal challenge, but certainly isn't an easy person with whom to share leadership. Adama is beloved by all his officers, even his occasionally rebellious son, Major Lee Adama, but Admiral Adama is plagued by personal fears and doubts and feels the loss of every colonist or crew member personally.

Darkover, Marion Zimmer Bradley, *Heritage of the Hastur* (1984) CL, AP, BK
Regis Hastur must battle to save his own culture from stagnation and inbreeding, yet preserve it from the Terran who've put a spaceport next to his capital, all while

trying to rule a fractious feudal empire that doesn't really want a ruler but needs a strong leader. The newest Darkover book, written from Bradley's notes (she died suddenly in 1999), *The Hastur Lord* (2010) is also about Regis' struggle with leadership and his powerful inherited role in traditional Darkover society.

Ender, Orson Scott Card, *Ender's Game* (1985) YA, BK, GN

At six years old, child genius Ender Wiggins is sent to a military academy to learn to fight the Buggers, aliens who invaded Earth many years ago and will soon return in force. Ender's story is continued in *Ender in Exile* and in a related series from the point of view of Bean, a fellow Battle School classmate. Together, their story is currently being told in graphic novel format. Originally an adult novel, it has become a teen favorite.

Firefly (2002) AP, SH, TV, MV, GN

Mal is supposed to be the captain of the ship *Firefly*, but his crew is not particularly subordinate. Maybe as a release from his independent crew, Mal frequently takes the law into his own hands, delivering frontier justice on the barren moons and crowded space stations. Mal has a soft spot for underdogs and women in distress, which leads to serious difficulties in "Mrs. Reynolds" and near death in "Golden Heart," but he always means well, and with the help of his crew, manages to eventually save the good guys (or gals), dispense justice to the bad, and escape in his ship *Firefly*. The *Firefly* television series is continued in a graphic novel *Those Left Behind* and in the movie *Serenity* (2005).

Honor Harrington, David Weber, *On Basilisk Station* (1993) AP, BK, AB, UAB

From lowly lieutenant to admiral of the kingdom of Manticore, Honor is an inspired and dedicated leader. She not only effectively leads her ships through brutal encounters with the enemy Peeps, but mentors and teaches the young officers serving under her. There is little not to admire in a leader of this caliber, especially when reading of Honor's struggles with personal attractiveness and loneliness. Captains of starships can't have lovers among the crew, even when it is months between home leaves. Honor survives devastating attacks of the naval forces of the People's Republic of Haven, pirates in Silesia, personal enemies among the nobility and in the admiralty, and fanatics on Grayson.

Old Man's War, John Scalzi, *Old Man's War* (2005) SH, RS, BK, UAB

John is more of an everyday guy than the fearless leader, but that doesn't stop him from earning the respect of his fellow soldiers in the Colonial Defense Forces. Rising rapidly in the ranks of the CDF, as much a result of high casualties as of planned advancement, John eventually retires, but not for long as he first takes a job as a village ombudsman and eventually agrees to lead a new colony.

Pegasus, Anne McCaffery, *Pegasus in Flight* (1990) YA, BK, UAB

You don't have to be big and strong to be an inspired leader. Quadriplegic Peter Reidinger not only pioneered machine-assisted telekinesis to move his paralyzed body, but helped build Earth's first space station to send out the first colony ships

Seaquest (1993) TV, BK, YA

Reluctantly leaving retirement, Bridger becomes the captain and commander of the new exploratory undersea vessel *SeaQuest* in this 1990s TV series. Bridger sometimes conflicts with his superiors on land, but he gets on with all his crewmembers and has their love and respect from the first day on board. Bridger provides confident and inspired leadership to this happy band of undersea explorers, even serving as a substitute father figure for gifted (and obnoxious) teen passenger, Lukas (played by former teen heartthrob Jonathon Brandis).

Vorkisigan Saga, Lois McMaster Bujold, *Warrior's Apprentice* (1991) BK, UAB, YA, SH

A neurotoxin attack on his mother before his birth made Miles deformed and crippled on Barrayar, whose cultural mores proscribed the killing of mutant babies. Miles is eventually accepted in the military, but his career is going nowhere until he invents an alter ego, Admiral Naismith, and a mercenary army. Miles' madcap adventures across the space as the manic and magnetic Naismith are as much an illustration in the power of charm and talk as they are in fighting, because Miles would much rather talk his enemies to death.

Unstoppable Heroines

Early science fiction may have been dominated by male characters, but since Princess Leia defied Darth Vader, strong women have become an important character type. The women in these stories aren't just strong; many of them are positively unstoppable.

Alien (1979) MV CL

First released in 1979, Alien was in part a response to *Star Wars*. When a mining ship picks up a distress call, it unwittingly picks up an alien life form that is clearly inimical to humans. Ripley (played by Sigourney Weaver) is the sole human survivor (along with Jonesy the cat) of the original alien attack. But the aliens aren't done with her yet.

Battlestar Galactica (2004) AP, TV

"Starbuck" is the call sign of Capt. Kara Thrace who certainly considers herself the best pilot on Galatica. And she may be right. Starbuck survives battle after battle with the Cylons, including the cunning and deadly Scar. But like every character in this excellent drama, Starbuck isn't perfect—she has an occasional drinking problem and can't decide which man she really wants.

Ghost in the Shell, Masamune Shirow (2004) AP, MN

Major Motoko Kusanagi leads Public Security Section 9, Japan's elite covert anti-terrorism squad. A full cyborg (a human mind in a mechanical body) since childhood and an expert hacker, nothing can keep her from completing her mission.

Lt. Leary, David Drake, *With the Lightnings* (1998) BK, UAB

Adele has been an orphan ever since her parents were executed as traitors while she was studying on another world. In order to survive, Adele has become both an unstoppable hacker (she used to be a librarian) and a deadly markswoman. She can never miss because patriotic assassins would love to kill her as the last surviving member of her famous family. But that's nothing compared her new life when she joins up with Lt. Daniel Leary. She has to fight off pirates, terrorists, and rebels just to make it off planet and keep herself and Daniel alive.

Skolian Saga, Catherine Asaro, *Primary Inversion* (1995) AP, BK

Soz Valderia is the Prime, the lead pilot for a fighter group of telepathically connected pilots, and the half sister of the Fist, the emperor of Skolia. Soz goes heads-up with the Fist and defies his orders, sneaks covertly around the Skolian Net hiding her tracks from her psychically talented family, and does things with her ship that no one considers survivable.

Star Wars, *Episodes 1–3* (1999) MV, BK

It's clear where Princess Leia gets it from, as her mother Padme is at least as tough and as deadly a shot as her daughter. Queen of Naboo at 13, and an imperial senator before she is 20, Padme fights off the Trade Federation and survives multiple assassination attempts and a secret marriage to Anakin Skywalker.

Star Wars, *Episodes 4–6* (1999) MV, BK, YA, SH, CL

Princess Leia is the original unstoppable science fiction heroine from Star Wars. Leia is a diplomat, rebel leader, and excellent shot. She never misses with her blaster or gives in to torture. She's not even scared of Darth Vader. Featured in Episodes 4–6 (the original trilogy), and in many of the Star Wars books.

Terminator (1984) MV, TV, AP

Sarah Connor was one of the very few to survive the first Terminator's attack; she defeats the machine and escapes to Mexico. Ten years later, Sarah breaks out of a mental hospital to confront the new Terminator. *Terminator: The Sarah Connor Chronicles* was a TV show from 2008 to 2009.

Tower and the Hive, Anne McCaffrey, *The Rowan* (1991) BK, UAB, YA

When she was three years old, her parents were killed in a mudslide and she was buried for nearly a week. Rowan may be one of the strongest Talents ever born, but first she has to survive growing up as a "white-haired freak." At 18, she's in charge of her own Tower on Callisto, but terribly alone. Until she talks with Jeff on Deneb, a man whose psychic powers may match her own. Rowan must conquer her agoraphobia and fight the aliens to save Jeff, Deneb, and her whole civilization from the deadly Hivers.

Vorkisigan Saga, Lois McMaster Bujold, *Shards of Honor* (1986) BK, UAB, SH

From facing down the Butcher of Komarr (her husband-to-be) to dodging assassination attempts and plotting to overtake the throne, nothing slows down Captain Cordelia Naismith, except maybe when she finds women on Barrayar don't even know what uterine replicators are.

Weber, David, *In Fury Born* (2006) BK

Alicia DeVries survives relatively unscathed through several years as an imperial marine (one of the youngest ever) and then becomes a member of the emperor's imperial commandos. She's one of seven survivors of a mission that was compromised by a spy and suffered 95 percent casualties. That's all before the pirates attack her family's homestead.

Rogue Good Men (and Women)

On the side of right, but not necessarily the right side of the law, these men and women are a staple of science fiction. Most often found in space operas, these are complex characters with internal conflicts and a burning desire to do what is right.

Bujold, Lois McMaster, *Falling Free* (1986) BK, UAB, AP

Leo Graf has always thought of himself as an everyday guy, just an engineer with no desire for heroics or derring-do. That is, until he met the Quaddies, a genetically engineered human variation designed for free fall, with four arms and no legs. But the Quaddies are deemed property and worthless property at that when Beta Colony invents a usable artificial gravity generator, and free-fall workers are no longer needed. Leo sees Quaddies as human beings with every right to freedom and determination and changes the entire course of his life to help them realize their dreams.

Kris Longknife, Mike Shepherd, *Kris Longknife: Mutineer* (2004) BK, UAB, YA
Kris is one of the Longknife; her father really is prime minister and her grandfather is now a king, not to mention the rest of her wealthy and powerful relatives. But all Kris really wants to do is join the Space Navy. On her very first deployment as an ensign, Kris finds her family's morals coming into direct conflict with a superior officer's order and must decide whether to do what's right and risk her entire career or just follow orders.

Mad Max, *Mad Max* (1979) MV, CL
Max Rockatansky was a loyal cop, despite the difficulties of life in a society teetering on the edge of collapse, until his closest friends and family are harmed by the violent road gangs that terrorize near-future Australia. Once Max has nothing left to lose, he commandeers the fastest and most powerful car the police department owns and sets off on a mission for justice.

Star Wars, *Episodes 4–6* (1999) MV, BK, YA, SH, CL
Han Solo is a mercenary, smuggler, and occasional pirate, and while he claims not to be the least bit interested in politics, he soon finds himself entangled with the Rebel Alliance and must decide whether to stick to his principles or chart a new course for his life.

Starship, Mike Resnick, *Starship Mutiny* (2005) BK, UAB
Wilson Cole has had a long and decorated career, but he's also notorious for being demoted for insubordination. Now his latest superior has gone too far and Cole must decide whether he can risk mutiny or the death of millions of innocents. Cole's adventures, along with the loyal crew of the *Teddy R,* continue across four more books.

Vatta's War, Elizabeth Moon, *Trading in Danger* (2003) BK, UAB
When Ky Vatta's family is killed and their company is blamed for the shutdown of interplanetary communication, she sets out to clear their name and take revenge on the killers. But the only way for her to turn the family merchant business into a tool for revenge is to become a pirate.

Cats and Dogs

As long as humans have been in space stories, their faithful companions have been along for the ride. Only in space, cats aren't always just cats anymore. Cats and dogs can be found in all types of science fiction, from near-future thrillers to far-future space operas and everything in between.

Alien (1979) CL, MV
If only they had listened to the cat. Jonesy is the only one who can reliably detect the alien, and he's one of the few to survive and appear in the sequel *Aliens.* Jonesy is an average orange tabby, and like any self-respecting cat, can detect things humans can't

see or hear, which in this case are killer aliens. Jonesy has few lines, but they are memorable, and without him Ridley would never have escaped. Bonus: apparently space cats also travel in plastic carry crates.

de Crecy, Nicholas, *Glacial Period* **(2007) GN**
Hulk is a genetically modified dog that discovers the Louvre after an ice age buries most of Europe. He also nurses a serious crush on a human member of the expedition.

Ghatti's Tale, Gayle Greeno, *Finders Seekers* **(1997) YA, BK**
On a lost human colony deprived of technology, civilization has redeveloped around the truth-seeking powers of the native Ghatti, medium-sized cats that travel with human companions, the Seekers Veritas, to seek truth and pass judgments. Books 1 to 3 are about stubborn and responsible Doyce and her loving and concerned bond-mate Khar'pern. Books 4 and 5, Ghatten's Gambit, feature their children, feline and human. The lost colony setting lends it a more fantastical tone, but these colonists have not completely forgotten their pasts.

Graham, Brandon Scott, *King City* **(2008) MN, YA**
Earthling J. J. Cattingsworth is not just a cat. With the right injection of "cat juice," Earthling can be anything his handler needs him to be—from a machine gun to a periscope to a skateboard. Not to mention he's probably smarter than all of the people he meets.

Honor Harrington, David Weber, *On Basilisk Station* **(1993) BK, AB, UAB, AP**
Nimitz, a six-legged, empathic tree cat from Honor's home world of Sphinx, has been her loyal friend and companion since they bonded when Honor was 11. Sticking close by Honor throughout her military career, Nimitz is one of the best (and sometimes overlooked) secondary characters in this outstanding space opera series, growing up along with Honor and eventually learning sign language to better communicate with his best friend. Nimitz is no soft housecat; he protects Honor and her friends from enemies and assassins and never hesitates to use deadly force.

Mad Max, *Mad Max* **(1979) CL, MV**
In post-apocalyptic Australia, where gangs have taken over the roads and fight for the last remnants of oil, the Road Warrior's loyal and intelligent sidekick is an unnamed Aussie mutt dog who shares Max's Dinki-Di dinners and has some of the best scenes in the movie. Unnamed Dog rides in the back of Max's V-8 Interceptor and will attack anyone who threatens to Max, even if it means losing his own life in the bargain.

Morrison, Grant, art by Quitely, Frank, *We3* **(2005) GN, YA**
Household pets are kidnapped and made into cyborg super-soldiers in this comic. In some ways, it reads as an homage to *The Incredible Journey*, only with a bunny and heavy weaponry.

Theme: Technology

What themes are popular with science fiction consumers? Why is theme a key part of the appeal of science fiction media? How do themes traverse different media? How do you talk to science fiction consumers about theme? What's the big deal with technology?

Cyborgs, Computers, and Robots Come Alive

Since Stanley Kubrick's epic movie *2001*, everyone has understood the dangers of self-aware computers. But this was not a new idea to science fiction, and continues to be a popular plot type for fans to explore. As science fiction has developed, these stories have moved beyond single computers like Hal to person-based computers, androids, and other artificial intelligence creations. There is some overlap in the section "What does it mean to be human?" because as artificial intelligences evolve, many take on human characteristics, and the lines between human and machine become blurred.

Appleseed, Shirow Masamune (2007) MN, MV

Bioroids—highly advanced androids—and humans coexist, but not always peacefully. Human Dunan Knute, her cyborg boyfriend Briareos, and the bioroid Athena are at the center of the hunt for the data known as Appleseed. The file has the power to turn an already-turbulent society upside down, and whoever finds it first will control the shape of the world to come.

Astro Boy, Osamu Tezuka (2003) MN, MV

In this iconic series, Japan's "god of comics," Osamu Tezuka, spins the tale of a very human robot with the power to save the world.

Battle Angel Alita, Yukito Kishiro (2004) MN

The city of Tiphares floats over the immense Scrapyard, where poor humans scrape livings from the city's trash and the remains of an earlier civilization. Bounty hunter and cybernetics expert Ido finds the amnesia-stricken cyborg girl he names Alita among the debris. Alita is no ordinary cyborg, not with her instinctual knowledge of martial arts. To regain her lost memories, she must journey through the Scrapyard, learning about the people who exist there and about herself.

Charon, Catherine Asaro, *Sunrise Alley* (2004) BK, UAB

A brilliant biotech engineer has retired to a remote house after having ethical disagreements over her company's use of her artificial intelligence work, and one morning she finds a man shipwrecked on her beach. He claims to be Turner Pascal, but the real Turner is dead, and it is soon revealed that he has non-human abilities and Samantha is the only one who may be able to help him.

Chobits, CLAMP (2002) MN

In the near future, the "persocom" is the hottest necessary accessory for modern life. These human-shaped computers are more like advanced personal computers than true androids, but their existence raises questions about humanity and love, especially for the technology-impaired Hideki, who may just have found a legendary, incredibly powerful persocom in the trash.

Dick, Philip K., *Do Androids Dream of Electric Sheep?* (1968) BK, MV, UAB, CL

Dick's classic book was made into the critically acclaimed movie *Bladerunner*. It is the story of bounty hunter Rick Deckard, whose job is to hunt down and "retire" the androids who keep trying to come to Earth to escape their role as chattel. Built to make life on Mars easier for the colonists, androids are forbidden from coming to the wrecked remains on Earth. Set after World War Terminus, when the few remaining humans on Earth are gradually being poisoned by radiation, Dick asks many big questions about what it means to be human.

Geodesica, Sean Williams, *Ascent* (2006) BK
The Archon is an artificial intelligence that destroyed the Bedlam system on its way to taking control of Geodesica. A pilot on a revenge mission, a post-human AI, and a human searching for ancient secrets ally to destroy it.

Ghost in the Shell, Masamune Shirow (2004) AP, MN, MV
Major Motoko Kusanagi leads the elite antiterrorism squad of Japan's Public Security Section Nine. The major is a full cyborg—a human brain in a completely mechanical body—while the rest of her team have different degrees of cybernetic parts. Their current mission is to track down and capture the master hacker known as the Puppeteer. But when they find the elusive hacker, they are forced to rethink some of their preconceived notions about a world where the boundary between man and machine is increasingly unclear.

Portal and Time Travel

Time travel has been a common plot since the early 1700s and really caught on after H. G. Wells's book *The Time Machine* was published in 1895. We want to focus here on technology-based time travel rather than those plots in which the character simply steps into another dimension. Using technology such as a portal or some sort of time machine is what makes the story science fiction rather than fantasy. Time-travel stories are often good choices for readers who enjoy historical fiction.

Bill and Ted's Excellent Adventure **(1988) CL, AP, MV**
Southern California teenagers Bill and Ted want only to play really excellent music. When a history project threatens break up the band and failing will get Ted sent to military school in Alaska, they are saved by Rufus, a time traveler from the twenty-fifth century, where Bill and Ted are huge stars whose music has brought peace to the galaxy. Rufus sets up Bill and Ted with a time-traveling phone booth, and they travel through history gathering historical figures. Possibly Keanu Reeves' best-ever acting.

Company, Kage Baker, *In the Garden of Iden* (1998) BK
The Company is a secretive group from the twenty-sixth century whose goal is to save species of plants and animals from total extinction. To do this, they use time-traveling agents who also happen to be nearly immortal and send them on missions across time. Baker's first Company novel, *In the Garden of Iden*, finds new agent Mendoza on her first mission after being rescued from the Inquisition. A dedicated botanist, she is sent to sixteenth-century England to gather rare samples from the gardens at Iden; but this is a very dangerous time, in the midst of the Counter-Reformation, and the Spanish visitors raise suspicions.

Crichton, Michael, *Timeline*, (2003) BK, MV, UAB, SH
A wealthy and powerful scientist creates a time machine to the fourteenth century as part of his mission to build an authentic medieval theme park. The chief historian sends a distress call back from 1357, and a group of young historians is dispatched on a rescue mission. But the fourteenth century is an extremely violent and nasty place; for one, it's right in the middle of the Hundred Years' War between England and France.

Crosstime Traffic, Harry Turtledove, *Gunpowder Empire* (2003) BK, YA
In the late twenty-first century, pollution is eliminated by the simple expedient of exploiting the resources of nearby alternate worlds. The Solter family spends summers in a land where the Roman Empire never fell, but the parents must leave the teenagers on their

own when the mother requires medical care. Problems with the portals leave the teens facing war and hardship, which is much worse than they ever could have imagined.

The Matrix, *The Matrix* (1999) MV

Neo, a rebellious hacker, thinks he lives in 1999, but to his surprise, he finds that his world is just a virtual reality created by machines in the future that control all human thoughts and actions. Neo breaks free of the matrix with the help of Morpheus but soon finds himself being targeted by deadly government agents. With lots of action, the time traveling and virtual reality mark this as science fiction that will particularly appeal to cyberpunk fans.

Stargate, *Stargate* (1994) MV, TV, BK, VG, GN

This long-running franchise first debuted as a movie but soon expanded into several popular TV shows, *SG-1*, *Stargate Atlantis*, and the newest, *Stargate Universe*. Stargate stories also have appeared in books, graphic novels, and video games. All the entries work around the same idea, an alien-made ring-shaped device creates wormholes that link the numerous gates, often across great distances. Many of the gates open into preindustrial human societies, creating opportunities for time-travel stories.

Tsuruta, Kenji, *Spirit of Wonder* (1998) MN

This cute manga deals with the adventures of a scatterbrained inventor and his apprentice. The bumbling but brilliant duo live above a struggling teahouse and build amazing contraptions, often to get out of paying the rent. Most impressive is the portal-creating device that allows them to hide from their adorable landlady and travel to the moon to impress her. This is especially great for fans of steampunk.

Willis, Connie, *Doomsday Book* (1992) BK, UAB

Kivrin, a history student at Oxford in 2048, is sent back in time to a medieval village at the height of the Black Death. Willis has received many accolades for her historical accuracy and details, and in *Doomsday Book* she deftly balances Kivrin's dangerous adventures in the past and the story of her colleagues back at Oxford as they face their own plague, a flu pandemic, and struggle to ensure her safe return. *To Say Nothing of the Dog* is another excellent time-travel novel by Willis.

What Does it Mean to be Human?

Pondering big ideas and asking questions is a key element of science fiction. One of the most important questions it considers is what it means to be human. Human variations as well as tech-enhanced humans are routinely considered, as well as more subtle manipulations caused by nanotech. Since Mary Shelley first wrote about the monster Frankenstein, this is a question that has dominated science fiction.

Andromeda (2000) TV, AP

Star Trek's Gene Rodenberry left some storylines that after his death his wife produced as this television series. Set in the far future, the story revolves around a ship stranded at the edge of a black hole being towed back into the time line. The ship's captain, Dylan Hunt, along with the ship itself, *Andromeda*, whose powerful artificial intelligence is also a main character in the series, are salvaged by a crew of misfits who join Dylan's cause and try to bring peace to the universe by creating a new commonwealth of nations. Of course, it's not an easy road, with several different races across different galaxies. Over the course of the series, Rommie, the ship's avatar, will struggle with just what it means to be intelligent and whether or not intelligent machines can have feelings. It is an interesting ride that takes us through the long night, where "on the starship Andromeda, hope lives again."

Bujold, Lois McMaster, *Falling Free* (1988) BK, UAB, AP
Falling Free is the 1988 Nebula Award-winner that introduces the Quaddies, a human variant designed for null gravity with four arms and no legs. Engineer Leo Graff is assigned to Cay Habitat, home of the Quaddies, and discovers that they are virtual slaves with their entire lives controlled by the company that designed them. As Leo becomes better acquainted with several individuals, he realizes that they have the same fears and desires as any other humans.

Cassandra Kresnov, Joel Shepherd, *Crossover* (2006) BK
Cassandra Kresnov certainly thinks of herself as human, and in fact the reader isn't even aware she's a cyborg until several chapters into the story. She's not only a cyborg, but is on the run from her creators, looking for her own identity and attempting to fit into human society.

Farmer, Nancy, *The House of the Scorpion* (2002) SH, BK, YA, UAB
Are clones people too, or just creations to be used for organ transplants? These are the key questions in *The House of the Scorpion*, when the border region between the United States and Mexico is a separate country controlled by drug lords and is the home of Matt, a clone of the 142-year-old drug lord, El Patron. But clones are raised for one purpose only—to serve as replacement bodies for the very rich and powerful.

Flynn, Michael, *Eifelheim* (2007) BK, UAB
In this historical time-travel novel, two modern-day scholars, historian Tom and his theoretical-physicist girlfriend, are determined to discover why the small German town of Eifelheim disappeared in 1349, right in the midst of one of the worst outbreaks of the plague. What they don't yet know is that the village priest had the first contact with a strange alien race in 1348.

Ghost in the Shell, Shirow Masamune (1989) AP, MN, MV
Major Motoko Kusanagi leads Public Security Section 9 as they hunt for the Puppeteer, a hacker thought to be able to manipulate national economies. In this future Japan, the line between human and machine has blurred thanks to brain-augmenting computers, commonly available cybernetic parts, and increasingly sophisticated artificial intelligences. The major, who has a fully cybernetic body, must examine her definition of "human" as the team comes closer to learning the identity of the Puppeteer. This is a classic of both the media in which it appears.

Gunslinger Girl (2003) MV, MN
Critically injured young girls are rebuilt as cyborg governmental agents as part of a secret program. The girls are controlled through brainwashing, drugs, and an encouraged dependence on their male handlers. Are the girls machines to be used until they break, or are they human children? The different handlers vary in their thoughts and approaches to the project in this thought-provoking series. *Gunslinger Girl* is also an anime series. The anime is oddly paced and is perhaps more frustrating than interesting.

Cyberpunk to Steampunk

Technology is the basis of most science fiction, whether it's the computer and Web-based technology and virtual worlds of cyberpunk or the steam-based machinery of steampunk.

Both of these are distinct subgenres that rely on a specific set of technologies and are popular with certain subsets of readers, and there are many overlaps as fans seem to be transitioning from cyberpunk to steampunk. Today steampunk may be more popular, but cyberpunk classics like *Neuromancer* still tell a fascinating tale and have a dedicated audience.

Cyberpunk

Ghost in the Shell, Masamune Shirow (1989) MN, MV, AP
In a near-future Japan, everyone's brain has been augmented with an onboard computer and cybernetic body enhancements are commonly available. In this world, Major Motoko Kusanagi and the rest of Public Security Section 9 are tasked with tracking and capturing terrorists, both through information networks and in the physical world.

Gibson, William, *Neuromancer* (1984) BK, VGM
The classic that started the cyberpunk trend is not to be missed. Written more than 20 years ago, it is still a timely novel, as Gibson's wordsmithing makes it enduring. At the same time, it seems familiar and far in the future, with action-oriented and thought-provoking scenes of urban grittiness. The dark and edgy tone is classic to cyberpunk as is the technology-infused storyline. A movie is in the making.

Stephenson, Neal, *The Diamond Age, or, a Young Lady's Illustrated Primer* (1995) BK, AP
Far in the future, people modify themselves daily to be stronger and look prettier, and can insert weapons into their temples as nanotechnology has evolved and literally makes everything now. Society has devolved further, so the gap between rich and poor is much more profound. A young thete, a member of poor illiterate tribes who belong to no one, ends up with a newly developed prototype book that teaches her to use her mind. The book follows several characters who have vital parts to play in the culmination of the story. This is literary cyberpunk with multiple plotlines that come to a conclusive and intriguingly complex ending. It will draw you in with its harsh reality and pull you along as we see Nell grow into the hard-edged young lady she will become. This is an edgy classic that is both philosophical and haunting in its portrayal of the future.

Stephenson, Neal, *Snow Crash* (1992) BK
Stephenson's first real cyberpunk novel follows in the footsteps of Gibson's *Neuromancer*. Hiro, a pizza delivery boy and virtual warrior, gets caught up in events that merge the real and online worlds of the future in a sarcastic and suspenseful way. Action-oriented and character-centered, this evocative political thriller moves at a breakneck speed, throwing in sword-fighting and ecoterrorism just for fun. This book is a cult classic.

Steampunk

Steampunk is currently experiencing a spike in popularity and seems to be finding a home among teen and adult readers. Steampunk is an excellent example of integrated advisory as it is more than just a book-based phenomenon. Parties, museums, and conventions are dedicated to steampunk, and dressing up is an important part of this emerging subculture.

Gibson, William, and Bruce Sterling, *The Difference Engine* (1991) BK, CL
In this steampunk classic, in 1885, Charles Babbage created the Analytical Engine, and the computer age arrived in the midst of the Victorian Age. This is a detective

story, a historical thriller, and one of the first steampunk novels from one of the masters of cyberpunk.

Girl Genius, Folio, Phil, and Kaja Folio, *Agatha Herotodyne and the Beetleburg Clank* **(2002) MN**
Agatha Heterodyne has the Spark, the creative power to invent fantastic steam-powered machines. And the Spark gets her into more adventures than could reasonably be considered sane in this fun-filled series.

Hollow Fields, Madeline Rosca (2007) YA, MN
A young girl finds herself accidentally enrolled in a school for budding criminal masterminds. Will she survive a place where no one ever comes back from detention?

Keys to the Kingdom, Garth Nix, *Mister Monday* **(2003) YA, BK, UAB, AP**
Arthur has asthma and can barely run, let alone complete the cross-country course at his new school. But a near-death experience on the course completely changes his life when he became the Heir to the Architect, the supernatural being who created all the Secondary Realms (including Earth) as well as the House, the true center of the universe. Arthur eventually realizes he must not only gain each of the seven keys, but must accept that he is the Heir to the House and the Will. A near-future setting and the steampunk environs of the House make this a fantastical but essentially science fiction story.

McMullen, Sean, *Souls in the Great Machine* **(1999) BK, AP**
This alternative future by Australian science fiction author Sean McMullen takes us to a world that has suffered a major catastrophe in its past and now all those who are in the educated and administrative classes are required to carry handguns as symbols of their power and judgment. World communication is by hand or beam flash, electricity no longer exists, steam power is outlawed, and most highly developed societies use wind power. It is detailed and complex with an epic scope as to how society works, with lots of foreboding, adventure, and imagination thrown in to keep the reader interested. From crazy gun-toting librarian mathematicians to religious zealots and warring tribes across barren deserts, this is an intelligent and sophisticated classic.

Moore, Alan, *The League of Extraordinary Gentlemen* **(2002) GN, MV, AP**
Heroes from Victorian literature are brought together to fight a menace facing Great Britain and the world in this well-paced adventure. It's worth the cover price for the fun of playing "spot the reference" throughout the pages. And it is oh-so-much better than the movie of the same name.

Steamboy, Katsuhiro Otomo (2004) MN, MV
Young Ray Steam must find a way to stop the ultimate weapon, a fortress-sized ship invented by his father and grandfather.

Westerfelt, Scott, *Leviathan* **(2009) BK, YA, SH**
World War II is reimagined, with Britain (the Darwinists) fighting with animal-based machines, while Germany and Austria (the Clankers) fight using steam-based machines. Prince Aleksander, a Hapsburg prince, escapes Austria at the outbreak of the war and is on the run in a small Clanker. Meanwhile, Deryn, disguised as a boy, becomes a midshipman in the British Air Service and is assigned to the *Leviathan*, a great whaling ship, for a secret mission. With fascinating descriptions of the two

competing technologies and exciting action scenes, this is a perfect choice for those new to steampunk.

Making Connections

Science fiction can be intimidating and is one of the less often read genres, but as evidenced by the popularity of science fiction movies (*Star Wars* and *Terminator*), science fiction stories have wide appeal. In the next section, we explore science fiction for those who identify with other genres.

Action and Adventure: Near-Future Thrillers

Science fiction fans are not the only audience for science fiction stories; near-future thrillers can be great recommendations for library patrons who enjoy thrillers and action-adventure stories. Many of these get made into mainstream movies, so they are good to know about, even if you're not ready to tackle the rest of the science fiction world.

Anderson, Barth, *The Patron Saint of Plagues* (2006) BK
In Anderson's near-future thriller, delicate peace negotiations in Mexico are threatened by a deadly virus that could decimate North and South America. Only Henry Stark, leader of a team from the U.S. Centers for Disease Control, can prevent an epidemic. But first he has to be smuggled over the unstable U.S.-Mexico border.

Conviser, Josh, *Echelon* (2006) BK
This is a fast-moving read about Echelon, the organization that controls and monitors everything, often playing god, and those who decide that it is better to just let things happen than to control them. Intriguing characters are often conflicted with moral dilemmas. Echelon also mixes in biotech advances that seem very possible in the near future and that add interesting twists. Action, suspense, violence, and intrigue make this a compellingly suspenseful read.

Farmer, Nancy, *The House of the Scorpion* (2002) YA, SH, BK, UAB
This story is set in the near future, when the border region between the United States and Mexico is a separate country controlled by drug lords and is the home of Matt, a clone of the 142-year-old drug lord, El Patron. But clones are raised for one purpose only—to serve as replacement bodies for the very rich and powerful, and it is nearly too late when Matt realizes his intended fate.

<u>Halo</u>, Eric Nylund, *Halo: The Fall of Reach* (2001) AP, YA, BK, VGM
Released in conjunction with the first video game, *Halo: Combat Evolved*, this book is really a prequel for the video game. It follows the story of the Master Chief or Spartan 117, John to his fellow Spartans. The Spartans are a unit of cybernetically enhanced humans trained from a very young age to be marine soldiers. They are stronger, faster, and have various enhancements such as superhuman hearing and sight that make them the ultimate ground warriors. This story follows the creation of the Spartan unit along with the escalating war between the human race and a group of aliens known as the Covenant that are bent on wiping out people from the universe. This highly successful series of books and video games may also see the production of a movie in the near future.

Moore, Alan, *V for Vendetta* **(1982) CL, GN, MV**
England has survived the nuclear war that wiped out the rest of the world, and its new government runs the island as a police state. It's a state where Motown records are illegal and citizens live in fear of being arrested by corrupt police. But one person has a vision of freedom and a plan to bring it about.

Morgan, Richard K., *Market Forces* **(2004) BK**
This high-energy techno-political thriller is set in the near future where corporations have taken over the political machinations of nations and rebellions. It is a mix between Mad Max-type futuristic road-rage battles and a Tom Clancy-esque world of politics, espionage, third-world revolts, and economics. The major character, Chris, struggles with the ethics of being good in a corporate world gone bad. Excellent character development reveals his struggle between being good and getting sucked into a world gone rotten. Morgan has created a dystopian world, and there is very bloody graphic violence and strong language throughout.

Sawyer, Robert J., *Flashforward* **(1999) AP, BK, TV**
The idea of the flashforward, or jump ahead in the time line of a story, has been used since the 1960s. This book takes that idea one step further in trying to come up with a plausible scientific basis for an actual flashforward event that everyone on Earth experiences. Intertwining complex physics with personable characters with ethical dilemmas, Sawyer asks, what would you do if you knew what was in your future? Blending introspective and philosophical moods with sophisticated scientific ideas and classic futuristic science fiction elements, this is not one to be missed. It was the basis of a television series.

Science Fiction for Fantasy Fans

As there is some significant overlap in the appeals of science fiction and fantasy, and many readers enjoy both, there are many possible suggestions, and those listed below work equally well for teen and adult readers. Long-established fan favorites, both Darkover and Dragonriders of Pern have been the gateway for many new science fiction and fantasy readers and are examples of world-building and historical and cultural development in science fiction.

Darkover, Marion Zimmer Bradley, Deborah J. Ross, Adrienne Martine-Barnes, and Mercedes Lackey (1958) BK, UAB, CL
Since the late 1950s, the late Marion Zimmer Bradley and her collaborators have written more than 25 full-length novels and dozens of short stories set on Darkover, a lost and then rediscovered colony. Over thousands of years of isolation, it developed a complex culture and mythology that includes a wide variety of psychic abilities and a pantheon of powerful deities. *The Bloody Sun*, originally written in 1964 and rewritten in 1979, is a good choice for new readers, as it is set only a short time after Darkover is rediscovered by the Terran Federation. Readers who wish to start at the beginning would want *Darkover Landfall* (1972), about the crash landing and the first terrible years in Darkover's brutal climate.

Dies the Fire and The Change, S. M. Stirling, *Dies the Fire* **(2004) BK, UAB, YA**
A sudden disaster causes all electronics and firearms to quit working, leading to a rapid breakdown of society. Some of the survivors are led by Juniper, founder of Clan MacKenzie, a non-violent agrarian group, and others are led by Mike, a former

pilot, and form the Bearkillers, with the help of Society of Creative Anachronism members who teach them how to use ancient weapons. Despite their dreams of peace, a history professor has gathered a group of rogues and criminals in downtown Portland; they are determined to recreate feudal society.

Dragonriders of Pern, Anne McCaffrey, *Dragonflight* (1968) BK, UAB, YA, SH
Anne McCaffrey's dragons may have scientific origins but that will not dent the appeal for fans of dragon fantasies. In the 2,500 years since the original colonization, much has been lost, but the dragons have more than reached their full potential as the main weapon against the deadly and voracious Threadfall. Fantasy readers should start the series with the Hugo- and Nebula-winning *Dragonflight*, the first novel of Pern, which introduces Lessa, her queen dragon, Ramoth, and their mates F'lar and his dragon Mnementh.

Heris Serrano and Esmay Suiza, Elizabeth Moon, *Hunting Party* (1993) BK, SH
Fans of fantasy similar to Elizabeth Moon's female-oriented Deeds of Paksenarrion series (1988) will find it easy to transition to her science fiction series. Older readers might want to start with *Hunting Party*, the first in a series about middle-aged and unemployed Heris Serrano, who takes a job as the captain of a rich elderly woman's private yacht out of desperation after losing her military career.

Marukami, Haruki, *Hard-Boiled Wonderland* (1991) BK, UAB
Often a bizarre or even surreal look at how we define ourselves and thus interact with the world around us, this will definitely appeal to fans of Philip K. Dick or Neil Gaiman. There are two separate but parallel narratives going on flipping from chapter to chapter. One takes place in an alternative version of Tokyo and the other in a town not unlike Wall in Neil Gaiman's *Stardust*. Full of comedy, satire, drama, and moments of terror, this book will stay with you for a while.

Moore, Alan, *The League of Extraordinary Gentlemen* (2002) GN, MV, AP
Heroes from Victorian literature are brought together to fight a menace facing Great Britain and the world in this well-paced adventure. It's worth the cover price for the fun of playing "spot the reference" throughout the pages. And it is oh-so-much better than the movie of the same name.

Pratt, Tim, *The Strange Adventures of Rangergirl* (2005) BK
This book is an interesting mix of modern-day, Old West, and fantasy fiction. It is set in current-day Santa Cruz and based around the story of a young woman working in a coffee shop. But, of course, it isn't just any coffee shop, but contains a link in the storeroom to an alternate reality where the comics the young woman draws in her free time come to life and try to take over California. It is steadily paced with eccentric characters, a mixing of a small-town feel with a stark desert feel to its descriptions, and a gritty, moody edge to the tone, with a story that we all know the ending to before it happens.

Stephenson, Neal, *Crypotnomicom* (1999) BK, UAB, AP
An epic tale of code making and code breaking, mixing historical fiction and near-future science fiction, Stephenson's book takes commitment. At more than 1,000 pages long with sometimes-meandering plotlines, parts of the novel get very technical, but this densely written story is worth the effort. It won the Hugo award in 2000 and draws in readers of contemporary fiction, thrillers, and historical novels, in addition to fantasy fans.

Vatta's War, Elizabeth Moon, *Trading in Danger* (2003) BK, UAB
Ky is sent off to escort a nearly derelict ship to the scrap yards after being thrown out of the military academy, but while she is off the planet, her wealthy and powerful merchant family is attacked. As one of the few survivors, she leads the hunt to track down the killers.

Science Fiction for Romance Readers

Romance readers who enjoy the many recent paranormal and speculative stories are ripe for introduction to science fiction stories with strong romantic elements. While romance authors like Susan Grant have only recently ventured into this field, romantic space operas have long been a part of science fiction. Catherine Asaro and Anne McCaffrey frequently wrap love stories into their science fiction, but they are not the only ones.

2176, Susan Grant, Kathleen Nance, Liz Maverick, and Patti O'Shea, *The Legend of Banzai Maguire* (2004) BK, AP, SH
This romance-shared series is set in 2176, when global warming has greatly altered the landscape. Pilots Bree "Banzai" and Cam "Scarlett" are shot down in North Korea in 2003, only to be frozen by a rogue scientists and reawakened in 2176 when the United States they loved has become the United Colonies of Earth. While each book has a strong romance plotline, the future setting is well described and scarily realistic, making the series an excellent science fiction/romance crossover.

Asaro, Catherine, *Skyfall* (2003) BK, UAB
Skyfall is part of Asaro's sprawling Skolian Saga, several of which feature love stories. Skyfall is the least technical of the series as it takes place almost entirely on a recently rediscovered and technologically backward world. It details the meeting between Eldrinson, the ruler of a primitive planet, and Roca, a beautiful dancer and mother of the ruthless imperial heir, Kurj. Both Roca and Eldrinson are powerful psions, individuals with telepathic powers, and their mental abilities account for their unexpected attraction for each other. Historically, Skyfall is the earliest in the Skolian series and is a good introduction to it.

Brain and Brawn Ships, Anne McCaffrey, *The Ship Who Sang* (1969) BK, UAB, YA
Helva was born too crippled to survive, so her parents grant permission for her to become one of the ship people; her brain is encased inside a ship and she becomes its computers. Helva delights in her new body, particularly her ability to sing in all possible ranges, and adores her human partner. Each book explores a new brain/brawn relationship.

Freedom, Anne McCaffrey, *Freedom's Landing* (1996) BK, UAB, AP
This is the story of Kris, a college student at the University of Denver, and her attempts to survive when she and a few hundred other humans are kidnapped by aliens and dumped on a new planet to test its prospects as a colony. But the humans are not alone; Zainal, a Catteni noble, has also been dumped as punishment, and as Kris is one the few humans who will work with him, they gradually develop a close relationship, even as they come to love their new home.

Star Wars, Episodes I–III (1999) SH, MV, BK, UAB
The ultimately doomed romance of Anakin Skywalker and Senator Amidala plays out over several years, from their fateful meeting during the embargo of Naboo, to their reunion at the outbreak of the Clone Wars and the birth of their children Luke

and Leia during the fall of the republic. While some fans complain of clumsy dialogue, their romance is one of the key elements in the Star Wars universe, and both are unable to live without the other.

Tower and the Hive, Anne McCaffrey, *The Rowan* (1991) BK, UAB

When she was three years old, Rowan's parents were killed in a mudslide and she was buried for nearly a week. Rowan may be one of the strongest Talents ever born, but first she has to survive growing up as a "white-haired freak." At 18, she's in charge of her own tower on Callisto, but terribly alone, until she talks with Jeff on Deneb, a man whose psychic powers may match her own. Rowan must conquer her agoraphobia and fight the aliens to save Jeff, Deneb, and her whole civilization from the deadly Hivers. Rowan's descendants continue the fight against the Hivers.

Vorkosigan Saga, Lois McMaster Bujold, *Shards of Honor* (1986) SH, BK, UAB

Cordelia Naismith is a survey captain for the peaceful Beta colony when her landing party is driven off by mutinous Barrayaran soldiers and she is captured by their former leader, Aral Vorkosigan, also known as the Butcher of Komarr. As Aral and Cordelia trek through the wilderness, they come to understand each other and fall in love. After their respective home planets declare war, is there any chance for their relationship?

Literary and Mainstream Science Fiction

Sometimes mainstream and literary authors write science fiction stories, and sometimes science fiction authors write a story that gets picked up by mainstream readers. Regardless, these are the books that get talked about by all types of readers, often win awards, and end up on school reading lists. They are often made into movies as well. These aren't always the best science fiction stories, as big social issues and/or mainstream stories can crowd out the science fiction elements, but they have enough science fiction to make them science fiction stories, regardless of what their authors say (and we're talking about you, Margaret Atwood!). Sometimes these stories use the framework of science fiction as a tool to comment on modern society.

Atwood, Margaret, *Oryx and Crake* (2003) BK, UAB

A cautionary tale about the end of civilization told from the point of view of Snowman, who just might be the last true human left on Earth as he takes care of a group of experimental human-like creatures whom he calls the Children of Crake. *Year of the Flood* (2009) takes place at the same time and tells about some of the same events.

Burgess, Anthony, *A Clockwork Orange* (1962) BK, MV, TV, UAB

In a not-too-distant future, teenagers run rampant and leave society teetering on the edge of collapse. Scientists perform an experiment on one of the worst offenders to determine if he can be eventually completely turned off from violence. An excellent example of classical conditioning, the book was made into multiple movie and TV versions, including the well-known and controversial movie by Stanley Kubrick.

Dick, Philip K., *Do Androids Dream of Electric Sheep?* (1968) BK, MV, UAB

Dick's classic book was made into the critically acclaimed movie *Blade Runner*. It is the story of bounty hunter Rick Deckard, whose job is to hunt down and "retire" the androids that keep trying to come to Earth to escape their role as chattel. Built to make life on Mars easier for the colonists, androids are forbidden from coming to the wrecked remains of Earth. Set after World War Terminus when the few remaining humans on Earth are gradually being poisoned by radiation, the book asks many big questions about what it means to be human.

McCarthy, Cormac, *The Road* (2005) BK, MV, UAB, AB

This is a grim, post-apocalyptic father-son story that focuses on the desperate search for hope and survival in a bleak and brutal world. The father and son trudge across the ash-covered landscape, devoid of all life except for bands of cannibalistic thugs; McCarthy renders difficult scenes with spare and searing prose. An Oprah Book Club pick, it was also made into a movie starring Viggo Mortensen.

Moore, Alan, *V for Vendetta* (1990) GN, MV, CL

England has survived the nuclear war that wiped out the rest of the world and its new government runs the island as a police state. It's a state where Motown records are illegal and citizens live in fear of being arrested by corrupt police. But one person has a vision of freedom and a plan to bring it about.

Moore, Alan, *Watchmen* (1987) GN, MV, CL, AP

This classic of the medium posits a world in which the United States and the Soviet Union teeter on the brink of nuclear war while a group of former "costumed adventurers" (essentially superheros without superpowers) struggle to figure out who is killing their former enemies and comrades. In the end, the mystery is solved and war is averted, but at what cost? This thought-provoking story set a new standard for "heroic" graphic novels.

Orwell, George, *1984* (1949) BK, TV, MV, UAB, CL, SH

Since its publication in 1949, *1984* has been one of the most widely read science fiction books and is frequently assigned in schools. Set in future London (1984), Winston Smith is a government worker and lives under the constant surveillance of Big Brother. *1984* is worth consuming to appreciate all of the terms and concepts that have pervaded modern thought. In addition to the many television and movie adaptations, *1984* has also been adapted for the stage and for radio.

Conclusion

Science fiction's audience will continue to grow as mainstream movies like *Avatar* draw in record-breaking crowds and teens devour novels like *Hunger Games* and *Life As We Knew It*. Science fiction TV shows will continue to be popular and may even gain larger audiences, especially character-driven dramas like *Battlestar Galatica* that appeal to a wide audience.

Over the next several years, libraries are likely to see an increased demand for science fiction manga and graphic novels. Since these illustrated formats are especially popular with younger readers, as they age and become the main users of the library collection, they will continue to want their science fiction in illustrated formats. Anime versions of manga series will also likely be in demand as fans will want to see their favorite characters on the screen.

Libraries will also need to increase their collections of science fiction TV shows as these are almost always shown on cable, which not all library users have access to. Just because they can't see the shows when they initially air on TV doesn't mean that they won't want to see them a few months later on DVD. It will be especially important to keep up with new and emerging shows; if they gain a larger audiences after the first or second season, fans will want to check out and watch the missed episodes.

In terms of books, they will continue to thrive and have a dedicated readership. Don't forget to suggest some of the excellent YA titles to adult readers; science fiction fans are some of the most likely to be willing to read across age barriers as long as they are guaranteed a good science fiction story. E-books will likely be in demand by science fiction readers as they are early adopters and many may already have e-book readers and will be looking for material. Regular library users will expect the library to provide e-book collections just as they do print book collections, so these should not be overlooked.

This is an exciting time for science fiction and integrated advisory as science fiction is thriving in all formats and science fiction fans are quite amenable to not only moving beyond books for their leisure needs, but most are more than willing to discuss science fiction preferences in terms of a variety of media.

Resources for Librarians

Turn to these resources for help when practicing science integrated advisory.

Fantastic Fiction: http://www.fantasticfiction.co.uk/
> With an emphasis on writers of genre fiction, the Fantastic Fiction database is a wonderful resource that features author photos, brief author bios, book jackets, and plot summaries for more than 25,000 writers. Don't have time to linger? Search by author or title to get a quick bibliographical list of titles arranged in publication order.

Internet Movie Database: http://www.imdb.com.
> IMDB is your one-stop shop information on films and television. If a novel or short story has been adapted for the screen, even if the title has changed, you'll find it here. There's a wealth of information, including plot summaries, movie stills, and extensive information on the actors and those behind the scenes of any given production. Most TV shows have per-episode plot summaries.

Rough Guide to Sci-Fi Movies by John Scalzi. London: Rough Guides, 2005.
> Science fiction author Scalzi has written the definitive guide to science fiction movies. Reviewing hundreds of movies, from 1950s B movies to classics of the genre, to overlooked newer releases, this is an excellent source.

SciFan: http://www.scifan.com
> Web sites for readers of fantasy. abound, but with more than 70,000 books and 20,000 writers, surely the most comprehensive is SciFan. Devoted to science fiction and fantasy books, the site includes information on new and upcoming releases while maintaining a staggering amount of information about older titles. When practicing integrated advisory, be sure to refer to their many thematic lists ("Crosswords," "Steampunk," or "Indonesia," for instance).

Strictly Science Fiction: A Guide to Reading Interests by Diana Tixier Herald and Bonnie Kunzel. Westport, CT: Libraries Unlimited, 2002.
> The single best source for information on science fiction books published before 2002, it is broken down into subjects based subgenres and categories.

Wikipedia: http://www.wikipedia.org.
> Though the world's most famous online encyclopedia has its faults, it is often the fastest, easiest, and sometimes only place to find information. (If reliability is crucial to your search, you can always confirm or deny the information from Wikipedia in a second source.) When practicing integrated advisory, Wikipedia can be especially helpful because articles will typically

indicate the different types of media to which a story has been adapted. It is one of the best places for finding information on complicated multiformat series and quite useful for understanding science fiction terms like steampunk or cyberpunk.

Endnotes

1. Palmiere, JoAnn. "Chapter 10: Science Fiction: Essay." In *Genreflecting: A Guide to Popular Reading Interests, 6th ed.* Westport, CT: Libraries Unlimited, 2006.

2. "Science Fiction Magazines." Wikipedia, http://en.wikipedia.org/wiki/Science_fiction_magazine.

3. Baen Books, Webscription E-books, http://www.webscription.net/.

8

Everything Street Literature
Rollie Welch

In this chapter, Rollie Welch covers the emerging genre of street lit and defines this elusive and controversial genre, including its appeal to teen readers. Plots and characters in street fiction are tied closely together, and these sections may appear to overlap. The "Plots" section focuses on stories about the drug culture, living with and overcoming poverty, and the allure of the hip-hop music industry. In "Characters," you'll find lists of people determined to rise to the top (no matter what it takes in some instances), street lit relationships, and powerful females. A major theme of street lit is betrayal, and this section also includes a special list on teens and disloyalty. Lastly, in "Making Connections," you'll find street lit titles for mystery fans, GLBT readers, and an extensive list of titles with teen appeal on the topics of crime, poverty, drug abuse, and violence.

Introduction

The publishing business and the general public continue to struggle to understand the exploding world of urban lit, a literary subgenre with interchangeable names ranging from urban lit, street lit, to ghetto books (or ghetto stories) and gangsta lit. The wide variety of labels compounds the confusion.

Defining Street Lit

So what is street lit? In a nutshell, street lit is a fiction subgenre that spectacularly portrays many issues and situations that people living in the inner city deal with on a daily basis. But that's only part of the story.

Street lit has the unfortunate reputation of being pornographic, glorifying the criminal life, promoting sexual conquests and the abuse of females, misogyny, or romanticizing violence that cheapens life. These qualities do apply to some street lit, but a more general characteristic is the explicitness of its sex and violence. Street lit is also widely read by inner-city citizens, including teens. The stories hit hard and are more plot-driven than in-depth character studies. That's not to say that the characters bursting from the pages of street lit are stereotypical or one-dimensional. In fact, street lit fans often comment on how the genre's characters struggle with doing the right thing while trying to "keep their head up."

Outside of inner-city life, there are several other elements common to street lit stories. Street lit can involve crime, often leading to the violent murder of enemies of the protagonist. Many titles' storylines pivot on fabulous wealth gained by dealing drugs, running a gambling operation, or other legally questionable pursuits. Street lit authors are often adept at creating incredibly graphic sexual scenes. Indeed, many titles focus on sex, not crime. But the bottom line is, true street lit always has a core forged in the inner-city streets and depicts the tough challenges and choices faced on a daily basis by the people who live there.

Stories Linked to Inner-City Streets

Let's start with a firm explanation of what street lit is all about. First and foremost, the stories must be rooted or connected to the streets. Not all of the action has to be centered in the ghetto, but street lit must have some connection to harsh lessons learned on the streets. These lessons can be forced onto characters during their developmental years, their teenage years, or even at some point in their adult lives. No matter what action or conflicts are presented in an urban lit novel, the problems, solutions, advice, and decisions reflect the experiences the characters gleaned from living harsh realities on the streets.

Lessons learned in the streets almost always have direct bearing on street lit's climactic scenes and can be as straightforward as "don't trust anyone outside of your immediate network." This network can be family, friends, or a gang. Individuals hovering inside the borders of the network often are childhood buddies, girlfriends, sex partners, or close relatives. Outsiders may be social workers, teachers, police officers, and other members of the legal profession. These are people with a stake in the main character making a difficult, but ultimately positive, life choice.

Another common "lesson" is that life is cheap in the inner city. Many street lit plots begin with the characters inexorably caught in a no-win situation. Characters are generally unemployed or underemployed. Home is a crumbling house or apartment projects stacked closely together with neighbors of questionable mental or moral stability. Early on in most street lit stories, a tragedy occurs to reinforce the cheapness and severity of daily life. Police may gun down a drug dealer as unsullied youth, former reflections of the story's main characters, witness the death. A drive-by may take an innocent life, usually someone close to the main character. These tragedies serve the purpose of hardening the main character, who later on may give no quarter to his or her rivals.

Money is of paramount importance in these stories. Characters are born and raised in poverty with their parents, or more likely a single mother, struggling to make ends meet. Understanding what economic hardship is all about often drives street lit story lines. Why not make easy cash slingin' rock if that is the quickest way to escape poverty? Materialism—gathering enormous amounts of money and spending it on expensive consumer goods, is another trademark of the genre. Urban lit novels are often laden with expensive and recognizable brand names. Automobiles are generally Bentleys or Mercedes-Benz or, in cases of lavish wealth, Maybachs. Women's accessories and clothes are always expensive labels—Gucci, Louis Vuitton, Jimmy Choo, Armani, Versace, and Prada. Even more common attire has brand names. Guys roam the streets wearing Sean John, Rocawear, or Timberlands.

Street lit characters often move from the ghetto to an upper-middle-class setting or a high-profile wealthy environment. But no matter where they settle, their decisions, actions, and thoughts are based on the lessons of trust, mistrust, and avoidance of poverty learned during their formative years on the streets.

Street Lit, Storytelling, and Parables

Street lit titles follow the basic concept of ancient oral storytelling; the primary purpose is to entertain the listener or, in this case, the reader. This explains the outrageous plot elements of crime, sex, and money. Readers connect with the easy path to incredible wealth, a concept that is one of the major complaints about street lit; it glamorizes a "get-rich-by-any-means" mindset. For readers, part of the appeal is to read about characters raised in poverty who find ways to gain wealth that enables them to cruise in a Benz, purchase clothes exclusively from Gucci, or tip valet parking with $100 bills. These stories are updated versions of Horatio Alger's "rags-to-riches" stories of the nineteenth century.

Like most good storytelling, seeds planted early in the tale have direct bearing on the final result. A childhood bond may lead to unexpected repercussions between adult friends or adversaries later in life. A young child may observe a parent's desperate struggle to provide for the family and vow never to leave loved ones in want of anything. A favor that seems unimportant early on becomes the key component to save a character from a major disaster later in the story. Street lit authors mine this concept and layer plots around it. The common theme of teenagers bonding, then taking separate paths in life, and reconnecting after tragedy or conflict is one plot that draws inner-city youth to read adult street lit titles.

As in famous parables retold over centuries, there are often cautionary or moralistic themes laced throughout street lit titles. For example, movement in the drug trafficking trade results in one of three consequences: the character is either murdered or seriously injured, the character may be incarcerated for an extended period of time, or the character becomes addicted to their own merchandise. Think of Tony Montana, Al Pacino's character in the movie *Scarface*, who embarks on this exact path of destruction. In its most simple form, street lit offers a setting and an action and then shows readers the results. These three components are melded into an urban backdrop along with current slang, and occasionally the stories are predictable and formulaic. However, street lit authors at the top of their game avoid this trap and write with a fresh voice, crafting intricate plots with layered characters.

Urban lit plots make great use of the traditional rags-to-riches tale. At the beginning of the story, a character is poor, and after hard work, grim determination, and an unlikely spot of luck, a set of related circumstances opens the door to fabulous wealth with a caveat. These traditionally glitzy tales come with hard lessons learned, as do many street lit titles. Like television ads promising to easily change a problem, the situations in these stories are usually too good to be true. The resulting fall from grace, power, and privilege is grim. Final resolutions may include loss of the big money, incarceration, or even a violent death. Think of street lit's storylines like the first big roller coaster hill. The climb to the top is full of excitement and suspense, but the sudden plunge is swift and often furious.

Authentic to Inner-City Life

Urban lit readers gravitate to stories that take place on inner-city streets of major U.S. cities. No bucolic small towns or tranquil beach villages here. Many locations where authors choose to set their tales are notorious for crime. Thus Harlem, Brooklyn, the Bronx, Compton, East Baltimore, and North Philly are all popular settings.

Life revolving around crime, either by directly breaking the law or existing near criminal activity, is a key component of street lit. The most often committed crime in street lit is drug dealing. Illegal drugs, ranging from marijuana to, cocaine, crack, and heroin, all have been included as plot catalysts in street lit. One thing that makes urban lit appealing is authentic representations of these drugs. Marijuana is often used as an icebreaker between two potential adversaries or as a "get-to-know-you" dating ploy between men and women. Cocaine is usually viewed as an expensive plaything that leads to addiction, thus destroying relationships. Crack and heroin physically alter characters into beings resembling zombies.

The realism is further accentuated in street lit by use of the slang terminology that hammers home drug use. Marijuana is smoked in "blunts," and often a paragraph is inserted into the story about the correct method of slicing the cigar, removing the tobacco, and stuffing in the pot. Copious amounts of pot are smoked in street lit titles, often before characters set out on an important errand, such as confronting a rival intruding on another character's turf. Authors go into great detail about the preparation of drugs for recreational use or business sales all while using the colloquial language of dealers and users.

The more accurate the slang, the more appeal to the story. Thus, "moving eight balls" or "slangin' rock" are phrases with higher street lit reader appeal than "selling drugs on the corner." Many authors simply group drug dealing into a general statement of their characters "selling product."

Name-dropping is another way authors bring immediacy to their stories. Hip-hop artists and song lyrics flood the pages, lending the stories a vibrancy connected to the streets. But use of hip-hop references is a double-edged sword. Authors on the cutting edge of new music may alienate readers who may not recognize the latest talent on the market or quickly date their own novels as these hot artists fall out of favor as they fall off the charts. A "right-now" feel is brought on by listing artists such as Jadakiss, Fabolous, or Young Jeezy, but older readers may not get the connection. Street lit authors tend to set the time frame of their works to their own preference and familiarity with music. If authors are more in tune with Tupac and Biggie, then the story is set in the mid-1990s. The same qualifications of authenticity come into play with brand names of shoes, dresses, jeans, automobiles, credit cards, and movies.

Shocking and Bold

Many books mention sex, crime, drug use, hip-hop music, and brand names. What separates street lit from more mainstream titles is the outrageousness of events.

If a simple crime is committed, often it becomes the impetus that fuels a major criminal or his gang. For example, a convenience store holdup might happen on a rival's turf and a stray bullet kills a relative. Retribution is quickly determined, and a major shootout highlighted by a high body count soon follows. Group murders actually do happen in today's inner cities, but not at the almost military firefight level with a dozen or more deaths often described in street lit novels. Drug dealing is done on the level of millions of dollars changing hands. If a nickel-and-dime operation is working, it will either be snuffed out or the players will parlay their business into locking down the entire neighborhood. Shopping sprees in street lit novels have women (and sometimes men) casually pulling out platinum cards and purchasing single items listed at thousands of dollars. An easy lifestyle with seemingly no consequences and a bottomless supply of cash is often the setup at the beginning of the street lit story. Higher quality, more readable street lit titles connect this fabulous wealth and these shocking plot twists to an earlier life laced with abject poverty and a brutal life growing up on the streets.

How is street lit different from other novels containing high levels of violence? While fiction titles by many authors contain instances of crime and murder, street lit takes these themes to a different level. Keep in mind that the extreme nature of the crimes and other actions are a main draw for street lit readers and gangs, and their crimes are staples of the genre. What distinguishes street lit is once a conflict or betrayal is uncovered, revenge comes fast and hard. Snitches are not simply removed, but die agonizing deaths, often while the story's main character gives a "hast a la vista" speech before the final dispatch. And the victim expects no mercy. Bravado gushes from the soon-to-die victims as they snarl in the face of death.

Revenge may not be limited to a single individual. Several members of a rival gang may be wiped out in a gloriously bloody exchange of gunfire. Shootouts in crack houses with high body counts are common scenes. Drive-bys at block parties show who is the boss. By vividly describing bullets tearing into flesh, blood spurting in firework patterns of liquid red, the temporary loss of hearing and adrenaline rush of close proximity to high-powered weapons, authors make sure readers understand the brutality of revenge and how clemency is a foreign concept.

Because urban lit is all about life in the streets, it must necessarily emphasize harsh realities. It stands to reason that relationships between men and women keep in step with this grim reality. There are very few demure and decorous fadeouts at the end of chapters when couples begin to get it on. Authors tend to write these scenes with an all-seeing lens. Sexual encounters occurring in street lit have been compared, usually in an unfavorable way, to erotica, soft porn, and sometimes hardcore pornography. As stated earlier, street lit authors depend on their stories having some shock value in order to sell, thus sex scenes, like violence and glitz, are amped up to a scandalously outrageous level. The sexual act generally lasts for hours. Women challenge men to give more. Men demand that women submit to their power. The graphic dialogue shouted during sex features a variety of harsh slang terms for sexual acts and body parts. This language gives street lit its most notorious reputation. To borrow a street term, the sex between these pages is often grimy.

In this genre, there are more instances of physical abuse between men and women than there are of actual criminal rape. Rape, usually against a beloved family member, is more often a motivator for revenge. The crime usually happens off the pages or happens at a time before the novel opens.

The exaggerated sex scenes may explain one of the appeals street fiction has for teenagers. Adolescents beginning to explore their sexuality read the inflated sex scenes in street lit novels and become shocked and titillated. They'll quickly share the juicier passages with their friends. These teens may never engage in such an over-the-top sexual encounter as they have read in these novels, but that is part of the fantasy. The connection between readers interested in discovering their own sexuality and their reading graphic sex scenes in street lit novels is easily made. Not only is the raw sex intriguing, but it also explains the concerns many adults and educators have about teenagers clamoring to read these sexy urban dramas, often ignoring recommended reading put in place by libraries and schools.

Not all characters in urban lit engage in explicit casual sex. There are noble characters who see sex and romance as a means to a happy-ever-after lifestyle. But frequently the sex lacks romance; it is usually depicted as a rough, nasty, and powerfully intense experience. In some street lit titles, such as K'wan's *Still Hood* and *T.H.U.G. L.I.F.E.* by Sanyika Shakur, male criminals are steadfastly loyal to their women and will make great personal sacrifices for them. Other titles featuring female protagonists show the women as tough, shrewd, and resourceful people who see right through a man's feigned interest to his real motivations.

Popular Street Lit Authors: A Suggested Starting Point

Street lit has definitely arrived in popular fiction. Reserve lists quickly grow long in urban libraries' catalogs. But what is a librarian to do if there aren't enough titles in the collection to meet patron demand? Below is a sampling of street lit authors who have written multiple titles. Consider this list a starting point for a core collection. Most of these authors have name recognition, and patrons eagerly await their next publications. These names are the leading authors in the street lit world and seldom write a boring story. With information about the biggest authors and suggestions for starting titles, this section is also a good place to start for readers and advisors new to street lit.

Chunichi   From Alabama to Virginia Beach, Chunichi lived her own fast lifestyle similar to the drama in a street novel's plot. Professional athletes were counted as friends along with other sports figures who introduced her to a lavish luxury. As she grew older, Chunichi earned a nursing degree and began fictionalizing the dramatic high points from her real life. Chunichi's writing always features a strong female character who has been wronged. These girls run with the big boys and set themselves up to take over their drug business. *California Connection* is her hottest title and its sequel, *California Connection 2*, was released in November 2009.

Clark, Wahida   Originally from New Jersey, Wahida Clark admits to spending some years in prison. While in prison she began her writing career. Is it any surprise that her writing is marked by tough females caught up in raw situations and balancing relationships with thugs? Clark's stories take readers right down to the streets where betrayal leads to murder. Her 2008 work, *Payback With Ya Life*, left readers clamoring for more.

Holmes, Shannon   Bronx native Shannon Holmes wrote his first novel while in prison for various drug charges. Although he only had a GED, Holmes stormed the street lit world with no prior writing experience. So far, he has produced several best-selling novels that have reached lofty sales numbers. Holmes is noted as a mentor for up-and-coming street lit writers. His 2008 book *Bad Girlz 4 Life* takes readers into a pay-for-sex corporation catering to VIPs.

K'wan   His full name is K'wan Foye and this author's writing consistently improves with every publication. Marked by extremely violent scenes, K'wan's writing connects readers with his characters. Authentic street slang and up-to-the-minute knowledge of street life make this author's works invaluable to street lit collections. K'wan has settled in with his favorite characters Lou-Loc and Gutter, who first appeared in the 2003 novel *Gangsta*.

Relentless Aaron   Relentless Aaron is the pseudonym of Dewitt Gilmore, a man who started writing while incarcerated and now enjoys large contracts with major publishing houses. Many of Aaron's works read like a male sexual fantasy wherein the women eagerly wait to be serviced by the men. Most often the guy is struggling to make ends meet until he meets an upper-class woman of refinement who cannot resist the hero's charms and must sleep with him, a decision that changes both lives in an instant.

Souljah, Sister   Her original name was Lisa Williamson and she's from the Bronx. In the early 1990s, Sister Souljah earned modest fame as a rapper. However, she burst into the spotlight by publically criticizing Bill Clinton's remarks about her views on race. Although she's shifted her focus to activism, Sister Souljah is still widely known for her books about male/female relationships and growing up on the streets. She has the distinction of writing both fiction and nonfiction. Her work *No Disrespect* is the story of her own life. *The Coldest Winter Ever* and its prequel *Midnight: A Gangster Love Story* are companion novels.

Stringer, Vickie   The founder and CEO of Triple Crown Publications, Vickie Stringer has taken her company to the heights of street lit. Many patrons don't refer to street lit as a genre, they simply request Triple Crown books. Not only a successful businesswoman, Stringer has firsthand knowledge of the drug game and her writing provides cautionary tales about falling into the drug trap. Stringer makes an effort to take time from the publishing arm of her business and keep her hand in the writing game. Her most recent novel is *Still Dirty*, published in 2008.

Turner, Nikki   This author now living near Richmond, Virginia, writes something along the lines of urban fairy tales. But her characters refuse to sit around and wait for their princes to ring doorbells. They would rather take matters into their own hands, charging ahead regardless of the consequences. Turner has founded her own imprint, Nikki Turner Presents. Her 2006 title, *Riding Dirty on I-95*, not only has a double meaning of carrying product and sex, it is one of the more recognizable single titles in all of street lit.

Zane   Known for introducing sexy and erotic tales featuring African American characters, Zane's books may not fall exactly into the street lit category. After all, the sex doesn't necessarily refer to street life. The sex is excessively rough and sexual encounters throughout the story become more and more disturbing. Nevertheless, many inner-city patrons pile up reserves on the next Zane book and impatiently wait their turn. Perhaps a more telling testimonial is that many new urban erotic tales fall under the heading "Zane Presents."

Origins of Street Lit

To paraphrase a Hollywood promotional statement, street lit is an overnight sensation years in the making. What we can pinpoint is that street lit was first written and read in the last 25 years of the twentieth century but only truly burst onto the literary landscape in the past 10 years.

As mentioned earlier, street lit has a connection to the streets, with roots in realistic situations that authors embellish with hyperbole. Magazines such as *Black Mask*, *Argosy*, *Dime Detective*, and *Spicy Detective* enjoyed a tremendous boost in circulation during the Great Depression. These stories were usually lurid, and their sensational cover art beckoned readers. Crimes were committed and women caught in the crossfire waited for men to rescue them. Sound familiar?

The detective magazines faded in the 1950s to be replaced in popularity by mass-market pulp paperbacks. Once again, sensationalized cover art drew readers into the garish tales. What the early magazines and the pulp paperbacks did was cash in on the kinds of stories readers were clamoring for: sex, crime, tough-guy dialogue, and larger-than-life characters.

Yet, there were few if any African American characters. This changed by the late 1960s and 1970s. Robert Beck, more famously known as Iceberg Slim, wrote a hard-hitting book called *Pimp: The Story of My Life* (1967). Having served multiple prison sentences, it wasn't until his last that Beck turned his life around by writing about it. *Pimp* was a groundbreaking work, borrowing elements from the pulps and adding those from the gritty world of inner-city streets. A seminal work of street fiction, *Pimp* is a classic and has never gone out of print.

The other benchmark author, Donald Goines, also drew from his own life experiences for his perennially popular works. He too began a writing career while serving a prison sentence. Following in Iceberg Slim's literary footsteps, Goines wrote his own semi-autobiographical work, *Whoreson: The Story of a Ghetto Pimp* (1971). Goines' works included rough characters such as pimps, prostitutes, dope fiends, and thieves. Unable to kick his drug habit after getting out of jail, Goines was murdered in 1974 along with his wife in what is believed to be a drug deal gone wrong.

In 1999, street lit found a powerful voice in Sister Souljah with the publication of *The Coldest Winter Ever*. This hard-hitting title established many basic conventions found in current street lit. Souljah introduced the aggressive, smart, and ruthless woman who knows her way around the streets. Other titles considered forerunners of the genre are Omar Tyree's *Flyy Girl* (1993) and Teri Woods' *True to the Game* (1999). These pioneering authors established street lit as a genre and have ushered in such widely known authors as Vikkie Stringer, Shannon Holmes, Anthony Whyte, Relentless Aaron, K'wan, Wahida Clark, and Nikki Turner.

Differences Between Street Lit and Other African American Fiction

Too often street lit is grouped into a general category labeled "African American fiction" or "black fiction." Due to lack of shelving space, many libraries shelve these urban dramas alongside the more literary works of Toni Morrison, James Baldwin, and Maya Angelou.

Regardless of where titles written by African American authors are shelved, distinctions between street lit and mainstream fiction are evident. Street lit is a subgenre of fiction, similar to romance and western novels. Nobody would think of separating books by dissimilar authors such as Danielle Steel and Louis L'Amour and regrouping them together due to the authors' race. The content gap between Steel and L'Amour is the same as K'wan's works and those of Toni Morrison. Nor should street lit be compared to fiction written by African American authors. To state that a typical street lit novel falls short in literary quality when compared to an award-winning fictional title is merely stating the obvious. Street lit should be evaluated as a genre. There are varying levels of quality within that genre, and voracious readers of street lit will easily determine titles that rise to the top.

Although street lit first exploded in the African American communities and remains the dominant characterization, not all street lit is African American. Latino street lit is establishing a foothold in the market. Jerry Rodriquez, author of *Devil's Mambo*, and Jeff Rivera, author of *Forever My Lady*, are two emerging authors, and Daniel Serrano's *Gunmetal Black* is a violent crime story featuring a Latino protagonist released from prison and determined to recover his money. The common denominator for street lit is a crime and the street atmosphere and thus is not restricted to the African American community.

The next section examines basic characteristics currently dominating this genre.

Sensationalized Cover Art

It's no secret that street content, as graphic as it can be, is accompanied by cover art that is also sensational. There are two types of images commonly seen on street lit covers. Sexy models striking poses clad in satin negligees (or less). These covers appeal to readers of both genders who glean that a sexy ride is waiting for them. Street lit with a focus on violence, gang activity, or crime will feature tough-looking muscle-bound men, often wearing shades or glaring menacingly from a title emphasizing weapons, chalk out-lines of bodies, or something else to suggest something illegal awaits the readers. Cover art also hints at the setting. Backdrops usually include a city skyline in the background, the main character pictured in the foreground on a deserted and litter-strewn street. Other props also make an appearance and can tell a reader or library staffer something about the story contained within: hundred-dollar bills, flashy jewelry, or a shiny fender of an expensive car all hint at the high stakes the characters are willing to risk for a piece of the luxurious pie.

No matter which general theme adorns street lit covers, the artwork can cause a con-siderable problem for some library staff and occasionally booksellers.

What needs to be understood among readers, readers' advisors, and booksellers is the fact that the cover doesn't lie; there really is no false advertising. The conundrum is how much does a cover that appears to glorify violence and promiscuous sex matter in a gen-eral library collection? What if those materials are appealing to teens? The best defense is to get the backing of the library's board, administration, and collection-development pol-icy. Make certain that frontline staff all know how to handle an infuriated parent shaking a lurid book cover in their faces. Be aware of circulation statistics, hold ratios, and requests the public makes for particular titles and/or authors. Know which patrons to solicit for sup-port at board meetings that involve book challenges. When the people speak, the board lis-tens. When the people spoke in support of street lit by sinking many dollars into this new biblio-industry, publishers were very happy to take note and "give 'em what they want."

In order for street lit to have the same respect given to other subgenres of fiction, library staff must be able and willing to defend its presence on the shelves and their patrons' rights to read it.

Teen Appeal of Street Lit

While street lit may not be targeted toward teens, there are many teens who can't wait for newest title to hit the shelves. Teen readers like the same things in these adult urban dramas that older readers do. Some reading experts have speculated that African American teens gravitate toward street lit due to a dearth of young adult books for African American teen-agers. There's no question that the majority of characters in young adult literature are white; however, it's very likely that if asked, a black teen will tell a library staffer that he or she has already read all of the Walter Dean Meyers or Rita Williams-Garcia and will probably rattle off a list of other titles with white and black teen characters by white or black authors.

Teen readers, like most adult readers, want books that speak to their experiences or take them away from a recognizable world and have likeable, realistic characters involved in inter-esting situations told in a compelling manner. Street lit appeals to teens because most of the characters are young men and women barely out of their teens if not teenagers. The urban set-ting is easily identifiable, and the stories grab the reader and don't let go until the last page is turned. The language is realistic and the situations, though grim, may be hauntingly familiar.

Integrated Advisory: Street Lit Style

Street lit is exploding but the dominant format remains trade paperback titles. However, as demand increases, publishers are beginning to produce titles that have a street lit feel in different formats. The release of the movie *Precious* in November 2009 gave a huge lift to stories set in the streets. *Precious* is based on the novel *Push* (1996) by Sapphire and contains many elements of street lit, including abuse, harsh language, and survival. The audiobook, recently published by Books on Tape, is enjoying huge popularity. Several established publishing houses, such as St. Martin's Press, are now promoting street lit authors. Nevertheless, each month dozens of self-published authors try their luck with getting their stories out to the public.

Audiobooks

While urban libraries struggle to keep print copies of street lit titles on their shelves, there is a contrasting lack of street lit titles offered in other formats. Libraries have urged audiobook and e-book vendors to secure the rights to street lit titles and make them available for purchase. While there's an overall "wait-and-see" attitude from vendors, there are only a handful of street lit titles currently available in CD format. Titles for teens (such as *Monster* by Walter Dean Myers) are more common than adult titles in audio format, despite the much larger adult book market, possibly because street lit like teen stories are becoming increasingly accepted part of young adult literature.

Books on Tape has taken the initial lead. Three titles are available in CD format from this company. Two are authored by Nikki Turner: *Forever a Hustler's Wife* and *Ghetto Superstar*. Another title available through Books on Tape is Treasure E. Blue's *Keyshia and Clyde*. An alternative audiobook format, a pre-loaded digital device comes from Playaway, a company which at the time of this writing had made available the single title, *Ride or Die Chick* by J. M. Benjamin.

Kindle and Audible have taken notice of the popularity of street lit and the most well-known authors are available in digital downloadable formats for the Kindle e-reader or MP3 player.

Music

Without question, the closest media connection to street lit is the hip-hop music industry. Rarely does a street lit title in print format fail to mention some sort of hip-hop artist or song. Hip-hop titles may be old school or the most recent hits, depending on the time setting of the story. Rapper 50 Cent has lent his name to a set of street lit titles called the G-Unit series. Several well-known street lit authors have partnered with 50 Cent to write for the series, notably K'wan, Mark Anthony, and Relentless Aaron. In many stories, music provides a background and sets the tone and scene of the book. Beyond this, however, it is difficult to make direct connections between the books and music as there are significant differences in the types of stories being told, as well the length and narrative style.

Movies

Street lit characters, plots, and themes easily make the transition to film. If everything is bigger than life on the page, it's even more so on the silver screen. Without going into a long analysis of blaxploitation films, it's safe to say that a few of these over-the-top productions might appeal to readers of street lit, especially those titles that have been adapted for film. Donald Goines did not live to see the two adaptations of his novels, *Crime Partners* (2001) and *Never Die Alone* (2004), but Iceberg Slim did. *Trick Baby* was released in 1972, five years after its initial publication.

Blaxploitation films suffer the same critical drubbing as street lit—stereotyped characters, extremely graphic violence and sex, strong language, flashy lifestyles obtained illegally, and glorification of a criminal lifestyle. However, viewers and readers understand the difference between cinema fantasy and street reality, and lately have had more realistic fare to view at the cineplex or on DVD.

Start with *Hustle and Flow* (2005), an Academy Award-nominated film about a pimp who tries to rise out of the drug trade to become a rapper; *Menace II Society* (1993); or *New Jack City* (1991). Other films that explore the difficulty of getting out of the drug trade are *Sugar Hill* (1994) and *Bluehill Avenue* (2001).

The critically acclaimed and Academy Award-winning *Precious* (2009) is shining a light on the life of women from the streets and showing viewers there are poignant, complex stories amid the grit. *Fresh* (1994) explores the harsh realities of being a child drug runner. Adding verisimilitude are films featuring rappers playing urban street toughs who want to leave the harsh street life for the glitz of the hip-hop world. 50 Cent made his debut in *Get Rich or Die Tryin'* (2005) and Eminem in *8 Mile* (2002). Fictional biographies of rap stars brought down in their prime also exhibit the same appeals as street fiction. Consider *Notorious* (2009) or *Tupac: Resurrection* (2003).

There are some intriguing documentaries that would also appeal to readers of street fiction. Don't look past *The Hip-Hop Project* (2006), *Tupac Shakur: Thug Angel* (2001), *Rap Sheet: Hip-Hop and the Cops* (2006), *Bling: The Blood Diamond and Hip-Hop* (2007), and *Hoop Dreams* (1994). And anyone who thinks purveyors of the street life don't know how to find the funny should have a look at *Katt Williams: The Pimp Chronicles Part 1* (2006).

The movie industry has also produced films that incorporate street lit themes such as betrayal, drug trafficking, crime, and loyalty. Many street lit plot lines closely parallel gangster movies such as *The Godfather*, *The Godfather: Part II*, and *Goodfellas*. Al Pacino's character from the movie *Scarface*, Tony Montana, is mentioned in many street lit novels, and at times even quoted accurately. In the 2006 film *The Departed*, Leonardo DiCaprio and Matt Damon bring to life the lies and deception that are so prevalent in crime stories from the streets. Released in December 2009, the film *Armored* contains strong language and intense violence. The crime connection is the big score of stealing $42 million dollars. These elements can make a logical connection to street lit that often involves thefts of tremendous amounts of cash, yet none of these are true street lit stories and many are a better fit for the crime genre.

Television

Street lit is rarely seen on TV due to the coarse language, sex, violence, and drugs. But there are a few series, usually produced for cable channels in order to preserve as much of the gritty reality as possible. The best example is HBO's award-winning show *The Wire*, which in five seasons explored all aspects of the drug trade in Baltimore, from the cops investigating murders to turf warfare to the intricacies of getting enough product into the city to satisfy demand. Other series that exhibit qualities that might appeal to fans of urban dramas are *Oz*, HBO's dark drama about life inside a maximum-security prison; *Prison Break*, a cult hit on the Fox Channel about two brothers with an intricate plan to break out of a fortress of a prison; and *Homicide: Life on the Street*. This police procedural puts just as much focus on the victims and perpetrators of crimes as it does on solving them.

Graphic Novels

Life on the streets and the crime that drives the need to survive is beginning to show up in a handful of other media. Only a couple of graphic novels have emerged. One, *High*

Rollers by Gary Phillips, features glossy artwork and the allure of dealing crack. It must be noted that because a format contains African American characters, that does not necessarily place the item in the street lit category. *The Boondocks*, created by Aaron McGruder, originated as a comic strip with episodes bound into a graphic novel called *A Right to be Hostile*. On the surface, this story has elements of street lit with harsh language, and the youths have moved from Chicago's South Side to the fictional suburb of Woodcrest. The work has been made into an animated series on cable's Adult Swim. Yet the story is not true street lit but a satire on race relations and pop culture.

Graphic novels feature only a handful of African American characters. Paving the way in 1972 was Luke Cage, a black man released from prison. Also called Power Man, Luke suffers an accident that leaves him with rock-hard skin and superhuman strength. The character has appeared in graphic novel series as recently as 2006. Luke experienced prison but again, his story does not fully mesh with street lit themes.

The Black Panther is a graphic novel series that first appeared in 1966 and was one of the earliest graphic novels to feature an African American. The Black Panther holds a PhD in physics and is considered one of the eight most intelligent humans on the planet. He fights evil rather than promoting it, and the violence involves magical artifacts rather than weapons found in street lit.

Magazines

Magazines promoting the hip-hop music culture are struggling to survive. *Vibe* closed its doors in 2009, leaving only *XXL* and *The Source* as the two major magazines showcasing hip-hop culture. Most information about hip-hop music and street lit can be found online. An especially extensive Web site featuring authors and reviews of street lit is http://www.streetfiction.org. Created by librarian Daniel Marcou, this site gives up-to-date information about various happenings in the street lit world. Marcou has also recently launched a companion Web site for teens, http://www.teenurbanfiction.com.

Video Games

The notoriously violent video game *Grand Theft Auto* and its various installments (four versions are currently available) have consistently been criticized for glamorizing crime and violence. Violent scenes occurring in street lit novels are visually shown in *Grand Theft Auto*. Other video games focusing on crime are available. *Scarface*, *The Godfather*, and the mafia all are portrayed through video games. Arguments against street lit are often repackaged in similar criticisms of violent video games, i.e., they promote crime, violence, and abuse toward women.

Street Lit and Non-Book Media: Summary

To summarize, several pop culture formats feature African Americans who are involved with some elements similar to those found in street lit and they may draw interest from street lit readers. However, it cannot be emphasized too much that these stories should not be automatically considered to contain the same type of outrageous plot and characterization as street lit novels. Sharing similar elements does not necessarily mean that they share the same appeal factors; librarians need to keep this in mind when conducting integrated advisory.

Trends

Street lit is still relatively new in the literary world. Authors and publishers are more concerned about establishing themselves rather than forming a directional plan for their work. Still, there are several emerging trends in the street lit world. More works are being written in the present rather than setting the story in the early 1990s. Authors are moving away from incorporating the early days of hip-hop and violence of the 1990s' drug wars in their stories. Several authors are concluding their stories with more glimmers of hope and less resignation. Occasionally authors will reference Barack Obama being the first African American president and how they hope his influence will bring change to inner cities.

Nothing works like success. Recurring characters are showing up even though the books are not numbered as a series. K'wan, Teri Woods, and Kiki Swinson have all written multiple stories with the same protagonist. Readers are becoming familiar with authors and want to know more about these characters.

The use of regional settings is growing in street lit stories. Five to seven years ago, the majority of street lit was set in Harlem, Brooklyn, or the Bronx. Now the action moves from city to city, East coast to West coast. The concrete jungle is no longer the sole location. Parties and action can happen anywhere from Virginia Beach to Atlanta to the Caribbean Islands. The majority of street lit showcases assertive female characters. The reason for this trend could be to fit the readership profile that in our experience in libraries is predominantly female. There are fewer stories about men forming a crime organization and more stories focusing on women gaining power either in a relationship with a crime figure or taking over as the head of an organization. Remaining strong are scenes of graphic sex, distrust of police or any authority, and the accumulation of lavish wealth. These traits do not seem to be going away.

The street lit industry seems to be squeezing out rushed titles that have little plot or characterization; however, readers have grown weary of loosely strung together scenes of sex and/or violence. The plots created by top authors such as Miasha, Jason Poole, Mark Anthony, and Deja King are becoming more intricate, with many twists and compelling climatic scenes. In other words, the cream is rising to the top, but demand has resulted in the publication of poorer quality stories, just like in any popular genre.

Plots

Drug Dealing and Drug Use

Drug dealing is a main source of income for inner-city denizens both in real life and in street lit novels. Some of the more realistic scenes created by street lit authors feature details on selling, processing, and using a variety of drugs, from pot to heroin. Although appearing to glamorize the drug industry, a more accurate characteristic is a cautionary tale as authors often show drug-using characters taking a hard fall.

Ashley and JaQuavis, *The Cartel* (2008) BK, RS
The cartel controls cocaine arriving through Miami, and the Diamond family holds almost all of the cards. When Carter Diamond loses his life, it's up to Carter Jones, his illegitimate son, to continue the legacy. Entering the drama is Miamor, a hit-woman determined to fulfill a contract until she meets Jones.

Dane, Dana, *Numbers* **(2009) BK, AP**
Numbers, aka Dupree Reginald Wallace, is a clever math protégé who can count cards and work all the angles. His concern for his cancer-stricken sister and his poor mother forces him to seek more cash by dealing for Coney, a local mover of product. Numbers is in love with both his ride-or-die chick Waketta and Rosa, a Latina pregnant with his child. His running partner Jarvis always has his back—or does he?

Givens, David, *Betrayed* **(2008) BK**
Control of Waterloo, Iowa, and a piece of the midwestern drug trade comes down to the Sandman's Get Money Crew versus four other street gangs in vicious battles that see dozens of soldiers getting their wigs split. Then there is Sherrice, a stripper with a bangin' body who needs money but wants a Prince Charming. Who knew Iowa was so wild?

King, Joy, *Stackin' Paper* **(2008) BK, SH**
Genesis works the Philadelphia streets trying to push product by any means necessary. He searches for a way to take his drug game to the next level until he meets the gorgeous Talisa Washington, who has connections to take his ambitions beyond simply pushing drugs.

McCaulsky, Marlon, *Pink Palace* **(2008) BK**
Cruising through Atlanta's Pink Palace strip club are tough guys with weaknesses for sexy women. Damien is a stone killer accompanied by his sidekick, Tommy, and they both want to sleep with Mo'nique and Nikki, strippers who came to the club's stage because of rough times. The guys are set to swing a coke deal that will lock down Atlanta, but first they must contend with King, the big man in charge.

Swinson, Kiki, *Playing Dirty* **(2009) BK, AP, SH**
Yoshi Lomax is a 34-year-old half-Korean, half-African American attorney with a Brooklyn swagger who has set up shop in Miami. She never misses an opportunity to be on TV while charging clients $2,500 per hour. Knowing that rappers and crime bosses are bridges to the real money, Yoshi contacts rival top drug suppliers and adds them to her client list. Yet her kryptonite is cocaine, and once she reaches the top, her fall comes hard and fast.

Clawing a Way to the Top

In 2008 and 2009, the economy collapsed. So what? This is nothing new to many inner-city inhabitants. Many street lit titles begin in poverty and characters struggle to reward themselves with wealth by any means necessary. Of course, get-rich schemes don't always come with a happy ending.

Clark, Wahida, *Payback with Ya Life* **(2008) BK, CL**
Shan, pregnant by a married man, decides to move to Detroit. Desperate to leave the fast life, she's ready to become a stronger person, but old conflicts flare up and a high-stakes turf war will leave only a few people standing. Shan is determined to be one of them.

McNair, E. R., *The Hood Rats* **(2008) BK, RS**
Bre, CeeCee, Nesha, and Nicky are four girls who are no strangers to the streets. They find their bond of friendship tested by lies, deceit, and tragedy. The girls know all hood rats try to do what they can with anything they have. That includes sex, drugs, and changing minds about trust.

Phillips, Gary, *High Rollers* (2009) GN, RS
This street lit story is presented in a graphic novel format and contains all the grittiness of street lit written in prose. Cameron "CQ" Quinn, who listens to the audio version of *The Art of War*, is a stone-cold executioner with an eye to taking over drug lord Trey Loc's business. His climb to wealth is sidetracked by a gambling addict and a crackhead attorney.

Swinson, Kiki, *I'm Still Wifey* (2009) BK, CL
Kira has to scramble when she learns she has a baby on the way and it's not her husband's. Word on the street travels fast, but how can Kira keep her pregnancy secret? The stakes climb as she enters the game of survival of the fittest.

Tyson, Alex, *Compton Chick* (2007) BK
Jackie Smalls' family struggles to get by in the daily grind of poverty-stricken projects in Compton, California. Roadblocks to success are teenage pregnancy, death, neglect, drug abuse, and separation of the family. Painfully real in its setting, in this story Jackie's family pushes on to redemption.

Woods, Teri, *Alibi* (2009) BK, SH, AP, UAB
Nard, who murders three people during a holdup, needs an alibi; Daisy, a stripper with a desperate need for money agrees to provide an alibi for $2,000, testifying that she was alone with Nard at the time of murders. At first Daisy sees only the quick cash, but easy money always comes with strings attached. As more and more people become interested in her, Daisy bolts the wild life and attempts to find peace in rural Tennessee.

Hip-Hop Music
Sometimes the presence of hip-hop music in street lit is a simple a matter of name-dropping; other times it becomes a driving force for a novel. Top street lit novels feature actual hip-hop artists' music either by name or a sampling of lyrics. Mostly it provides a background rhythm, but at times the hip-hop industry drives a novel's plot.

Hustle and Flow (2005) MV
Djay, a small-time hustler and pimp, thinks he finally has the chance at a big break when he hears that former local and rap superstar Skinny Black is coming to town. Djay pulls together a crew and makes a demo tape that he hopes will be his ticket to stardom.

K'wan, *Still Hood* (2007) BK, SH, AP
A large crew gathers in Harlem to shoot a music video for the up-and-coming artist True, including his slick managers Black Ice and Don B., whose morals are questionable as they may be there just for the quick cash. But the biggest challenges are for security man Jah when it becomes all too clear that someone is out to kill True.

Mattison, Booker T., *Unsigned Hype* (2009) BK, RS, YA
Fifteen-year-old Tory ("Terror Tory") Tyson is thinking of dropping out of school to hit it big in the hip-hop world. Talented at mixing beats, he wins first place in a New York radio station's Unsigned Hype demo show. But Internet buzz brings Tory more complications than he can handle. Although lacking the usual sex and profanity, this debut YA novel still flashes strong street cred and fills a void for teen readers seeking fiction that is not quite as raw as adult street lit.

Turner, Nikki, *Ghetto Superstar* (2009) BK, SH, UAB
Fabiola Mays, an innocent girl from Virginia, wins New York City's Hot Soundz contest, but before she can collect her $50,000 prize, the company goes belly-up. Neighborhood gangster Mr. Casino comes to her family's aid with quick cash, but Fabiola never gives up on her dream of becoming a star. She finds an enemy in Mr. Wiz, a recording mogul famous for ushering starstruck girls to his casting couch. Nikki Turner is the queen of hip-hop lit and proves she knows all about the music industry.

Washington, Jesse, *Black Will Shoot* (2008) BK
The story of two brothers, up-and-coming New York City writer Marq, with a new dream job at the magazine *Fever*, and his older brother Dontay, a failing producer with street smarts and a crack problem. Marq and Dontay alternate the narration.

Williams, K. Roland, *Cut Throat* (2008) BK, AP
Quincy Underwood is willing to do anything to be the next big thing for the Cut Throat hip-hop record label—including associating with deadly music industry rivals Raymond James and Victor Sweet. Raymond, who sports a long scar on his neck from a botched murder attempt, parlays his club's business by moving cocaine. Williams gives readers a realistic, behind-the-scenes view of a volatile business where talent is manipulated, then discarded.

Williams, Wendy, with Zondra Hughes, *Ritz Harper Goes to Hollywood!* (2009) BK
Ritz Harper reconnects with her longtime producer, the flamboyantly gay Chas James. She's willing to do almost anything to have her own television talk show, but in California, ugly racism gets in the way of her grabbing the brass ring. It's all about ratings, and any scandal will do, including sleeping with the enemy. The hip-hop community will instantly recognize the author, who is also a New York City radio DJ.

Characters

Determined to Rise to the Top
The flip side of extreme poverty is fabulous wealth, i.e., outrageous wealth, stacks of cash wealth, leave $100 tips wealth. At times, a wealthy setting appears almost like a fantasy world to the characters. These are not extra windfall income supplements, but more like the high society of the Roaring Twenties. To gain entrance to this lavish lifestyle, characters are ruthless and driven with a dose of obsession. In short, they seek wealth by any means necessary. Their obsession to be wealthy is often their tragic flaw. The key here is the way they obtained wealth and how many strings are attached. Many strings are attached to danger.

50 Cent and Derrick R., *Pledger* (2008) BK
The Diamond District. Flush with male testosterone, D. J. and his crew the League party hard, accumulate scores of women, and drink to excess. Yet they figure out a scam to boost diamonds and launder them for quick cash at a corrupt jewelry shop. What could go wrong? Maybe their newfound wealth is just a bit too flashy and draws the wrong attention.

Dixon, Gregory, *The Cake Man* (2009) BK
As a seventeen-year-old, Chris King enters Houston's drug game after his father, Big George, is arrested by the feds. Big George left a comfortable lifestyle that Chris

must abandon to deceive the authorities. Ruthless, he begins the long climb back from small-time street hustler to druglord. With a high body count, this title shows one man's climb to the top of a city's drug trade is marked by violence.

Dutch, *Thug Politics* (2008) BK, AP
Maurice Sebastian comes up with a plan to become mayor of Newark, New Jersey, and will stop at nothing to achieve his goal. With his thug connections, he aims to put the city on lockdown. Assisting him on his grassroots campaign are the lower denizens of society. The people elect him and he enjoys the prestige of office. But his wife Keisha, aka Queen Diva, is a rapper with high-level drug connections. Seemingly pulled from newspaper headlines, this street lit novel shows how thugs can also be adept at the corruption game.

Poole, Jason, *Victoria's Secret* (2008) BK, SH
Babyface is kind to his girls and they feel he's the best pimp in the business. His best girl is Victoria and she's the catalyst for money pouring into their bank accounts. As the pair hits the money spots of Atlanta, Chicago, Memphis, and Washington, DC, Babyface develops strong feelings for Victoria and wants to marry her. Unfortunately, Victoria's heart of gold and Babyface's urge for vengeance threaten their romance.

Simmons, Jacki, *Shot Glass Diva* (2008) BK
Honey Davis finds herself without the bucks from a trust fund set up by her parents. She checks her skills and finds out her taste for booze will attract men. Then she can peek into their bank accounts and see if they're the real deal with money. Her high-wire act threatens to come tumbling down when instances from her past resurface.

Wright, Ana'Gia, *Loving Dasia* (2009) BK
Dasia Warrington has been literally stood up before she can walk down the aisle. Depressed, she is desperate to make her next move but doesn't know which way to turn. Enter the fabulously wealthy tycoon Grimarious Guatreaux. Their romance explodes, but her man has a secret other life that may bring the glamorous vacations and expensive lifestyle to a crashing halt.

Hardened Criminals In and Out of Prison
It makes sense that if realistic crime is a staple of street lit, then jail should also be a part of it. Lessons are learned while on the inside, and once released, characters are thrust back into the game. Their personalities are changed by the time spent inside. Their survival instincts are razor sharp and they are on a mission to get what they can as fast as they can. They often establish tight running crews who move product. What has changed is that prison has made them even more hardened and ruthless, traits that often set violent confrontation in motion.

Carter, Quentin, *Stained Cotton* (2008) BK, AP
Qu'ban Cartez plays three different women and there are setups on top of setups in this story. The law catches up with Qu'ban, but he's able to run his game from prison with the help of a female guard. Marked by hard-core, brutal sex scenes, this is an example of street lit at its grittiest.

Freeze, *Against the Grain: A Novel* (2008) BK
A bank job goes very wrong, and Arkadian "Kay" Frost pulls nine years in prison. Once outside, he quickly establishes himself as a major player in Baltimore's drug

industry. Working the cocaine side of business is Mike, a supposed friend. Or could the sexy Shu-Shu be Kay's kryptonite? Nobody can be trusted, and Kay realizes how fast loyalties can change.

Poole, Jason, *Larceny* (2004) BK

Bilal takes the hit for his "brother" Jevon and does time for manslaughter. While Bilal is in prison, Jevon enjoys the hustle on the streets. Jealousy leads to backstabbing in this story where snitching cannot be tolerated.

Scott, Lena, *O. G.* (2007) BK

After doing a 20-year bid in prison for a crime committed when he was a teen, Abel Diggs now has to decide if he should settle the score. His decisions become complicated after meeting Tish, a doctor with some issues of her own. More of a romance than a hardened street novel, this title is laced with references to old-school music from the 1970s.

Serrano, Daniel, *Gunmetal Black* (2008) BK, AP

This title features tough Chicago ex-cons who encounter police corruption, betrayal, and shocking violence. Eduardo "Eddie" Santiago is released from prison but quickly runs into nasty police who lift the $40,000 he accumulated while serving time. Bent on revenge, Eddie vows to recover his money while giving no quarter.

Seven, *Gorilla Black* (2008) BK

Bilal Cunningham, aka Gorilla Black, has pulled seven years in jail for vengeance for his brother's murder. Upon his release, he moves to become the main cocaine dealer in Richmond, Virginia. His sexy girlfriend can't stay away from the blow and becomes involved with men who may be responsible for Bilal's brother's death.

Relationships, Street Lit Style

Guys and girls interact throughout all street lit novels, but that is not to say they always get along. The trail of love sometimes is a bumpy road marked by crime, abuse, drug use, and a host of inner-city issues. It's enough to make readers wonder if these characters truly love each other or are misplaced people who wander into each other's orbits.

Anthony, Mark, *Reasonable Doubt* (2008) BK, SH

Snipes is a charismatic dealer who draws New York University coed Katrina into his world. They set off on a crime spree that includes murdering a cop, abusive sex, and fast cash. The moral is that crime leads to death or incarceration, and Katrina must fight for her freedom.

Blue, Treasure E., *Keyshia and Clyde* (2008) BK, UAB

Clyde figures he can make quick cash by robbing drug dealers, and Keyshia falls into selling herself on Harlem's streets. The pair hooks up and set off on a spree of sex, drug use, and murder. The Bonnie-and-Clyde theme finds these lovers in a courtroom with Keyshia set to free Clyde with a pair of nine-millimeter pistols.

Miasha, *Chaser* (2009) BK, AP, SH

The opening scene of this street lit novel has Leah's boyfriend, Kenny, beating her almost to death. Flashing back five months, readers learn that Leah is fed up with Kenny's dumb get-rich-quick schemes. She strikes up a saucy affair with Nasir, one of Kenny's supposedly loyal partners. Everyone is on the grimy side, but the drama of trying to get ahead by using each other makes this fast-paced story a fascinating read.

Phillips, D. Y., *Love Trumps Game* (2009) BK

Gangster Topps Jackson is pure evil and wants his kids back. Neema, his children's mama, is out partying with her best friend cocaine, so it falls to 49-year-old grandmother Hattie Sims to protect the youngsters. The male-female relationship here is between a powerful thirtysomething drug dealer and a grandmother who believes in the strength of family.

Stecko, C., *Brooklyn Brothel* (2009) BK

Bo Rice physically forces Chantel onto a bus, ordering her to "make us some damn money." She leaves Pittsburgh and arrives in New York City with a new street name, Co-Co, and sets to making money as a hooker in a nasty brothel, a place where the smuttier the sex, the bigger the tip. Why does she put up with this abuse? Chantel needs cash to show the courts she is a worthy mother for her son.

Whyte, Anthony, *Ghetto Girls Too* (2004) BK, SH

Deedee and Coco keep things moving in the hood, but Eric Ascot, music producer and Deedee's uncle, gets hooked up with the mob. Determined to avenge the rape of his niece, he crosses a line. Deedee and Coco also get caught up in the danger and there seems to be no way out.

Powerful Females

In chess, the queen has more power than the king. So it seems in street lit. Men may have physical strength and are armed with weapons, but women also know the score. Characters may be ambitious, vicious, and conniving, but they also are gorgeous and know exactly how to use their sexuality . . . for their own gain, of course.

Clark, Wahida, *Payback With Ya Life* (2008) BK, SH

Shan is ready to leave the fast life in her rearview mirror after becoming pregnant by a married man. But her brother is targeted for revenge as he tries to rise up in the drug game, and Shan may end up caught in the crossfire. A turf war erupts and Shan is determined to survive the violent outcome.

King, Deja, *Bitch* (2006) BK, CL, SH

Precious Cummings has a cache of weapons; that is, her beauty, sexy body, and slick street smarts. She meets benefactor Nico Carter and she's determined to hold on to her new status as a hood queen. Spinning a web of deceit, Precious may not be able to escape the betrayal she sets up, which includes the man responsible for her elite status.

Miasha, *Sistah for Sale* (2008) BK

Sienna uses her stunning beauty and sexiness to become one of Miami's top prostitutes. When she learns that the guy running the game is responsible for her parents' murders, she is determined to increase her value and break free no matter what it takes.

Souljah, Sister, *The Coldest Winter Ever* (1999) BK, CL, SH, AP

This is the mothership that all street lit with powerful female characters evolves around. Winter Santiaga is 16 and knows only that she wants her lavish lifestyle back. Her family lost everything when her drug kingpin father was sent to prison. Winter is foolish, conniving, and ruthless, and her only weapon is sex, which she uses to get her way.

The Street Life Series, Weeks, Kevin M., *Is It Passion or Revenge?* (2008) BK
Hanae Troop is a no-nonsense cop in Washington, DC. Her case is to find out why the city's top male exotic dancers are being murdered. Teco Jackson is a former snitch and her number-one suspect, but she cannot decide to protect him or arrest him.

Woods, Teri, *True to the Game II* (2007) BK, SH
Gena is sitting on a pile of money stashed away after her drug-dealing lover Quadir is killed. Her freewheeling spending alerts Jerrell, who is attracted to both Gena and her money. Problems? Yep, she doesn't realize Jerrell is her former lover's murderer.

Theme: Betrayal

By far the most common theme in street lit is the concept of betrayal. Betrayal can come in many forms, from lovers cheating, lifelong friends becoming self-centered, or simple greed being more powerful than any relationship. Betrayal brings up the most intriguing question; what would it take for you to give up a friend?

Black, Shawn, *Stick N Move* (2007) BK
Yasmina loses her parents to senseless violence initiated by Jamaican druglords. After moving in with her grandmother, Yasmina meets and falls for Scorcher, a dude with money and power. Once deep in the drug-dealing lifestyle, Yasmina discovers her lover is the one responsible for her parents' death. Her decision comes down to keeping wealth or extracting revenge.

Carter, Quentin, *Amongst Thieves* (2007) BK, AP
Ramon Delay answers only to himself. After serving a 15-year prison sentence, Ramon ruthlessly pursues his version of the American dream, running a game on Montel Murphy, taking over the old man's hotel, and transforming it into Resthaven, Kansas City's premier casino and resort. Soon, he has it all, including $86.9 million in his bank account. Ramon is blinded by the outrageous sex he has with a pair of sensual women, which raises the question, is the player being played?

K'wan, *Gutter: A Novel* (2008) BK, SH
Kenyatta Soladine, aka Gutter, has problems. His girl, Sharell, is pregnant, and Gutter looks forward to having a son. But first he has business to handle following the murder of his partner Lou-Loc. Gutter's thirst for revenge takes him from Harlem to Los Angeles. But who is minding his business while he is away? And who will handle Major Blood, a stone-cold killer sent to execute Gutter?

Lennox, Lisa, *Crack Head II* (2008) BK
Laci and boyfriend Dink are recovering from drugs and street life as undergraduate students at Boston University, but hood habits pull them back. Laci thirsts for, and is consumed by, her need to retaliate against the South Bronx Bitches for making her a crackhead. She returns to the hood and puts in motion a revenge plot against her old girl gang.

Reign, *Shyt List* **(2008) BK, UAB**
Yvonna's ghetto-fabulous world is rocked following her boyfriend's murder at the hands of her own father. That's bad enough, but her friends were guarding secrets about her boyfriend and her best friend. After moving back to Washington, DC, from Baltimore, Yvonna and her friends hatch plans for revenge for folks on her "shyt list."

TeKay, Rumont, *Ruthless Dictator* **(2009) BK**
Adon is slowly winning the street game but his right-hand man, Shamrock, has been tagged as a Judas by Nitty Calhoun. Adon has sworn allegiance to Nitty and feels he has no choice but to take fatal action against his only friend. But was Nitty giving advice or setting Adon up? Now, betrayal must lead to revenge.

Teens and Betrayal

During adolescence, teens naturally become suspicious of adults. Authority is often questioned and there is almost constant rebellious behavior by many teens. But underlying this difficult-to-deal-with behavior is the teens' apprehension, and perhaps fear, of being betrayed. During their teenage years, youths face the harsh reality that not all adults are there to nurture their progress. These titles present the theme of betrayal in an inner-city environment, a trait that is also a cornerstone of adult street lit. The betrayal can originate from adults or from other teens. As the old song says, breaking up is hard to do.

Booth, Coe, *Kendra* **(2008) BK, RS, YA**
Fourteen-year-old Kendra Williamson deals with her absentee mother and the neighborhood boys' increased interest. She falls into a hush-hush sexual relationship with Nashawn, a guy her best friend Adonna has her eye on. Kendra's problems are her own until Adonna discovers the betrayal of their friendship.

Flake, Sharon G., *Who Am I Without Him? A Short Story Collection about Girls and Boys in Their Lives* **(2004) BK, SH, YA**
Flake presents a set of cautionary tales that show the benefits and drawbacks of being head-over-heels in love. By concentrating on showing rather than telling each situation, the author allows girl readers to debate about who is being stupid and who cannot help themselves because they are so in love with a guy. Of course, several guys in the collection pride themselves on having more than one girlfriend.

Precious, *The Ab-solute Truth,* **Platinum Teen Series #2 (2005) BK, YA**
Christopher Abdul Parker, whose basketball moniker is the Ab-solute Truth, is caught up in serious drama with his formidable girlfriend Porsha. They are deep into a he-said, she-said argument as their friends wait to offer their take on the situation. Realistic inner-city teen issues of drug dealing, sex, and violence mark this title about a player who may also be being played.

Volponi, Paul, *Black and White* **(2005) BK, CL, SH, AP, YA**
Marcus and Eddie are tight friends and two of the top high school basketball players in New York City. Marcus is black and Eddie is white, but they are way past that being a problem. Desperate for cash, they begin robbing people at gunpoint. Their last holdup goes completely wrong and the cops arrest Marcus. Volponi's intriguing theme is simple: Would you give up your best friend?

Woods, Brenda, *Emako Blue* (2004) BK, AP, YA

Emako Blue was a golden child with an outstanding singing voice but her quick rise to stardom is cut short by a random South Central Los Angeles drive-by. In flash-backs, her high school friends and community reveal the jealousy and betrayal that was going on before her tragic death.

Zarr, Sara, *Story of a Girl* (2007) BK, AP, UAB, YA

Although this title's setting is not in the ghetto, inner-city teens will nod in acknowl-edgement of Deanna Lambert's dilemma as she copes with being labeled the school slut. She avoids the guy she was caught with in a car's backseat until he also gets a job at the same pizza joint. The intertwined teenage relationships are realistically pre-sented, especially when Deanna kisses her friend's boyfriend. In this title, betrayal happens before the story begins when everyone turns their backs on Deanna.

Making Connections

Street Lit for Mystery Readers

Lovers of mysteries may wish to take a peek at street lit. There are several titles that contain the basic components of a mystery. Of course, a street lit "mystery" is more in line with the hard-boiled detective novel rather than a cozy. Expect blood, a high body count, and plenty of suspects. These aren't your grandmother's Miss Marple tales.

Brown, Tracy, *Snapped* (2010) BK, UAB, RS

Brown writes of a family dynamic that is full of marriage betrayals and gangsters. Frankie feels loyalty to a drug boss who raised him, but the boss's daughter is just a bit too friendly for Frankie's wife. Camille wonders if her marriage is on the rocks, but when violence explodes, her feelings take a backseat to revenge. The mystery in this story deals with Frankie leading a double life.

Stephens, Sylvester, *The Nature of a Woman* (2009) BK

Dr. Johnny Forrester is a psychologist in Atlanta with his own disorder, erotomania, a mental condition in which he believes others are in love with him. His actions are dangerous to his marriage and so is his affair with sexy Anise. Their love affair is unpredictable, but she becomes something of a mysterious stalker similar to Glenn Close's character in *Fatal Attraction*.

The Street Life Series, Kevin M. Weeks, *Is it Rages or Riches?* (2009) BK

A psychotic killer named the Paradox who leaves G-strings on his victims' bodies returns in the latest in Weeks's self-published Street Life series (after *Is It Suicide or Murder?* and *Is It Passion or Revenge?*). A combination of mystery and police pro-cedural is told from the cops' point of view. Bloody executions and a wild, climatic shootout mark this violent tale.

Woods, Teri, *Alibi* (2009) BK, UAB

This title was mentioned earlier but reappears here as an example of street lit with mystery appeal. A botched robbery, bodies on the floor, and an innocent girl with a questionable past on the run all come together in a fast-moving story. Crime bosses who want to know where their money went? Sounds like a hard-boiled plot to me.

GLBT Characters in Street Lit

Street lit is drenched with testosterone and men climbing to get the upper hand on their business. It is a zig to the expected zag, but street lit has several titles with gay characters. These homosexuals are usually portrayed as secondary characters, but in all the cases they do manage to play an important role to the plot. Quite often they are scene-stealers. Although homosexuality is a controversial topic in the African American community, in these stories the gay characters are not judged by the authors.

Edwards, Mia, *Love Lockdown* (2010) BK

Kanika is married to drug kingpin Tyrell and they are never far away from the drug game. Lurking for her chance at stealing their wealth is Kanika's stepsister Tiffany. Willing to do anything to disrupt Kanika's life and to bankroll her own lifestyle, Tiffany begins a lesbian relationship with the wealthy and powerful Rasheeda. This is more about using sex as a weapon and Rasheeda's Achilles' heel is her love for Tiffany, who only cares about one thing, grabbing easy money.

Nero, Clarence, *Too Much of a Good Thing Ain't Bad* (2009) BK

Johnny is a reformed convict trying to make it big in Washington, DC. He meets a woman who is suspicious of men after several failed relationships. She meets Johnny but is unaware of his secret lover James. An interesting sidebar has Johnny pledging a college fraternity that shuns homosexuals. The author has strong feelings about discrimination against gays and that passion is personified in James' mother, who will fight in a minute if she believes her son is being disrespected.

Nicole, Anya, *Corporate Corner Boyz* (2008) BK

Christopher Black and Brandon Brunson are business partners with a tight bond. Chris has always watched Brandon's back on the streets, and Brandon has Chris covered in the boardroom. Co-owners of Indigo Records, a label that discovers hip-hop talent in North Philly, the men are also playas who satisfy their hearty sexual appetites. Both men seek the best of both worlds in their women—sexy and loaded with cash. They also are guarding a close secret, their own bisexuality.

Relentless Aaron, *Platinum Dolls* (2009) BK

The lesbians in this story are there for the sexual pleasure of Stew Gregory, the master of the Web site Platinum Dolls. Stephanie, his right-hand woman, seduces new girls for Stew's viewing pleasure, but she is not there for woman-on-woman sex. Someone is trying to disrupt his porn empire and Stew can rely only on Stephanie's loyalty. The lesbian sex described in this story is not sensual, but designed to be rough and filmed as porn videos.

Williams, Wendy, with Zondra Hughes, *Ritz Harper Goes to Hollywood!* (2009) BK

This book features the scene-stealing Chas James. His witty running commentary carries the story's first half. Chas is loyal to Ritz Harper but he is also concerned about himself and his own love interest. He's the one who ends up sleeping with the enemy in a gay affair.

Titles with Teen Appeal

The elephant in the room when discussing street lit is the audience. As stated earlier, teens are drawn to adult street lit because this genre fills a perceived void in their reading tastes. The other argument is that the harsh content of adult street lit is too rough for impressionable teens. Librarians and other adults who work closely with teens and reading often become stumped when a teenager asks if there are any more books like this one while holding up a street lit title with provocative cover art. Included in this section are teen titles that pack a punch and may be used as alternatives to adult street lit. Be warned however, these are not squeaky-clean stories. In these titles, characters are confronted with similar issues as adults, but they approach them from a teenage perspective. Titles below include both urban lit written for teens and more mainstream teen literature that will appeal to readers of urban lit.

Crime

Deciding to commit a crime is a situation confronting more inner-city teens than we would like to admit. These titles show teenagers caught up in that very same situation. How they cope with what happens will draw teens to read about a character not unlike themselves.

Kuklin, Susan, *No Choirboy: Murder, Violence, and Teenagers on Death Row* **(2008) NF BK, SH, YA**
Kuklin includes portions of actual interviews with teens sentenced for murder. The set of narratives reads like a novel as teens describe events leading up to their crimes, how prison works, and how they still try to maintain a life. Kuklin also includes commentary on America's legal system, in which teens could be sentenced to death up until 2005.

Mowry, Jess, *Babylon Boyz* **(1997) BK, AP, YA**
Dante and his small group of friends form a posse because that's how protection works in their crime-infested neighborhood. What they don't expect is a suitcase full of cocaine falling into their laps. Their decision of what to do with the valuable drugs can mean escaping their tough environment or adding to their community's addiction to drugs.

Myers, Walter Dean, *Monster* **(1999) BK, UAB, CL, YA**
On trial for murder, Steve Harmon deals with the reality of his potential sentence and court trial by imagining the whole atmosphere is a movie and he's the director. Myers' groundbreaking style of writing the novel as a movie script, including scene changes and different camera angles, emphasizes Steve's desperation. *Monster* was the winner of the first Michael L. Printz Award in 2000.

Porter, Connie, *Imani All Mine* **(1999) BK, CL, YA**
Tasha is a 16-year-old girl trying to keep her life together and raise her baby Imani. Imani was conceived following a rape, a crime Tasha keeps hidden inside her mind. But the drug dealing in her neighborhood makes it an extremely difficult place to safely nurture a baby. Tasha's hopes and dreams are achingly contrasted by the poverty of her home.

Sitomer, Alan Lawrence, *Homeboyz* **(2007) BK, AP, YA**
Teddy Anderson is bent on avenging his little sister's death following a random drive-by shooting. She simply was in the wrong place at the wrong time. Arrested for attempted murder, Teddy is put in prison but gains probation and is assigned to tutor Micah, a young gangsta wannabe who knows a lot of what's going on in the streets.

Van Diepen, Allison *Street Pharm* **(2006) BK, YA**

Ty Johnson knows the streets after taking over his father's drug business at age 16. What school has not prepared him for is the daily grind to get ahead and survive. He remains in school, but things become complicated when he falls for Alyse, a young mother who is dead set against drugs.

Poverty/Abuse

The inner-city climate typically mixes poverty, drug use, violence and alcoholism into a recipe for abuse. Abuse can hit teens sexually, physically, emotionally, or by all three types. In teen novels featuring abuse, caring adults often intervene. However, the abused teens must first learn to survive by themselves. Poverty is a starting point for many street lit titles and these teen novels also feature teens caught up in poverty that leads to abuse.

Make Lemonade Trilogy, Wolff, Virginia Euwer, *Make Lemonade* **(2006) BK, UAB, YA**

Le Vaughn figures working for money will help her escape the projects and enter college, so she accepts a babysitting job. What she doesn't count on is Jolly, a 17-year-old unwed mother with two children and not much of a future. Le Vaughn realizes Jolly is helpless and what starts as a simple job turns into a full-blown drama when Jolly is fired from her factory job.

McCormick, Patricia, *Cut* **(2000) BK, SH, UAB, YA**

The abuse in this story is self-inflicted. Callie is housed in a treatment center, a place she has been sent because she cuts herself with sharp objects. Slowly, details of her dysfunctional homelife are revealed; the ending will have readers hopeful for her eventual recovery.

Monroe, Mary, *God Don't Like Ugly* **(2006) BK, YA**

Annette Goode's mother works long hours as a domestic to support her daughter. Left alone, seven-year-old Annette falls victim to their boarder, Mr. Boatwright, who begins a series of repeated rapes upon the child. After years of the sexual abuse, Annette's friend Rhonda decides the rapes must be stopped. Marketed as an adult novel, this title will engage teens with its flamboyant characters that accent the serious plot.

Pelzer, Dave *A Child Called It* **(1995) NF BK, CL, AP, SH, UAB, YA**

Pelzer's autobiographical account of the many abuses he suffered at the hands of his alcoholic mother hits home with many inner-city teens. Poverty, desperation, drug use, and alcoholism are all prevalent in the ghetto and suffered by Pelzer. It became a perfect storm for abuse which many inner-city teens know of firsthand.

Sapphire, *Push* **(1997) BK, MV, SH, CL, AP, UAB, YA**

Precious Jones has been abused, is HIV-positive, and is now pregnant for the second time, with her own father's child. This rough and gruesome title has a high cringe factor, but ultimately becomes a novel of redemption for the teen as the semi-literate Precious grows with the help of mentoring by caring adults. She begins writing a therapeutic journal and takes her place in a support group of incest survivors. A film based on the book was released in November 2009 under the title *Precious.*

Strasser, Todd, *Can't Get There From Here* **(2005) BK, RS, YA**
A group of runaway teens bands together in an attempt to survive on New York City's harsh streets. They all form aliases and would rather take a chance anonymously begging for enough money to eat rather than return to their abusive homes. Narrated by Maybe—she uses that word to answer questions—the different levels of abuse are revealed with stunning clarity.

Drug Use/Abuse

The drug game is the fuel that drives street lit and is also prevalent in realistic teen novels. It is as if anything an adult can do, so can a teen. These titles reflect the harsh reality of drug use and its consequences. The cautionary message remains the same: entering the drug game can only lead to problems that very few can escape.

Booth, Coe, *Tyrell* **(2007) BK, AP, YA, RS**
Tyrell moves between two worlds, one living in a homeless shelter with his addicted mother and being responsible for his younger brother. The other world is where his middle-class girlfriend lives; he visits for sexual encounters and what he believes is love. Unfortunately, he feels pressured to make money selling drugs as did his incarcerated father. Booth presents a story about an engaging inner-city teen struggling to do the right thing.

Draper, Sharon, *Tears of a Tiger* **(1994) BK, SH, YA**
This title has become the catalyst for encouraging inner-city middle school teens to read. Although a cautionary tale, it packs a punch about the decision to drive under the influence of alcohol. Andy Jackson was behind the wheel and drunk when a crash claimed the life of his teammate and friend, Robert Washington. Andy's hard journey to reconstruct his life and deal with survivor guilt is this novel's sobering message.

Gantos, Jack, *Hole in My Life* **(2002) BK, CL, UAB, AB, YA**
Gantos relates the true story of his youth, when he made the reckless decision to help smuggle a large shipment of marijuana into New York City. Unsuccessful, he is sent to federal prison as a 21-year-old inmate. His narrative accurately portrays a young man in a situation way over his head and the grim consequences of being involved with drug trafficking.

Hopkins, Ellen, *Crank* **(2004) BK, UAB, YA**
At one time a perfect daughter, Kristina Georgia Snow falls for a charismatic boy who turns her on to crank. She's immediately addicted. The drug becomes the driving force of her life and she is willing to trade everything for the next high. This title is the first in a series by Hopkins that features extreme downward spirals of drug use presented as novels in verse.

Koertge, Ron, *Stoner and Spaz* **(2003) BK, AP, AB, UAB, YA**
Ben Bancroft has a mild form of cerebral palsy—he's Spaz. Colleen Minou is a girl willing to try any drug at any time and plays the role of Stoner. A chance meeting leads to a friendship and something of a romance. Opposites attract, but is the pull of drug use too powerful to allow the pair to achieve their dreams? Koertge's story of star-crossed lovers is one of the more realistic teen titles dealing with the seemingly unbreakable cycle of drug abuse.

Nolan, Han, *Born Blue* **(2003) BK, YA**
Janie has been neglected by her mother and thrust into foster care. There she's essentially sold for drug money. Throughout her many shocking trials—including rape

and pregnancy—Janie doesn't lose sight of her goal of becoming a famous singer. This intense title shows one teen's repeated cycled of drug abuse.

Conclusion

Street lit has burst onto the literary scene as a genre that almost defies description. Characters in the stories are predominantly African American, but other minorities are included. The settings are typically in major cities. Although characters are raised in poverty, ostentatious wealth is easily gained and lost. Rough sex is a trait of many street lit titles; yet there are characters for whom a fierce love is a driving emotion and earns respect from street colleagues. Ultimately, the true benchmark for street lit is its connection back to the urban lifestyle. Traits common throughout street lit are betrayal, overcoming poverty, materialism, drug dealing, ruthless violence, hip-hop music references, and explicit sex. All that said, the major appeals of street lit titles are fairly simple: sex and violence, extreme situations, and intricate plot developments that keep the pages turning.

The future of street lit is unclear, even though sales are up and demand is high. It's possible that street lit will lose its roots and its appeal as major publishing houses sign authors such as K'wan, Tracy Brown, and Relentless Aaron to lucrative contracts. Because there are so many authors self-publishing, it is becoming more difficult for a self-published author to break out of the pack. By shunning self-published authors, street lit risks losing its authenticity, a trait that made readers first embrace the genre. As mentioned earlier, street lit had early ties to the drug wars of the late 1980s and early 1990s. That era has been mined dry and a story set in that time would come across as "been there, done that" for readers. Readers seem to be gravitating to stories relevant to their lives today.

Meanwhile, publishers are beginning to invest a cautious amount of money into street lit audiobooks. Patrons seem to have some initial interest, but the format has been slow in taking off. While the explosion of downloadable e-media titles is expanding daily, one wonders why no street lit titles have been packaged in this format. It cannot be a wariness of explicit content, as steamy erotica is a major genre for downloading. However, street lit publishers need to understand there is more to this game than selling a small print run of 1,500 copies and moving on. Deals need to be made with producers of other formats. The public is demanding much more.

One current trend that is welcome is the overall improvement to plotting. Descriptive writing is also improving, with grammar mistakes being edited out. Five to 10 years ago, simple errors such as using the wrong form of "to," "too," and "two" were common in street lit novels. Now as far as grammatically correct, street lit has become a cleaner product. But will the raw power and bold writing be tamed by corporations interested in moving street lit out of the inner city and into bookstores located in middle-class neighborhoods? Yes, street lit is all about sex and crime, but there is no denying the passion of which the top authors write about life on the streets. It would be tragic if that power were homogenized by the publishing world.

Resources for Librarians

Barnard, Anne. "From the Streets to the Libraries." *New York Times*, October 23, 2008.
Brehm-Heeger, Paula. *Serving Urban Teens.* Westport, CT: Libraries Unlimited, 2008.

Honig, Megan. "Takin' it to the Street: Teens and Street Lit." *VOYA* (August 2008): 207–211.

Kilgannon, Corey. "Street Lit With Publishing Cred: From Prison to a Four-Book Deal." *New York Times*, February 14, 2006.

Malone, Tara. "Balancing Act With Books: Schools Try to Find Right Mix to Keep Students Interested." *Chicago Tribune*, October 19, 2008.

Millner, Denene. "Limited Options: The Dearth of Books Written for African American Teens is Glaring." *Publishers Weekly* (September 8, 2008): 54.

Pattee, Amy. "Street Fight." *School Library Journal* (July, 2008): 27–30.

Wright, David. "Streetwise Urban Fiction." *Library Journal* (July 1, 2006): 42–45.

Zabriskie, Christian. "The Challenges of Serving Urban Teens." *VOYA* (October 2008): 316–317.

9

Everything Teen: Stories of the Teen Years

Heather Booth and Nicole J. Suarez

In this chapter, Heather Booth and Nicole Suarez present an overview of the wide and fast-growing world of teen stories, including the appeal of teen stories to adults. In the "Characters" section, you'll find lists on various types, including the brain, male and female athletes, the basket case, princesses, and criminals. The "Plots" section covers the quest to fit in, teens dealing with adult issues, and clashing with parents. The theme of this chapter is rites of passage; it covers teen love, drugs and alcohol, and new identities. In the "Making Connections" section, you'll find teen titles for paranormal fans, romance fans, and stories of teenage mutants. There is also a special section on trends, which covers titles that deal with technology and daily life, adult/teen crossovers, and graphic memoirs.

Introduction

Definition and Appeal of Teen Stories

For this chapter, we based our definition of teen stories and criteria for inclusion on Heather Booth's General Qualities that Identify Young Adult Literature as we functioned on the concept that the content and creator's treatment of the content is what holds the appeal, whether the patron is a teen or adult. These qualities work especially well for the selections listed here because they are specific to the works themselves, not to their origins, such as the publishing house division or age rating, which are sometimes used to divide YA from other materials in library collections.

1. The protagonist is a teenager, as are most of the key players.
2. The protagonist is close to the experiences, not reflecting back on time gone by as an adult.
3. The book's (or other media's) issues and conflicts are relevant to the life of a teenager.[1]

Rarely do we reflect back on the teen years with ambivalence. Whether we loved high school or hated it, this brief life phase is fraught with great emotion. This connection accounts for part of the appeal of stories about teenagers and their lives. Teen stories are emotional stories. The moment the ball sinks through the hoop is the most exhilarating in the history of sport. That kiss is the most romantic (or disappointing) thing to ever happen. The declined invitation is the most devastating social slight. For teens dealing with more than the usual dramas of daily life, the potential for an even more emotionally charged environment exists. Pregnancy, sexuality, violence, loss, discrimination, and being true to one's self when it runs counter to a family's or society's expectations are very adult topics that many teens must and do deal with on a daily basis.

The years between 12 and 20 are pivotal in many ways. At first glance, teenagers may appear to be leading carefree lives, unbound by the responsibilities that come later: work, family, finances, and the like. Some popular teen stories play up this free-and-easy phase, emphasizing only one element—usually romance or sports. Readers looking for a little bit of escapism may prefer this lighter fare, as in historically popular movies like *Grease* (MV, 1978) or TV sitcoms. But don't forget about Rizzo's pregnancy scare, or the friend *Family Ties'* Alex P. Keaton lost to a drunk-driving incident. Behind the well-lit and laugh-tracked teen story we think we see while watching teens hang out, serious work is going on that lays the groundwork for the rest of their lives. This stuff goes on our permanent record! Bodies develop and brains expand, we reach away from our families and seek out peers for our main social connections, and we delve deeply into our own personal philosophies and beliefs as we begin to define our worldview. Teen stories touch on these defining moments in large ways, like in *Whale Talk* (BK, 2001) when T. J. struggles to break free from the many stereotypes that define him and his teammates; and in smaller ways, like *My So-Called Life*'s (TV, 1994) Angela Chase staking her claim on a new life by dying her hair a vibrant red.

A "teen generation" spans a relatively short time period. By the time today's high school freshmen are in college, the new batch of freshmen will have notably different hairstyles, favorite television shows, and technology. Because of this, teen literature and media is able to focus more heavily on current trends, using names of popular bands, actors, or fashion styles, without the same fear of dating the material that adult-targeted materials might. This makes teen stories feel immediate to our contemporary lives and may help us feel connected to the youth of today—whenever today may be.

Recently, I asked a group of teens at my library what then-newly elected President Obama should know about being a teenager in America. Two particularly poignant comments appeared: "We want to be treated like citizens, too," and "You'll get over it." And herein lies the conflict that makes stories of the teen years so appealing. Teens are taking on the awesome task of defining themselves, setting the stage for the lives they will lead as adults. Sometimes they look and act like adults, and sometimes they look and act like kids. They are struggling to stake their claim on their futures. And they have precious little time to do it.

History

Teens in Movies   Teens have nearly always had a place in popular motion pictures. In the movies of the 1930s and 1940s, the teen point of view was usually represented in high-profile, lighter fare, which also focused on family life, such as the teen Andy Hardy movies of the late 1930s, *National Velvet* (1944), and *The Bachelor and the Bobby Soxer* (1947). *Rebel Without a Cause*, released in 1955, broke the mold of happy-go-lucky teens in mainstream film, focusing instead on teen angst and loneliness. *Blackboard Jungle*, released the same year, highlighted the rage of troubled juvenile delinquents at a tough New York school. Movies portraying idealized teen experiences were, of course, still being made, but were not particularly influential.

In almost direct opposition of those two groundbreaking movies, the popular teen movies of the 1960s seemed to shy away from serious topics and focused mainly on romance and zany hijinks. The Beach Party series of movies starring Annette Funicello and Frankie Avalon, including *Beach Party* (1963) and *Beach Blanket Bingo* (1965), depicted fun times. Interestingly, in the 1970s, the most popular and influential movies featuring the teen experience were actually set in different eras. *American Graffiti* (1973) and *Cooley High* (1975) are set in the 1960s, while *Grease* (1978) was set in the late 1950s.

The 1980s are widely considered the golden era of teen movies, with subject matter ranging from broad, coarse comedies to grittier themes of crime, teen apathy, and violence. Sexuality and losing one's virginity is a big theme for both guys and girls in movies like *Little Darlings* (1980) and *The Last American Virgin* (1982), as well as in many other teen films. Social status and cliques are also a thoroughly explored theme in the comedy/drama genre. A girl from the valley dates outside her own social clique when she meets a "dude" who is actually a punk from feared Hollywood in *Valley Girl* (1983). Every group is represented at Saturday detention in John Hughes's *The Breakfast Club* (1985); and in *Fast Times at Ridgemont High* (1982), drug use, casual sex, and abortion take place among the cliques in one year at a high school based on Cameron Crowe's fact-based book by the same title. Writer/director John Hughes also helped define the 1980s teen experience with comedic films like *Sixteen Candles* (1984), *Weird Science* (1985), and *Ferris Bueller's Day Off* (1986), and romances like *Pretty in Pink* (1986) and *Some Kind of Wonderful* (1987). Benchmark films with mature themes, featuring teens with real problems from this era, include *My Bodyguard* (1980), *The Outsiders* (1983), *Bad Boys* (1983), and *River's Edge* (1986).

In the 1990s and beyond, movies geared toward a teen audience and featuring the teen experience continued to be a lucrative genre. Popular movies included reworkings of novels by classic authors: *Clueless* (1995, Jane Austen) *Cruel Intentions* (1999, Choderlos de Lacos), and *She's The Man* (2006, Shakespeare) to name a few. Possibly inspired by the ultimate "one day in the life" teen movies of the 1980s (*Sixteen Candles* and *Ferris Bueller's Day Off*), movies with this popular theme with included *House Party* (1990), *Dazed and Confused* (1993), and *Can't Hardly Wait* (1998). Serious themes were not ignored with groundbreaking movies such as *Boyz N The Hood* (1991), *Menace II Society* (1993), *Kids* (1995), and *Thirteen* (2003).

Teens on Television   Teens and their experiences have also had a special place in television history. Despite the potential for corny plots that seem to get resolved relatively quickly, the teenager-centric plots provided reassurance of the normalcy of teen experiences and/or angst. *The Adventures of Ozzie and Harriet* debuted in 1952 and starred the real Nelson family, which was comprised of parents Ozzie and Harriet and their sons, David and Ricky. After a few years, Ricky was clearly the breakout star, with the show often ending with him performing a song. Other benchmark television shows soon followed that focused on teenagers and their point of view, such as *Dobie Gillis* (1959).

In the 1960s, *The Patty Duke Show* and *Gidget* highlighted the teenage girl experience. In the 1970s, shows like *The Brady Bunch*, *The Partridge Family*, and *Happy Days* also centered on teens and started touching on issues such as puberty and serious dating relationships. ABC also began airing the *ABC Afterschool Special* in 1972; these programs generally meant to inform teens about serious issues such as drinking and drug use. In the 1980s, wildly popular shows that featured teen characters again went a little bit further in addressing teen issues. In one episode of *The Cosby Show*, Vanessa

Huxtable deals with getting her first period; *Blossom* touched upon make-out parties and virginity; and *Degrassi Junior High* (a spinoff of *The Kids of Degrassi Street*) broke new ground by exploring nearly every issue that a teen could face, from teen pregnancy to drug use to eating disorders. *Degrassi Junior High* was so popular and acclaimed that the show continued as *Degrassi High*, following some of the same characters and introducing new ones while still tackling tough issues faced by teens, including a controversial storyline involving a student contracting HIV through unsafe sex.

This trend of truthful storytelling continues today. Groundbreaking reality television programs showing unscripted real-life teen experiences include *Juvies*, *Engaged and Underage*, and *16 and Pregnant*, all produced by MTV. Many of the most popular and enduring teen shows in the 1990s and beyond were not sitcoms, but dramas with touches of humor. Just a few of these shows include *Beverly Hills 90210*, *My So-Called Life*, *Party of Five*, *The O. C.*, and *Gilmore Girls*.

Teens in Graphic Novels and Manga   With the rise in popularity of comic strips in the daily newspapers and the introduction of comic books in America in the 1930s, reading graphic stories became acceptable for everyone, from kids to adults. The most famous sidekick in comics' history, Robin, was introduced as a teen who assisted superhero Batman in fighting crime in Gotham City. The Archie comics, which featured teen Archie Andrews, perpetually torn between Betty and Veronica, and his gang of high school friends attending Riverdale High, continues to be published today. Reading comics became more of a leisure hobby associated with children and teens in the 1950s and 1960s, even though they didn't necessarily highlight the teen experience.

Superheroes fighting evil forces remained the most popular and dominant subject matter until the late 1960s and 1970s, with the adult-oriented underground work of Robert Crumb and Harvey Pekar breaking new ground by focusing on their own lives in titles such as *Zap Comix* and *American Splendor*. The 1980s and 1990s saw the rise of the graphic novel, with more thoughtful and darker subject matter being explored by Alan Moore (*V for Vendetta*), Frank Miller (*Sin City*), Neil Gaiman (*The Sandman*), and Art Spiegelman (*Maus: A Survivor's Tale*).

The introduction of Japanese manga to the American consumer ignited new interest in graphic storytelling. Manga features its own vocabulary and unusual twists in storytelling not seen in traditional American graphic storytelling, which appeals to many teens.

Manga also seems to have bridged the gender gap, with many girls reading epic series that are written specifically for them. Shojo manga was created and is marketed specifically to girls and young women using the familiar manga style but focusing on the emotional and relationship-based stories that appeal to this demographic.[2] Groundbreaking series of this type include Sailor Moon, Mars, and Fruits Basket. American publishers took notice and produced graphic novels specifically marketed towards a teen female audience. Publishers have also developed specific imprints geared towards children and younger teens featuring popular superheroes as younger versions of themselves.

The format of visual storytelling continues to grow and evolve with the publication of graphic memoirs and the conversion of bestselling books into a graphic format. Laurell K. Hamilton, Stephen King, James Patterson, and Dean Koontz have authorized graphic adaptations of some of their most popular books. A new trend may be emerging with the continuation of the popular television series Buffy the Vampire Slayer as a graphic novel series.

It is important to remember that graphic novels and manga are widely read by patrons of both genders and all ages; and it isn't unusual to see adults and teens perusing the same shelves in libraries and bookstores.

Magazines   Like the formats mentioned above, magazines fill an important need for teens. Whether perennial best-selling magazines like *Seventeen* or underground and locally published zines, these publications remind teens that their experiences are normal and that their interests and concerns do matter. Teen fashion magazines have served an important function in the lives of many teen girls as they validate (and may unfortunately exacerbate) their concerns about such topics as body image, dating, and physical development. Magazines are also a useful tool for teens who are exploring extracurricular interests, whether in sports, hobbies, or current events as they read up on their topic of concern and read about other teens who have similar focuses.

Computer and Video Games   Computer and video games give teens a chance to have experiences as someone other than themselves. They also give teens an opportunity to try on different roles and to be great in the areas in which they wish they could excel. Games that offer multiplayer functionality allow a group of teens to collaborate, interact, and focus on an activity together in a virtual arena during this age when in-person social interactions can feel awkward and uncomfortable.

Teens in Books   Adolescents have long held an important place in literature. The heroes and heroines of nineteenth-century bildungsroman novels such as *Jane Eyre* and *Great Expectations* were introduced as children and the reader saw them grow to the brink of adulthood as they sought autonomy and carved out a place for themselves in their world. However, although coming-of-age stories are a classic literary motif, teens as teenagers are a relatively recent occurrence in the span of the written word. Holden Caulfield of J. D. Salinger's classic *The Catcher in the Rye* (1951, BK) is the grandfather of today's angsty teen seeking meaning in his life that we so often read about in contemporary literature. Since then, teens began appearing with greater frequency, and not just in decades-spanning coming-of-age stories, but in works highlighting the specific tasks, challenges, joys, and sorrows of the teen years. The late 1970s and 1980s saw a significant increase in teen novels as well as teen movies, and as teens became greater consumers of the media, publishers responded. During this time, many of the foundational works of young adult literature were written, and it has been called the golden age of teen literature.[3]

Today, teen fiction is no longer relegated to a dusty corner behind the picture books in the library or bookstore. In 1996, the National Book Foundation changed its children's book award to an award for young people's literature, and in 2000, the first Printz Award for Excellence in Young Adult Literature was granted, bringing prestige to the literature of teen lives. We are now widely considered to be in the second golden age of teen literature. Today the genre includes a great diversity of formats, from novels in verse and cerebral, meaty tomes to graphic novels, in addition to representing a broad range of viewpoints: homeless and wealthy, victim and aggressor, the outcast and the social climber, the farm kid and the urbanite, the gay and straight, and everything in between.[4]

Aren't Teen Stories for Teens?

Teen stories are indeed for teens. Teens read and watch teen stories in addition to a number of different genres. But they are also for the teenagers in all of us—the ones we were, the ones we avoided, and the ones we wanted to be. Just as watching a child's unbound joy on the playground can bring us back to those rosy childhood moments, reading teen stories allows us to relive the angst and fear, drama and excitement of the teen years. Who are the readers of teen stories? They tend to be on the younger end of the age spectrum of general library users, though many seniors can and do appreciate historical or gentle teen stories that hearken back to simpler times. Those who grew up in the 1980s are prime non-teen consumers of teen stories. This was the golden age of the teen movie and an overall rich time period for teen stories. Coming of age in the 1980s will likely make them more open to teen stories, as they grew up watching their lives unfold on screen.

Who Likes Teen Stories?

The Reminiscer   The nostalgia factor is strong for tales of adolescence. Some consumers of teen stories relish the heightened emotional tenor of teen stories and delight in reliving the victories and defeats of their own teen years—or someone else's. Adult women who enjoy impassioned romantic novels are ideal candidates for teen romances, as evidenced by the Twilight craze among the mothers of the series' original audience. Currently, more moms are waiting to sink their teeth into the overwrought "I'd die for you—literally!" vampire romance than teens. Former athletes may fall into this category too, as adults think back to their years on a team, winning or losing the big game, and forming lasting relationships with their teammates and coaches.

The Romantic   As mentioned above, readers who enjoy emotional romantic stories are ideal candidates for teen material. First love and sexual awakenings are common themes in teen stories. Most teens, not having been through the difficult work of adult relationships, often have a fresher, more optimistic view, and more of a sense of wonder about their romances, which brings a different perspective to the romance reader. Though many teen romances differ from traditional romances in that the couple very well may not end up together by the story's end, even if this happens, a hopeful tenor leaves the reader or viewer with the feel of a happy ending. Some may steer readers looking for a sweet or gentle romance toward teen fiction. This may work, but beware as it can backfire dramatically! Teen emotion can be raw, and as these characters are just beginning to understand their sexuality, some scenes may cause even a seasoned romance fan to blush.

The Humorist   As evidenced by the tremendous popularity of teen movies like *Superbad* (2007) or the American Pie series, it is clear that the appeal of teen humor expands far beyond the teen years. Adults who can laugh while they cringe at the inevitable awkwardness of adolescence are great consumers of this genre. Evidenced by the widespread popularity of teen "gross-out" films such as those just mentioned, many adults, even those into their thirties and beyond, enjoy the escapism as they relive the best and worst moments of their teen years from the safety of adulthood. Patrons who are fans of teen humor on film may also enjoy the memoir-style graphic novel as authors explore all the gory details involved with growing up, as well as some of the lighter teen novels—humorous teen novels make great vacation reads for those looking for a break from the "serious novel" or the latest blockbuster thriller.

The Parent   Many parents of teens read and watch teen media. Some read their teens' classroom assigned books in order to stay informed of the curriculum and potentially offer assistance at homework time. Others use it to get the inside scoop on their kids' preferences and contemporary experiences. Reading the same book or watching the same drama can provide a safe but excellent jumping off point for discussing relationships, sensitive topics, or feelings with a teen. And of course, some enjoy it simply because it appeals to them for the well-written plots, character development, or any number of other factors.

The Coming-of-Age Fan   Coming-of-age stories abound in literary fiction. Those who enjoy coming-of-age plots or the theme of finding oneself will likely enjoy teen stories since most, if not all, involve some element of self-reflection and growth. An added benefit for those who enjoy a coming-of-age story, but prefer a quicker, more plot-driven read, is that many teen novels do what fewer general-market books do: tread a careful line between being purely character or purely plot-driven. As self-possessed as teens might be, their stories are not typically endless introspection. An event moves the story along. These books and movies are about something in a way that a lot of literary fiction isn't! Self-awareness comes through a catalytic event rather than a slow dawning of consciousness.

The Reluctant Reader   The blend of character and plot-driven stories is one of the points that recommends teen stories to the reluctant reader. Someone who has been away from books for a time might not be sure if she prefers character to plot and may not give a book very much time before deciding that it's not working out. Teen novels are known for their hooks. Nancy Pearl's Rule of 50 (read the first 50 pages and if it isn't grabbing you, quit it and read something else) works great for well-rounded, experienced readers, but a teen novel has to pass a rule closer to 25.[5] Teens are a tough crowd, ready to bang the gong at a simple misstep. If the first chapter is a dud, the audience is lost. Once the story gets going, the reluctant reader will enjoy other perks in a teen novel: ample white space, more dialogue, and brief chapters. And since teens are people too, it's possible to find a teen book or movie on just about any topic of interest to the general reader, from crummy jobs to humorous romance to foreign vacations; there's a teen book for everyone.

Integrated Advisory: Teen Stories Style

For today's teens, the so-called "digital natives," the idea of advising on only one format may be as foreign as an 8-track tape or a slide rule. Stories for them have always crossed formats, with favorite books being made into popular movies, which are then translated into video games. Additionally, teens pay attention to the characters they admire: the Web sites they frequent, the books they are reading, and the movies they discuss with friends. A prime example of this is Rory Gilmore, the teenaged protagonist in *Gilmore Girls* (2000–2007, TV) who was an avid reader. The character's book selections were featured on the network's Web site, spawning local teen book clubs that exclusively discussed her reading choices.

For patrons interested in teen lives, the variety of formats helps to fulfill the wide range of appeal elements. Books typically allow a more intimate glimpse into the inner workings of the character's emotions and motivations, with manga and graphic novels benefiting from the incorporated visual element. Television shows may offer a broader perspective on teens within their peer group and environment. Movies can strike a balance between the intimacy of a novel and the visual splash of television and can push boundaries in a way television cannot. Video games tend to focus on the plots of teen life rather than the character development in other formats. Magazines are uber-current, offering a nearly as-it-happens look at trends and pop culture from a teen perspective. Because each format offers a different way of looking at the teen experience, more than one format is often desirable for the patron who simply enjoys teen stories. The question isn't "Why would we advise on more than just books about teen lives," but "Why on Earth would we limit ourselves to just one format?"

Trends

As mentioned above, each format can offer something different, but there are common current trends that can be found across the formats featured. The cannon of teen stories has always had its edgier elements, but boundary-pushing content is becoming more commonplace and reaching down to feature younger protagonists in movies like *Thirteen,* graphic novels like *Emily the Strange*, and even TV shows such as *Degrassi: The Next Generation.* Light-hearted looks at the teen years can still be found, but today's teen stories are much more *Rebel Without a Cause* than *Beach Blanket Bingo.* Also, teen stories are more and more frequently entering "crossover" territory, where the intended market may well be adults or adults and teens.

The Harry Potter phenomenon made it OK for adults to publicly admit to indulging—and really enjoying—the stories of teen and pre-teenaged protagonists, and the ball is still rolling. Movies featuring teen stories are commonly released with R ratings, meaning no one under 17 will be admitted to a theater showing of the film without a parent. By the letter of the law, this cuts out a significant portion of the teen market, and movie houses count on their adult patrons to fill the seats, which they happily do. As book marketers get savvier, teen book covers are looking more similar to adult covers in parallel genres, allowing readers to seamlessly float from one to another. TV shows are increasingly incorporating teens as significant characters in ensemble casts on shows with otherwise adult main characters, such as *Heroes* and *Glee.*

Our final trend, alluded to above, makes the concept of integrated advisory even more important. Just as content is crossing appeal lines, it is also crossing format lines. At this writing, 20 of the titles featured here include two or more formats, not including audiobook versions of novels, as fans scramble to get their hands on as much content with their favorite characters and stories as possible.

Characters

From the greasers and the socs in S. E. Hinton's *The Outsiders* (1967, BK; 1983, BK) to the goths and plastics of *Mean Girls* (2004, MV) teens have been typed and classified and plunked down into tidy character categories for generations. In John Hughes's modern classic *The Breakfast Club* (1985), the five teens quarantined in Saturday detention begin the day believing the stereotypes they had about one another, just like the principal who assigned them the task of writing about just who it is they think they are. The group breaks down walls and forges new understandings of themselves and others, finally concluding that "You see us as you want to see us: in the simplest terms and in the most convenient definitions. . . . But what we found out is that each one of us is a brain. And an athlete. And a basket case. A princess. And a criminal."[6]

The Brain

We may remember the valedictorian, but most of the "brains" we knew in high school faded into the woodwork. They always showed up, they cleaned up at awards night, and they might have helped you with your calculus homework, but they're no one you spent your Saturday night with. These are stories of the brains who shone through, whose lives are defined not just by their intelligence, but by their individuality. This is the inside scoop on life as a brain.

10 Things I Hate About You (1999) MV, AP
It is well known at Padua High School that cute Bianca Stratford isn't allowed to date until her sister Kat starts dating. Prickly feminist Kat prides herself on not being distracted by the opposite sex and focusing on academics so she can attend Sarah Lawrence College. When a new student hires delinquent, bad boy Patrick to woo Kat in order to date her sister, will Kat actually fall for him? This is an updated take on Shakespeare's *The Taming of the Shrew*.

21 (2007) MV, *Bringing Down The House* (2002) BK
It's every brain's dream: your smarts get you the girl, the glamour, and the cold hard cash. But students at MIT bite off more than they can chew when, led by a charismatic teacher, they form a cadre of blackjack card counters that take on Vegas with a complex scheme. Based loosely on a true story *Bringing Down the House: The Inside Story of Six M.I.T. Students Who Took Vegas For Millions* by Ben Mezrich, this film version starring Kevin Spacey glosses over some of the details and has been criticized by some for its stereotypical depictions of minority characters. However, the geek-to-chic story is fast-paced and entertaining.

Anderson, Laurie Halse, *Catalyst* (2002) BK, UAB
High school senior Kate is an excellent student. She is an exceptional runner. She is good at nearly everything. But when her Holy-Grail school, MIT, rejects her college application, she finds her life seriously derailed and unable to talk to anyone about it. Kate is, in many ways, the epitome of the "brain" character type as her identity as a scholar-athlete has trumped all other aspects of her life, including forming a relationship with her father or dealing with the death of her mother. When a former bully moves into Kate's home after a house fire, elements combine to form a catalyst that accelerates events leading to Kate's unraveling and the eventual realization that there is life after death and MIT.

Gilmore Girls (2000–2007) TV, AP, CL
Rory Gilmore is accepted into Chilton, an exclusive prep school that can only help her chances of getting into an Ivy League university. The only problem is that her mother is now forced to ask Rory's grandparents for assistance with the tuition, grandparents Rory has rarely seen. This show features the signature rapid-fire banter between Rory and her mother Lorelei, as well as countless pop-culture references in each episode.

Green, John, *An Abundance of Katherines* (2006) BK, UAB
Upon graduating from high school and getting dumped by the nineteenth girl named Katherine he has dated, Colin realizes that since he was a child prodigy, and is now no longer a child, his life is suddenly void of focus and meaning. Colin and his best friend Hassan hit the road on the classic post-high school cure-all, an aimless road trip. Finding themselves in a small town in Tennessee, they find jobs interviewing townspeople, and Colin begins a friendship with Lindsay, the daughter of their boss, while trying to create a mathematical theorem to explain love and relationship success. Colin and his peers revel in their "geekdom," and Colin finally begins to find meaning in life outside of his prodigy status.

Moriarty, Jacklyn, *The Murder of Bindy MacKenzie* (2006) BK
Bindy is the girl everyone loves to hate, the one who would remind the teacher of a scheduled quiz with just enough time left in class. And someone certainly does hate

her—enough to murder her measure by measure. As Bindy struggles to grasp the importance of the new required course, "Friendship and Development," her classmates work to solve the murder-in-progress. This is a breezy read despite its length as it is told through a series of notes, journal entries, classwork, and more. The goofy murder mystery element turns the tables as the brain needs the help of lesser creatures to solve a crime in which she is the victim.

Nancy Drew (2007) MV, VGM

After they move to California, Nancy promises her dad that things will be different when she starts going to Hollywood High School—no more investigations! But when Nancy doesn't fit in with the girls at school, she soon finds herself back to her sleuthing ways and investigates the death of the famous movie star who once owned their house.

Never Been Kissed (1999) MV

Nerdy twentysomething Josie, a copy editor at a newspaper, is assigned to go undercover and write an exposé about high school life. Still traumatized by her own awful school years, Josie must rely on her brother to make her cool and get her in with the popular kids in her second try at high school.

Portman, Frank, King Dork (2006) BK, UAB

Tom, a brainy 14-year-old outcast, occupies his time inventing names for an imaginary band and scouring the cryptic notes in the margins of his late father's copy of *Catcher in the Rye* for clues that would illuminate his death. Was it really an accident? A smart kid who feels ostracized by his peers and can't wait to graduate and move on is a character that many who remember their teen years with a cringe will understand.

Ryan, Sara, Empress of the World (2001) BK, UAB

Nic, 15, is spending the summer at a camp for gifted students. One would think that the archeology student would finally feel that she fits right in, but she is surprised to find that she still often feels on the outside, and she is even more surprised to find herself attracted to a girl, Battle, for the first time. Nic tries to apply the same studious nature with which she undertakes all other elements in her life to her relationship in this love story of self-awareness and understanding.

Veronica Mars (2004–2007) TV

Veronica finds herself on the fringes of high school society after her best friend is killed and her father, a county sheriff, seemingly botches the investigation. She hones her detective skills solving cases while working for her father, who starts a private investigation business to make ends meet.

The Athletes (Guys)

Remember Queen's song *We Are the Champions*? The athlete is not just a jock. The jock is generally portrayed as a brainless thug, following the crowd while pretending to lead. The athlete is a different being all together. He cares about his sport with a passion and is often torn between his dedication to the team or his own success and his outside obligations. He often turns to sports as a venue in which he can succeed after running into difficulties at home or in the academic realm. These athletes are driven and complex in a way that makes them appealing characters to learn about even if we'd never sit through two minutes of their sport of choice.

Crutcher, Chris, *Whale Talk* (2001) BK, CL, AP

Tao Jones (TJ) is a naturally gifted athlete who wants nothing to do with high school organized sports and its competitive posturing. But incited to action after seeing a jock bully a mentally-challenged student wearing his late brother's letter jacket, TJ enlists this student and several other freaks and outsiders to form a swim team, proving that the letter jacket is something for anyone with the drive and dedication to earn it. Filled with humor, soul searching, joys, and tragedy, this is a gracefully well-rounded sports novel.

Life of Ryan (2007–2009) TV

This MTV reality show follows Ryan Sheckler, a professional skateboarder who just happens to be a teenager. Viewers watch as Ryan competes professionally while dealing with the recent divorce of his parents and juggling business ventures and his personal life.

The Lords of Dogtown (2005) MV

In Venice Beach, California, during the 1970s, a ragtag group of teens become infatuated with skateboarding. Soon, their skill and innovative skating style change their lives and the sport forever.

Lupica, Mike, *The Big Field* (2008) BK, UAB

Hutch aspires to baseball greatness for his own satisfaction but also to please his father, a one-time pro who was benched due to injuries. When Hutch's team acquires a hot new talent that bumps him from his prized position as shortstop and also begins to garner Hutch's dad's tips and attention, it pushes him to try harder and contemplate alternatives that would get him a spot playing in the state championship, under the lights on the "big field" where major-league teams play their spring-training games.

O (2001) MV

Odin, or "O" as his teammates call him, is the star basketball player at an exclusive prep school and the only African American student. Hugo, the jealous son of the basketball coach, plots to destroy O. This is an updated, teen version of Othello.

Real, Takehiko Inoue (2008) MN

Tomomi, Hisanobu, and Kiyoharu couldn't be more different. These three young men, all struggling to make sense of life after tragedies, share one thing in common—their love of basketball.

Roll Bounce (2005) MV

Set in 1970s Chicago, Xavier and his friends are disappointed when their only source of entertainment, the neighborhood roller rink, gets closed down. Showing off his skills while hanging out with his friends helped "X" from thinking too much about the recent death of his mother. When the boys decide to start skating at the fancy Sweetwater rink, they enter a skate-off competition to win $500.

Skateboarder, Thrasher Magazine

These two magazines treat skateboarding as a serious sport and are written specifically for skateboarders. They also promote the skateboarding culture.

Slam Dunk, Takehiko Inoue (2008) MN

Hanamichi Sakuragi is hard to miss, as he is extremely tall with a shock of red hair and very unlucky with the opposite sex. When Haruko, a cute girl just his type, asks him if he happens to play for the school basketball team, Hanamichi becomes determined to make the squad. Whatever he lacks in basketball fundamentals, he makes up for with eagerness and natural athleticism.

Smith, Roland, *Peak* (2007) BK, UAB

After being arrested for scaling a building, avid climber Peak Marcello is sent to live with his father who owns a mountaineering outfit. Together, the two set a goal of Peak becoming the youngest to scale Mount Everest. But the further Peak gets into the journey, and the more he learns about his father's business and selfish motives, the less confidence he has in the project, leading to some difficult decisions at critical moments along the trek.

Stomp The Yard (2007) MV

When his brother is killed in a fight after a krump dance competition in L.A., DJ gets a second chance when his uncle gets him enrolled at a prestigious African American university in Atlanta. DJ gets pulled into another rivalry after he makes an enemy out of the star step dancer on campus and joins a fraternity that could threaten their championship title.

Sweeney, Joyce, *Headlock* (2006) BK

Formerly a gymnast, Kyle quits the team to pursue his dream of becoming a professional wrestler. He is the youngest in his class at the Hard Knocks wrestling school and must compete physically and mentally with some twice his age and twice his size. At home, he is the main caregiver for his aging grandmother, and when her health takes a turn for the worse, he wrestles with the difficulty of letting his estranged mother become involved in his life once again. This book is illuminating in its portrayal of amateur professional wrestling and a young man's sense of duty.

Varsity Blues (1999) MV

When the Coyotes' star quarterback gets badly injured during a game, backup quarterback Mox finally gets a taste of being the town hero. Mox soon finds himself at odds with the coach's desire to win at all costs.

The Athletes (Girls)

Female athletes in teen stories are often stigmatized, but differently than their male counterparts. Either they are ultra-feminine (the cheerleader, the gymnast) or too masculine (the tough girl who went out for quarterback). Additionally, female athletes often overcome familial or social barriers in their search for success on the court and in the spotlight. These teen athletes are complex and strong as they fight convention and strive to be the best player and best person they can be.

American Cheerleader Magazine

This monthly magazine is written for teen cheerleaders at all skill levels and features articles on current pop culture, nutrition advice, and fashion.

Bend it Like Beckham (2002) MV, CL

In this feel-good movie set in London, 18-year old Jess idolizes soccer icon David Beckham and knows she has the talent to play the game. Going against her traditional Indian parents, Jess tries out for and gets invited to join an all-girl soccer team, but her joy soon fades as she realizes she is upsetting her family.

Bring it On **(2000) MV, CL**
In this wildly popular film, the cheer squad at Rancho Carne high school is used to competing at the national cheerleading championships—and winning. Torrance, the captain of the squad, tries to do the right thing when she learns that all of their routines have been stolen from an inner-city high school.

Carey, Mike, *Re-Gifters* **(2007) GN**
In South Central L.A., Korean American Dixie and her friend Avril both practice hapkido competitively. As the girls pursue their sport, Dixie becomes distracted when she develops unrequited feelings for another hapkido student, Adam. The black-and-white graphic format accentuates the martial art moves and illuminates the emotion in this upbeat blend of sports, friendship, and romance.

***Crimson Hero*, Mitsuba Takanashi (2001) MN**
Tomboy Nobara Sumiyoshi is 15 years old and dreams only of playing volleyball. Her mother is convinced that Nobara must give up any notions of playing the game and instead do her duty and become hostess of the family restaurant. With the help of her aunt, Nobara refuses to give up her dream and enrolls at Crimson Field High School, which is known for its excellent boys volleyball program.

Esckilsen, Erik E., *The Outside Groove* **(2006) BK**
Seventeen-year-old Casey is irked by the unequal attention her racecar driver older brother gets. And now, adding injury to insult, she may not be able to pursue her career of choice or go to college because family funds are all being sunk into Wade's racing. So with the help of an understanding uncle, Casey becomes the first female stock car racer at her brother's track, where she finds racing and bucking convention more difficult than she imagined.

Girl Got Game, Shizuru Seino (2004) MN
Kyo Aizawa's father had hopes of playing professional basketball until he was injured. When Kyo is accepted at a new high school, she discovers that her father has enrolled her as a boy so she can fulfill his greatest dream of playing basketball. For Kyo to succeed with the charade and play on the boy's basketball team, she must live in the boy's dormitory and keep her sex a secret. To complicate things, she is forced to room with competitive Chiharu, who can't stand Kyo.

Girlfight **(2000) MV**
Diana Guzman has a reputation in her high school for fighting, a bad attitude, and her hair-trigger temper. After picking up her little brother Tiny from a boxing lesson, Diana sees a way to redirect her aggression.

Murdock, Catherine Gilbert, *Dairy Queen* **(2006) BK, UAB**
D. J. is a strong teen in a small town, having taken over most of the heavy lifting on her family farm after her older brothers moved out and her dad was injured. Then she shocks first her family and then her community when she tries out for the guys' football team. A genuine voice, a little-told perspective, and a gentle romance accentuate this female athlete's trials and triumphs.

Save the Last Dance **(2001) MV**
Dancers may be artists in their hearts and minds, but in body, they're exceptional athletes, too. After her mom's death, ballerina Sara moves in with her dad and transfers from a suburban school to one on the south side of Chicago where she takes up

hip-hop dancing thanks to Derek, the brother of a friend, who becomes much more than an after-school dance tutor.

Shull, Megan, *Amazing Grace* (2005) BK

After years on the circuit as a tennis prodigy and celebrity athlete, Grace "Ace" Kincaid decides she has had enough. The fame and fortune and celebrity treatment are quickly eschewed in favor of the simple life in a backwoods Alaskan hideout with a friend of the family, a former FBI agent, who orchestrates her mysterious disappearance. Living as regular girl Emily, Grace seeks to redefine herself as an individual, not a brand, and finds true friendship and love along the way, with an outstandingly supportive network of family and friends.

Stick It (2006) MV

After walking away from competitive gymnastics, teen Haley Graham has a lot of fun getting in trouble. After getting caught one too many times breaking the law, Haley is sentenced to mandatory attendance at a gymnastics academy, where her bad attitude is not appreciated. Eventually Haley and the other members pull together as a team to take a stand against harsh judging.

The Basket Case

The guys who hang out behind the bleachers, the girls who sit in the corner, the kids who cut class and sometimes themselves, these are the basket cases. Adolescence brings out the awkwardness in already awkward people, and as teens grow into their new physical shapes and try to stay on top of their constantly shifting emotions and interests, feeling like an outsider even in one's own skin is not uncommon. Some of these teens are supremely self-reflective, some to the point of obsession, but others may be unaware of their own neuroses until a final climactic event.

Anderson, Laurie Halse, *Wintergirls* (2009) BK, UAB

Lia and Cassie were best friends but their own worst enemies, too, as they egged each other on in contests that became obsessions that became deadly psychoses on the quest to become the thinnest. Now, Cassie has died a painful and gruesome death as a result of her bulimia and Lia is tortured by her ghost. As she wastes away ounce by ounce, trying to deceive everyone around her, she totters on the brink of oblivion.

Chappell, Crissa-Jean, *Total Constant Order* (2007) BK

Numbers are always running through Finn's head. They are a way of life for her. But her parents' divorce and a move add to the anxieties she has, and her obsessive-compulsive disorder becomes unmanagable without medication. But that doesn't feel right to her, either. Finn's struggle to understand herself and overcome her compulsion enough to carry on a livable life is empathetic and illuminating.

Crazy/Beautiful (2001) MV

Even though they both attend the same high school, Nicole and Carlos couldn't be more different. She's the wild daughter of a congressman who loves to act out, and he's from East L.A. and is only concerned with getting the best education possible. When they start falling in love, Nicole's self-destructive habits threaten to tear them apart.

Emily the Strange, Rob Reger, *Lost, Dark, and Bored* (2006) GN

A snarky and darkly humorous series of vignettes featuring Emily the Strange, the ultimate antisocial 13-year-old, and her four black cats.

Emo Boy, Steve Emond, *Nobody Cares About Anything Anyway, So Why Don't We All Just Die?* **(2006) GN**
Emo Boy constantly ponders his existence, his feelings, his inability to dance, his emo superpowers, high school, and even his own sexuality. He overthinks and analyzes every iota to the detriment of his own happiness.

Friesen, Johnathan, *Jerk, California* **(2008) BK, AP**
Despised by his stepfather because of his Tourette's syndrome, Sam is forced out of his home shortly after high school graduation and reluctantly finds a new home with the town's "old coot," an old friend of his late father's. Just as he is settling in and finally feeling wanted, his new friend dies and Sam is once again left alone until beautiful, conflicted Naomi enters the picture and the two embark on a trip to California, Sam to seek the windmills his father built, and Naomi to run away from the inevitable.

Mad Love **(1995) MV**
Focused student Matt becomes infatuated with the new girl in school, Casey. When Casey is hospitalized after attempting suicide, Matt decides to help her escape, but is completely unprepared for the depth of her mental illness.

Napoleon Dynamite **(2004) MV, CL, VGM**
Annoyed and aggravated by nearly everyone in high school and at home, awkward outsider Napoleon finds true friendship with new kid Pedro and patient Deb.

Rosenburg, Liz, *17* **(2002) BK**
Prose poems explore the inner life of 17-year-old Stephanie who, in addition to the usual joys and sorrows of the teen years, harbors a deep-seated fear of inheriting her mother's debilitating mental illness.

Slade, Arthur, *Tribes* **(2002) BK**
Emulating his deceased anthropologist father, Percy survives his last year of high school by viewing everything and everyone around him with a scientist's eye, analyzing the various tribes around him without belonging to any tribe himself. This psychological novel is brief but meaty, and a final twist at the end will have readers viewing Percy in a whole new light and skipping back to the beginning to read the book again with this greater understanding.

Ucci, Carol Plum, *What Happened to Lani Garver* **(2002) BK**
Claire tries her best to hide her basket-case side—the side where she is a leukemia survivor, or a musician, or has an eating disorder. She just wants to be normal and fit in. But when androgynous and mysterious Lani Garver moves to town, Claire is pulled in by him and starts to open up secrets that she has long locked away. For Claire, Lani seems too good to be true—is he even real?

The Princess

The princess is often the one we love to hate. Many of these stories are told, at least in part, from the perspective of an outsider to the princess clique who alternately aspires to be like and is burned by the group. The princess is beautiful, wealthy, and stylish, and gets the car, the crown, and the guy. She is the foil to the heroine in many contemporary teen stories, the one our girl finally gets the best of as the rest of her peers finally take notice of the person they should really be idolizing. And granted, sometimes princesses exist in teen stories just for that reason. But sometimes the princess is just as complex and storied as the "regular girl." Sometimes, on the inside, she really is a regular girl.

The A-List, Zoey Dean, *A List* (2003) BK

Stories of princesses often include a fish out of water. This time, though, she's new to Hollywood's hijinx. Anna is quite familiar with the ways of the rich, having transferred from Manhattan to live with her dad. Similar in tone to *Gossip Girl*, this series has inspired a spin off of its own, *A-List: Hollywood Royalty*.

The Au Pairs, Melissa De La Cruz, *The Au Pairs* (2004) BK

Three New York teens summer in the Hamptons, caring for the children of a wealthy couple by day and partying by night. The babysitting, along with the Hamptons' glitz and glamour, sun and sex keep regular girl Mara, down-on-her-luck Eliza, and Brazilian socialite Jacqui busy through several books in this popular series.

Baldwin Hills (2006) TV

This reality show filmed by BET follows a group of privileged African American teens living in the exclusive Baldwin Hills community of Los Angeles. Gerren, Roqui, and Garnette are just three of the teens in the show whose posh lives are quite different from that of Staci, who lives in a lower-middle-class neighborhood.

Clueless (1995) MV, CL, AP

Wealthy Beverly Hills teen Cher Horowitz begins to do good deeds to help the less fortunate and clueless people in her life after being chastised by her ex-stepbrother Josh for being selfish. Realizing she enjoys helping others even if things don't go as planned, Cher begins to wonder if she is the clueless one. A fun, updated reimagining of Jane Austen's *Emma*.

Cosmogirl Magazine

This teen variation of popular women's magazine *Cosmopolitan* features advice articles on relationships, beauty, and fashion.

Gossip Girl (2007) TV, BK, UAB (2002)

Based on the popular series of books by Cecily Von Ziegesar, the series gives viewers a peek into the lives of wealthy and popular teens attending an exclusive private school in New York. Blair Waldorf and Serena Van der Woodsen are the queen bees of the social elite. The all-seeing "gossip girl" narrates each episode, tracks the activities of the privileged few, and makes it a point to report the juiciest gossip to the entire school.

Hannah Montana: The Movie (2009) MV, VGM

Miley Stewart is used to living a double life; she becomes the famous pop singer, Hannah Montana, on stage. When Miley starts to let fame and the perks of being a star get too important, her dad brings her back to Tennessee to remind her what really matters in life.

Kare Kano, Masami Tsuda (2003) MN

Yukino is the smartest, prettiest, and most helpful girl in school, and she knows it. She is consumed with making sure that everyone thinks the best of her, even though it is not deserved. Soichiro is new in school and excels at everything that Yukino is used to claiming for her own, except he is sincere in his desire to help others and get good grades. Yukino burns with jealousy and vows to stop Soichiro from receiving the praise and accolades that she deserves.

Laguna Beach (2004–2006) TV

This show is filmed reality style by MTV and follows a group of privileged high school students in Laguna Beach. It was originally billed as "The Real O.C." to distinguish the show from the Fox scripted television show *The O.C.* LC and Kristin are the privileged princesses who battle over Steven. Hookups, conflicts, relationship drama, the prom, and saying goodbye to leave for college are par for the course on this show.

The Prince and Me (2004) MV

Girl meets boy, girl falls in love with boy, boy turns out to be the prince of Denmark and must convince his family that he should be allowed to marry outside of his royal sphere, girl decides to go to medical school instead—but he'll wait for her, so there's a happy ending after all. Julia Stiles stars in a lighthearted romance where she gets a chance at the Cinderella dream so many girls have and sees the reality behind the crown.

The Princess Diaries, Meg Cabot, *The Princess Diaries* (2000) BK, MV, SH, UAB

Mia Thermopolis is a quirky, artsy vegetarian whose biggest problem is her widowed mother's relationships, until she discovers that she is the crown princess of Genovia. Mia chronicles the upheaval in her life caused by this revelation, in addition to her relationship and friendship struggles though a series of diaries in the book series. The movies (2001, 2004) keep the same general storyline but with some significant departures.

Private, Kate Brian, *Private* (2006) BK, UAB

At her new private boarding school, Reed aspires to more than her working-class background. She desires the academic and social success she sees around her, especially in the elite Billings Girls clique. Treachery, gossip, tests of loyalty, and romantic entanglements ensue along the way as Reed tries to work herself into the position she desires. Those who enjoy the drama and tension of *Gossip Girl* antics may enjoy having another series to follow.

Seventeen Magazine

This is the gold standard for magazines targeted toward teen girls. It features articles on beauty, fashion, celebrities, relationships, and fitness so that every girl can discover her inner princess.

Teen Vogue Magazine

A teen spin-off publication of the high-fashion *Vogue*, this publication also features the standard fare of pop culture and beauty articles, but strongly emphasizes style and fashion trends.

The Criminal

Just as the princess gains status mainly by others' perceptions of her, the criminal often does as well. It may not be what they have done but what those around them think they have done that accounts for their status. The criminal is the bad kid, the dangerous one, the one your parents warned you about. Likely as not though, they are more complex than you might assume. Maybe they have good reasons for the things they've done. Maybe they are just as conflicted about their actions as you hoped they would be. And maybe they really didn't do anything at all.

Brooks, Kevin, *Martyn Pig* (2003) BK, RS

Martyn didn't mean to kill his father. It was an accident. Not that the guy didn't royally deserve it. Distrustful that the authorities would believe his story, Martyn tries to cover up the death by enlisting his crush Alex's help. She and Martyn try to hide the body and keep on as usual, and Martyn is almost ready to breathe a sigh of relief when the tables turn dramatically.

Cromartie High, Eiji Nonaka (2005) MN
Takashi Kamiyama vows to prove that one can indeed learn anywhere by enrolling at Cromartie High School in Tokyo. Cromartie is a school with quite a reputation—not for academic excellence, but for having a student body of juvenile delinquents!

Donner, Rebecca, *Burnout* (2008) GN
When Danni's mom finds a loser boyfriend for them to move in with, Danni becomes intrigued with Haskell, who may soon be her stepbrother. Danni is drawn to Haskell, even though he seems to be hiding a secret and sneaks out at night. Someone is spiking the trees in the forest to prevent logging; is it just a coincidence?

Giles, Gail, *Shattering Glass* (2002) BK, UAB
With echoes of *The Chocolate War*'s psychological suspense played out in the social strata of high school, *Shattering Glass* examines how and why a group of "good kids" could find themselves beating a classmate to death. From a vantage point of five years after the fact, narrator Young tells how charismatic Rob moved to town, ascended to high school royalty, and then used his power to manipulate those around him to horrific acts. This is a dark page-turner.

Gipi, *Garage Band* (2007) GN
Four troubled boys have only one thing to look forward to in their lives, jamming in a borrowed garage if they can stay out of trouble. They believe that making a demo tape of their songs is their ticket to fame and they have a hard time passing up the premium equipment being housed in a nearby church basement.

Gridiron Gang (2006) MV
A group of delinquents, mainly from L.A.'s street gangs, have carried their allegiances and prejudices with them to Camp Kilpatrick, a probation facility that is the last chance these young men have before being moved to the youth prison system. A young probation officer decides to start a football program, hoping to instill in the teens the values he learned from playing. Though the teens struggle with their personal issues and anger, they eventually come together in the spirit of teamwork. This is based on a true story.

Juvies (2007) TV
This MTV reality series follows teens who have been incarcerated in the juvenile detention system. Some are here for the first time, and some are very familiar with the legal system from a young age. It is viewable online at http://www.mtv.com/ontv/dyn/juvies/videos.jhtml.

Manning, Sarra, *Let's Get Lost* (2006) BK
Isabel is not a nice girl. She has reached her perch at the top of the pecking order at school and at home by being the "biggest bitch" around. Her abrasive personality and deceitfulness are partly traceable to her unsettled feelings over her mom's recent death, but she spirals out of control with nearly tragic consequences before hitting bottom and reconciling with her past.

Myers, Walter Dean, *Monster* (1999) BK, UAB
Steve Harmon is about to go on trial for his involvement in the murder of a convenience store clerk. He claims he was just the lookout and didn't really know what was

going on. The prosecution believes otherwise. Steve, an aspiring filmmaker, uses the opportunity to create a screenplay of his experience from his perspective. Is he telling the truth? Or does it just make a better movie this way?

Proulx, Joanne, ***Anthem of a Reluctant Prophet*** **(2007) BK, AP**
In the midst of a drug-soaked day of hanging out in the basement with his buddies, Luke suddenly pipes up with an eerie prediction about the death of one of the guys. The very next day, it all happens just as he foresaw. And then he does it again. As Luke struggles with what his responsibility for the deaths might be, he becomes obsessed with trying to find a missing girl and is pursued by a drug-pushing doctor and a fundamentalist Christian preacher, all the while searching for meaning in his own life.

Sachar, Louis, ***Holes*** **(2003) BK, MV, CL**
Stanley Yelnats is pretty sure his family is cursed with bad luck. A misunderstanding lands him in a desert boot-camp-style juvenile detention center, where he and the other boys are forced to dig and then fill giant holes day after day. Here, he bonds with the other misfits, breaks free with one of them, sets out on a quest through the desert, and confronts his preconceptions about his family and his fate.

Strasser, Todd, ***Give a Boy a Gun*** **(2007) BK, UAB, RS**
Two teens plan a Columbine-like massacre at a school dance. In an exposé style, the narrative is shared by many of those involved in the incident, probing deep into the motivations and psyche of the perpetrators going back to middle school. Fiction that reads like nonfiction, the book also includes many statistics and facts about gun control and gun violence.

The United States of Leland **(2004) MV**
Inspired by Albert Camus' *The Stranger*, teenaged Leland senselessly kills a mentally retarded boy, the brother of a friend of his. As those around him try to understand the crime, including his distant father and a teacher in the detention center, Leland journals about his feelings and experiences.

Plots

New Kids on the Block: The Quest to Fit In

Stories featuring the "new kid" are popular and appealing in teen media for a few good reasons. If the story is told from the perspective of the new kid, as in most of these, the reader or viewer sees the way a community reacts to an outsider. The new kids in these stories usually fall into one of two categories: the outsider who will remain an outsider because new is weird and different, or the outsider whose foreign appeal rockets him or her to popularity. In reality, new kids are going to fall somewhere in the middle. But for anyone who has ever changed schools in the middle of the year, the dream of the celebrity new kid is an awfully appealing fantasy.

Alexie, Sherman, ***The Absolutely True Diary of a Part-Time Indian*** **(2007) BK, UAB, AP, RS**
Arnold Spirit (Junior) was born poorer than poor on a Spokane Indian reservation. By high school, his intelligence far outpaces the opportunities his local tribal school

can offer him, so he makes the 22-mile trek to the nearest "white" school in hopes of creating a future for himself that will get him off the reservation. But Junior isn't prepared for what he finds at his new school, Reardon High: he is suddenly kind of popular. Nor is he ready for what faces him when he returns home, suddenly an outsider: he is looked upon with mistrust and scorn by many. This semi-autobiographical novel shines in its harsh realism and humor as Junior struggles to make the right choices for his future while honoring his past.

Beverly Hills, 90210 (1990–2000, 2008–) TV, CL

In both versions of this television show, premiering in 1990 (with twins Brandon and Brenda Walsh) and 2008 (featuring siblings Annie and Dixon Wilson), teens from the midwest must adapt quickly to the wealthy and image-obsessed West Beverly High School in California.

Boys Over Flowers, Yokio Kamio (2003) MN

As if attending a new elite school wasn't stressful enough, quiet Tsukushi Makino incurs the wrath of the F4, the four most powerful boys in school, when she stands up for her friend. Tsukushi stays strong and vows to be a "weed" when the entire school shuns her.

Castelluci, Cecil, *Plain Janes* (2007) GN

After a terrorist attack in the city, Jane and her parents move to a "safe" and boring suburb. Soon Jane meets three other Janes who have nothing in common except for their shared name and the desire to do something different in their town.

The Clique, Lisi Harrison, *The Clique* (2004) BK, VGM

Claire's family moves into the guesthouse owned by Massie's family while in the process of relocating from Florida to Westchester, Massachusetts. Though the girls are the same age, Massie sees little else that they share in common because Claire lacks the money and status of Massie and her friends on the Pretty Committee. The series is full of brand-name-dropping, backstabbing, and social climbing as Claire attempts to stake a claim among the popular in her new community.

Dramacon, Svetlana Chemkova (2005) MN

Christie goes through a roller-coaster ride at her first anime convention. Promoting the manga she created with her jerk of a boyfriend doesn't go exactly as planned. Meeting a strangely confident boy named Matt who seems to figure her out pretty easily makes the bad weekend worthwhile.

Griffin, Adele, *Amandine* (2001) BK

Lonely and isolated in her new school, Delia is fascinated by fellow freshman Amandine, the first person to show any interest in befriending her. Amandine is unlike anyone Delia has ever met. She is creative and shocking and, Delia soon finds out, more troubled and dangerous than she could have imagined.

Malkin, Nina, *Swoon* (2009) BK, UAB

Candice (Dice) is Swoon, Connecticut's newest resident, living across the street from her cousin but largely on her own as her parents work in New York and are gone most of the week. Dark-haired and broody, Dice doesn't fit in well with the country-club set, but when her cousin's near-death experience brings back a maligned character from Swoon's past, the town's newest resident changes by awakening buried passions and turning everything on its head.

Mean Girls (2004) MV
Cady, the new girl in school, has been homeschooled by her zoologist parents while living in Africa. Completely unprepared for the cruel nature of high school life, Cady agrees to help two outsiders by spying on and sabotaging the most hated and popular clique, the Plastics.

St. James, James, *Freak Show* (2007) BK, AP
Cosmopolitan transplant Billy Bloom is ready to take on his new small backwater Florida town with style and verve, meticulously planning every detail of his outfit for the first day (involving more shimmer and glam than any of his classmates have ever seen on a guy). But his reception is less than warm, and despite his best efforts, he becomes the victim of a vicious attack that, though it damages his body, doesn't quash his individuality. A truly unique voice and one of few drag queen characters in teen literature make this novel a real treat for fans of the genre.

Yang, Gene Luen, *American Born Chinese* (2006) GN, AW
Jin Wang is the ultimate outsider: not only is he the new kid in school, but is one of just a few Asian American students. He stands out even after he has been there for what seems like forever. Jin's differences cannot be forgotten by his classmates or himself. Tactfully told and filled with anguish, the author integrates a Chinese fable and another story of Danny, an American teen shamed by the yearly visits of his cousin Chin-Kee, with Jin's experiences.

Teen Lives, Adult Issues
At some point during the teen years, most teenagers decide that they are essentially adults, know better than their parents, and feel that they should be able to make their own minds up about major and minor life choices. But there are some times when decisions and events occur that trump the conversation. Pregnancy, death, abandonment, or military service pushes teens into a forced position of adulthood, and whether or not they are truly ready for the consequences, they are at points of no return. The teen then exists in a middle space, not quite an adult, but required to make adult decisions; they are still a teenager, but lack the freedom to explore and grow like their peers.

16 and Pregnant (2009) TV
This reality show produced by MTV documents the struggle of a different girl in each episode through the end of her pregnancy, the birth of her child, and the first few months of motherhood. Viewers see the real, adult decisions and situations each girl faces, with happy endings not necessarily guaranteed. These teenage mothers must juggle school, learning the skills to care for newborns, and shaky relationships. Full episodes are viewable online at http://www.mtv.com/ontv/dyn/16_and_pregnant/series.jhtml.

Budhos, Marina, *Ask Me No Questions* (2006) BK
It wasn't a big deal that Nadira's family was in the United States illegally from Bangladesh, having overstayed their visas. Everyone did it. And then the 9/11 terrorist attacks changed everything. Nadira's father is detained while trying to seek asylum in Canada, and Nadira returns to New York with her perfect older sister, who quickly begins crumbling into a shell of her former strong character. Young Nadira must hide her family's predicament and work to find a way to get her father released in this contemporary, realistic immigration story.

Engaged and Underage (2007–2009) TV
This reality-style show produced by MTV follows young adults preparing to get married. Most of the couples featured in this series are going against the wishes and advice of their parents or close friends. It is viewable online at http://www.mtv.com/ontv/dyn/engaged_and_underage/series.jhtml.

Fienberg, Anna, *Borrowed Light* (2000) BK
Bright but lonely, 16-year-old Callisto is pregnant and on her own to make the most important decision of her life. Her slacker surfer boyfriend is out of the picture, her parents are too occupied with their own passions, and her steadfast brother Jeremy is only five years old. When she decides to get an abortion, Jeremy has to come along, but when he goes missing during her procedure, the family tumult that ensues is revealing. Rich with a pervasive astronomy metaphor (Callisto feels like she is a moon, just "borrowing" light from those around her) and lyrical, self-reflective prose, this novel tackles difficult topics maturely.

Going, K. L., *St. Iggy* (2006) BK, UAB
Iggy was born drug exposed, a crack baby, and though he tries to move beyond his troubled past, it is an unavoidable part of who he is. Poor and virtually parentless, Iggy is largely alone in the world. After being suspended from school once again, Iggy becomes determined to make a difference, to do something that counts. But his attempts, earnest though they are, do not have the consequences he envisioned.

Hornby, Nick, *Slam* (2007) BK, UAB
Sam is floored when he finds out that his almost-former girlfriend is pregnant, but he sticks by her and tries to do the right thing for his child. Hornby brings his lively voice to this story full of humor and heart, authentically portraying the experience of a teenaged guy in way over his head with the burdens of parenthood and school, friends, skating, and romance.

Johnson, Angela, *First Part Last* (2003) BK, UAB, CL
Sixteen-year-old new father Bobby is overwhelmed by his new duties and his love for his daughter Feather. The fast-moving story alternates between Bobby's time as a new father with the story of how he came to be raising Feather all by himself. This emotional story leaves a lasting impression that will impact readers of all ages.

Juno (2007) MV, AP
After losing her virginity to her best friend and sort-of boyfriend, offbeat teen Juno MacGuff decides to give up her baby for adoption when she realizes she is ill-equipped to raise the child properly.

Krulik, Nancy, *Dawn's Early Light* (2006) BK
Her boyfriend Tim is shipping out for basic training in 24 hours. The day should be filled with meaningful talks, last kisses, and farewell parties. And though Sarah goes along with the motions of what she thinks Tim needs, she is struggling with the news that her brother, currently stationed in Iraq, is missing.

Myers, Walter Dean, *Sunrise over Fallujah* (2008) BK, UAB
Full of patriotism and seeking to make a positive difference, Robin enlists in the army just before Operation Iraqi Freedom instead of going to college. Just like his uncle before him (Richie Perry in 1988's *Fallen Angels*, about a teen enlisted in Vietnam), Robin soon finds that the war is much more complex and devastating than he had imagined. His job in a civil affairs unit becomes increasingly more combat-oriented, and Robin struggles to reconcile his beliefs and morals with his patriotism and duty.

Rabb, Margo, *Cures for Heartbreak* (2007) BK

Mia is shocked when her beautiful, healthy mother falls ill and dies after a brief illness. Shortly thereafter, her father is also hospitalized with serious health problems. Mia is left depressed and constantly fearful, taking brief solace in dark humor and doing everything she can to keep the household running and her dad healthy. Episodic in nature, this novel is raw with emotion, both exhilaratingly happy and unbearably sad, and inspired by the author's own experiences as a teen.

The Secret Life of the American Teenager (2008) TV

Fifteen-year old Amy Juergens struggles with the knowledge that she is pregnant after losing her virginity in a one-night stand at band camp. She dreads informing her parents and friends, and knows she will have to make a difficult decision about her pregnancy. Full episodes are viewable online at http://community.abcfamily.go.com/watch/9/full-episodes.

Talbot, Bryan, *Tale of One Bad Rat* (1994) GN

After years of abuse at the hands of her parents, teenaged Helen runs away to live on the streets of London, with her vivid imagination, beloved Beatrix Potter books, and pet rat to keep her company. As Helen draws more and more parallels between her life and that of her favorite author, she also draws closer to confronting the tragedies of her past and gaining closure before moving forward with her life.

White Oleander (2002) BK, MV

When her mother commits a crime of passion, 15-year-old Astrid finds herself vulnerable and adrift in the California foster care system.

The Generation Gap: Clashing with your Parents

One of the major tasks of adolescence is breaking away from one's family of origin and coming to an understanding of oneself as an independent individual. Start with a few less-than-understanding parents, add in a generation gap and a dash of teenage rebellion and you've got the conditions for a volatile disconnect. The characters in these stories represent a diverse group, displaying that this disconnect is something that transcends stereotypes and has the potential to impact any teen.

Anderson, Laurie Halse, *Twisted* (2007) BK, UAB

Tyler expects a triumphant return to his senior year after a graffiti prank lands him a summer of muscle-building landscape work. But his grades are never good enough and his relationship with his dad's boss's daughter is threatening enough, and a final drunken evening with a tremendous misunderstanding leaves Tyler and his father at dangerous odds with one another.

Davis, Tanita, *A la Carte* (2008) BK

Lainey is dedicated to her goal of becoming the first vegetarian female African American TV chef, but her motivation suffers a blow when her childhood friend asks for a favor that puts her in a delicate position, and ultimately puts her at odds with her mother. Lainey soon finds out that once trust is damaged, it is slow to recover.

Garsee, Jeanine, *Say The Word* (2009) BK, AP

The misunderstandings go both ways here. Shawna is deeply hurt by her mother, who abandoned the family to live with another woman when Shawna was seven. For 10 years she struggled to please her perfectionist father, but when Shawna's mom dies and she sees the damage that her dad is doing to her partner's life and family, she must reconcile who she is with what she knows is right, even if it means coming to terms with who her idolized father really is as well.

Mackler, Carolyn, *The Earth, My Butt, and Other Big Round Things* (2003) BK, UAB
Virginia discovers the ugly truth about her idolized older brother and grows to embrace herself for who she is, but she does so in the face of her distant and judgmental psychologist mother and executive father.

Mizuki, Hakase, *Asian Beat* (2007) MN
This collection of short stories involves lonely teens just trying to survive. Parental abandonment, trying to support younger siblings by selling drugs, and bullying are the serious themes touched upon in this stark manga.

***The O.C.* (2003–2007) TV**
Troubled Marissa Cooper has everything a girl in Newport Beach could ask for: a cute boyfriend, great clothes, an unlimited spending allowance, and an awesome best friend. To her mother's great displeasure, Marissa finds herself drawn to Ryan Atwood, a juvenile delinquent who moves into the neighborhood after being taken in by the Cohen family.

***The Rage in Placid Lake* (2003) MV, AP**
Placid Lake is the only son of uber-hippie parents who are too occupied with their New Age search for enlightenment to realize that Placid, despite being raised with every opportunity to embrace his inner self, is deeply unhappy. Deciding that his parents' way is not for him, Placid, who has just graduated from high school, gets a haircut and a desk job at an insurance company, sure that embracing conformity will cure what ails him. This quirky satire provides a clever counterpoint to the types of teen rebellion we are used to.

Thomas, Rob, *Rats Saw God* (1996) BK, UAB, CL
Steve's dad, a famous astronaut, expects a lot of Steve, a lot more than he is apparently capable of, especially after his heart is broken by his first love. Steve's grades have plummeted and he has one chance to pass English and graduate: write a 100-page essay. This is Steve's essay; he examines where he is and how he got there, and comes to some conclusions about his father and their relationship along the way.

Themes: Rites of Passage

Separating the major theme of teen stories—rites of passage—from plots is a murky distinction. However, as the overarching motif in teen stories is a self-awareness, it is often borne through these three rites of passage: learning (or not) from mistakes associated with drugs and dangerous behavior, forays into first love, and confronting or embracing one's true self.

Teenage Wasteland

While not part and parcel of every adolescent experience, the allure of drugs and alcohol and the intrigue surrounding them are strong influences on teen life and in teen stories. Cautionary tales abound right along with comedic send-ups in the form of the "stoner flick" and both are hugely popular with their intended audience. Whether living vicariously through the dangerous behavior of others, gobbling up the drama of the situations a la the after-school special, or trying to glean insight into the behavior of those around, stories about kids who do bad stuff are long-standing staples in the realm of teen lives.

13 (2003) MV

Who knew that 13 could be such a dangerous age? Vulnerable good girl Tracy falls under the spell of Evie, her popular, wild, and manipulative classmate. This captivating transformation was co-written by Nikki Reed, who plays Evie.

Anonymous *Go Ask Alice*, ed. Beatrice Sparks (1972) BK, CL

A rite of passage in and of itself, *Go Ask Alice* is a fictional diary purported to be by an anonymous teen counseled by the editor, Sparks. In it, the unnamed narrator details her rapid descent from a good girl to a strung-out junkie runaway. Whether it is read as a didactic cautionary tale or a juicy account of the dark side, teens have been clamoring for this book since its original publication in 1972.

Brick (2006) MV

Reminiscent of a classic film noir, a group of teens in an affluent California suburb lose one of their own to a drug-related death, and Brendan attempts to solve the crime in hopes of setting things right.

Cruel Intentions (1999) MV, CL

Spoiled, privileged Kathryn plots to corrupt naive Cecile and bets her stepbrother Sebastian that he will not be able to seduce pure, virginal Annette. A modern, updated teen spin on *Les Liaisons Dangereuses*.

Dazed and Confused (1993) MV, CL, AP

It's the last day of school in 1976 and as soon as the last bell rings, the tradition of hazing that the new seniors inflict on the fresh-faced incoming freshman begins. For some of next year's seniors, the beginning of the end of their last year of high school is confusing and maybe even bittersweet. For the new freshman, it's all about finding out which clique you'll end up in, cruising, and finally being invited to the kegger in the woods.

Freaks and Geeks (1999–2000) TV, AP

Siblings Lindsey and Sam represent the spectrum of outcasts in a Michigan high school in the early 1980s. Lindsey, eager to shed her mathlete image, decides to start hanging with the pot-smoking, burnout freaks. Sam's best friends are the geeks of the school, too eager to please, and the doormats of the student body.

Going, K. L., *Fat Kid Rules the World* (2003) BK, UAB

While Troy stands at the edge of the subway platform and contemplates jumping, live-wire Curt, a classmate and high school punk-rock god, steps in to interrupt him and invite him to be the drummer in his band. Troy reluctantly accepts and is quietly thrilled by the attention Curt pays him. But Curt's manic behavior soon reveals a heavy reliance on drugs, and it becomes Troy's job to return the favor and save Curt.

Hopkins, Ellen, *Crank* (2004) BK, UAB

A dark and gripping novel in verse, Kristina grapples with an all-encompassing addiction to crystal meth. As she spirals downward, she becomes the victim of violent crime and ends up pregnant, despite the best efforts of those close to her. Kristina's story is continued in *Glass*.

Kids (1995) MV
This highly controversial film follows a group of teens in New York. Telly's favorite pastimes are relieving girls of their virginity and hanging with his best friend Casper. After getting tested for STDs, Jennie discovers she is HIV-positive after sleeping with Telly only once.

That 70's Show (1998–2006) TV
Point Place, Wisconsin, is a pretty boring town to live in, but Eric Forman's basement is the best place for his friends to hang out and avoid parents, schoolwork, and responsibility.

Teen Love
Stories of first love are quintessential to teen life. Falling in love as a teenager is truly the best and worst of times. Never having had the experiences before, a casual brush of the hand across the back or a gaze that lingers just a little longer than usual can set hearts racing and shivers down spines. Teen love feels like it has to last forever—how could it not? But inevitably, the love will dissipate or change, and our protagonists will experience the saddest emotions and the lowest lows. Fortunately, they will get up and move forward, and sometimes, when the reader is lucky, find love again before the story's close.

Crazy Love Story, Vin Lee (2004) MN
Shin Hae Jung is devastated over the death of her mother and doesn't seem to care about anything. She and her boyfriend Jimmy have a temperamental and dysfunctional relationship. When Hae Jung's classmate Sung Moo decides to act on his crush for her, he gets drawn into their games. Which boy will win Hae Jung's heart?

Davidson, Dana, *Jason and Kyra* (2004) BK
Jason can have anyone he wants, and as he tires of the beautiful but shallow Lisa, he is paired up with intelligent Kyra, an individual with a great dedication to school and a knack for knowing what is under Jason's showy surface. This is a common storyline but is notable for its setting in a well-to-do suburb of Detroit and a mainly African American cast—the type of book we hope to see more of in the future.

Dawson's Creek (1998–2003) TV
Budding film director and tenth grader Dawson Leery finds himself torn between Joey, the girl he has known all his life, and Jen, the new girl next door.

Friedman, Aimee, *Breaking Up* (2007) GN
It's junior year for Chloe Sacks and her three best friends at "Fashion High," and everyone thinks it will be their best year yet. When her friends MacKenzie, Erika, and Isabel start getting pulled in different directions and no one seems to be connecting like they used to, Chloe falls in love with a geek. Hiding the relationship from her supposed best friends can only last so long.

Freymann-Weyr, Garret, *My Heartbeat* (2002) BK, UAB, AP
Ellen admires her older brother Link and develops a serious crush on his best friend, James. But she suddenly realized that Link and James may be more than just best friends. After asking if they are, as she suspects, a couple, the two become distant and James begins to date Ellen. This is a sensitive portrayal of the complexities of family, love, and sexuality, true and poignant in its emotional examination of first love.

Katcher, Brian, *Playing with Matches* **(2008) BK**
One of the amazing things about loving someone else is how it shows us corners of ourselves that we were unaware of before. Leon is a confirmed geek, lusting after beautiful Amy. He relies on his sense of humor and inadvertently draws the attention of Melody, a bright, funny girl ostracized by her peers because of the severe burns covering her face. Leon fears what his buddies will think if they find out he and Melody are dating, but plunges ahead anyway. Mistakes are made, hearts are broken, and Leon emerges a better version of himself.

Korman, Gordan, *Son of the Mob* **(2002) BK, UAB**
As if falling in love wasn't hard enough, Vince chooses the most perfectly wrong girl. She's the daughter of a respectable FBI agent. And Vince? He's the son of a mob boss. In the midst of the humor generated from this modern-day *Romeo and Juliet* pairing, Vince and Kendra attempt to overcome their differences and find romance.

The Man in the Moon **(1991) MV, CL**
Just 14, Dani falls hard for Court, the handsome new boy who moves in next door. When Court finds himself attracted to Dani's sister Maureen instead, the sisters become rivals. Reese Witherspoon makes her film debut as Dani.

Raising Victor Vargas **(2002) MV**
Arrogant teenager Victor knows he can get any girl he wants. He lives with his grandmother, brother, and sister on the Lower East Side of New York. When he sets his sights on Judy, Victor learns a few things about relationships.

Soryo, Fuyumi, *Mars* **(2002) MN**
Kira, artistic and quiet, unexpectedly runs into her classmate Rei outside of high school. Bad-boy Rei, known for racing bikes and breaking hearts, finds himself drawn to Kira's talent and sensitivity. The unexpected attraction between Kira and Rei surprises not only themselves, but their classmates as well.

The Real Me

As teens grow into adults, they often come to know themselves in all-new ways. Whether it is a realization about goals, sexual orientation, religion, or something as seemingly simple as hobbies, these revelations can sometimes cause upheavals in one's family or social circle. Teens in these stories all deal with moving into their new identities—some more gracefully than others.

After School Nightmare, **Setona Mizushiro (2006) MN**
Handsome freshman Mashiro Ichijo attends a prestigious school and is admired by many of his female classmates. No one knows he is a hermaphrodite who is terribly ashamed of his secret, until he participates in a strange mandatory after-school class in which his true self is revealed.

Degrassi: The Next Generation **(2001–) TV, CL**
This highly popular updated version of *Degrassi Junior High* highlights the struggles of teens to discover who they really are and how to navigate life. A few key storylines involve the struggles of sexual identity, turning goth after being the preppy good girl, and the diagnosis of mental illness.

My So-Called Life (1994–1995) TV, CL, AP

Introspective sophomore Angela Chase questions the kind of person she wants to be and feels disconnected to the friends she's had all her life. After becoming friends with the wild Rayanne and not quite out-of-the-closet Ricky, a different side of high school becomes her reality. Drama ensues, especially when brooding Jordan Catalano begins to finally notice Angela. Family life and serious issues like alcoholism and violence are also explored.

Only the Ring Finger Knows, Satoru Kannagi, *The Lonely Ring Finger* (2002) BK

Wearing matching rings to proudly declare your true love for another is all the rage at school. When Wataru realizes his ring actually matches the ring of arrogant and handsome Yuichi, he begins to wonder if they belong together. This is primarily a novel, with manga illustrations. (As of this writing, three volumes have been published, with two more scheduled.)

Paradise Kiss, Ai Yazawa (2002) MN

Yukari, a diligent high school senior, is taken aback when she is approached by two students from Yazawa School for the Arts. The first student, Arashi, is a punk rocker with a fake British accent, and the second, Isabella, appears to be a beautiful transvestite! They, along with two other students from Yazawa, wish to make over Yukari and use her as their model for the line of clothes they are creating, Paradise Kiss.

Peters, Julie Anne, *Luna* (2003) BK

Regan has always loved and supported her older, transgendered sibling Liam. When Liam announces to her that he is ready to transition to become Luna, Regan has a whole new set of worries. How will Luna be received by family and friends? What if it is too difficult and Luna harms herself? As Luna transforms and Regan observes, a sensitive and touching relationship between the siblings is revealed, along with the person Luna has always longed to be.

Saved! (2004) MV

Born-again Christian teen Mary becomes pregnant after having sex with her boyfriend in order to "save" him from his suspected homosexuality. Doubting that the Jesus she loves would allow this to happen, Mary begins to lose her faith and bonds with a cynical group of teens at her school and tries her best to hide her pregnancy. While satirical in nature, the film presents several teens' journeys of self-awareness and how they reconcile their faith with their realities.

Vivian, Sibohn, *Same Difference* (2009) BK

Emily is accepted into a prestigious university summer art program just a commuter train ride away from home. Excited to develop her skills, she is also anxious to expand her horizons and spend some time away from her bland suburban hometown, including her long-time best friend with whom it seems the past is all they have in common. She is a total outsider, but as she gets to know the ins and outs of the art world, she is able to find a middle ground that feels more comfortable, taking the best of both worlds and making them her own.

The Wallflower, Tomoko Hayakawa (2004) MN

Four trendy, handsome teen boys are offered free rent for three years in a beautiful mansion near their prestigious school . . . if they can convert the landlady's niece into a proper young woman. Everyone fears 15-year-old Sunako; she loves horror movies, resembles the scary dead girl from the movie *The Ring*, and barely speaks to anyone. Will the boys ever be able to transform Sunako?

Making Connections

Since teens actually are people, their stories appear in just about any popular genre. Readers of romance, speculative fiction, and vampire stories may be perhaps more suggestible when it comes to offering stories of teen lives because of the wealth of interesting teen stories in these subgenres.

Death by High School: Teen Stories for Paranormal Fans

Invincibility, beauty, strength, charisma, powers . . . vampire qualities are nothing if not appealing when in the awkward, ugly trenches of adolescence. Teen vampire stories are nothing new, but they are enjoying a renaissance thanks both to cult hits like *Buffy the Vampire Slayer* and blockbuster success stories like the Twilight series. The current popularity of this niche market has created an abundance of vampire/werewolf/zombie/witch romance stories, and these are some patrons are most likely to enjoy.

Buffy the Vampire Slayer (1997–2003) TV, MV, GN, BK, CL, VGM
Buffy Summers is your average teenager attending Sunnydale High in California, with just one exception . . . she's the chosen one. Unfortunately, the town is built on a Hellmouth, a gateway between Earth and hell. Buffy is the lone guardian preventing vampires, demons, and other dark forces from taking over. Though most popular in its television incarnation, Buffy's story is available in multiple formats.

<u>Chibi Vampire</u>, Yuna Kagesaki (2007) MN
Karin is not a typical vampire like the rest of her family. She attends high school and instead of biting victims, she produces more blood that results in nose bleeds if she doesn't get rid of it by giving it to others. When Karin's blood unexpectedly reacts to the new transfer student Kenta, she knows that her secret may be revealed.

Klause, Annette Curtis, *Blood and Chocolate* (1997) BK, AP
Vivian is not afraid of her wild side—she's not just a beautiful girl, she's also a werewolf. When her romance with "meat boy" Aiden endangers both their lives, as well as the security of her pack, Vivian must take action. This book is notable for a female main character with a real awareness of her sexuality. A movie version of the book was widely panned and had several drastic departures from the original story.

<u>Twilight</u>, Stephenie Meyer, *Twilight* (2005) BK, MV, SH, UAB
Though it wasn't the first, it is certainly the most popular teen vampire romance currently around. *Twilight* starts the saga of Bella Swan and Edward Cullen, the young vampire who alternately loves her and thirsts for her blood. The ultimate in star-crossed romances, Bella is faced with a grave decision: would she really give up her life for her love?

<u>Vampire Academy</u>, Richelle Mead, *Vampire Academy* (2007) BK, UAB
Rose and Lissa attend St. Vladimir's Academy, a boarding school for vampires. Rose is Lissa's protector and friend, and the two are deeply entangled in the dangerous,

dramatic, sexy world of vampires, dhampir, Strigoi, and more as they fight for love and for their lives.

Vampire Kisses, Ellen Schreiber, *Blood Relatives* (2007) MN, BK
Goth girl Raven is an outsider at school, but she could care less. Her biggest dream came true: her boyfriend Alexander is a real vampire. She can see him only at night, but it is a small price to pay for absolute happiness. When Alexander's cousin Claude arrives with evil intentions, Raven gets drawn into their rivalry.

Vampire Knight, Matsuri Hino (2007) MN AP
Yuki and Zero attend the prestigious Cross Academy during the day. They are also guardians of the school, protecting the day students from the attractive students who attend class only at night. Yuki and Zero are the only day students who know that the night class is comprised entirely of vampires.

Velez, Ivan, *Dead High Yearbook* (2007) GN
This compilation of horror stories is styled as a high school yearbook with vignettes featuring teens in various storylines with zombies, monster pets, and vampires. Beware, high school can get you killed!

The Agony and the Ecstasy: Teen Stories for Romance Readers

Again we are reminded that teen stories are emotional stories. Love and romance weigh heavily upon the minds (and plots) across the genre. This creates a natural bridge to romance readers and romance titles. Many teens happily devour adult market romances for their dream fulfillment, satisfying endings, and, let's face it, the dog-ear-worthy sex scenes that get passed around in the locker room.

Bridget Jones, Helen Fielding, *Bridget Jones's Diary* (1996) BK, MV, UAB, AB
An early teen/adult chick lit crossover, Bridget Jones is a heroine teens can relate to: clumsily stumbling over herself, attracted to the wrong guy, and determined to come out on top. The diary format also appeals to many teens who may have first encountered and been entranced by it in *The Princess Diaries* or other teen fiction.

Cohn, Rachel, and David Levithan, *Nick and Norah's Infinite Playlist* (2008) MV, BK, UAB, AP
Nick is heartbroken and can't seem to get over his ex-girlfriend, Tris. When he's convinced by his bandmates to go out and play a gig, he sees her with another guy in the audience. Norah, a classmate of Tris, asks Nick to pretend to be her boyfriend for five minutes in front of her, not realizing that Nick is the guy who can't stop making mix CDs for Tris.

Dessen, Sarah, *This Lullaby* (2002) BK, UAB
Dessen's romantic stories resonate with teens and adult readers who identify with the strong, complex female protagonists. *This Lullaby* features a cynical main character whose experience with love and romance is colored by her mom's disastrous relationships.

Jessica Darling, Megan McCafferty, *Sloppy Firsts* (2001) BK
Jessica Darling is 16, has been abandoned by her best friend, has parents who may as well be aliens, and is about to fall in love. Beginning in her junior year in high school and following her into college and beyond, the series is notable for Jessica's pithy observations and her genuine reactions to the romantic entanglements she encounters.

One Tree Hill (2003–) TV
The first four seasons of this popular television show chronicled the rivalries and romantic relationships of a group of teens attending high school in Tree Hill, North Carolina. After graduation at the end of the fourth season, the series jumps forward four years ahead in the future for the fifth season to follow the more mature concerns of the characters, now adults.

Sparks, Nicholas, *A Walk to Remember* **(2002) MV, BK, UAB**
Unpopular pastor's daughter Jamie Sullivan befriends rebellious Landon Carter even though they have almost nothing in common. After Landon refuses to acknowledge their friendship publicly and humiliates her, Jamie refuses to have anything to do with him. Soon Landon realizes Jamie is the only person among his friends who is worth knowing and eventually learns that Jamie has been keeping a secret from the entire school. This film was adapted from the book of the same name published in 1999 by Nicholas Sparks.

Teenage Mutants

Bodies are changing, emotions are running amok, even beliefs and values can shift during the teen years. There's much to relate to in tales of mutants, alter egos, and superpowers. Some of these take place in the world we know, others in an alternate reality. All of these teens are alternately blessed and cursed by their "mutant-ness," a feeling most teens can relate to while enduring the unique pleasures of puberty.

Avatars, **Tui T. Sutherland (2006) BK**
With echoes of the popular TV show *Heroes*, the Avatars series focuses on five teens from around the world who, for unknown reasons, are the only ones of their era shuttled 75 years into the future in what seemed like a day to them. After being mysteriously drawn to New York City, the teens find one another and set about trying to salvage what they can in spite of giant crystal monsters and technology gone haywire.

The Craft **(1996) MV**
New student Sarah is befriended by Bonnie, Nancy, and Rochelle, the outcast "witches" of St. Benedict's Academy. The four girls discover they can combine and use their skills to cast spells, but are unprepared for the dangerous side effects of having so much power.

Invincible, Robert Kirkman, *Family Matters* **(2003) GN**
Everyone knows it's not easy being a teenager, but imagine being the teen son of a powerful superhero from another planet. Mark Grayson, whose superpowers begin to develop when he's taking out the trash, renames himself Invincible and helps his father fight evil.

Kyle XY **(2006–2009) TV**
Naked and unable to speak, a 16-year-old boy without a navel finds himself in the forest with no memories or knowledge at all. Stumbling into town, he is arrested by the authorities, and is soon taken in by a psychologist who vows to figure out who or what Kyle is.

Maximum Ride, James Patterson, *Maximum Ride* **(2009) MN, BK, UAB**
A group of kids who were bred to have special talents escaped from the "school" where they were raised. When the youngest, Angel, is kidnapped and taken back to the school,

Max and the others vow to rescue her. Based on the novels also by James Patterson, the winged children were first introduced in Patterson's adult novel *Where the Wind Blows*.

Runaways, Brian K. Vaughn, *Pride and Joy* (2003) GN

A group of very different teens with nothing in common are always forced to come to their parents' annual meeting that raises money for charity. When the kids witness their parents sacrifice a young girl, they realize their parents are evil superheroes and must be stopped at all costs, and soon learn of their own burgeoning superpowers.

Smallville (2001–) TV

Teenager Clark Kent knows the reason he is different from everyone—he wasn't born on Earth. After a meteor shower, he was discovered and taken in as a youngster by a kind couple, Martha and Jonathan Kent. Now in high school, Clark struggles to fit in with his friends and keep his superhuman powers secret while helping those who are in danger.

Terminator: The Sarah Connor Chronicles (2008–2009) TV

The fate of humanity rests on the shoulders of young John Connor in the war against the machines that seems unavoidable in the future. Defended by his mother and a reprogrammed Terminator, John must stay alive to ensure that humans will have a fighting chance.

Uglies, Scott Westerfeld, *Uglies* (2005) BK, UAB AP

Until you turn 16, you're an Ugly, but on that magical birthday, everyone undergoes massive beautification surgery and is allowed to cross over into "Pretty" territory. Tally isn't so sure this is the way to go—these Pretties seem awfully dull. She finds a group of like-minded people, the Uglies, and finds that there's more to the Pretties than just looking beautiful.

X-Men (2000) MV, GN, VGM

The discovery that many people are being born with mutant abilities results in a congressman trying to pass legislation that would require mutants to identify themselves and their powers. Rogue, a teen girl, runs away from home after she cannot control her superpowers and is soon drawn into the brewing war between the mutants who want to take over the world and those who wish to live in peace with humans.

The Future: Trends, Themes, and Authors to Watch

Where are teen stories heading? Here are our best guesses as to the future of this exciting and volatile genre.

Technology in Daily Life

Today's teens are digital natives and content creators. Technology, whether the integration of cell phones and chat into the narrative of a book, or moving the consumer between various mediums (book to phone to Web), is becoming more ingrained in the way we consume stories.

Anderson, M. T. *Feed* (2002) BK, UAB

The feed is implanted in people's brains as a way to convey educational information, but quickly becomes much more encompassing than that. And when a feed is removed, the consequences can be devastating.

Clark and Michael (2006) WebTV

This is a Web-based series created by Michael Cera and Clark Duke, real-life friends who began the project as a college thesis. The series was subsequently bought by CBS but aired exclusively online. Though Cera has gained acclaim as an actor, this is an example of the types of low-budget, user-created content that teens will be contributing much more of as time goes on. Information is available at http://www.clarkandmichael.com.

Doctorow, Cory, *Little Brother* (2008) BK, RS

A tech-savvy teen fights back after his life is turned upside down by the government's invasive monitoring of his every movement after a terrorist attack. Knowledge is power as he subverts an unjust system with his foresight and skills.

Fred, WebTV

Hyperactive kindergartner Fred Figglehorn is actually high school freshman Lucas Cruikshank who writes, films, edits, and stars in this high-pitched, high-energy Web TV show doled out in brief episodes on YouTube. Cruikshank's site has grown to be one of the most popular on YouTube, and all because his mom bought him some video-editing software.

Green, John, *Paper Towns* (2008) BK, UAB, AP

A secondary character is obsessed with updating a Wikipedia-like online source. The same source becomes instrumental in the main character solving the mystery of his missing friend thanks to the information, Easter eggs, and clues buried in the many layers of information.

Myracle, Lauren, *ttyl* (2004) BK

Groundbreaking in its delivery, the entire story of a group of friends' trials with guys, alliances, betrayal, and support is told through the instant messages they send to one another rehashing their daily events.

Plummer, Louise, *Finding Daddy* (2007) BK

The Internet connects a teen to her long-lost father after she seeks him out. The reunion is less than sweet when she realizes the true reasons her mother has kept his identity a secret for so long.

Stewart, Sean, and Jordan Weisman, *Cathy's Book: If Found Call 650-266-8233* (2006) BK, UAB

Cell phones are instrumental in the unfolding mystery, and the reader has an opportunity to get involved as well by calling numbers listed in the book to hear messages and uncover clues.

Adult/Teen Crossovers

As teen literature and movies continue to develop, the reader-viewership is broadening to include more adults on a regular basis. Likewise, the teens who are enjoying the bounty of great stories about people their age are reaching outside of the YA area and finding coming-of-age stories in the general collection. These titles gracefully blur the line between genre and readership.

American Pie (1999) MV

Tired of being made fun of for being inexperienced virgins, high school seniors Oz, Kevin, Jim, and Paul decide to be proactive about their status. The four make a pact to lose their virginity before graduating and overcome amusing obstacles along the way.

Chbosky, Stephen, *The Perks of Being a Wallflower* **(1999) BK, UAB, CL**
Charlie's coming of age and reconciliation with some tragic events in his past are set to a 1990s soundtrack blaring out of a car radio. Published by MTV Books, Charlie's story, told in letters to an anonymous friend (could it be us?) is an ideal example of a crossover title and a contemporary cult classic, the kind of book that appeals to bibliophiles and nonreaders alike.

Everybody Hates Chris **(2005–2009) TV**
Set in 1980s Brooklyn, Chris is the only African American in his all-white junior high, he can't seem to catch a break with his classmates, his parents are strict, and his family is always struggling to make ends meet. Through it all, everybody seems to hate Chris. This sitcom is narrated by comedian and producer Chris Rock and loosely based on his adolescence.

Friday Night Lights **(2006) TV, BK, MV**
For the Panthers, the high school football team in the tiny town of Dillon, Texas, every game is the big game. Expectations for the team are nothing less than absolute perfection. Losing a game means not just disappointment to the coach and teammates but to every single person in town. The TV show is based on the nonfiction book published in 1990 and the film released in 2004.

Galloway, Gregory, *As Simple As Snow* **(2005) BK, UAB**
A loner, a mysterious girl, a disappearance, and a burgeoning self-awareness are part of this book. Our unnamed narrator embarks on a curiosity that turns into a romance that turns into a mystery in this Alex Award winner.

Hairspray **(2007) MV**
This musical set in 1960s Baltimore follows plump teen Tracy Turnblad, who vies to be a dancer on Corny Collins' television show. Along the way, Tracy becomes even more infatuated with her crush Link, despite his snotty girlfriend Amber, and vows to stop the racial segregation of the dance show. The movie is based on the film of the same name released in 1988.

Real Women Have Curves **(2002) MV**
Living in East L.A., Ana Garcia knows what her mother wants for her now that she has graduated high school: stay a virgin, work in her sister's garment factory making dresses she could never fit into, and lose weight. Instead, Ana chooses to experience love, applies to Columbia University, and accepts her body while encouraging her co-workers to do the same.

The Sisterhood of the Traveling Pants, Anne Brahsares, *The Sisterhood of the Traveling Pants* **(2001) BK, MV, UAB**
This story features four girls, four summer destinations, and one pair of magical pants that fits them all and makes them feel like their best and most alive selves. Published for the teen market, the title quickly gained favor with adult women who relate to the power of female friendships in supporting one another through difficult and happy times alike. The stars of the original movie have gone on to garner more adult fans, bringing them back to both the books and the movies.

Smith, Dodie, *I Capture the Castle* **(2003) MV, BK**
Set in the English countryside in the 1930s, intelligent Cassandra lives with her eccentric family in a drafty, deteriorating castle on an estate. She often feels drab compared to her beautiful sister Rose, who only wants to marry someone wealthy to get away from their family's current misfortunes. When the estate is inherited by a wealthy American family with two eligible sons, the sisters become rivals.

Superbad **(2007) MV**
High school seniors and best friends Evan and Seth are far from popular. Scoring an invitation to a party and vowing to try to lose their virginity before they go to college, they enlist the help of their even geekier friend Fogell to buy them booze with his fake ID. Nothing goes as planned during a memorable night.

The Virgin Suicides **(1999) MV, BK, AP**
Set in suburban Michigan in the 1970s, a group of boys becomes obsessed with the four beautiful Lisbon sisters after one commits suicide. The boys witness the tragedy that unfolds when the girls feel they cannot escape the state of isolation imposed on them by their parents. The movie is based on the novel by Jeffrey Eugenides.

Graphic Memoirs

The authors of the following graphic novels allow readers a glimpse into their formative years and beyond, while bringing new acclaim to the format.

B., David, *Epileptic* **(2005) GN**
The author vividly chronicles the lengths his family went to in order to treat his brother's severe and unpredictable epilepsy.

Barry, Lynda, *One Hundred Demons* **(2002) GN**
This semi-autobiographical graphic novel includes vignettes that touch upon themes of loneliness, drug use, and contentious family relationships. The author begins the introduction of each new demon with personal collages.

Bechdel, Alison, *Fun Home: A Family Tragicomic* **(2006) GN**
In this unflinchingly honest memoir, the author recalls her obsessive-compulsive tendencies and a dysfunctional family life with a father who is secretly gay and having affairs with much younger men.

The High School Comic Chronicles of Ariel Schrag, Ariel Schrag, *Awkward*; *Definition*; *Potential*; **and** *Likewise* **(1996–2000) GN**
These four graphic novels recount each year of the author's experiences while attending Berkeley High School in the 1990s. There are no holds barred as the author writes and illustrates losing her virginity, experimenting with drugs and alcohol, and coming out as a lesbian.

Landowne, Youme, and Anthony Horton, *Pitch Black* **(2008) GN**
Artist Landowne brings to life Horton's experiences of homelessness and their chance meeting in the New York subway system. Abandoned by both his parents and his foster-care family, Horton lived in shelters until finally discovering the dark passageways in the subway tunnels below the city. This is a short and powerful memoir.

Satrapi, Marjane, *Persepolis: The Story of a Childhood* **(2003) and** *Persepolis 2: The Story of a Return* **(2004) GN, MV**
In the first volume, the author skillfully recreates the uncertainty of growing up under a repressive religious regime in Iran during the Iranian Revolution in the late 1970s. In the second volume, Satrapi remembers her rebelliousness as a teen after being sent to Vienna to escape the strict religious regime and her eventual return to Iran. These graphic novels were made into an animated film released in 2007.

Schrag, Ariel, ed., *Stuck in the Middle: Seventeen Comics from an Unpleasant Age* **(2007) GN, AP**
In this semi-autobiographical anthology, 16 authors (plus the editor) delve deep into their memories of middle school to compose painfully honest and occasionally funny tales of their awkward years.

Small, David, *Stitches* **(2009) GN, RS**
In this powerful graphic memoir, the author shares his experiences of growing up in a cold and mostly silent household. At age 14, he wakes up from surgery unable to speak with a gruesome scar, unaware that he most likely developed cancer because of the many x-rays he was given by his radiologist father.

Thompson, Craig, *Blankets* **(2003) GN, AW**
The author provides a touching depiction of his strict Christian upbringing, his relationship with his brother and parents, and the joy and pain involved with falling in love for the first time.

Weinstein, Lauren R., *Girl Stories* **(2006) GN**
The author touches upon universal experiences in a teen girl's life. As a 13-year-old, she is secretly ashamed for still playing with Barbies and she desperately attempts to be cool. In high school, Lauren decides to be completely original and get her navel pierced, starts really making out with boys, and wonders if she is fat.

Conclusion

Teen stories are enduring in their popularity due to the universality of the experience. If you've made it to adulthood, you were, at some point, a teenager. Whether hearkening back to our glory days, vicariously experiencing something we missed out on, or cringing at the agony of it, there are many points of connection with the entertaining stories of teens in print or on the screen. Even so, library teen collections are often marginalized either in space, budget, or service.

The teen materials collection should be made accessible to all patrons while respecting that teenagers themselves deserve a dedicated space. Additionally, knowing the collection should be the responsibility of everyone in the department. While there may be a resident teen "expert," staff should not rely solely on that individual for their integrated advisory needs, especially since it's not just teens that are interested in this genre. Our hope is that this chapter has assisted librarians in seeing the diversity of material available for those patrons who enjoy teen stories and inspires them to continue to seek out additional items that they can suggest. Teen stories are everywhere, and being attuned to new material can only benefit our patrons.

Resources for Librarians

Booth, Heather. *Serving Teens Through Readers' Advisory*. Chicago: ALA Editions, 2007.
Herald, Diane Tixier. *Teen Genreflecting: A Guide to Reading Interests*. Westport, CT: Libraries Unlimited, 2003.
Pearl, Nancy. *Book Crush: For Kids and Teens: Recommended Reading for Every Mood, Moment, and Interest*. Seattle: Sasquatch Books, 2007.

Endnotes

1. Booth, Heather. *Serving Teens through Readers' Advisory*. Chicago: ALA Editions, 2007, p. 32.
2. Thorn, Matt. "Shôjo Manga—Something for the Girls." *The Japan Quarterly* 48 (2001): 3.
3. Booth, Heather. *Serving Teens through Readers' Advisory*. Chicago: ALA Editions, 2007.
4. Herald, Diane Tixier. *Teen Genreflecting: A Guide to Reading Interests*. Westport, CT: Libraries Unlimited, 2003.
5. Pearl, Nancy. *Book Lust: Recommended Reading for Every Mood, Moment, and Reason*. Seattle: Sasquatch Books, 2003.
6. *The Breakfast Club*. Universal Studios Home Entertainment, 1985, 2008.

10

Everything Women's Stories
Kaite Mediatore Stover, with Rebecca Vnuk and Jessica Zellers

This chapter covers the wide world of women's stories, including fiction and non-fiction. "Plots" includes love, women's places, and different cultures. Characters covers mothers and daughters, sisters and friends, women without men, and working girls. The theme of this chapter is women's lives and relationships. It covers such diverse topics as birth, death, coming of age, marriage, family, friendships, and community. In the final section, "Making Connections," the authors suggest women's stories for fantasy and science fiction, mystery, and historical fans.

Introduction

In a way, the term "women's fiction" is both too liberal and too limiting for readers and readers' advisors. Any fiction book featuring a female character could come under this moniker—a science fiction book with a female captain fighting rebels, a mystery with a tough woman detective, a thriller focusing on a sadistic female serial killer, a fantasy surrounding the women of King Arthur's court, or a western about a saloon keeper in skirts. Women's fiction, by this general definition, reaches into all the genres of fiction, and could easily lay claim to over half of it. Yet the phrase can also be too narrow, implying that women's fiction is to be written and read by women about only women.

"Women's fiction" is the catchall term used by readers and library staff to quickly describe a type of fiction, and while the specific definition may go unspoken much of the time, both know exactly what is meant by the phrase. There are no genres, per se, in the literature of women's lives and relationships. Instead, these works gravitate toward more emotional, character-driven stories with steady pacing, which can be compared to the rush of a good cup of coffee shared with a friend. Reader preferences lean toward more contemporary titles that address issues and concerns of the readers' time. Some novels from the 1970s and 1980s have aged well, but many have not as they have fallen victim to changing times and trends.

The fiction and literature of women's lives and relationships focus on the experiences, both extraordinary and everyday, of female characters and their many-layered relationships with spouses, parents, children, friends, and community. Some books employ a romantic tone and others will inject a sense of adventure, mystery, or suspense, but the primary theme of these novels is that of the female protagonist facing and transcending the crisis at hand. One current trend is to employ a lighter, sometimes even tongue-in-cheek tone. But overall, emotions and relationships are the common thread between books that can be classified in this genre. The two primary elements of appeal for this genre are character and storyline, which tend to be intertwined. Often, readers enjoy women's fiction and nonfiction because they can identify with a character (or sometimes, it's a feeling of relief that they are not like a particular character!). A large part of the appeal of these books is one of recognition—feeling as though you are that character, you know that character, or you recognize what that character is going through. Even nonfiction gets lumped into this category as most memoirs of women's lives focus heavily on their relationships with others and their own coming of age.

Nor are women's stories limited to fiction. Stories of women and their lives and numerous relationships tackle recognizable themes in both fiction and nonfiction: birth and death; love and marriage; grief and loss; and identity and aging. Readers are attracted to multifaceted women who may or may not be trying to solve problems readers are familiar with, but offer assurance that these issues can be faced and, if not completely resolved, then endured with grace. These works can be counted on to have primarily female leads, but that's not absolute. Old, young, rural, suburban, sophisticated and educated, earthy and plain spoken, the characters in the literature of women's lives and relationships come in all shapes, sizes, and colors. They take on the roles of those female figures most prominent in the lives of all readers, mothers, daughters, sisters, wives, and friends. Relationships are very prominent in these works and are important to many female readers.

Women's stories in the visual media tend to be more dramatic, and television offers more opportunities to explore women's lives in depth, due to the extended life of some television series. As in literature, the emphasis is always on the relationships, and those are developed and demonstrated through the interactions, conversations, dialogues, and monologues between all the characters. There's a reason *Gilmore Girls* had more dialogue than almost any other series broadcast for the time. Viewers loved the warm and witty banter between the edgy youthful mother and her serious and studious daughter, and it is only through their rat-a-tat conversation that viewers got to know these two loveable people.

It should also come as no surprise that many novels that are aimed at women make easy transitions to film. Emphasis is, again, always on the relationships and much of the story may be related through dialogue. The movies can be giddy or grave, depending on the tone, in the same way the books might be. *Steel Magnolias* couldn't be less similar in tone and execution than *Terms of Endearment*, although both are about the relationship between a mother and daughter heading in a heartbreaking direction. *Somewhere Off the Coast of Maine* and *Divine Secrets of the Ya-Ya Sisterhood* examine the lives of two groups of friends that span many years, yet both books take strikingly different paths to tell the multiple stories, one employing more pathos and the other more humor.

Fans of women's fiction and nonfiction will try any other form of entertainment as long as it possesses the characteristics they enjoy. Format is not the primary concern. Films and television aimed at a predominantly female audience have learned to deftly mix drama and comedy among the numerous characters who populate the multilayered stories. *Sex and the City*, easily one of the most successful television series for women, triumphed by identifying what most appealed to women in entertainment—smart, likeable, flawed heroines with real-life problems and issues that were sometimes solved and sometimes unanswered but always addressed with intelligence and wit. Please note that these young women were not the first group of friends to trade quips and advice about men, friendship, fashion, and work. *The Golden Girls* paved the way for the younger set and showed that these issues are ageless. Witness also the success of such television networks as Lifetime and Oxygen.

Making generalizations about those who enjoy books, films, and television using women as a focal point isn't easy. There are plenty of men (whether they'll admit it or not) who enjoy these types of entertainment. The appeal is multicultural and multigenerational, and no one is checking gender IDs at the door.

Integrated Advisory: Women's Stories Style

Few other types of literature cross genres or formats as easily as women's stories. Women are avid readers, moviegoers, and television-watchers and they like entertainment that covers a variety of subjects and topics and genres. Popular and thought-provoking books that are made into solid films will find double the audience, first in readers (and likely book-group attendees) and then in the movie theater. Subjects that interest women and that are given top-notch production values will find faithful television viewers and radio listeners. It's all in the storytelling and the characterization. Create characters that women can identify with or recognize and place them in intriguing situations and women will tune in, turn a page, or buy a ticket. Format isn't the driving force when women make a decision about entertainment: it's the content.

Print Books

Women will continue to outread and outspend men in the print arena. Publishers of literature aimed at a female audience know this and will continue to seek out authors who can tell an emotionally gripping and intellectually respectful story with believable characters in realistic situations. Books that lend themselves well to discussion will be especially popular. Women who are pressed for time like to combine as many leisure activities as possible. Why not organize a friendly book group that discusses the salient points while enjoying a pedicure? And after that, they'll go see the theatrical version of the book. Consider *Brick Lane* for this type of outing.

Movies and TV

Movies and television have long recognized the importance of the female character, and we've come a long way, baby, from expendable girlfriend to spinster district attorney to curmudgeonly Miss Daisy. Film producers (and the people who give them money) are beginning to notice that women want movies and television in which women are smart, resourceful, independent, clothed (fashionably is preferable), and strong enough to save the hero or the day (whichever needs it most). Insert *The Closer* or *Buffy* here.

Graphic Novels

Women are discovering the charms of graphic novels, too. While the majority of the female reading public are not storming the shelves for the latest mutant superhero, they are seeking out the currently popular graphic memoir and graphic nonfiction. Writers and artists are taking note of the issues and themes of importance and interest to women and using them as fodder for the graphic format.

In short, women's lives have always been full of fascinating and challenging topics that make for great reading, film, television, and art. What's new is the increase in interest *everyone* is taking in women's lives.

Trends

It's hard to pinpoint trends in women's stories since many of the subjects and topics have been written about since women put nib to parchment. Family, friendship, love, marriage, work, education, birth, and death, just to name a few. What readers have seen, and can expect to see more of, are stories that continue to focus on women at all stages of life. Readers should be aware that authors and artists are exploring the graphic literature format and keep an eye out for more illustrated stories in both fiction and nonfiction. Memoirs continue to explode as a genre and women are tackling this literary form with gusto and guffaws. Humor is working its way into much of the literature that appeals to women. Mixed with drama and romance, it's a heady combination that more accurately reflects women's lives than the glitz-and-glamour novels of the 1970s and 1980s and the over-the-top sentimentality of soap operas. Look for subjects that reflect women's growing interest and power in politics, health care, the environment, and other matters of social importance.

Plots

The stories most commonly found in fiction appealing to women will place the heroine in both extraordinary and ordinary circumstances requiring strength of character to surmount the situation. Experiencing love, both true and tragic, is a topic universal to everyone, not just women. In addition to discovering the value of a loving relationship with another, the protagonist usually discovers the value of loving herself. The search for a place to call home, whether geographic or psychological, is another common story in much of literature, and may involve a journey as arduous as trekking across tundra or a psyche. History has a way of shaping and being shaped by the women who contribute to it and, frequently, it's not until many years later, if at all, that the women learn of the impact they've had on their times. Stories of women in unfamiliar surroundings can be dramatic or comic, usually depending on the outlook of our erstwhile heroine, and often there's a smattering of both.

Women in Love

Looking for love is a common theme in women's fiction, particularly the related genres of romance and chick lit. The search for a satisfying relationship will drive some gals to courageous heights, tragic depths, zany predicaments, and revolting developments. These titles celebrate the many ways women will look for love, usually in the wrong places. What sets them apart from the romance genre are the focus on the female protagonist's appreciation of herself first and a mate second. This topic is listed first before all others because it is unquestionably the most popular and prevalent topic in the fiction of women's lives. The titles listed below are not necessarily the best or the newest or the most well known. In selecting these books and films, the goal was to find those hidden gems that deserve a wider audience. And there is no doubt there are additional treasures out there that await happy discovery by eager readers and viewers.

Ashley, Trisha, *Singled Out* (2004) BK, UAB, YA

It's goth-tinged chick lit in a rural setting starring a fortysomething heroine. Ashley takes all the typical elements of a chick lit novel and gives them a pleasantly daft twist. Cass, a successful romantic horror novelist, is gravely concerned that Max, her lover of 20 years, won't marry her now that his wife is gone. She laments this fact at a local pub with her delightfully kooky friends, Orla and Jason. To take her mind off her romantic matters, Cass enters a charity slave auction and finds herself the object of a bidding war. The winner is Dante Chase, handsome mysterious stranger in residence. The age-old conundrum of "who should she choose" is presented in a fresh style. There are lots of quips, witty conversation, and amusing asides.

Bosnak, Karen, *20 Times a Lady* (2006) BK

For all the women who have ever wondered about the "one that got away," Delilah is willing to do the research for you, complete with footnotes. After reaching her self-imposed limit of only 20 inappropriate men in one lifetime, Delilah experiences the typical single gal meltdown and goes on a road trip to interview all the guys she's loved and lost, never realizing that Mr. Right is right beside her. Just when Delilah is ready to give up the search, guess who she finds? Her wacky adventures are told with warmth and all the regulars are present—quirky pet, bossy mother, calm and understanding guy, breezy pace, and hopeful tone.

Cook, Claire, *Must Love Dogs* (2002) BK, UAB, MV, SH

How desperate does a woman have to be to find a date? Desperate enough to answer a personal ad, but not so desperate she'll date her own widowed father. Sarah likes to think she has some standards and she is constantly reminded of what they are by her lovingly boisterous and interfering Irish family. She makes the attempt to date again and meets a man closer to her own age, who, like Sarah, loves dogs but doesn't own one. It might be a match made in newspaper heaven, if only Sarah's well-meaning family would trust her enough to go on a date alone. With a wide cast of loveable and realistic characters, this book about ordinary people cast adrift in the dating pool was made into a movie starring two of the most attractive actors in motion pictures. Hard to believe Diane Lane or John Cusack ever had trouble finding a date.

Down With Love (2002) MV, AP

Barbara Novak is through with love and she's written a book all about it. She's going to conquer the Big Apple circa 1960, and in the process make mincemeat out of Catcher Block, ladies' man-about-town. Of course, this seemingly diametrically opposed couple is destined for true love once they reveal their inner agendas. The movie is a frothy send-up of Doris Day-Rock Hudson movies that relies completely on witty double-entendres and clever conversation for plot and sex appeal.

Girl Meets Girl, PC, YA

Sienna and Toast, two gals living in Hawaii, talk about being gay, Asian American, vegan, singer-songwriters and their relationship. Funny and inspiring, it is free from iTunes.

How to Marry a Millionaire (1953) MV, CL

A classic film with classic performances from some classy dames who know exactly how far they'll go to get the guy. Lauren Bacall, Marilyn Monroe, and Betty Grable play three gal-pals who pool their meager earnings to rent a posh apartment and snag rich men into marriage. Just as the trio decides that they can't marry for money when love is at stake, they get another twist in the tale. We all know how this ends, it's the great dialogue and zany set-up that brings all the charm to this romantic comedy.

Meaker, Marijane, *Highsmith: A Romance of the 1950s, a Memoir* (2003) BK, NF

In the early 1950s, Patricia Highsmith was a dark-haired beauty just beginning a career as a writer of psychological thrillers. Marijane Meaker was a tawny-haired beauty also about to embark on a lifelong writing career. And for two wild years, both writers were lovers, taking the literary scene of New York City by storm. This is Meaker's memoir of their affair, told in her fast-paced, gripping, artfully crafted style; it is also a biography of Highsmith, a fascinating but often unlikable character. The overall tone is bittersweet—the 1950s romance ultimately dissolves, and a reunion in the 1990s reveals Highsmith to have become a bitter woman and a callous anti-Semite—but the characters and setting are fascinating, and the romance, though doomed, is brilliant while it lasts.

Niffenegger, Audrey, *The Time Traveler's Wife* (2003) BK, UAB, MV, YA

What has love done to Clare? It's made her wait and worry, caused anger and stress, and brought her joy and sadness. Clare is constantly waiting for Henry, the man she is destined to love but whose own destiny won't allow him to stay in one place long enough to establish a normal relationship. The story is full of love and longing and has a poignant quality that will have readers asking themselves "what will a person do for love?"

Simmonds, Posy, *Gemma Bovery* (2005) GN

Flaubert's classic gets an update and a makeover in this graphic retelling of a young woman who rises from poverty and a wretched relationship with grit and determination to make a new life with a new love and ultimately throw it all away. This is a clever and colorful tale of love in all the wrong places for all the wrong reasons.

The Truth About Cats & Dogs (1996) MV, YA

This feather-light romantic comedy of mistaken identity is boosted by smart performances from actresses Janeane Garofalo and Uma Thurman. Garofalo plays Abby, a talk-radio vet with confidence in her abilities to diagnose but not accessorize. When a listener-fan asks to meet Abby, she panics and describes herself as a tall, willowy blonde, just like her ditsy neighbor, Noelle (Thurman). This offbeat update of Cyrano will please fans who want some brains with their beauty in their love stories.

Whitaker, Robert, *The Mapmaker's Wife: A True Tale of Love, Murder, and Survival in the Amazon* (2004) NF BK

Science journalist Robert Whitaker skillfully blends a variety of nonfiction genres—science writing, travel writing, true romance, and true crime—into this fast-paced narrative, but the book is, above all, an adventure story of the highest order. During the Enlightenment in Europe, a group of French scientists decided to test their theories about the contours of the planet by mapping equatorial South America. While on their cartographical mission, one of the Frenchmen, Jean Godin, fell in love with an Ecuadorian girl, Isabel Grameson. The two were married, but turbulent political realities forced the couple apart. Twenty years later, the bride undertook a perilous journey through the rain forest in hope of a reunion with her long-lost husband. So dangerous was the 3,000-mile trip that all of her companions died, but Isobel persevered until she found Jean.

A Woman's Place

The search for place is a common theme in women's fiction and nonfiction, no doubt because it has been a common quest for women in history. The journey can take a woman around the world, through time and cultures, and usually leads right back to herself. Once the protagonists find their places within, it makes no difference where they are. However, in their inimitable fashion, these women make the journey an entertaining and enlightening one, and this is the element that appeals to most readers. The ending is all but assured; our heroine will make the sacrifice, learn the lesson, or find the inner serenity that will carry her through the rest of her life no matter where she goes. It's the adventures and obstacles along the way that draw us in and provide hope that we will also find the way to a place of confidence, peace, and wisdom.

Abel, Jessica, *La Perdida* (2006) GN, YA

Carla turns her back on her upper-middle class life and travels to Mexico City in search of a more "authentic" life. She is on a quest for she knows not what. Her innocence helps her appreciate the beauty of this international city and her heritage, but her ignorance puts herself and others in danger. She becomes involved with a group of politically active students and soon finds herself in the midst of an international plot with dark repercussions.

Blum, Arlene, *Annapurna: A Woman's Place* (1980, 1998) NF BK

In 1978, Arlene Blum led a group of 13 women from various countries to the top of Annapurna, the world's tenth-highest mountain. With descriptive, evocative prose, Blum recounts the compelling story of the first expedition of women to scale the Himalayan mountain. While the book certainly contains the nail-biting elements you'd expect from a narrative about a radical mountaineering expedition—avalanches, unbelievably cold temperatures, and dangerous interpersonal conflicts—it also focuses on the friendships, teamwork, and logistics involved in planning and executing an unprecedented adventure. Dramatic events make this a real page-turner, while the successful triumph over nature's most brutal obstacles makes it an inspiring read.

Felicity (1998–2002) TV, YA

Newly graduated from her high school in Palo Alto, California, Felicity Porter makes the first daring decision of her life: skip Stanford and move to New York City to follow her high school crush, Ben. Once there, Felicity makes additional rash but life-changing decisions—she pursues her interest in art instead of medicine, begins a relationship with a resident advisor, and makes friends with the most unlikely people. Through her four years at New York University, Felicity will question herself and reevaluate her entire life, relationships, and future. This dramatic and heartfelt series is full of realistic, likeable characters, true-life conundrums, and the memorable moments that make up the most formative years in a young woman's life.

Gilbert, Elizabeth, *Eat, Pray, Love: One Woman's Search for Everything across Italy, India, and Indonesia* (2006) NF BK, UAB, YA, AP, SH, RS

Gilbert was a woman with a mission: following a dissatisfying lifestyle and an unpleasant divorce, she wanted to recapture her *joie de vivre*—and as the legions of fans of *Eat, Pray, Love* can attest, she did it with style. Purposefully choosing travel destinations that would revitalize her body and soul, Gilbert went hunting for fulfillment. In Italy, she feasted on succulent pizzas and wines; in India, she meditated on mental wellness; in Indonesia, she balanced her appetites for physical and mental health while entering into a passionate romance. With an engaging style and captivating story, Gilbert's memoir mixes the best of travel writing and spiritual contemplation.

Hope Floats (1998) MV

Birdie Pruitt thought she knew her place—at the top of a very small heap. But the former beauty queen is toppled off her complacent hillock on a nationally televised talk show when her best friend reveals a longtime affair with Birdie's handsome husband. With her daughter, meager belongings, and bruised pride in tow, Birdie heads back to the last place she felt safe—her tiny hometown in Texas. Watch Birdie's transformation from smug young married to devastated divorcee to mature and responsible mother. Her grief for the loss of her old life and confidence is palpable and her earnest efforts to make amends with school chums she once treated callously is wincing. But Birdie discovers a surprising reservoir of inner strength to carry her forward. Actress Sandra Bullock is an Everywoman many women can cheer. She isn't afraid to show the ugly side of tragedy and the tentative side of survival.

I've Loved You So Long (2008) MV

Recently released from prison for an unspeakable crime, Juliette Fontaine is claimed by her long-estranged sister, Lea, and Lea's warm, yet wary, family. As Juliette carefully enters the "outside" life, searching for a job, friendship, peace, and salvation, her gregarious parole officer, Lea's inquisitive daughter, and a teacher colleague of Lea's aid her along the way. Juliette's anguished struggle to carve out a new place for herself will not be complete until the heinous nature of her crime is finally revealed and Juliette learns that Lea, unlike the rest of Juliette's family, never stopped loving her.

Kidd, Sue Monk, *The Dance of the Dissident Daughter: A Woman's Journey from Christian Tradition to the Sacred Feminine* (1996) NF BK

Perhaps you know Sue Monk Kidd for her best-selling novels *The Secret Life of Bees* and *The Mermaid Chair*; possibly you even remember her Christian spiritual nonfiction writings from early in her career. Now discover *The Dance of the Dissident Daughter*, the remarkable story of her spiritual journey from Southern Baptist Christianity to a pagan approach, one that embraces the feminine and dispenses with traditional patriarchal paradigms. Readers who know Kidd only through her fiction will be delighted to recognize the same powerful storytelling and evocative prose that distinguishes her novels in this compelling, deeply personal story of paradise lost and faith rediscovered.

Tyler, Anne, *Earthly Possessions* (1977) BK, UAB, MV

Charlotte is ready to chuck her safe and quiet life. One morning, she goes to the bank to withdraw enough money to escape and finds herself forced to take a trip to an unknown destination. As the hostage of the bank's robber, Charlotte finds plenty of time to contemplate her life and choices on the way to Florida in a stolen car. Readers who have ever dreamed of ditching it all but needed a little push will find an ordinary woman on an extraordinary voyage. The story is contemplative and touching.

Wendy and Lucy (2008) MV, YA
All Wendy Carroll has ever wanted is a chance. She gets one when she hears about a job in Alaska and she embarks on a journey full of tribulations that would rival those of Odysseus. With her loyal dog, Lucy, by her side, Wendy suffers the first of many mishaps; her car breaks down in a small town in Oregon and she loses Lucy. This quiet character study is a portrait of love and desperation and what those two emotions will drive a person to sacrifice.

Williams, Kayla, and Michael E. Staub, ***Love My Rifle More Than You: Young and Female in the U.S. Army*** (2005) NF BK
It was tough, explains Iraq veteran Kayla Williams, for "us females to get our work done without having guys insinuate that 'blow jobs' was part of our Advanced Individual Training. It totally sucked, pun intended." If you prefer to avoid racy language, then steer clear of Williams' book: the dirty, difficult side of war comes through loud and clear on every page—but of course, that is her intent; it is this edgy, raw tone that makes her narrative effective. Visceral and provocative, this is the story of a soldier who had served as an Arabic interpreter in the U.S. Army since 2000; when America went to Iraq, it was inevitable that she would be deployed. Discover the gritty terror of combat and the complicated sexual politics of the modern military in this fast-paced, eye-opening war memoir.

Woolf, Virginia, ***A Room of One's Own*** (1929, 2005) NF BK, CL
Though best known for her fiction, Virginia Woolf produced several remarkable pieces of nonfiction, including one of the early classics of feminist writing, *A Room of One's Own*. Dealing with both class and sex, this lengthy essay criticizes the unfair distribution of money and power under the patriarchal system, arguing that "a woman must have money and a room of her own if she is to write fiction"—or, indeed, to express herself in any creative way. In a particularly memorable passage, Woolf creates a fictional sister for Shakespeare, Judith, who has all of the bard's talents but none of his opportunities due to her sex and lower economic status. If you already know Woolf from her other, frequently difficult works, you may be pleasantly surprised to discover the accessible style and engaging tone of this landmark feminist essay.

Different Cultures, Similar Lives

Female readers enjoy stories of women of other cultures experiencing similar daily challenges. Even life's big events demonstrate that everyone is treading common ground no matter where in the world you are or what language you're speaking. Whether it's wedding jitters, parental clashes, troubled childhoods, or workplace woes, these situations cross cultures faster than two women comparing meddling mother-in-law stories over cups of tea.

Banerjee, Anjali, ***Imaginary Men*** (2005) BK
Lina's caught in a terrible dilemma—she lied and told her family at a gathering in India that she was engaged, but the truth is that she doesn't even have a boyfriend. Despite her renown for recognizing the "shimmering thread" of romance in other couples, Lina can't find love for herself, leaving her to face her family who are all excited to meet her fiancée.

Fernandez Barrios, Flor, ***Blessed by Thunder: Memoir of a Cuban Girlhood*** (1999) NF BK
Author Barrios was born while a hurricane raged in Cabaiguán, Cuba, just a few years before Castro came to power—and yet her dramatic entry into the world was

only a portent of the drama that little Flor would face as she grew up in communist Cuba. With vivid, lyrical prose, Barrios recounts her troubled childhood: the political nightmares that rocked her family, the labor camp where she was forced to pick tobacco and sugar cane, and her eventual exile/escape to the United States. Read this not only for a glimpse into the history of Cuba, but also for the tender story of the author's spiritual connections with her family both during and after the harrowing trials of her childhood.

Hachemi, Latifa and Chékéba Hachemi, *My Forbidden Face: Growing Up under the Taliban: A Young Woman's Story* **(2001) NF BK, YA**
In 1996, Latifa (not her real name) was a normal 16-year-old girl, busy with going to school, watching movies, and listening to music—and then the Taliban came. Suddenly, the Kabul that Latifa knew and loved was gone, transformed into a city of nightmares. No longer could she leave the house unless escorted by a close male relative, and even then she had to cover her face and arms with a chadri; failure to obey could result in stoning. With vivid, disturbing details and a compulsively readable prose style, this memoir paints a horrific picture of Afghan women's lives under the Taliban. Haunting and all-too-realistic, Latifa's is a story you won't forget.

Hidden Kitchens **(2004) PC, NF BK, UAB, YA**
Perhaps nothing draws people together more than food and the language of cooking is one many women speak. Nikki Silva and Davia Nelson travel the United States and find the hidden kitchens of fading cultures, political movements, and historical significance for their weekly NPR radio program. This is free from iTunes.

Larkin, Alison, *The English American* **(2008) BK, UAB, YA, RS, AP**
Pippa Dunn has always known she is not quite the perfect fit in her adopted and posh British family. Her suspicions are confirmed when she discovers her birth parents are American southerners. Pippa goes across the pond to get to know them and discovers she is more British than she thought, even though all her quirky traits are obviously American. Laugh-out-loud situations arise as British Pippa tries to fit in with redneck American culture.

McFadden, Bernice, *Nowhere Is a Place* **(2006) BK, UAB, SH**
In this multigenerational saga, 38-year-old Sherry, a wanderer, is always looking for a place to belong. She sets off with her estranged mother, Dumpling, on a days-long road trip to a family reunion in Georgia. Along the way, Sherry gets Dumpling to tell her family stories, from slavery to the present, and uncovers family secrets. This leads the women to discover who they really are and what kind of relationship they need to have.

Masuda, Sayo, *Autobiography of a Geisha* **(2003) NF BK**
Perhaps you're familiar with the fictionalized narrative of the geisha experience in Arthur Golden's *Memoirs of a Geisha*. Now turn to *Autobiography of a Geisha*, written not by a Western man with a vivid imagination but by Sayo Masuda, who at the age of 12 was sold to a geisha house for a paltry sum. If you're expecting glamour and romance, think again: Masuda's life as a geisha is marked by violence and despair. She is abused both physically and verbally; she suffers from depression and attempts to kill herself; and even when she does escape the geisha lifestyle, she finds herself struggling to survive in World War II Japan. The narrator's candid, intimate voice, translated from the Japanese by G. G. Rowley, makes this a compelling albeit grim read.

Monsoon Wedding (2001) MV

A large family scattered across the globe comes together for a traditional Punjabi wedding in New Delhi and typical familial mayhem ensues against the backdrop of a lavish and chaotic ceremony. The bride has been having an affair with a married man, a cousin is determined to reveal the patriarch's sexual abuse in order to prevent it from happening to a younger relative, a son struggles with his father's disapproval of his career choice, and even the wedding planner adds to the bedlam by falling in love with the family's maid. Recognizable characters and situations make this colorful movie suspenseful, funny, and romantic.

Myhre, Lise, *Nemi* (2008) GN, YA, RS

Nemi is a lively, opinionated, sexy, hard-core goth chick from Norway. Nemi struggles with the typical challenges of a twentysomething looking for direction in life. She spends time at the pub cracking wise with her goth pals, visits museums to view vampire art, and has no qualms about shocking children and senior citizens. Readers will recognize the universal themes of young adults looking for a place in society (or not) in this feisty collection.

Pradhan, Monica, *The Hindi-Bindi Club* (2007) BK, YA

Three young women share the story in this charming novel. First-generation Americans Kiran, Preity, and Rani like to mock their Indian mothers for their old-fashioned notions. The mothers simply want what they think is best for the girls—marriage to a nice Indian young man. Two cultures collide as the women find their own romances and career paths. Indian recipes, shared by the mothers, are dotted throughout the breezy narrative.

Sukkar banat (Caramel) (2007) MV

The lives of five Lebanese women converge in a Beirut beauty salon. One woman worries about the impact her affair with a married man will have on her future, another frets about growing old, one harbors a secret affection for another, and the last has devoted the best years of her life to caring for an older sister with a mental illness. Viewers will recognize all of these situations and identify with the warm, open, honest portrayals of these Middle Eastern women with universal problems.

A Thousand Years of Good Prayers (2008) MV

A Chinese daughter and father are trying to overcome years of estrangement in this quiet drama. The daughter has recently gone through a divorce and her father wants to help her overcome her recent tragedy; however, the more the father pries into his daughter's life and the reasons for her divorce, the more she pulls away. A heated confrontation brings up misunderstandings they both try to reconcile with limited success.

Characters

While it's safe to assume that the majority of characters in women's literature will be female, there's no predicting what type of woman a reader is going to get until the spine is cracked. However, the numerous roles that women play in society are always rich in comedy and tragedy. There will always be conflict between mothers and daughters, sisters and friends, and husbands and wives. There's drama to be found in the workplace as women seek to carve out a piece of the professional pie for themselves. Forging a new life whether it's minus a spouse in a familiar hometown or in a foreign environment with plenty of associates makes for intriguing and insightful reading and viewing rich in story as well as character.

Mothers and Daughters

Perhaps no relationship is as fraught with drama as the one between a mother and a daughter. The friction in the fiction is a tale oft told, but it never ages. These stories help readers and viewers make sense of their own mother-daughter ties. Some of the characters are frighteningly familiar and some are women only a mother, or daughter, could love.

Bombeck, Erma, *Motherhood: The Second Oldest Profession* **(1983) NF BK, YA, CL**
Though written in the early 1980s, *Motherhood* is still as funny today as it ever was. As in all of her books, humor columnist Erma Bombeck expertly blends comedy and poignancy in *Motherhood*, giving zest to the experiences of everyday life. A mother of three and a prolific writer, Bombeck had a wealth of background to draw on ("I once spent more time writing a note of instructions to a babysitter than I did on my first book"). With humor that is gentle but not bland, universal but not generic, this is a timeless read, perfect for anyone who wants a laugh about the trials of motherhood.

Chang, Jung, *Wild Swans: Three Daughters of China* **(1991) NF BK, UAB**
This epic family story begins starkly—"At the age of 15 my grandmother became the concubine of a warlord general"—and it does not relent for another 500 pages. Absolutely gripping in its style and story, this powerful family history tells the story of three Chinese women: the author, her mother Bao Qin, and her grandmother Yu-fang. Experience the dynamic, tragic history of China in the twentieth century—the Communist Revolution, the Japanese occupation, and the tyranny of Chairman Mao—through the eyes of these three women as they and those they love grapple with hardships such as foot binding, death, slavery, and insanity. This is an eye-opening account of life in China during several decades of tumultuous political upheaval, made poignant and personal by the excellent rendering of the three heroines.

Cook, Claire, *Multiple Choice* **(2004) BK, UAB, YA**
March is about to embark on a new college life, just like her daughter Olivia. They don't share any classes or majors, but they do wind up sharing an internship at the local radio station. When a DJ observes the mother-daughter duels in person, he decides it will work better on the air. Now the pair is airing all their grievances for their loyal listeners. Can they keep the folks at home entertained without losing their own connection? This feisty tale of mother-daughter conflict retains its warmth and charm in the midst of the dust flying.

Gilmore Girls **(2000–2007) TV, YA**
Television's favorite mother-daughter team used more dialogue than almost any other scripted show during its run. Youthful Lorelai Gilmore is frequently mistaken for daughter Rory's sister instead of her mother. Lorelai and Rory live in the bucolic town of Stars Hollow with a host of quirky characters who bring additional drama and comedy to this family-friendly show that appealed to teens as well as adults.

Lipman, Elinor, *Then She Found Me* **(1990) BK, MV, UAB, SH**
When 36-year-old April's adoptive parents die, her birth mother shows up out of nowhere. Brassy Bernice, a local TV talk-show host, intends to publicly create a mother-daughter relationship with April. The two women are as different as night and day, and April never really had any curiosity about her birth mom to begin with.

This is a wry and moving portrait of an instant family. The movie cast Bette Midler and Helen Hunt as Bernice and April and made a few changes in the story to focus more on motherhood as a theme and less on the mother-daughter reconciliation.

Moriarty, Laura, *The Rest of Her Life* (2007) BK, UAB, YA

Leigh's own dysfunctional childhood colors how she deals with her family, especially her golden-girl daughter, Kara. When Kara is involved in a traffic accident that results in the death of a classmate, Leigh must confront her troubled relationship with her daughter as well as revisit the willful neglect of her own mother. It is the story of lifelong strained relationships and the means to which the injured parties will go to ease them.

One Day at a Time (1975–1984) TV

This groundbreaking situation dramedy tackled many serious subjects involving a newly divorced woman and her two teenage daughters. Behind the breezy one-liners and comic predicaments are thoughtful treatments of teen suicide, pregnancy, and sexual harassment at school. The clothes and slang may seem dated, but the emotions and challenges of single motherhood are not.

Porter, Connie, *Imani, All Mine* (1999) BK, YA, AP

Tasha is a 14-year-old unwed mother whose world revolves around her daughter Imani. There is nothing apologetic or preachy about Tasha and her situation. The only example she wishes to serve is to her daughter. The poverty and violence in Tasha's life do not keep her from being the best mother she can be, which includes going to school and parenting classes. But Tasha is also a young teen who wants to date and dream about her future. An unexpected tragedy changes Tasha's neighborhood and her own life journey. Readers will find much to admire in Tasha's strong and inspiring story.

Sebold, Alice, *The Almost Moon* (2007) BK, UAB

Helen resents her duty as caretaker for her senile mother, Clair. One evening, having had it with the stress and tediousness, she suffocates Clair and then doesn't quite know how to cope with the aftermath. Helen unravels the story of her life and her mother's descent into mental illness. The relationship between Helen and her mother is revealed at a slow pace but gives the reader much insight into how it turned Helen into the person she has become.

Strout, Elizabeth, *Amy and Isabelle* (1998) BK, UAB, MV

Isabelle shares a close relationship with her teenage daughter, Amy. When Amy falls in love with her high school math teacher, Isabelle becomes furious not only at the teacher, but at her daughter, for enjoying a life she herself has never known. As the scandal hits their gossipy small town, Isabelle finds herself at the center of judgment. This is an intense look at the bonds of love and jealousy between mothers and daughters.

Terms of Endearment (1983) MV, BK, UAB, YA, CL

It almost seems as if Emma sprang from the womb itching for a fight with Aurora. Although a classic tearjerker, there are plenty of laughs as Emma and Aurora square off about everything from clothes to men to medical treatments. Every argument is only hiding what the women can't seem to say out loud—how much they love each other. The movie is a deft adaptation of Larry McMurtry's novel.

Walker, Rebecca, *Baby Love: Choosing Motherhood after a Lifetime of Ambivalence* (2007) NF BK

How does a bisexual, biracial, famous Third-Wave feminist decide to be come a mother? It is no easy thing. Acutely aware of society's conflicting messages about career and identity versus motherhood, Walker struggled with the choice to reproduce before conceiving a child with her male partner. On one level, this is a memoir of Walker's personal journey through pregnancy and motherhood, including her tumultuous relationship with her own mother, Alice Walker; on another, it is a reflection on the larger societal issues of motherhood and all it entails, including topics such as health care and reproductive options. The book's lyrical prose and wrenching honesty illuminate the complicated, conflicting nature of motherhood in a way that will leave readers thinking.

Sisters and Friends

Some of the strongest relationships that sustain women are those shared with sisters and friends. These are the companions of the heart who love in spite of the flaws and quirks and have shoulders big enough to cry on, closets big enough to dress any occasion, and a loyalty that is fierce enough to make the greatest sacrifices.

Arnesen, Liv, Ann Bancroft, and Cheryl Dahle, *No Horizon Is So Far: Two Women and Their Extraordinary Journey Across Antarctica* **(2003) BK NF, YA**
One day, Ann Bancroft, a schoolteacher from Minnesota, contacted another schoolteacher, Liv Arnesen—a woman she'd never met—to propose a joint trek, on foot, across the Antarctic. It's not as crazy as it sounds: both women had prior experience exploring the continent, and both agreed that it would be a great way to engage students. So, armed with food, supplies, skis, laptops, and really heavy sledges, they set out in 2000 to become the first women to traverse Antarctica. Frostbite, injuries, brutal temperatures, and blizzards all threatened the explorers, but, as this riveting account shows, they ultimately prevailed.

Beverly-Whittemore, Miranda, *Effects of Light* **(2005) BK, YA, RS**
A mysterious package compels Kate Scott to return to her family home and confront the secret history she shared with her sister, Pru, as child models for a controversial photographer. As Kate sorts through her deceased father's effects, she uncovers the truths that led to her decision to change her identity.

Brashares, Ann, *The Last Summer of You and Me* **(2007) BK, UAB, YA, RS**
Shy, sweet Alice and her headstrong, sporty sister Riley come of age at their summer house on Fire Island, along with their best friend, Paul. Both girls are childlike in different ways—Alice is naïve while Riley is something of a female Peter Pan. Paul and Alice have a secret, strong attachment growing, while Riley shuns any talk of romance. When Riley becomes seriously ill, childlike Alice is torn between her conflicting feelings for Paul and loyalty to her sister and realizes they all need to finally grow up.

Girls Night In, **PC**
Maggie, Jaime, and Rachel review movies, answer wacky questions, and talk about all the things women talk about on a girls' night in or out. A Talkshoe production, this is free from iTunes.

Graham, Laurie, *The Future Homemakers of America* **(2002) BK**
Five wives of air force pilots meet in England at the end of World War II, and this novel follows their friendship over 40 years. They encounter marital strife, money woes, and bouts of illness, but their one constant is a strong bond of friendship. Nicely drawn characters and humor make this a good choice in the female friendship category.

Hernandez, Jaime, *Locas: The Maggie and Hopey Stories* **(2004) GN**
The lives of lovably insecure Maggie and wild-child Hopey span over 15 years as the two women experience many adventures (some fantastically unbelievable) through their on-again, off-again relationship. They have a wide circle of friends involved in everything from the New Wave punk scene in L.A. to street gangs and women's wrestling. Heroine Maggie grows up along with her creator's artistic talent.

Kelly, Cathy, *Best of Friends* **(2005) BK, UAB**
Four Irish best friends band together in this charming novel. Divorced Lizzie worries about being alone; TV star Abby frets about growing older; beauty salon owner Sally is always too busy; and Erin is obsessed with family secrets. When Sally is diagnosed with breast cancer, the women realize their problems are insignificant, and Lizzie, Abby, and Erin rally together to support Sally.

Landvik, Lorna, *Angry Housewives Eating Bon Bons* **(2003) BK**
Five housewives in small-town Minnesota meet in the turbulent late 1960s and form a book club. There's socially and politically active Slip; young widow Kari; meek and shy Merit; sexy and audacious Audrey; and transplanted southerner Faith, who's not too thrilled with the Minnesotan tundra. The book follows the women to the present day as they form close ties and act as sounding boards, partners in crime, and rescuers for one another.

Mapson, Jo-An, *Bad Girl Creek* **(2001) BK**
Beryl, Nance, Phoebe, and Ness come together to take over Phoebe's newly inherited flower farm. As they work to overcome the farm's problems, they support each other to defeat their personal problems. Phoebe is wheelchair-bound due to congenital heart problems; Ness is out of work and fears she may have a serious illness; Nance is down on her luck and lonely; and ex-convict Beryl has just been evicted from her home. These women from such different backgrounds and experiences form a tight bond and realize that they can overcome anything as long as they have their friends along for the ride.

Mystic Pizza **(1988) MV, YA, AP**
The bond between sisters Daisy and Cat and their best friend Jojo is strong. All support one another during comic, stressful, and heartbreaking situations. Jojo faints at the altar during her wedding. Daisy warily dates a wealthy boy from a snobbish family. Cat struggles with three jobs to earn enough money to go to college, yet jeopardizes it all when she falls in love with one of her employers. Funny, warm, and emotional, the three young women may test their relationships, but never waver in their love for each other.

Pink Acres, **PC**
A suburban mom and her city sister share differences and similarities in opinions, experiences, friendship, and sisterly bonds.

Robinson, Elisabeth, *The True and Outstanding Adventures of the Hunt Sisters* **(2004) BK, UAB**
Olivia Hunt, a Hollywood screenwriter whose career is dragging her down—she works with incompetent writers and egotistical directors and stars—is just about ready to throw in the towel. But when she finds out her younger sister Maddie has been diagnosed with leukemia, her life seems golden by comparison. Maddie, newly married and determined to keep a cheerful face, needs her sister's help. At turns funny and sad, this story is never overly sentimental.

Sex and The City (1998–) **TV, MV, BK, UAB, AP, CL**
Candace Bushnell's newspaper columns begat a book that spawned a hit television series and a movie. The TV series is the most well known of all the formats. Carrie, Miranda, Charlotte, and Samantha are friends who consider themselves family. They are fearless, beautiful, accomplished, neurotic, talented, single, and, on occasion, desperate. All four are looking for love and success in New York City and encounter many setbacks and roadblocks, but always have each other to turn to.

Weiner, Jennifer, *In Her Shoes* **(2002) BK, MV, UAB**
Slightly frumpy and very dependable Rose allows her extremely pretty and very flighty sister Maggie to move in with her when Maggie loses yet another job. But Rose hits her limit when Maggie steals her shoes, her credit cards, and her boyfriend. The sisters are finally brought back together when the grandmother they never knew comes to seek them out. Weiner's novels are funny, smart, and touching, and this one doesn't disappoint in its portrayal of two very different sisters who think they don't need anyone discovering that they truly need each other.

Willett, Marcia, *The Children's Hour* **(2004) BK, UAB**
Nest and Mina, sisters in their 70s living on the English coast, are worried when their ailing older sister Georgie comes to live with them. Georgie is on the brink of Alzheimer's and threatens to spill long-dormant family secrets. The book has complex characters and a riveting family saga from British author Willett.

Women Without Men

"A woman without a man is like a fish without a bicycle." No doubt there are many women who would disagree with that old adage, even as there are plenty of women who prefer to live their life by it. The following books and films tell stories of women who have perfectly fine lives without men or women who are abruptly left alone and to their own devices. These characters are all redefining themselves and learning that life on one's own terms is still a life worth living.

Ahern, Cecelia, *P.S., I Love You* **(2004) BK, MV, UAB, YA**
Holly discovers a year's worth of letters that her late husband Gerry left for her to read after his untimely death. Feeling that he is still close by keeping watch, she embarks on reclaiming her life. Holly's family and friends also play a large part in her growth. This is a sentimental story but not sappy.

Anshaw, Carol, *Lucky in the Corner* **(2002) BK**
Permanent student Fern, her lesbian mother Nora and her lover Jeanne, and her cross-dressing (straight) uncle Howard are featured in this fun novel, a look at a slightly dysfunctional but very loving family. The most stable family member is Lucky, Fern's dog. When Fern discovers her mother is cheating on Jeanne, the family dynamic is rocked. This book is well-paced with realistically drawn characters and great Chicago detail.

Asher, Bridget, *My Husband's Sweethearts* **(2008) BK, UAB**
Lucy is not quite a widow, but she's grieving all the same—after discovering her husband was cheating on her throughout their marriage, she leaves him, only to be called back home when he realizes he's dying of heart failure. Needing closure, she decides to call all the women in his little black book and have them come to say

goodbye. Humorous yet poignant, this is an interesting look at a woman who gets time to make amends and get used to being a widow before her husband's gone.

Baldock, Kirsten, and Fabio Moon, *Smoke and Guns* (2001) GN, YA, AP
Sometimes looking to shake things up a bit is all the adventure a girl needs. It appears to be all Scarlett requires to keep her life lively. A licensed cigarette girl for District 5, Scarlett and her sidekick Annie find themselves in hot water when they enter District 6, territory of the Broadway Belles, a rival cigarette-girl gang. This is a stylized graphic novel crossed with the noir films of the 1950s, the violence of Dirty Harry, and the turf toughs of *The Warriors*. The send-up of riot grrl pop culture is hilarious and empowering. This is the perfect antidote to a bad day at the office.

Forney, Ellen, *I Love Led Zeppelin* (2006) GN
There's nothing Forney can't do on her own, and these wildly imaginative and witty short comics demonstrate that fact. Eclectic, compelling, funny, mundane, and sometimes delightfully disrespectful stories are told in clean lines and vibrant colors with unpredictable emphasis on unusual objects. Just like life.

Ganahl, Jane, *Naked on the Page: The Misadventures of My Unmarried Midlife* (2007) NF BK
"Where art thou, astrologically perfect, sexually compatible man of my future?" asks *San Francisco Chronicle* writer Ganahl near the beginning of her book. This rollicking memoir details Ganahl's attempts to answer that question over the course of her 49th year. With lots of friends, a great daughter, and an exciting, lucrative career, she's ready to embrace the final missing ingredient in her life, romance—but what she ends up embracing is a series of awful matches. In some memoirists' hands this would be tragic, but Ganahl's knack for humor turns her luckless dating into laugh-out-loud comedy, while her reflections on middle age round out her engaging life story.

Jessop, Carolyn, and Laura Palmer, *Escape* (2007) NF BK, UAB
When she was 18 years old, Carolyn Jessop became the fourth wife of a man nearly twice her age. She didn't ask for the marriage, but her opinion didn't matter in the eyes of the Fundamentalist Church of Jesus Christ of Latter-Day Saints (FLDS), the sect whose followers broke away from mainstream Mormonism so that their men could practice polygamy. Every aspect of Jessup's life was controlled by her psychologically abusive husband—when and if she would have sex with him, how her children would be raised, and how the money she earned from teaching would be spent. Jessup wanted to leave, but not at the risk of losing her children—but 17 years into the marriage, she managed to escape with all eight of them. Disturbing, vivid, and evocative, this page-turning memoir shows us how one woman managed to single-handedly defy the insular world of the FLDS community.

***The L Word* (2004) TV**
This smart and sexy drama is peopled with glamorous, intelligent, and passionate women dealing with the typical everyday concerns of career challenges, relationship conflicts, and family pressures. They just happen to be lesbians.

Samson, Lisa, *The Living End* (2003) BK, UAB
When Pearly's husband Joey dies from a stroke after 35 years of marriage, she is devastated. Thinking she could never live without him, she contemplates suicide—but then finds a tattered note in one of his jacket pockets. Titled "While I Live, I

Want To . . . ," she realizes it's a list of things he always wanted to do but never had the chance. She decides to fulfill his wish list herself, including getting a tattoo and visiting the pyramids. Along the way, she meets many quirky characters who convince her that life is worth living, even without her beloved husband.

Truly, Madly, Deeply (1990) MV

Nina suffers the devastating loss of the love of her life, Jamie, and cannot cope with it. She is paralyzed with grief and soon her apartment falls into a state of disrepair requiring a parade of quirky, amorous repairmen to troop through and make attempts to bring Nina out of her sorrow. It doesn't work, and one day, in her profound heartache, Nina sits down at the piano to play a duet, and the strains of Jamie's cello join her. Life without Jamie wasn't worth living, but life with dead Jamie isn't much better. This is a very honest depiction of life after a loved one dies and the small pockets of humor and tenderness that get one through.

Winston, Lolly, *Good Grief* (2004) BK, UAB, SH, RS

When 36-year-old Sophie Stanton goes from newlywed to widow after being married only three years, she learns there are actually 14 stages of grief, rather than five: denial, Oreos, anger, bargaining, depression, ashes, lust, waitressing, mentoring, dating, baking, acceptance, goodwill, and Thanksgiving. After a brief breakdown when she loses her job for showing up in her robe and bunny slippers, Sophie sells her house and moves to Oregon to find herself and lose her grief.

Working Girls

Every woman has a second family, one that is lazy, whiny, sloppy, needy, and critical. The office can be similar to the one found at home. But the workplace also affords women a place to find accomplishment, make contributions, and receive recognition. Occupational hazards abound and make for comic and tragic situations in which women not only make decisions that save the business day, but those that save their sanity.

9 to 5 (1980) MV, CL

This is a bubbly comic fantasy about committing the ultimate workplace revenge—murdering a sexist, insensitive boss. The over-the-top film features three enduring comediennes, Jane Fonda, Lily Tomlin, and Dolly Parton, and a rollicking theme song.

Albert, Alexa, *Brothel: Mustang Ranch and Its Women* (2001) NF BK

The world's oldest profession is still practiced in Nevada. Author Albert was given unfettered access to one of the most popular cathouses outside of Las Vegas and learned some eye-opening truths about these career "professionals." Many simply view themselves as working wives and mothers; however, they are kept virtual prisoner behind the iron bars of the Mustang Ranch gates and are treated with dismissal and disapproval in society. This is a fascinating and sympathetic look at legalized prostitution.

Bagshawe, Louise, *The Go-To Girl* (2005) BK, YA

London script-reader Anna desperately wants to make it big in the film industry, but she's just too mousy to get ahead. She's not good at sucking up to the boss or flirting with the bigwigs. Having two supermodels as roommates isn't helping her confidence much, either. But when a hot new director uncovers her screenwriting talent, she may be on the way to bigger and better things.

Browne, Hester, *The Little Lady Agency* **(2006) BK, SH**
When serious and stable Melissa finds herself out of work and bored, she decides to start her own business, lending her skills to single men in need of those tasks that only a woman can perform—picking out clothing, buying gifts, and going to company parties. To keep her personal and professional lives separate, she takes on a new persona, Honey, and becomes London's most sought-after bachelorette.

Chisholm: Unbought and Unbossed **(2004) MV, NF, YA**
Shirley Chisholm was the first black woman elected to Congress and the first African American to seek the presidential nomination. This documentary of her life, filmed the year before her death, chronicles her extraordinary life in politics and the harrowing challenges she faced from fellow politicians, women, and African Americans as she campaigned on the Chisholm Trail in the summer of 1972. This is a rousing documentary of a woman who never lost her dedication to public service and may inspire the same in viewers.

The Devil Wears Prada **(2003) BK, UAB, AP (2006) MV**
Although the best-selling book differs from the smash-hit movie, both address the conundrum of selling one's soul to the career demons—in this case the superficial, backstabbing world of high fashion. The "devil" as portrayed by Meryl Streep is a character for the ages, and Streep manages to find the smidgeon of heart in this soulless and beastly editor-in-chief. Anne Hathaway turns in a star-making performance as the relentlessly dumped on Andrea. This is a Cinderella story with a killer makeover montage.

Gold, Robin, *Perfectly True Tales of a Perfect Size 12* **(2007) BK, YA**
Delilah White, an aspiring Martha Stewart, is up for a promotion that could make her a star. She's confident she'll get it—she's got personality, experience, and skills—but she finds herself thwarted at every turn by a rival determined to get the promotion herself at any cost. Scheming and sabotage abound in this funny story filled with appealing and realistic characters.

Greenlaw, Linda, *The Hungry Ocean: A Swordboat Captain's Journey* **(1999) NF BK, UAB, YA**
Linda Greenlaw is gritty, resourceful, courageous, and matter-of-fact—and no wonder, as she is the world's only female captain of a swordfish boat. She is also a gifted writer, as we see in *The Hungry Ocean*, her chronicle of one month at sea. Greenlaw and her fishermen have a successful fishing expedition, but not without their share of adventure. The accommodations on the boat are meager, the weather is a continuous threat, on-the-fly health care must suffice for injuries and illness, and infighting among the crew whittles away at everyone's sanity. It's hard to say which is more fascinating, the glimpse into life on a fishing boat or the captivating narrator herself.

Maddox, Brenda, *Rosalind Franklin: The Dark Lady of DNA* **(2002) NF BK**
Students in schools through out the world learn that Watson and Crick discovered the model for DNA. What students rarely learn was that Rosalind Franklin, the assistant to Watson, did the real work and whose scientific research and photographs revealed the famous double helix. Whereas Watson and Crick won the Nobel Prize for their "discovery," Franklin was relegated to the back pages of history. In this thought-provoking biography, Maddox restores Franklin to her rightful place,

showing how a combination of sexual discrimination and anti-Semitism conspired against her and how her untimely death from ovarian cancer shunted her out of the spotlight she deserved. Based on Franklin's letters and records, this biography paints a portrait of a fascinating woman, and Maddox's clear language makes the science accessible to the lay reader.

Moran, Lindsay, *Blowing My Cover: My Life As a CIA Spy* (2005) NF BK

"My father," writes Lindsay Moran, "was certain the CIA would never take me." "You're not their type," he said. "They look for people who've been the president of the Young Republicans Club." But it has been Moran's life-long dream to be a spy, so she sent her résumé to the CIA. It turns out her father was wrong; Moran was hired and she eagerly embarked on her career, itching to uncover plots and catch bad guys. Except, as it turned out, spying wasn't nearly as fun as she had expected: her work environment was a mix of mind-numbing bureaucratic work and sexist colleagues and it put a major crimp in her social life; it's very hard to date someone when you can't tell him what you do for a living. Forget James Bond: this is a memoir of what espionage is really like, of the inherent loneliness and thrilling but infrequent adventures, related in Moran's enjoyable, fast-paced style.

Murphy Brown (1988–1998) TV, CL

Murphy Brown is a recovering addict who is determined to continue her success as a television news journalist even if her zany coworkers and the current political administration are driving her back to drink. Critics and viewers loved this realistically flawed, acerbic, tough, yet caring, single mother experiencing the same challenges as all professional women everywhere. Just as funny as *The Mary Tyler Moore Show*, but certainly less dated.

Nelly Don: A Stitch in Time (2006) MV, CL, AP

Nell Donnelly Reed was not a devil in Prada by any stretch, but a feminist fashion maven in her own right. Nelly Don was one of the twentieth century's first and most successful self-made millionaires. She designed and sold more dresses than any other person in the United States at the time. She led an exciting and dramatic life—she was kidnapped in 1931, prompting her lover, Missouri Senator James A. Reed, to threaten the current mob boss of Kansas City with national exposure of his vice crimes if Nell was not found unharmed. Twenty-five cars of gangsters combed the city's underworld to find her. This is a documentary drawing on the Reed family documents to tell a classic tale of the American dream.

Paul, Caroline, *Fighting Fire* (1998) NF BK, UAB, YA

While casting about for something to do after college, Paul was encouraged to take the San Francisco Fire Department exams. She passed both written and physical tests and not long after became the lone woman in her station house. This is her memoir of adapting to a physically demanding life and the psychological challenges she endured as well. It is an insightful look inside an inner-city fire station and the lives of all who are "the bravest."

Working Girl (1988) MV

Unlike *9 to 5*, the boss in this working gal flick is a steely, conniving woman who appropriates a lucrative idea from her beleaguered and ambitious secretary. Melanie Griffith earned raves as the doe-eyed baby-doll-voiced career girl who temporarily adopts her boss's life in order to get meetings with honchos at rival companies, but

Sigourney Weaver steals every scrap of celluloid as the power-mad corporate shark. Harrison Ford is the man-candy they do battle for. This is a Cinderella story for the executive set that packs a more poignant punch when watched in the current economic climate as viewers realize many of these workers likely lost their jobs when the 1980s bubble burst.

Zimmerman, Jean, *The Women of the House: How a Colonial She-Merchant Built a Mansion, a Fortune, and a Dynasty* (2006) NF BK
In 1659, 22-year-old Margaret Hardenbroeck set out from Holland to seek her fortune in America; by the time of her death, some three decades later, she had become the richest woman in New Amsterdam, having amassed a stunning empire based on business and real estate. In *The Women of the House*, you'll discover how a shrewd colonial businesswoman ambitiously traded goods in a man's world (though many readers will be disappointed to find that she participated in the slave trade). With excellent research and an engaging style, Zimmerman's book brings Hardenbroeck to life along with the female heirs who followed in her footsteps.

Theme: Women's Lives and Relationships

Common themes in women's literature follow the major milestones in a woman's life. Birth and death are traditional themes explored in fiction and nonfiction, but in women's lives, these events immediately bestow a change in societal role, from maiden to wife, wife to mother, wife to widow, and daughter to matriarch. These significant events can bring on heartache, anguish, laughter, and satisfaction. Stories that address these issues are usually set in a contemporary time and place. The problems may be universal, but the solutions and reactions are generally modern. Happy endings are not required elements in most women's literature; however, a satisfactory ending is. The protagonist must achieve a personal change or gain a piece of knowledge that will have an enlightening impact on the rest of her life, usually for the better.

Birth, Death, and Other Journeys

Women make many journeys in a lifetime and some include staring death in the face until death blinks first. The books and media on this list pay tribute to the strength of women who take that first step on a path that may have unfavorable destinations, insurmountable challenges, or final resting places that fall completely off the map. Some characters never stop traveling and find the journey is where the heart is.

Albert, Elisa, *The Book of Dahlia: A Novel* (2008) BK, YA, AP
Dahlia, a pot-smoking, unemployed slacker, is diagnosed with a terminal brain tumor at age 29. She endures seizures, grueling radiation treatments, and a support group. She comes across a lightweight self-help book called *It's Up to You: Your Cancer To-Do List* and tries to live by its principles, but her bitter sense of humor and anger at the universe prevent her from accepting her illness. Sometimes harsh, sometimes humorous, this is a decidedly non-weepy look at cancer.

Askowitz, Andrea, *My Miserable, Lonely, Lesbian Pregnancy* (2008) NF BK
Most women get pregnant the old-fashioned way, but that plan presented a hitch for Andrea Askowitz; being a lesbian is not generally conducive for introducing sperm

to egg. But she wanted a baby, and she finally conceived, thanks to a fertility donor—and immediately she found herself in pregnancy hell. This is the darkly funny memoir of nine months of hormone swings, hideous underwear, and bodily aches and pains, told in Askowitz's acerbic, acidic tone. She is grouchy, she is bitchy, she is whiny, and she is laugh-out-loud funny because of it. Read this for a hilarious accounting of one lesbian's foray into nine cranky months of childbearing.

Beaches (1988) MV, BK

A friendship that can span 30 years can handle any challenge—including motherhood, betrayal, and death. From the time they meet under an Atlantic City boardwalk, CeeCee and Hilary know they are connected, even as each attempts to sever the connection in multiple ways when they grow older. The two women take divergent paths through life but each one leads them back to each other. The ultimate test of their friendship is when Hilary asks a life-changing favor from CeeCee. The film is a fine adaptation of the popular novel by Iris Rainer Dart.

Berg, Elizabeth, *Talk Before Sleep* (1994) BK, UAB

Reserved Ann and gregarious Ruth are unlikely best friends. When Ruth is diagnosed with breast cancer, Ann, a former nurse, throws herself into caring for her friend. Ravaged by the disease as the cancer spreads to her brain and lungs, Ruth depends on Ann's skills and her unwavering friendship. A trio of other friends helps Ann keep Ruth's spirits up in her last days as all renew the bonds of friendship and prepare for inevitable sorrow.

Escandon, Maria Amparo, *Gonzalez & Daughter Trucking Co.* (2005) BK, AP, YA, SH

Incarcerated in Mexicali Women's Prison, Libertad refuses to give away any information about herself or her crime. Instead she forms a library club for the other inmates and starts weaving a tale of a young woman, her political fugitive Mexican father, her beautiful deceased mother, and the many adventures they have as a trucking family. In between Libertad's stories, the inmates tell their own tales of love, regret, and loss.

Hall, Meredith, *Without a Map: A Memoir* (2007) NF BK, YA

It is 1965. Sixteen-year-old Meredy Hall falls for a boy and, being sexually naïve, she unwittingly conceives a child. She is kicked out of high school, thrown out of her mother's home, sent to live with her father, and forced to give up her baby. The loss casts a shadow on her life; as she grows into adulthood, she shuns the familiar and escapes overseas, moving in loneliness from one country to another. Much later, having returned to America, she receives a phone call out of the blue: her son wants to make contact. Lyrically written, this is a profoundly moving story of the pain of forced adoption and the power and healing of reconciliation.

Immediate Family (1989) MV

Infertility, unwanted pregnancy, and adoption get a mature and thoughtful treatment in this serio-comic film with some heavy-hitting actors and straightforward storytelling. James Woods and Glenn Close portray a professional couple who have had 10 years' worth of difficulty in conceiving a child. Mary Stuart Masterson and Kevin Dillon play a young teenage couple who know they are not equipped to care for a baby, yet yearn to keep it anyway. Strong, touching, and believable performances from all the actors make this story a tearjerker in all the best ways.

Kuebelbeck, Amy, *Waiting with Gabriel: A Story of Cherishing a Baby's Brief Life* **(2003) NF BK**
"'You have a beautiful baby,' the ultrasound technician said quietly. She was studying the flickering images on her screen, staring intently at the shadows of the tiny heart. I think she had already seen that our baby was going to die." These three sentences form the first paragraph of Amy Kuebelbeck's heart-wrenching memoir of her doomed pregnancy. It was during her second trimester that she learned that her undelivered son, Gabriel, suffered from hypoplastic left heart syndrome: essentially, her baby had only half of a heart. While in the womb, his mother's placenta would sustain him, but upon delivery, he would have days, at the most, to live; in fact, Gabriel survived only a few hours after he was born. But the impact he had on the lives of his mother, father, and two sisters was tremendous, as we see in this beautiful, poignant tribute to an infant who changed his family forever. This is a story of religious faith and spirituality, of living through and recovering from pain.

Marchetto, Marisa Acocella, *Cancer Vixen* **(2006) GN, YA, AP**
In vibrant colors and strong lines that accent the *Sex in the City* tone, the author details every step of her discovery and treatment of breast cancer. Marisa starts her story with the day she discovers a lump—only three weeks from her wedding day. She then flashes back to life BC, "before cancer," as a single, fashionable, socializing cartoonist for *The New Yorker* who starts dating an up-and-coming restaurateur. The artist goes into detail regarding her many doctor visits, chemo treatments, insurance woes, wedding preparations, and the fabulous shoes she wears to all medical appointments. Our heroine is eminently likeable and sympathetic. Readers will be drawn to her humorous warmth and petrifying fear.

Mayes, Frances *Under the Tuscan Sun* **(2003) BK, MV, UAB, SH**
Although the memoir by Frances Mayes was a bestseller, it's not surprising that the slightly altered movie is the greater favorite among most female viewers and readers. The movie opens with Frances being dumped, deserted, and divorced, unceremoniously, and then going a on an all-gay tour of Italy. While there, she falls in love with a decrepit villa and purchases it, the first impulsive thing Frances has done in many years. Frances's renovation of the beautiful but crumbling villa is a metaphor for the renovation she does on her own spirit, and viewers will appreciate how Frances gets all she wished for, even if it arrives in unusual packages.

McClure, Tori Murden, *Pearl in the Storm: How I Found My Heart in the Middle of the Ocean* **(2009) NF BK, YA**
Don't look for a Hemingwayesque tale here. McClure is making more than a physical journey across the Atlantic in a rowboat (the first woman to do so). Her quest for this title is only the smallest part of what she gains once the adventure is concluded. The forced isolation and the threatening ocean storms encourage an inner soul-searching and emotional honesty that make for a thrilling and inspiring narrative.

Samantha Brown, **PC**
Sponsored by the Travel Channel, Samantha Brown's television show *Great Weekends* is condensed to podcast form. Brown shows how to travel on a dime to great places, where to eat delicious local food, how to find activities and landmarks off the beaten path, and chats with the residents who make each location a unique treat. It features unique commentary on places near and far and is free from iTunes.

Thelma & Louise (1991) MV, YA, AP, CL

An Arkansas waitress and her best friend take off for a weekend getaway, shoot a rapist, and spend the rest of the weekend trying to elude the authorities and escape to Mexico. This is not just a "two dames on the road" movie. The two women embark on a spiritual journey that separates them and then brings them closer together. Louise is struggling with the trappings of a life spent "doing what's right," while Thelma is rebelling against her suffocating life as a housewife. The ending packs a wallop that will have viewers on their feet cheering.

Coming of Age

The loss-of-innocence story is a familiar one in women's literature and is not limited to tales featuring youthful characters in love. Our heroines learn universal truths about parents, friends, and life in a myriad of ways.

Abby's Road, PC, YA

High school senior Abby Laporte and guests offer fresh perspectives on sex, friendship, drugs, parents, money, and other topics of teen interest in this weekly podcast that is free from iTunes.

Angelou, Maya, *I Know Why the Caged Bird Sings* (1970) NF BK, UAB, MV, SH, AP, YA

Maya Angelou, a tremendous force in the American civil rights movement of the 1960s, wears many hats: among other things, she is a poet, a professor, an actress— and, as we see in the enduring classic *I Know Why the Caged Bird Sings*, she is a voraciously talented autobiographical writer. Hers is an emotionally difficult story to read, but her painful experience growing up as an African American girl in a racist and sexist America is essential reading for anyone who wants to understand the bitter climate of the country in the 1930s and 1940s. Trauma is the hallmark of the first 17 years of Angelou's life: she is raped by her mother's boyfriend; she goes mute when she feels guilt after her rapist is murdered; she endures an unplanned, out-of-wedlock pregnancy; and throughout, she struggles against the twin specters of racism and sexism. This is a grim book, yes, but beautifully written, with examples of love and hope that shine in spite of everything.

Bank, Melissa, *The Wonder Spot* (2005) BK

Sophie, a witty, self-deprecating suburban child, grows up into an astute young woman. Over the course of 20 years, she struggles to define herself throughout Hebrew school, college, and her first job. Her family plays a big role in the story as well, including her grandmother's descent into senility, her quiet father and high-strung mother, and her two brothers.

Bechdel, Alison, *Fun Home: A Family Tragicomic* (2006) GN, YA

This mesmerizing graphic memoir traces Alison's formative years living with her family in the same location as the family business, a funeral home. Alison's father looms large in this memoir and had the most impact on her life. When Alison finally comes out to her mother in a letter she writes from college, her mother replies, "so was your father." The pounding surf of memories that wash over Alison with that news alters almost everything she remembers about her father and yet does not lessen him in her memory. This is a powerful and emotionally complex story.

Chambers, Veronica, *Miss Black America* **(original title:** *When Did You Stop Loving Me?***) (2004) BK, YA**
Angela is happy growing up with her passionate yet volatile parents in 1970s Brooklyn until the day she comes home from school to discover her mother Melanie is not there and her father Teddo won't (or can't) tell Angela where her mother has gone. Left with her magician father, Angela is raised to be proud of her heritage even while the family of two struggles to keep food on the table. Teddo takes Angela to the hedonistic discos of New York City while he looks for work, and she maintains her innocence in the midst of all the debauchery. A chance meeting with Muhammad Ali changes Angela and leads her to decisions about locating her mother and choosing her own path.

Fitch, Janet, *White Oleander* **(1999) BK, MV, YA**
Astrid, 13, is bounced around through the foster-care system after her flighty mother is sent to prison. Her first foster mother is Starr, a born-again former abuser whose middle-aged boyfriend seduces Astrid. When Starr finds out, her jealous rage leads her to send Astrid to her next foster home, with the tyrannical Marvel, and from there to the sadistic and neglectful Amelia. When she finally lands with a "dream" family, yuppie couple Claire and Ron, there is trouble in that home as well. How Astrid gets through her ordeals and grows up into a mature young woman makes for an absorbing read.

Hissinger, Amy, *Nina: Adolescence* **(2003) BK, UAB, YA**
In an effort to draw her artist mother out of a deep depression that has set in after the death of Nina's little brother, Nina offers to pose for her mother. Marian gladly accepts this persuasion to take up her art again and has Nina, 14, pose nude. Soon the series of "Nina" paintings make their way to a gallery, where Nina, now almost 16, is embarrassed to be viewed by the public. Her father is furious that his wife would display their child in such a manner. Confused, angry, guilty, and curious, Nina embarks on an affair with an older art critic, a former lover of her mother's. The turmoil of adolescence is perfectly captured in this debut novel.

Kominsky-Crumb, Aline, *Love That Bunch* **(1990) GN**
With loose lines and splashes of riotous color, respected and lauded comic artist Kominsky-Crumb tells the story of her formative years as a misfit growing up in suburban Long Island. Nothing escapes her keen eye and wit—the humiliations of fat camp, the befuddled banality of her family, and the headiness of Greenwich Village in the 1960s. This is a visual memoir of laughter, tears, and ultimately triumph.

The Man in the Moon **(1991) MV, YA, CL, AP**
The movie that put Reese Witherspoon on the map is an unsentimental look at the crushing blows and ethereal highs of first love for two sisters during a 1950s summer in a small Louisiana town. Fourteen-year-old Dani is waiting for her life to begin and it does when 17-year-old Court Foster and his family move to the farm next to Dani's. Dani and Court become fast friends, but it is Dani's older, beautiful sister, Maureen, who catches Court's eye. Watching Dani suffer heartbreak and betrayal will remind every viewer of the power of first love. The tragic incident that will eventually draw the sisters back to each other is not clichéd and viewers will experience the pain and comfort Dani and Maureen give each other without feeling manipulated.

McCandless, Sarah Grace, *Grosse Pointe Girl: Tales from a Suburban Adolescence* **(2004) BK, YA**
Set in a wealthy Michigan suburb in the 1980s, this story follows Emma from the summer before sixth grade to her high school graduation. Emma goes through typical

adolescent rites of passage, such as getting her first bra, being bullied by the popular girls, experiencing unrequited love, getting fake IDs, and adjusting to her parents' separation. Told as episodic reflections in the first person, this is a quick and enjoyable read that will appeal to anyone who grew up in the era of Madonna and Michael Jackson.

My So-Called Life (1994–1995) TV, YA, SH

It only lasted one season, but this cult TV series still has legions of fans who want to know what happened in the season finale when Angela found out that Jordan didn't write the letter that captured her heart, geeky neighbor Brian did. This show is still worth checking out for the extremely realistic depiction of what teen life is actually like. The speech, the clothes, the excessive mood swings, and the snotty and angst-ridden tones of voice. Even the adults are treated well. They are exasperated, supportive, and bewildered with these young adults and their tribal ways. It is a classic show and it's a crime that it was cancelled.

Simons, Paullina, Tully (1994) BK, UAB, YA

The bond between three teenage girls forms the core of this sprawling, absorbing novel. Abused by her mentally ill mother and her uncle, Tully barely survives her wretched adolescence in 1970s Kansas. Julie, who comes from a large Hispanic family, is determined to do better for herself. And Jenny, moderately autistic, wants to escape her overprotective parents. As the three unlikely friends struggle against their origins and circumstances, their lives take uncharted paths marked by both destiny and choice.

Souljah, Sister, The Coldest Winter Ever (1999) BK, YA, AP, SH, CL, RS

The world of spoiled urban princess Winter Santiaga crashes around her the day her druglord father's Long Island mansion is raided and he's taken to jail. The authorities seize all of the Santiaga's possessions, including the home. Winter's mother is shot in the face by a rival drug gang, and the state takes Winter and her three sisters into protective custody. Winter returns to the hard streets of Brooklyn to reclaim her place as a daughter of the privileged streets. Her ruthlessness and intolerance for weakness are qualities that serve her well in the drug trade but hinder any attempts at a new and different life. This is an extremely popular coming-of-age tale for urban youth with a grave message.

Marriage and Family

As women age, marriage and family become two great definers of their lives, in some cases completely redefining a woman's sense of herself. These stories explore how women view themselves in the role of wife, matriarch, and sibling, and how a place is carved out in newly created families or firmly established ones. Liberal doses of humor, a strong backbone, and the flexibility of a bendy straw are always required elements in the characters.

bandele, asha, The Prisoner's Wife: A Memoir (1999) NF BK

By many accounts, asha bandele had a blessed life: a college-educated young African American woman from a good family, she was moving beyond an unfulfilling former marriage and growing in her identity as a poet. It was her poetry, in fact, that led her to her destiny in the one area of happiness that her life lacked: romance. While reading her poetry to a group of inmates, bandele met Rashid, a man serving time for second-degree murder. *The Prisoner's Wife* is the unlikeliest of love stories, tracing the romance between bandele and Rashid through their initial tentative attraction, their growing love, and their eventual marriage—even while he was still behind bars. bandele's gift for poetic language recalls the bittersweet emotions, the struggles, and the triumph of joy in unexpected circumstances in this moving narrative.

Brothers & Sisters (2006) TV

Jockeying for position in a family doesn't stop once the siblings become adults. This lively, warm, and intelligent family drama features the Walker family, closely knit but very different individuals, and the challenges they face in their professional and personal lives. The standout women are Norah, Sarah, and Kitty, the matriarch and her two daughters. All are emotional, loyal, smart, and conflicted. This is a standout drama about a twenty-first century American family and how they make it all work.

Chitchat Moms, PC

Two moms talking about nothing, anything, and everything in between—kids, money, sex, family, work, and relationships. This podcast is free from iTunes.

Cleage, Pearl, *What Looks Like Crazy on an Ordinary Day* (1997) BK, UAB, AP, RS

Unlike other Oprah's Book Club selections, this title comes with more humor than the others even though the subject matter is equally serious. Ava Johnson, recently diagnosed with HIV, is headed to her hometown in Michigan to stay with her older sister, Joyce, recently widowed. It may seem as if Cleage is overstuffing her novel with social problems: suicide, drunk driving, pregnant teens, crack-addicted babies, and domestic violence. However, in her sharp and witty hands, this novel is inspiring and thoughtful.

The Family Stone (2005) MV

Tightly wound, conservative Meredith is trying to prepare herself to meet her boyfriend's laid-back and liberal family at the Christmas holiday. After completely blowing the first impression, she calls in reinforcements in the form of her younger sister, Julie, who immediately bonds with the family and charms Meredith's boyfriend. There's not much to the movie's plot; it is more of a situation and character study of a very realistic family, their unusual ways of dealing with each other and outsiders, and the secrets families will keep in order to maintain a positive atmosphere during a stressful holiday.

Haigh, Jennifer, *The Condition* (2009) BK, UAB, YA

This is an earnest novel about a family that thinks its dysfunction is due to the medical condition of one of its members. If the children of Paulette and Frank haven't turned out quite the way their parents wanted, it may be the fault of Paulette's compulsive need for control or Frank's constant distraction instead of Gwen's Turner syndrome. While Gwen struggles to mature in a body that never will, her older brother Billy wrestles with his sexuality and her younger brother Scott leads a directionless life. Twenty years later, all will gather for a reunion and start to understand their places in this damaged clan. The book is leisurely paced with layered characters.

Lurie, Allison, *Truth and Consequences* (2006) BK, UAB

Two marriages go under the microscope in this quietly compelling novel set in the world of elite academics. Jane and Alan have been married for more than 16 years, when one day Jane looks at her husband and does not recognize him. This innocuous event sets in motion the inevitable, but it gets a boost from a self-centered critically acclaimed visiting poetess whose beauty exceeds her poetic talent. Alan is a respected professor of architecture suffering from a near-debilitating back injury; Jane is merely a lower-level university administrator when she is not taking care of Alan. Delia is a diva-esque visiting poet-in-residence with her husband Henry, whose sole purpose is to take care of Delia. Jane and Henry first connect over their spouses' medical ailments and then over the demands and shortcomings of academic life. This is an interesting novel about the life choices some couples make and what it takes to correct the errors.

My Big Fat Greek Wedding (2002) MV, YA

Before this movie gets to all the wedding trimmings, viewers are first introduced to Toula's big, loud, loving, and meddling Greek family. They are not pleased when Toula falls in love and plans to marry a man who is not Greek. As Toula struggles to please everyone around her (much to the amusement of the audience), she learns that she will have to reshape her place in her extended family and refold her cultural heritage to include her non-Greek husband.

Newman, Catherine, *Waiting for Birdy: A Year of Frantic Tedium, Neurotic Angst, and the Wild Magic of Growing a Family* (2005) BK NF

When her first child is two-and-a-half years old, Catherine Newman becomes pregnant with her second child. This situation is not exactly unprecedented in the history of humankind, and yet Newman manages to tell the story of her second pregnancy in a way that is fresh and magical. Journey through the joys, anxieties, and anticipation of pregnancy with the mother, father, and brother-to-be as they anticipate and finally meet Birdy. This quirky humor on every page ("I didn't understand that having a baby would be like falling in love, but like falling in love on a bad acid trip") blends with the tender warmth of maternal love in this unexpectedly compelling memoir.

Once and Again (1999–2002) TV

Two fortysomething single parents try to manage their new romantic relationship while juggling the demands of estranged spouses, children, siblings, jobs, and parents. This family drama moves seamlessly between romance and comedy as well. While the time is evenly split between both families, the more memorable plots involve Lily, her sister Judy, and Lily's daughters Grace and Zoe. Judy, especially, is struggling with the notion that it's possible she has frittered away her life before getting serious about settling down and having a family, things she has always wanted.

Picoult, Jodi, *Mercy* (1996) BK, UAB, SH

Jamie McDonald has just killed his beloved yet terminally ill wife Maggie and confessed the crime to his cousin, Cam McDonald, the local police chief. Cam's wife Allie takes Jamie's side in the ensuing criminal trial, believing Jamie has committed the ultimate act of love and sacrifice. Cam's strong sense of justice compels him to arrest and testify against his cousin, yet weakens in the face of his wife's new flower shop assistant, Mia, with whom he begins a torrid affair. Marriage vows are defied and defined in this compelling story of two couples' enduring love.

Rachel Getting Married (2008) MV

A taut and tense drama about how a family reacts to an unspoken tragedy and the one member with an insatiable need to address it. Kym is being released from rehab for the weekend to attend her sister Rachel's wedding. During the stressful wedding preparations, old family conflicts surface, and Kym is usually the catalyst. She both longs for and rebels against her place in her offbeat family and slowly realizes she must be the one to redefine it.

Friendship and Community

Rare is the story of a woman's life that does not include interactions with friends and community members. Frequently these relationships are stronger than familial ones, much more diverse, and provide the love, support, and understanding that might not be found in a family. The universe of a female character's friends and community can shape the character's thoughts and actions in interesting ways and provide some of the best content in the following books, movies, television shows, and podcasts.

Addison, Sarah Allen, *Garden Spells* (2007) BK, UAB, YA, AP, SH
After years following in her vagabond mother's footsteps, Sydney returns to her suffocating small town of Bascom, South Carolina, with her daughter, Bay. Sydney hopes to start a new life in her grandmother's home, now inhabited by Sydney's older, reclusive sister, Claire. The Waverly women are well known in Bascom, Claire for her edible flowers and delicious catering, Sydney for her talent with hair and makeup, and family matriarch Evanelle for giving people things they need before they know it. All of these women will touch the residents of Bascom, but not everyone is enamored of this magical family. Emma Clark harbors a talent of her own and is using all of it to protect her marriage and family from the Waverlys.

Binchy, Maeve, *Circle of Friends* (1991) BK, UAB, MV, YA
Binchy transports readers to a 1950s Irish village to tell the story of Benny, overweight and shy; her best friend Eve, an orphan; and a host of colorful local characters. The girls grow up and endure the conservative decade, heartbreak, and the betrayal of friends. More than just a charming coming-of-age tale filled with memorable characters, *Circle of Friends* captures the religious and social flavor of Ireland in the 1950s with almost picture-perfect detail.

Brown, Rita Mae, *Southern Discomfort* (1982) BK
In 1920s, Montgomery, Alabama, the city teems with an excitement, bustle, and tension that touches all walks of life. Hortensia Reedmuller Banastre is a restless and intelligent woman trapped in a loveless marriage to one of the city's wealthiest residents. She falls in love with the black son of her housekeeper and the two must hide their ill-fated relationship from everyone. On the other side of town, Banana Mae Parker and Blue Rhonda Latrec are plying their trade as successful soiled doves and trading barbs with the local reverend who is trying to bring them to salvation. These two worlds collide when Hortensia discovers that Banana Mae is her husband's mistress and Banana Mae learns Hortensia's scandalous secret. This is a passionate and witty novel of different social strata that eventually intersect, for better, worse, and laughs.

Cook, Claire, *Wild Water Walking Club* (2009) BK, UAB
Noreen Kelly wakes up the day after she accepts a buyout offer from her company to face the fact that she is jobless, dumped by a fast-talking co-worker, and directionless. She connects with Tess and Rosie, and the three women start walking together and sharing their concerns about parenting, aging, and finding and sustaining relationships. They interact with a cast of multi-generational characters up to some

bizarre suburban hijinks in the neighborhood, and as they find sustenance in each other, their other problems are solved in unusual ways. This is a gentle, quirky novel.

Designing Women (1986–1993) TV

Four strong southern women come together to run an interior design company and bring their wildly different personalities with them. Sure, it's dated (1980s big hair, padded shoulders, and excess), but the dialogue is whip-smart and the characters believably flawed. The show tackles some issues of the day, including sexual harassment, racism, and single parenting. The women remain firm friends and stalwarts in their sometimes-misguided community.

Flagg, Fannie, *Fried Green Tomatoes at the Whistle Stop Café* (1987) BK, UAB, MV, CL, AP, YA

Ninny Threadgoode, a spry 86-year-old, recounts her adventures in 1930s-era Alabama to Evelyn, a visitor at Ninny's nursing home. The Whistle Stop Café, run by two outspoken women ahead of their time, forms the central setting for Ninny's funny and heartwarming stories of courage, love, and friendship.

Jackson, Joshilyn, *Between, Georgia* (2006) BK, UAB, YA

Nonny has not one, but two dysfunctional families, and now she's stuck in a family feud that began the night she was born. Her biological family, the Crabtrees, are the poor, lawless outcasts of their rural Georgia town; her adopted family, the Fretts, are the upper-crust, can-do-no-wrong type. Her adopted mother is blind and deaf, her rocker husband is always half out the door, and her biological grandmother sets her Dobermans on anyone she doesn't like. Funny and poignant, this is a story of two polar-opposite families with more in common than they think.

KnitPicks, PC

Host Kelley Petkun chats with knitters about knitting problems, interviews craft book authors, evaluates yarn, needles, and other knitting tools and techniques, and does "charity knitting." The segment "Cry on Kelley's Shoulder" is a popular one with listeners. The show is free from iTunes.

Naylor, Gloria, *The Women of Brewster Place* (1982) BK, UAB, MV, CL

Brewster Place is the walled-off and decrepit rental housing for seven strong diverse black women who support each other during devastating personal disasters over three decades. Poverty, rape, homosexuality, and murder are only some of the events in the women's lives that they must overcome. The powerful final scene of the wall tumbling down is the women's demand for recognition and acceptance. This is a moving and thought-provoking work.

Satrapi, Marjane, *Embroideries* (2005) GN, YA

You may already be familiar with Satrapi thanks to the two-part memoir of her girlhood, *Persepolis*, but even if you've never encountered her before, you're in for a treat with this lovely gem of a book. The setting is simple: a group of Iranian women—Satrapi as a young woman, some of her female relatives, and their friends—are gathered for tea and company. What unfolds through their various stories is a glimpse into women's lives in the Middle East in the latter part of the twentieth century: through the course of their conversations, they discuss issues such as marriage, faith, family, love, and—of course—sex. Satrapi's straightforward black-and-white illustration style makes this an accessible graphic novel, even for those who are hesitant to read books in a graphic format.

Steel Magnolias (1989) M, YA, CL

This is a classic among female movie fans who all have a favorite character to identify with. The six women cover the spectrum in age, demeanor, and social position but remain fiercely devoted to each other in the face of setbacks and tragedy. As one character states, "I can't tell these things to my husband." Laughter, tears, and outrageous situations that could only be found in a quirky southern town have made this movie a staple on the top ten lists of many viewers. Interesting note: the movie was directed and written by men.

Women of a Certain Age

Entering the twilight years can be one of the most traumatic events in a woman's life. Yet many women find renewed purpose, liberation, and a stronger sense of self once the wrinkles set in. None of the women below have lost their sense of humor as they age. Most have honed a sharper wit with so many years of life experience behind them.

As Time Goes By (1998–2002) TV

British favorites Judi Dench and Geoffrey Palmer play former lovers who are reconnecting after 38 years. They had a great romance during the Korean War and then lost touch with each other, going on to live separate but full lives. This lively and witty series follows the pair as they face all the challenges of a mature romance that comes with adult children, in-laws, impending retirements, new careers, and establishing a new household together. This is a mature, intimate, and intelligent series about rekindling love in late middle age.

Calendar Girls (2003) MV, AP

Helen Mirren and a cast of delightfully daft women's club members show viewers that sexy is all in the mind, not the body, when they bare all for a charity calendar to raise money for cancer research. Once the women get used to the idea of "baring some, not all" for the camera (a hilarious sequence that addresses all the insecurities of aging, beauty, and nudity), they embark on an inventive and empowering photo shoot that causes a public sensation, raises oodles of money, and brings the ladies more notoriety than they expected.

Cohen, Paula Marantz, *Jane Austen in Boca* (2002) BK

This is a loose adaptation of *Pride and Prejudice*, updated and set in a Florida retirement village. May is a gentle woman in her 70s, Lila is a merry widow in search of a rich husband, and Flo is a sassy retired librarian. When men enter the picture, you can bet there will be discord among the friends. Social commentary abounds in this fun look at the modern retirement scene.

Ephron, Nora, *I Feel Bad about My Neck and Other Thoughts on Being a Woman* (2006) NF BK, UAB

Never mind all those cheerful books about aging; writer Nora Ephron has a much snarkier perspective, thank you very much: "Every so often I read a book about age, and whoever's writing it says it's great to be old. It's great to be wise and sage and mellow; it's great to be at the point where you understand just what matters in life. I can't stand people who say things like this." In this wickedly funny collection of essays on aging, Ephron reveals the pitfalls of growing old: she can never find her reading glasses, she has to devote more and more time to maintaining her appearance, and—of course—there is her traitor neck, which one day decided to stop being attractive, and now there is nothing she can do about it. Whether you're young or old, you'll find yourself snickering at Ephron's droll wit and deliciously jaded perspective on life.

Gelman, Rita Golden, *Tales of a Female Nomad: Living at Large in the World* **(2001) NF BK, YA**
It's the year 1985. Gelman is leading a charmed life: she writes children's books for a living, and her husband's job brings her into contact with celebrities and gala events. But her marriage of 20-plus years is feeling some strain, and she yearns for something different. This memoir is the story of Gelman's remarkable transition from urban sophisticate to career adventurer. Shedding the shackles of the modern American lifestyle, Gelman becomes a bona fide nomad: with no plan, no schedule, and no one to answer to, she moves freely to Mexico, Israel, Indonesia, anywhere that strikes her fancy, staying as long as she wants. Meet fascinating people and cultures as Gelman's wanderlust propels her across the world.

Golden Girls **(1985–1992) TV, CL**
Perhaps no other television show in the history of American popular culture demonstrated that life truly began after 60. Four south Florida seniors share a home, heartaches, backaches, and quips during their golden years. The traditional sitcom situations also arise: romance, friendly conflict, and screwball situations, and also more serious ones: crime, death, and job loss.

Ironside, Virginia, *No! I Don't Want to Join a Book Club: Diary of a Sixtieth Year* **(2007) BK, UAB**
About to turn 60, Marie looks forward to relaxing and being comfortable, unlike some of her friends, who want to take up hang gliding or go on African safaris. She's also excited about her new grandson and sees no reason to want to "reclaim her youth." But when her dear friend Hugh is diagnosed with a fatal disease, she realizes she doesn't want to get too comfortable, and she decides to seek out an old crush.

Mass, Leslie, *In Beauty May She Walk: Hiking the Applachian Trail at 60.* **(2005) BK NF**
Few people have the stamina, health, and courage to hike the entire Appalachian Trail. At age 59, Leslie Mass decided to see if she was one of them. In her memoir, *In Beauty May She Walk: Hiking the Appalachian Trail at 60*, Mass describes the physical and mental challenges of hiking the trail from beginning to end, with special emphasis on the trials unique to women and seniors.

Ray, Jeanne, *Julie and Romeo* **(2000) BK, UAB, SH**
Dueling rival florist families, the Cacciamanis and the Rosemans, have been engaged in verbal warfare for years, but no one quite remembers why. When Julie and Romeo meet at a small-business seminar on keeping a small business afloat, the sparks immediately fly between the sixtysomethings and get even hotter when their respective parents and children discover the secret romance. As the book is populated with plenty of eccentric and likeable characters and an engaging storyline, readers will wonder why it was never adapted to film.

Ross, Ann B, *Miss Julia Speaks Her Mind* **(1999) BK, UAB, RS**
Recently widowed after 44 years of marriage to a minister, proper Miss Julia discovers that her late husband left her not only his estate—but a surprise nine-year-old son

as well. When the boy's mother skips town, feisty, opinionated Julia discovers she has the mettle to take charge of events and turn her idle life into an eventful one.

Yglesias, Helen, *The Girls* **(1999) BK**
Four sisters cope with growing old gracefully. Jenny, Flora, Naomi, and Eva range in age from 80 to 95 and have come together to live in Florida and take care of one another. Jenny, the youngest, realizes that even in old age she has not overcome jealousies and hurt feelings from childhood. Flora, a geriatric sexpot, still bickers with her sisters as though they were teenagers. Naomi struggles with cancer, and Eva slowly fades. This is a sumptuous character study.

Making Connections

The elements of women's literature have long been present in other genres and bring an added depth to them. Focusing on female characters, themes, and storylines within a particular genre has provided some of the most compelling storytelling and memorable characters within the realm of mysteries, fantasy, and science fiction.

Fantasy and Science Fiction

The fantasy and science fiction genre is a great place to find strong, independent, intelligent heroines who can take care of themselves and anyone else who comes along. Even readers who can't suspend enough disbelief to relate to the otherworldly settings will cheer for these heroines, who bring twenty-first century sensibilities with them wherever they go, whether it's the future, another planet, King Arthur's court, or the local cemetery for some vampire annihilation.

Alien **(1979) MV, CL**
What do women like about this classic science fiction/horror film? The ass-kicking heroine, Ripley. This is an intense, tension-filled action picture that expertly manipulates the emotions of the viewer. The sole survivor Ripley is perfectly portrayed by Sigourney Weaver in this and subsequent *Alien* films. A rousing and empowering story even as it scares viewers right out of their seats.

Battlestar Galactica **(2004) TV, YA**
A sci-fi series with complex and layered storylines, strong and believable characters, and smart commentary on social issues of the day, *BSG* has been a cult favorite among men and women. Due in part to the outstanding female lead characters, brainy and thoughtful President Laura Roslin and hotheaded hotshot pilot Kara "Starbuck" Thrace. In addition to the action-packed plots, President Roslin deals with breast cancer and Starbuck must confront mother issues.

Bradley, Marion Zimmer, *Mists of Avalon* **(1982) BK, UAB, MV, CL, AP, YA, SH**
The King Arthur/Camelot story gets a rich and layered retelling in this version told exclusively from the viewpoints of all the women in his life. His half-sister Morgaine takes a prominent role in this story as she struggles to protect a magical land and ancient religion from the pious and ultimately successful persuasions of Gwenhwyfar, Arthur's Christian queen. This is a sumptuous reinvention full of historical detail, complex characters, and intriguing plots.

Buffy the Vampire Slayer (1997–2003) TV, YA, CL

For all the world-saving and monster-slaying, viewers really tuned in for the hip and snappy dialogue, excellently paced stories, and wholly believable teen characters who were just trying to grow up, lead predictable teen lives, and go to the school dance. There is an excellent meld of the paranormal, abnormal, and normal in a series that was always trying to stretch the boundaries of genre.

Contact (1997) MV, BK, UAB, YA

Carl Sagan's science fiction classic gets fine treatment in this film starring Jodie Foster. Dr. Eleanor Alloway believes she has received a signal from an alien life form bidding humans to build a mysterious machine. An intelligent exploration of science, religion, politics, and human nature at a crossroads converge in Ellie.

Weber, David, *On Basilisk Station* (1993) BK, UAB, YA, SH

Science fiction and fantasy are full of gutsy, smart heroines, but few are more appealing or have a larger fan base of both genders than Commander Honor Harrington. *Basilisk Station* is Honor's thrilling ride of a debut. In disgrace, Honor is sent to a dismal outpost with a meagerly outfitted rig, the HMS *Fearless*. She proves her worth to the fleet when she staves off an attack on the space station in her ragtag vessel. She is a heroine for all readers, young and old, and male and female.

Mystery

The mystery genre allows its female characters to employ all their smarts to solving the crime, taking down the villain, and sometimes saving the hero. What makes this genre even more attractive to female viewers and readers is the heroine's juggling of home and career life with a dead body to avenge or a riddle to solve.

Alias (2001–2006) TV, YA, AP

Another powerful, vulnerable, and inspiring heroine-centered series featured Jennifer Garner as Sidney Bristow, an operative for a secretive government agency. In addition to keeping up appearances as a student with a dull bank job, Sidney must juggle life with a roommate, her roommate's boyfriend woes, her tense relationship with her secretive father, and the flirty attentions of a pal from her college days. But first, she has to disable a bomb and take down a hostile government. In high heels. This is a thrilling roller-coaster ride of a series that employs the best elements of a soap opera to keep viewers coming back.

Grindle, Lucretia, *Night Spinners* (2003) BK, UAB, YA

Susannah and Marina are twins with a special talent. They can nightspin—send their thoughts, conversations, and laughter faster than light over enormous distances to each other. But as Susannah grows older, she tires of having someone who can read and penetrate her own thoughts. She shuts herself off from Marina. But then Marina is brutally murdered and Susannah finds herself haunted by inexplicable events: someone delivers a funereal flower arrangement to her home; she hears an obscure song from her childhood emanating from her basement; and most shocking, one morning she wakes up to find a lock of her hair taped to the bathroom mirror. Clearly someone is trying to scare Susannah, but she becomes ever more frightened when she learns the exact same things happened to Marina just before she died. This is a taut thriller with a satisfying conclusion.

Jagged Edge (1985) MV

Most women will sympathize with lawyer Glenn Close's dogged defense of Jeff Bridges's grief-stricken husband accused of murder. But as the clues mount up, the attorney starts thinking she may be falling for the wrong guy. This is a tense legal drama in which the heroine solves the crime and saves herself.

Neely, Barbara, *Blanche On the Lam* (1991) BK, YA, AP
Finally, a black working woman's heroine. Blanche is a hired domestic who can recite 10 things about you just by looking at your dirty house. When we first meet this sassy and savvy woman, she is standing before a judge listening to a lecture on passing bad checks before being sentenced to 30 days. Blanche can't have that and soon finds herself a fugitive from the law and working as a live-in housekeeper for a strange family that may be plotting against each other in order to inherit a fortune. A cast of offbeat characters, a liberal dose of feisty sleuthing, and enough red herrings keeps readers turning the pages that feature a woman who can see past the dust to the truth.

***Prime Suspect* (1992–2004) TV, SH**
Helen Mirren perfectly captures the frustration, work-fueled obsessions, and vulnerability of DCI Jane Tennison, leading her first murder investigation and suffering much antagonism from her squad, highers-up, and boyfriend. This is a rich series that deftly shows the difficulties of balancing career and personal life.

Historical

History is full of women who misbehaved enough to make it instead of tolerate it. The best historical novels, movies, and television shows emphasize the progressive natures of these heroines without sacrificing the historical accuracy of their times and culture.

Baker, Ellen, *Keeping the House* (2007) BK, YA
Baker does double duty, telling the story of a family from 1896 through the end of World War I and the parallel story of a woman named Dolly bucking convention in the 1950s. Dolly, a free spirit, doesn't have much in common with the coffee-klatch women in the small Wisconsin town her husband has dragged her to live in. She becomes obsessed with the abandoned mansion on the hill and the family secrets hidden there. Both stories showcase fine detail of their respective time periods and the social mores of the day.

***The Buccaneers* (1995) MV, BK, AP, SH**
The Edith Wharton novel becomes an opulent BBC miniseries with pointed commentary on money, marriage, and the plight of women of the nineteenth century who needed one in order to have the other. Three young American women, deemed too *nouveau riche* for elite New York society, travel to London at the behest of their governess in order to participate in the season and catch the eyes of eligible titled (impoverished) bachelors. All marry, but none well. The BBC screenwriter has invented an ending to Wharton's unfinished novel that may satisfy some viewers and rile literary academics. No matter. This is a feast for the eyes and intellect.

***Iron-Jawed Angels* (2004) MV, YA, AP**
"Votes for women" is the rallying cry of this period piece that pulls no punches in its depiction of the clash between suffragettes and police. The women are arrested and jailed on trumped-up charges. Impeccably acted by Hilary Swank, Angelica Huston, and Frances O'Connor, this well-researched film is a fair and accurate portrayal of the struggle for the right to vote and the passage of the Equal Rights Amendment.

Jiles, Paulette, *Enemy Women* **(2002) BK, YA, SH**
This is an affecting, promising debut novel of one woman's personal rebellions during the Civil War. Marauding soldiers arrest Adair Colley's father. On a journey to seek his release, the women are arrested and Adair is accused of being a Confederate spy. Instead of offering up information, true or false, Adair writes out her life story, pulling in legends and fairy tales, much to the bemusement of the interrogating officer, who finds himself falling in love with her. Part love story, part historical novel, the book is never sentimental.

Merkle, Judith Riley, *Vision of Light* **(1988) BK, YA**
A compelling fictional account of the dictated memoirs of fourteeth-century Englishwoman Margaret of Ashbury, this novel is charming and fast-paced and the first in a series. Margaret, certain she has been commanded by a mysterious voice to record her memoirs, dictates them to unfrocked Brother Gregory who is hired for the purpose since Margaret cannot read or write. Gregory is scornful of the daily women's minutiae that Margaret insists on including but is soon won over as she recounts her violent marriage, survival of the black plague, and accusations of witchcraft.

Waters, Sarah, *Tipping the Velvet* **(1999) BK**
In this historical novel set in Victorian England, Nancy falls in love with a male impersonator, Kitty, and follows her to become part of a cross-dressing music hall act. When an ashamed Kitty marries their manager, Walter, Nancy runs away and struggles to survive the gritty streets of London. This is a fascinating look at the effects of a repressed era on the lives of women who dared to be different.

The Future of Women's Stories

No matter how serious the lives of women may become, many of them know that the very small daily dramas experienced are entertainment for Friday night cocktails with the girls. Women know that the darker the situation, the more humorous the story and the more urgent the need to share it. This is the way women make sense of their lives, solve their problems, share their stories, and maintain their friendships and sanity. No one understands the daily drudgery, inanity, and life-changing seriousness of the lives of women better than other women.

The media love to report that's it's a surprise to Hollywood when a movie with female leads and about female concerns that would appeal only to females breaks box-office records—*My Big Fat Greek Wedding* or *Dirty Dancing*, anyone? (And you didn't have to be Greek or a dancer to get it.) If the studio execs would only grasp that women have many disposable dollars to spend and we like to dispose of them at the movie theatre with our friends, they'd be raking in the dough and the recession wouldn't even be a blip on their radar.

It's no wonder that women have figured so prominently in all forms of entertainment. At the heart of it, women are the storytellers—of their own lives, their families, their communities, society, culture, and history. Women will always be readers and talkers, and the entertainment industry recognizes this by publishing numerous titles year after year that are suitable for book groups and movies and television series that have casts of women of various cultures, ages, and socioeconomic backgrounds.

The literature of women's lives and relationships is a rich and layered one that also spans ages, socioeconomic backgrounds, and cultures. With such a far reach and wide appeal, these stories have only to worry about the room to hold them all.

Resources for Librarians

Hill, Nanci Milhone. *Reading Women: A Book Club Guide for Women's Fiction*. Westport, CT: Libraries Unlimited, 2010 (note: this title is forthcoming).

Maltin, Leonard. *Leonard Maltin's 151 Best Movies You've Never Seen*. New York: HarperStudio, 2010.

Vnuk, Rebecca. *Read On . . . Women's Fiction: Reading Lists for Every Taste*. Westport, CT: Libraries Unlimited, 2009.

Vnuk, Rebecca. *Women's Fiction Authors: A Research Guide*. Westport, CT: Libraries Unlimited, 2009.

West, Beverly, and Nancy Peske. *Cinematherapy: The Girl's Guide to Movies for Every Mood*. New York: Dell, 1999.

West, Beverly, and Jason Bergund. *TVtherapy: The Television Guide to Life*. Surrey, UK: Delta, 2005.

Zellers, Jessica. *Women's Nonfiction: A Guide to Reading Interests*. Westport, CT: Libraries Unlimited, 2009.

Index

About the Contributors

HEATHER BOOTH, a graduate of the University of Illinois Graduate School of Library and Information Science, is the author of *Serving Teens Through Readers' Advisory* (ALA Editions 2007) and a co-author of *The Hipster Librarian's Guide to Teen Craft Projects* (ALA 2009). Heather is currently the teen-services librarian for Thomas Ford Memorial Library in Western Springs, Illinois, and previously worked in the readers' advisory department at Downers Grove Public Library in Downers Grove, Illinois.

CHRISTY DONALDSON is media librarian at Utah Valley University and a lifelong science fiction fan. She received her MS degree from Drexel University and her MBA from Philadelphia University and previously worked as a reference librarian at Montana State University. A 2008 ALA Emerging Leader, Christy is currently chair of the Science Fiction and Fantasy Interest Group (Imagineers) for the Library and Information Technology Association of the ALA.

NANETTE DONOHUE is the technical services manager at the Champaign Public Library in Champaign, Illinios. She graduated from the MS program in library and information science at the University of Illinois at Urbana-Champaign in 2003. She has written book reviews for *Library Journal*, *Historical Novels Review*, and *Public Libraries*.

KATIE DUNNEBACK is a lifelong reader of romances. She has served on the American Library Association's Reading List Council, which recognizes excellence in genre fiction, wrote the practitioner's section of "Serving the Romance Reader" in *Research-Based Readers' Advisory*, is a contributor to Romancing the Blog, and is a member of the Romance Writers of America. She also writes romance fiction under a pseudonym. Currently, she works as a consultant at Southeastern Library Services in Bettendorf, Iowa.

GARY WARREN NIEBUHR is the library director for the village of Greendale in Wisconsin. His book *Caught Up in Crime* (Libraries Unlimited) was published in 2009. He is the author of *Read 'Em Their Writes: A Handbook for Mystery and Crime Book Discussions* (Libraries Unlimited, 2006), and several other popular mystery guides. Gary received the 2002 Don Sandstrom Memorial Award for Lifetime Achievement in Mystery Fandom ande was the Fan

Guest of Honor at the 2004 Bouchercon: The World Mystery Convention and at the 1995 Magna Cum Murder. He received the 2005 Margaret E. Monroe Award from the American Library Association in recognition of his contribution to the development of adult services in libraries. Gary is a contributing writer to Book Group Buzz, a *Booklist* magazine blog, at http://bookgroupbuzz.booklistonline.com. Visit Gary at http://www.garywarrenniebuhr.com.

RICK ROCHE is the author of *Real Lives Revealed: A Guide to Reading Interests in Biography* (Libraries Unlimited, 2009) and is an adult-services librarian at Thomas Ford Memorial Library in Western Springs, Illinois. He graduated from the University of Texas at Austin and has worked in public libraries in Texas, Missouri, and Illinois. Rick is interested in promoting reference services and the reading of good books and blogs at http://www.ricklibrarian.blogspot.com.

KAITE MEDIATORE STOVER is the head of readers' services for the Kansas City (Missouri) Public Library. She holds a master's degree in library science and a master's degree in literature from Emporia (Kansas) State University. Co-editor of *The Readers' Advisory Toolkit* (ALA Editions 2010) Stover is also the She Reads columnist and an audiobook reviewer for *Booklist*, a contributing writer for NoveList, and has contributed articles to *Reference and User Services Quarterly*. In 2003 she was named one of *Library Journal's* Movers and Shakers.

NICOLE J. SUAREZ is an adult-services librarian at the Frankfort (Illinois) Public Library District. Previously, she was a readers' advisory librarian in the Readers' Advisory and Audio Services Department at the Downers Grove Public Library.

MARY WILKES TOWNER, MA, MS, is an adult-services librarian at the Urbana (Illinois) Free Library. She is an adjunct lecturer at the University of Illinois Graduate School of Library and Information Science, where she teaches both on-campus and online versions of a course on adult popular literature.

REBECCCA VNUK is the author of *Read on . . . Women's Fiction* (Libraries Unlimited, 2009) and *Women's Fiction Author: A Research Guide* (Libraries Unlimited, 2009). A longtime reviewer and writer on collection development for *Library Journal*, she was named Fiction Reviewer of the Year in 2008. She was a previous chair of the Adult Reading Round Table, and is the current chair of the RUSA CODES RA Committee. Rebecca blogs at Shelf Renewal, http://www.libraryjournal.com/blog/1760000776.html, and in 2010 was named a *Library Journal* Mover and Shaker.

ROLLIE WELCH is teen coordinator of the Cleveland Public Library System. He has worked as a librarian, mostly with teens, for 26 years in both school and public library settings. A frequent presenter at local library workshops throughout his home state of Ohio, Rollie has served on the YALSA book selection committees, Quick Picks for Reluctant Young Adult Readers and Best Books for Young Adults. He has also chaired *VOYA's* Top Shelf for Middle School Fiction committee. He is a reviewer for *Kirkus Book Reviews*, *VOYA* magazine, *Library Journal*, and the *Cleveland Plain Dealer* and is the author of *The Guy-Friendly YA Library* (Libraries Unlimited, 2007) and the upcoming second edition of *Core Collection for Young Adults* (Libraries Unlimited, 2010).

JESSICA ZELLERS is the electronic resources librarian with the Williamsburg Regional Library in Virginia. She helped found the library's award-winning book review blog, Blogging for a Good Book (http://bfgb.wordpress.com) and writes Author Read-Alikes for NoveList. She enjoys writing for her own Web site, http://thelesbrarian.com, and reads a lot of graphic novels, ostensibly for professional development. Jessica is the author of *Women's Nonfiction: A Guide to Reading Interests* (Libraries Unlimited, 2009).